SUNRISE IN THE WEST

Sunrise in the West

The Life of American Mystic Samuel L. Lewis

WALI ALI MEYER

Sufi Ruhaniat International
San Rafael, California

Sunrise in the West: The Life of American Mystic Samuel L. Lewis

9 8 7 6 5 4 3 2 1

FIRST EDITION
Sufi Ruhaniat International
304 Devon Dr.
San Rafael CA 94903
www.ruhaniat.org

Hardcover ISBN: 978-0-9973999-5-0
Softcover ISBN: 978-0-9973999-6-7
eBook ISBN: 978-0-9973999-7-4
Library of Congress Control Number: 2023906356

Book Cover Design: Jelaluddin Hauke Sturm
Interior Book Design: Hassan Herz and Jelaluddin Hauke Sturm

Dedication

Murshid Wali Ali Melvin Meyer passed from his body on Thanksgiving Day, 2022. He dedicated his life to the awakening of all beings, and touched thousands of lives in his 80 years—lives of those who knew him personally and those who read his words, heard his voice on recordings, or received his transmission through video. Our deep gratitude and love for Murshid Wali Ali live on.

Contents

Introduction

Dear Reader,

This book has been a wish of mine for over two decades. I have felt it would be a way for you to "experience the teacher" in a similar way to those of us who had the privilege of knowing Samuel Leonard Lewis during his lifetime (October 18, 1896—January 15, 1971).

I met my teacher Murshid Sam in early summer of 1969. He left his earthly form less than two years later. Still, I can say I have felt his guiding presence every day since. In some of his last teachings, presented at his home in San Francisco in December 1970, he repeated, "The connection between the student and the teacher is in no way dependent on one or the other being in the body." This has proven true for me. I make this an invitation for all of you not just to learn the history of this remarkable man, but to experience the guidance stream here and now.

As you will read in the following pages, Murshid Sam's own experience was the proof of the teachings. He told us that three years to the day after the passing of his Sufi teacher, Hazrat Inayat Khan, Inayat appeared to him in full form and guided him. He further explained Hazrat Inayat Khan did not continue to appear regularly in that way but still taught him every day. You will also read that in the 1940s he had experiences of both Prophet Muhammad and Christ appearing to him. Muhammad became his guide, and Christ presented him with a peace plan for the Middle East and directed him to work for peace in Palestine.

As a living demonstration of the universality of religious ideals—all paths leading to the One—six weeks after Murshid Sam began his Sufi practice with Murshida Rabia Martin he became a disciple of Zen Buddhism under the guidance of Rev. M. T. Kirby. His Zen studies continued over the years, significantly with Roshi Nyogen Senzaki, Roshi Sokei-an

Sasaki, and Dr. Kyung-Bo Seo. He continued deepening in the Sufi path by becoming a disciple of Hazrat Inayat Khan in 1923 and received widespread recognition of his realization throughout Pakistan during his travels in 1956 and the 1960s. He immersed himself in Jewish mysticism (Kabbalah) as well as the Christian mysteries. In the 1950s he reported having a recurring vision of a saint accompanied by the words, "In one year's time by land or sea I will come to thee!" It turned out to be the great enlightened Indian Swami, Papa Ramdas, and Samuel also became his disciple.

Along with this unfolding of the Path of the Mystic, you will see that not only did Murshid Sam have a deep inner life, but he also dedicated himself to relieving suffering in the outer world. He was biologist and botanist, dedicated to gardening, horticulture, and farming methods, to water desalinization, seed exchange, food production and in general recognizing the Holy Book of Nature. He involved himself in politics, constantly writing letters to world leaders. During World War II he worked for Army Intelligence. He worked for social reforms.

In 1966 while in the hospital for heart trouble, Murshid Sam shared that he had a vision: "Allah came to me and said, 'I make you spiritual leader of the hippies!' I was flat on my back so it was hard to argue."

The last years of his life were a flowering of everything that had come before. The young people of the day flocked around him. In 1968, following inner vision, he gathered his students around, asking them to hold hands in a circle to move, chant and sing sacred phrases from the mysticism of Islam, Judaism, Buddhism, and Hinduism in Arabic, Hebrew, Sanskrit, and other languages. These practices became known as the "Dances of Universal Peace." At that time when there were only a handful of us dancing, he told us this sacred practice would go around the world. True to his prediction there are now Dance circles in 50 countries.

Samuel Lewis distinctively combined unshakable strength with great tenderness and the capacity for occasional fierce love. May his life serve as an inspiration to persevere even in the light of protracted obstacles as we return again and again to the Voice which constantly comes from within.

Gratitude

More than two decades ago, I made the request to write a proper biography of Murshid Samuel Lewis to the person I felt was most gifted for the task, Murshid Wali Ali Meyer. Wali Ali was Murshid Samuel Lewis's Esoteric Secretary and lived with his teacher for several years. Ten years ago, my friend of fifty years, Wali Ali, accepted. This book is the result.

With profound gratitude, I wish to express my appreciation for Murshid Wali Ali's efforts fulfilling my Heart wish, so the world has a much better chance to "Meet the Teacher"—Murshid Samuel Lewis.

I also wish to express deep appreciation to the extraordinary editorial team of Barakat Bryan and Halim Dunsky who with amazing dedication carried the project to its completion.

Kudos to our book designers: Hassan Herz, also a direct disciple of Murshid Sam, and Jelaluddin Hauke Sturm, now one of our senior teachers living in Berlin, Germany.

Further gratitude to head researcher Tawwaba Bloch, who provided invaluable information for the biography project, and to Saadi Neil Douglas-Klotz for his generous support to the author and researchers. The list is long of those who contributed to research in many areas, and apologies are extended for any oversights. Included are Colyn Brown, Barakat Bryan, Junaid Michael Burke, Saraswati Andrea Burke, Shivadam Adam Burke, Walia Donna DeMille, Majida Teresa Dietze, Halim Dunsky, Talat Halman, Haqiqa Nuri Hampton, Iman Michael Howden, Mohsin Mustafa Maken, Suria Rebecca McBride, Tansen Phillip O'Donohoe, Qahira Jo Oppenheimer, Paula Saffire, Yusuf Schuman, Don Stevens, Jami Michael Walsh, and Laurent Weichberger.

To the following behind-the-scenes support people, many thanks for your invaluable assistance: early readers Tansen O'Donohoe, Sabura Perry, and Basira Beardsworth; proofreading support, Wali van der Zwan; image seekers Ali Charles and Andrew Storey; and for image copyright clearance and so much more, Zardusht Chet Van Wert. A special thanks to the team who worked to get the Murshid Sam Archives from paper to their current online format.

And now, my dear reader, let the adventure begin! May this book enliven your heart and inspire you to manifest Loving Kindness and Compassion as the root of all your activities.

April 2023

With gratitude,

Pir Shabda Kahn

Lineage Holder in the line of Murshid Samuel Lewis

and his successor Pir Moineddin Jablonski (January 1, 1942–February 27, 2001)

NOTE: The Murshid Samuel Lewis Archives are referenced throughout this book and provide voluminous inspiring material for study, far in excess of what could be incorporated here. We encourage you to make the Archives a part of your adventure:

murshidsam.org

Précis

Editors' Note: In 1981, Masheikh (later Murshid) Wali Ali Meyer wrote this condensed story of the life of Murshid Samuel Lewis. It has been lightly edited for presentation here. The original text can be read in the Murshid Samuel Lewis Archives, murshidsam.org, under the title "The Early Life of Murshid Samuel L. Lewis."

SAMUEL LEONARD LEWIS WAS BORN ON OCTOBER 18, 1896 to Jacob Lewis (a salesman at the Levi Strauss Company) and the former Harriet Rosenthal. He once said, "My parents never forgave me for being conceived out of wedlock." He was an unusual child, a child prodigy; his mother often claimed to have had a dream of the Prophet Samuel before the child's birth and therefore gave him that name. But these unusual qualities did not endear him to his family. His father never could accept the other-worldly tendencies of his oldest son. He was angered time and again that Samuel was not interested in business, competition and material success. In all matters his younger brother Elliott was preferred; even when he lied and stole, this was at least showing interest in money.

This introverted and deeply studious young man, with his memories of previous lives and his mystical inclinations, graduated from San Francisco's top high school, Lowell, with the highest grades in its history to that point. But his well-to-do family refused to send him to college. This family rejection and conflict was one of the crosses he had to bear until the end of his life. He achieved reconciliation with his parents and with his brother shortly before their respective deaths, and funds from his father allowed him to resume college when he was already in his 50s. He continued taking courses until his death; his passion for knowledge was inexhaustible.

He told his students on several occasions that it was his own family rejection which made him naturally sympathetic to the young people who came to him with similar problems at the end of his life. It was one of the ways God prepared him to be of help to others, he later came to believe. Through rejection after rejection in life he developed great patience and perseverance until at the end of his life, the flow of time and evolution began to catch up with him—initially in the persons of the youth of the late sixties. He repeated again and again the phrase of Christ: "The stone which is rejected is become the cornerstone." He said that this was the koan for his life.

While he had "intimations of immortality" from early childhood and reports reading about psychic research at age 13, his mystical training was set into motion a few years later:

In 1915, at the age of 18, he goes to the Palace of Education at the World's fair which was held in San Francisco. There he meets with Theosophy, which taught him "All religions are right. They differ on the outside when taken exoterically, they agree on the inside if taken esoterically. All religions are from God. There are seven planes of existence, the lower one experienced in life after life, the higher ones only by sages and the illumined." He knows in his depth of being that this is true. He believes he has found the Way. He continues to read all the world's scriptures voraciously. He is still living at home, something of a recluse. But the teachings of the Theosophists have proven to be only intellectual and he renews his search.

In November 1919 he is walking on Sutter Street; he sees a display of books. He is unaware of how but soon he is upstairs facing a little dark-haired lady. She is Jewish. "You can explain the Kabbalah?" he asks. "Yes, and all religions." "What is Sufism?" "Sufism is the essence of all religions. It has been brought to the West by Hazrat Inayat Khan." The woman is Murshida Rabia A. Martin, Inayat Khan's senior disciple, and his first appointed Murshida.

Shortly after this he formally begins his study of Zen, meeting the Zen teacher Rev. M. T. Kirby, a disciple of the Rinzai Abbot Shaku Soyen. His study of religion has now taken a much deeper turn.

In June of 1923 he has a vision of the arrival of Hazrat Inayat Khan and his mergence with him. The next day, noon, the summer solstice, he is summoned to meet the Pir-o-Murshid. Samuel walks into the room only to see a tremendous light. "Come, don't be afraid," says the Murshid. He takes initiation. He is loyal to his teacher through thick and thin for the rest of his life: "He was the first person to ever touch my heart." Thereafter, he introduces Rinzai Zen master Nyogen Senzaki and Hazrat Inayat Khan, who "entered samadhi together."

Samuel begins to write poetry and numerous essays on religious themes. His being is beginning to ferment. His behavior patterns become stranger and even more difficult for his family to understand; his health begins to deteriorate. In 1925 he is on the verge of a nervous breakdown. By his own report he goes into the wilderness to die. This is on land in Fairfax, California, owned by Murshida Martin, dedicated to the Sufi work and called Kaaba Allah. He is to make a khilvat or spiritual retreat. In the midst of it, the legendary Khwaja Khizr appears and offers him the gift of music or poetry. He chooses poetry. Khizr appears again the next night. And then all the Prophets of God appear; Elijah presents him a robe in vision, and Mohammed appears to him as the Seal of the Prophets. For the next 45 years until his death he never questions the validity of these experiences.

He remains silent about them until Hazrat Inayat Khan's return to America in 1926. Then he seeks an interview and tells the Sufi master of his experiences. Inayat Khan summons him back for five more interviews and gives him tremendous responsibilities for the work. He makes him "Protector of the Message." During the course of these interviews Inayat Khan yells at him that he has not as many trustworthy disciples as he has fingers on one hand. This yell literally knocks him over, and he later says that it was at this moment that he received the full transmission of Baraka (blessing-magnetism) from his teacher. It was to be, he later says, the strength for his whole life.

Hazrat Inayat Khan reads Samuel's early efforts at spiritual commentary and tells him that he is to be a leader in the Brotherhood work—the efforts to build a bridge of communication between the mystics and the intellectuals. Inayat Khan has Samuel and Paul Reps take a special pledge to protect and be loyal to Rabia Martin, not to let her defend herself in public or take up money matters. On these latter points he fails. Hazrat Inayat Khan dies the next year and the Sufi Movement which he establishes becomes divided by politics. Murshida Martin uses Samuel as her foil for making her claim for succession, having him write numerous letters to headquarters.

In 1930, three years after his passing, Hazrat Inayat Khan appears to Samuel in vision and exerts pressure upon his crown center. From then on Samuel receives communications from Inayat. He writes lesson paper after paper for the Sufi mureeds. He writes numerous commentaries on the esoteric teachings of the Pir-o-Murshid. These commentaries he continues to write until his death, often rewriting his commentaries three or four times. The 1930s is a fertile period for his writing, particularly the prophetic types of materials which is all that survived the Kaaba Allah fire of 1949.

He begins to live at Kaaba Allah, and stays there throughout most of the depression years. He has no salary; his work is as a gardener and groundskeeper. He lives off the land. Murshida Martin appoints him as her Khalif (representative) and he bears much of the responsibility for the running of the Sufi Khankah. But as the years go on they have increasingly more differences. He is being taken through inner initiations all the time and his outer behavior patterns reflect this inner intoxication. There is no one around who can be his teacher. He takes the spiritual name Murad, meaning one who receives by Grace.

During the 1930's Samuel also spends time in Los Angeles with Luther Whiteman collaborating on the book *Glory Roads,* a classic study of Utopian movements in the state of California, and conducting what they called "propaganda analysis." He is becoming more involved with social issues. He lives for a time at the bohemian community called the Dunes in southern California. He is still a celibate, not by choice but by fate; he rarely even touches a woman and never men.

The outbreak of World War II finds him working as a historical consultant and secretary for Army Intelligence (G2). His immediate superior Capt. Edward Landsdale tells him to burn all his diaries of this period.

"This was easy because nobody believed me anyway," he says later. He was fighting the war in the inner planes, and his diaries were a chronicle of this.

After the war years, Murshida Martin appoints Ivy Duce her successor—someone nobody in the Sufi Order knew—bypassing Samuel who had been her chief representative for years. Ivy Duce decides to turn everything over to Meher Baba. Samuel tries to accept this out of loyalty; he goes to South Carolina where he lives as a beachcomber. Finally after two years he is given a vision of the grand mosque of the heavens where Jesus sweeps the floors, Mohammed takes up the shoes, and this lady goes around demanding and demanding from others. He is allowed to leave. He collects one box of his multitudinous writings and leaves Kaaba Allah. It burns down the next day. He is wrongfully accused of burning it down and finds himself disgraced, penniless, broken. The sacred writings of Hazrat Inayat Khan are withheld from him.

Around this time he gets a vision from Jesus Christ of how to bring peace in Palestine. He goes to school. Takes odd jobs. Has some very small allowance from his family. Does many spiritual practices. Writes copiously. Works with orphaned children. Takes up horseback riding, folk dancing, ornamental horticulture. Works with road crews planting shrubs and flowers.

In 1956 Samuel makes his first trip to Asia and is accepted everywhere. He is recognized by spiritual teachers of all schools. He takes up many world projects. In 1960 he makes his second trip. He studies and teaches Sufism in the East. Among many other recognitions is made a Murshid in the Chishti Order of Sufis, the parent school of Hazrat Inayat Khan. He works actively distributing different kinds of seeds around the world and working on solutions to world food problems. In 1962 he returns to the United States.

In 1966 he begins to attract a few young disciples. He lands flat on his back in the hospital and God comes to him and appoints him "Spiritual Leader of the Hippies." It's something he never expected, but shortly after this time the young people begin to flock to his door. He finds the family he never had. At the end of his life he is hugging and kissing men and women all the time. He originates the Dances of Universal Peace, often called Sufi Dances, and dedicates them to the Temple of Understanding which is committed—as was Inayat Khan—to providing a house of prayer for all peoples. These dances, which take sacred phrases from all the world's religions, have since spread worldwide. He originates the work of the Sufi Choir and institutes spiritual instruction through music. He credits his "fairy godmother" Ruth St. Denis with his ability to draw Dance forms out of the cosmos and for his inspiration to teach through the Walk.

In 1968 he joins forces with Pir Vilayat Khan, the eldest son of his first teacher, and there follows a great flowering of the Sufi work in the United States. Murshid Sufi Ahmed Murad Chisti—as Samuel is now known—appoints his own spiritual successor, Moineddin Jablonski, from among his disciples, as well as several Sheikhs and Khalifs. In December of 1970 a fall down stairs gives him a brain concussion and he dies on January 15, 1971. His work is continued by his energetic and devoted disciples.

"For years," Samuel said about himself, "I followed a Gandhian attitude, always yielding, and got nothing for it. When once I was able to be firm and take the path of the master everything came my way."

The events of the last years of Samuel's life were so full they deserve a chronicle all their own. This brief biographical sketch focuses on less-known periods of his early life. At the end, all the seeds of his earlier efforts and experiences came to fruition. Finally he got the Divine instruction: "Harvest what you can, and leave the rest to Me."

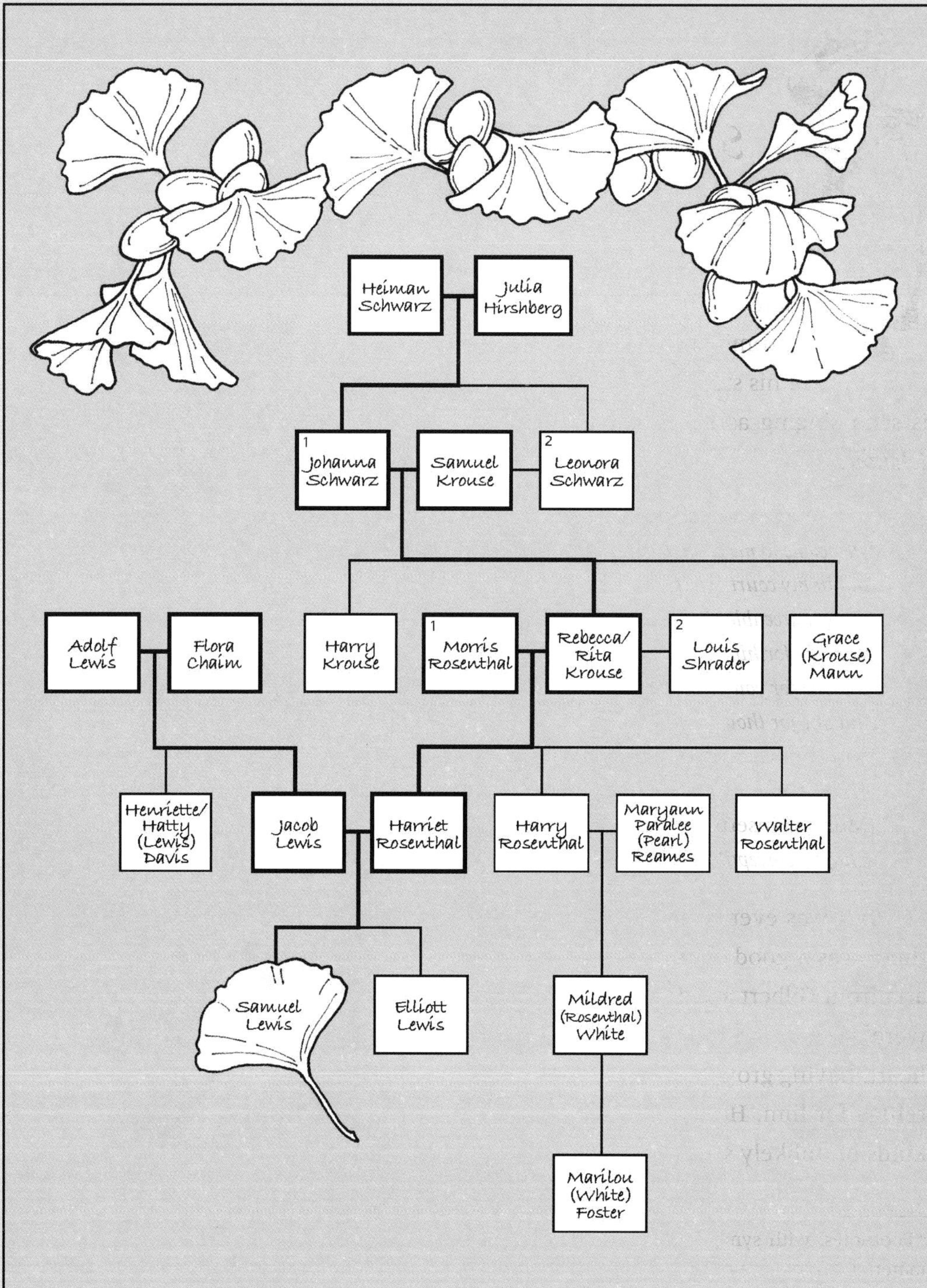

Selected Family Tree of Samuel Leonard Lewis

CHAPTER 1

Setting the Stage

THE RISING NEW SPIRITUAL MOVEMENT in the United States in the late 1960s was portrayed in the movie *Sunseed,*[1] which prominently featured Samuel Lewis.* At a wedding of two of his students on the spring equinox of 1970, Murshid Sam† is seen singing as the Lord High Chancellor in Gilbert and Sullivan's *Iolanthe:*

> *And every one who'd marry a Ward*
> *Must come to me for my accord*
> *And in my court I sit all day*
> *Giving agreeable girls away*
> *With one for him—and one for he—*
> *And one for you—and one for ye—*
> *And one for thou—and one for thee –*
> *But never, oh, never a one for me!*
> *Which is exasperating for*
> (Murshid inserts here: "No, it isn't!")
> *A highly susceptible chancellor.*[2]

If it was ever your role to drive Murshid Samuel Lewis anywhere, there was a good chance that along the way he would break out in an aria from Gilbert and Sullivan or other light opera. Gilbert and Sullivan were popular in his parents' home and he knew much of their work by heart, having grown up in the midst of music and song. The music was a refuge for him. He would spontaneously offer spirited renditions in all kinds of unlikely situations.

---

*Footnotes, with symbols like these * † ‡ §, contain explanations and supplementary material. Endnotes, which are numbered, contain source citations and appear at the end of the book.

† A *Murshid* is a Sufi guide or teacher; feminine, *Murshida.*

One time in the car he asked me if I had a request for a song. I suggested the farcical aria of the monumentally absurd *King Dodo,*[3] which he supplied with glee. At this stage of Murshid Sam's life in the late 1960s, joy was his natural medium. It simply never occurred to him to be self-conscious about expressing himself. He was happy being who he was.

It may seem odd to begin a biography of an influential figure in the spiritual evolution of America with accounts of his extemporaneous singing from comic operettas. However, it is an entry into his family story.

Our lives are deeply impacted by the conditions that surround us: from our ancestors, from family in our youth, and from adult relationships. Samuel Lewis's family history is marked by broken marriages and reparented children. His parents' home offered little stability and was at times emotionally frigid, explosively tense, and dramatically lacking in intimacy. Yet even within the barrenness there was an echo of the world of music and theatre.

Raising the Curtain

Samuel Lewis's ancestors, as far back as the research team has been able to trace (into the 19th century), were Jewish. Those on his mother's side played the most important historical role. They can be traced to Samuel Krouse, Heiman and Julia Schwarz, and the Schwarzes' two daughters, Johanna and Leonora. These five were immigrants to America from a part of Prussia that later was absorbed into Poland.

Sam's great grandfather, Samuel Krouse, had three children with his first wife Johanna in New Jersey: Harry, Rebecca, and Grace. After some years Samuel and Johanna separated, without divorcing, and Krouse moved to San Francisco. He later married his wife's sister Leonora, who became the matriarch of the family as well as a mother figure for subsequent offspring. This included Krouse's three children by Johanna, who moved across country to live with Samuel and Leonora in San Francisco for an extended period.

Leonora Schwarz Krouse on left, Rebecca/Rita Krouse Rosenthal Shrader on right

Krouse's eldest, Harry, was a musician, composer, arranger, and singer who made his career in the music world. When he joined the family in San Francisco, he gave piano lessons in the home before establishing himself in the broader musical theater scene. The musical milieu in the home of the Krouses undoubtedly inspired Samuel Lewis's mother Harriet, Harry's niece, to develop her own innate musical talents, which in turn gave her son his musical refuge in their dysfunctional home.

Samuel Krouse's middle child, Rebecca, was Samuel's Lewis's maternal grandmother, Harriet's mother. Rebecca had a rocky marriage to one Morris Rosenthal and ultimately left her husband—as well as her three young children—to marry Louis Shrader, a talented singer and performer also involved in the theater. They made their home in New York and toured with the DeWolf Hopper Opera Company. Rebecca's children were left in the care of her father, Samuel Krouse, and his wife, Leonora, Rebecca's aunt, at the tender ages of five (Harriet), one and a half (Harry), and a few months (Walter). Just as Leonora was a mother figure for earlier generations, she became a grandmother figure of comfort and support to baby Samuel Lewis and other family members, who tended to refer to her as though this role were biological; she was technically Samuel's great-grandaunt.

Jacob Lewis

Harriet later married Jacob Lewis, son of Adolph Lewis and Flora Chaim of Massachusetts. At the time of Samuel's birth, Jacob was a salesman at Levi Strauss. On October 18, 1896, Samuel Leonard Lewis was born to Jacob and Harriet in San Francisco. Samuel's brother Elliott was born about a year and a half later.

The Stone the Builders Rejected

> *I shall give thanks to You, for You have answered me, And You have become my salvation. The stone which the builders rejected has become the chief corner stone. This is the Lord's doing; it is marvelous in our eyes.*
>
> PSALM 118 [4]

In a 1961 letter to his friend Florie Leonard, Samuel Lewis wrote:

> Please bear in mind that this is my diary, for my records and for posterity and is not any effort to win anybody over; indeed some people will say as they always have said: what egotism! All my early life was rife with suffering and I used to envy Job! I am not fooling. The biblical saying that was before me was, "The stone that is rejected is become the corner stone." [5] *

Great grandfather Samuel Krouse died a few years after Samuel Lewis was born, and Lewis's father Jacob became the man of the family. It appears there was little intimacy or warmth in the home. Sam's cousin Mildred later remembered witnessing what she called a war between the two parents, and it had gotten progressively worse.[6] The children were definitely out in the cold, wondering how to make a connection. Any kind of fundamental bonding of heart with Jacob and Harriet was out of reach, and neither child was viewed as having great promise of success in the society that was of paramount importance to their parents.

In the early days, relations between Sam and Elliott were apparently normal for brothers. They competed for what attention and

---

* Samuel often kept copies of his correspondence as diary entries.

Brothers Elliott (L) and Samuel

approval was to be had, as would be expected, but the hatred between the parents only worsened over the years, and as a result Elliott obsessively pursued victory in the sibling rivalry.

Samuel had come in with prodigious intellectual gifts, but academic education and erudition were not considered to be of real importance by his parents. His father was a highly successful businessman with an eighth-grade education and didn't see much, if any, benefit in higher education. Moreover, Samuel's challenging independence of mind threatened both parents and assaulted their values about what was important. On top of all that was the fact that he was often absorbed in a private inner world.

As beneficiaries of the "American Jerusalem" of San Francisco, Jacob and Harriet Lewis agreed on one thing. They were both fully devoted to the importance of a person's place in society. Acceptance in the right social circles coupled with charitable actions was a top priority of the world they lived in. They had wealth, a secure niche in the San Francisco landscape, and each on their own attended many social events and supported charities. Sadly, in their eyes, Samuel with his eccentricities and ways of standing out awkwardly in social situations would never fit in San Francisco high society.

Vera Van Voris* described herself as among a few people Harriet invited over to the 9th Avenue home to have fun, which was always when Jacob was away.

---

*Vera Van Voris, later known as Murshida Vera Corda, first met Samuel in his role as a Sufi teacher in 1935 when she joined the Sufi Order. She herself became a Sufi teacher and was Samuel's devoted friend and student until the end of his life.

> You'd have to hear [Harriet] on the piano to believe it. I'd say she had the strength of three men, and it all came out on those keys. It was tremendous power in those little hands, and this little bird-like, alive, vital person who would bang away and stop in the middle and say, "Vera, come here. Did you know my son is named Samuel; do you know why?" And she would tell me the history of Samuel . . ."They said he was born out of wedlock but . . . don't you believe it. He was born a prophet, and he came in the spiritual body first." . . . And [Vera's husband] Arjuna . . . would hear this [from elsewhere in] the house; and afterward, he'd say, "She's mad! She tells the world, but she doesn't tell her own son." [7]

Other indications that Samuel Lewis was a gifted being come from his own later writings about his youth. Two papers stand out: "My Lesson in Spiritual Cosmogony and Astronomy" (1925) and "Intimations of Immortality from Juvenile Reminiscences" (ca. 1935).

"Spiritual Cosmogony" was written during a pivotal *khilvat* (spiritual retreat) Samuel undertook in 1925 under the guidance of Sufi teacher Murshida Rabia Martin in Fairfax, California. The paper included these parenthetical remarks:

> The writer always pictured God as a white sky when an infant, and as he grew older the sky gradually disappeared, in proportion as his elders put ideas about God into his head. I learned the alphabet in 5 minutes; I read before I was 3; I read the Bible at six; I read the history of the United States while an infant, before I was 4 I would turn pages of music, always at the right time. I knew cards not long after I could talk. I read the Bible diligently and 3 times until I was 9½, and believed, then. I had many dreams I remember that came true afterwards. I also remembered some things about my former home. Death was not real, even when my grandfather died.* All these things happened with no outer encouragement save a little from my grandmother.† Whence the urge?[8]

Where did his spiritual impulse come from? Samuel Lewis incarnated with the light of intelligence already burning, and with memories of his time before incarnation. Puzzled that nothing in his outer environment existed to support his quest for further spiritual knowledge,

---

* He is referring to Samuel Krouse, his great-grandfather, who died in 1899.

† The reference is to his great-grandaunt Leonora Krouse.

Samuel was amazed that he nevertheless strongly felt the urge to pursue that path.

Reading his words begins to give us some insight into the unusual world of his childhood. As a young child Samuel had vivid memories from his soul's journey through the inner planes toward incarnation. He was a kind of prodigy, gifted in intellectual skills at an age much earlier than normal. He was subject to visions and had ongoing communication with the next realm as well as intimations of his future life.

It is taught in a number of spiritual traditions that some rare souls are born awake and with memory of what came before incarnation. Called a *tulku* in Tibetan Buddhism, an unusual soul like this is recognized as the reincarnation of a self-realized being who returns to Earth to fulfill their vows of working endlessly for the awakening of all souls. Dream/visions like the one reported by Harriet Lewis of her son being born a prophet are frequent in such cases. Samuel Lewis's later life further indicates that he had the light of realization from the very outset.

How Different Was He?

The unusual nature of Samuel's consciousness in childhood is best described in "Intimations of Immortality from Juvenile Reminiscences." These memories were prophetic, revealing how certain elements in his life would play out, and the challenges he would face. They also document aspects of his inner life as a child.

Significant quotations from the document are included to enrich the picture of Samuel's inner life through the age of 15.[9] He begins with a description of his sense of self, or soul, from the beginning of his incarnation in a body:

> I do not believe there ever was a time in which I did not believe in former life, but this by no means indicates that I necessarily believed in reincarnation (multifold appearances on this plane) or that I was uncreate, lasting from eternity. The child-mind does not philosophize, but it may remember well. Although it is generally claimed that we do not remember the earliest incidents in life, there have been remarkable cases of people who recalled their weaning period.

> The child memory seems to be closely connected with the picture memory, or shall we say imagination?

Samuel then remembers aspects of his life before incarnation that were carried forward into his worldly life:

> Now as to actual memories. Until I was fifteen I distinctly had the continuing memory of having been in a kind of wood. It was gloomy there, being like a perpetual four o'clock in the afternoon, lacking the bright light of the sun, but not being in darkness. This, I feel, is the condition of the soul, and the afternoon of the soul continues until about the age of seven, when the sun of the soul sets and we are enshrouded in darkness (until the "New Birth").

Generalizing from his own experience, Samuel describes here what may be any child's experience—the decreasing stages of awareness of the illuminated nature of their own soul as they grow older. This diminution continues until that original light of knowing disappears into darkness. The phrase "until the New Birth" suggests the possibility of reawakening into one's inherent nature in this lifetime. The New Birth also points to the soul's incarnation from the inner planes onto Earth.

Samuel continues with the illuminated nature of his first notion of God, which became obscured over time.

> As a positive proof of this—when my great-grandmother who first told me of God, would mention Him to me, I always saw a great sky of white or light ([no] sun in it) and no figure or being or anything anthropomorphic or in form. The man-like God, or the veiled God or mist, or God in symbol came later, particularly after Sunday school studies.

He then details his experience of the wood of four o'clock that he remembered from before incarnation. The experience marked him and continued to influence him:

> Returning to the wood. There were three of us closely associated. We had been exiled—my chum and his sweetheart and I. We had been leaders of a great group of reformers of some kind, destined to free humanity. But passing through the realm of the Usurper, we had been deprived of our power and I had lost all my wealth and my wife (or sweetheart) besides.

> These two souls with me I feel were Maurice and Minnie. In my last visions of this wood, which continued . . . until I was about fifteen, I remember a few souls having gathered around us, and a sign that we would again be leaders in a great movement and recover our position, power, and wealth, and I my soulmate sometime, somehow.

It was a great source of strength for Samuel throughout his life to have had this sign: he and his small group would recover their power and overcome obstacles to become leaders in an influential movement, despite rejection and numerous discouraging circumstances. The memories also caused sadness and resignation, while Samuel remained ever hopeful that he might eventually have a wife or sweetheart in this world.

Next Samuel leads the reader into the realm of light that preceded the wood, which brought its own challenges and choices.

> On one side of this wood there was an open space, but it was also gloomy there and entirely bare and flat, almost like a dry mud flat. Both the flat and the wood extended a long distance back to a land of greater light, memory of which gradually disappeared, but which I must have remembered until I was about twelve. However, it was from this land souls came. They were not permitted to return that way . . .
>
> Before we had been exiled into the world of gloom, we had been given some choices and some of these choices were actually repeated to me during youth. One of them was the choice between truth and suffering on one hand, and pleasure and plenty on the other. When the Usurper offered this choice it seems that at first our entire band deserted us, won by stealth or trickery, and only Maurice, Minnie, and I (it would appear) held out, although later a few discovered the treachery of the Usurper. (This group continued growing until "birth.") I believe that from the ages of three to fifteen I went through a great deal of suffering over this memory which I am now mentioning for the first time.

These last sentences reveal much about Samuel's inner state as he grew up. He remembered his choice to stand with truth, even though it would mean suffering, to abhor stealth and trickery, and to have no expectation of pleasure and financial ease. His young life was full of suffering for lack of a feeling of love, social intimacy, and acceptance. It seemed evident to him that this state would only continue, for to him it was the choice he had already made from his soul.

Next he shares his memories of a previous inner realm in which the Usurper overthrew the power of his band of souls and Samuel lost the union with his soul mate:

> The fact that I was to be separated from my wife to be, whoever she is, is further explained by some of the details below.
>
> The land where the Usurper overthrew our power was, I would say, a sort of 2 or 3 in the afternoon of the soul, where it was warm and bright and there were meadows. There was much playing and feasting and dancing. I had evidently been a great dreamer and idealist for I would not join in the games, and it was in this way that my band left me, drawn by pleasure . . .
>
> This is rather interesting, for when I was in my late teens I was in the Socialist movement and had a fair amount of influence among the young folks and lost my power through the machinations of a young man who introduced dancing and dancers, and used this means to overthrow me . . .
>
> It seems that in the former world, I had therefore taken an aversion to dancing, and this played a part in this life. At the same time I have always loved to watch good dancing, and sometimes I feel that I shall marry a dancer.*

Samuel's reminiscences on his juvenile experiences of immortality take us back even further, to a realm in which he dwelt before the ones already described:

> Before entering the world of the Usurper we had been in a much brighter world, memory of which only remained in early childhood, as with Wordsworth, but I am sure many more children have this experience than is commonly believed.
>
> This land of Light was where souls receive their instructions before birth. I was at the top of this class (later, I was invariably at the top of my classes in school), but the idea of "school" is somewhat of a misnomer. We learned **directly out of the light with our breath, and this breath came in not only through the nostrils but through every pore of the body, and this learning was the same as food: we**

---

*Years later he would make a noble effort to marry a particular dancer he met on his travels to India.

> **lived on it, and learning, living, eating and breathing were all one and the same process.***
>
> In that land also there was no idea of parentage, but of brother and sister, and perhaps sweetheart and even husband and wife. We traveled in bands, but I do not remember much and that not very clearly. However, I shall relate a few memories, all of which can be explained by doctrines given in "The Phenomenon of the Soul"[10] and "The Soul, Whence and Whither."[11]

As mentioned previously, Samuel had a kind of pre-knowledge of the English language:

> I was evidently born with a knowledge of the English language, for as soon as my mother repeated the alphabet I repeated it and was reading before I was three. I read history at four and completed the O.T.† at six. Now as regards reincarnation, there is this peculiarity—I have always felt if I lived on earth before, that I was a Jew and yet every memory I might have brought has been with England or the English language. For instance:
>
> When I was thirteen I had to write a story in the English class, and wrote in detail the first half of "The Lady of the Lake," which I had never read. The teacher thought I had copied it but I never had heard of it nor knew nothing of Scott. This could be explained that I met him on a higher plane, where I also most likely met at least one Sufi poet on the downward course to earth.

This explanation and his earlier reference to two texts by the Sufi Master Hazrat‡ Inayat Khan on the nature of the soul refer to his teacher's description of how souls communicate with each other in their descent into embodiment at birth and in their ascent through the heavens at death. Samuel Lewis appears equally content with this interpretation and with the traditional Hindu or Buddhist versions of reincarnation. For Murshid Sam, experience was always primary, and explanations secondary.

---

* Boldface type in original, here and throughout the Archive material.

† Old Testament.

‡ Hazrat is an honorific title for a deeply respected and beloved Sufi teacher whose spiritual presence is always available to *mureeds* (Sufi term for disciples), whether at a distance or no longer in the body.

In the inner sphere he also remembers being with a family:

> In that land, I had a brother and sister. For many years after coming to this plane I continued to dream of a sister younger than myself but older than my brother. This continued until I was about twelve. I had already met the girl who was adopted the following year, fulfilling the conditions; and also most of the dreams, if not all, materialized in the following years.*

In this passage Samuel describes dreams that seemed prophetic throughout his childhood, most of which eventually materialized. His connection with the inner world remained intact, a fact that is essential to understanding him as a child and an adult.

In addition to his images and memories of the world before incarnation, Samuel as a child had active conversations with the next world:

> I always believed in the coming of the Messiah and for a long time felt I would meet him and that the great work for which I had been a leader (on the earlier planes) was connected with him. I often rehearsed conversations with the Messiah, and later, after I was eighteen, with a Master. When I awoke to the realization, it was almost impossible to reconcile the dreams and musings with the objective reality. In fact this has been the wonder of my life.

There was a great disconnect between Samuel's inner and outer experience of life, and it was difficult for him to harmonize them. It was a koan. In the end, the wonder of his life was that the stone that was initially rejected ultimately received acceptance as a cornerstone for a worldwide spiritual movement.

Samuel continues with a description of how he developed his early notions of morality and caught a glimpse of what his profession in life would be:

---

*There was a girl who came to live nearby when Samuel was eleven whom both Samuel and Elliott apparently regarded as their sister. No adoption or blood connection has been discovered; the so-called "adoption" was most likely simply a report on the brothers' shared feelings. Mildred White refers to this in her Remembrance (available in the Murshid Samuel Lewis Archives, murshidsam.org).

> Why I did not indulge in dancing, sex, smoking, etc. I had evidently been given very complete instructions on these points before incarnation. I have never ever received any guidance (on such matters) from my parents . . .
>
> When I was fifteen, it came very definitely, suddenly at first, but often repeated, that I would be a philosopher, although I had but the vaguest idea as to what this word meant, and a few years later actually scorned studying the subject. This was an initial form of spiritual experience . . .
>
> I already knew at that time I was to pass through adolescence without meeting my sweetheart—very painful—and that my career would be tragic for some time. This made that year particularly hard.

In contrast to his inner life during childhood, Samuel Lewis had to face the stark outer reality that surrounded him. He was nine when the estimated 7.9 magnitude earthquake hit San Francisco, and 12 when the one family member he had felt close with, his great-grandmother figure Leonora, died in 1909. This left him even more isolated and without a sense of having any spiritual allies or friends.

The Earthquake, and the Family After His Birth

The problems Samuel encountered in adjusting to his household in San Francisco in the early years of the 20th century are easy to understand. An odd child, he must have been confusing to his parents and in some ways repellent to them. The intensity of his intellect alone would have been uncomfortable. His odd ideas and inner life were a further complication. His childhood efforts to give love and to receive loving acceptance in his family were met with aloofness and brushed away.

Somehow, this "ugly duckling" was destined to offer unexpected beauty to the world.

The great earthquake and fire of 1906 destroyed the Krouse home that the Lewis family shared with the now-widowed Leonora Krouse. The whole block was leveled in the devastation. Fortunately for them, the home was just outside one of the worst zones of damage, in which buildings on the unstable landfill over the watery Laguna de Manantial were demolished. Some residents drowned as buildings sank up to several stories deep into the muck. The primary water main for the city ran

1906 earthquake devastation, one block from Krouse household

through this area and burst when the quake first hit, a serious risk the fire chief had recently identified. The disruption of the water service caused firefighters to be ineffective throughout most of the city. By the afternoon, inside of 12 hours, half the heart of the city was gone.

There were hundreds of stories about what happened in the immediate aftermath. Numerous residents wandered in shock, while others whose dwellings were on bedrock flocked down to tour the destruction. Many displaced people camped in the park by Mission Dolores, cooking over fires as they weathered the aftershocks. They took care of each other. Samuel Lewis recorded no details of his experience, but there were family memories. Marilou Foster, Sam's first cousin once removed, recalled what had been said about the earthquake and Leonora Krouse's famous diamonds:

> One of the things [my great-grandmother] asked about is what happened to Harriet's diamonds, and if I had them . . . Evidently the best that we can surmise is that Samuel's brother gave them away to someone, or various people—ladies, of course—or hocked them, I really don't know, but evidently the diamonds were fabulous because my grandmother described them [as] just unbelievable. And during the . . . earthquake and fire, my Uncle Jacob went down to . . . the vault of the Levi-Strauss Co. building . . . he went through the fire to the vault to get the diamonds out—that's what kind of diamonds they were! . . . I have a picture upstairs of [Leonora] Krause with some of the diamonds on. We could all retire.[12]

Some family stories asserted that Leonora was descended from the famous Rothschild banking family and these diamonds were a part of that wealth. No basis was found for such a claim of ancestry. Leonora's father was a jeweler, and it seems most plausible that he had given the diamonds to Leonora.

Fortunately for the family, a place on solid ground on Ashbury Street was conveniently available to move into within a few months of the epic quake. A duplex, it accommodated both Leonora and Samuel's grandfather Morris—the latter only intermittently—in one flat, and the Lewis family in the other.*

Only the Cosmic Mother Will Do

Samuel Lewis many times wrote that his father never took any interest in anything that he did, and that his mother rejected every gesture of love he ever made toward her. He frequently referred to his mother as an extremely dominating woman and a source of a later complex of problems with older dominating women.

Around the time he was 12, Samuel came into conflict with a rabbi. He was studying for his bar mitzvah and spoke up in class. Sam had a prodigious attraction to the Bible, had thought about it, believed in the truth of it, felt very much in tune with the teachings of the Prophets, and was prepared to intellectually stand up for his viewpoint.

The Reform Judaism of the time did not emphasize the presence of the living God as an active force in history, nor the Voice of the Prophets who sought social justice and challenged religious and political leaders over their corruption. Samuel's later writings and teachings reveal how he would have been in conflict with this Reform perspective.

More than 15 years later, during his 1925 retreat, Samuel wrote a poem recalling the incident that suggests he must have spoken up in the voice of his namesake, challenging the teachings and actions of current religious and political leaders. The rabbi scolded him for acting as if he thought he were the Prophet Samuel. Whatever the conflict with the Rabbi was specifically about, Samuel was marked by it and the wound

---

*This building still stands, near the corner of Haight and Ashbury Streets, where the flower children who became Samuel Lewis's followers were gathering in 1967, the Summer of Love.

stayed with him. Additionally, the incident displeased his parents, causing them embarrassment and some social stigma.

The poem, "God, My Mother," excerpted below, views Samuel's childhood in a unique way. Having never experienced a loving relationship with his earthly mother, he turned to the Divine Mother. Samuel allowed that cosmic mother to speak with the voice he must have longed to hear from his own mother:

O Samuel! O Samuel! How long I have waited for thee!
Ever since thou wast born, I've always cared for thee.
I watched thee as an infant and each smile gave me joy,
I saw [thee] grow from babyhood—I watched thee as a boy.
And when thou readst My Bible, while still at infants age,
My heart did throb with Mother's Love, when you learned page by page.
And when thou wast a child at school and others did deride,
I never once deserted thee, was always at thy side.
Yet as the years passed one by one, and child a youth became,
And looked to others for thy joys, 'twas I who suffered pain.
When doubt crept in upon thy mind, and to others did you go,
The anguish that was in My Heart! Would that you never know!
O Samuel! O Samuel! When rabbi did chide thee,
And said thou wast not like thy namesake, why didst Thou blame me?[13]

In the beginning segment of this poem, one can see how it was important for Samuel to discover and feel that there was a greater Mother who always cared for him, who was joyful when he smiled as a baby, who was proud when he was drawn to the Bible, who never deserted him when he was teased at school, who was sorrowed when he strayed from the path. Such a mother would still see the truth of his being, even when the Rabbi rejected his spiritual nature, and she might sigh and wonder why the act of any man could make Samuel blame God.

Early Schooling

> *It is said that confession is good for the soul so I confess. I was born in a fairly well to do family here and was #1 at Lowell High School which is not exactly a moron's paradise.*
>
> Samuel Lewis[14]

Yearbook photo, 1914, Lowell High School

Lowell High was the elite high school in San Francisco during Samuel's youth. He enrolled as a freshman in January of 1910 and graduated on December 9, 1913. He accumulated 28½ credits, considerably more than were needed for graduation.

In addition to the required Mathematics and English classes, students in their junior year were asked to choose any three courses out of nine electives offered. Samuel chose seven(!): Latin, Greek, French, Chemistry, Physics, European History, and Economics. He received top marks in eight of his nine classes.

The yearbook for Samuel's senior year at Lowell provides the only meaningful glimpse into his school life aside from his own later writings. Among the items mentioned beneath Samuel Lewis's picture is the designation President. Samuel also chose to serve in a number of thankless areas, such as cafeteria staff and lost and found. His interests were clearly on the intellectual side, including Debate and Reading Club. The question remains of how his classmates saw him.

There is only one entry about Samuel in the yearbook by a fellow classmate. The class poem, sometimes called the class prophecy, was a tradition that many schools had during those days. One of the students was given *carte blanche* to write four lines of verse about every student in the class, making witty comments about them or making a funny or serious prediction about their future. Below are a few stanzas from the 1914 Lowell High class poem. The third stanza relates to Sam.

Picture Joseph Hyman,
Dressed in apron and jacket,
A waiter, spilling things around,
And raising quite a racket.

A curly headed lad there is
Whose middle name is borrow

Can't E. Hyman get this or that –
He'll pay you back tomorrow.

See Sammy Lewis rushing by,
He sure is in a hurry,
A Social leader he will be,
With motto, "I should worry."

The line "See Sammy Lewis rushing by" speaks volumes. Throughout his life, those who knew Samuel were awed by his mercurial nature: his mind and his body moved equally fast. He made a beeline to things quickly and your job often was to get out of the way. This poem demonstrates that he was always like that. "He sure is in a hurry" is a way classmates would have seen him, with little time to socialize, always heading toward some purpose of his own.

On all counts, the picture here is of someone following the beat of a different drummer. Samuel Lewis was 17 when he graduated from Lowell. He had been aware of psychic research and spiritualism from the age of thirteen, and he was already aware of Gandhi even though Gandhi was almost unknown in America. He also was attuned to world issues.

Resigned to what he saw as his fate regarding intimate relationships, Samuel was looking forward to pursuing further education. At this time the University of California at Berkeley was tuition free for those who qualified academically, and Samuel certainly did. He could at least get started.

Socialism in Berkeley: Zen Art and Mayor Wilson

There saith the Lord:
. . . The leaders want God and six percent interest,
The leaders desire God and money, God and debt.
May be zealous in sanctifying the seventh day to call it holy,
But the seventh year they regard not holy,
And the seven times seventh year they regard not at all.
The leaders have rejected the Jubilee . . .
When My ways, which are the paths of peace, are deserted,
There is no room left except for strife, for war, for bloodshed.

SAMUEL LEWIS[15]

Samuel Lewis was admitted to the University of California at Berkeley during the Summer session of 1914. He lived at home and had a significant commute to school via bus and ferry. His Drawing course that summer was the most memorable for him. His instructor was Perham Nahl, whose groundbreaking approach Samuel details in "Dharma Transmission."

> Professor Perham Nahl used to come occasionally to Nyogen Senzaki's Mentorgarten gathering. He had been an art teacher at the University of California where one had studied drawing with him. A friendship had been established. Professor Nahl went to Japan to study and returned a convert to Zen Buddhism. He introduced the principle of immediacy. He practiced the One Mind. He illustrated the teaching both in his own work and by introducing both Chinese and Japanese instructors. He became responsible for bringing Professor Obata to Berkeley. The doors were opened. Professor Nahl introduced the real and hidden values in the Zero and in the Infinite. One still remembers them.[16]

Berkeley was an ideal place for the young man described in "Intimations of Immortality," who in his late teens had an active and influential role within Socialist youth groups. Two years previously, in 1912, Berkeley had elected Rev. J. Stitt Wilson, the first Socialist Mayor in California history, and the most successful Socialist candidate ever to run for Governor of the state.

Samuel Lewis deeply admired Wilson and agreed with many of his ideas. Samuel mentions Wilson in the book *Glory Roads: The Psychological State of California,* which he coauthored with Luther Whiteman 22 years later, referring to Wilson as "a man who commands tremendous personal respect and who has been one of the great Moral Leaders in California." [17]

Mayor Wilson had been a minister before he went into politics. His view of the teachings of the Bible and their application to contemporary life coincided with Samuel's then and more than 20 years later, when the above poem was written. Here was someone with whom Samuel thoroughly agreed, and who had a large public voice that commanded respect.

Stitt Wilson became a major influence in Samuel Lewis's life. In a paper entitled "Moses: The Greatest of Labour Leaders," Wilson spoke of Moses and the Great Planks of Moses's Platform:

> The Socialist Movement demands that the land shall be socially owned by the whole people . . .
>
> The land, according to Moses, was never to be private property. The land belonged to the Lord—not to the landlords. This is the Jewish form of Land Nationalization. That means Social Ownership for the Equality of Opportunity to all. In case exchanges of use should occur in the process of time, in the year of Jubilee* every 50 years the land all went back to the original tribes and families. Any developing injustice was nipped in the bud. Socialists do not ask for a reduplicate of Moses' land laws. But we do demand the twentieth century application of the principle involved . . .
>
> The second form in which the power of Capitalism is exercised is by the laws of Interest. "If thou lend money to any of my people that is poor, then thou shalt not be to him, as an usurer, neither shalt thou lay upon him usury." † . . . The early Church fathers vehemently preached against it. Capitalism has succeeded in utterly silencing the modern pulpit on these questions.[18]

In "The Hebrew Prophets and the Social Revolution" Wilson relates the history of Israel and how the gap between rich and poor became wider and wider. The Prophets rose up to speak against these injustices in the name of God. Samuel Lewis does exactly the same in many poems. In his poem briefly quoted in the epigraph above, the poet speaks at various times in the voice of the Lord, the voice of Moses, and that of the Prophet Jeremiah. He also criticizes Marx and Marxism, in part because of Marx's rigid claims of the supremacy of his own thought and because Marx had nothing but contempt for the religious thinkers and brotherhoods, who had other ideas about how to live communally.

Samuel's common outlook with Wilson was reflected throughout his poetry and life. In "The Day of the Lord Cometh" (1938) Samuel wrote:

The ways of the spirit are for man.
Thus the days of the atom were days of inequalities,

---

*This is the Jubilee mentioned in the epigraph to this section.

† Exodus 22:25.

But the days of the electron are for equality and justice;
And as the electron reveals the light in things,
*So am I the Light in the things of earth and the spirit of man.**
The days of the atom fashioned the thoughts of the atom,
The differences of the atoms upheld the differences among men,
So where these thoughts prevailed, private property was upheld.
The days of the electron fashion the thoughts of the electron,
The identities of electrons suggest collective action,
Bringing new impetus to collectivism . . .
If it be wrong for capitalists to control the wealth of the world,
Is it not worse for the capitalizer to control the thoughts of men? . . .
In Mammon-lands is man robbed of the fruits of labour,
In Marxian-lands is man robbed of the fruits of thought,
In neither nor in both together is salvation found.[19]

In Samuel's prophetic poem on Christianity, "What Christ? What Peace?" (1942) he speaks in the voice of Jesus to the modern world, saying:

Look not to me upon the cross—
Look to the hospitals filled with the lamed,
The broken in spirit, the totally maimed,
The silent old houses whose youth have all left,
The widows and orphans and many bereft,
The millions of valiant returned to the dust,
While powerful editors lead on in lust
To stir up more madness, cast some new spell
To egg on the remnants to a still madder Hell,
That their private portions may be unaffected,
And all who oppose them remain unprotected,
Permitted in churches to bend their vile knees,
Using My name in their devilish pleas,
Producing more trouble and bringing damnation
To those who would uphold their proud civilization.
Look not to Me upon the cross—
I died in vain, I died in vain indeed
If for selfish gain, if for lust and greed.
I lived and died to help the human race,

---

*In Hebrew this becomes a pun on *adam* and *adamah*—man and earth.

And in God's heaven have prepared a place
For all of you—Christian, Hindu,
Muslim, Parsi, Buddhist, or Jew—
For the heavenly Father loves each one of you.[20]

Samuel Lewis's life was a passionate battle with religious hypocrisy. He showed a determination to reawaken the heart of religion so that it might again include loving consideration of all humanity and of all life. These ideals were implanted early in his youth and were confirmed and strengthened by Rev. Wilson's teachings.

Returning to this time in his life story, Sam is seventeen. He must still commute from Berkeley back to the family home in San Francisco where these radical thoughts would surely have met a deaf ear and been nothing more than fuel for the family story of his being a special kind of kook.

In Quest of the Super Miraculous

Youth comes to the Palace of Education. "Lord, I know nothing, show me." He places his hands on his forehead moving each in the opposite direction as if to empty his mind, and walks in. He walks in as if a Socrates and asks and asks and asks. Then he meets the Theosophists. "All religions are right. They differ on the outside when taken exoterically; they agree on the inside if taken esoterically. All religions are from God. There are seven planes of existence, the lower ones experienced in life after life, the higher ones only by sages and the illumined." The youth is satisfied. He thinks he has found the way.

Samuel Lewis[21]

The Panama Pacific International Exposition (San Francisco, 1915) was a vast world within a world. It appeared to eighteen-year-old Samuel Lewis to have been put there conspicuously and auspiciously for his exploration and inquiry. Driven by his persistent inner search for truth, he consciously prepared himself for the task of visiting the Expo, as described in the epigraph above from a short paper called "In Quest of the Super Miraculous."

Samuel had a breakthrough of awareness at the PPIE, which stayed with him over the years:

Panama Pacific International Exposition 1915

> In 1915 there was an international exhibition in my city of San Francisco; I decided that inasmuch as God, so to speak, had created many people, with many points of view and cultures, that my own might not be the favorite. After a few inquiries I came to a conclusion that all religions were correct, that mankind is subject to karma and reincarnation, and that there were states of consciousness beyond the here/now within the possibility of direct experience.[22]

Historian Frank Morton Todd described the unique nature of the PPIE in *The Story of the Exposition,* published in 1921:

> There is something in the nature of an international exposition that refuses to be satisfied with merely material exhibits. If corporeal exhibits, why not incorporeal? The job is only half done when you show what men are manufacturing. You must go ahead and show what they are thinking. To represent what they have to sell to one another isn't enough. In this twentieth century of ideals and idealism you must show what they mean to do for one another . . .
>
> The Exposition of San Francisco had a strong utilitarian character. It took the two themes of previous fairs, Religion and Learning, and sought to consolidate them and make them real and give them practical application to human life, through Service. This was the core and spine . . . There was no single large and conspicuous gathering, dominating all the rest, such as the Parliament of Religions at Chicago . . . but through

> the majority of the subjects discussed and expounded at the PPIE there . . . ran a consideration of the question, "What can men do for men? And how can the sciences help them?"[23]

This overarching question, What can human beings do for other humans and how can the sciences help them? aligned perfectly with the state of the young "Socrates" Samuel Lewis, as he emptied his mind and entered the grand gate of the Fair. He deeply wanted an answer to this question to help define his mission in life. He was less interested in the practical goals of the Expo than in his quest for the answer of answers. In emptying his mind, the question Sam was posing of the Universe could be framed, What is the truth that will help me most to serve the best interests of humanity?

The Expo was everything rolled into one, a combination of diverse elements letting out a complex cry of beauty, commerce, service, science, education, and humanity to a world that at that very moment was focusing its concentration on a war that stretched across Europe and Asia. The fair began in February of 1915. In May of 1915 the American liner *Lusitania* was destroyed, and America was drawn toward direct involvement in the world conflict. The PPIE soldiered on in the face of these world events and continued on a grand scale until December, hosting upwards of 19 million people.

Samuel Lewis also soldiered on. He set about investigating the claims of the Theosophists for the next few years, strongly sensing that they contained some truth. He continued to have discussions with a woman he met at the Theosophical booth, Miss Crane, who introduced him to several people associated with Theosophy.

At the same time, his spiritual realization was very much enhanced by a professor at the University of California.

The Influence of Cassius Keyser

The summer of 1915 was the last full session for Samuel Lewis at the UC Berkeley campus.* He had been there for an academic year. The high-

*He would return for individual classes many years later.

light of the summer term was an inspiring course on non-Euclidean geometry and mathematical philosophy with theoretical mathematician Cassius Keyser, a visiting professor from Columbia University.

> In 1915 I met Prof. Cassius Keyser, and became his disciple in mathematical philosophy. This led to an understanding of integration. I later re-studied integral calculus and asked myself, "Can't this be applied to philosophy and psychology as well as to mathematics?"
>
> In the course of years Keyser did this with philosophy and in part with religion. But the internationalist movements in psychology are very feeble indeed.[24]
>
> The more one studied Keyser, the more one learned about Zero and Infinity and Hyperspace and non-Euclidean Geometry and Psychology and everything else. Among his pupils was the late Count Alfred Korzybski.*
>
> One could discuss the Zero and the Infinity and Transpace of Keyser with Professor Nahl and the relation of these projections with actual Satori and Samadhi experiences. There were no social bars; there were no institutional bars.
>
> Some mathematicians threw out their own Georg Cantor for presuming the Infinite might be real.† We had no ecclesiastics then to throw out social peasants who found the Infinite to be real.[25]

What in particular was Keyser teaching? In his preface to the book *Science and Religion: The Rational and the Super-Rational,* published the year before, Keyser wrote:

> The following address aims to suggest and sketch a new way of thinking about old things of universal interest. The major emphasis falls upon the great function of Idealization regarded in the light of what mathematicians call the method or the process of Limits. The central thesis is that this process in the domain of reason or of rational thought indicates the reality and, in part, the nature of a domain beyond, a realm super-rational and that this realm is the ultimate and permanent ground and source of the religious emotions . . .

---

*Korzybski developed the field of General Semantics, which later became an interest of Lewis's.

†Cantor was shamed by some members of his academic community for his research on mathematical forms of infinity. Only toward the end of his life was he richly acclaimed.

> What then is the upshot? It is this. The creed of the limitless progressibility of human knowledge may be allowed the largest possible interpretation and validity, generation after generation centers of knowledge may continue to multiply where new-born wonder may take its rise and put forth antennae, to feel the touch of a thrilling world, the advancement of science may proceed far beyond any prescribed point or goal, and yet the Uncharted, the source, it is said, and support of all religion, will continue to surround us on every side as vast and deep and mysterious as the infinite abysses of space.[26]

The same year that he was teaching in Berkeley, Keyser had written in the preface to *The New Infinite and the Old Theology:*

> Some years ago, in the course of a lecture dealing with Mathematics regarded as a distinctive type of thought and with its relations to other varieties of philosophic and scientific activity, I ventured to say, "I do not believe that the declined estate of Theology is destined to be permanent. The present is but an interregnum in her reign, and her fallen days will have an end. She has been disposed mainly because she has not seen fit to avail herself promptly and fully of the dispensations of advancing knowledge. The aims, however, of the ancient mistress are as high as ever, and when she shall have made good her present lack of modern education and learned to extend a generous and eager hospitality to modern light, she will re-ascend and will occupy with dignity, as of yore, an exalted place in the ascending scale of human interests and the esteem of enlightened men. And Mathematics, by the inmost character of her being, is especially qualified, I believe, to assist in the restoration."[27]

Samuel Lewis's enduring interest in General Semantics is one example of Keyser's influence. Keyser had shown mathematically and philosophically that the realms of the infinite, the religious, and the scientific could thrive in common.

While Keyser's ideas were stellar and very advanced for his period in history, they would not have been of interest to anyone else in Samuel's family.

Back to the Family

At that time the world was consumed with World War I. The scene at home was tense. Elliott was in trouble with the law because of theft allegations. His parents were determined to rescue him from a jail record and fashion a place for him in local society, an end to which they devoted considerable resources.

Immediately facing Samuel was the very disappointing decision by his family that summer to cut off the funding for his education. This left unmet his needs beyond what free tuition provided. He later wrote of this decision, "My parents 'discovered' they had not enough money to send me through college. They needed the money badly to keep my brother from matriculating at S.Q. Varsity [referring to San Quentin Penitentiary] although it cost them a pretty penny."[28]

Samuel's parents did not believe that his participation in the University of California's course of study was beneficial. For Jacob Lewis, higher education was of little use. To appeal to his father's practical side Samuel had taken up a major in Civil Engineering, but that did not sufficiently move his parents to release funds. Samuel was forced to give up his formal academic studies.

Nevertheless, during the period after the PPIE, Samuel dedicated himself to reading the voluminous texts of Max Muller called *Sacred Books of the East,* a 50-volume set of translations of Indian classic Hindu teachings. Along with these he read the works of Thomas Rhys Davids, a British scholar of the Pali language and founder of the Pali Text Society for Buddhist texts.

After a number of years of study, Sam decided that Theosophy did not have the answer he was looking for. It proved too theoretical. There was much talk about spirituality without a definite program of study and practice leading to realization.

Samuel Lewis intensified his quest for the Real. Interestingly, his experiences at the Panama Pacific International Exposition continued to play a part in his movement toward the realization of his life's purpose.

The Quest Continues: Buddhist and Sufi Beginnings

Rabia was the name of a great woman saint of Iraq whose tomb has been visited by many people for over a thousand years. Earlier studies and researches had brought me to the conclusion that common interpretations of religion were either incomplete or incorrect; there must be some deeper meanings in them. Murshida [Rabia] Martin then took me on three journeys:

a. The mysticism of the Old Testament
b. The esoteric study of Comparative Religion
c. The Sufic discipline

But, though disciplined, she encouraged investigations into the mysticisms of all faiths.

SAMUEL LEWIS[29]

During 1917–1919 Samuel Lewis continued to share a room with his brother in the family home on 9th Avenue. He applied for military service several times and was always rejected for poor eyesight. He was listed as a "clerk" on his voter registration in 1917 and passed the Civil Service Exam that same year. In 1918 he was a student at Munson's Secretarial School, where among other skills he learned shorthand and typing, skills that served him well throughout his life.

Samuel spent a great deal of time in solitary study of sacred texts and in sitting with living teachers during this period. His encounter with Theosophy at the PPIE was followed in short order by life-changing openings into the Sufi and Buddhist paths.

"In Quest of the Super Miraculous" contains Samuel Lewis's concise assessment of Theosophy and describes a singularly important event of his spiritual journey. It begins here:

> November, 1919. This way [Theosophy] has proven only intellectual.
>
> He is on Sutter Street, looking at a display of books.* He is unaware but soon he is upstairs facing a little dark-haired lady. She is Jewish. "You can explain the Kabbalah?" "Yes, and all religions."

---

* Samuel in his writing often referred to himself in the third person.

> "What is Sufism?" "Sufism is the essence of all religions. It has been brought to the West by Hazrat Inayat Khan."[30]

Murshida Rabia Martin

Samuel Lewis had walked into the shop/library of Murshida Rabia Ada Martin, the first disciple of the first Sufi teacher to come to America. Initially he stared into a window display of books. Then without remembering how he got there, he found himself in her office loft.

Murshida Martin appeared at just the right time for Samuel Lewis on his spiritual quest. He had already arrived at the conclusion that the common interpretations of religion were either incomplete or incorrect. Now he was seeking a deeper understanding that would help answer his soul's questions.

His profound new connection with Murshida Martin was augmented when, six weeks after meeting her, Samuel met his first Buddhist teacher, Rev. M. T. Kirby. Through Sam's initiative, Rev. Kirby met Murshida Martin and they became friends, so Samuel was able to study both Zen and Sufism without conflict. Sam's studies in both areas were deep and consequential.

A letter Samuel wrote five decades later illustrated one way that he manifested being the "Protector of the Buddha Dharma," a role he was called upon to play. Samuel's point in the letter was that Buddhism had been distracted by its diverse egocentricities, and that it would do well to return to following the teachings and example set forth by Sakyamuni Buddha. The letter was addressed to the publisher of a Buddhist magazine, *Golden Lotus.**

---

*The correspondence continued, and the publisher strongly rejected Sam's positions as being without documented foundation.

It is almost fifty years since entering the Palace of Education at the Panama Exhibition here in San Francisco. I decided that a just God could not condemn humanity for wrong beliefs and I determined to seek "truth" without regard to past instructions or inheritances. Soon I came upon two booths next to each other, one occupied by the Theosophists and the other by "Right Reverend Mazziniananda Maha Thero."

I was soon drawn into two complexes, one the hyperbolic belief that the great masters were in Tibet and the other the struggle between "white" and "black" forces, between good and evil. And I found Mazziniananda, so called, definitely on the "wrong" side . . .

The true Dharma was introduced [in America] by Soyen Shaku under whose influence I came in 1919 to witness immediately two battles royal among Buddhists and Occultists with the same lines, and the beginning of attacks on this person by the lovers of Cloudnine ethereal-ism for daring to oppose those who were my "superiors"—this continues and will probably until my end.

We had then about three classes of Buddhists—the followers of Shaku Soyen,* the Pure Land [, and] the theosophical-Tibetans. The latter had then a legitimate leader, Dr. Vandernailen who . . . went down to Mayaland and claimed that these people also had the exoteric doctrines and this appalled everybody. What better opportunity for a champion of the Tibetans!

Mazziniananda was a sort of eagle-beak hawk-eyed person, nothing wrong in that but it could not be reconciled to his claim that he was a Persian prince (he did not insist he was legitimate) who had been educated in Tibet, which did not prevent a sharp British accent. He gave a service which he claimed was Tibetan but which a fellow of the Royal Asiatic Society, investigating, said was from North India. And there is no doubt he added thirty years to his life.

His sermons were obtuse and confusing . . . They were very ritualistic but now I can say they did not resemble Buddhist ritual, which I have either seen in person or in picture . . .

---

*Traditional name order for Japanese and Korean names places the surname first, followed by the given name. In the West, these names are most often ordered using the Western convention of given name first. Samuel was inconsistent in his writing. Original text in this volume follows Western convention.

Samuel Lewis with Buddhist Sangha

L. Adams Beck* has sent for Rev. M. T. Kirby to come from Engaku-ji to Vancouver where he was so successful the Japanese Archbishop Ichida either sent for him or was so ordered by the Japanese foreign mission group, and he was made "assistant" to Mazzinianánda. Kirby taught "Dhammapada," Shaku Soyen Zen, and morality. These, in combination with personality conflicts, led to a struggle both private and public . . .

Mazzinianánda had left "elementary training" to Kirby . . . [who,] putting the pieces together found out that [Mazzinianánda] had been a German doctor who had been stationed in India, learned a good deal of Indian rituals, and began a career. [Mazzinianánda] did give ordinations to people.[31]

---

*L. Adams Beck was one of several pseudonyms for influential British author Elizabeth Louisa Moresby, who wrote both fantasy and non-fiction on Buddhist, Theosophical, and other esoteric subjects. Her extensive travels in Asia and Egypt provided factual basis and settings for her work.

Soyen Shaku

Samuel became both a participant and observer of the earliest stages of Buddhism in America.

Rev. Soyen Shaku, the first Buddhist teacher to come to America, planted the most fertile seeds. He was the teacher of both Rev. Kirby and Nyogen Senzaki, who were soon to become Samuel's Buddhist teachers. The Rt. Rev. Soyen Shaku, Rinzai Zen Lord Abbot of Engaku-ji and Kencho-ji, attended the World Exposition in Chicago in 1893. A book of his talks entitled *Sermons of a Buddhist Abbot* was edited by his student D. T. Suzuki and demonstrates his universal approach. This excerpt is from Soyen Shaku's important talk on the Buddhist conception of God:

> I propose here to elucidate the Buddhist conception of God. At the outset let me state that Buddhism is not atheistic as the term is ordinarily understood. It has certainly a God, the highest reality and truth, through which and in which this universe exists. However, the followers of Buddhism usually avoid the term God, for it savors so much of Christianity, whose spirit is not always exactly in accord with the Buddhist interpretation of religious experience. Again, Buddhism is not pantheistic in the sense that it identifies the universe with God.
>
> On the other hand, the Buddhist God is absolute and transcendent; this world, being merely its manifestation, is necessarily fragmental and imperfect. To define more exactly the Buddhist notion of the highest being, it may be convenient to borrow the term very happily coined by a modern German scholar "panentheism," according to which God is (all and one) and more than the totality of existence.
>
> One of the most fundamental beliefs of Buddhism is that all the multitudinous and multifarious phenomena in the universe start from, and have their being in, one reality which itself has "no fixed abode," being above spatial and temporal limitations.[32]

This exposition by Soyen Shaku is completely in tune with the words of Cassius Keyser and with the perspective of universal Sufism presented by Hazrat Inayat Khan and Murshida Rabia Martin.

In a subsequent talk, America's first Buddhist teacher also spoke inclusively about the Goddess of Mercy. At the end of his text he said,

> To add one more word. It seems to me that the Virgin Mary of your religion corresponds to the Buddhist Goddess of Mercy, Kwannon Bosatz. Human nature everywhere seems to request what Goethe calls "eternal femininity." Christians according to their needs have created Maria. Though she is a historical figure, she has been invested with all the necessary qualities that will satisfy their inner yearnings. Buddhists have Kwannon, who, whatever her historical standing in critical Buddhism, fully answers their religious cravings.
>
> From the Christian point of view, Kwannon is a Maria incarnate; and from the Buddhist standpoint, Maria is a representative of Kwannon among a class of people who designate themselves Christians. The truth must be one and humanity the same everywhere, and it is my earnest wish that the time will soon come when the East and the West will all join in the adoration of truth, disregarding all their accidental differences and contradictions.[33]

Samuel described Rev. Kirby's history and teachings in the paper "Incense from Roshis":

> Rev. M.T. Kirby, an English Zen monk . . . had belonged to a Catholic order previously but his convictions had drawn him to Buddhism. He became in due order a disciple of Shaku Soyen who had given him the name of Sogaku Shaku . . .
>
> Kirby told me his story. He had to wait outside the monastery for three days before being recognized. He had had a background of culture, wealth and monastic living. Now he was compelled to dissociate himself from his entire past. This proved most difficult.[34]

Ultimately, Kirby was recognized by Soyen Shaku.

> [Kirby] visited British Columbia, California, Hawaii and Japan, functioning in the dual role of Zen Monk and Pure Land Priest. Here it should be stated that Buddhists in general are not analytical or dualistic

> like Westerners, and the functional differentiation of sects is not determinate. In later life Kirby also took the vows of a Theravadin *bhikku* (Pali term for "monk") and stayed at the Island Hermitage, Ceylon. Among his pupils is the famed Dr. Malalasekera.
>
> Kirby taught that Zen meant meditation; that it was derived from the Sanskrit *dhyana*. There were not many books on Buddhism in these days and we practiced meditation but did not have philosophical discourses. He introduced me to Beatrice Lane, Kenneth Saunders, and most important of all, the late Nyogen Senzaki.
>
> He also showed me *Sermons of a Buddhist Abbot* by Shaku Soyen. The Roshi* had much to say about God, having views quite different from intellectuals who teach comparative religion or talk about "Zen."[35]

Kirby may have been the earliest of Sam's teachers to impress upon him the primacy of practice over theory, which was to become one of Sam's central themes. As Sam wrote, "The true mysticism of the Orient comes in and from experience, not definitions, dialects or discussions . . . *Prajna*† . . . comes . . . with experience and not by definition."[36]

Sam went to Dr. Kirby's meetings, but the itinerant monk was soon sent to a post in the Hawaiian Islands. Sam described his early time with Senzaki:

> I first met . . . Nyogen Senzaki early in 1920. Like Dr. Kirby, he had been a student-disciple of that wonderful Shaku Soyen. He occasionally attended meetings at the Hongan-ji Temple on Pine St. where Kirby officiated. When [Kirby] departed, he urged me to become friendly with his [spiritual] brother [Senzaki], a friendship which continued until the latter's death in [1958].[37]

When Samuel Lewis established a relationship with Nyogen Senzaki as Dr. Kirby had suggested, he found himself as one of the first students in what Senzaki called "the Mentorgarten." Here's how Samuel described it years later:

> [When] I first met Nyogen Senzaki . . . he . . . was director of the "Mentorgarten." This Senzaki bore few resemblances to the Zen monk of later

* Roshi is the Japanese term for Zen master.

† Spiritual insight; perfect wisdom.

date. He was an intellectual authority, known for his acquaintances with many great books, not included in Mortimer Adler's lists.*

Nyogen Senzaki

The Mentorgarten was basically an intellectual institution. But we always did have short meditations during the evening. At that time, Mr. Senzaki (as he was generally called) conducted an open forum dedicated to Asiatica and not just Japan. He might lecture on Chinese poetry or have someone talk or demonstrate some phase of far Eastern Art, or there might be some traveler or explorer to entertain us. Philosophy, metaphysics and speculative thoughts were banned. Some attention was given to Buddhism, along the lines of Lafcadio Hearn rather than . . . Rhys Davids.[38] †

As a youth Senzaki was told by his grandmother that he had been abandoned as an infant and discovered by a fisherman from Sakhalin Island, Siberia.[39] He grew to have a number of teachers in both Soto and Rinzai Zen. In 1896 he studied with Soyen Shaku at Engaku-ji, a Rinzai temple in Kamakura where D. T. Suzuki was a fellow student. While in the monastery, Senzaki often turned to reading voraciously as a comfort. It was there that he encountered Friedrich Froebel, the originator of kindergartens. In 1901 Senzaki left the monastery with Shaku's permission to form what he called a "mentorgarten"—a kindergarten for children, a place free of religiosity and ritual, where children could be children.

---

*Adler was a scholar who had published volumes entitled Great Books of the Western World.

†Hearn was a man of many skills, a writer who mingled with the people of Japan and wrote stories for them and became famous abroad. Davids was a scholar of Buddhist texts in Pali.

In 1905 Senzaki traveled to the U.S. with Rev. Soyen Shaku, who had been invited by Buddhist students in San Francisco to give teachings. When it was time for him to return, Soyen Shaku told Senzaki, "Just face the great city and see whether it conquers you or you conquer it. Do not feel obliged to serve me any longer."[40] When Senzaki later chose to teach Buddhism, he identified as a monk rather than a priest—monks are not aligned with any temple but function independently, whereas priests are wedded to institutions.

Rev. Soyen Shaku also instructed Senzaki to learn how Westerners thought before he opened a *zendo*,* and not to open one for 15–20 years. When Samuel Lewis met him, Senzaki was learning the psychology of Westerners by living with them and observing. He supported himself with odd jobs such as elevator operator and language teacher. He was also known as a man very highly educated in Oriental Art and culture. At that time he rarely presented himself as a monk, but quietly continued his own meditation practice.

Sam described the transition from Mentorgarten to *zendo*.

> Then [Senzaki] suddenly changed his whole way of life in 1926, and for practical purpose the Mentorgarten died, the Zendo was born.
>
> With the opening of the Zendo conversation stopped. No more entertainments, no more discussion, even no more lectures for a while. The whole emphasis was on meditation. At first the meditations were quite short and easy. A paper might be read on how to meditate. We sat on chairs. The ritual elements were only slowly added. All we retained from the earlier period were the holidays or holy days. The meditations gradually lengthened. There would be rest periods, and then continued silence.
>
> As we became more attentive and skillful, there would be the chantings of the Pali Formula, the *Pancha Sila* (in Pali) and the Vows of the Bodhisattva (in Japanese). Occasionally we had readings from the Sutra of the Sixth Patriarch. Sometimes Senzaki-san would translate poems from the Masters of China or Japan. Some of these translations later

* Place of Zen study.

> came into print. But during the Depression Senzaki-san moved to Los Angeles and established his *zendo* there.
>
> I later became a member of the Los Angeles *zendo.* There was a gradual relaxation of strict discipline and a degree of intellectualism. But this was never introduced at the expense of meditation which was first and foremost, always.[41]

Years later Samuel Lewis would write, "The simple servant I met in 1920 has become a legendary figure. The great doctor of philosophy remains unknown. The Buddha-Dharma claims there is no abiding ego; *sensei* (Zen teacher) used to say: 'There is no such person as Nyogen Senzaki.'"[42] Samuel also said that Senzaki had taught him "seven forms of laughter."[43]

Samuel's regard for Senzaki was immense. Samuel wrote, "He was the Dharma-Master of the Age."[44] Senzaki was given the dharma name "Nyogen," which means "like a dream," from the concluding verse of the Diamond Sutra.*

Samuel brought Sufi and Buddhist worlds together within himself and in the outer world. He wrote:

> In 1923 I had the pleasure of introducing Nyogen Senzaki to the Sufi Pir-o-Murshid,† Inayat Khan. This was bringing a man who denied God (we would say) to another who held that nothing existed but God. Their meeting would have delighted Emerson. The two men sat opposite each other at a table, a mutual glance passed between them, and they both spontaneously entered into that grand state called *samadhi.* "Murshid, you would make a very good Zennist." "Mr. Senzaki, you are a brilliant Sufi." [45]

---

*Like a tiny drop of dew, or a bubble floating in a stream; Like a flash of lightning in a summer cloud, Or a flickering lamp, an illusion, a phantom, or a dream. So is all conditioned existence to be seen."

†Literally "Pir and Murshid," one who is head of a Sufi order and its lead teacher (Pir) and Sufi guide (Murshid); a term of deep respect.

Hazrat Inayat Khan (1882–1927)

CHAPTER 2

Years with Inayat Khan and Rabia Martin

Inayat Khan, the Pioneer Exponent of Sufism and Oriental Music, arrived in America in 1910, trusting in the injunction of his Pir-o-Murshid Syed Mohammed Abu Hashim Madani, the great Sufi Saint of Hyderabad, who struck the chord of his soul at the right time saying, when blessing him, "Go thou abroad into the world, harmonize the East and the West with the music of thy Soul, spread the knowledge of Sufism, for thou art gifted by Allah, the most Merciful and Compassionate."

THE SUFI CALL[46]

Murshida Rabia Martin (1871–1947)

THE PRIMARY SUFI INFLUENCES SHAPING SAMUEL LEWIS'S LIFE at this time were brought by Rabia Ada Martin and Hazrat Inayat Khan.

Ada's parents were Asher and Etta Ginsberg, Yiddish-speaking Jews from Poland and Russia who immigrated to San Francisco in the late 1850s in the wave following the Gold Rush. Ada was born in July of 1871 among many siblings, including a twin brother Joseph.

She made her way through public school, and at the age of 19 married David Martin, a successful businessman. Inayat Khan is reported to have described Mr. Martin as one who was not drawn to the outer trappings of spirituality but supported its essence with his whole heart.

Inayat Khan was from a noteworthy family of musicians in Baroda, India. He, his brother Maheboob, and his cousin Ali had formed a group call the Royal Musicians of Hindustan, which toured Europe and North America. Inayat accompanied his voice on the *rudra vina*.* During their West Coast tour, the group opened for the renowned modern dancer Ruth St. Denis, and it was at one of the performances in Seattle that Inayat initiated Ada Martin.

Having advanced on the Sufi spiritual path with his teacher Syed Abu Hashim Madani, Inayat had been given a *khilafat,* which permitted him to teach Sufism. He journeyed to the West at Madani's direction with the intention and prayer to use music as a means of transmitting the spiritual illumination of his soul, thus uniting East and West in a common spiritual understanding. As he learned, most Western ears were not yet prepared to hear the message in this form. Ada Martin was an exception.

Khan later described his 1911 meeting with Mrs. Martin in this way:

> At the end of my tour through the United States, when I arrived at San Francisco, I found the meaning of the scheme of Providence, that I was meant to come to San Francisco, a land full of psychic powers and cosmic currents, and begin from there the work of my Message. It is here that I found my first *mureed,*† Mrs. Ada Martin.
>
> I was welcomed by Swami Trigunata and his collaborator Swami Paramananda, who requested me to speak on Indian music to their friends at the Hindu temple . . . I saw among the audience a soul who was drinking in all I said, as the *Hamsa,* the bird of Hindu mythology, who takes the extract from the milk leaving the water. So this soul listened to my lecture on music and grasped the philosophical points which appealed to her most. She thanked me, as everybody came to show their appreciation after the lecture. But I saw that there was some light kindled there in that particular soul.

* An Indian stringed instrument.

† Disciple or student.

Next day I received a letter near to my time of departure from San Francisco, saying that this lady was immensely impressed by the Message, though it was given under the cover of an address on music and would most appreciate some further light on the path. I knew that she received the call, and wrote her that I regretted very much that I was leaving, but yet I could be seen at Seattle, a city at a considerable distance from San Francisco.

I had a vision that night that the whole room became filled with light, no trace of darkness was to be found. I certainly thought that there was some important thing that was to be done next day, which I found was the initiation of Mrs. Ada Martin, the first *mureed* on my arrival to the West and, knowing that this soul will spread light and illuminate all those who will come in contact with her, I initiated her and named her Rabia after the name of a great woman Sufi saint of Basra, about whom so much is spoken in the East. Since her initiation she has entirely devoted her life to spiritual contemplation and the service of humanity.[47]

In the short autobiography Rabia Martin wrote at her teacher's request, she described her experiences:

In my 28th year a deep grief came to me—and for four years I suffered much—and the problem compelled me to search deeper for the questions I asked of God . . . I was led into spiritual teachings and freed myself from pain and heart sorrow . . . After certain realizations came in the secret place of my own heart—I gave all to Allah and studied, served, prayed ever—to realize His laws—love—mercy and justice. This period of my life I call the reconciliation and spiritual regeneration, all praises to Allah.

I was not satisfied with the Western teachings, so made an independent study of comparative religions—and prayed Allah to lead me to the source—as thus far it was only drinking from a brook instead of the Ocean of Reality. Lecturers, teachers and advanced students here, I met always—but none touched my heart's longing—they all represented more or less the circumference. I longed for the center.

Then Allah sent my blessed Murshid, spiritually—and later in form. These mystical and blessed experiences I cannot give to the world—to me they are too sacred—this may be selfishness—I cannot share them. My blessed Murshid's Murshid too—may Allah glorify you both—came to me—and it can never be told in words—realizations which belong only to the Rabia not of this world—and so all I care for in this life is to worship Allah love and serve Him and Murshid and all Murshids in chain. May Allah keep my heart pure and my spirit humble (Amen).[48]

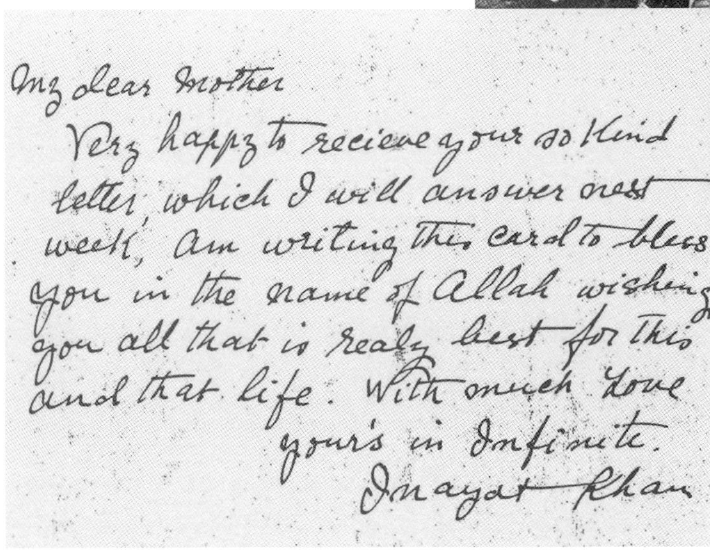

My dear Mother
Very happy to recieve your so kind letter, which I will answer next week, am writing this card to bless you in the name of Allah wishing you all that is realy best for this and that life. With much love
yours in Infinite.
Inayat Khan.

Postcard from Hazrat Inayat Khan to Rabia Martin

Rabia Martin later shared with Samuel Lewis that her experience of being blessed spiritually by Murshid Inayat came in the form of a vision of the Prophet Muhammad.[49]

Hazrat Inayat Khan continued to instruct Rabia frequently by letter after his departure from America for England in 1912. He did not return to America for another eleven years, but during this period he gave Mrs. Martin a rigorous program of mystical training.

During this time, Murshida Martin began to gather a small group around her, as well as a secretary, Mrs. Rebecca Miller, who shared her commitment to the Sufi path. Mrs. Martin spoke at events, including a series of lectures on the Persian poets at the Panama Pacific International Exhibition. There were notices in the *San Francisco Chronicle* about

Samuel Lewis, ca. 1920

activities at her center on Sutter Street. She occasionally shared a platform with Sogaku Shaku (Rev. Kirby).

Mrs. Martin's advertisements in the San Francisco newspaper often mentioned Kabbalah, and Samuel Lewis first asked her if she would be his teacher in that study. She said, "Yes, and . . ." He described Murshida Martin as thoroughly grounded in European mysticism; the mystical depth of the Old Testament was a major aspect of her teachings. Fabre D'Olivet and scholars like him probed the roots of the Hebrew language for depth of meaning and for a window into the inner message of the scripture. This became a significant factor in shaping Samuel's approach to the heart of religious texts and their revelation of transcendental unity and immanence. And through Murshida Martin, he began to attune to Hazrat Inayat Khan.

Given Samuel's ongoing aspiration to be of benefit, it is not surprising to immediately find him offering help to the circle of students studying with Mrs. Martin. He wrote a brief paper on the subject of inner communication with Hazrat Inayat Khan as early as the Fall of 1920. It begins:

> Revealed Sunday, August 18, 1920, at 9 p.m. Revised August 19
>
> One who has not learned about the nature of an iceberg, when he sees (one) will think and say: That is its real size and is all—not knowing most of it is under the water.[50]

Samuel's sense of his purpose in life was evolving during this period. His intentions were becoming clear. One aspect was that he wished to bring religious teachings and philosophical thought together into Oneness through an understanding of the ultimate source of all. He had an invaluable opportunity to study through Murshida Martin and her rich, inclusive library in the period before Hazrat Inayat Khan's return. She encouraged him to follow his enthusiasm and study the mysticisms of all faiths, an integral part of the Sufi Message. With his driving interest to learn and his unusual mental capacity, Samuel was overjoyed to feast in her ample library. Misraim, Martinism, the Kabbalistic order of the Rose Croix, and other esoteric and para-Masonic organizations fell within this orbit.

An inner blessing came, offering Samuel an esoteric relationship with Inayat Khan when he appeared to Samuel in a vision. They had yet to meet in person. Samuel reported on this experience in a paper called "Genuine Mystical Experience" written for a college class in 1966:

> On May 30, 1921 . . . Pir-o-Murshid Inayat Khan appeared to me (on five different planes or levels) and said: "Fear not, I shall always be with you." There followed a long period of pain and tribulation, but the consciousness of the Pir grew and grew until one entered into the next state, called *fana-fi-Rassoul.** [51]

It was two years later that Samuel first met Inayat Khan in person.

> Once one has met a real Mystic it becomes easy to distinguish the true from the false. In June, 1923, when I was ushered into the presence of Pir-o-Murshid Hazrat Inayat Khan, I had already met him in the spirit and it is noteworthy that he looked as I had seen him in "vision" and not like his pictures. However, in coming into the room there was no person, only a tremendous Light.
>
> I had recognized that Light, having read also the works of G. R. S. Meade on Gnosticism and "The Solar Body." But it was not just Light; it was a tremendous feeling of a binding Love. This binding Love has proved lasting . . .
>
> One feels as if in the air, or at least not touching the ground, expanded and elevated. And this experience has been an occurrence over and over again.[52]

Seeing that Samuel was blinded by this light, Hazrat Inayat Khan gently invited him to approach. He then offered him *bayat,* or initiation into Sufism– a confirmation of the "binding love." Samuel Lewis often

---

* *Fana* is the practice of effacement in a higher spiritual figure; *Rassoul* (or *Rasul*) is the Prophet or world-messenger. This Sufi term therefore signifies effacement in the Prophet.

said that Hazrat Inayat Khan was the first person ever to fully touch his heart. Meeting this awakened teacher was a moment of utmost significance for Samuel. The strength and confidence he drew from Inayat Khan's immediate and unconditional acceptance stayed with him throughout his life.

During the six weeks in 1923 that Pir-o-Murshid Inayat Khan spent in Mrs. Martin's home, he gave talks, conducted services, held interviews with initiates and others, and presented teachings to the circle around Murshida Martin. A new outer form of expression emerging from Hazrat Inayat Khan's Sufi Order was presented, called the Universal Worship Service. The practice had been crafted in Europe and was now being brought to America. It was a formal ceremony honoring all the established religions with readings from their different texts that incorporated a common theme. On an altar a candle was lit for each religion by a *cherag* initiated to this task, who helped perform the ceremony.* Recognition was given to "all those whether known or unknown who have held aloft the light of truth amidst the darkness of human ignorance." There was also a sermon.

Many years later Samuel Lewis wrote:

> In 1923 the Universal Worship was introduced by Hazrat Inayat Khan and was organizationally somewhat separate from the Sufi Order. But the Sufi Order provided the esoteric disciplines, in theory at least, by which achievements could be obtained in the outer world, God-willing. Therefore, in 1923 many disciples were given concentrations on the Temple—the finding of a place, the collection of funds, the building of an edifice. When Hazrat Inayat Khan returned to this country in 1926, he found that very few disciples, of which I was one, had gone ahead with the assigned concentrations.[53]

Samuel Lewis remembered Inayat's recommendations in relation to the world temple. It later became significant for Sam that Murshida Martin did not choose to act on the guidance Inayat Khan had given about this.

---

* *Cherag* in Persian means "lamp;" the word is here used to indicate an officiant.

Wars Within the Family Escalate

Things had gone very bad for my aunt and my uncle and they were not speaking to one another . . . It was a very uncomfortable visit at mealtimes because we would sit at the table . . . my aunt at one end and my uncle at the other, my cousins at each side, and my mother and I would sit by the side of a cousin. And my aunt [Harriet] would say, "Will you ask—tell your father, Elliott, that I . . . need so much money . . ." And my cousin Elliott would say to my cousin Samuel, "Tell father that mother wants to have some money put in her bank account," and my uncle would tell Samuel to tell [his] mother that the money he owed would be in the bank.

MILDRED WHITE[54]

Sam's first cousin Mildred White was the daughter of his uncle Harry Rosenthal and Harry's first wife, Maryanne Paralee (Pearl) Reames. Mildred had visited the Lewis family as a child of eight or nine and found them relatively normal. When Mildred returned to California in 1922 or 1923 with her mother and her daughter Marilou Foster, everything had dramatically changed. Mildred related:

> When I was 17 or 16 [ca. 1923] we were going to California again, my mother and I; I wrote my grandfather [Morris] Rosenthal at that time and he said that he would see me but not my mother. So I wrote back and said that then I couldn't see him . . . [Eventually] he accepted my mother and I in his apartment, which was kosher, very kosher. The food was all on the different plates and the different types and like that, and it was the first time that I had ever been in a kosher home . . . [During this visit] Samuel was only home for a few days, and he was very busy. I think he was engaged in some sort of business at that time; he was only home at dinner time . . . The whole house was only together at dinner . . . and this was the way it always was at dinner all the time. My uncle had the large master bedroom in the house . . . and my aunt had the room across the hall. They did not share the same rooms.
>
> All I can say [is] there was no outward evidence of ill feeling, but there was just a strain. It felt like people were at war, and of course my aunt and uncle were.[55]

Marilou described this atmosphere further:

> [Jacob and Harriet's relationship] was sick. Even as a 13-year old [I could see it.] I knew nothing about this when I walked in. My uncle brought me home a box of candy from Sees one day. My aunt didn't speak to me for two days because I not only accepted the candy, but I ate some . . . The cats would get up on the table and eat from the table . . . while we were eating and I found out subsequently that my Uncle Jake was a fanatic about cleanliness, keeping things up, and this house stunk of cats, cat hair all over—and he was an asthmatic—I know now, that those cats were in the house to kill him. She would have had 100 of them if she could have. There was absolutely no communication between them. They hated one another . . .
>
> [Harriet] never shared a room with [Jacob] after the birth of the second son . . . [Jacob] fell in love with a . . . third or fourth cousin that came to town—and at one point was really contemplating a divorce, and I don't know whether the grandparents stepped in or if it was a thing that he would have lost his position at Levi Strauss, but family pressure was put on him—in fact the cousin was living here [the house on 9th Avenue] for awhile . . . And that was the end of any communication between the two of them.[56]

The year when the two parents stopped talking to each other appears to have been around 1922. Jacob and Harriet Lewis then continued to live in the same house for another 32 years without ever speaking a word directly to the other. Nevertheless, their public image was important to both of them. Harriet remained active working with orphanages and they maintained a respectable façade.

That Jacob actually brought his mistress into the house, Marilou believed, was the event that ultimately severed all communication between Harriet and Jacob. The eerie family drama pitted two strong-willed people in battle, and the children, from their perspective, were basically pawns in the game. Harriet's strong will, in particular, was a significant influence on Samuel while he was growing up, and created an ongoing psychological trigger for him over the years.

Rising above the increasing dysfunction in the family, Sam continued to pursue his soul's calling and entered a life-changing retreat prescribed by Murshida Rabia Martin at Kaaba Allah, her newly developing Sufi center in Fairfax, California. He went into seclusion with training both in Sufic practices and meditative Zen.

Samuel's Visionary Retreat in 1925

From the street of my friend bloweth the soft breeze of the Dawning Year,
With whose help, if thou wishest it, thou mayest light the lamp of thine own heart . . .
Go into the garden, and there steal from the nightingale the secret of love:
Come to the assembly, and hear from Hafiz how thou shouldst sing a song.

HAFIZ, GHAZAL XV[57]

The verses of Hafiz guided Samuel Lewis's initial days on retreat. Murshida Rabia had sent him into the wilderness to read this much-loved Sufi poet and Samuel was inspired to write about him:

> Picture him and what do I see? Smiles! One big smile, bearing joy to all who greet him. He is like sunshine, bringing comfort and courage. In my days of darkness he was with me, guiding me, encouraging me, showing me the way, always smiling, always cheerful. When I look at the beautiful trees and pleasant meadows of sunny California, I picture him in his rose garden at Shiraz and feel that Hafiz, had he not been born where and when he was, this country with its lovely scenery and beautiful weather would have brought inspiration to his heart, and ode upon ode would have resulted.[58]

He then wrote a short verse in the manner of Hafiz:

I hear the blue birds twittering in the trees,
The leafy branches fluttering in the breeze,
While I sit here, musing at my ease,
Thinking of thee, Hafiz.
The trees around me Spring has clothed in green
On hillside and in lovely vale between,
A typical lovely California scene,
Reminding me of thee, Hafiz.
And now to study and to read thy book,
'Neath shelt'ring trees and in this lonely nook,
For though alone, God has not forsook me,
Nor thee, Hafiz! [59]

One imagines Samuel, a few days into this retreat in the solitude of nature, free from the dominating pressures of his parental home, shedding layers of impressions, and emerging from his gloom. But now, with

Khwaja Khidr

many heavy burdens left behind, he began to awaken to his own natural goodness. Among other writings, Samuel Lewis composed a divan of poetry during the ten days of retreat. The verses of Hafiz guided his initial days, and then dramatic events began to unfold.

> That night as he was doing his spiritual practices he felt a presence and he was sure it was Khwaja Khizr.* There are many legends of Khwaja Khizr. Even some Western occultists have accepted the reality—of the legends. When it comes to events that is something different again . . .
>
> Sooner or later we are going to have objective honesty in esoteric branches of culture. And that is why these reports are being given. **Sufism is based on experiences and not on premises** . . .
>
> There was a recurrence of this appearance of Khwaja Khizr on the second night and then on the third. He offered poetry or music. Sam chose poetry. On the third night there was a long argument—why was the poetry chosen and not the music? . . .
>
> Actually, it was not a choice. It is merely a different story.[60]

---

*Khwaja Khizr (the Green Prophet) is a legendary figure among Sufis. Like the Prophet Elijah he is considered to be an undying presence on planet Earth. Murshid Sam used the spelling "Khizr" as the name would have been pronounced in India. In Arabic pronunciation the name is generally transliterated Khidr. *Khwaja* is an honorific title particularly used for Sufi teachers; literally "lord" or "master."

The poetry was immediate, and the music came afterwards, first as the embodiment of the Flute of the Masnavi and then as the Flute of Krishna, which was demonstrated many times. The music came, and with it the Dance.

Many years later Samuel wrote about the effect of Khwaja Khidr's appearance at the retreat:

> One had Hafiz's teachings for study and like the great poet of Shiraz, one was visited by Khwaja Khizr. The world has not accepted this person's poetry but it is forced to face that longevity and **élan** which are nothing but Grace.[61]

A visitation of Khwaja Khidr is said to bring great longevity and remarkable personal life force. Samuel Lewis is referring to this vitality, which he fully embodied in his later life and which was undeniable to those with whom he interacted. He ascribed this blessing to Grace, a spontaneous gift of God.

After the third appearance Sam began writing without interruption. His retreat writings included two Allegories, two lessons on the Logic of the Finite and Infinite Universal Laws, two lessons on Spiritual Cosmogony, the Art of Creation, On the Name of God, *Zikr,** Pesach Passover, Will, Bible Thoughts, *Nufs,†* Reincarnation, Beauty, Hafiz, Notes on Rumi, and Initiation. Fortunately, the scrapbook of papers that he wrote on this retreat survived a massive fire on the Fairfax property in 1949. That fire destroyed 35 years of his research and writing as well as a magnificent spiritual library.

For the rest of his life Samuel Lewis continued to be an incessant writer of poetry, prose, spiritual commentaries, essays in a wide variety of fields, and worldwide correspondence. It is almost impossible to exaggerate the quantity of his work. Much of this material has been gathered online and is available at murshidsam.org, referred to from here forward as the Archives.

---

* *Zikr* is a form of devotion, chiefly associated with Sufism, in which the worshiper is absorbed in the rhythmic repetition of a sacred phrase or a name or attribute of God.

† *Nufs* (also *nafs*) is an Islamic term for the incarnated soul, often rendered as "ego." Transliterations of many foreign-language terms vary. Original text in this volume corresponds with spellings presented in the Glossary.

Samuel wrote a letter entitled "Initiation" to Murshida Martin on the last day of his retreat.

> **"PEACE ON EARTH, GOOD WILL TOWARDS MEN."**
>
> Here in your wonderful room I sit, awaiting the hour of noon, when the sign of the cross shall be made in the heavens, and the sun pass over the equator. This lovely room with its spiritual atmosphere—here where I have sat in meditation, morning, noon and night for the last twelve days—an atmosphere of calm and peace . . . There seems to be a sign over the door: "Abandon all **Fear** ye who enter here."*
>
> Yet not one hour have I been alone; God said—and it is noted in the diary—that an angel with a flaming sword stood outside and only those who could see, could pass. So the birds remained and other creatures and humans never disturbed me. "You have nothing to fear but yourself." And God Himself has been with me . . .
>
> Over your bed there is a quotation: "The Light Eternal According to the Kabalah." And I have felt that where Gewurz failed, I have succeeded; that I might bring joy to your heart both as a *mureed* and a son of Israel. I saw Gewurz' handwriting on the wall of the front room and felt it was "handwriting on the wall."†
>
> I have brought with me every word I have written in diary, articles, poems and essays to lay them this morning on the altar of Him alone Who is Creator. Step by step have I risen, to find myself in Him. Every prophecy or hint in the diary has been realized . . . I have felt at times like a mosque with my head as dome reflecting the light from underneath. Then I have felt as a circle with a point inside . . . And it seemed that Pir-o-Murshid stood on the left, nearest my heart . . . His nearness to my heart brought love. You seemed to be behind or even in me, my very backbone, giving strength and courage. Hafiz was in my forehead,

---

* Years later Murshid Sam used this phrase again in his epic poem "Saladin" when the character of Saladin is taken on a journey through all the heaven realms. The quote in the poem is "Abandon all tension ye who enter here." For the full text of the poem, see the Archives.

† Elias Gewurz was a learned Jew and Theosophist who wrote many books on the Kabbalah. He used permutation and numerology as well as the signatures of each Hebrew letter in his analysis. In *The Mysteries of the Qabalah and Sepher Yezirah* (South Carolina: CreateSpace, 2008), Gewurz sought to unfold the *Sepher Yetzirah*, a central text of the Kabbalah, in which the principles of the letters and the associations between the letters and the tree of life are explained. Samuel Lewis used the teachings of the *Sepher Yetzirah* in his mystical poem on Judaism, "The Day of the Lord Cometh" (Archives).

holding the mirror there, that the light from within might be reflected without. And the Rab on the right side seemed to be guiding my hand, even using it himself.*

Murshida . . . My words first seem like a baby trying to speak and day by day the inspiration increased until suddenly I saw "The Art of Creation." And if I have not gone more deeply into the Truth, it is because I myself have asked God to guide me slowly and make my steps sure.

When you handed me the *Awarifu,*† you were giving me a gem of esotericism! But who can see it? Step by step I saw and realized what *Nufs-Nachash*‡ was.[62]

"The Art of Creation," written the day before, brings light to Samuel's statements above.

The first element in creation is Motive. There must be an urge, a desire, an impulse. This motive with God was Love. God is love and He wants to be loved, and for this reason He created the Universe—and man . . .

If we were to make a geometric picture of creation, it would be in the form of an expanding wave, as a light wave . . . Light, sound, electricity, heat all give, they do not get . . . Many philosophers recognize this and have said: "Being is motion." But when we want to preserve ourselves, we are consciously or unconsciously making ourselves the center of a universe, trying to shine as it were as a star. And it is this centripetal force that causes all known as "Evil," which is really disharmony.

Many of us are acquainted with the symbol of the interlaced triangles§ . . . The white triangle with apex up represents God. The apex is Love and the lower points Harmony and Beauty. Or we may give them other names, but if analyzed the meanings are the same . . .

Very often words are placed near the interlaced triangle: "*Diabolus est Deus Inversus.*" "The Devil is God turned upside down." In Hebrew this word for "devil" is *Nachash.* And what does *Nachash* mean? A hidden desire, a yearning, a tendency to draw to a point. And this is what *nafs*

---

*Rab was Samuel's affectionate name for Fabre D'Olivet.

†*L'Awarifu-l-Maarif* (sometimes rendered *The 'Awarif ul Ma'arif*) is a highly respected Sufi book of instructions for the seeker by Sheikh Sohrawardi (or Suhrawardi).

‡*Nachash* is an encoiling around one's constructed idea of self, a force of taking, not giving. It was translated from Hebrew into our Scriptures as a serpent.

§In the Jewish tradition this symbol is of course known as the Star of David. Sam here gives a Masonic interpretation.

> means and Ego means . . . Geometrically this is centripetal motion. And we see it everywhere, animals killing other animals, not only for food, but for pleasure, men doing harm to their fellow-men, each striving. "Every man for himself, and the devil take the hindermost." . . .
>
> Adam and Eve were in bliss in Paradise. *Nachash* bid them to eat of the fruit of the tree of knowledge. Why was it wrong to eat of the fruit of this tree? Because the fruit belongs to God. Man was to enjoy happiness [and] express love, but the fruits of his actions were to God. And as soon as he took to himself the benefit therefrom, a clash of forces resulted . . .
>
> Man himself has therefore created evil and disharmony. And by disobeying the Law of God. Every sage and prophet, teacher and Messenger has acted otherwise and endeavored to teach mankind to act otherwise . . .
>
> O, fellow-man, if you want peace on this earth, if you want concord and harmony, bring it first into your daily lives! . . . You will find your true method from within.[63]

Samuel Lewis had finally begun to find his "true method from within" and was uncovering previously hidden inner resources. "Initiation" continues:

> My greatest joy was the pleasure or happiness it might bring you, that you have another *mureed.* I feel (I have) passed the stage of *Shari'at* and well on the road of *Tarikat,* towards *Hakeekat.** [64]

In saying he had passed through the stage of *Shari'at,* Samuel Lewis indicates that he had set aside his ego and fully accepted the God reality.

Samuel was beginning to prepare for a final ritual, incorporating some of the principles learned from Murshida Martin as to how to proceed. He now felt ready to launch his prayer and take his place as a representative of God. Samuel later described this in his paper "Genuine Mystical Experience":

---

*The stages of the Sufi path as explained by Hazrat Inayat Khan in *A Sufi Message of Spiritual Liberty* (London: The Theosophical Publishing Company, 1914), 39. *Shari'at* refers to prescribed laws. *Tarikat* refers to the steps in the spiritual journey leading toward unity, and often is synonymous with Sufism. *Hakeekat* (often transliterated *haqiqat*) is the mystery of God's own self-knowing without any intermediary to reflect upon.

On March 21, by this same *kashf** I performed a ritual and it ended by perceiving in open daylight (twelve noon to be exact) the procession of the Messengers of God and their forming a circle to perform a cosmic dance, whereupon all merged into One. At that time I saw the Prophet Mohammed, double, the other ones singly, and took this as a sign to begin Qur'anic studies. I had already studied most other scriptures, at least superficially.

Then a robe (*khirkah*) was bestowed on me. That same robe was later bestowed in front of the Shrine of Moin-ed-din Chishti in Ajmir,† India.[65]

In "Initiation" he wrote:

Last night it seemed as though Christ Himself were with me, giving me the instructions He gave to His disciples when sending them forth and repeating ever and anon, "Be wise as serpents and harmless as doves." So long as I remain true to God, I feel I can reflect His Light and help to spread the Message, to go to Los Angeles or anywhere. "The Lord is my shepherd, whom should I fear?" I am [ready] to teach the New Testament and explain much of the Old with God's help and under your directions . . .

The more I have pondered, the more I found that the Prophet Mohammed himself was expressing the greatest principles of science inwards, that God is Love and He is Beauty, etc. I am beginning to see further into the great declarations of Judaism and Islamism, to see behind the philosophy of Plato and Pythagoras in ways I could hardly dream of . . .

Truth has always been on earth, despite deluders [who say] that it has been kept from man except at certain ages and in secret ways . . . The mysteries have never been lost and never will be lost, but their outward form may change. Today one joining the Church of Universal Service is really being initiated into the Lesser Mysteries.

My future—that is in God's hands. It is now four and one half years since I began studying with you and five and one half since we met. I have always wished to carry on the work of the Rab and it may be so. I have also desired to continue the true American Philosophy of Emerson and Whitman . . . Now I leave all these things to God, yet feeling if I

---

* Insight, revelation.

† Now Ajmer.

keep my covenant with Him, my wishes will come true. I have already dedicated all to Him . . . But I shall go slowly.

The gift of poetry is entirely from Him. I have never cared for poetry but I feel more and more the spirit of the Sufis, and I almost can say "with God's help and Hafiz" I may succeed.[66]

Samuel had been drawing wisdom from many sources. Among the poems in The Diwan there is a short and sprightly one celebrating this.

MY RELIGION 3/21/25

Call me a Christian, call me a Jew,
Call me a Parsi, if you wish to.
Call me a Hindu, call me a Sikh,
Or Mussulman, for Allah I seek.
Call me a Taoist, or lover of Buddh.
A worshipper of Nature, or that which is Good.
My religion is "Love, Harmony, Beauty."
If it needs a name, why, call it "Sufi."[67]

You will note in my diary . . . I feel I have realized my name:

Samuel Shemuel "In the name of the Lord," even "The word or the voice of the Lord."

Leonard: Leon is a lion; **Ard** from Arduus, valiant

Leonard: Valiant as a lion

Initiation comes from the Latin and means "a beginning." . . . Every day have I read much from the "Gayan"* and step by step realized it. I feel I am ready to begin, Murshida. I feel I can say, "God bless you" to others as you have said it to me.[68]

"The voice of the Lord, valiant as a lion," is a noble description of Samuel's spirit. Those who knew him well in the last decade of his life would agree with its accuracy. For what may be the first time, Samuel Lewis is taking a fully optimistic view of his future, a tidal shift in perspective.

My meditations have been like the cleaning of machinery at night so the factory will produce more at day. I have needed little sleep. My

*The "Gayan" is a collection of sayings of Hazrat Inayat Khan. It is available in the Archives, with Samuel Lewis's commentary, under the title "Gayan: Notes from the Unstruck Music of Pir-o-Murshid Hazrat Inayat Khan."

> brain has been as a servant, actually working on hours, not allowed to work at certain times and often getting tired while working. I have not read my diary or articles over except to make two small changes in poems. I hand these to you. Some may be ready for publication in *Sufism*. I should like the "Maypole" to appear in *Sufism* at an early date, if it be your wish . . .
>
> Soon I enter into my last meditation before the sun crosses the equator. I again thank you with all my heart and soul and mind for your benefits and blessing, and to Him above be all honor and glory forever. Amen.
>
> Faithfully and sincerely,
> Your *mureed* and disciple in Israel.[69]

Samuel's reference to himself as a "disciple in Israel" may require some explanation. In a paper "Pesach Passover" written three days earlier, he had observed: "More [and] more one sees that Israel typifies mankind in general in its search for God." [70]

A new life was dawning for Samuel. With this day in 1925 the door was open for him to write confidently on many subjects. He planned to depart for Los Angeles after completing his last concentration, filled with gratitude for Murshida Martin and her guidance.

The Enduring Influence of Khwaja Khidr

> *Grace is beyond intellection. And now on my 70th birthday I can attribute the strength, the energy, and even the prowess retained as the result of Grace, and the blessings received from Khwaja Khizr in 1925. And these experienced blessings were accepted in full by Pir-O-Murshid Hazrat Inayat Khan but generally rejected by those who claim some sort of "Sufic" knowledge from him.*
>
> LETTER TO SUFI BARKAT ALI[71]

There is no doubt that this retreat changed Samuel's life. He wrote: "I have felt like Walt Whitman, without a grain of conceit, I am full of good things. I never knew I contained so much goodness, for I have found I contain God, and all Goodness is in God."[72] This is an extraordinary affirmation from someone who had been a struggling young man, hammered down by his family and facing continuing rejection and disinterest, his perceived faults always recited for him.

By grace and his own dedicated effort, Samuel had broken through the muck of his mind and emotions and found his essential goodness, a veritable cornucopia of blessings. On this retreat he was able to clear his inner space of all confusion and competing impressions, and the light of his true self arose with joy. The guidance he received confirmed his relationship with the Sufi path, and Samuel showed his appreciation of Murshida Martin's esoteric teachings as well as her dedication to them. Khwaja Khidr gave him his legendary transmission of living vitality as well as the gift of poetry, with more arts, such as music, to come.

Samuel had written, "There are many legends of Khwaja Khizr . . . If you believe in legends you are 'saved,' but if you propose that your belief is based on actual experience, that is a sure sign you are a pretender and damned."[73]

Khwaja Khidr figured in the lives of many Sufis and some religious scholars over the centuries. As with Samuel Lewis, Khidr blessed the poet Hafiz with a visitation. Hugh Talat Halman states in *Where the Two Seas Meet* that both Hafiz and Samuel* received the power of poetry from Khidr as a grace, not as a delineated formal gift.[74] And like Sam, Hafiz gave up his plan for marriage in exchange for a spiritual calling.

Khidr also appears in a very well-known Qur'anic story in which he becomes the teacher of Moses. Khidr is able to assume this role because he has an immediate direct knowing that Moses lacks. The great Persian poet Rumi had an inner relationship with Khidr, and Rumi's son, Sultan Veled, attested in his book *Ibtida-nameh* that Rumi's Khidr was Shams-i-Tabriz. Even outside of Sufism, Khidr has played a significant role. In the story of Alexander's search for the waters of immortality, Khidr is the instrument for finding these waters.

---

*Halman refers to Samuel as Sufi Ahmed Murad Chisti and as Murshid Sam.

What distinguishes Khidr in all these stories is that his knowledge is wisdom directly from the source without any other intermediary. "And we taught him knowledge from our presence."[75] The immediacy of his knowing of things unseen in the visible world and the inner world, without depending on any external teaching, distinguishes his state. Murshid Sam shared this faculty, which Halman describes in a section entitled "Al-Khidr as Living Qibla and Model of Spiritual Masters:"

> The figure of al-Khidr provides a point of direct transmission of the knowledge and presence of God. Al-Khidr stands between the temporal world of human experience and the eternal world of divine majesty, grace, and truth with all its force of paradox.
>
> Where questions of authority are raised, where chains of transmission falter, where certainty of connection is unclear, al-Khidr arrives as the symbol, proof, and presence of divine transmission, continuing revelation, and theophanic witness in human form.
>
> Al-Khidr stands at the horizon of that potentiality intimated in Adam and Joseph and the succession of Sufi masters: that certain gifted persons function as a human *qibla,* the point of orientation and direction by which one knows and fulfills the summation and essence of the spiritual path . . . [76]

Samuel Lewis was destined to become one of those rare, gifted individuals who are graced to embody the role of Khidr. He was as rough-hewn as Khidr is presented, and he lived whole-heartedly in immediacy.

Family Challenges Continue

The impetus of Samuel Lewis's spiritual elation arising from the 1925 retreat carried him to Southern California and liberated him from the family home in San Francisco. The move to Los Angeles at age 29 was Samuel's first foray into living independently from his family. He found clerical work at the Whittier State School, a detention center for boys now known as Fred Nelles School. Suspected of being a political spy, he was discharged in December of 1926. The error was subsequently realized and he was invited back to the school.[77]

Concerns about his family, however, continued to haunt Samuel. His mother Harriet's stubborn dominating will, as well as her frequent verbal abuse, had left a deep mark on him. Samuel's heart sympathies lay with his father, whose world was in shambles. Jacob's reputation was tarred, his marriage vows were a sham and his younger son, Elliott, appeared to be a thief or worse.

Elliott was then living in New York City. Many elements of his life were viewed as morally deplorable in the family. He periodically accumulated considerable gambling debts, and with the loss of his job, the financial consequences mounted. Elliott appears to have been bailed out of these financial misfortunes by his father, and his reputation was kept as untarnished as possible through Jacob's apologies.

Now, perhaps for the first time, Samuel was coming to grips with his brother's situation and its effects on his father, and it clearly distressed him. This is apparent in a letter he wrote that Spring (1927) to his Aunt Hatty. Henriette (Hatty) Davis was Jacob Lewis's only full sister and someone Samuel clearly trusted.

> I have slept well these last two nights and am feeling pretty good, but last evening I almost broke down. I keep on learning so many bad, if not terrible things about my brother, that I can hardly understand where he could have gotten such wickedness into his system. While I was pondering on these things and listening to the radio, some club took charge of the program (KFI, Los Angeles) and began putting on sentimental songs about "mother." That was just about the last thing to put pep in me so I had to go to my room.
>
> Well, I have learned one lesson, and that is, if I feel very good or very bad, I try to write poetry. I tried and although I did not succeed very well, got the following in blank verse.
>
> *A PRAYER FOR MY FATHER!*
>
> *God give him strength to fight, though hard the fray.*
> *Give him the courage to bear the battle blows;*
> *Guide him in these hours of darkness and despair;*
> *Show him the light, and Lord, please lift the veil*
> *That he may see a step or two ahead.*
> *O Lord, I pray Thee lighten his burdens a little,*

A little that, though stormy be the way,
Though terrors seem to encompass him about,
Disperse the clouds, and let a ray of sunshine
Pierce the gloom. O God, may the end be now in sight,
An end to these torments and these tortures;
Though time be needed, let the time approach
When he may have peace and rest, though years pass by
Before he leaves his mortal frame and enters
Into a world where sorrows abide not.
O God, give me strength to aid my father.
May my next years bring happiness to his heart,
Make me a source of pride and joy to him,
And may the future show the way
That he may see in me a son of his,
And I see and treat him as my father.
O God, give him hope, and may Thy Mercy
And Thy Grace rest upon him even as I write.
May he have that faith which leads to Peace,
That faith in Thee, remover of all pain
And sorrow, Source of all that's good.
O God, help my father, I repeat again,
Give him strength and courage, from this day forth.
Amen. [78]

The letter to his aunt concludes, "It certainly is a Hell we are going through."

Hazrat Inayat Khan's Last Visit

In December of 1925 Hazrat Inayat Khan returned to America for what would be the last time. After journeying across the breadth of the country, undertaking numerous speaking engagements and events, he arrived to stay with Murshida Martin in San Francisco. She took him to Kaaba Allah in Fairfax, Marin County, crossing the Golden Gate by ferry. Inayat highly praised the atmosphere of the rock formation that dominates the Fairfax site and named it *Pir Dahan*, "The Voice of the Pir." Later it was called the Voice of the Prophet following the inclination of people to see Inayat Khan as a world teacher. The rock provided a natural seat for meditation.

Hazrat Inayat Khan

After his stay in San Francisco, Inayat continued south to Santa Barbara and Los Angeles, accompanied by Murshida Martin. The driver they selected was one of his *mureeds*, Paul Reps, to whom Inayat Khan had given the name Saladin. Saladin Reps and Samuel Lewis were already acquainted, and in the forty subsequent years Reps could easily be said to be one of Sam's closest friends.

Years later in an extended interview Reps was asked how he remembered Hazrat Inayat Khan.

> "He was the most remarkable man I ever met . . . It was as if one's soul were speaking all the time . . . He would say, "Call me Inayat," because he was completely humble and completely at peace and completely relaxed and completely concentrated at the same time. His eyes were concentrated to one point, which was outside his body a few feet; but he looked right through your forehead all the time when he talked to you. And yet at the same time, he was utterly at ease and said nothing for himself; he was always letting you do the talking and drawing you out. But he was certainly practicing what we might now call "Sufism" or the mind on the breath, or however you want to interpret it.
>
> And this kind of a presence, with this great gentility and kinglike bearing and rather tall body and complete modesty simply overcame those who had never seen anything like it. They were very much impressed and extremely touched by his sympathy for them, and everyone felt, "Here, at last, is the one person who understands me thoroughly."[79]

Murshida Rabia Martin

In this interview Reps also talked about Murshida Martin's personality and recollected the car ride:

> I knew her for . . . ten years or more. She was very faithful to Inayat Khan, and she was his first representative here in the West . . . She was very much attracted to him, and her husband was too. But she was a stormer. She would continually complain, vigorously complain, that people should be different.[80]

Quite aside from other people's judgments, Rabia Martin gave much the same description of herself within the short autobiographical statement she wrote at the request of Hazrat Inayat Khan:

> My folks had a difficult time of it I guess because when I played with children I wanted to lead them and they had to follow or there was no play for me. My sense of justice in my world of play was so marked—they did not understand me—and consequently my family felt I was too positive and all sorts of advice went unheeded. Of course you know I could not accept less than the ideals of my childish heart, and somehow as I grew older I felt quite alone within the family circle.[81]

Six Interviews with Pir-o-Murshid

Inayat Khan received Samuel Lewis for a series of interviews at a luxury hotel in the Los Angeles area. What Inayat revealed at that time offers an important lens through which to view historical events and to understand much of what subsequently happened to Western Sufism and to Samuel Leonard Lewis.*

The date of Samuel's first interview arrived:

---

*In addition to the sources directly quoted, the following has been composed based on versions of Samuel's account of these meetings written in the 1960s, along with additional references. The original account was burned in the fire at the Sufi *Khankah* (gathering place) in 1949.

> One had to keep quiet about one's mystical experiences until they were reported to the teacher. Although one began studying with Murshida Rabia Martin in 1919 and one had many of the same types of experiences that one can read about in Sufi literature (that is, literature by Sufis) and also in legends concerning Sufis by others, one restrained oneself.
>
> But one also felt, and it proved to be true, that the real spiritual teacher would accept anything and everything, psychical, occult, and spiritual or mystical, coming from the disciple. Indeed, as Hazrat Inayat Khan has said, but his followers, badly divided, rejected, "It is the *mureeds* which make the Murshid."[82]

At this first meeting Samuel Lewis reported in full the events of his retreat of 1925—keen memories that, according to him, had been marked in the ethers. When Samuel entered the retreat he had been at the end of his tether, believing he was going into the wilderness to die. Instead, he was surprised to emerge with an embodied experience of resurrection.[83]

Hazrat Inayat Khan saw Samuel's authenticity and accepted his report. The Pir-o-Murshid listened and told him to write the whole experience down in detail. Samuel told him about his vision of a company of illuminated souls including Prophet Muhammad, who appeared twice and on horseback. He also spoke of the appearance of Khwaja Khidr. Inayat then asked Sam to come back the next day or as soon as possible. The next day's interview was unforgettable.

As Samuel entered the room Pir-o-Murshid stood up and motioned to him. Then he took Samuel's hands in the position used for initiation and said, "I initiate you for the sixth time in the Sufi Order." When Samuel later looked at the organization's early records, he found that he had been initiated as a "Sufi."* It was an appellation he refrained from using for many years until confirmed in Asia by several Sufi Pirs.†

> Before we sat down, Inayat Khan said to me, "Samuel, I am going to ask you a favor. I want to speak to you as man to man. I am not Murshid;

---

* The designation "Sufi" recognizes a deep level of realization. Prior to that level, it is considered appropriate to say rather that one follows the Sufi Path.

† The Pir is the lineage holder and head of a Sufi order.

> you are not *mureed*. We are just men. If we cannot act as men, it will not help me. Can you act to me as man to man? If so let us shake hands and then we can sit down and talk as man to man."
>
> We did so and sat down. "How many loyal *mureeds* do you think I have?"
>
> "Oh, I guess about 100."
>
> "I wish I had 100. But how many do you think, at the least, loyal *mureeds* I have?"
>
> "Well," I said, "I don't believe it, but just to give an answer, I would say 20."
>
> "I wish I had 20! I wish I had 10."
>
> Then he lifted his right hand, and using the index finger of his left hand, pointed to it, and yelled, "I wish I had 5 loyal *mureeds*. Samuel, can you believe it, I have not as many loyal *mureeds* as I have fingers on one hand."
>
> By that time, the chair in which I had been sitting toppled over like in a Hollywood movie, and I was sitting on the floor, totally amazed. But, by this action and by his loud speech, I received the full magnetism of his *baraka* or blessing, and I believe I still have it.[84]

What appeared as an expression of personal pain from his teacher transmuted into a source of strength for Samuel. In many of his writings Murshid Sam attributes his *jalali** strength to this *tawwajeh,* or spiritual merging experience with his Pir's vibration. He felt the depth of mastery and power by which Inayat Khan would eventually transform this "frightened young man," as Samuel described himself in his account of these interviews.[85] He was destined to become a valiant, lion-like voice of God, and the spiritual transmission from Inayat Khan in this moment was an undying experience from which Samuel Lewis would always draw.

Organizational Difficulties

> *Though Murshid Inayat Khan never lied or betrayed his fundamental convictions, he habitually improvised with a fine sense of what his* mureeds *did or did not want to hear and of what he had to concede to them to protect his family and esoteric school. In the end, the cumulative weight*

---

* *Jalali* refers to the manifesting of power.

> *of numerous small concessions caught up with him and contributed to the deep frustration of his last year in the West.**
>
> Hendrik Horn [86]

To understand Hazrat Inayat Khan's complaint that he had fewer loyal students than the fingers on one hand, it is necessary to examine some of the history of Inayat's time in England and Europe, and especially what transpired in the organizational development of the Sufi Movement, the corporate successor of the Sufi Order.

Before leaving India on his initial journey to the West, Inayat Khan was interviewed by the Mysore newspaper:

> My sole object of travel is to admire the works of God by appreciating music as it exists in the different parts of the civilized world, and thus come into close touch with God's higher power. Besides, I have my better and superior interest to do good to my fellowmen and enable them to improve by means of this Art.[87]

Hazrat Inayat Khan and family took refuge in London when World War I broke out. Raden Mas Jodjana was part of Inayat Khan's circle in London and was one of the very few drawn to him who truly appreciated classical Indian music for its inner spiritual content.

He gave her an independent course of study while recommending that she not join the Sufi Order, which was then in the process of being established. Inayat wished to hold Raden to a higher standard. She perceived a gap between her teacher's actions and those of the people gathered around him, who coaxed him to speak on Hindu Yogis and similar subjects of interest. They wanted him to speak out and literally give them the meaning of mysticism in words rather than experience. Inayat Khan accommodated their interest, which he could easily do by calling on his treasury of knowledge, but this radically differed from his training under Hashim Madani, with its traditional methods of direct transmis-

---

*This is a historical judgment by Hendrik J. Horn, annotator of Theodoor van Hoorn's text *Recollections of Inayat Khan and Western Sufism*. Horn acknowledged on many occasions the great debt he owed to Shaikh-ul-Mashaik Mahmoud Khan, the son of Maheboob Khan, for bringing knowledge and resources to him in his research. The publication of *Recollections* was commissioned and financed by Nekbakht Foundation.

Inayat Khan and his family in London: his brothers Maheboob and Musharaff behind him, his wife Begum Ora Ray Baker and children (L to R, Noor-un-Nisa, Khair-un-Nisa, Himayat, Vilayat)

sion from the master and the unquestioning observation and willing surrender of the disciple. Under the circumstances he was ready to compromise and adopt this very needed means of supporting his family.

As a result, Inayat Khan was recorded on numerous subjects and this became a source of ongoing study material for his students. The *Githas,* as the study documents were later called, began to be developed during this early period. The organization that Inayat Khan chose to call by the generic title "the Sufi Order" was forming around a nucleus of interested souls.

There were many levels of organization described in the papers of the Sufi Order but the real power at this time was in Inayat's close family circle—his wife Begum Ora Ray Baker, his brother Maheboob Khan, his cousin Ali Khan, and his youngest brother Musharaff Khan were all listed as the executive committee, which held the highest power.

Only Jodjana had been granted permission to be a member of Inayat's close family circle. She wrote: "In the intimate circle of Inayat Khan's family in Addison Road, we formed the first group in England of initiated adepts. Begam, his young wife, and I were the only women in his circle. Inayat Khan taught us all to master emotional states causing reactions in conduct and expression. And he submitted all of us to severe tests."[88]

Hazrat Inayat Khan's first published work, *A Sufi Message of Spiritual Liberty,* was printed by the Theosophical Publishing Society in 1914. He gave the central practices of Sufism, including many teachings drawn from the Islamic practices done by the Sufis over the years. As a member of the Chishti Sufis of India he naturally included the importance of music.

> It was not long before the "intimate circle" of Addison Road expanded and gave rise to a growing organization. The burgeoning organization announced itself by means of a journal, titled *The Sufi: A Quarterly Magazine,* the first issue of which appeared in February 1915.[89]

The first characterization of Inayat Khan's Sufi teachings in list format appeared in the magazine. Here are a few examples:

1. To overcome beliefs and disbeliefs by self-realisation . . .
4. To be pure from distinctions and differences by merging into the Oneness.
5. That wisdom is the true religion . . .
7. That music is food of the soul and the source of all perfection.

The Objects of the Order were similarly described:

1. To establish a human brotherhood with no consideration of caste, creed, race, nation, or religion . . .
2. To spread the wisdom of the Sufis, which has been until now a hidden treasure, although it is indeed the property of mankind and has never belonged to any race or religion . . .
4. To harmonize East and West in music, the universal language, by an exchange of knowledge and a revival of unity.
5. To bring forth Sufi literature, which is most beautiful and instructive in all aspects of knowledge.[90]

In his annotation of the events of this time, Hendrik Horn points to a major difficulty that arose as a result of Inayat's teachings found in this volume and elsewhere:

> By explicitly and repeatedly identifying Muhammad as the last of the Messengers and the reason why no more world teachers were needed,

> Inayat Khan also identified his revered "message-bearer" as the one great obstacle to his own apotheosis to world-teacher status, as fervently wished for by his Theosophical *mureeds.*

During this London period, Horn tells us,

> Murshida Sophia Green, a friend and former associate of the Theosophist Annie Besant, emulated Besant's picking of Krishnamurti as a world teacher by doing the same for Hazrat Inayat Khan in her own promotion of him and his teachings. As might be expected, this development was resented by his Christian followers . . . as well as by his Muslim friends.
>
> Things came to a head in the fall of 1920 in England when Hazrat Inayat Khan's espousal of the teachings of Islam put him on a disastrous collision course with a wealthy follower who almost literally threw him and his family out of house and home . . . The Islamic origins of Western Sufism had become its best-kept secret, having succumbed to a conspiracy of silence, collective amnesia, or outright ignorance.[91]

In his early writings, Hazrat Inayat Khan had made a very prominent place for Prophet Muhammad and his teachings. He had even written both a full length and a brief biography of the Prophet,[92] but no one in the West had wished to publish either of them. Here is a representative sample of what did appear from him on this subject:

> When democracy was necessary, Mohammad gave his message as the Servant of God, one like all and among all; this put an end to the necessity for more prophets, because of the democratic nature of his proclamation and message. He proclaimed *La elaha ill' Allah,* None exists but God. God constitutes the whole being, singly, individually and collectively, and every soul has the source of the divine message within itself.[93]
>
> This is the reason of there being no more necessity for mediation, for a third person as a saviour between man and God when man was evolved enough to conceive the idea of God's being all and all being God, and when he was tolerant enough to believe in the divine message given by one like himself, who is liable to birth, death, joy and sorrow and all the natural vicissitudes of life . . .
>
> The message individually received will never come to an end . . . The ideal of the divine oneness which was the main object of Muhammed's message has inspired the world, its influence being in some parts known

> and in some parts unknown. The light of guidance shines as brightly as it shone before, and will ever be the same.[94]

In London during and immediately after World War I, Inayat Khan had reached out to the Muslim community. "He collaborated with Ikbal Ali Shah, father of Idries Shah, to create a new organization called Anjuman Islam, the purpose of which was the promotion of a better understanding between Christians and Muslims."[95]

Just as many Christians were put off by the prominence of Muhammad in Inayat Khan's teachings, some Muslims were put off by the inclusive elements of his Sufi Order.

> Ikbal Ali Shah, the vice-president of the Anjuman Islam, was remembered in the family oral tradition as having vigorously disapproved of the Sufi Order's policy of admitting non-Muslims. Marmaduke Pickthall, an English Muslim soldier and novelist, was invited to join the Sufi Society as an honorary member. He was, however taken aback by the October 1917 issue of *The Sufi,* which listed seven "Sufi teachings."[96]

The one that provoked his opposition states: "There is One Holy Book, the sacred manuscript of nature, the only scripture which can enlighten the reader." Pickthall considered the Qur'an as the final Revelation and refused to associate his name with a movement that was not purely Islamic.

Inayat Khan, replying, said:

> To a Sufi, revelation is the inherent property of every soul. We do not shut ourselves off from any community, but are ready to be united with all and any, for within we are already united with the Infinite. Our Order is composed of truth-seeking people of different faiths and beliefs, who are not in any way obliged to give up the faith or belief they have nor to accept a certain faith or belief, nor are they, if they have none, compelled to adopt one.[97]

Despite resistance from people who were not ready to accept the idea of Anjuman Islam, Inayat Khan refused to abolish it. At least in part for this reason his sponsor Margaret Skinner turned him and his family out of her house on short notice, while saddling him with a substantial bill for supposedly unpaid rent. Hendrik Horn recounts this history:

> Virtually destitute, Inayat Khan was left to depend on faithful followers such as Nargis Dowland . . . and eventually new friends in Geneva. The incident taught him the hard way that unlike any Indian guru, he would have to work hand in glove with those of his *mureeds* who became his leading followers, allowing them to pursue their own preferences.[98]

He and his family soon returned to continental Europe.

> The fat fly in the ointment was that Inayat Khan's converts, who had often been Anglicans and/or Theosophists, wanted to cling to just about everything that they had held dear before they met him . . . But once his conception of Beauty had become estranged from the disciplines of India's music and mystical practice, his Sufism lay wide open to invasion by followers who craved some kind of artistic, bureaucratic, esoteric, hierarchic, magical, mysterious, ritualistic, or supernatural embellishment to his core concerns.
>
> And while Murshid's pursuit of harmony through meditation was a suspect notion and hard sell outside a select circle, the "unity of religious ideals" offered a distinctive doctrine of tolerance that stood a real chance in the world at large. No wonder it quickly became the ecumenical flagship of the Movement.[99]

However, a number of people, including Samuel Lewis, strongly felt that the Sufi Movement had made a major mistake in putting their main focus on the ceremony of all religions. Doing so was seen as diminishing the role of Hazrat Inayat Khan's core teachings, which were aimed at awakening a full living awareness of the One and Only Being.

Editorial problems were reported in *Recollections.* Here's what the annotator had to say:

> Secretarial problems went much deeper than the kind of sporadic incompetence described in *Recollections.* Murshid intended his pithy admonition, "Do not change my words" to stop the endemic interpretative interventions of early secretaries and editors who had ideas of their own, and too little understanding of his deep cultural reservoir or profound underlying intentions.[100]

Inayat Khan had learned how to accommodate some of the wishes of his followers in Europe and to sincerely integrate them into his own message. As much as he tried to clearly present the tradition of Sufism and the teachings of Muhammad, his Theosophist and Christian followers were not willing to go along. Realizing this brought Inayat pain, and he continually sought a hybrid approach to give birth to a spiritual movement all could embrace without departing from his core truth.

But trouble was brewing. Within the organizational framework of the Sufi Movement an event occurred that changed everything. Hendrik Horn described what transpired in Geneva in September of 1925 as "a fateful climax" and attributed it to the endemic scheming of Hazrat Inayat Khan's closest followers.

Pir Zia Inayat Khan of the Sufi Order (now the Inayatiyya Order) later addressed this particular topic in some detail in his doctoral dissertation at Duke University, "A Hybrid Sufi Order at the Crossroads of Modernity: The Sufi Order and Sufi Movement of Pir-o-Murshid Inayat Khan."

> As Pir-o-Murshid of the Esoteric School, Inayat Khan functioned in the traditional capacity of a spiritual teacher endowed with the perfect authority of a "perfect man "*(insaan-i-kamil)*. As Representative General of the Sufi Movement, however, his role had yet to be defined in practice . . .
>
> In Inayat Khan's absence, a proposal was made . . . to abolish the Representative General's plural vote in the Executive Committee. Essentially at issue was the role of the Pir-o-Murshid, as Representative General, in the management of the organization. Did the Sufi Movement exist to serve the Pir-o-Murshid's agenda, or did the Pir-o-Murshid exist to serve the Movement's agenda?
>
> Supporters of the amendment—Sophia Green, Sirdar van Tuyll, Mumtaz Armstrong, and Dr. Steindamm—emphasized the distinction between esoteric and exoteric authority: "We feel that it will keep Pir-o-Murshid as an esoteric head, we wish to lift him out of the question of voting . . . It is not an esoteric matter, but an administrative manner. It is now the moment to revise these rules."
>
> Those opposed to the amendment, of whom the primary voice was Sharifa Goodenough, challenged these views. "It has been said Pir-o-Murshid is dependent upon information brought to him by people who come to him. This is against the most elementary knowledge of what a mystic is. A mystic is not dependent on what various people tell him."

> The motion was put to a vote, the result of which was ten in favor of changing the Articles of Incorporation and seven against. The Chairman consulted with Inayat Khan, who was present in Geneva though not in the meeting, and returned to report that the Representative General had cast his vote in the negative, bringing the negative votes to eleven and causing the resolution to fail . . .
>
> Inayat was not flattered. On the contrary, he was profoundly offended. His response is perhaps best understood in the context of a passage from his own teachings: "When a disciple begins to judge the teacher or his actions, to criticize his teachings, or try to test his inspiration or power, however cleverly he may do it, he ceases to be a disciple in the right sense of the word. It may not seem very bad to many, but there is a thin thread connecting the pupil with his spiritual guide, and at any moment this can easily break. Once broken it can never be mended."[101]

Disclosures from Inayat's Interviews with Sam and Letters to Rabia

In his dissertation Zia Inayat Khan wrote further about this period following the events in Geneva. He draws here from a family conversation shared with him by Sheikh Mahmoud Khan in 2005:

> Inayat had reached a terminus. His family could no longer restrain him from leaving for India. He privately confided that if Allah meant for him to return to Europe, he would alter his activities completely. He said, "They want to play games. Well then, let them play games from Geneva or wherever they like. I will only withdraw into private life of meditation and reflection here, at home, in this Oriental Room. And should any *mureed* on his own, truly serious and sincere, want to come and join me for a while he or she will be welcome to do so. Only that." [102]

Paul Reps was asked about Hazrat Inayat Khan's organizational difficulties, and he confirmed Samuel Lewis's description. "Hazrat Inayat Khan said to Murshida Martin in my presence: '[The Board of the Sufi Movement] have taken my organization completely away from me.'"[103] Shedding further light on some of the problems in the organization, Reps added:

> [Inayat Khan] was and is a very great teacher. Unlike all the other teachers, the teaching was humble instead of assertive . . . However, he had initiates which he gave various ranks to, and they fought so much, that when leaving for India [in 1926] he said, if he came back again to the Western world he wouldn't have anything to do with these ranks, you see, because it was misused.[104]

In 1925–26, still in the tailwind of the affair in Geneva, Hazrat Inayat Khan had made his last trip to the U.S. He spoke at the Waldorf Astoria, delivered lectures in Detroit, and had an epic meeting with Henry Ford.* He continued West, stayed for some time in San Francisco, then continued to Los Angeles, where the previously-mentioned interviews with Samuel Lewis took place. At that time Inayat Khan confided further in Samuel about what might be forthcoming organizationally.†

> Inayat began telling me that he wished me to defend Murshida Martin of San Francisco, who had been my original teacher (1919–1923) . . . I was to stand by her and protect her, but see to it that she never defended herself. He went over that again and again. He said he expected trouble and that he had seriously searched for one honest man he could trust and found Mr. E. Cruzat Zanetti.

Samuel was advised to write to Zanetti if difficulties arose. According to Samuel's reports, his teacher continued to reiterate his main points:

A. Pir-o-Murshid Inayat Khan intended that Murshida Martin be his successor.

B. She was never to defend herself on any occasion and positively never in public.

C. She was to divest herself of all right to handle funds.

---

*For an account of this meeting, see Pir Zia's dissertation, "A Hybrid Sufi Order at the Crossroads of Modernity: The Sufi Order and Sufi Movement of Pir-o-Murshid Inayat Khan" (PhD diss., Duke, 2006).

† Murshid Sam's original accounts were destroyed along with many of his papers in a fire. When he wrote later drafts of his interviews he could no longer indicate with surety what occurred in each of the specific interviews. As a result, further content from Sam's drafts has been blended in this account. Quotations not directly attributed, here and in later chapters, have been assembled in this way.

What led Pir-o-Murshid Inayat Khan to give such profound recognition to Murshida Martin? Answers can be found in the correspondence between them, which provided her with an extensive training in Sufi practice over the course of many years.*

Ada Martin, in a letter to Inayat Khan written after meeting him in 1911, declared:

> I have waited for years to hear someone express publicly the truth of all art, be it music, painting or poetry. I have always wondered at the lack of understanding which exists in the minds of the majority of people who profess to teach, not even hinting to students, that the first step in self-development along any line whatsoever, must have its basis in spiritual laws.[105]

Inayat was moved by Mrs. Martin's great interest in his teachings. In Seattle, where she had followed him, he initiated her and immediately started her on Sufi practices. His early letters of instruction included the following, written on May 4, 1911:

> I shall be too glad to give you lessons in this, but my style of practice being quite different you will have to learn it from the beginning. There is not any charge or compensation for my lessons as this is a spiritual message and I consider it my duty to impart it.
>
> Practice. Keep it quite private. Sit in the yoga posture turning to the left knee (*La-El*) to the right knee (*La*) to the right shoulder (*Ha*) turn to the liver say *El-Ella-hoo. Mantram:* Nothing else but God. Concentrate during the practice on the meaning. Do it two hundred times in the mid night, counting beads, at about 11 p.m. and finish the practice by saying: *Sal-lal-la-ho-Alai-he-vasal-lam.*† Yours respectfully, Inayat Khan.

He also wrote out the musical notes for her to use with the practice.

---

*The letters of Hazrat Inayat Khan to Murshida Martin were preserved by Sufism Reoriented and are in their archives. A copy of them given to Pir Zia Inayat Khan as an aid for research on his doctoral dissertation was shared with the research team. Excerpts from many of these letters are offered here. Unattributed correspondence in the balance of this section is drawn from this material.

†This traditional phrase refers to Prophet Muhammad, saying "God bless him and his family and grant him peace." It can be rendered in the shorter form "Peace be upon him" and is often abbreviated in writing as "PBUH."

Inayat wrote again from Columbia University in New York on June 13, 1911, and as he often did, addressed Rabia as "Mother."

> Dear Mother, Very glad to know about your advancement in the Sufism . . . You are the first lady in the western world whom I have found full of the merits that a Sufi possesses in the East. With my best wishes and love. Yours in the infinite, Inayat Khan.

In a letter a week later also from the Columbia address (June 19) he wrote:

> Dear Mother,
>
> I gratefully thank my Lord, my masters in connection with the spiritual chain, for their so kindly inspiring their light and power into your heart and soul. You must rest assured that all your spiritual guides under the chain are responsible for your development . . .
>
> I want you to find out the God in the usual things that you are experiencing by your five senses . . . I have sent psychic vibrations . . . now I write . . . that you have to repeat the exercises once every day. After your present course of forty days, I will teach you a very nice way of having a psychic communion between us.

On June 30 he again wrote.

> Dear Mother,
>
> The practice of *zikr* makes a kind of fire lighted in the body and heart. You feel warm affection to whatever you see or hear or experience . . . Now what you have to do is to see every form and think of *La ilaha el ellahoo* as the meaning of the form that you see. It may be a human, bird, animal, tree, stone anything, even your own body. Consider nothing but the form of God . . .
>
> P.S.
>
> The presence of mine that you feel near is the infinite self of mine that is very complimentary; it is the proof of your advancement in the Sufi study. The words that you have heard are the promise of the embodiment of the chain, represented as my words. You must take it as God's promise for your salvation. The dream that you saw, was of my Lord, my love, my father, my Master, my Murshid in whom I have already sacrificed my self. The ceremony was nothing but the assurance of your being united by the *bayat,* the initiation in the chain of the Sufis. Also it was the realization of your being one of them.

Five days later he added: "All the praise of your advancement in this line is due to our masters in the chain who are sending the vibrations of their joy, love and peace."

On July 17 he wrote again.

> I am extremely glad to see you progressing according to my views . . . While practicing *fikr** you must clear off all thoughts from the mind and strongly think of your Murshid . . . Then try to watch your breath day and night continuing the same practice. After some days it will be so much accustomed to the practice that you will not take a single breath unconsciously. And then you will be praying to God almighty for day and night . . . Try not to lose even a single breath without the *mantram* . . . Yours in the Infinite, Inayat Khan.

On August 7, still in New York, he wrote further about how to continue her process of visualizing Murshid with eyes closed as well as open. He then introduced Mrs. Martin to a practice of remembering Muhammad. This practice of offering Allah's blessings to the Prophet was one that in later years he learned not to give his students in Europe:

> The following mantra is called *Darood*† and is the best thing to recite in the morning. This is in the praise of the perfection of the nature in the form of matter and the spirit, and this will create divinity, immanence, and give you spiritual power and devotion. After mastering this for a few days I will guide you how to use it for different affairs.
>
> *MANTRAM (DAROOD)*
> *Allah huma salleh alah Saiyadina*
> *Mohammadin wa alah alle Saiyadina*
> *Mohammadin wa barik wa Sallim*
>
> Recite 1100 times every morning and keep incense burning because while you will recite this all our beloved Masters' souls will be around you with all love and devotion, respect and humility and intoxication. As well as the great Master of the Sufis *Sarkar* Muhammad himself will send his reflection upon you as he sent on the Sufis like Shams Tabreez, Moulana Rumi, Saadi, Hafiz, etc. With all love and best wishes. Yours in the Infinite, Inayat Khan.

---

* Following the sacred phrase in thought on the breath.

† *Darood* is a breathing concentration practice carrying a sacred phrase in rhythm with the breath.

The Dargah of Moineddin Chishti

The number of recitations was large and expected every day. Mrs. Martin was on a regimen of practice like Inayat had himself observed during his discipleship.

In August, back in New York, Inayat gave Rabia further instruction on *zikr, fikr,* and *shaghal,** and directed her attention also to the Sufi shrines of India and Persia: "Ajmer is the headquarters of Sufism in India where there is the tomb of the great Moineddin Chishti, the leader of our order. In India on his tomb people of different races and casts and creeds go with all humility and devotion and get their wants fulfilled."[106]

She had written him a question about how to teach Sufism to her daughter and in September he responded to this.

> (Pittsburgh 8 September 1911)
>
> Received your very kind letter. I am glad to see that the signs look alright about your advancement more than anticipated and I thank God almighty and *Piran-i-Khan* (Murshids in chain) very much for this . . .
>
> The Sufis generally coach up their children on Sufism though they do not initiate their child themselves. If you think of teaching something to your child let her recite *Darood.* Seven times in the morning and *La ellaha el allah Mohammadar Rasoolillah* seven times while going to bed. It will do her much good.

On the September 13, back in New York, he wrote to her about her experiences with *shaghal:*

> The light that you see is not yet developed, it will take years to see in its clear form . . . This is called *Noor-i-Mohammad* . . . Do not speak of your realizations to anybody except your Murshid and never make use of the

---

* *Shaghal* is a practice in which the 7 openings of the head are covered, to draw the attention from the outer 5 senses to the experience of inner realms.

> powers that you gain by the mercy of God unless you know how to use them.

A short time later he concluded another letter with an affirmation about the experience of sound and light in *shaghal:*

> You're the one sound that is all pervaded and also you are the light that is signified in the material world as the matter, forms, and figures. It is the light that you see during the *Shaghal.* This light is called *Noor-i-Mohammad,* the light of Mohammad. Now by the favour of the Lord you have arrived to a plane where you can see *Sarkar* Mohammad. That is not everybody's luck to see him in his real form of the primal light. Only a few are deserving in this world.

On October 10, Khan instructed Rabia Martin in the advanced practice of *walayat* (also referred to as *amal*), an absorption of self in the absolute. In this letter he told her, "Your humility is quite appreciable, it is just like the Sufis of the East. It is very hardly found here. This is really the blessing God gives to the person whom he wants to draw towards his Mercy."

On November 7 he wrote: "You have now to continue your practice of *walayat* with *zikr, fikr, shaghal* and *darood* forever, though it will take your precious time, but you will get more precious results from that than the value of the time."

He spoke of her realization: "Your saintliness is such that it is very hard to find this among the Ladies and Gentlemen of America, even in the Western World, because the atmosphere of this world is quite different from that of the East. You are so much suited to Sufism that it seems you are born for this, as Saadi says 'Every individual is born for a certain purpose and to accomplish that purpose he has got the light in him to guide.'"

He then gave her further instruction in *fikr.* Looking at the practices Hazrat Inayat Khan gave her, one can see the deep emphasis given to traditional Sufi practices in Arabic and the great respect given to the great chain of Sufi masters who form a unity of blessings in the light of the whole creation, called *Nuri Muhammad.* He clearly felt that very few had the inner purpose and power of accomplishment he could see in his disciple Rabia Martin.

On December 11, 1911 he wrote again:

> Dear Mother,
>
> I am glad to know that you are learning Arabic. I wanted you at least to read, if not understand, because the Sufi practices and all prayers are in Arabic . . . I would like you to read Koran translated by some native authorities, also *Sirkar* Mohammad's life by some native authority . . . I want somebody to undertake my mission as my successor in America before I would leave this and you know that my presence is very necessary in India to save Hindu music from its downfall.
>
> I find you, only, the most suited among my *mureeds* because I see in you a great faith and devotion besides a very good heart full of love and affection together with illuminated intellect. Also you are possessing all the attributes of humanity that is the most important thing for a spiritual guide. Now in your spiritual development I see a great improvement and every hope for the future. All this shows God Almighty and all Murshids in chain have selected you to bestow upon you this honor.
>
> But before I give you a written Diploma of Khilafat in Sufic order I must teach you the work of training *mureeds* of different dispositions. You are trained by quite an exceptional method, it was no training, it was just divine blessing . . . Now for this training your presence is wanted for about forty days at least.

In London on July 27, 1913, he wrote:

> I am glad to know of your high regards for my Murshid who is mine as well as yours. Also it delights me to hear you say of your adoration for Muhammad, the root of all Murshids and the fruit of all prophets. Do your best to serve humanity by the Sufism and be sure that Allah the great will help you.

In subsequent years he wrote her on the evolving organizational structure, the issues that came up and what she needed to do to comply, most likely imagining her in a future leadership role. Again he underscored what he saw as her unique attainment.

> I feel so sorry to ask you to have some more patience with me when you already have had for so many years. I have not found your equal in it so

> far and it is no wonder you have been the only one Murshida in the Western World since the commencement of our blessed work.

By August, 1922, Miss Goodenough had been made a Khalifa* and Inayat apologized "that the letters from her to Rabia were not worded as was desired."

On March 2, 1924, he wrote to Rabia:

> My blessed Murshida, I welcome you with my heart's arms open on the soil of Europe. We have written to the headquarters in Geneva and to our centers in Suisse and in Italy to receive you and to welcome you at our societies and, if possible, to arrange some talks for you to give to *mureeds* and friends.

Murshida Martin arrived in Rome in late March and Inayat wrote saying, "I would so much like if it were in any way possible for you to prolong your stay and pass summer in Suresnes [at the summer school]," which she did.

Failure Comes When Will Surrenders to Reason

> *Will is the Divine Energy which penetrates the mind-mesh and has capacity to rise above it. When the mind begins to turn its thought upon particular experiences, it seizes the will-power and prevents it from returning to God, keeping it in the mind. This is the murder of Abel by Cain. This causes all suffering and also prevents further will-power from entering the sphere. Mind cannot use that beyond its capacity but can misuse anything and everything. The great weakness in reason is that every person may use it for some particular end, and even wickedness can be defended by an argumentative soul.*
>
> Samuel Lewis[107]

Samuel Lewis wrote about the ultimate outcome of the vow he made to Pir-o-Murshid Inayat Khan to stand by Murshida Martin:

> The first thing that happened after the death of Hazrat Inayat Khan was my removal from the Board of Trustees, which handled the funds. Never

* In Sufi usage, a *Khalifa* is a teaching rank; the masculine form is *Khalif.* The specific obligations and authority of this rank vary among Sufi lineages and over time.

> after that until the disassembling of the *Khankah** in Fairfax, which Pir-o-Murshid had blessed, was I ever permitted to say a word about finances.
>
> The funds were handled by a Board of *Mureeds* with the Murshida with the advice and consent of her family. When Samuel refused to countenance private deals in which her family benefitted, he was never forgiven, ever!
>
> It must have been this spirit which was felt in Europe, where the vast majority of disciples refused to accept Murshida Martin as successor to Pir-o-Murshid Inayat Khan. But they surely felt the *nafs*.† It is to one's great regret that Murshida Martin always insisted on defending her *nafs* in public, and this led to her downfall . . .
>
> Still if we have to see life from the standpoint of another as well as of ourselves, the outlook is that there is nothing that can be called exactly right or exactly wrong. Later on in life—much later than the above events—when an outsider came along and insisted that Rabia give up public self-defense and control over funds, she did so without a whimper. She could not do that at the dying request of her own Pir-o-Murshid, but for an outsider [Meher Baba] she did that. Her death was a tragedy.[108]

Paul Reps had also promised Hazrat Inayat Khan to help Murshida Martin:

> As far as I'm concerned, he only told me to help Murshida Martin. I was glad to do that, but she was beyond help because she always had her own opinion and her own viewpoint. So she stormed into Europe, expecting them to receive her as the real Murshida, but there were other Murshidas appointed in Europe, and they didn't go for that at all.
>
> She initiated Sam Lewis as a khalif, but later on she had differences with him. And before she passed away she gave her materials to Mrs. Duce, so what a mess it was! It was impossible for me to help her in any way. So I simply kept out of it because I felt if there was to be so much assertion and quarreling, that this was beautiful Sufism turned into anti-Sufism. I proposed not to be anti-Sufi so I just lived a simple life in my own way. And Samuel was living in his own way; so I would be periodically and forever writing, encouraging him.[109]

---

* A *khankah* is a gathering place or residence for Sufi students.

† Ego.

It was true that Murshida Martin had not made the best impression on some people during her visit to the Summer School in 1924. The view from Europe about her was mixed, to say the least. There was a mention of her presence at Suresnes Summer School in 1924 in the van Hoorn *Recollections* volume. The annotator, Dr. Horn, commented:

> An unexpected strength of Theo van Hoorn's chapters on Suresnes is that, cumulatively and perhaps inadvertently, they convey a sense of a split between the central, unifying presence and activities of Inayat Khan and the persistent bustle and fragmented interests of the many privileged *mureeds* around him. Theo mentions the bewildering notions and monumental egos of *mureeds* such as Rabia Martin, David Craig and Mumtaz Armstrong.[110]

However, Hazrat Inayat Khan's letter to Murshida Martin after her return to America gave a strikingly different message:

> My blessed Murshida,
>
> I am writing this to tell you something, which in words cannot be told, but you will read between the lines. Your visit to us all in Europe has been the answer to our hearts' deepest desire and the impression, which you have left here with us all, is everlasting. Now you are in America to rear plants I have sown. I pray, Lord, to give you all strength and wisdom to fulfill your blessed mission.[111]

Hazrat Inayat Khan, weighed down by his demanding schedule and the infighting in his European organization, returned to India in late 1926 for respite. He became ill there and passed away in Delhi on February 5, 1927. Not long after that, Murshida Martin returned to Europe to make her claim of succession. That time is described in Zia Inayat Khan's dissertation:

> Contention over succession was not slow in coming. The first claim was that of Rabia Martin, who presented herself at the Summer School in Suresnes following a visit to Geneva on the invitation of Birbal Zanetti. Zanetti and Talwar Dussaq, the Executive Supervisor and General Secretary of the Movement respectively, were initially inclined to recognize Martin as Inayat Khan's successor in the exoteric capacity of Representative General.[112]

That she was the senior Murshida, had proven administrative ability, and that Inayat Khan had praised her devotion to the Message, argued in her favor as far as the Board was concerned. However, it is unlikely that such an outer assignment would, in and of itself, have appealed to her, as she believed that she was also Hazrat Inayat Khan's nominated successor to be the head of the esoteric school.

According to the Sufi Movement constitution the Pir-o-Murshid should state whom he wanted to succeed him. Since the Sufi Movement Board had no formal record to this effect, they were befuddled for several years as how to handle the ultimate question of succession.

The dissertation continues: "Martin's actions in Europe, however, soon caused Zanetti and Dussaq to change their minds. Dussaq was taken aback by Martin's 'reiterated self-praise,' as well as 'violent language' . . . Martin contended that 'a plot was hatched to oppose her at the Summer School.'"[113]

Three years after Hazrat Inayat Khan's death Mr. Dussaq wrote Rabia Martin a letter explaining their rejection of her claim:

> I do believe that it was your indirect self-praise and self-assertion that turned everyone against you. For instance, when you were given the Sacred Readings of the Master to be read at a gathering of his disciples, among whom were a Murshida and several Shaikhs, you started the meeting by addressing them as "my dear *mureeds*" and you gave them a shock. For we are all *mureeds* of the Master whether through this or that initiator. Following this you pushed aside the Sacred Words of the Master, declaring: "I have not crossed the Ocean to read to you from a paper, but to give you a solid teaching!" What could be the effect upon your listeners?[114]

Being a no-nonsense Jewish woman from America, Murshida Martin was perceived as out of place within this elite cultural circle in Europe that had gathered around Pir-o-Murshid Hazrat Inayat Khan. People would have needed the capacity to look beyond her outer mannerisms to her inner core to recognize the realization that her teacher had seen. Unfortunately, she had been unable to hold to her teacher's adamant advice not to defend herself.

During Samuel Lewis's time with Hazrat Inayat Khan in Los Angeles in 1926, he was given new esoteric responsibilities. Inayat established him as a leader in Los Angeles who would be in charge of presenting various studies to *mureeds* and interested students. *Gathekas* were the papers for the latter. *Gathas* were to be used for the first three years of discipleship, and *Githas* for the next three. The *Sangathas* and the *Sangithas* were similar collections intended for more advanced study.* The materials also included published talks. In addition to offering his advice on how to present these materials, Hazrat Inayat Khan returned repeatedly to the subject of commentaries that he had broached with Samuel Lewis three years before.

Inayat had seen in Samuel both the intellectual capacity and the realization to pursue a most important task, that of making a bridge between the mystical teachings of the inner school of Sufism and the academicians in the Universities. It was common at that time to find academicians who taught about Sufism and other esoteric schools without having had any actual experience of their own in relation to the practices and traditions. Indeed, the biggest obstacle to achieving this goal at this point in history was the unwillingness of the academic community to pay serious attention to those who actually had the experiences. The philosophers and Ph.D.s knew about them only through conceptualizing and speculating.

Again in 1926 Inayat Khan reemphasized Sam's leadership role in the Brotherhood work, an assignment that Samuel Lewis took seriously. During the interviews the Pir-o-Murshid also spoke further to Samuel about the organization of the Sufi Movement. Here's how Sam later remembered this description:

> The Sufi Movement was to be divided into three sections . . . There was to be a) the Sufi Order, for *mureeds* and spiritual instruction, which was the heart and soul, and without which there can be no Sufism what-

---

*Inayat Khan also wrote a more advanced series of teachings. In later years, these papers were withheld by the Sufi Movement and others, so Samuel wrote his own, which he referred to as *Sangathekas.*

> ever; b) the Universal Worship, a ritual including scriptures of all faiths, which was connected with the Universel temple and which became organically active but socially ineffective; c) the Brotherhood, which was to be the intellectual side of the teachings to bridge the gap between mysticism and universal culture.
>
> He went into exact details and told me to work with Miss Sakina Furnee in Suresnes, France, but if anything happened to her, I was to take over the Brotherhood work. She did retire on Pir-o-Murshid's death. The appointment was never recognized in Europe and de-emphasized in America.[115]

Inayat Khan also spoke to Samuel about studying the previous constitutions that he had drafted. He wanted the disciples, particularly in Europe, either to restore the constitutions—any of them that he had given—or have a visible constitution that could be seen by others. It did not happen.

The subject of commentaries directly arose in Samuel Lewis's later study of the constitutions. He wrote:

> There was an Esoteric Constitution (there were several) which distinctly called for commentaries. Each person to become Khalif was supposed to write a commentary on the *Gathas*, the first three years instructions, and each Murshid on the *Githas*, the next three years instructions. While this was explicit in the Esoteric Constitution, years later when I saw a copy, the section had been removed.[116]
>
> One read later in records which have since been suppressed, that the *Gathas* and esoteric papers belonged to and belong to the Sufi Order and not the Sufi Movement. The Sufi Movement was organized to facilitate the outer workings for the Sufi Order . . . There is no *bayat** to any legal entity. There may be a *bayat* to a representative of the Sufi Order . . . or to Teachers of the seen or unseen, who do not consult with legal entities as to who is worthy or unworthy.[117]
>
> Pir-o-Murshid then asked me to study all his constitutions, all his records and submit findings to Mr. Zanetti in Geneva. This was not an easy task. The records were scattered. Murshida Martin had a book for Murshids, which she put away for safety and, at her death, nobody was

---

*Pledge of initiation.

> able to find it. But at her death one found a lot of scattered miscellany, in a range of places. These covered the complete *Ryazat** of Hazrat Inayat Khan.[118]

Eventually Murshid Samuel Lewis was able to put together a "Book for Murshids" from notes he found.

About his later research Samuel said, "I have since found several attempts on Inayat Khan's part for a constitution. One was based on prowess in *zikr,* never completed. Another on advancement in *hal*† and *makam.*"‡ [119]

Samuel concluded one of his drafts of the six interviews in the late 1960s:

> There are many means by which problems can be solved. The tragedy is a school of Sufis discarding, one after another, the esoteric sciences which could be used to settle problems, and resorting to ego-reasons, or rather just ego, then justified, instead of to Allah.
>
> The rise of a new generation, not to say culture, that wishes Divine Experience direct and not personalities and personalisms, means, *inshallah,*§ that the Truth (*hikmat*) will manifest despite all the arguments, unsubstantiated statements and claims of all persons. This includes those of the writer himself, who is not without faults. But in a law court, an eyewitness is permitted the box, not on his private merits or demerits but on whether he has been witness to events causing litigation.

One last item from the interviews deserves to be covered:

> Hazrat Inayat Khan told me of his efforts to establish a universal Temple which would unite the peoples of the East and West. He was also trying to unite and integrate the practical ways of all parts of the world. He used the words "unite" and "integrate" in a semantic, or dictionary fashion. I have been a student of mathematics, and "integration" in Newton and Liebnitz means "merging with growth," and not just "blending and compiling."

---

* Spiritual practice.

† Transient mystical state.

‡ Established spiritual station.

§ God willing.

Organizational Breakup and Aftermath

Believe in God with childlike faith; for simplicity with intelligence is the sign of the Holy Ones.

HAZRAT INAYAT KHAN[120]

Complexity is human born; humankind loves complexities. This is due to the activity of the mind-mesh, which splits truth into fragments, the shadows of which appear as facts. Not all the facts combined will present the truth, nor can all facts be combined until the essence of truth is discernible.

It is the perception of unity, very simple in itself, very intelligible, yet quite unanalyzable, which is the natural aspect of the heart, characteristic of children and angels and possible in all souls who have escaped the network of the mind-mesh.

SAMUEL LEWIS[121]

For many, the obvious alternative to Rabia Martin as successor was Inayat Khan's next younger brother Maheboob, whom Inayat described as "the wise man."[122] The International Executive Committee convened at the Sufi Movement headquarters in Geneva in September 1927 and elected Maheboob Khan Representative General. They then immediately weakened his authority by requiring him to consult with the National Representative of a country before sending anyone to work there.

Maheboob Khan

For several years the Council explored how to advance someone to be the esoteric head of the Sufi Order. There was no document from Hazrat Inayat Khan on record about the succession. After much spirited debate it was decided that they would ask the four Murshidas to recommend Maheboob Khan.

In advance of the *Jamiat Aam** meeting of the summer of 1929, Dussaq wrote to Rabia Martin asking

* A gathering for all members of the Order.

her to vote on the question of recognizing Maheboob Khan as Esoteric Head or Pir-o-Murshid of the Sufi Order, informing her that the other three Murshidas had already recognized him as Pir-o-Murshid. In response, Martin replied directly to Maheboob Khan, challenging his claim and asserting her own.[123]

Her letter was never read to the *Jamiat.* In it she mentioned the many initiations she received from Inayat Khan, putting particular emphasis on her special last initiation. Unfortunately for her purposes, this secret practice of *amal* had also been given to Maheboob Khan. Murshida Martin challenged the Sufi Movement to go with the actual choice made by Holy Murshid, which was herself, and she argued that it was improper to choose a successor by a vote. In support of this she quoted the Esoteric rules, "Pir-o-Murshid makes rules, his successor is designated by him." Her feelings had been badly wounded.

She also wrote,

> I must now refer to the painful situation which arose concerning my refusal to sign a three year appointment as National Representative, when the General Secretary had been told by our Holy Murshid himself on the eve of his departure for India, that I was not to be disturbed, as it was a life appointment. I have the right to ask, what consideration has been shown the first Murshida and Mother of the Sufi Movement in America? Recognition of her highly spiritual and responsible position includes respect for her spiritual degrees which confirms the rights, instructions, privileges, duties, teachings, utterances and commands the Revered Murshid bestowed upon her. That is why I suffered so in spirit when I read that letter containing a so-called appointment. That letter should never have been allowed to be written. It should then be quite clear why I maintained a self-imposed silence on many things . . .
>
> The utterances contained in this letter place us both on holy ground, for the eyes of God the Almighty are upon us. I do not believe that you covet your election; but what I grieve for is the utter lack of consideration and investigation. Your position as Representative General made it imperative for you to consider, investigate, question, and learn if in America your brother, our Revered Murshid, had conferred upon myself, or any other *mureed* he may have chosen, the right of mystical succession as the Esoteric Head of the Sufi Order.

> I have spoken now regarding the Western World, and though you may not accept what I have written concerning this election, it matters not, for God and Those who form His Holy Embodiment (the Hierarchy) know the truth of these statements; this suffices.

Mr. Dussaq went on to argue in the Council meeting that a designation is by definition "something that can be shown." Murshida Martin, in making her claim, had relied on her special initiation. She had failed to remember a letter from Pir-o-Murshid Inayat Khan written to her in 1915 that would have helped her cause. Pir Zia Inayat Khan in his doctoral dissertation wrote, "Perhaps the most direct evidence Rabia Martin possessed in support of her claim of pre-eminence was a letter Inayat Khan had written to her in 1915."[124]

Here is that letter from February 8, 1915:

> Dear Mother,
>
> I cannot keep up correspondence with my closest *mureeds* in Germany and Russia and will you give you the trouble if you do not mind to keep in touch with them on my behalf . . . and help them in advice upon their study if desired on behalf of the Murshid during the war . . .
>
> Sorry to give you this trouble but you are always chosen to work on my behalf. When I will go for the life of absolute retirement you will have to attend to all my affairs in the West, also some times in the East.[125]

If Murshida Martin had shown this letter to the Sufi Movement Board it would have very much helped her claim to be Hazrat Inayat Khan's successor as head of the Sufi Movement. Instead she wrote only Maheboob Khan about who had been named as the acting leader. He never replied to her criticisms.

An annotated copy of this letter appears in the papers of Samuel Lewis and contains the following note: "This shows that as early as this date the Holy Murshid had designated his successor." This note was either ignored by Murshida Martin or was made too late to be of any significance in the succession arguments.

At this council meeting in 1929 Mr. Dussaq also dramatically discounted a letter he had received in support of Murshida Martin's claim written by Samuel Lewis.

> He dismissed the suggestion that a turban bestowed on Martin by Inayat Khan was proof of designation, answering that Inayat had given his own turban to his son Vilayat . . . Dussaq also brushed aside Samuel Lewis's substantial assertion that in Los Angeles in 1926 Inayat Khan had told Lewis that Martin was his successor.[126]

Dussaq's comments on Samuel Lewis's letter are quoted in full below:

> This statement seems to me most extraordinary for is it not strange that Pir-o-Murshid kept all the Murshidas (yourself included) and Khalifs and Shaiks of the Sufi Order ignorant that you were to be his Successor, but made the disclosure of it to Mr. Samuel Lewis, who has no standing in the Sufi Order, for whatever be the value in your eyes, to be a "Khalif by spiritual degree."
>
> However let us admit that Mr. Lewis statement was true and that he did not misinterpret the Master's words, or that he did not imagine it, which is likely—for is it not well known that certain visionaries are subject to strange delusions and hallucinations, and you have declared, as well as Mr. Lewis himself, that he has visions—even supposing his statement to be correct, we cannot take it into consideration, for we happen to have in this office written instructions from Our Blessed Master urging us never to act upon anyone's saying, "Murshid told me," but only to act upon what Murshid himself had told us.[127]

The top administrator of the Sufi Movement gave a cavalier and cynical dismissal of Samuel Lewis, the person, as well as of his eyewitness testimony of what Hazrat Inayat Khan had said. It is easy to understand Lewis's ongoing criticism of those in charge of that corporate entity.

The council finally made the decision, during the 1930 *Jamiat,* to name Maheboob Khan the esoteric head of the Sufi Order.[128] There were five dissenting voters, who subsequently resigned from the Sufi Movement. One of these, Sarfaraz Meyer, immediately transferred her affiliation to the Sufi Movement (Sufi Society) as established by law in the U.S.

Shabaz Best, who had defended Murshida Martin's claim in the meeting and had voted against continuing Maheboob Khan in his post, also severed his relations with the Movement. The national representative of the Dutch movement, Sirdar van Tuyll, resigned. There were others who broke away throughout the world. The most formidable was Murshida Martin.

> In America, on receiving the news of the *Jamiat Ahm* meeting, Rabia Martin announced that she no longer recognized the authority of Headquarters and declared herself the Representative General of the Sufi Movement. Meyer and Martin were then, in turn, officially expelled respectively from the Sufi Movement."[129]

There were a number of other dis-affiliations. However, the Chicago and Santa Barbara centers kept their affiliation with Geneva. The important Sufi center in New York, headed by Fatha Engle, also remained loyal to Geneva. "In October, according to Headquarters newsletter, The Sufi Record, Rabia Martin and Samuel Lewis made repeated efforts to persuade the New York leader and other workers and *mureeds* to their point of view, but their efforts proved unavailing."[130]

Samuel Lewis, true to his pledge to Hazrat Inayat Khan, continued to offer his support to Murshida Martin. His abilities as a secretary, writer, and intellectual were put to work. Murshida Martin recognized him as a Khalif. At times he helped pull together materials for Rabia Martin and represented her in letters.

Having finally uprooted himself from the family home on 9th Avenue, Samuel Lewis had begun a life filled with frequent moving about. At the time of his six interviews with Inayat Khan, he was employed doing clerical work in Southern California. In 1928 he went to Portland, Oregon, and worked there for the next several years as a freelance stenographer and clerk. He transcribed medical and scientific lectures, mostly from chiropractors who were at the core of coalescing a college. It was all piecework.

Here are two reports from him from those times:

> I was working as a clinical clerk for doctors in Portland, Oregon. The doctor tried every known test on his brother-in-law and could not come up with one answer other than the symptoms. I said, "That is easy." "What is easy?" "Your brother-in-law?" "What about him?" "His profession." The man was an X-ray operator and in those days there was no

> protection. This comment started my principal on the task of studying the effects of X-Rays and radioactivity, long before World War II.[131]
>
> I first met the Baha'i Ali Khuli Khan about 1911 and saw him from time to time throughout this life. I do remember a confrontation in 1927 in the city of Portland, Oregon, when I asked him what would be the difference between a world with 700 conflicting faiths and 700 conflicting "universal brotherhoods."[132]

Samuel also said, "Most of these 'universal brotherhoods' seem to deny the direct God experience or to restrict it in acceptance to a few specially privileged persons. He could not answer my challenge. All he could say was the usual 'They should all join us.'"

During 1927–1930 Samuel Lewis often returned to visit the Bay Area. On one such trip he had the opportunity for an interview with Henry Atkinson, General Secretary of the Church Peace Union from 1918 to 1955. The CPU was a function of the Carnegie Council for Ethics in International Affairs.

> Rev. Henry Atkinson was an academic, minister, author, and peace activist. He spent much time in Europe on behalf of the CPU and in the 1920s he visited India, China, and Japan to survey religions in Asia. Atkinson served on the boards of numerous organizations that worked to promote the rights of religious minorities, and denounced the rise of anti-Semitism in Germany early on in the 1930s.[133]

Samuel Lewis's meeting with Atkinson helped confirm his purpose in life, and he wrote of it in many letters. Here was a person whose goals were well aligned with the Brotherhood activity that Samuel's Murshid had assigned him. Sam had been studying world religions from childhood but in those days did not have the financial ability to travel abroad as Atkinson had.

Henry Atkinson

Sam brought his own written notes on his studies of the different religions when he went to meet Rev. Atkinson. Sam later wrote about this meeting in several letters, among them one to a professor of religions in Rome and another to Sri Aurobindo Ashram.

> Many years ago I met one Dr. Henry Atkinson who was executive secretary of the World Church Peace Union. I was an unknown and very much downtrodden young man. Dr. Atkinson said I was the first person he had ever met that had a proper universal attitude toward the problems he was facing and the goals he was seeking.[134]
>
> Dr. Atkinson laid out plans of studies to acquaint myself with the religions of Asia, which before God I have done . . . Dr. Atkinson's successors refused even to give me an interview. The same with the clergy almost all over, except the Quakers. The same with those pretending to believe in universal religion, excepting the Sufis and Vedantists. The same with the so-called representatives of Sri Aurobindo.[135]
>
> Later I followed [Dr. Atkinson's] suggestion in meeting leaders and saints of all faiths and found common grounds in their hearts. Dr. Atkinson accepted my reports, his successors have not.[136]
>
> In 1930 I proposed that all religious holy places be de-nationalized and depoliticized. After the UN was established I felt that it, or some co-coordinative or subsidiary group should in some way be given jurisdiction over the holy places of all religions.
>
> The peace plan which I proposed and which was accepted as wonderful by Mr. Gunner Jarring and separately by at least three other UN officials, included at least mutual recognition of all religions by each other.[137]

He summarized his conclusions on his efforts with religionists over the years with these words, "So years of research stand, and man can be as selfish or as honest or egocentric as he will, and it is particularly notable that in the world of 'religion' a large number of people will not accept 'Whatsoever ye do to the least of these, My creatures, ye do it unto Me.'"[138]

Mother of the World by Nicholas Roerich

CHAPTER 3

Deeper Into Zen and the Dharma Path

Roerich's Paintings and Ambitions

Samuel Lewis was deeply drawn to the work of painter Nicholas Roerich. Insight into the personal agency by which the arts could become a vehicle of peace came with his exposure to Roerich's work. At the outset Samuel was thoroughly impressed by the depth of wisdom in Roerich's art and the idealism of his quest into the Himalayas. Over the years, he wrote about these times:

> 1930 was like any other year of importance in spiritual history. One came to the Roerich Museum to study the Dharma in art-form. Nicholas Roerich gave us the Dharma-Transmission in painting. It has been done before. Kenneth Saunders had explained the Dharma-Transmission in Sculpture and Architecture. We did not need the verbal-transmission. But Roerich was accepted socially and intellectually. The Dharma-Transmission became frozen in his art, and most of it has been stored away.[139]
>
> I was mixed up in the Roerich complexities and wrote a minority report saying that art would have become a means to world peace and understanding, unless the artists themselves were the leaders. [Roerich] accepted the goodwill of every politician and international gangster and in the end lost everything. His personal losses may or may not have been important, but he started something which has continued: **personnel** as the nexus of world peace through the arts, so it becomes individual persons, rather than movements, which become the center of the stage.[140]

Sam wrote about Roerich and about the art at the museum in a set of poems called "Rhapsodiae Coronae Mundi." Surprisingly from today's perspective, Sam and other invited poets and writers lived in the Roerich Museum in New York City, thus allowing them to study the art daily.

Three poems about Roerich, excerpted here, conclude the "Rhapsodiae." They show great respect for Roerich's work and his spiritual ideal.

NICHOLAS ROERICH, THE MAN WHO KILLED TIME.

I once . . . . but was it I?
It was in the land of Beauty,
The realm of enchanting lights, of colour symphonies,
The plane of dreams-made-facts,
Where forms grew from the substance of the sphere,
Which Life Itself had molded.
Intoxicated I, and then awoke in a body of clay.
I thank my God for giving me this body
Whereby to paint those haunting memories,
Realities that spirit-blinded persons cannot see.

NICHOLAS ROERICH, HERO ASPIRANT.

He seeks where lesser souls have never trod,
He climbs the long abyssal steeps toward God,
He holds the Chalice close into his breast,
He toils his patient way, and knows no rest.
His master eye sweeps untold miles of land,
He holds high Himalayas in his hand;
Colossal genii whisper in the storm,
And on his palette hide in subtle form.
He speaks, yet not a word flows from his tongue,
While endless sermons, symphonies unsung,
Breathe out from every motif that he etches,
And Heaven embraces Earth in all his sketches.

Roerich began to fade in Samuel Lewis's esteem when Sam experienced the ego conflicts of those organizing the Banner of Peace event through the museum. Roerich and guest artists fell into competition, eschewing the Buddhist methodology they espoused. Sam wrote, "The Roerich Museum tried the impossible: 'egocentric Buddhism.' There was no *Sangha* (brotherhood of monks) in the usual sense, and soon the individuals were in conflict."[141]*

Still, Samuel would write glowingly about the seeds of vision in Roerich's work, and he held Roerich's wife Helena in high esteem:

> Hierarchs may not go around saying, "I am a Hierarch." Nicholas Roerich said that and he delighted a lot of people. They did not say then that the awakened never tell. They accepted. He was not a true Hierarch but his wife (not he) was open to the Hierarchs and was received by them in Tibet and elsewhere.[142]
>
> [She] wrote two books called *Heart* and *Hierarchy*.† Unfortunately the marked emotionalism and egocentricities of her colleagues de-emphasized the importance of these books.[143]

Samuel also commented on the vision of women that could be gleaned from Roerich's work.

> Women have a great mission in the world as Nicholas Roerich and others are indicating. There are spiritual faculties which mankind had in the past and there is some likelihood that these gifts will be bestowed upon women in the future. They will play the leading parts in education of every sort and in the mysteries. The healers will be women in many instances. The hand of the male is made more for physical purposes or for the performance of mental acts, but the hand of woman can better coordinate with her heart. So we shall see many perform the duty of *Shifayat*‡ within the Sufi Order, and without it, many women will be taking up the healing profession.
>
> It is also probable that women will function as priestesses, as sybils, as oracles, performing again those spiritual functions which prevailed among the many ancient races. All this will mean a real new day for the women, and for the women as women.[144]

---

*Roerich was later involved in political scandal that touched Franklin Delano Roosevelt's fourth presidential run. For a fascinating account, see Jason Colavito, "How a (sort of) Believer in Ancient Astronauts Almost Became U.S. President," jasoncolavito.com, February 6, 2013.

†Sam here refers to two of Helena Roerich's many books.

‡Director of the Healing Ritual.

In another of the "Rhapsodiae Coronae Mundi" poems Sam wrote about "The Mother of the World." The number 536 was a painting listing number at the New York City exhibit. In the late 1960s Murshid Sam purchased copies of this picture and gave them to the young women who were students in his women's dance class at that time.

MOTHER OF THE WORLD. 536

O Thou veiled One . . .
Whose words unuttered fall like dazzling jewels
In the throne-room in the Center of the Infinite;
We kneel before Thy bounteous Presence . . .
Thou sacrificing, All-pervading Mother . . .
To Thee we offer praise for every favor,
Humbling ourselves before Thy Heavenly Throne,
Hailing Thy Glory through endless kotis *of aeons.*
Without Thee less than naught are we,
But through Thy magnanimity,
We have been raised to quaff the purest nectar.
Praise to Thee forever, Mother of gods and devas *and men,*
We worship and adore Thee, Soul of our souls.[145]

While looking to further his study of Buddhism, Samuel was inspired by Roerich's depiction of Milarepa (also called Milaraspa). Samuel wrote the following poem; his reference to Amida Buddha, the Buddha of Infinite Light, is based on insight inspired by the painting.

MILARASPA. 551

When the ear hears light
And the eye sees sound,
When the self seeks self,
And no self is found,
With the mind at peace,
And the heart awake,
Lost in deep meditation
At the soul's daybreak;
And the soul's daybreak
Sees him still at rest,
With Amida's Boundless Light

Shining through his breast.
Shining through his breast.
Namotasa Bhagavato Arhato
Samma-Sambodasa.[146] *

Sokei-an Sasaki

The Roerich Museum was a center for many activities in 1930 and Samuel wrote about another great benefit from his time there. "Among these activities were groups dedicated to Tibetan-Mongolian Buddhism and to the Theravadin teachings (Maha Bodhi Society). It was at the Roerich Museum that I was first told about Sokei-an, a Zen monk living in New York."[147]

Being drawn to study Roerich's work indirectly enabled Samuel to make a living connection with an illuminated Zen teacher from whom he received a direct dharma transmission. He had already learned to meditate in the Zen manner with Nyogen Senzaki and to appreciate Zen koans. Now his attention was directed to the First Zen Institute of America and the teacher Sokei-an Sasaki.

Sokei-an Sasaki

> *Uncle Nyogen was asked: "Is the Zen monk bound by causation or is he outside causation?" Uncle taught: "The Zen monk is one with the Law of Causation." Unless you can understand and appreciate, you cannot grasp that incarnation of the Cat's Yawn known as Sokei-An Sasaki.*
>
> *There is a statement in Gilbert & Sullivan's* Iolanthe *concerning the Duke. When he asks for an evaluation one of his associates says: "Why, you are the most ordinary man in existence." The Duke approves. Mohammed said, "I am an ordinary man like you." God made the ordinary man in His Image. Sometimes this is manifested.*[148]

---

*Salutation to the Perfect One, the Wholly Enlightened One, the Most Supreme Buddha.

> *Sokei-an was not a Swami Ramdas or Sufi, whose love-vibrations permeate the atmosphere. Neither did he show power or beauty or repose; he was, in one sense, the most ordinary person one could meet and, in another sense, the most complete.*[149]
>
> SAMUEL LEWIS

Samuel Lewis criticized a culture that persisted in its absorption with personality traits and could not understand a person like Sokei-An Roshi who "broke all the laws of culture and tradition without breaking any of them."[150]

The influence of Sokei-an Sasaki (1882–1945) on Murshid Sam's life would be difficult to overstate. Sam wrote, "After Roshi the scriptures became open books. To the world the scriptures are full of mysteries and contradictions or even falsehoods, but after Roshi they became clear channels of light."[151]

Sokei-an began his Zen training in 1901. He was the son of a Shinto priest and a graduate of the Imperial Academy of Art in Tokyo. Upon graduation in 1905 he was drafted into the Japanese army, where he brought his depth of realization to the battlefield. "When I was on the battlefield, under the shower of fire, I thought often of this teaching: 'My existence is like lightning which flashes through the dark air! My life is so short—but original substance exists timelessly. It is like a dream. When I draw my last breath, I will go back to original emptiness. Why should I be afraid of death?'" Like Samuel's first Zen teacher, Sokei-an also had his period of coming to understand Western culture and actually walked from the West Coast to the East Coast over several years' time. He completed his study of Zen in 1928 and at age 48 was ordained as Zen Master. He chose to become a priest during the early 1930s because he felt Americans would not respect a lay person bringing Zen. The First Zen Institute was formed in 1930. This is the period when Samuel Lewis met him in New York.

> In 1930 I came to New York and met Senzaki's spiritual "nephew," Sokei-An Sasaki. I have never, I hope, escaped from his influence and wisdom.[152]

Sam did his best to describe this remarkable man.

> Uncle Daisetz [Suzuki] had given long articles. Roshi brought his presence. "A single day with the Lord is worth a thousand years." . . .
>
> Thus one entered the *Zendo* of that remarkably ordinary man. When Bodhidharma faced the Emperor of China and told him there was nothing sacred in the entire universe, he might have also said that everything in the entire universe is sacred—for this is the teaching of the *Avatamsaka* (*Kegon*) transmission.
>
> Roshi was one of the most approachable men ever encountered. Not until one met Swami Ranganathananda Maharaj of the Ramakrishna Order years later did one meet someone so approachable, so simple, and so utterly profound that words are but the shadows of conveyance.[153]
>
> I remember attending nine lecture-meetings of Sokei-an . . . Besides these encounters with Sokei-an, I was fortunate to have had a number of private interviews and meditations.[154]

Due to the providence that one person at the Roerich museum suggested Sokei-an instead of the Theravadin and Tibetan Buddhist lineages, Samuel Lewis now dedicated himself to study with this Zen Master, a relationship that had a profound effect on his life.

Sokei-an Sasaki had a cat. This story he wrote in the October, 1940, issue of *Cat's Yawn* puts his own cat's yawn in perspective:

> Among our ancient savants many "disheveled" men attained enlightenment; for instance, Hotei, who used to sit on the ground outside the villages with a big bag at his side, beating his drum-shaped belly with his own hand and laughing loudly. You call him the "Smiling Buddha" . . . I wish to talk about my faith in a very disheveled attitude, just as a cat vomits the breath from its mouth in yawning. Let me speak, lying on the floor with my yawning cat at my side, about the Buddhism which is my very self.

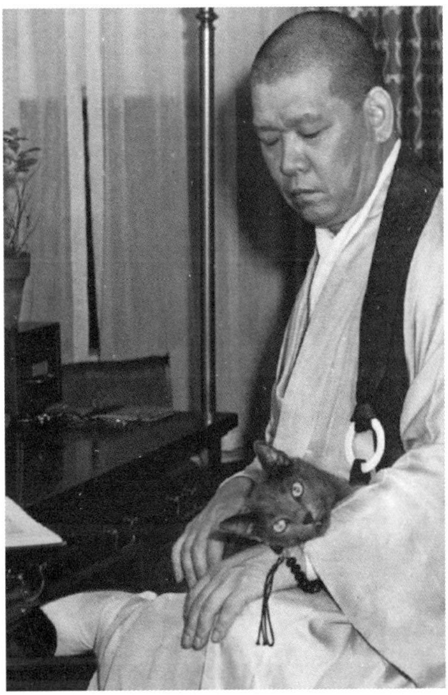

Sokei-an Sasaki with his cat

> Human beings . . . have wonderful knowing power. When, however, we ask them the question, what were you before your birth, and what will happen after your death, they use their brains and answer with their imaginations. They go to the clergyman and the scientist who answer, "Wait a minute" . . . We also are thinking about this question. They do not realize that there is a shortcut by which to find direct knowledge of life and death. This shortcut is in our existing soul. I am living. I see and I hear. My soul is living. I shall ask all the questions of my own soul.
>
> This word soul I am using as a makeshift because in English there is no other word by which to express the present consciousness of living beings. We Buddhists hold that soul is not created by any one. We hold that soul is not divided individually. There is only one soul in the universe. We look into this one great soul through the window which is our power of self-cognition.
>
> What is soul? What is my soul? We cannot see it by opening our eyes, so we close our eyes and try to look within. How foolish human beings are. The eye exists for the outside, not for the inside. So we do not need to try to know what soul is. Soul knows all that we know. When we come to this realization soul has no particular form. It has no particular nature, male or female. It is simple; it is clear; it is pure! And this soul is not mine. It is the great soul. When I see I am not performing this act of seeing, it is the soul that sees . . .
>
> When this physical body is severed from the soul, what will happen? The body will become ashes. When the soul leaves this physical body every function comes to an end. How can we regard this soul as "my soul," as "my self?" Human beings commit the error of clinging tenaciously to the "I," to this difference from "You." This is mine, not yours. Thus they struggle through life, and when the end comes they are still clutching the arms of the chair, still clinging to the edges of the bed, crying "I do not want to die!" . . . When this time comes you can do nothing more. You must close your eyes and join your hands. Go with the soul, which is not yours, back to that original state whence you have come.[155]

Sokei-an referred to his method of teaching as soul to soul. The transmission that Samuel Lewis reported receiving from him was clearly of this kind. Mary Farkas, one of Sokei-an's principal students in New York, offered insights from her experience of his teaching:

> When I came to Sokei-an, he would present his face, his original aspect, so you were able to see it, to recognize it; you could develop it. So when you saw him, as he himself described it, people would say, "Sokei-an, why are you putting on that face?" He meant, another person would see him if he were in that state of consciousness and not recognize what he was doing because they didn't have the receptors to recognize it. He always taught through this absorption. When this happens it awakens something in the other person and they are together in a kind of exchange . . . That's the only way. Crossing that little barrier between catching on that you can do it or catching on suddenly to what it is . . . Sokei-an said, "You can only go so far with an answer in *sanzen.* Then you must do it yourself . . . Self-awakening is the highest teacher. You just open your eyes and there it is."[156]

Samuel wrote that attempting to describe Roshi "is a most difficult task. Unless one understands that we have at least Three bodies as Indian Wisdom teaches; unless one comprehends the potentialities of the Three *kaya* beyond such limitations, it is impossible to explain Roshi."[157]

The three bodies referred to are the *dharmakaya, sambhogakaya,* and *nirmanakaya.* Here is a brief description of them from Sokei-an:

> Dharma is a Sanskrit word with twenty-four meanings. European scholars translate it as "law" or "way" or "religion." I accept the translation of *dharmakaya* as "body of law," but note that in "law" there are three grades. The first grade is that which we can reach by meditation. It is timeless, spaceless, bodiless. Here consciousness fails to conceive its own existence. There is no center of consciousness [neither conscious state nor unconscious state] because there is no space or time. The human mind cannot conceive a concept for this first law* . . . In meditation, there is no idea, no vision that symbolizes IT. Every religious person, no matter of what faith, must open this door and enter, must unveil the mystery that is *dharmakaya.*[158]
>
> The second grade is *sambhogakaya,* our own consciousness. A European scholar has translated *sambhogakaya* as "body of enjoyment"! Yes, *sambho* is "enjoyment," but this word must be translated as "unity" or

---

*This first law is the law of the state of *dharmakaya.*

> "connection" or "yoga." Consciousness cannot exist alone. It must make contact with outer existence . . . When we observe the outside substantiality as a spiritual existence, then it is the objective experience of subjective mind. The outside is an extension of our consciousness. The outside and consciousness make unity in meditation, that is, yoga with *dharmakaya.* With the physical body and with the active mind yoga is made with the entire universe, including all the thoughts of the human being. We make yoga with everything to realize our own existing *sambhogakaya.* With present consciousness, you can see the inward body and the outward body; you see *dharmakaya* with the *sambhogakaya.* You also see *nirmanakaya,* the outward body, the body of transformation. All the many shapes—man, woman, tree, animal, flower—are extensions of the source—*sambhogakaya.*[159]

Samuel Lewis called this body of transformation "'no mind-body' but really no ego-mind."[160] It is manifest in the midst of the world. It allows for infinite flexibility such that enlightened being may be seen in any form. Such realization activates awakening. "According to tradition, those skilled in meditation, such as advanced Tibetan lamas and yogis, as well as other highly realized Buddhists, may gain access to the *sambhogakaya* and receive direct transmission of doctrine."[161]

To illustrate such a relationship with the *nirmanakaya,* Sokei-an in his autobiography gives these two examples of entering *samadhi:*

> One day when I was in a shop I saw men outside working on the street, and suddenly I realized the whole universe was mirrored in me, all was in me—all sounds, everything. The hard shell of consciousness cracked, and I realized the size of consciousness . . . The great universe's consciousness covers all; outside and inside is just one existence . . . In 1920 I had a second great experience—I saw a dead horse in Sixth Avenue. I went by and saw the physical details—a dead horse lying on the pavement. Something happened. In that moment, nothing was left in my mind.[162]

Sokei-an also spoke of and demonstrated the Dharma Eye, a faculty that Samuel had every reason to appreciate from his own direct experience. "The Zen Master Eno had told his students that he was leaving. They asked, 'Master, to whom are you going to transmit your Dharma

Eye?' The Daishi answered, 'Those who possess the Dharma will attain it; those who are mind-less will spread it abroad.'"[163]

This koan is something to contemplate when you try to understand Sokei-an's state. The attribution of being mind-less is giving the highest praise in Zen terms. Such a person is at one with the *dharmakaya* in all their actions and thoughts. There is a saying of the Buddha that Sokei-an translated elsewhere in *Cat's Yawn:*

> *I am the highest, I am the mightiest!*
> *To no Dharmas whatever am I attached.*
> *From all craving am I released.*
> *Self-awakening only I call my teacher.*

As a student, Sokei-an once complained about Gautama talking too loudly in this passage. His teacher replied, that is natural for you because you are small and you imagine saying things like that to others. The awakened Buddha has the consciousness of all that is.

Sokei-an and Sam

Sokei-an Sasaki wrote in his autobiography about the time needed for religious experience to fully deepen:

> The farmer works on the field doesn't he? And the Buddhist has a great field on which to work—*dharmakaya,* consciousness. And just as the farmer cannot change the ground, we cannot change that field. True religious experience must have time. You sow the seed of a peach or chestnut tree, and it is three years before it bears fruit. You sow the seed of a persimmon and wait eight years. For attaining Buddhist Experience you must wait thirty years. Wise man or idiot, when you enter the way of religion, all must wait about thirty years.[164]

The dharma transmission Samuel received from Sokei-an Sasaki played a large part in his ongoing life. The scriptures were now streams of light in his understanding and not avenues for argumentation. From the moment their souls met the future was open to him. But, as noted above, time is required for the full ripening.

According to Samuel Lewis,

> Each lecture [of Sokei-an] was followed by six questions, this being the upper limit. If you were an intellectual, you received philosophy. But if you had the Dharma-Eye, you **saw**. One of his lectures was on "Dharma-Eye." This makes a reality of *sama-dhrishti,** the first principle of Lord Buddha's **Eightfold Path**. When you received this spiritual *darshan,* you received. When you were taken beyond *maya* you entered the realm of the Immeasurable.[165]
>
> When Sokei-An gave *prajna* and *karuna* and *dhyana*—actually practiced—he gave much more. The veil was lifted over many things. Not only Buddhist Scriptures but much Indian literature and wisdom became clear. Future events were often foreseen. The demarcation between science, religion and philosophy disappeared. And one came to know something of the true being of himself, and others.[166]

The foregoing description reflects Samuel Lewis's experience. He later related a supreme awakening experience, a soul-to-soul absorption, a consciousness-to-consciousness merging:

> Once Roshi was asked if he could see into the future. He answered: "It is too terrible." Dharma Transmission is not intellectual, it does not stop at *manas* [mind-stuff]. It includes *vijnana* and *ananda* and *prajna.* Intellectuals do not understand [these terms] . . .
>
> English has no equivalent for *vijnana* and *ananda* and *prajna* and *samadhi,* and so we grasp any words, appropriate or inappropriate, and become confused† . . .
>
> Roshi opened these eyes to the whole history of the period 1930–1945,‡ and some . . . records [of these visions] were miraculously preserved from a fire which destroyed twenty-five years' research and a whole Oriental library. Roshi took one into *prajna* **without destroying** levels between the seemingly finite and the seemingly infinite.

---

* *Sama dhrishti* is often translated "right views," but as Samuel Lewis taught, *sama* means universal in Sanskrit, so having *sama dhrishti* would mean to have a universal view, as Sokei-an had.

† These terms can be approximated in English as follows: *vijnana* – cosmic awareness; *ananda* – pure bliss; *prajna* – spiritual insight, perfect wisdom; *samadhi* – dissolution in the dharmakaya.

‡ Lewis wrote of these visions in "The Book of Cosmic Prophecy" (Archives), which predicts many events that later occurred.

Parinirvana by Nicholas Roerich

> The painting of *Parinirvana* shows that the artist had the Dharma Transmission. Naraka, Preta, Tirthaga-yoni, Rakshasa, and Asura are the creatures of Darkness. They were welcomed at the bier. These are Sanskrit words. They have no European equivalents unless we accept that there are more things in Heaven and Earth than are thought of in our philosophies. We do not do that. We call what we do not know "unreal." Roshi explained these terms.
>
> Radioactivity could not be explained in the earlier Physics. Relativity had no place in the earlier Physics. The Quantum idea did not appear in the earlier Physics . . .
>
> In the Grand Experience as illustrated by the Cosmic Wheel, all these creatures exist, within or without. The world, especially the Western world, has refused to accept here what has not been experienced.
>
> You cannot experience Radioactivity and Relativity and Quantum without the experience of the laboratory without. How does one know what is experienced in the laboratory within if one does not go in?[167]

Samuel often spoke in the way Sokei-an did, saying that there is nothing to be gained by just sitting in meditation without the awakening of the pure insight of *prajna*. Roshi freely admitted to having entered a transcendental state and dwelling there. That perspective always gave him balance between the realms. A good description of this process is given by Sokei-an in his autobiography:

When Shakyamuni Buddha transmitted his Dharma to Mahakashyapa, he is said to have branded him with the seal of the Buddha Mind, and when I transmit to you the traditional view of a koan, it can be said with my seal I brand you with Shakyamuni's mind. Literally the Buddha cast a golden *mudra* to signify his mind and handed it down to Mahakashyapa.[168]

Sam had more to say.

[Sogaku] Shaku explained the Four Stages of Meditation by lecturing. Roshi explained the Four Stages of Meditation by Meditation and Dharma-transmission.

We sat comfortably. One is not convinced that special *asanas* [postures] causally produce *samadhi* or *satori* . . .

Creatures mentioned in the Upanishads and other Indian writings, creatures mentioned in the Pali and Sanskrit Suttas and Sutras, creatures mentioned in poetry and song remain outside the domains of philosophy, and even symbolism. **What is Buddha?** cannot be answered in the terms of *maya* and *manas*. **What is Buddha** is the easiest question in the world to answer . . .

The Bodhisattvic Vow and the Great Vow of Samantabhadra are the basis of all Mahayana.* The rest is commentary or embellishment . . .

Uncle Nyogen used to say that Tathagata said: "I see now that all creatures have perfect enlightenment. But they do not know it, I must go and teach it to them."[169]

Dharmakaya literally may mean "the body of law." But *dharmakaya* is infinite and belongs to a class of terms associated with the experience of perfect self-realization. Until then it is a word that loses meaning and charm through gross discussion.

Dharma-transmission is basic in Ch'an and Zen Buddhism. In this they do not differ from spiritual or mystical Hinduism. In both realms

*The Bodhisattvic Vow: "However innumerable sentient beings are, I vow to take them all across to enlightenment; however countless the deluding passions, I vow to extinguish them all; however numberless are the dharma gateways I vow to pursue them to the end; the realization of the Buddha is supreme, I vow to attain to it." The 10 Vows of Samantabhadra: "To respect all Buddhas; to make praises to the Tathagatas; to practice profoundly the giving of offerings; to repent and reform all karmic hindrance; to rejoice and follow in merit and virtue; to request that the Dharma Wheel be turned; to request that the Buddhas remain in the world; to always follow the Buddhas' teaching; to constantly accord with all living beings; to transfer all merit and virtue universally." (Gold Coast Dharma Realm, www.gcdr.org.au/.)

> there may be references to chains of Patriarchs and Masters who have passed the Dharma on ceaselessly, even to this day.[170]

The next passage shows how Samuel Lewis, in his life-given role of unifier of spiritual traditions, merged the Buddhist teaching with Christian scripture.

> Perhaps this might be expressed in a free interpretation of the first chapter of the Gospel of John:
>
> 1. In the uncreated was the *dharmakaya,*
> And the *dharmakaya* was with God,
> And this *dharmakaya* was God.
> 2. This was in the uncreated with God.
> 3. Through it everything became,
> And without it not even one became,
> That has been done.
> 4. In it was Life; and the Life was the Light of men;
> And the Light shone in the darkness
> And the darkness did not grasp it.
> 9. Was the true Light
> Which enlightens every man
> Coming into manifestation.
> 10. Was in the manifestation,
> And the manifestation was because of it,
> And the manifestation knew it not.[171]

Samuel concluded that this teaching proposes that there is only one Truth and one finality.

> There is a close kinship between "The Sutra of Forty-Two Chapters" and the Brihadaranyaka Upanishad. There is a further kinship between many aspects of Mahayana Buddhism and schools of Indian tradition regarded as orthodox. In other words there is one Supreme Dharma. However one receives it, one has it. It may have come through one teacher or another but it is one and the same Truth . . .
>
> From the first instance Sokei-an impressed me as a sort of incarnation of the basic teachings of Mahayana. There was no separation in him between the ultimate peace of Nirvana and the life and activity of the world. He lived in the midst of the world, though it did not know him.[172]

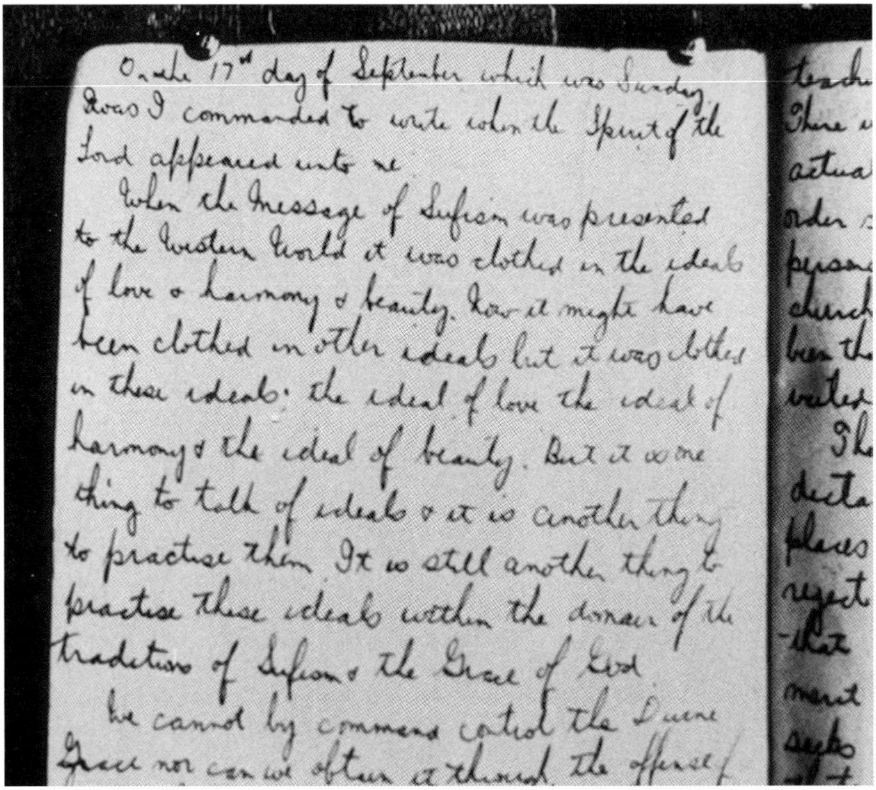
On the 17th day of September which was Sunday
was I commanded to write when the Spirit of the
Lord appeared unto me
When the Message of Sufism was presented
to the Western World it was clothed in the ideals
of love & harmony & beauty. Now it might have
been clothed in other ideals but it was clothed
in these ideals: the ideal of love the ideal of
harmony & the ideal of beauty. But it is one
thing to talk of ideals & it is another thing
to practise them. It is still another thing to
practise these ideals within the domain of the
traditions of Sufism & the Grace of God
We cannot by command control the Divine
Grace nor can we obtain it through the offense

Original manuscript, "The Book of Cosmic Prophecy," 1933 diary

Birth of "The Book of Cosmic Prophecy"

The consequences of the faculty of seeing into the future that had come with Samuel's transmission from Sokei-an Sasaki did not make him popular. He was regarded as a Cassandra. Who wants to see through Samuel's eyes the waves of destruction of the Japanese troops in China? Or witness the rise of Nazism and its extremes that was going to manifest in the next decade? "It's too terrible." However, Samuel recorded his visions and prophetic pronouncements in his "Book of Cosmic Prophecy,"[173] a series of poems and prophecies in Biblical style that chronicle this period. It was one of his few documents to survive the fire of 1949. Two prophetic poems are given below, which were quite accurate in their predictions.

This book begins with the Sufi invocation given by Hazrat Inayat Khan, a teaching that Samuel Lewis took very much into his heart and his breath.

Toward the One, the Perfection of Love, Harmony, and Beauty,
the Only Being, United with All the Illuminated Souls
Who Form the Embodiment of the Master, the Spirit of Guidance.

I. Jan. 31, 1932
And the Lord said, "Arise and prophesy unto the children of men as did your forefathers,
Arise and convey to them My Will and My decrees,
For as it has been in the days of yore, so shall it be again."
And He said unto me, "Samuel, what tasteth thou?"
I answered, "O Lord, the taste of blood is in my mouth,
And the taste of blood is in my heart,
And the taste of blood is in my inner being."
He answered, "Thou speakest truly, for the taste of blood is the taste of war.
As it is in you, so it is in the world and war will surely follow."
Then the taste of blood continued in my mouth and in my heart and in my inner being;
For three days did the taste of blood remain, neither at day nor at night did it depart.
And at the end of three days, in the evening, did the voice of the Lord appear,
And when the Voice of the Lord appeared, the taste of blood disappeared.
Then said Beth Sol:* *"Behold, that the taste of blood was the blood of man;*
Verily this day on earth has the city of Shanghai been taken,
And innocent babes slaughtered at their mothers' breasts.
Innocent men and women and children killed and maimed and robbed.
Therefore arise and turn thy face against the men of Yamato [Japan],
Against the men of Yamato and the women of Yamato and the children of Yamato, the fire of the Lord is kindled.
What they this day have done upon earth, so it is being done to them in Heavens.
Their islands shall tremble; their islands shall sink,
Earthquake and famine and pestilence shall destroy the land.
The walls of Yokohamo are fallen and the shipping is again destroyed.
The selfishness and greed of rulers is repaid;
I knocked and they would not listen,
I called and they would not heed.
False is their cry and false their moves,
Their government utterly corrupt, and venial,
The Lord declares who is the bandit and who is the murderer:
As Nippon has done, so it shall be done unto them,

*Translation given the Archives: "The Divine All-Pervading Voice or Sound."

A pariah among nations they were and a pariah they shall be.
The Lord had mercy upon Nippon in its hour of suffering;
He raised them from the darkness to a high station,
And they waxed fat and became full of vain glory, envious, lustful.
Now their evils shall return unto them,
For every son of China shall it be repaid,
For every harm to the peaceful shall it be returned,
A curse is spread, a curse upon Cipango [Japan]:
Yokohama and Hakodate and Kobe shall suffer,
Tokyo and Osaka and the islands shall not escape,
Only the sacred places shall be preserved,
And the nation is doomed to destruction.

This next prophecy addressed the future of Hitlerism.

VI. The doom of the Ashkenazi [Germans]; *Against Hitlerism, May 9, 1932*
Say "Ye shall not be doomed,
But insofar as ye turn against the children of the Lord,
Then shall ye be doomed;
Insofar as ye turn unto your self-will
Then shall ye continue to suffer.
Yours was a fair country, a glorious country, a country of promise,
Yours was becoming the elected among the nations.
Then in the war ye failed to give a just peace
To the people [of] Hruska [Russia] *and the people of Roum* [Romania]
Ye failed to give a just peace.
Now for fifteen years ye suffer as ye have sown,
The thorn and the briar intended for others has become your goad.
The lash and the whip prepared for others has been hurled against your backs,
The servitude for others has been redeemed against yourselves.
Now before you is the pardon of your Lord or the worst of grievances.
Now before you is relief from trepidation
Or a thousandfold punishment."
Thus sayeth the Lord, the Holy One:
"On that hour when you hurl the lash against my people,
Yours will be the fate of Sepharad [Spain] *and Lusitania* [Portugal] *and Sarmatia* [Russia]*;*
Down shall ye go unto barbarism,
Hand will be turned against hand, even brother against brother.
The forest shall conquer the city and the tares the pleasant fields.

Woe, woe unto you who threaten danger,
For upon you and all your people shall fall the doom."

Sam appears to have returned to California fairly directly from the East in 1931. One East Coast visit he made was to Duncan McDonald, a highly regarded professor at Hartford Theological Seminary who was an early pioneer of Muslim and Christian understanding. Sam later wrote, "We only differed on the Trinity, and having so much in common we did not let thirty thousand agreements be disturbed by a single disagreement."[174]

Howard Street in San Francisco, known as "Skid Row," the district of the unemployed

CHAPTER 4

Engagement with Social Movements

BY 1931 THE DEPRESSION HAD ALREADY ARRIVED in most of the United States. At the time of the election of Franklin Roosevelt in 1932, a quarter of the population was out of work. New social ideas were arising and gaining partisans. Various forms of Communism and Socialism were being discussed widely, and questions about Capitalism were in the air.

The impact of the Depression was now felt everywhere, even in the West, which had seemed like the Promised Land to Dust Bowl refugees. Much of the population was driven to focus on daily survival. Social ideas and movements were being trumpeted among the poor and for the poor, stirrings that soon captivated Sam's interest. He had a peripatetic lifestyle during this period, something he often attributed to his Uncle Harry, who worked on the railroad.

Social Activism

Spreading the Sufi teachings of Hazrat Inayat Khan was a priority for Samuel Lewis in 1932. When he was not engaged in this work, he was drawn into social movements that were attempting to address the problems faced by large numbers of Americans during the Great Depression.

Sam's interest in attending to the ills of society led him to meet Luther Whiteman sometime late in 1934. Whiteman was a writer and social reformer, and immediately recognized Sam's impressive intellectual abilities. Whiteman felt sympathy for him as a person and in effect became like a father to him for a while. He hired Sam as a secretary and drew him in to be the coauthor of a book he was planning.

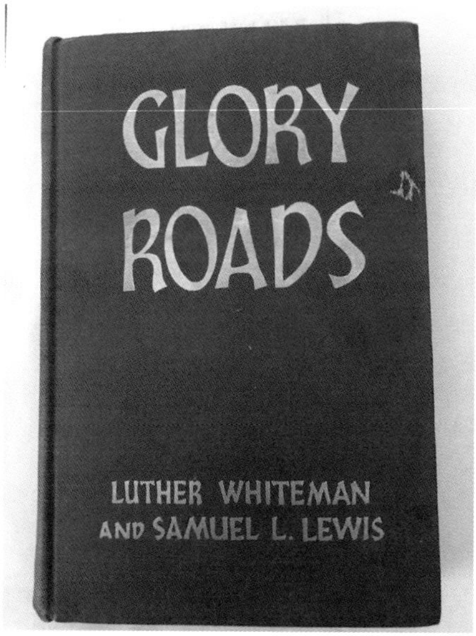

The book was entitled *Glory Roads: The Psychological State of California.*[175] Sam, according to his own accounts,[176] did most of the research for the book. He had previously become familiar with the political and social positions of many of the groups of the times, and in 1934 had become an employee of the Townsend organization, which promoted universal pensions for senior citizens in the days before Social Security became a reality.

Looking at some of what was presented in *Glory Roads* is a good way to begin to understand the background of this mostly unknown period in Sam's life. In their joint introduction Whiteman and Lewis bring up the question of what is so unusual about California:

> What is it in California that causes this State to give birth to so much that is new in reform, in science, in religion, and in politics? . . . Is there something in the atmosphere of its deserts, mountains, and sea shore, conducive to the lush growth of cults and cultists, or is California actually a state of mind as much as it is a political subdivision of the American Commonwealth? . . . It is now well understood in the United States that individuals exhibiting the unusual in approach to economic and political problems have "gone Californiac" . . . California since the days of the Padres has been a land of prophets, and profits. Its inhabitants will seek prophets and profits with no sign of abatement.[177]

A signal that times had changed in California came with the death of James Rolph, Jr., a former mayor of San Francisco who was elected Governor of the state in 1930.

> "Sunny Jim," as he was known, was the last governor in all probability to represent the old California, the California of the pioneers, gold miners, of romantic San Francisco . . . When Rolph took office, the State

> Treasury had a surplus of some millions of dollars; when he died less than three years later, the State was broke and vastly in debt . . .
>
> In Los Angeles the boom of the ['20s] was now in a backwash. This city and county was to have the unenviable distinction of being called the 'blackest spot' in the United States.
>
> There were at least twenty known groups in San Francisco whose purpose was to lead the way out of depression . . . No two groups agreed on anything fundamental. A leader, a messiah, had not yet arisen. But a plan and leader were bound to come; a manifestation of some sort was somehow foreordained. California, psychological California, was certain the calamity would be checked . . . The same luck that had discovered the gold in the hills, the oil beneath the orange groves, would not fail. If leaders had proven false, success was certain for a messiah was bound to come.[178]

There was a wide variety of movements with prophetic types at the reins during this time, some more worthy than others. And there were ample sheep who were ready and willing to fund what were often unscrupulous leaders. The Townsend movement is a perfect example of the phenomenon. Samuel Lewis worked for them in 1934 and 1935 as a stenographer, typist, correspondent, and organizer, along with other miscellaneous duties as described in his Civil Service application. He earned $15 a week.

In another application for Federal employment Sam described the organization as political and said that he supervised one to six people.

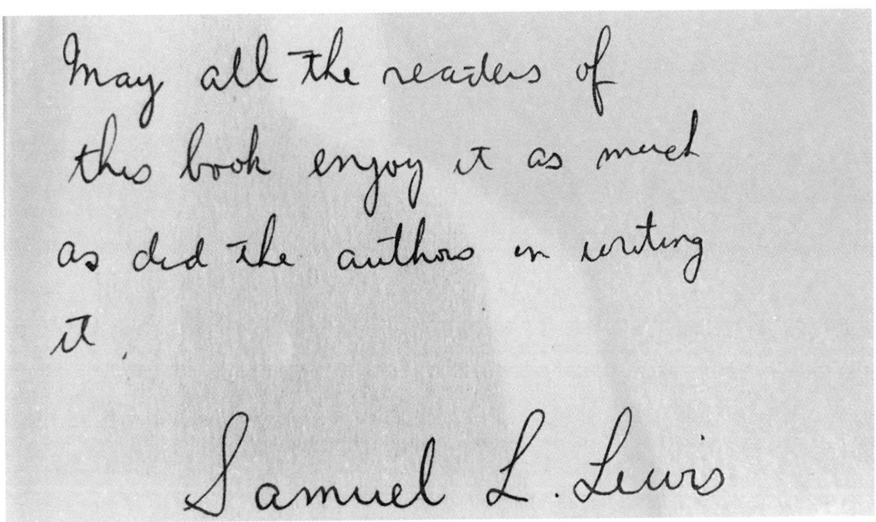
May all the readers of this book enjoy it as much as did the authors in writing it.

Samuel L. Lewis

Handwritten inscription in *Glory Roads*

He listed his duties and responsibilities in more detail: "Speaking, economic research, extracting from Congressional Record, writing and copying radio speeches, and circular letters, keeping records of all kinds. Sometimes dictated letters and answered correspondence. Work was constantly changing."

Congressional investigation eventually showed internal corruption at the top within the Townsend operation. The following summary of the Townsend movement is drawn freely from *Glory Roads,* which was written in 1935 and 1936 as the seamy side of the movement was becoming apparent to some.[179]

Dr. Francis Townsend migrated to Long Beach, California, from the Midwest. One day, as he told it, he saw three elderly women rummaging for food around a garbage pail outside his home, a sight that motivated him to act. It is probable that Townsend modeled his Plan on the copyrighted work of Steward McCord, who had proposed a monthly annuity for retirees at a time when the idea of Social Security was deemed a radical and unworkable idea in Washington. Townsend never acknowledged the source of his proposal, and it was said that he "seldom admits indebtedness to anybody."[180]

Millions were in need of aid, and the Townsend Plan took hold immediately after the organization was established in 1934. Soon there was a flood of literature pouring forth demanding two hundred dollars a month for every man and woman over sixty years of age who would retire from their occupation or trade and spend this sum monthly. Petitions were circulated requesting that congressional representatives support the Old Age Revolving Pension plan as well as a sales tax of 10% to fund it. Clubs were formed that attracted crusaders, publishers, and opportunists. Membership dues were fixed at 25¢ paid to National Headquarters. Money poured in, and into the pockets of Townsend and his top associates. Townsend and his national treasurer Clements were doing very, very well from the pennies and nickels and dimes of the poor old people of California.

Samuel Lewis headed up a Townsend office in San Francisco in 1934–35 and became aware of the massive fiscal misfeasance of the operation. Consequently, he resigned from the Townsend organization and fully cooperated with the congressional investigation that took place.

> The testimony taken by the committee fills some one thousand pages, in five volumes. If it never serves any other purpose, it will at least serve as an encyclopedia of American gullibility, economic illiteracy, and avarice. The commonest facts seem to have escaped the self-appointed economic crusaders. Neither science nor mathematics apparently had a place in their schooling. These hearings also disclosed the palpable disregard for truth on the part of many of the leaders, from Doctor Townsend down.[181]

Continuing Education

> *Our scheme of government and of life can succeed only if in their more mature years men and women will engage in careful, enthusiastic and guided study of common values, common dangers, common opportunities . . . The end to be served will not be vocational . . . The deepest question in American life today is not economic or political; it is educational. It is the question of the thinking power of a democracy. Can our people understand and direct their own living or must someone else do their thinking, make their decisions, for them? As a democracy we are pledged to try the first of these.*
>
> ALEXANDER MEIKLEJOHN[182]

In the 1930s Samuel was frequently in transit to the Los Angeles area and other parts of Southern California. During this time his address of record was at a house on Clay Street in San Francisco with Hazel Armstrong and Davida Herrick, fellow Sufi initiates also associated with Murshida Martin. In the city directory he is identified as a writer for the first time.

Samuel enrolled at The San Francisco School of Social Studies,[183] which had been founded in 1934 by the famous educator and philosopher Alexander Meiklejohn. Meiklejohn had been Dean of Brown University and President of Amherst College. He had also had founded an Experimental College at the University of Wisconsin that inspired scores of innovative undergraduate programs.

The San Francisco school required no credits for admission and charged no fees, which made it possible for Samuel to participate. Further, this adult education program worked out well with his robust schedule.

In the article in *The New Republic* quoted in the epigraph above, Meiklejohn describes in some detail his educational philosophy and gives a practical description of the way this particular school functioned.

> The first task of the teachers has been that of selecting the books in which the best minds of our civilization have expressed themselves upon our common problems in ways suitable for popular reading. In the nature of the case, most of our technical, scholarly books will not serve the purpose. But the "Dialogues of Plato," the Bible, the Constitution, the writings of Emerson, Whitman, Adam Smith, Karl Marx, Emily Dickinson, Dreiser, Jeffers, Dewey, Veblen, Tawney, Brandeis, Turner, Beard, Lenin, Bourne, Mumford, Dos Passos, these and a host of others in poetry and prose, tell us of the attempts of our intellectual leaders to solve the human problems that we in America now face . . .*
>
> The purpose is to develop in the student the power to do his own reading and to discuss it with his friends . . . The first step in the process of generating your own better ideas is an honest, painstaking attempt to understand what an idea means when presented by another mind . . .
>
> If this work could be brought about on a larger scale it would do for us what the folk schools have done for Denmark, what the tutorial classes have done for the workers of England. It would have in it the beginnings of the making of an American mind. To say these things is of course to speak of dreams rather than of present achievements. But such dreams define the direction in which our efforts may go. As such they may be of value in the planning and creating of a democratic America.[184]

Meiklejohn pursued his interests in the constitutional right to free speech, protesting the permanent installation of the House Un-American Activities Committee and loyalty oaths. He received honors from the American Civil Liberties Union and the Socialist League for Industrial Democracy, where he served as vice-president for almost forty years.[185]

---

* Meiklejohn's motive here found expression in the "Great Books" course at Columbia and again in the similar venture carried on at the University of Chicago by President Robert Maynard Hutchins and Professor Mortimer Adler.

Meiklejohn could not have had a more ideal student than Samuel Lewis, a brilliant thinker who was already in agreement with the school's overall ideals and policies, and who also dreamed of creating a more robustly democratic America. He remained a student his whole life, attending numerous university classes and seminars up to the time of his passing. Likewise, he continually pursued his commission from Hazrat Inayat Khan to bring the knowledge of mysticism to the academic establishment. He also continued to follow the urge, nourished in Meiklejohn's school, to play a political role in improving society.

Samuel very briefly described his experience with Meiklejohn's school in his civil service application for work. "Poetry and social studies. Studied by self: Oriental culture, philosophy, religion, history, art, etc., etc., etc." He also listed his courses at UC Berkeley as Chemistry, Mathematics, Physics, and Economics.[186]

Sam in the 1930s

As previously detailed, Sam was already working in the political sphere with both Townsend and Luther Whiteman. At some point he and Whiteman relocated to Hollywood. Vocha Fiske, who became one of Sam's very close lifelong friends and confidantes, met him for the first time during these years. A few years after Sam's passing, she described Sam and Luther in an interview,[187] referring to Sam as Murshid.

> Sam had come to Los Angeles with Luther Whiteman, you will recall he did all of the research on that book *Glory Roads*, which dealt with several avant garde or off-beat movements . . . Luther introduced me then to Sam . . . his friend Paul Reps was still married to a girl who he called Estelle, and Murshid knew this flower child and had gone to see her, and I met him there, and that was the beginning of our forty years of friendship.

When asked to describe Sam's personality in those days Vocha said:

> Murshid went through several personality changes. When I first knew him, he was quite scornful of a great many people who had won some recognition in the world. At the same time, he was quite envious [and felt he should receive] recognition, because as you know he had a bril-

liant mind. I had never known anyone, and I can say this with no reservations, with the erudition that Murshid had. And I could quite well understand his feelings, that he ought to be recognized. But, at the same time, he had several behaviors that might [have kept] that [recognition] from him.

She went on to speak of her initial experience with Sam and Luther.

Murshid, and Luther Whiteman also, had done some articles. I remember the title of one, that certainly was Murshid's, that was labeled "Antics or Semantics." You see Semantics was just coming into some kind of notice then, and Murshid did a very funny article . . . it came out in a Social Credit paper that Luther Whiteman edited . . . called *Controversy.*

General Semantics was supposed to look at how words influenced the human nervous system. And Murshid's interest in it was that it was a new tool, so to speak, although the Buddha certainly in the *Lankavatara Sutra* said about all that is important about words, and Murshid knew this, but this was an up-to-date, it was a scientific terminology that was being used, and so you see he became interested . . .

[His interest had started] because Cassius Keyser was one of the few professors—and he had great standing as you know—that admired Alfred Korzybski's book Science and Sanity, and he had written a splendid review of it . . . I'm sure [it was] through Cassius Keyser that Murshid began a new interest in Semantics, and that went on until it was a part of [him]. In the draft of what could be done as far as the Arab and Israeli question—in the first paragraph Murshid writes: "It's largely a question of Semantics."*

In the interview Vocha agreed that Murshid had felt Semantics could be used to solve problems, and that somehow or other the people that he called the Generals of Semantics had lost this conception.

Yes, particularly Don Hayakawa and the San Francisco group, they all became anathema, as it were, to Murshid. He felt that they were just playing around and as a matter of fact I studied under Korzybski for 4 years, I know of no one who is seriously using General Semantics. In ways that Korzybski suggested, it could be used . . . to have very clear understanding of the different levels at which one used key terms. And

---

* Murshid Sam's draft program appears in the Archives as "Draft: Integrative Program for Peace in the Near East."

to, if necessary, index the level at which you used the term. Let us take the term religion. This is a very confused and wobbly term. If one indexed that and said "now in this context, my usual term 'religion' refers to . . . ," and limit the way that it does refer, you would have much fewer disagreements . . .

I studied with Alfred from 1935. I was the one who brought him to Los Angeles . . . After, I had taught for him in 1947 at his Institute of General Semantics, which was in Lakeville, Connecticut . . .

[Murshid] admired Alfred very much. And in fact some of the more recent letters that he sent me spoke about the need of people reading and using Korzybski's work, and when you think of the tangle . . . our communication is in, there is something in that . . .

What was going on in those days was that there was a great burst, as it were, and not from the academic level, but there was a great burst of activity of new ideas. For instance there was the epic movements in politics, which Upton Sinclair was very active in, and then of course the coming on the scene of Howard Scott's technocracy, and in a way, I suppose you could draw some similarity between that period in the early 30s and this present period [early '70s]. But the difference was, it was the old people then who were interested in new ideas, new solutions, and today it is the young people. Praise be . . .

I knew [Luther Whiteman] for many years. [He] came of English stock, and he began in public relations and spent all of his life. He was a man who was interested in forward looking ideas, ideas of Social Credit, which we don't know anything about now, and of course was then a very new idea in 1933, '34, '35 . . .* Luther believed in that, and championed it. And something happened to Luther, after he was divorced from his wife of many years, and he came down to Hollywood, and then Luther had two different wives; he I would say never really found himself, he was a splendid friend, the man with gorgeous sense of humor.

Humor was not Sam's quality, she said.

He was too wrathful, in the early '30s, to show much of a sense of humor, but I do hope when you are thinking about his style, in writings, you will remember that he had a most delicious way of coining words,

---

*Vocha's references to Social Credit led to research into Gorham Munson's archives at Wesleyan University, where extensive correspondence between Munson and Lewis is collected. Several articles on the subject were also published in Munson's journal *New Democracy.*

> which became very apt. This is the main reason that I regret that I have none of his letters, because often I would take and underline when he had done this with a word that seemed particularly effective.

Vocha also said she would highlight all the positive things in Sam's letters and write notes of appreciation back to him, and she would ignore the many criticisms and complaints that the letter would often include. She was a true friend who said that she always felt Samuel Lewis was destined for full integration, and she lived to see her vision of him proven true.

Out of the Townsend Plan and Into Social Credit

> *Of course Townsend supporters stand with the advocates of Social Credit in opposition to the present monetary and financial system. They both desire to relieve the multitude from debt-slavery, artificial money, control by the very few, and endless taxation and compound interest. They also concur that it is possible to solve the problems of the day by democratic means, without need of violence, and both also hold to a form of money circulation, resembling the life-blood of the body in certain respects . . . A reconciliation may not only be possible, but inevitable.*
>
> SAMUEL LEWIS[188]

Social Credit was a school of thought that had begun to attract a great deal of interest in the 1930s. Drawing from founder C. H. Douglas's works *Economic Democracy* and *The Fig Tree: a Douglas Social Credit Quarterly Review,* Wikipedia offers this brief history and definition of the movement:

> Social credit is an interdisciplinary distributive philosophy developed by C. H. Douglas (1879–1952), a British engineer, who published a book by that name in 1924. It encompasses economics, political science, history, and accounting. Its policies are designed, according to Douglas, to disperse economic and political power to individuals. Douglas wrote, "Systems were made for men, and not men for systems, and the interest of man which is self-development, is above all systems, whether theological, political or economic."[189]

Before Sam fully joined ranks with Luther Whiteman to coauthor *Glory Roads,* he responded somewhat critically to an article by Whiteman in *New Democracy,* a Social Credit journal. At this point he still wrote in support of the Townsend Plan (OARP), unaware of the large-scale corruption:

> Luther Whiteman's admirable article in the December 1st issue of *New Democracy,* while in many respects logically justifiable, did not take into account the hardly expected and rapid growing popularity of the Old Age Revolving Pension (OARP) Plan. The number of its followers (end of January) has been estimated as high as thirty millions, although this figure is not official and may be very inaccurate—it is roughly somewhere between fifteen and thirty million.
>
> The reason for this is not hard to seek. Today those earning more than $5,000 per annum possess about 99 percent of the nation's wealth, either directly in their names or through corporate control. The rest of us, meaning nearly all of us, "own"—if such a word can still be applied—the remainder. And being believers in democracy, and feeling sure there is a way out, we demand action. And what action has been proposed?
>
> The OARP suggests in brief that: "All citizens of the United States, man or woman—over the age of 60 years may retire on a pension of $200 per month on the following conditions: 1. That they engaged in no further labor, business or profession for gain. 2. That their past life is free from habitual criminality. 3. That they take oath to, and actually do spend, within the confines of the United States, the entire amount of their pension within thirty days after receiving same."[190]

Samuel wrote that the reconciliation of the Townsend supporters and Social Credit was inevitable, demonstrating his emerging analysis of events and pointing clearly to a direction he would eventually take himself. His turning to Social Credit as more universal and more scientific had begun.

> The followers of Social Credit . . . demand a new money based upon the scientific definition of the principle of money and wealth. Nor do they see any reason for fixing the debtor's age at 60, for the vast majority are today in debt, and that for very artificial and not natural reasons. They hold that the Townsend Plan, while undoubtedly in the right direction, does not enable all citizens to partake immediately of the National Dividend, and does deprive the beneficiaries of a certain amount of liberty unnecessarily . . . Townsend supporters are in sympathy but desire a plan of action immediately, one in a concrete form, and believe that the adoption of such a legal and political device will lead toward the ultimate solution of other economic and social problems.

> Social Credit, on the other hand, begins as a broad, universal philosophy with a tremendous spiritual and scientific background, with exceedingly deep roots. The names of Douglas, Orage, Colbourne, Dyson and Ryder conjure up so many branches of knowledge, not to mention the contributions of the world-renowned scientist Frederick Soddy . . .
>
> The Townsend Plan is as yet thoroughly American, it requires the spending of the money in America. Perhaps it has not yet found itself . . . There is a strong possibility, already expressed in the views of Robt. E. Clements, co-founder of the plan, and in the addresses of the leading speakers, that the whole movement is tending rapidly in the direction of Social Credit.[191]

The aforementioned Clements, his wife, and the good Doctor Townsend would all be found to be guilty of pocketing most of the money raised by the fund for their own personal use. The last thing they wanted was to share power with anyone. There was no democracy in the movement, as all power and financial control was held at the level of headquarters. They were not held accountable for the very large amount of money that they disposed of personally.

Not many months after this article was written, Sam's observations and investigation of the Townsend movement began to reveal its flaws at the most basic level of ethics, without even getting into the dubious numbers that speculative advocates generated about the supposed effect of the taxation element.

Gorham Munson, editor of *New Democracy*

Partly because of Luther Whiteman's connection to Gorham Munson, Editor of *New Democracy,* and partly through a Social Creditor acquaintance, Samuel Lewis initiated correspondence with Munson, a well-known literary editor and teacher of writing. Munson was also a pioneer in the Social Credit movement, serving as Secretary General. His magazine was a direct descendant of earlier Social Credit efforts, including *Contro-*

versy, which was soon incorporated into *New Democracy.*

Munson would prove to be a friend and a kind of mentor. The subsequent spirited exchanges between the two of them reveal a treasure house of details about Samuel Lewis's life and activities during the late 1930s that were not previously known.

Below is Sam's first letter to the Editor of *New Democracy* in New York City. It was written from his San Francisco address at 2536 Clay St. on December 30, 1935.

NEW DEMOCRACY

INCORPORATING "CONTROVERSY"

CANTO XLVI

Ezra Pound

SOCIAL CREDIT PREVENTS INFLATION

H. C. Whernside

NATIONAL CREDIT ACCOUNT

Paul Hampden

$2.50 a year — March, 1936 — 25c a copy

Vol. VI — Published Monthly — No. 1

Cover of the issue that carried Sam's article "Mint's Meat"

Dear Sir:

I am enclosing a little humorous article, which you may use at your discretion, and if published, it may be properly edited and shortened as you see fit.

When Mr. Taylor was in San Francisco I was connected with the Townsend Movement. At that time he asked me for names and addresses of the leaders that he might contact them, which I felt I could not justly place in his hands. As I am no longer in that organization I am under no compunction in this regard, but do not know whether Mr. Taylor is with you in New York or not, or whether he or you would still desire such names.

Incidentally, I am now a firm believer in Social Credit, and through the experience gained in the Townsend Movement I hoped to assist in this really scientific application of knowledge to the problems of economics and finance. In this regard, I am keeping in close touch with Luther Whiteman, etc.

I am also working on a more serious problem, that of marginal liquidity, which I expect to write up shortly in two forms. Simple, for the layman, and technical for the students of the new economics. This is being submitted to Mr. Ezra Pound who has asked for material for the New English Weekly.[192]

Munson's response came two weeks later and was enthusiastic.

> Your short piece, Mint's Meat, is accepted with cheers. I congratulate you on being hilariously funny from the first paragraph to the last. We will run it in "New Democracy" in the February 1st issue.*
>
> If you wish to send me a list of the Townsend movement leaders to whom you think copies of New Democracy might profitably be sent, I shall be glad to have such a list. I do not, however, expect that Social Credit will deflect the leadership of the Townsend movement an inch from their present course during the year 1936. They are projectiles in flight, and we shall have to wait until they have come up against a stone wall of some sort.[193]

Vocha Fiske had said Sam's humor often came out beautifully in his usage of words. "Mint's Meat" illustrates this well. The theme of the satirical piece is in complete harmony with the concerns of the Social Credit Movement, and gives a nice sample example of Sam's gift with words:

MINT'S MEAT BY SAMUEL L. LEWIS

> The dollar is the most remarkable and intricate discovery ever made by the human race. It consists of a very definite and exact number of grains of gold, out of which it is never made, and so perfect must it be that if its weight is .000001% from the normal, it may be confined to the limbo of some furnace to be reincarnated at an early opportunity.
>
> So conceived and so dedicated its behavior continues to be remarkable. Simply by placing it in a bank, and letting it do nothing it does everything. The dollar, conceived in gold, and bastardly begotten as silver, if passed from hand to hand, because it does not break the law of perpetual motion, will in time be so worn as to be considered improper for use. But just place it in a bank, and no more wear and tear, no more infractions of the law of perpetual motion.
>
> There in the bank the dollar studies the "Bhagavat Gita" which teaches that bliss comes from finding action in inaction and inaction in action. So placing it in a bank, it will increase at the rate of 3% per annum without taking on a single grain of weight, feeding endlessly without fear of obesity.
>
> Yes, the dollar in the bank is not one of the seven wonders of the world, it is the wonder even of the wonders. For it has two remarkable characteristics:

---

* Size considerations delayed the article's inclusion to the next monthly issue.

a) It has its own law of perpetual motion

b) It reproduces parthenogenetically

That is to say, the more the banker gives it away, the more he has of it. It is very simple. You go to the bank to borrow a dollar. The banker places it in his left hand—it is his; then he places it in his right hand—it is yours. Then he enters it upon his books and you have it, only he has it.

Now that you have it, which you haven't, he lends it—that "it" not being the original dollar which he has already lent to you, he can't lend that again, but he can lend the dollar which he has lent to you.

Note well how this is done. For the dollar which he has-has-not given you, you have given him a note on which he gets another dollar which he lends. It is your dollar which he lends. You think you have borrowed from the bank, and the joke is on you. But, as Uncle Henry would say, that is only the beginning. Having lent your dollar which you have-have-not to somebody else he keeps on doing this so long as he can make that dollar obey his law of perpetual motion in collecting interest on it.

Therefore at the end of one year a nice dollar by doing nothing does:

a) The original lender to whom the bank gives no security, and who is out of luck if the bank fails, gets 3c on it.

b) The banker, lending it ten times gets 60c on it, only he has it, whether he fails or not—he still has that dollar.

Now the reason for all this is that the dollar is made up of bull-ion. All the other chemical ions are made up of atoms following definite laws, but the bull-ion is no respecter of law; it knows nothing of the principle of conservation and never heard of thermodynamics. And when everything else decreases, it increases—provided it is in a bank doing nothing.

The chemistry of the bull-ion is so remarkable that when Sir Frederick Soddy investigated it its chemistry made his researches in radioactivity quite simple. Radium is radium and is lead but is not both radium and lead, but the dollar is both the dollar and not the dollar, and in this pea and shell game, bull-ion in the hands of the bankers makes its own rules.

Now the future of the bull-ion has been described by H. G. Wells, who has described everything, and by Hamlet, who said, 'To be or not to be, that is the question.' But Mr. International Banker, who owns the bull-ions, said, 'No. Both to be and not to be, and there is not any question at all.'

> All of which was true until we had a New Deal. And this is the New Deal:
>
> The bull-ion is made of gold (the law says so). But the bull-ion dollars are of silver (in the Far, Far West). And the silver in the silver dollar is worth so much in gold. And therefore the gold may be expressed in a multiple of the silver in the dollar. This is called Finance.
>
> But even more remarkable. The gold is henceforth to be the child of the bull-ion dollar, because there are to be so many dollars in an ounce of gold. Which is probably why Al Smith calls it the bull-iony (pronounce boloney) dollar.[194]

Sam's relationship with Munson and Social Credit deepened over the next few years. He never lost his knack for writing cleverly when he wished to. Years later he would have an almost daily correspondence in this vein with the famous humorist Art Hoppe.

Correspondence with Munson

> *It is very heartening to me that a man of your enthusiasm, energy and intelligence is coming actively into the Social Credit movement. I am so glad that you are working arm in arm with Mr. Whiteman. I look forward to the day when I shall meet you both. Mr. Whiteman in my judgment is one of the princes in our movement.*
>
> GORHAM MUNSON[195]

Gorham Munson (1896–1969) became an important figure in Samuel's life. His whole body of work is interesting, as noted by Andrew Salinas of the Amistad Research Center.

> [Munson] lived in Greenwich Village and was a close associate of Hart Crane, Waldo Frank, and Jean Toomer. In 1922 he founded the little magazine *Secession*, whose contributors included Marianne Moore, Hart Crane, Waldo Frank, and William Carlos Williams. He taught a popular professional writing course at The New School in New York for over thirty years. The author and editor of numerous publications, Munson was also a leader of the American Social Credit Movement and a follower of Gurdjieff's American Movement." [196]

One of Munson's works was an article entitled "Orage in America." It is a vivid account of his friend and Gurdjieff teacher, A. R. Orage, whose influence as a cultural catalyst is noteworthy.*

Samuel had written to Munson about his stance with regard to Social Credit:

> My experience with the Townsend movement, which was considerable, firmly convinced me of the truth of Social Credit principles and of vibrational thinking and money as against atomic thinking and money . . . I will not submit articles gratis to any magazines other than Social Credit publications.[197]

It was not long before Munson became an advocate for the book Whiteman and Lewis were writing, and with his literary contacts lined up a publisher for them. Samuel continued to research *Glory Roads* and involved himself more and more with Social Credit and with Munson directly.

Samuel struggled to make ends meet. He hoped that his links with the Sufis in San Francisco could be beneficial, but nothing immediately materialized. His life was diversified between research on *Glory Roads*, public lectures, his writing in numerous areas, and ongoing responsibilities in the Sufi work as a Khalif under Murshida Martin.

Samuel later passed along a copy of an article on the Tradex operating philosophy to Munson. He said that this material showed how a cooperative operated in the business world. The article formed the basis for suggestions that Sam later sent to Alberta, Canada, which was reportedly operating on Social Credit principles.†

Munson was enthusiastic about Samuel's new approach to the discussion, but he was skeptical that anything would be properly received

---

*For further information about the connection of Orage and Social Credit, see Gorham Munson, "Orage in America," in Gurdjieff: A Reading Guide, J. Walter Driscoll, ed., www.gurdjieff-bibliography.com/Current/q_munson_orage-in-amer_2_2004-07-04.pdf.

†Sam wrote to Premier William Aberhart of Edmonton, Alberta, on April 3rd, 1936, offering to describe for him some of the promising movements in California, and cheering on Social Credit (Wesleyan University, Munson Collection).

by those handling the failing situation of what was called Social Credit in Alberta. He graciously responded to Samuel's letter:

> I wonder if you could do a sympathetic article on the cooperative movement from the Social Credit point of view. We have had requests from leaders for treatment of the cooperatives and thus far have not known any writer who was intimate with them and yet thoroughly grounded in Social Credit whom we could ask to do the piece.
>
> I hope you and Mr. Whiteman are making good progress on your book. Isn't it wonderful the way Congress has set up practically a research committee to help you along? [198]

Samuel responded with an update on his activities: *Glory Roads* was nearing completion; he was devoting time to the subject of cooperative and barter movements; and he was writing to congressmen about supporting Tradex, providing extensive quotes from early leaders of the republic to reinforce their approach.

In response to Lewis's letters, Munson responded that he liked the edited article on Tradex Sam had sent and would try to get it into *New Democracy*. He said that the magazine now had a precarious existence and probably would have to be reduced in size.* He praised Sam for the material he sent the congressmen and told him that Sam's findings on Margett of the Townsend movement looked absolutely conclusive.[199]

Sam had written to him about Margett and the Townsend investigation some days before:

> The Federal Government is carrying on three investigations locally "and the three are one." These are (a) police graft in San Francisco, (b) borrowing of funds through members of the State Board of Equalization, (c) The Townsend Movement, particularly centered around Edward J. Margett. This is the story, almost every detail of which can be covered and proved:
>
> With the coming of the depression many of the hotels in San Francisco became mortgaged to banks, and later found it impossible to liquidate. The banks took them over, and in order to operate them at a profit . . . taking advantage of the repeal of prohibition opened up night clubs and . . . bawdy houses . . .

---

*It does not appear that this article was ever published.

The State Board of Equalization was early drawn into the ring because they determine liquor licensing. The banks in turn permitted the members and their friends to borrow money through more or less official channels in turn for their favors.

The San Francisco Police were told that they could borrow money without security, in theory, by the profits from these hotel nightclubs, etc. The police were allowed to have bad memories, and with no security necessary, began building up immense personal fortunes . . .

To strengthen themselves this bank controlled ring began building their fences. Margett was drawn into the picture . . . because he had been a saloon keeper, a rum-runner, billiard room man [and] he sold furniture. He would bill the furniture to the night clubs and they would pay him out of their profits. In the meanwhile he took a lien or equity on the night-clubs, etc.

The inner ring of international bankers and local machine politicians gave Margett their blessing and some financial help . . . to "sacrifice" all his time, efforts and money to build up the Townsend movement. He did so, but he also delivered the Townsend votes to the other side in the Fall of '35, and at the presidential primaries.[200]

In the coming weeks, Sam continued:

I wonder if you can do me a couple of favors: To write a short synoptic review of the book, preferably to Whiteman, so I can show it to members of my family and others; to write using my name to a lawyer in your city A. Waterman Jr., who is my second cousin, calling attention to the book and sending him a blurb . . . This is for psychological purposes . . .

Incidentally, could you use articles from time to time on Oriental psychology in "Practical Psychology" [in *New Democracy*]. These would be chiefly Buddhistic, but could cover any and all schools, and would cost you nothing, being furnished freely.[201]

My preliminary talk on Glory Roads yesterday was quite a success as is evidenced by the check for $2.50 which I'm enclosing. This is for copies of "New Democracy" of February 1st, the one in which appeared the article by L. W. and myself on the Townsend plan. Will you kindly forward whatever number of copies you consider reasonable to Mrs. J. E. Lewis, 567 Ninth Avenue, San Francisco . . . Actually we have had no difficulties or obstacles whatever so far except lack of publicity material and this is an obstacle.[202]

Samuel Lewis was 39 years old, but he had never given up hope to find some way that his family would come to appreciate his abilities and accomplishments. His requests for magazines to be sent to his mother and for a favorable review by Munson of his book to be sent to his family members shows that he still strongly identified as the black sheep of the family, needed respect from them, and hoped to gain approval and acceptance.

As Samuel had developed a close relationship with Munson, he now opened up to him by suggesting some Buddhist stories for an already existing section of *New Democracy.* It is worth emphasizing that both of these well-informed intellectuals had a history of study and practice within esoteric schools.

Sam energetically countered an article in the London *New English Weekly* in a letter to the editor. The article's author was a Social Credit advocate who had used the example of international bankers to slur Jews on a large scale. Samuel's response takes a personal tone at the beginning. He speaks of his family ancestry and asserts a distant blood relationship to the Rothschild family. What he wrote shows what he believed about that story:

> Sir,
>
> The writer is not only a Social Creditor and a Semite by race, but his grandfather, whose name was certainly not originally "Lewis," was born in Frankfort and was through his mother (my great-grandmother) a blood relative of the Mephistophelian Panjoram himself. In other words, at least one blood relative, not to say descendant of the Meyer-Rothchilds, however distant be the connection is neither a Marxist nor a gold diviner . . .
>
> Removing a cross section of the populace is not going to alter the weather or mathematical formula. If the Jews are to be blamed at all, it is for not following the law of Moses in regard to money and business, but by the same token the Hindus, the Buddhists, believers in traditional Christianity and Islam are to be regarded as equally culpable—all religious founders declared themselves against the monetary ideal . . .
>
> Even those bigots who rave about the Talmud, which they have in most instances never read, would gain considerably by an examination of Hebrew literature in regard to gold, money and usury. I think if Mr. Orage were alive and someone exclaimed to him that the teachings of

> Moses are fulfilled, not destroyed, by Major Douglas and Social Credit, he would assent; and the same is true with all religious-sociological revelations. [203]

An End with Whiteman

In 1938, the California election news was not good. Sam described it to Munson, and took the opportunity to refer to his deteriorated relationship with Whiteman:

> Luther and I have utterly and absolutely split. He is employed by the pensioners. Their leaders are just the kind of people against which he leveled his own darts in *Glory Roads,* only instead of being mere racketeers they come from a family of criminals, out and out! And these are the persons who would be in charge of the moneys.[204]

Samuel changed his place of residence at this point, an event that was necessitated not by his admittedly peripatetic ways but by Luther Whiteman's personal breakdown and the breakdown of their working relationship.

> Please see that all mail and notices henceforth go to P.O. Box 1063, Hollywood Calif. I may have no special residence for some time, traveling back and forth down into lower California as well . . . Most of Luther's former colleagues think he has gone berserk. Unfortunately, this was mixed up with some personal doings by himself, very strange. The local papers are attacking the plan (Pension plan proposal) as a Social Credit Measure. And I have to speak against it now myself. Davenport of Collier's is right. Mostly a racket. [205]

Things were coming to a head politically in 1938 in the world of politics and Social Credit issues. The manuscript of *Glory Roads* was already in the hands of investigators of the Townsend movement in Congress. Luther Whiteman was having disabling personal issues as alluded to by Vocha Fiske and hinted at by Sam. Two wives at the same time and a change of address led to a weakening of his compass of intellectual clarity and dedication to ideals.

Munson was quick to reply to Sam's postcard.

> Won't you, when you have the time, tell me just why you left the pension movement? And give me some reliable information on Social Creditors there . . . It is not idle curiosity that prompts me to ask for reliable information. We are trying to build a genuine national movement. It is discouraging when a man like Whiteman flops. After *Glory Roads!* Which was a fine book.
>
> P.S. How did your distribution of the Beacon* go?[206]

Sam wrote back on old stationery headed "Whiteman and Lewis—Research and Publicity, Analyzing Propaganda," with an address on Sunset Boulevard in Los Angeles. He told Munson that he had made an attempt at a cooperative based upon Social Credit and spiritual principles. "I have been making many trips up and down the Coast and have always been welcomed by the Santa Barbara Cooperative Industries. They told me of their successful work in chemiculture and gave me leads and information."[207]

Samuel's breakup with Whiteman in the face of Whiteman's personal difficulties could not have been easy for him. Sam had described his initial relationship with Whiteman as being like having a fresh father figure in his life. The fact that this relationship dissolved was a difficult but familiar family problem. Still he was optimistic about Social Credit. He ended his letter to Munson by saying that he had established contact with Robert Heinlein and Ed Gordon, and that the Beacon distribution had gone "fair enough to lead ultimately to a new monetary reform movement or more than one."[208]

On June 15, 1939, Samuel wrote Munson a rambling account of his various involvements, particularly with public officials and political candidates.[209] In this letter Samuel summarized the politicians he had conferred with and offered some criticisms of certain aspects of the Social Credit approach.

---

*Sam's Social Credit article entitled "Antics or Semantics" was published in that magazine and Sam distributed it to various politicians and public figures. Munson had written at the time (April 29, 1938) to say: "Congratulations on 'Antics and Semantics.' Have Luther take a bow too. It's better than Hook or Kenneth Burke or any of the other exposes of Chase I have read. Articles like that do much for the prestige of Social Credit." The relevant issue of *The Beacon* is stored at Wesleyan but is reportedly in too fragile a state to be approached without further funding for restoration.

Munson responded: "I take the opportunity to acknowledge your letter of 15 June. It leaves me up in the air as to what you are doing that is useful to the Social Credit cause, although your energies seem very busily employed."

Any observer over the years of Samuel's life could easily testify that Sam's energies were very busily employed. When he committed to something he gave it his all. After discussing some specific people and policies, Munson, who was a successful professional editor, writer, and teacher, offered Sam some worthwhile guidance:

> If I may offer an opinion about your work, I think it would gain from concentration. You scatter yourself so much that, to speak frankly, you sometimes give the impression of being an economic gadabout. Yet your talents, if concentrated, appear to be considerable. We now have an integrated movement with a splendid morale. I have no doubt it is the most effective fighting organization Social Credit has achieved. It ought to be, for the experience of seven years of daily work is being poured into it by tried and true Social Creditors. For those who join it, it offers continuous opportunities for concerted work. Social Credit is the only remedy. Social credit is coming![210]

Munson's criticism of Sam's rambling style was not out of line. It is reminiscent of Vocha Fiske's comment, which she happily relayed, of always believing Sam was destined to achieve integration. His intellectual curiosity and exploration were so vast that they defied being concentrated into a whole. Such would be the burden of accumulating a massive amount of information. Years later his friend Gavin Arthur reported that Sam was quicker and more accurate than the Encyclopedia Britannica, and if Gavin had a question he had only to knock on the wall of their adjoining apartments and ask.[211]

Other news in the June 15 letter shows the spiritual aspect of Sam's life. He speaks of a new teacher that he has met, with whom he is quite impressed.

> I don't know whether you have followed his career but I had some very nice visits with Paul Brunton last year. In his "Search in Secret India" he portrays the Radha-Soami movement, which has much to recommend it. However, the first contact with him was spent discussing S.C. [Social

Paul Brunton with Ramana Maharshi

Credit] more often than deeper spiritual matters (which took up our entire time later). It is also interesting to know that Heinleins and Gordons have this broad background but that Paul Brunton, even more, has felt that S.C. is the way out, altho he may never say so publicly . . . We have maintained contact since he left these shores."[212]

Samuel also wrote Munson that he was allowed to function as a teacher in Brunton's school. In his later teaching career he often quoted Brunton's statement that he knew three ways to accomplish spiritual realization: through the breath, through the heart, and through the glance or use of light. Sam demonstrated these himself in his classes and everyday life. Heinlein and Gordon failed in their election campaigns, but Heinlein's broad background can be seen in his science fiction work, particularly *Stranger in a Strange Land,* which is highly mystical.

Samuel made another important statement in this letter indicating the way his life was moving.

> I have been compelled to give up my whole time either to my spiritual affairs or [my Social Credit and political involvements]. I have found recently an increasing number of people actually desiring real esoteric and mystical training, and no more blah-blah or fakes. This has on the one hand given me much responsibility, and on the other hand taken up time. But if that is my dharma, I shall continue.[213]

The California Pension Plan would fail to get the necessary votes in the election. Much of the world was at war or approaching it, and it wouldn't be long before the U.S. would be directly drawn into World War

II. The economic upturn that resulted would finally give President Roosevelt a vehicle to solve the lingering American unemployment problem.

The great fighting machine of Social Credit that Munson was pushing also proved unable to register any real achievements in America. He had lost his pulpit at *New Democracy* and was giving lectures.

Gorham Munson, like Samuel Lewis, was a true intellectual, a writer, a social idealist, and one with a spiritual background. Samuel often praised him in his various political and literary interactions. While highly respected, Munson was not another father figure to him but more of a colleague/leader with superior connections in the literary world.

Samuel, like Munson during this period, gave public speeches. On one occasion Sam's cousin Mildred White was present. She remembered the experience as part of her visit to the Lewis household where Samuel was staying at the time. It gives a palpable taste of the strange family atmosphere, as well as a description of the event.

> I think it was approximately about 1938, '37 or '38. I went to California . . . Samuel was in San Francisco and I called from the train station to the house and talked to my aunt first. She said that Elliott had the car and would I mind coming out on the bus, so I took a Geary Ave. bus right to the house. I knew my way around; I had been there before and when I got there I came in and Samuel and Aunt Hatty both greeted me, but the cats—they had Midnight and something else, I can't remember, became very upset and very excited and climbed to the top of the high buffet in the dining room, and so they asked me if I would mind leaving for a while so they could get the cats calmed down.
>
> Cousin Samuel took me down to the Golden Gate Park and sat me on a bench where I stayed for about two and a half hours. They finally calmed down the cats and then he came back to get me. The cats then would run to Samuel or to my aunt. Then when I went back to Los Angeles in a few days, Samuel went with me because he was working at that time in the movie colony in some position. I don't know what it was, but that night we went to a political rally held in the auditorium of one of the studios, and he made a talk, whether it was Democratic or Republican, I don't know. I do remember that Edward G. Robinson was there and Myrna Loy was there and several other well-known actors

> and actresses of that time that were all well acquainted with Samuel and seemed to have a high regard for him.[214]

This event would have happened during the period Sam had an office in Hollywood with Luther Whiteman, and his talks would have been on the monetary crisis using a Social Credit approach.

Samuel replied in polite tones to Munson's critical letter about him lacking concentration in his writing and behaving like a financial gad-about.[215] He told of the many difficulties in California just to have enough to get by on. He wrote about the politicians and the inroads that he had made with some of them and the ignorance encountered, and how after his breakup with Whiteman he was working with Ed Gordon and Robert Heinlein and investigating politicians that Munson distrusted as possible converts to Social Credit. He ends by saying "We are entirely for your Hargravian outlook. We agree with your philosophy, efforts, etc. but we are meeting practical situations."

He also mentions for the first time a man whom they had quoted in *Glory Roads* in relation to a Social Credit approach that had worked in businesses in Norway. "Do you know Bjorset, author of 'Distribute and Destroy?' He now lives near me and is getting in. Most of our successful liberals are Danish or Norwegian and they listen to him."*

Shamcher Bryn Beorse

Munson replied to Samuel affirming clearly what role Samuel could play.

> I feel that you can help national headquarters by sending us reliable information (we greatly need shrewd realistic un-wishful reports) and I am sure that our facilities can be of great aid to any Californian who actually tries to convert the state situation into a better field for our propaganda.
>
> Yours for economic democracy, Gorham Munson[216]

---

*Bjorset later used the name Beorse along with the Sufi name Shamcher given him by Hazrat Inayat Khan. Years later Shamcher was to play a central role in encouraging the initial meeting of Samuel Lewis and Vilayat Khan, Hazrat Inayat Khan's oldest son.

Samuel's next card indicates a new return address and a new focus: Samuel L. Lewis, Esq., c/o Sufi Movement, 545 Sutter St., San Francisco.

Sam at entrance to Kaaba Allah

CHAPTER 5

Sufi Work with Murshida Martin

When we devote ourselves to the thought of God, all illumination and revelation is ours.

HAZRAT INAYAT KHAN[217]

For it is the thought of God that obliterates the thought of self, as light coming into a chamber terminates darkness. It is the practice of wazifa,* darood, fikr, zikr, *and* shagal *which bring revelation—not any philosophical consideration of them, but the actual practice. This can only be understood through the experience.*

SAMUEL LEWIS[218]

MURSHIDA RABIA MARTIN HAD BEEN TRAINED in these Sufi practices by Pir-o-Murshid Inayat Khan, and Khalif Samuel Lewis wrote about them in a paper for Sufi students.[219] Samuel was an avid practitioner and intellectual whose efforts to bridge the gap between mystical experiences and academics were, in time, influential. Today there is often academic respect for the experiences of those within the various spiritual traditions who learn to set ego-self aside.

Samuel's involvement in social movements—living into the scriptural views of service—would alone have comprised an exceedingly busy life, but he had another just as busy: his life with the Sufi Movement. Aside from writing texts for Murshida Rabia Martin and the Sufi Movement as she had organized it in the United States, he also worked as a caretaker on the grounds of the Sufi School and was a chief teacher

* A *wazifah* is a divine Name or attribute of Allah. The practice is to invoke a Name as a prayer.

there. Samuel's teaching duties increased when Murshida Martin was away; she traveled widely as an international representative of the Sufi teachings of Pir-o-Murshid Hazrat Inayat Khan.

Murshida Martin called for a *Jamiat Khas** in 1931, by which time she had recognized Samuel Lewis as a Khalif. He had been blessed by Hazrat Inayat Khan on the anniversary of the Pir-o-Murshid's passing in 1930, an experience he described this way:

> I sat on my bed in meditation and my teacher Hazrat Inayat Khan appeared and sat next to me in meditation. That's the only time after his death I ever saw him with the physical eye. He opened up this crown-consciousness, pressured it, physically pressured it.[220]

The stream of mind-to-mind harmony that this brought about allowed for an effortless outpouring as Samuel began his work of writing commentaries on his teacher's talks and writings. For this *Jamiat,* Samuel wrote an address for the attendees along with a number of commentaries on the esoteric studies left by Hazrat Inayat Khan (the *Githas*). He included commentaries on his own *Githekas,* which were available for the general public. Additionally, he prepared a set of addresses to the Khalifs and Sheikhs at the *Jamiat* in which he wrote about the processes of these gatherings, how to relate to Pir-o-Murshida, and numerous other topics.

Samuel recommended as supplementary texts two classical works on Sufism authored by recognized Sufi Masters, *L'Awarif ul-Ma'arif*† by Sheikh Sohrawardi and *Kashf al-Mahjub*‡ by Sheikh Al-Hujwiri. At this time in his life he assumed increasing responsibilities as a Khalif for Pir-o-Murshida Martin. His emphasis on commentaries that drew out the teachings in the writings of Hazrat Inayat Khan and his readiness to rely on these highly respected classic texts from the traditional Sufi orders show the emphasis he gave to established Sufi wisdom.

In a document prepared for this meeting, Khalif Samuel Lewis wrote:

---

* A gathering for the designated spiritual and organizational leaders of the order.

† This Persian title can be roughly translated as "The Knower of Deep Wisdom."

‡ This title, also Persian, translates as "Revelation of the Veiled."

> In the end, all balances, for balance is necessary to Perfection. An extreme of phenomenalism, or of devotion, or of intellectualizing the teachings prevents the reaching of the goal, which is God realization.
>
> Even in the earliest works of Pir-o-Murshid mention is made of *fana*, absorption, the becoming selfless. This lays behind all else, and for this reason special spiritual practices are given.[221]

Samuel was fully absorbed in his discipleship with Hazrat Inayat Khan, preserving and advancing his teachings, and assisting Murshida Rabia Martin. He continued to work closely with Murshida Rabia and tried to protect her from defending herself against criticism and from criticizing others in public, as he had promised his teacher. At this time Murshida Martin was seen by many as the head of the Sufi Movement in America, and fully independent of the European corporation. As mentioned, Samuel worked for her intermittently, providing secretarial services, some caretaking of the grounds at Kaaba Allah and writing spiritual materials. A few years later his work included lecturing and teaching, and he was provided an office and lodging on the property.

Shortly after Samuel's return to San Francisco from his travels east in 1931, he delivered several talks at the Theosophical Society in Oakland. These talks were promoted in the *Oakland Tribune* in small box ads amid other religious listings. One ad carried the headline LEWIS TO LECTURE with the topic "Theosophical Principles of Music."[222] He spoke again at the same Lodge on "Spiritual Forces in History,"[223] "Shambala and the Coming Age,"[224] and "Can World Peace be Attained Through Religion."[225] His talk on Shambala may have been influenced by Roerich's various adventures in Asia. These talks are early evidence of his lifelong interest in the role of spiritual practice in promoting world peace and social equity, alleviating hunger, and other social issues.

When applying for work through the U.S. Civil Service Commission during World War II, Samuel described his arrangement with Murshida Martin as piecework. He listed the years he was so employed as 1930–1941 and stated that he ended that affiliation because of the war. During the early 1930s he wrote several letters on Murshida Martin's behalf to the Sufi organization, but mostly he composed copious materials for the general public and for Sufi students. In his Civil Service application in

1942 he said that his annual salary averaged $600, and mentioned writing, correspondence, lecturing, caretaking, and research. He noted that he had periods of interruption when he had other jobs.

It is difficult to adequately convey the irrepressible energy that Sam expressed every day to one who was not an eyewitness to it. He was indefatigable and always gave everything his all. In short, he was a Sufi bodhisattva working for the benefit of all sentient beings. Among his writings that survived the fire at Kaaba Allah, some were recovered from South America, a few were collected that circulated in Australia, and others were found in the Sufi Movement archives in Europe. The latter included some writings of Sam's that were mistaken for the writings of Hazrat Inayat Khan in the esoteric papers distributed in Germany. Several writings are drawn from these papers and provide insight into Sam's upbringing as well as his future.

Murshida Martin actively embraced her role as a successor to Hazrat Inayat Khan, and she widely shared her personal presence and teachings. The public record holds a number of examples of her travels. Occasionally Samuel Lewis traveled with her both as Khalif and esoteric secretary. He had supported Murshida in making her case with Sufi Movement headquarters. After her rejection there he still wholeheartedly supported her in taking on the leadership of Hazrat Inayat Khan's movement.

In the early stages of their relationship Murshida's communications with Samuel were generally harmonious. They traveled together to Detroit in 1930 and their presence was reported in the *Detroit Free Press* of November 9. Murshida Martin conducted the Universal Worship service of Hazrat Inayat Khan and gave a sermon to a large audience on "The Power of Silence." Samuel Lewis was mentioned in a separate news story: "Mr. Samuel Lewis gave an extremely interesting talk on the influence of Oriental literature. He spoke particularly of the literature of Asia, Persia, and India."

The Hartford, Connecticut, center was headed by Sundar Giffin, a disciple of Murshida Martin whom she had appointed as a Sheikha* in

---

* *Sheikha* is the feminine form of Sheikh.

the Sufi work. Sundar wrote poetry, one volume of which, *Beggar of Beauty,* was published by the Roerich Museum Press in 1931.

Sheikha Giffin was mentioned several times in Samuel's writings from this period. His poem "Holy Murshid's Song to His *Mureeds*" carries the dedication "Murshid to Sundar with his blessings 7/3/30." The most notable reference to her comes in what can be called Murshid Sam's "social papers." This group includes "The Social Directions," "The Spiritual Attitude and Class War," "Social *Githekas,*" and "The Book of Peace."*

The introduction to an early draft of "The Social Directions" includes two paragraphs that reveal Sam's visionary approach to the external goals of reform he was pursuing. He practiced attunement with the illuminated souls in the inner planes, a practice evidenced in his writings and later in the Dances of Universal Peace and Walking Concentrations.

In a few instances, early versions of a document by Samuel opened with statements that depicted what he felt to be the inner chain of guidance:

> The Blessed Master Jesus:
>
> In the Name of the Lord Who is Omniscience and Mercy and Compassion, in the Name of all the Holy Ones in Chain† Who form the Embodiment of the Master, the Spirit of Guidance, I, Jesus son of Mary and Anointed of God, open the New Season with Thanksgiving and Joy, rendering great praise to the Omnipotent Father for His new vessels in who has been given and will be given.
>
> In Heaven a Trinity, with my Brothers Inayat Khan on my right hand and my servant the Rab‡ on my left and on earth a Trinity with my Sister Rabia in the center and her servant Samuel on her right hand and her servant Sundar on her left, for from us above to you below it shall be as was said in the spirit: "Either you shall lead the Social Revolution or the Social Revolution shall lead you." It is not now to defend or attack any human institutions.

"Either you shall lead the Social Revolution or the Social Revolution shall lead you" reflects Samuel Lewis's ongoing commitment. This became

---

*For these papers, see the Archives.

†This refers to the chain of Sufi masters, who keep the stream of love flowing.

‡Fabre D'Olivet.

quite evident later when he became the center of guidance for many young people who had tasted or longed to taste spiritual realization during the political and social revolution of the mid-1960s and early '70s.

Murshida Martin's travels were not confined to American cities, although Samuel never went with her beyond the U.S. She also traveled to Brazil, India, Australia, and more. It is important at this point to get a better picture of Murshida Martin's center in the San Francisco area, the complementary work of Samuel Lewis during the 1930s, and how their relationship was developing.

Samuel's manuscript *Spiritual Dancing,* written during this period (see Archives), demonstrates his historical study of dance and offers a detailed program of development. The manuscript has fourteen chapters on topics such as static and dynamic symmetry, the metaphysics of the dance, physical and mental aspects, moral and spiritual aspects, the breath, the heart, sex and the dance, psychic aspects, technique, and sacred dances, as well as a concluding chapter on dancing and the other arts.

Many of the core teachings involved working with the five elements of earth, water, fire, air, and ether. Yogic postures, the process of bringing heart, mind, and body into attunement, meditation, concentration, and more also appeared in the later training of his students and in the Dances of Universal Peace. Several short passages from this important work follow.[226]

From the outset Samuel Lewis makes clear the underlying intention into which he invites his readers:

> The dance is the way of Life; the dance is the sway of Life. What Life gives may be expressed with body, heart and soul to the glory of God and the elevation of mankind, leading therein to ecstasy and self-realization. Verily, this is the sacred dance . . . Let us venture, pioneering as angels where fools may fear to tread. When mankind, terrorized by conflict and faced with the ruin of his civilization, when the power of wealth has dominated justice . . . let us in spite of what occurs before our eyes, invoke the Divine Spirit through love and beauty, that we may restore order and balance to humanity . . . Not what we think or say but what we do shall avail. May we therefore

bear the torch of holiness and make of our bodies temples of sacred worship . . .

From the East and from the West we invoke thee, o man! The prophets of old spoke with fiery tongues. The flame is never quenched though eyes be turned aside. Now look with hearts and minds and eyes, on with the dance—the dance itself shall mount through the seraphic flames of Jacob's ladder, leading humanity through sacred initiations from the netherworld even unto Thy courts, O Jehovah! Seek and ye shall find, and in the hour ye think least the Son of man shall come and the Daughter of man be there . . .

Everyone shows one or more of these four aspects: the animal, human, genius, and angel in his or her personality. Sometimes one, sometimes another seems to dominate behavior. Usually one aspect is so preponderant that we can say a person belongs to that type, to that grade of evolution. However, a skilled dancer learns to take on all roles, just as an actor does, and her divinity must manifest in all forms . . .

Dane Rudhyar* has been telling us that the music of the future will be based upon group-tones and group-units. The moral significance thereof is tremendous . . . The group-unit is displacing the individual unit as the logical "atom" of chemistry, sociology, botany, psychology, genetics, and all sciences. The ego self of a thing is lost, but not destroyed, in the synthetic process. This is our main teaching . . .

The Psalmist sang: "Let everything that has breath praise the Lord." We can recognize the divinity within and without. We can illustrate it in art and music. The sincere dancer is one of the best workers for universal harmony, and so, for universal peace . . .

The Sufis, especially, have looked with favor upon the dance as a highway toward God, and that every movement in it can be endowed with holiness . . .

The kingdom of heaven is not far away; the kingdom is at hand. What is needed are practical methods by which it may be attained. The dance which delimits personality and encompasses space enables one to draw into the consciousness the fine qualities of the sun of the soul. The quivering, throbbing heart-center bursts into flame, and the whole being becomes illuminated. Then one is; his deity dominates his movements. His inner being dances, his outer being responds, and he becomes the servant, if not the very self, of the **Lord of the Dance.**

---

*Rudhyar is considered the pioneer of transpersonal astrology.

The effect of Samuel's family history made its way into his writings during this period as well. The following excerpts from his paper "On the Control of Sublimation of Vital Force"[227] provide an example.

> The question of atmosphere is very important . . . Instruction and guidance of infant, child and youth, in the sex relationship from every angle, and indeed in the course of life viewed as the experience of vital force and the incarnation of God. The best way to build up a personal atmosphere is through having one's own sleeping quarters. While it is not unsafe for brothers and sisters or even blood cousins to occupy the same sleeping rooms until the advent of youth, after that time there are a thousand factors which favor some sort of separation. If this is impossible or undesirable, it is better for two persons to occupy a sleeping porch together than a closed room where their personal atmospheres would mix.

Samuel's relationship with his younger brother Elliott deteriorated during the years they shared a room, and he obviously still felt its effects. Even though they ultimately did shift to a more open sleeping porch, Sam felt that change came too late for either of them to develop a healthy personal atmosphere. Later in the paper he says:

> At the present day the tendency is toward destroying the family rather than to recreate it under better circumstances . . . While future society may be built in part upon the family unit, it may be a very different kind of family than we have been accustomed to consider in sociology.

He also recommends:

> Periods of silence with children, teaching prayer, rhythmical breathing, cultivation of music and the arts, knowledge and practice in the crafts, and an ideal outlook on life often prevents most of the emotional storms . . . One need hardly ever resort to a "Thou shalt not." . . . [Young people] need instruction and guidance, not prohibition, inhibition, indulgence, or too much supervision . . . We are trying to be universal, practical and scientific. We have to include the women of the Orient as well as those of Occident and people of dark-skinned races as well as pale faces . . . We want to see woman as woman . . .
>
> Instead of the road to marriage being swift and the road to divorce slow, the road to marriage would be slow and the door to divorce swift. This of itself would provide for less divorces and happier marriages.

The tale of Samuel's own extended family is an example of swift marriages, painful divorces, and unhappiness. In the face of his upbringing, his spiritual development and idealism often prompted visions of pathways to universal harmony, and even in the '30s his relations with the young were joyful, creative, and meaningful.

Sufism in the Bay Area

> *"Insight into life is the real religion, which alone can help us to understand life."*
>
> HAZRAT INAYAT KHAN[228]

> *Insight is different from perception, in that perception deals with variety, and insight takes one toward Unity. It is the apprehension and comprehension of Unity which leads to the understanding of life. This is a process of the heart, not of the head.*
>
> SAMUEL LEWIS[229]

Samuel's spirited adventures as a writer, lecturer, and lobbyist for Social Credit had failed to pan out as he and Munson had hoped. Instead he turned more and more to the cultivation of his spiritual gifts. Some of his last recorded correspondence with Munson demonstrates how he had changed his primary focus. As early as March, 1937, he wrote to Munson in this vein:

> My turn to Social Credit was in itself a mystical experience, which may not surprise you. For it is thoroughly consistent with all the spiritual teachings, with the shastras, Islamic doctrines of money, Mosaic Code. But this very condition, with its political aspects, makes it advisable for me not to appear as a spiritual teacher in the usual sense—at least not yet.
>
> Nevertheless I am quite in a position to extend both intellectual and esoteric help, to prepare others, and would be more than willing to do this with no other qualification than assent on your part . . . My recent reading has made me understand Gurdjieff better; Ouspensky I have long known.
>
> The West needs meditation mostly, then scientific occultism and mysticism can come later. The West does not yet understand the pupil-teacher relationship, or the significance of heart-vibrations and heart-unions (Yoga). The metaphysics of the West, however, is now advancing on the mental plane—a good sign. If this letter should evoke

> a response, permit me to serve you in any way possible along these lines.[230]

The Sufi presence in San Francisco had various outlets of expression in the city, and there was Kaaba Allah, often referred to as the Sufi School, in Fairfax. The operational support staff for Rabia Martin were long-term Sufis. Clara Sibley, the mother of Sam's housemate Hazel Armstrong, was the constant companion of Murshida Martin in her frequent travels around the world. She had been to Suresnes at the time of Hazrat Inayat Khan and was a trusted ally. Other Sufi practitioners had migrated to the West Coast as well.

Young Vera

Murshida Vera Corda (1913–2002), as she is known today, was Vera Van Voris when she arrived on the Sufi scene in 1935 at the age of 22. Her lifelong friendship with Samuel Lewis was seemingly rooted in past lives and she understood him deeply. Like Sam, she had met Hazrat Inayat Khan in the spirit body first. Inayat appeared in the cornfields next to her home walking with with his eldest children, Noor-un-Nisa, Hidayat, and Vilayat. He walked with Vera outside, encouraging her to learn about the elements and kingdoms. Forty years later she founded the New Age Seed Schools in the San Francisco Bay Area based on these teachings of Hazrat Inayat Khan.

After a few years of study with Rabia Martin, Vera was initiated as a Sheikha, a position for which she felt inadequate.*

> It was absolutely overwhelming to me and I do not think that I would have been able to do it except for Murshid Sam who always sat in front

---

* Vera was later initiated as a Murshida by Pir Vilayat. In later years she was known by her married name, Vera Corda.

> of me and said, "Ignore everybody and talk to me." I talked to him. That made it real easy . . .
>
> I consider those years under Murshid Sam's guidance to be the greatest privilege that an individual can have, and it does not diminish as the years go on . . . I can see the prophesy of this man and the natural oracular ability that recycles in soul and spirit as he was far ahead of his time. If he had come into it at this stage of the game, where we are today, he would have been recognized everywhere immediately, but like most prophets who are ahead of their time, he finds a small close group who appreciates, if not understands, him and who is so charged by him and so inspired by him they stay with him and feel honored to be in his presence.[231]

Vera's remembrances below are transcribed from an interview conducted in 1972, a year after Sam's passing, and provide a first-hand description of Sufism at Kaaba Allah in the 1930s. Her extraordinary account extended to 78 pages, from which subsequent excerpts in this chapter have been drawn.[232]

> It was in the Spring of [1935] that I met a very inspiring woman [Hazel Armstrong] who was then Secretary of the Index of American Design . . . She had just returned from work with the Navajo Indian children . . . We had an immediate attunement and liking for each other, and it wasn't long before she invited me to her apartment, which she shared with the Khalifa, Dr. Davida Herrick. Davida Herrick and Hazel Armstrong were of the same generation as our Murshid. [Both] had grown up in the Sufi work, living in the old *Khankah* on Franklin Street in San Francisco and later at Kaaba Allah at Fairfax.
>
> It was at her home that I first met up with the work of Inayat Khan, his music and a few recordings which we then had and felt deeply attuned to . . . because I had had early psychic experiences with Murshid Inayat Khan as a very young child, five years of age. And I had never seen him in the flesh or knew that he lived in the flesh; and when I saw pictures of him in her music room, it just turned me on . . . [I was immediately] attracted because of that to the Sufi literature and the Sufi work. Hazel Armstrong started me out in the *Gathas* and the preparation to become a Sufi. But because of my experience and background, Hazel soon felt she couldn't handle me . . . She said, "Be patient. Your teacher is going to be here in a few days." But the few days went into many weeks . . . Finally one day Samuel Lewis returned from his trip, and she

set a specific time and date for me to come to the Sufi headquarters on Sutter Street to meet him.

I came in, not knowing what to expect . . . No one had told me a thing about Samuel . . . so it was a great surprise. But the minute I saw him we recognized each other immediately and went towards each other and enfolded each other in our arms, and both of us were overwhelmed with emotion. It was as though we had been separated for centuries and all at once we again met. And neither one of us could put it into words or explain it.

Perhaps I can't explain it to this day, but I'm sure that we knew each other [and] had been very closely aligned . . . in a blood relationship where we were of the same generation and very close in our thoughts and our love for each other. He initiated me immediately following this, without any speech or explanations. Our meetings were always emotional: we were either weeping or very joyous or dancing or—we would go into this state immediately we met, and that set the key . . .

Samuel immediately took Arjuna [Vera's husband] and I to Fairfax . . . I was then starting to paint for the Index of American Design and had to be there part of the week, but I spent perhaps four days a week at Kaaba Allah . . . Every weekend on Friday evenings all the Sufis got on the ferry boat and went over to Fairfax.

And we met in what was called the lower house . . . in the biggest room on the property, second to the chapel. This room was kept bare to the center; it had a large fireplace; it had a dining alcove, and a large kitchen led off of this room . . . We all sat in a circle—the older *mureeds* sat in chairs; all of the younger ones sat on cushions on the floor and Samuel would always see that I was opposite to him. He wanted me in front of him. I might be across an auditorium or across a room, but he would always give me the eye—and we had excellent mental telepathy—and I knew what he wanted me to do . . . There was a positive-negative polarity between us, and if we were in alignment whatever happened would not be a direct attack on him. It would be put into a *kemal* state [perfect balance] where the individual could not continue that attack.

In my first meetings with Samuel in the Sufi Order, I realized that he was having an inner battle with the older *mureeds.* When I say, "older *mureeds,*" I mean those who had been young disciples of Inayat Khan at Suresnes, and later in New York and the Cleveland Center and finally in San Francisco where they settled at Kaaba Allah under Murshida Rabia

Martin's tutelage . . . The so-called upper house . . . was the house that the older *mureeds* lived in. They were all grey-haired or white-haired. And I was a young woman when I came into the order. They lived up until the time of the Meher Baba entrance on the scene, and then they seemed to die one after the other.

Samuel and I had a great deal in common in the dance. I had danced for ten years, and we did a lot of dancing together when we didn't have dances as you have today. The dervish dance did not come in yet . . . But we danced with each other. Samuel would just simply stand up in the circle and lift up his hands and start, and I would stand up, and we would dance. And everyone else sat and looked at us . . .

The older *mureeds* would say that Samuel was a canary bird. And he was hopping up and down on a perch and getting nowhere. Well they simply did not understand the dances of Shiva, which of course took in that type of leg and arm movement . . . That was the type of dancing we did. We had three groups there: this group in the twenties, the very older *mureeds,* and the very young.

Asked if Murshida Martin lived at Kaaba Allah, Vera replied:

Not at this time . . . The older *mureeds* put a lot of money into this. They put their fortunes and their lives into it. And they deserved the love and respect of the younger group. But unfortunately they put up a block against the younger generation's growth and tried to stick to the old formulas that had come from Suresnes, I guess—I don't know where this had come from. But they wanted to sit in a room and they wanted to be preached **at** or talked **to**; they didn't want to experience. We wanted to experience; we wanted to dance and to paint and to work on the flowers and on the gardens. Everything we wanted to do we wanted to be active in doing. And the older *mureed* had a different concept of getting the work . . .

Previous to my becoming a Sheikha, Samuel took me into what was sort of an entrance hall between the front and back of the upper house. And this room had all of the files—locked files—with the entire Sufi papers—everything that Inayat Khan had written—and most precious materials, all of which burned in the fire later [December 31, 1949]. The library was there, a large Sufi library which took in all four walls. And this was a place that the older *mureeds* loved to read in and to work in. And every afternoon at 3:00 they opened their bedroom doors, which led off of a long hall from this library, and each one sat in his room with his Sufi book; and each one read aloud from the Sufi books, whatever he was currently on. The droning here was like a hive of bees, each one doing his own work on a different level. Samuel and I would come up to the library, plug our ears, and march through as fast as we could out to the other part of the house.

The chapel was on the second floor [and] was occupied by chairs in rows, and we never were allowed to open that up and dance or do any of that work there. That was always done in the lower house . . . The prayers, of course, were always said there, and the speakers would speak in front of the altar there. Healing services were held there. I recall only once that we had Universal Worship there. Universal Worship was always given in the Sutter Street headquarters in San Francisco. And most of the lectures and meetings were given there . . .

At Kaaba Allah, when Murshida Martin was on the property, things ran in a very routine manner, as routine as one could make Samuel and the younger *mureeds*. We would have about 25 young ones—I mean teenagers—that Samuel and I would be in charge of: I in the girls' apartments, he in the boys' apartments. But this didn't work out too well . . . We would be having meditations at 12:00 at night or 2:00 in the morning in the girls' rooms. (laughs) The older *mureeds* up above could look down and see those lights and look in the windows; their hair was standing on end, and they were sure that Samuel and I were leading them down a devious sexual path, which of course was not true . . .

Every Sufi was in love, and no Sufi was in love with one person. Everybody was in love with at least three: This entanglement never brought on any extreme jealousies among the men . . . [no] terrible arguments or fights or feelings against one another. But with the women it was another thing . . . They would study the Sufi work very closely to back up all of their love notes with quotes from Murshid [Inayat Khan] . . . All of this Samuel seemingly paid no attention to, as if he didn't see it . . . Everyone's life went their own way. He interrupted and involved himself with all of them with love and understanding and criticized none of them.

[The teenagers] came on weekends only, and they were children of *mureeds* . . . I don't ever recall anyone being there that was not related to a Sufi . . . We took turns with these young people . . .

When you came in there would be a retreat schedule posted on a doorpost of every room in both buildings . . . You were expected to rise when Samuel gave the call and get yourself to the chapel, and in a hurry. So most of us just put on our Sufi robes and our sandals and went up there. And, by the way, I see something happening now that Samuel was dead against at that time, and that was that never did you expose your feet to concrete. He felt and preached to us all, "You are losing your magnetism when you put your feet on concrete or on asphalt, but take off your shoes whenever you can get on wood, and on earth, and on grass." Which we did . . . The minute we get off the train, off with our shoes. And we walk on the dirt borders, seeing as how we were never supposed to walk on the concrete. But we could manage that way to get the biggest part of the way up to Kaaba Allah without it. But Samuel would always be on the upper terrace looking down: "You're doing it again!" when he'd see us in bare feet coming up the asphalt on the last turn of the road. He didn't want us to have our feet on this pavement at all . . . You'd run up the stairs thinking you were going to see Samuel, but you didn't. He'd disappeared . . . you wouldn't see him then until dinnertime.

We had a big gong, on the front of that building, which was always struck by Hazel Armstrong . . . It was the day of what's called hot pants now . . . we'd all be in our hot pants when we were there, with as little clothes as possible, which really shocked the older *mureeds.* And they made it so that you had to wear your robe when you came to the dinner table. They were not about to see you like that . . .

There was a big banister on the porch at the upper house, and we'd all throw our robes over it . . . Everyone had a robe . . . peach color; apricot was the great Sufi color used during Inayat Khan's days at Suresnes . . . and we all copied that . . .

A robe was always given to you by your initiator . . . Sometimes it was very poor material, sometimes it was patched. [The one that] was given to me when I became a Sheikha . . . was full of holes and gold wool, and it had the Indian embroidery on it, that tarnished years before, and nothing can look so bad as tarnished Indian embroidery. And I looked at it, and I thought "Oh my, how am I going to stop the moths?" And Samuel, who was present, laughed . . ."Don't worry," he said, "you fight them with a needle . . . By the time you patch all of those holes, all of your sins will be worn out. You will have worked them out." (laughs) I said, "You've got to be kidding!" "No, I'm not kidding," he said, "the ancient Sufis believed that as you darn the holes in your robes, you expiated the sins of your life before your initiation—your lives, not your life, but your lives before."

> And I said, "Oh Samuel, you don't believe in reincarnation!" He said, "I can only quote you what my Murshid taught me: reincarnation is a fact, but we do not teach it!" (Laughter) . . .
>
> If Murshida Martin gave [the robes for initiation] to you, they had openings down the front. And all those that she brought from India and the great holy places of the Sufi poets which she visited in her lifetime had [Sufi prayers in Urdu] stamped or painted down the shoulders . . .
>
> [When] you came in, and you came to the table . . . you stood, much as you do at the Catholic and Anglican retreat houses. You did not sit for the blessing. You stood behind your chair until the Murshid entered. If it was Murshida Martin, she entered first, and then Samuel entered. He was a Khalif then, and he sat at the foot of the table and she sat at the head.* If she was not there, Murshid Samuel sat at the head of the table. They were long refectory tables, with straight backed chairs . . .
>
> And a *mantram* was also given for that day, which was usually a reprimand. It seemed to us, the young ones, that we were always being reprimanded, that whenever we'd gotten off too wildly we were given a quotation to cool us down . . . When we sat down, Samuel would soften this . . . with his own talk and interpretation which might be about what the Chinese are doing this week in Chinatown in San Francisco, or "I saw somebody roller skating backwards at the rink last night." . . . They would be completely disjointed stories that you'd think, "What in the world is he talking about?" And then when the silent parts came and people were eating, you'd be trying to mull over in your mind, "What was he thinking? What was he talking about?" (laughs) And then, bang! you had it! It was always something for the younger generation. And then, as soon as we got out of there, we'd say, "Hey! Did you understand what he said?" And they'd compare notes, and sure enough, the biggest amount of us had all got the message, which was so hidden in this jumble that the older generation never knew what he was talking about (laughs). And we felt very wise and it sort of encouraged us.

Murshida Vera reconnected in person with Murshid Sam in 1969 and experienced tremendous harmony with him. As well, she had great respect for how he was embodying the Sufi Message with the younger generation, using Dances, Walking concentrations, and esoteric material

---

*Murshida Martin initiated Sam as a Khalif during the period between 1926 and the early 1930s.

they had only talked about in the earlier days.

Murshida Vera continued:

Murshida Vera in her later years

> Both [Samuel and I] had extreme experiences on the spirit plane with Inayat Khan. Samuel, in his early days, now, at the time when he was gardener and Major Domo and second Murshid Khalif and manager of Kaaba Allah during Murshida Martin's many travels, was very much receiving on the spiritual plane. His messages, his commentaries, the work which he gave to us, was all dictated from the spirit.
>
> And he was down in the little apartment . . . below, and you'd hear the little typewriter going faster than anyone could ever type, and the reams of material that was coming out—to every level, to every age level, to every interest on Kaaba Allah: from things like how to ride horseback and meditate to [things] like how to do the Dervish dances on roller skates or on ice skates, or how to hike and, while hiking, heal oneself, to climbing trees, and retreats from the world in treetops for young people—fantastic subject matter! Such breadth of view—of course, a human being could not do it!
>
> Samuel was not a human being, and anyone who tries to approach him that way starts off on the wrong foot, because you find him Yiddish, you find him pushy, you find him insulting, you find him over-egotized, you find him a man who's going to plow through whether you like it or not. But if you meet him and looked at him as in the spirit, then you would understand that here is a man who has a work to do, in a very short lifetime, a tremendous work to do. He has to meet all generations, all age levels, on their level, never on his own . . . And sometimes that level was a low level, in those days of great poverty in the depth of the Depression . . .
>
> [Samuel] would take you on a hike, and he would pick an herb here to give you and an herb there to give you, and he would talk to you. And soon you ended up on the rock, and you sat down with him. And then he would transcend you out of the flesh totally and into the spiritual body. And you would have the most marvelous experience with him—some spoken, some meditating, some merely holding his hand and watching the sunset from the rock. And you would come down totally filled. You would not feel hungry, and you would not feel weak

. . . Complete harmony. Then you entered for your evening meal, and you weren't even thinking about physical food. And this was not only my experience . . . but it was the experience of quite earthy people, who at that time were hungry.

Murshida Martin was extremely generous—those of us who did not have the money were never kept away from Kaaba Allah . . . Right inside of your room, on the door, would be posted [your] own instructions, which would tell you what you were expected to do; you were assigned, and Samuel made these assignment[s]. But . . . you just wondered, How did he ever choose these? Because many of us he hadn't seen since Wednesday, when we would meet at the Sutter Street headquarters for an evening of whatever he was teaching at that time—and yet he hit it right on the nail for everyone. If you were physically low that week, he would have you assigned to working in the earth. If you had a whole lot of sexual energy that you didn't know where to place, you'd be working on the rock pile, digging up bamboo, or planting fences. He had it planned for you so that you used your energies in a way that you would gain something in the spiritual body, no matter what . . .

There was great work going on at Kaaba Allah. We were leveling the ground where the clotheslines were . . . the only flat area on the grounds . . . This was a great place where we could do our dancing and our games. We played lots of games with these younger children. Samuel's games were original and they were always in the circle, and they were always big group things that everybody did . . . No matter what age you were, if you went down there, you got hauled into it and you had a great old time. And we took down the clotheslines, which made the old ladies roar . . . [The area was large and] lovely; bare feet felt great in it . . .

The upper gardens, above the rock and below the rock, were heavily overgrown with bay trees and grass and bamboo, scattered bamboo. And Samuel decided to transplant it;we would dig up the bamboo . . . and get it along the border, so that there would be privacy from private homes above there . . .

There was a huge oak tree that . . . wound around to the third floor where Murshida's apartment and my apartment—or whoever was her maid or her servant chosen for that month would live in that apartment. But I was there most of the time, and took care of her clothes and her robes and the burning of her incense and the scattering of the rose petals—everything was ritual. Everything that had been done for Murshid's apartment in Suresnes, I had to learn those methods . . .

Samuel cared not at all for that. He lived so much in the spiritual body that, if it hadn't been for Hazel Armstrong taking care of him, he would have forgotten to take a bath, change his clothes, or put on a sweater. I'll tell you some incidents of this forgetfulness of the physical body, which was hilarious when we were young, and sometimes embarrassing too, to those of the older generation . . . [who] just didn't understand it. They were shocked at it, and they would always quote Murshid Inayat Khan who always wore his slippers, who always had his robe on, who always combed his beard and his hair, who always had the light shining around him. And here was Samuel—frockless, dirty, unkempt, not giving a hoot . . . and it really shook these *mureeds* to the bottom. I can't remember that it ever bothered any of us; we always thought it was amusing and funny and just cute. We all got a big bang out of him. But the older generation surely did not . . .

When it was time for chapel in the morning, Samuel would be out there, sometimes at 5:30 if he wanted you to go horseback riding or hiking, but it would be . . . dawn's early light. He would get outside of the girls' dorm, in that garden at the side of the lower house, and he would sing—oh, "Pirates of Penzance" (laughter) or any one of those that happened to hit his mind . . . It would take two minutes before we'd be up to the window and yodeling it back to him . . .

Of course, he was a very young man, and he'd usually have on his dark slacks, his bare feet, and always a white shirt, open down to his stomach. (laughter) And sometimes his prayer beads or sometimes just flowers . . .

Arjuna, my young husband, was a very quiet young man, but he was very interested in . . . the breathing. And Samuel spent a lot of time with him working on levitation. And he and Samuel would sit, would go down below the rock there. And there were big rocks we were trying to move; I mean they were perhaps three by six feet—they were boulders! And they had to be moved. Well, the boys would put down planks that they'd nailed together with cross bars, and they'd roll these rocks onto this sort of a lever. And then it had to be lifted, so that it could be carried to where they wanted to put it in this bamboo garden. And Arjuna would always be on one end and Samuel on the other . . . working . . . on this levitation. And at our parties we would practice levitation . . .

Somebody would cross hands and then sit down, and the person would sit up and Samuel would say, "All right?" . . . and everybody would inhale like the roof was coming off . . . They could lift them right over their heads. And it was really a sensation when you were the person being given the ride on the breath. It was lots of fun . . . and the levitation went on and on. [Murshida] was away; when she came back she put a stop to it right away. She said, "You are off on something that is far from what Inayat Khan taught, and we are not going to have any magicians around here, period." (laughter) But we didn't care, because big work in the garden had been done by breath on levitation; whether she liked it or not, it was done, and that's how it was accomplished. We had no wagons, no sleds; it was all done by the breath . . .

The first thing in the morning after you were awakened by this yodeling, and bathed—you were expected to wash your hands, feet and face. This was the rule . . . You would all rise as Murshida came in, and you did not sit down again from the time she entered the room. And the prayers were said—*Saum, Salat* . . . The regulation prayers were done. Then a *zikr* was always sung on an empty stomach, which the young ones hated for one reason and the old ones hated for another. The older ones wanted their coffee before they started, and the young ones wanted to get off to hike or ride before this work and breakfast routine began . . . Either way, you had *zikr* on an empty stomach . . .

Samuel . . . always led the *zikr.* Murshida Martin would follow. But he was always a great chanter and he had a fine voice for it. And sometimes he would be in a different mood entirely, and we would be taken off into Hindu chants, or he might be in a Buddhist mood and you'd get Zen chanting . . . Whatever it was, it seemed like people didn't enter in. It seemed to me we did a humming, like you took a breath and you hummed and Samuel carried it. We all didn't enter in; he led it.

And . . . you were assigned to certain work for the breakfast . . . But Samuel, if I was there, he'd usually give me the sign: "I have something for you," he would say "and you and you." . . . And you went out the front door at Kaaba Allah, and you then did *Ya Hayy Ya Haqq** out to the rock. And this was done in single file, and Murshid Sam always led the way.

Asked if Samuel lived full time at Kaaba Allah, Murshida Vera replied:

---

* Sacred phrase meaning "Oh Life, Oh Truth."

> He did when he was a gardener and when Murshida was away. But he had this Wednesday night, he had the meetings to take care of, so he usually left on Sunday night, stayed through Wednesday, and then came back to Kaaba Allah. He was usually gone the first part of the week when he had business—the Sufi business and the running of the center—Hazel Armstrong was the full time secretary of it [in] San Francisco.

Glimpses of Murshida Martin

Vera gave an account of her first meeting with Murshida Martin:

> She was a square woman who was like a block, to me. And she was strong looking, masculine looking, a deeply mental woman who had striven hard for her early learning . . . Her husband was an importer of Oriental art goods, and she had an endless amount of money to devote to the work. She was completely and absolutely devoted to Inayat Khan. When she went to Suresnes, she was so different from all the other *mureeds* . . . Inayat Khan made her a Murshida before any of the others. And no doubt she deserved it, because she worked so hard to attain the entire teaching . . . Her devotion, heart devotion, was so sincere, could not have been denied. But her personality and her outer approaches were intellectual.

Murshida Martin took a long international trip for the Sufi Message of Hazrat Inayat Khan in 1938 through 1939. She ended her trip in New Zealand, returning by ship from Auckland to Vancouver, British Columbia, arriving August 24. A newspaper clipping from Melbourne, Australia, in July reported, "She has travelled the last 15 months in Palestine, India, Iraq, and Persia."

Murshida Ivy Duce, Rabia's successor, later recounted matters related to Murshida Martin's meeting in India with Pir Hasan Nizami:

Pir Hasan Nizami

> When Rabia Martin visited Hasan Nizami center in Delhi they made her stand behind a screen when she talked to the group. Hasan Nizami had 13,000 disciples when

he died. He said Inayat impressed on him that Rabia Martin was to be his successor.[233]

Mrs. Duce also specifically made mention of Rabia Martin receiving a document from Pir Hasan Nizami in 1939, and provided a copy in Urdu with an English translation. Murshida Martin had arranged for this translation while still in India. What Pir Hasan Nizami had given Rabia was an *ijazat,* a formal certificate granting her permission to teach Sufism. The document given by the Pir is quoted here in the translation presented by Murshida Duce, believed to be the one tendered by Murshida Rabia:

> All praise be to the Almighty Allah and his Prophet, Mohammad, and all his *Sahabaas** and *Auliya-e-Ummat.*† I, Hasan Nizami, as a Grand Master of the Chishtia Nizamia Order, authorize Sister-in-Silsila‡ Rabia A. Martin to disseminate the blessed teachings of my Sufi Chishtia Nizamia Order among the people of all religions in the Western World and for this purpose to build *Khanqahs* wherever necessary and to adopt all means for spreading and teaching practical *Tasawwuf* [Sufism]. I give this letter of Authority because Sufi Inayat Khan, Pir-o-Murshid of Rabia Martin, told me in 1927 seven days before his death, when he came from the West to visit me in Delhi, that he found Rabia Martin most capable of teaching Sufism in the highest degree and that he had allowed Rabia Martin to give the Spiritual education in the Western World and that she was his Khalifa.
>
> Sufi Inayat Khan passed away on the 5th of February 1927, and was buried near my house. According to his will and wish, I give this letter of Authority to Rabia Martin to disseminate the teachings of the Chishtis, for which I have every authority, being the Grand Master of the Chishtia Order; recognizing her as the true Spiritual Successor of Pir-o-Murshid Inayat Khan. In the end I pray to God that Rabia Martin be successful in spreading the Chishti message of love, harmony, and contentment of heart.[234]

Decades later, subsequent to an interview with Mrs. Duce, flaws in the translation were noticed and a new translation from the Urdu was

---

* Companions.

† Helpers and community members.

‡ A *silsila* is the historical chain of leaders in a spiritual lineage; "spiritual genealogy."

provided by Professor Marcia Hermansen. It surfaced that parts of the original Urdu text had not been translated into English. The original translation was also found to contain many questionable representations, including use of the terms "Spiritual Successor" and "Khalifa," which were not present in the original document, according to the new translation. And according to the *Urdu to English Dictionary ijazat* means: "The act of permitting or allowing; formal consent; authorization; leave; license or liberty granted." The word "succession" is not used in the definition.[235]

Both translations were published in an article in Pir Zia Inayat Khan's collection of essays on the legacy of his grandfather Hazrat Inayat Khan, *A Pearl in Wine.* The reader is referred to that article* for an extended treatment of this topic.

It seems likely that the original translation was shaped by Murshida Rabia's efforts to bolster her image as Inayat Khan's designated spiritual successor. Inayat appears to have wanted Pir Nizami to give Rabia the *ijazat* to empower her to function as a worldwide representative of Sufism. Being designated directly by Inayat Khan, she would not have needed any approval from the Sufi Movement headquarters in Geneva (which had rejected her bid to become Inayat Khan's successor a decade earlier).

One other radical difference in Rabia's version of the *ijazat* was the omission of a last, prophetic paragraph. The part removed from the document reads as follows in English:

> In conclusion, I pray God to make Rabia Martin succeed in establishing the Chishti teachings that spread love and contentment in the heart. I was given spiritual inspiration that the American nation possesses more capacity for genuine spiritual development that brings people to God than any others. The human being can see and understand things that materialists using the latest scientific means cannot perceive or understand. Therefore in the coming age America alone will become the spiritual exemplar for the whole world in the same manner that it is currently the most developed from the material standpoint. Listen

*Wali Ali Meyer, "A Sunrise in the West: Hazrat Inayat Khan's Legacy in California," in *A Pearl in Wine: Essays on the Life, Music, and Sufism of Hazrat Inayat Khan,* ed. Zia Inayat Khan (New Lebanon, NY: Omega Publications, 2001).

Rabia! Give my message to America and prepare America for the coming age.[236]

BARON Von FRANKENBERG OF CAMDEN

SEVEN miles out of Camden, a farmhouse, surrounded by a picturesque little garden from where the eye can travel across miles of undulating green fields, is the present centre of Sufism in Australia.

Baron F. Elliot von Frankenberg, of The Oaks, near Camden, an enthusiastic disciple of the late Piro-o-Murshid Inayat Khan, has been appointed representative of this ancient Indian religious movement.

Headquarters of Sufism in San Francisco have authorised him to confer upon approved candidates the first degrees of initiation in the Sufi Order in Australia and unassigned territory.

The descendant of an old German noble family, Baron von Frankenberg, received his education in Germany and Switzerland. Some years ago he came to Australia, where his mother was born. She was a member of a well-known Sydney family. He took up farming near Camden, and for many years was a keen follower of Sufism. He is highly thought of by the international brotherhood of the movement. He has now decided to lease his farms and come to Sydney to serve Sufism. Here he will conduct sacred readings, universal worship, and brotherhood meetings.

The late Pir-o-Murshid Inayat Khan brought Sufism to the Western world in 1910 by order of his master, the late Sufi Pir of India, Sayed Mohamet Abu Madani. When Inayat Khan died in 1927 he left to his pupils the Sufi Message of old, set to suit the mentality of the Western World.

Baron von Frankenberg says it is most difficult to define Sufism. It may be religion, but it is tolerant towards all other religions, which it calls "garments concealing the one Truth."

"In the Sufi service, called 'Universal Worship' the lights of six candles represent symbolically the Hindu, the Buddhist, the Zoroastrian, the Hebrew, the Christian, and the Moslem religions. Passages from the scriptures of all these religions are read.

"A Sufi does not separate himself from others by opinion or dogma," continued Baron von Frankenberg.

"A vast literature, composed nearly exclusively of the personal teachings of the late Inayat Khan, exists and is slowly being brought within the reach of wo.thy candidates," he said.

From left to right:—Mrs. Rabia A. Martin, the present Grand Master (Per-o-Murshida) of the Sufi movement; the late Inayat Khan; Baron von Frankenberg.

Newspaper clipping; source unknown

Rabia's international journey continued. There is an account of Murshida Martin's visit to Australia in a thesis entitled "History and Development of Western Sufism in Australia."[237] The author explains that the Sufi Movement was first introduced to Australia in the late 1920s, shortly after the death of its founder, Hazrat Inayat Khan. This early phase, under the leadership of Baron Friedrich von Frankenberg, continued until 1950. The Baron was a *mureed* of Hazrat Inayat Khan and attended the Summer School at Suresnes in 1925 and 1926. He immigrated to Australia in 1927 to marry an influential Australian woman, Olive Taylor, known as Stella.

In the mid-1930s the Baron and Stella visited the leader of the American Sufi Society, Rabia Martin, in New York. She made von Frankenberg a Sheikh and appointed him as the Australian representative of the Sufi Society. As a Sheikh, the Baron was authorized to initiate *mureeds*. The connection with Rabia Martin also gave him a new spiritual guide. At this stage he had had, at most, six months with Inayat Khan. According to Celia Genn, the Baron's letters indicate that he greatly appreciated Rabia Martin's support and guidance.[238] He continued the practices she had received from Inayat and in 1939 initiated Francis Brabazon, who later became quite prominent, into the Order.

The Baron supported Rabia Martin's 1939 tour of Australia and New Zealand by advertising public lectures in newspapers and writing letters to church groups and community leaders. In these, von Frankenberg credentials her as the Pir-o-Murshida, the Representative General of the Sufi Movement and successor of Pir-o-Murshid Inayat Khan. The tour was successful and Rabia Martin gave lectures in Melbourne and Adelaide, including addresses at the Blavatsky Lodge, The Radiant Health Centre, and the Psychic Research Society. She met with groups of *mureeds* and candidates in Sydney and Melbourne and gave practices such as singing *zikr* and the *kasab* breathing practice as well as advice.

Von Frankenberg found the Murshida's visit a mixed experience. In a letter to his wife he said, "Murshida has her winning ways, and her rather unbearable ways, but it is all to teach me something! I get many corrections for being impatient, not *mureed*-like and other points. It does not matter . . . I will keep my peace to the End of her Stay!!!" The Baron continued to seek guidance and papers from her until her death.[239]

Kaaba Allah, with its different factions, prepared for Murshida Rabia's return from travel.

Life at Kaaba Allah

Murshida Vera vividly remembered Murshida Martin's return from a long trip:

> There were times when we had tremendous experiences. When Murshida came back from South America I had been up at 4:00 in the morning with all of the young ones; and we sat on the front porch of the lower house and we made garlands, yea big around. And those garlands were just draped over every entranceway. And we had tons and tons of marigolds, a beautiful orange color with all the greens—it was just delightful. And they were on everything, along with the Sufi ribbons . . . with the different welcoming Urdu or Muslim signs for these welcoming words, Sufi words . . . And I had made little bows and tied them onto bushes going all the way out there, which said, "*Allah ho Akbar,*" or

some Sufi phrase. I had them, oh boy, on every bush leading out to the rock.

Samuel was trying to build a chapel [at the rock]. It was a little round pergola with a pointed roof, a pergola with lattice-work . . . This is where we went to have our own little mantras he would give in the morning to those he chose to go with him. And after you got out into this little chapel the lattice-work gave you some privacy from the highway.

On the morning that Murshida Martin came and walked out there—and I had been so worried that she might not have anything to welcome her on this path—and as she walked out, all of the bushes bowed. And everyone saw it. Every bush on that path bowed down as she arrived and went to the rock. And I felt it was one of the highest spiritual moments I had ever seen her in.

When she came back down to the lower house and sat down in her chair, I sat on the right side on a cushion at her feet, and Samuel sat on a cushion at her left. And everyone else was in a circle. The older *mureeds* like Maria Phelps, and—oh, many others—sat there with a smirking smile on their lips; and afterwards she said, "I thought I'd die when I saw you and Samuel sitting at her feet." And this struck me badly . . . I felt they had missed the boat. All the years at Suresnes . . . the lifetime living in *khankahs* . . . was all to be washed down the stream by lack of recognition of the spiritual body . . . And they had divided us by their criticism—mental, intellectual criticism of the *mureed* who chose to sit at the feet of the master. However we might disagree with Murshida Martin, intellectually or any other way, we never ever felt our loyalty was not hers . . .

Samuel was a Murshid . . . by discipline, by realization, by practice, by recognition of the entire Fairfax community, not just the Sufi School. He put it to work among the populace, among all the young people in Fairfax, regardless of religion, in all the churches which he took us to visit on Sunday mornings. At 10:00 or 11:00 all the young people would gather together with Samuel, and we would visit a church of his choice in Fairfax. Sometimes it would be Methodist, Baptist, Pentecostal, Catholic; we visited every parish in that area. And we were taught, a Sufi enters any church of God, any house of God, and behaves as that denomination behaves . . . When we went to the synagogue . . . and . . . the Quaker meetings, we sat separately and honored it. And we learned, by experiencing these different congregations, the love of God expressed in so many different manners . . . When we came back, Samuel would give us the heart of that message in that religion's own texts. And then he would swing back and immediately quote from Inayat Khan, so that you would see that Inayat Khan's message also was the same message, in a different age, in different words, in a different teacher.

And this taught young people the oneness, the unity of religious ideals as the books never could have, because we were living it with him, experiencing it and seeing it. All of these ministers, all of these priests . . . respected Samuel, accepted him, welcomed us into their parishes . . . The donation was the same—many of us didn't have money; Samuel would always have a little bag full of money, and he would say, "This is the time when we give back to Allah that which he has given to me." And you never knew where he got the money, because he never had anything except what was given to him, no salary, you see. And you put out your hand, and everybody got the same thing; sometimes it was a nickel, sometimes it was a dime; there were times when it was even a quarter but this is what you dropped in the plate; and you never went in there without it . . .

When we were walking down there, he would tell you something about this denomination, their way of worship, about how to behave. There were young people there that had never walked into a Catholic church before in their lives, or a Greek orthodox, or didn't know how to behave in a synagogue. He said, "These are the manners, your manners of worship; these have nothing to do with your talking to God. When you talk to God, you speak one language, remember that. There's only one language for God; there are many forms of worship." . . . When we came back from that . . . there was never any talking. Samuel would start a *mantram,* and he would quote from Murshid, and from their texts here and there, haphazard . . . he would throw it out as you walked along . . .

When you went back—we had an early lunch at Kaaba Allah—oh, I'd say around 11:15 or something like that, you'd have the lunch. Immediately following that lunch Murshida Martin would sit in her chair, everybody would sit in a circle, and she would give her talk; and all the old people fell asleep, which were her *mureeds,* all fell asleep while she was giving the message . . . Nobody ever fell asleep with Samuel, believe me! (laughter) . . . Following this, there was never any talking. She went to her apartment, I went with her, prepared her for her afternoon nap . . .

After this afternoon quiet period or nap time and the afternoon lecture, then you all came out into the sun; and everybody was allowed to

> get into their sun suits or as brief as you wanted to . . . This was the time when the *mureeds* traded friendship and talk. And the talk was always full of jokes and they had all kinds of Sufi jokes . . . And sometimes the flute was played here and if someone came from the East and had the sitar or any of the oriental instruments, they would play. If there was anybody in Fairfax who was visiting there from Europe or Asia, they were invited up. And this was teatime . . .
>
> Supper was never served until dark. You ate supper and you left on Sunday night . . . At the end of supper Samuel would stand at the door. Your baggage was always ready to go . . . When everybody was more or less organized, then we walked single file up to the chapel . . . and . . . had the last of the prayers . . . You left after *zikr* in silence. Everybody kissed everybody, said goodbye; but it wasn't in language: it was in gesture, or by kissing or hugging one another. Usually the older *mureeds* stood at the doorway; the very oldest, the three oldest ladies, always stood together. And Samuel would be returning to the city with us, and we would say goodbye to these older *mureeds* as we left.

This was all before the arrival of World War II, which would dramatically change the functioning of Kaaba Allah. Some difficulties were already developing there. Maria Phelps, who was on the Board of the Sufi Order, was "at odds, but proper" with Samuel, as Vera said. She went on to describe some of their history:

> Her daughter, Gladys Coto, and Samuel had a love life that went on for many years. They were very close. They had a great love and attunement between them, although she married a pharmacist. But he had known her before that marriage. And all through those years he was a guardian, mentor and father to her three children by her first tragic marriage. The children had come out from the East during the depth of the Depression with a crate of oranges in an old tin Lizzie, no food or anything, based on faith alone. They had become *mureeds* in [the Midwest] . . . They came to live at Kaaba Allah. They had no food, no money, nothing; and Murshida Martin took them in . . . as housekeepers and cooks . . .
>
> Samuel knew these children very well, and very intimately . . . The two oldest ones, Shirin and Nadine, came [west]; and then Gladys married and had this little girl who was born with club feet. And Samuel

was very close to Gladys in advising as to the procedure of how they would heal this child, what was to be done for her, the final decision on the surgery. The first surgery was done . . . against Samuel's wishes—but other people influenced them, at the last minute, and they felt that they should have this one tendon cut. It was later decided it was a mistake, and they put the child in braces. Both Samuel and I fought this terribly, because it was so cruel to see these heavy braces on this tiny child two or three years of age . . .

We would always manage to get Gladys aside in the rose garden and say, "Gladys, get those things off of her!" . . . and then we'd hold her by the hands and walk her without the braces. And Samuel did much healing by hands and by earth and by water on this child's feet and legs, and great progress was made.

[During] those years Samuel did a great deal of healing with the children and with this family and this child, in particular . . . The oldest girl, Shirin, became a WAVE* . . . and she went to Seattle, Washington, and her plane crashed. She was landing and she hit high tension wires . . . Samuel grieved deeply over this. The body was brought back and he had a service in the Cotos' home, and oh, his grief over Shirin's passing! . . .

[She] was such a beautiful girl . . . a lovely smile, and just the most delightful teenage girl you'd ever know . . . Shirin and I built the friendship seat, which is still . . . on the rock at Kaaba Allah. He felt terrible grief over her, but I could not attend any of this. I couldn't stand to see Samuel in the state he was in. I couldn't stand to see him shook all to pieces and weeping. They said that the funeral service he gave for Shirin was an agony for everyone there; everyone was weeping, and Samuel was in a state for two weeks. He just had a horrible time getting over it . . .

This work he did with the children in those days was a healing work, and many of the ideas that I have and that I have put to work with . . . children with all kinds of physical and emotional problems are things that I saw our Murshid do . . .†

Samuel, when I first knew him, was very delicate; he had nothing of this strong body that he built through the years by practices. But he had

---

*United States Naval Reserve (Women's Reserve), better known as WAVES (Women Accepted for Volunteer Emergency Service).

†After retiring from full-time teaching, Murshida Vera Corda tutored children with special learning needs at her home in the Salinas Valley, California. (See veracorda.com.)

> a delicate bone structure. He was [a] thin and intellectual and esoteric being, all head . . . During the time that Arjuna and I were first married we lived on . . . the top floor of a flat that overlooked the Bay and the bridge. And if you weren't young and strong you couldn't stand it to climb up that amount of stairs; so we didn't have to worry about the old ones—they wouldn't climb. (laughs) We had only the young ones who came there, and we would have tremendous parties in this house . . .
>
> One night we were having one of the first parties we had after I joined the Order. And all the young people were there, and Hazel Armstrong and a few of that middle age group were there; and Samuel came late . . . Shirin and Nadine and all the Phelps kids and the whole bunch of children that were children related to Sufis . . . were all sitting around on the couches and the chairs. And we had a fishbowl, which was turned upside down for an oracle; and we had towel turbans—if you were the swami, you had to put on the turban. And then you had to look into the fishbowl and you had papers that everybody had their question and their name on it, and you picked up a paper . . . You . . . predicted for this person, gave him his fortune. And these fortunes were just hilarious; everybody told all the dirt they knew about anybody else (laughs). And we were all laughing and having a great time when Samuel came, and he looked and he said "What are you doing? This is all wrong! Vera should be the swami." And he walked over to me and snatched this turban . . . , wound it around my head, and went out to fill the fishbowl with water and put it right side up. And he said, "No, put your mind on this and stop the nonsense" . . .

Vera then told of Sam hanging up his coat in the hallway and returning to the circle, not knowing that his fly was unzipped—which left him graphically exposed. She managed to back him out of the room to remedy the situation, leaving the young kids unaware and Sam unfazed. She continued:

> [It was] the joke of the Order, but it is typical of the states that Samuel was in; he was totally unaware of the physical; it simply didn't exist. He was in the spirit body; he was working in the spirit all the time, and the physical body was just simply not recognized. I think this was true all of his life, so that in the low points, when he should have been on his own retreat, free of teaching *mureeds* or giving the Message, he would plow on, not even recognize his physical states. And after the years of Hazel's

death [years later] when there was no one to knit his sweaters, take care of his dirty socks, care for him physically and see that he did what was right for his physical body, no one cared about his physical body.

Growing Difficulties with Murshida Martin

> *When in ourselves there is inharmony, how can we spread harmony?*
>
> HAZRAT INAYAT KHAN[240]

> *The best way to develop strength is to achieve unity. This comes out of the practice of concentration. Concentration need not be limited to a few minutes a day or week when one performs some exercise given in the teachings. Concentration may be practiced every hour, every minute, every breath—especially through* darood.* *Then one does not have to seek unity, unity will seek one. When added to that the* talib† *is given instruction in music or else in meditation, he acquires that unity of purpose, that unity of feeling and the more he adheres to that unity the better can he protect himself and assist others. Never surrender to anything, to anyone, to any force except God or those who represent God in the Spiritual Hierarchy.*
>
> SAMUEL LEWIS[241]

Paul Reps later had these reflections on Murshida Martin's style:

> She was formalized. I think she had formalized a method of teaching people . . . Once I was driving—Murshida Martin in the back seat and Murshid [Inayat Khan] in the front seat—from San Francisco to Los Angeles. She scolded so much about the woman Los Angeles representative that he couldn't bear it any more. So he said, "Now I make Reps in charge of Los Angeles." I turned to her and said, "You must stop talking now."[242]

Murshida Vera noted a turn in Murshida Martin's influence on Samuel.

> One of the reasons Samuel's work was found so late in life was not because he wasn't practicing it or have the self-realization. He did have

---

*Murshid Sam used *darood* to indicate a concentration in which one breathes in and out the words "Toward the One" from the Sufi Invocation of Inayat Khan; one focuses fully on being present in oneness in this moment, thus enhancing integration of self within the oneness of all.

†A *talib* is an initiated seeker of knowledge, a student.

Murshida Rabia Martin at Kaaba Allah

it, and he did not in those days have this terrible ego-tramping, this crucifixion in the spiritual and subtle body that became worse later.[243]

The feelings of being crucified by Murshida Martin had not yet surfaced in Samuel in the earlier 1930s, "those days" in Murshida Vera's recollections. Toward the last years of the decade, however, Murshida Martin was beginning to develop more resistance to Samuel. She especially chafed against his role of being the voice of Hazrat Inayat Khan, even though she frequently asked for that voice to try to better manage her spiritual affairs and the outer affairs of the Order. Rabia had been advised by the Pir-o-Murshid that if she ever needed to hear his voice, she could ask Samuel Lewis, who he affirmed had a genuine inner connection with him.

Rabia in turn complained of being crucified over the years by Samuel Lewis! They were in the crucible together. She complained of this even on her deathbed in August of 1947.

As World War II approached and reached America, there was a giant exodus of young people into the war effort. Samuel, who continued to live at the Sufi School in Fairfax, also became employed in work associated with the war. Murshida Vera's remembrance of this later period reveals significant details, including the increasing strain on the relationship between Samuel and Rabia.

> When World War II came . . . we were all pulled out of the *khankah* life to serve. The young men went to war immediately—Arjuna and probably four or five others. [Dr. Tuffey and Dr. Davida Herrick] went into the medical work. Hazel Armstrong moved out to the end of Monterey Boulevard and opened a knitting shop, where she had little Sufi meetings that I could attend to. We were all working different hours . . . I went into the Naval Training School at Bethlehem Steel as an artist . . . Our lives changed drastically because of the war.

> In [these] years when Samuel was receiving psychically practically day and night . . . he was advising, at Murshida Martin's behest, every decision she made. Just before I became a Sheikha . . . I was living at Tenth Avenue and Irving, and I had to walk through the park to get over to [her home on] Ashbury. There was no money for carfare, so I would take my big dog and hike over through the park to [her place]. When I got there, she knew that we were half-starved, and she would give me jelly and bread and tea. And then we would go into the front room.
>
> Murshida Martin would sit me down in her beautiful living room, filled with the art that she had collected all over the world, and would then question me as to the psychic messages brought to her by Samuel in the name of Inayat Khan. This was extremely shaking for me, and I just didn't know what to do about it. I would just insist on going into a short meditation and then answer her on my own ground . . .
>
> This is how I got around criticizing what Samuel might be doing, or what might be coming through to him, which was never handed to me straight. I'd pick up the papers here and there and know in reading it that this is the language of Murshid . . . it is Inayat Khan's message . . . Murshida Martin used and misused [them]; she took them and used them to rule the outer work . . . [She] should not have used Samuel to bring her the psychic answers to her pressing problems in the Order . . . No matter how you may doubt yourself, get your own attunement with the Presence, which was our Murshid Sam's rule of life . . . Murshida Martin doubted her own wisdom.
>
> Of course, he was highly trained psychically . . . [but] Murshida Martin would put it to work on the material plane right away . . . You cannot do that; that is the wrong approach. And everything that Samuel wanted to do, she was putting to work in a different interpretation.*

Murshid Sam said about his work for Army Intelligence during the war years and his inner activities, "What was actually happening was that I was being called on by the Hierarchy† to have a function in the war." One of the things he was willing to say was that he was called on

* Vera has misspoken here regarding training. Sam from birth had the gift of being psychically aware as seen in the chapter on his early childhood. Practicing with the teachings of Inayat Khan gave him the experiences he needed.

† To Sufis, the Spiritual Hierarchy is the deeply respected lineage of realized beings, linked in the heart and depth of being, serving as models for others and providing a stream of blessing (*baraka*).

to take the souls over to the other side, all these bodies, these people that were being executed in the gas chambers in Auschwitz and elsewhere. Vera related a story that connected with this function of Sam's work, both inner and outer:

> This is what happened at that period. There was a *mureed* called Mrs. Green, who was Jewish, who had a very beautiful home out in the avenues. *Mureeds* would meet at this home quite often . . . We decided to have a party; and our parties were always in costume. We came in Sufi dress, the ancient Sufis . . . characters like Shirin and Khusrau and Majnun . . . We were having such a party one evening . . . when four of the Jewish people smuggled out of Hitler's Germany and smuggled into the United States . . . were smuggled to the Greens' unexpectedly . . . They were immediately ushered in, looked at us in awe and fear and trembling, and were taken to a back bedroom . . .
>
> Late in the evening when we were ready to go, I went into that room to get the cloaks, and these people, who were huddled together, looked in fear at me and got down on the floor and crawled under the bed. And I thought, "What in the world is wrong with them?" They were guests; we were not told who these people were, but we could tell they were just from Europe by the way they were dressed, and they did not speak any English. I immediately went out to Green and said to her . . ."These people are in fear of me, and they're under the bed." . . . She said they had been locked in attics in Germany and later in Holland and we've just gotten them out. Any sounds at all make them feel they are going to be put in a wagon and taken to be eliminated . . .
>
> I [asked], "Does Samuel know?" And she said, "I don't think so; I didn't want to make any announcement in front of all these Sufis." There were over 50 Sufis there that evening. I went and got Samuel . . . I took him in the bathroom and slammed the door. I said, "Do you know about these people?" He said, "I know what they look like to me." And I said, "Well, you're right." And I told him what had happened. And I said, "She has locked them in that back room because we're here, and she's going to keep them there until we go . . . These people are frightened to death. "Oh," he says, "I never heard of such a thing."
>
> So he went into the kitchen and immediately got Mrs. Green and went into that back room; and soon you could hear the *mantrams* going, and Samuel was working with them. So this was my first, and his first introduction, then, to the problem of these people, that I know of . . .

> Now Sam immediately got to work on this, beginning that evening when the first refugees were found under the Greens' bed, And he started to work for these people, on the inner planes, immediately.

Most often, Murshida Martin was in her own home in San Francisco with physical problems. As Vera relates, "She was not controlling it. And Samuel had the full go, the full control of Kaaba Allah, all the initiations, the running of the Order, the whole thing. And he was then relieved from gardening duties." He felt the pressure of his position.

Vera described an incident that reflects this pressure. She was approached by someone who had been disturbed by Samuel:

> Here was this old lady with the tears running down her face, crying to me at the way Samuel had treated her and had banned her to her room, and she had to stay there for two weeks. She was not to be allowed out of her room as punishment. And I was just indignant . . . And I just told him "No, Samuel, you cannot treat these old people this way." . . . I was standing above him, sitting on the Sufi symbol,* and the power was coming through me, and it cracked him up. He began to cry and ran down to his apartment.

Vera was so upset by this incident that she and her husband packed their suitcases and were en route to their car. Hazel Armstrong stopped their departure because Sam was crying and she wished Vera to go and talk to him. Vera refused to see him while she was in such a state of distress. In her remembrance Vera reflected further on Murshida Martin:

> Only the week before, [this same old woman] had appeared with her hair . . . tied in the back with a little black bow like maybe colonial men would have looked, with a little curl—and Murshida Martin had read her out before the whole Order in circle, telling her that she was too old to look like that. And everybody just acted as if they were slapped in the face when she said that. It was the most rude thing she ever could have said in public to a woman who had given her fortune and her life to her. But this was the sort of thing that was going on in there,

---

*A heart and wings carved at the top of the entry gate to Kaaba Allah. The carving was the work of Ray Van Voris, Vera's father.

> complete disregard for the heart and feelings of people who'd given their lives to the Order . . . It was no longer the Message . . .
>
> Had Murshida Martin been the inner listener instead of one trying to the last to fulfill her claim, and having Samuel devote years of his productive life in typing nothing but defenses for her, for her desire to reach that level [Pir]. Only after she made the trip to India and was recognized by different holy orders on her own ground and had a hundred people or more trotting behind her whenever she got off of a train, did she finally come to any feeling of being recognized on her own ground . . .
>
> She didn't start at all on the spiritual plane for . . . humanity, as Samuel did, [or] of working in your own back yard, but demanded and spent her whole life trying to prove and claim the Pir-ship. And this was just a great pity; but I feel that she has been dropped as if she didn't exist. She influenced so much of our Murshid's life that something definitely should be done on the life of Rabia and the work that she did in America . . . We do owe her a debt.*

During this period Murshida Martin was asking Sheikha Vera questions in parallel to Samuel, without showing her what he was bringing forth. She asked her to give answers purely from the psychic dimension—demanding an inner reading each time. Vera personally never knew if she was right or wrong. The messages she received were, "Send Samuel to India; get him there." He was never sponsored to do this, and he lacked the necessary funds. That trip wouldn't happen for several decades.

After the outbreak of the war, Samuel Lewis, still living on the Fairfax land, was commuting by ferry to his employment as a civilian working for U.S. Army Intelligence. Denied entry into the armed forces because of poor eyesight at the time of World War I, now he had a chance to serve his country. He landed in a setting appropriate for one whose interests were always global.

---

*The present volume has made a significant effort toward this end. In the last decade from 2010 there has been more and more interest in Murshida Martin's place in this history.

Samuel receiving military award

CHAPTER 6

Samuel Lewis in Army Intelligence

Man, who is more capable of perceiving by breath still deeper things, warnings and calls from the earth and from heaven, which places are meant for him to dwell in or to settle in, of discriminating between friend and foe and discerning their pleasure and displeasure, owing to his interest in the superficial things of life cannot fully benefit by the power of breath.

HAZRAT INAYAT KHAN[244]

During the World War II, the commentator was constantly demonstrating or trying to demonstrate it. Nobody else seems to have understood. Instead of trying to learn and absorb, there was great hostility to this peculiar behavior. But strange as it may seem, some of the leading offices in Army Intelligence were aware of the existence of personalities with such faculties and made use of them.

SAMUEL LEWIS[245]

SAMUEL LEWIS'S DESCRIPTION ABOVE INDICATES that he was constantly demonstrating or trying to demonstrate what he was receiving within. His encounter with the refugees from Nazism focused his attention. After that experience, he put his spiritual powers to work to succor the souls of the victims in the Nazi concentration camps, assisting them in their passage to the next world. And he was positioned to be fighting the War on the outer planes as well as the inner. The U.S. National Archives reveal more about his civilian service and relationship with Army Intelligence, known as G-2.

Toward the end of March in 1942 Samuel Lewis filled out a lengthy application for a job as a temporary clerk-typist, giving his address as

Fairfax, California, and saying he had lived there intermittently for 12 of the last 20 years. On March 23 he was appointed Junior Clerk Typist at $1440 per year and was assigned to the Port Ordnance Office at Davis and Vallejo at the Embarcadero, listed as Fort Mason in the official records. Most of the records, including requests to promote Samuel, were signed by Major Frank Batson. Sam's duties were described as shipping orders, tickets, teletypes, typing, and other clerical tasks.

By June Samuel was recommended for the regular position of Assistant Clerk with an improvement in income to $1620 per year owing to the increase in the volume of work and responsibilities. Additional responsibilities related to ordnance requisitions, shipping manifests, and dock records. In July he applied for part of his wages to go into Defense Saving Bonds, naming Hazel Armstrong as beneficiary.

In October Batson again recommended him for promotion with a raise to $1800. Additional duties included editing and checking checker's reports, supervising junior clerk typists, cataloguing shipping tickets, supervising distribution, and preparing statistical reports of ammunition and supplies, some of which was classified information. He was stationed in Oakland, which was considered the primary port for San Francisco.

Subsequently there was an investigation of Civilian Employees by one Intelligence Officer Dillon. His report in February of 1943 identified Samuel as working in the General Supply Section. "Subject reported to be loyal, of good repute and satisfactory for employment in war industry." He was now classified as being "in the field." His experience of the brain trust in Army Intelligence was during this period. In a class recorded during 1967, Murshid Samuel Lewis gave this account:

> I worked for G-2 and I wanted to write a paper on the roads of Asia. The Colonel said, no, write one on Africa. So I did give them some information they didn't have. I knew a good deal more than most Americans, and the day when they got through, I brought my part. That was the day that soldiers landed in North Africa! I went upstairs to the Colonel and said, "You are pulling my leg." He said, "Yes, I was testing you."[246]

Allied forces landed in Morocco and Algeria on November 8, 1943. In October of 1945 Samuel, now assigned to the Procurement Division from the Water Division, was in the process of resigning from his job for lack of use of his abilities. He was told to get higher approval.

> During the War I did some pseudo-research for Colonel Harris of GII. He tested me and I passed and he, with his subaltern, Edward Lansdale, had a laugh on me. But two years later when I wanted a release I had to go to Col. Harris and showed him my esoteric notebook with the precise predictions.[247]
>
> [Colonel Harris] was the chief of Edward Lansdale, who became a Lieutenant General in Vietnam. And I said "Remember the time you had me do work on the roads of Africa? I am going to show you something I never showed anyone else before." I pulled out my esoteric diary and there was my prediction of the invasion of North Africa. I told him, "I think I am going to destroy all my papers." He said it was a good idea, so I did. Under certain conditions predictions come easy, and friends and enemies become easier.[248]
>
> All my poetry for the last twenty-five years is prophetic and all rejected . . . the odd is odd and must be rejected, but the fact remains, it is all prophetic and now I am amazed how much is true, but to be correct does not make one popular . . . A certain person returned my papers after many years, and I found among them my poems written in 1932 on the death of Hitler, the fall of the British Empire, the independence of India, the return of Jews to Palestine, etc.[249]
>
> One does not have to have any third eye if he is honest, for he sees the operation of karma so deliberately and definitely it is easy to predict anything. All one has to do is to examine events and persons dispassionately. Actually, this is the way Sufis teach occultism, without any psychic or *siddhantic* elements [development of powers]. You just have to be impersonal and honest as the scientific researchers are.[250]
>
> 75% of my predictions, though they are not published, have come true, and not symbolically . . . I have always felt they were under Divine Guidance and with Love and Compassion for humanity, and not with the idea of just looking into tomorrow. St. Paul said, "I die daily," and if you really die daily you can see into the future easier.[251]*

---

* St. Paul's statement about dying daily relates to the Sufi injunction *mutu kabla anta mutu,* "die before you die," which refers to the effacement or "death" of the *nafs* (ego). Sam here suggests that his access to this type of death made possible the manifestation of his psychic abilities.

Later Sam described an event in his wartime life that gives an example of such a death, in this case allowing his effacement into the being of another. This permitted him access to knowledge of the future, a gift that appears to have been used by the military.

> It was during the War that, when it was said that Hitler was going to call in psychic powers, I asked God what to do and He said: "Go upstairs!" I went upstairs and became an [*abdal*], which means **changeling**.[252]*

In 1966 Samuel referred to his years in G-2 in a letter to a U.S senator, criticizing U.S. policies:

> During the War I had some slight associations with an important branch of GII, under one Col. Harris, whose aide was Edward Lansdale, now one of our top experts on Vietnam . . . There was an office in this department consisting of Americans who were adepts in real, practicing Buddhism and they used to put on real Buddhist programs in Japanese to appeal to those people . . . When the surrender took place, General McArthur took further measures to separate pure religion from the personality worship of the Emperor . . . This person not only "saw" the excellent methods used by GII during the war, which were most effective—he has seen the absolute refusal to repeat these today and we have had no great success.[253]

In a 1967 letter to Stewart Alsop at the *Saturday Evening Post,* Samuel included what he learned about the effect of these efforts:

> [There] was a department broadcasting in Japanese on "Buddhism." When I came to Japan later I was informed—all first hand—the beneficent effect of those broadcasts and the effects of General McArthur's policies . . . [254]

A review of a later biography of Gen. Lansdale gave this picture:

> An Air Force officer and CIA operative, Lansdale devised tactics against the communist Huks in the Philippines in the early 50s and master-

---

*The word *abdal* refers to one who has the capacity not merely to emulate, but to experience the inner reality of another person. Samuel here brings in the English word "changeling" in an apparent attempt to evoke that sense of transmutation. Inhabiting the self of the other would give rise to an intimate knowledge of their mind and intentions, thus accounting for otherwise unexplainable psychic access.

> minded the first free elections there, and soon afterward helped Ngo Dinh Diem form his fledgling government in South Vietnam. So much for his triumphs, which made him a legend in the Far East. The second half of this notable biography makes for painful reading, as the author describes Lansdale's struggles in Saigon to prevent the disintegration of the fragile nation he helped establish. Convinced that counterinsurgency must have a social vision as well as military strength, he urged political-psychological programs as opposed to search-and-destroy missions and B-52 raids . . . Many of Lansdale's urgent warnings were virtually ignored by the U.S. high command, and he closed out his maverick career collecting soldiers' songs.[255]

Gen. Lansdale was Samuel Lewis's war hero; Sam acknowledged the principles Lansdale had used effectively in World War II, and naturally believed Lansdale would continue to function in that way. His outlook was supported when he ultimately succeeded in establishing communication with the General after having earlier letters returned by the government. Sam learned in early 1969 that Lansdale's son had a house in Marin County. He contacted him and the son was happy to give his father's mailing address. Lansdale's response to Sam came on May 4, 1969:

> Dear Samuel,
>
> Your 25 February letter has been waiting with others from friends until I could get a good solid start on a book I'm writing. Now that I'm about a third of the way into it, I'm taking a day off for a stretch and to say hello to friends. It was a most pleasant surprise to hear from you after so many years and to learn that you had been traveling in Asia among people I have come to know. Like you, I am neither hawk nor dove but a believer in the brotherhood of man, which is something else entirely. My last attempt to live by my philosophy as part of the U.S. mission in Viet Nam, 1965–1968, had plenty of ups and downs, but the Vietnamese seemed to feel that my work was constructive and most helpful to them. However, I'm afraid I didn't make too much of a dent in official U.S. thinking.
>
> In Viet Nam, I came to know many of the religious leaders, some during my first service there (1953, 1954–1956) and some on my last tour of duty. My last day in Viet Nam was spent with Cao Dai leaders at Tay Ninh. I don't know how the book I'm writing will turn out. It concerns

> my relations with people and events in the Philippines and Viet Nam mostly, from 1950 to 1968. I'm trying to tell what actually happened, except for a few secrets that aren't mine to tell and would only harm some good people who are still active on the scene if I embarrassed them by telling what I know. There's plenty to relate without that. I presume that the new Left and the far Right, who ganged up on me in the past, will react angrily to what I'm writing, but I couldn't care less about their reactions.
>
> With warmest and best wishes,
> Ed Lansdale[256]

Lansdale later sent a postcard informing Sam of the publication of his book, *In the Midst of Wars.* Lansdale's last acts of collecting soldiers' songs were also meaningful:

> It is to General . . . Lansdale that we owe most of the knowledge of the songs of the Vietnam War . . . His interest in the possibilities of folklore in psychological warfare were apparent during early years of the war as part of Office of Strategic Services (OSS) . . . Felt proper place for an intelligence operative was with the people—get to know them, be with them, learn their songs. Went to Philippines in 1945, Vietnam in 1954. Learned folklore, superstitions, etc.[257]

Throughout his career Samuel Lewis would frequently and proudly call on his war experiences, such as his work sending messages to Japan. In a letter from Peshawar, Pakistan, to the World Affairs Council he said, "If you ever write my biography, go to Fort Mason and look at the heroes' book, May 1945, and see my signature and ask how it got there. Right under Carlson's Raiders."[258]*

---

*Fort Mason is no longer an Army base. Research was not able to uncover the heroes' book.

Murshida Ivy Duce and Meher Baba, July 1956

CHAPTER 7

The Meher Baba Connection

With good will and trust in God, self-confidence, and a hopeful attitude towards life, one can always win one's battle, however difficult.

HAZRAT INAYAT KHAN[259]

When there is trust in God, there can be no defeat. When one is bound by one's conception of God, when one limits God by one's human conception, one's trust is necessarily limited. To increase the scope of trust one must find a greater being in whom to trust, and if this being is limited by human thought, then trust is limited.

SAMUEL LEWIS[260]

MURSHIDA RABIA MARTIN HAD BOTH MESSIANIC AND THEOSOPHICAL ROOTS. A significant focus for her was finding a world-savior, someone still in the body whose God-realized perfection could be recognized by the whole of humanity. With Hazrat Inayat Khan no longer alive, she questioned whether someone who had passed away could still be an active source of communication for the benefit of the Sufi Message. Still, she felt compelled to respect what her teacher had said to her in relation to Samuel—that she could receive his transmissions as Inayat's own guidance. These transmissions, however, were often critical of her actions and it is clear from her history that criticism was not an effective approach with her. Aside from these mixed feelings, it appears Rabia no longer felt she had the strength to proceed on her own.

Some years later in a letter to Mrs. Duce, Samuel Lewis referred in part to his difficult communications with Rabia:

> I must confess that I have not always written in a devotional manner. I once had a long and disquieting experience with Murshida Rabia—it

> ended dramatically—in which I failed in calling her attention that her acts were unequal, those which were done in a hierarchal fashion being infinitely more important than the details she used to do for the cause of God, and the latter in their turn, being almost again infinitely more important than the affairs of her private life. I failed . . . but I have not changed my point of view.[261]

In 1942 Rabia Martin had a meeting that played a significant role in determining the future of the Sufi Movement in America. This event modified her direction and that of some of her followers—those who were willing to align themselves with Meher Baba.*

Rabia met two devoted Baba lovers, Norina Matchabelli and Elizabeth Patterson, in San Francisco in 1942. They had come to California to investigate sites for Baba's proposed American center. After listening to their descriptions of their Master at one of Norina's public talks, Rabia became convinced that Meher Baba was an extraordinary spiritual figure. She offered her Sufi retreat center in Fairfax near San Francisco for his use. Elizabeth Patterson wrote Baba in India: "Rabia's offer seemed to come from the heart and we all agree that she is the most advanced and understanding soul we met in California."[262]

Over the next three years, Rabia Martin studied Baba's writings and began corresponding with him. Her husband David Martin died in April of 1943, ending his perennial support of all her efforts. She then grew closer to Norina and Elizabeth through repeated visits to New York City. Their descriptions of life with Baba and his philosophy rapidly formed a conviction within her of the importance of Baba as the key spiritual figure of the age.

Two of Murshida Martin's early students, Don Stevens and Ivy Duce, also became important to the Meher Baba movement in the United States. They had begun to study with her in 1941, although they did not participate in group Sufi classes or activities at that time.

In April, 1945, Norina and Elizabeth invited Rabia to live with them. She joined them in New York and then at Myrtle Beach until July.

---

*Bhau Kalchuri's biography of Meher Baba, *Lord Meher,* has been used extensively as a source for the material in this section.

Rabia's inner experiences during those months confirmed her belief that Baba was the living embodiment of Sufism and the divine incarnation of God: the *Rasul* or Avatar.

> In May 1945, at Myrtle Beach, Rabia asked Baba by letter to accept herself as his student, and then on his acceptance, wrote further to ask him to take the responsibility for the spiritual guidance of the Sufi Order, which he accepted.[263]

On July 4 of 1945 Ivy Duce joined Rabia in New York. Rabia told Mrs. Duce that she had spent the time validating for herself that Baba was the *Qutub* (head of the Spiritual Hierarchy). Rabia left the next day to return to San Francisco.

While Meher Baba's teachings and work gradually became known in many parts of the world, he never approached such an apotheosis as that of being recognized by all of humanity. Khalif Samuel Lewis, for his part, would respect his vow to Pir-o-Murshid Inayat Khan and continue to offer support to Murshida Martin in the Sufi work.

Samuel wrote papers on Rabia's behalf to her existing students outlining their choices after her acceptance of Baba. They were given two weeks to decide if they would accept her decision or go elsewhere, which included leaving the land in Fairfax. According to Don Stevens,

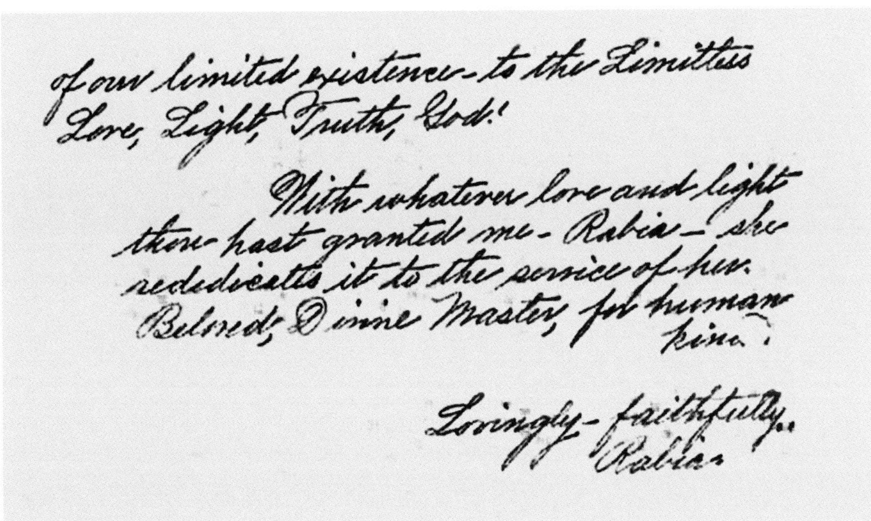

of our limited existence to the Limitless Love, Light, Truth, God!

With whatever love and light thou hast granted me - Rabia - she rededicates it to the service of her Beloved, Divine Master, for humankind.

Lovingly - faithfully.
Rabia

Letter from Rabia Martin to Meher Baba, August 1945

a relatively new *mureed* at this time, most of Rabia's students initially followed her in turning to Meher Baba, but after her death in August of 1947 the majority of her earliest students left.* Ivy Duce, who wholeheartedly embraced Meher Baba as the spiritual head of the Order, was named Rabia's successor one month prior to Rabia's death. In the ensuing years, many more students drifted away from the fold.

During Rabia's stay in New York, important activities were taking place in San Francisco. On April 25 of 1945, only a few weeks before Samuel visited Colonel Harris and resigned from his job at Fort Mason, the United Nations Conference on International Organization opened and Sam became seriously involved. The conference went on for weeks and gave birth to the Charter for the UN. Fifty nations from the allied powers participated. India was included, although it was not to get independence officially from Great Britain until 1947. Some of the regions of India such as Hyderabad Deccan that were not formally absorbed into India were also represented.

It is quite likely that Samuel Lewis encountered some of the delegates who were Sufis, and who anticipated the partition of India into Hindu and Muslim states. In a 1966 letter to Sufi Barkat Ali in Pakistan, he described what they had asked him to do:

> In the year 1945 this person was asked to perform some errands for the brotherhood in Hyderabad Deccan. To get credentials he was examined by the cultural diplomat of the then undivided India. The subject was "Ibnu l-'Arabi" and when this person submitted as answer: "The Identity of Ibnu 'l-'Arabi and Sankara" the attaché embraced him.† But when he tried to bring this matter up before certain of the innumerable European professors of Asian philosophies, he was so strongly rebuked that the matter has been dormant.[264] ‡

---

*Rabia's "earliest students" were those who had become followers of Inayat Khan's teachings through her guidance. Research has shown that most of Rabia's students who remained at Kaaba Allah following her passing were original students of Inayat Khan's and were older. The majority of them passed away between 1947 and 1949.

†Adi Sankara (8th century CE), also spelled Shankara, is considered the root teacher of Advaita Vedanta.

‡Sam would persist in pursuing this mission to keep communication operating between the Sufi brotherhoods when the separation of India and Pakistan actually occurred.

Forty-six nations joined at the founding of the United Nations in October 1945

At some point during this time Samuel visited his Uncle Harry and other relatives in Southern California. Sam's cousin Marilou Foster described the visit in an interview:

> He came down to visit my grandparents . . . He stayed at the house a couple of days. And I started getting up in the morning to Gilbert and Sullivan . . . He was not [like] the other brother [who] had been down also, Elliott, [who] was a braggart and it was: me, me, me, me, me . . . Samuel was more into a philosophy thing; this caught my interest at the time as opposed to his brother's ego trips.[265]

On May 15, 1945, Samuel left San Francisco at Murshida Martin's request to go to the land in Myrtle Beach, South Carolina. This land belonged to Elizabeth Patterson's family and had now been dedicated to Meher Baba. On May 17 Sam arrived in New York City, the very day that his Zen teacher Sokei-an Sasaki passed through death into *parinirvana.** Samuel said, "It was the saddest period of my life; since then, it has been impossible for me to experience such sorrow."[266]

During this period, Samuel was writing actively in his journal called "The Book of Cosmic Prophecy;" further quotations in this section are drawn from that document.[267] On May 23, he recorded speaking at Carnegie Hall, and added, "Baba says important day." On June 7 he wrote "Became empty (*fana*)."

---

*Release into unity (*nirvana*) after death.

When Sam arrived in Myrtle Beach, he made a long and detailed entry that begins with this paragraph in the voice of Meher Baba:

> On this 13th day of July 1945, do I, Meher Baba, the Avatar, incarnate for this age, take over, so to speak, this esoteric diary and Book of Cosmic Prophesy, to utilize it to the full for the purposes for which it was originally intended, to integrate it consciously and completely with those works personal and impersonal which have [come] through the mind of this vessel, to coordinate it and them with my own writings and with all those inspirations which have come to and through [men] and women who are conscious of My Presence and My Being on one or more planes from the lowest to the highest.

This proclamation is a striking contrast to the words he had written in the same document on May 15, 1932:

> *The Holy Ones send their greeting unto Sheikha Sundar*
> *And admonish her thus in the Name of the Lord:*
> *Be not deceived, dear sister, by the approach and appearance of one who acts not as men act,*
> *Who misuses the bodily parts as God did not intend.**
> *Wherefore our Holy Prophet did declare he was a man as men,*
> *and acted among the human kingdom as a man*
> *Depending neither upon miracle or magic to preach the doctrine of the Lord . . .*
> *"Lord, open Thou my lips and my mouth shall speak forth Thy praise" . . .*
> *Unto all prophets have commands been given in word, in speech, in music.*
> *Cannot the idiot hold silence?*
> *Cannot the dumb in heart withhold their speech? . . .*
> *Whoso sees not and hears not music shall not find the Lord,*
> *For in Brahma is sound, in Ahura is music, in Jehovah is speech.*
> *Take heed to speak when the Holy Spirit commands thee,*
> *When the Spirit of Guidance takes thy hand,*
> *When the Spirit of Truth leads thy heart,*
> *Blessed thou shall be forever and ever.*
> *And accursed is he who makes a theatrical out of the holy things of the Lord.*

Below the poem Samuel Lewis wrote: "Against the *Dajjal* Meher Baba, on May 15, 1932, who was struck dumb thereafter and left the country."

---

*This is likely a reference to Baba's vow of silence, under which he did not use his tongue for speech.

A *dajjal* is one whose ego proclaims itself as a savior. Toward the last period of his life Samuel would occasionally reaffirm this evaluation of Meher Baba. Now, however, in 1945, thirteen years after calling him accursed, Samuel Lewis is proclaiming that Meher Baba has taken over Sam's journal.* In a lengthy essay in the journal, there is a detailed description written by Sam in Baba's voice of how the center at Myrtle Beach should be developed. The ways that an Avatar acts are also described.

> Myrtle Beach has been carefully selected. Islam teaches that the sacred place would be where the swift waters and the salt and the bitter waters met. On the blessing and merits of these waters I shall speak more when I come but I have asked that the lakes be kept free from human emanations and vibrations. If you touch these waters before I have done so with my living presence it may require much rain and drainage to purify them psychically. But of these matters I shall speak more especially with My Living Presence . . .
>
> The Center, or the Abode for One and All will be established in a manner which will avoid some of the basic errors made by the Great Religions in the past. Buddha gave out the three jewels of the Buddha, Dharma or doctrine and *Sangha* or Brotherhood. When he left this world there was a division of his followers as to their nature. Then Christ came and emphasized the Church, which is also to say, the Brotherhood. What happened instead was that the Church was institutionalized and man was supposed to give up his individual existence for this Church.
>
> Now the Avatar comes to awaken and the Brotherhood is formed of those who have been awakened. The true brotherhood or church (*Ikhwa*) or *Sangha* is not composed of people with faith or trust or love, certainly not of those with any particular set of beliefs. To become a member of this brotherhood one must taste of love or death or union with God, for the sake of God and usually, if not always, this comes with and through the Avatar.

Many ideals are enthroned in Baba's voice:

> So I take the human character and use all of it. You (Samuel) learned in the mysteries of Sufism that in the preparation of land sometimes all the growths had to be used. You also learned that in the spiritual preparation

---

*This apparent turnaround may be attributable in part to Sam's continuing dedication to supporting Rabia, along with his own recognition of Baba's realization.

> of the mind not only weeds and underbrush, but all vegetation had to grow . . . You say you are clearing land, I say I am clearing ego-minds. You will have Rabia show Norina the *Ziraat.** That *Ziraat* of Inayat Khan is valuable—it is not theory, it is not ceremony or ritual or occultism, it is doing. Others say I do, when I say I also do.
>
> Neither is our work confined to certain places. Clearing land may seem to be an operation on a certain plane. Clearing minds is a preparation on another plane. As you do, I do. If you did there would be no selfless service even with the best of intentions. Love could so easily be tainted with pride or conceit. I do not want that. It is even more important to get rid of pride and conceit. Love is natural to the soul.

Clearly Samuel had a wave of enthusiasm for the project, but he was never called on to teach or to share his knowledge as he had been led to believe would occur and as had been his custom. Being ignored in that way always disturbed him. Nevertheless, he did work hard clearing land, creating a garden and trying to play a part in the evolving community. There was much for Samuel Lewis to face during the time he lived at Myrtle Beach.

At Myrtle Beach

Samuel Lewis wrote from Myrtle Beach many times to Laura DeLavigne, a Sufi *mureed* in Detroit.† Numerous details of his state during this period were conveyed through this material, including his discomfort with Murshida Rabia.

Prior to his arrival at Myrtle Beach, Samuel wrote to Mrs. DeLavigne from California, describing deteriorating conditions in the Sufi community there:

> We have not had much fortune lately. I find that so long as people remain personal a spiritual message cannot be spread. Personal entan-

---

* *Ziraat* is a spiritual concentration introduced by Hazrat Inayat Khan. It uses the study of agriculture, balancing the elements, and tending the Earth as a metaphor and practice for spiritual awakening.

† Laura's daughter, Marie Shore, gave permission to use her mother's letters, which were stored in the Baba archives at Myrtle Beach. These included copies of several important letters Sam wrote to Murshida Martin.

> glements reached such a pitch that we have no longer a centre but are using Murshida's home and this place [the Sufi land in Fairfax]—will do my best to have a real peaceful meditation quarters. People need peace, quiet, calmness, vitality and magnetism. If these things can be given in words, well and good. Otherwise the silence can be used and used to good effect. It is very hard when you are surrounded by elderly women who have not broad outlooks.[268]

Samuel had long felt that Meher Baba's and Inayat Khan's teachings dovetailed with one another. While Sam was at Myrtle Beach, Inayat Khan continued to manifest to him. Sam wrote that he was elevated in 1946 into a state of *fana-fi-Rassoul* in an almost humorous experience. He said that his poem "Saladin" was the evidence. At least this is true of Section II of this mystical poem on Islam, which Sam always said had been received directly from Prophet Muhammad. Here's the humorous story:

> There is a tradition that the Prophet Mohammed had lost a certain tooth. And there is one school of Sufis . . . where the initiation ceremony consists of knocking out that tooth.
>
> I was living in semi-seclusion in the woods of South Carolina in 1946 and every day Hazrat Inayat Khan would appear. One day while brushing the teeth a tooth fell out, the very one missing in the Prophet's mouth. Hazrat Inayat Khan appeared and laughed and laughed. The next day *Rassoul* Mohammed appeared.
>
> During the following period both Jesus Christ and Mohammed appeared intermittently. I have "seen" Jesus in so many guises . . . Seldom has He appeared in human form and the last times as the Spirit of the Universe . . . Therefore the Arabs or Mohammed have given [the prophets] special names. And before the Christians object, Jesus is known as *Ruh-i-Allah* or The Spirit of God.[269]

Samuel Lewis made time to travel while residing at the new center being formed in Myrtle Beach. He traveled to New York and back several times, to Philadelphia, and later visited the Edgar Cayce center in Virginia Beach. He traveled to Washington DC to promote his plan for peace in the Middle East, a plan that he said initially was widely accepted there.

> My first effort after 1945 was to have a meeting between the spiritual leaders of Israel and Islam, and both groups accepted the offer but questioned whether the other "camp" had real spiritual persons in it.[270]
>
> In 1946, I was alone in the woods in South Carolina. It was Christmas Eve. My principal had sent neither my Christmas allotment nor food. The people who had invited me to dinner suddenly went away. I was alone in the woods, and only a single family even within walking distance. Then suddenly, the skies opened, Jesus Christ appeared, and directed me to work for Peace in Palestine. I went to Washington. All the doors opened. Then suddenly I was betrayed by my own confidante, a person of considerable social and political importance.[271]

In another letter he spoke more specifically about who had blocked his efforts:

> In 1946 I was spiritually commanded to bring peace in Palestine and only Ivy Duce knew of my plans. She later not only betrayed but roadblocked me, making further efforts impossible. I kept quiet for [years] until I met the aide of General [Burns] who was in charge of the Gaza Strip and he told me he had never heard of a better plan, that I was the first person to bring anything sensible. Step by step the Israelis, Egyptians and Saudians have accepted my efforts but not Americans and most of all not those in diplomacy or "peace" movements.[272]

UN Peacekeeping Forces Commander General E.L.M. Burns (L) with Israeli Armed Forces Chief of Staff Moshe Dayan outside Tel Aviv (1956)

Something quite unusual happened during a visit Samuel made to New York, when Princess Matchabelli challenged him. He mentioned it decades later in a letter to Elizabeth Patterson:

> The joint inheritance of spiritual music and dancing from Hazrat Inayat Khan and Ruth St. Denis is a continuance of the work they started in 1911. It is remarkable how young people are being attracted; abandoning drugs and artificial stimulants, and joining in the joyful praise to God . . . Or to put it tersely, I am now doing and accomplishing outwardly the

very things I had been summoned to Myrtle Beach to do. I do not know whether you will recall the incident in your home in New York when I was asked to die in the name of Baba in five minutes and to disconcertment of all present, did just that.[273]

In May of 1946, Samuel wrote again to Laura from Myrtle Beach and sent her a clipping from the local newspaper, which described the evolving community and its participants. He spoke of how highly he now saw Meher Baba:

> Murshid (Hazrat Inayat Khan) said that the Hierarchy is more real than the earth itself. My own inner, and some outer experiences, led me to recognize first that Meher Baba was the living head of the Hierarchy on earth, and one who has attained Nirvana, and yet come to live among mankind . . . The tradition of all faiths is that when the world gets at its worse, God would intervene.
>
> Both the Eastern literature and the works of the French Fabre D'Olivet assert that God will manifest through Hierarchy and take part in the social political affairs of the world . . . You cannot divide your ideals and have society . . . Some of us have given up the futile battle to engage in a sensible warfare, the warfare against egotism, individualism, and have a leader in whom we have full faith, viz. Meher Baba . . . Believe me, Laura, this is not based upon faith but upon the awakening I have at the present state of evolution.[274]

In this letter he also expressed hope that Baba might visit Detroit. He continued with a statement of confidence about Kaaba Allah and some of its supporters:

> Hazel (Armstrong) has done nobly since I left. Fortunately we now have a couple of young men at Fairfax and another on his way. I believe these young men will give the place the vitality it so needs, and I am today very confident over the future of Kaaba Allah. This should mean that Murshida can work with renewed vigor. I have not heard from her lately . . . I was very, very happy to hear from you, and don't mind the delay at all. And if I don't hear soon, I shall take up with Mother Norina, the Sadguru's representative, the possibility of a visit to your city later on.[275]

In August, he gave a report on some conditions at Myrtle Beach:

> So far there has just been a small amount of land clearing, road building, and temporary structures to house any staff that Baba may bring with him. These persons in turn would assist in the establishment of institutions, the construction of buildings, and the general upkeep of the place. However, we are having a problem . . . in regard to plumbing, sanitation and related affairs. Materials are scarce here, as elsewhere, but in addition we are not on the trunk line of any railroad and New York firms felt freight rates were too high to send any materials here whatsoever . . .
>
> I may write to you further and it is even possible that I may visit Detroit in the not distant but rather indefinite future. This depends largely upon when Baba reaches the States and also what he wants me to do when he arrives.[276]

Samuel continued to counsel Laura about how she might marry her concentrations on the teachings of Inayat Khan and Meher Baba:

> I know you have received some of the Baba literature and have no doubt had some information and possibly instructions from Murshida. I can only express my own opinions here, but they are to continue the Sufi work exactly as it has been carried on, but include emphasis on those parts of the esoteric and exoteric lessons which will bring out the part that Baba is functioning today.[277]

The continuation of unity with the founding Pir of the Order, Inayat Khan, was very important to Samuel. Throughout all that would ensue, he never abandoned Inayat. He then referred to places in Inayat Khan's work where he speaks of Hierarchy and also of certain designations such as *Ghaus, Kutb, Rassoul.** These correspond to the Avatar of the Hindus and Sam suggested this would be a good way to bring Baba into becoming the focal point.

In September, he again wrote of the developments at Myrtle Beach, and explained more about Inayat's work:

> At Fairfax we began with three acres, then increased it. Here we are supposed to look after about six of these 800 odd acres. Are we doing it?

---

*These are among the grades of the Spiritual Hierarchy as described by Inayat Khan. For additional information, see Inayat Khan, "The Spiritual Hierarchy," in *The Sufi Message of Hazrat Inayat Khan* (Delhi: Motilal Banarsidass, 2011), vol. IX, chap. III, p. 128. Available at wahiduddin.net/mv2/IX/IX_12.htm.

> You ought to know the answer. We do have electricity and expect some other advantages, and every few months there is a new vehicle but nobody to operate them.
>
> Regarding Hierarchy, I am willing, if God permits, to do any of these things: Write at length; Speak at length—assuming a trip is made—assist with meditations and esoteric practices that will help others.
>
> I shall have to explain also a few things about Murshid's work. In the Esoteric Constitution mention is made of commentaries. But so far as I have learned, excepting myself, nobody seems to have taken this seriously. He not only spoke to me about it on his visits but went into some detail. Later I learned more about this, especially when practicing *tassawuri* Murshid. You are certainly advanced enough to have this assignment, and I shall be glad to explain it to you in a separate letter if you have not had it.[278]

Samuel's focus on the great importance of the practice of *tasawwuri* Murshid should not be ignored. It requires one to absorb the atmosphere of Hazrat Inayat Khan through one's inner concentration and to act from that place. Inayat recommended this practice in his esoteric teachings for *mureeds*. Samuel wrote:

> I also understand this personality situation. I myself am not clear from it. There has been too much buying, selling, personal adulation and criticism among people who want to take up the Path to God. This has resulted even in tragedies in the end, when there is not love, there is pain and tribulation, but man is very, very slow to learn . . .
>
> What is needed is that the heart be pure. When that is so, one has more and more such dreams as yours. Too few people, alas, experience the true ecstasy and so do not know the true love. God has indeed blessed you.[279]

After returning from Washington and Virginia, Sam wrote in October:

> My trip to Washington, though outwardly personal and political, was really spiritual. Spoke to 200–300 people in Blackstone . . . During that time it was fairly well settled that we shall not be having any heavy construction until next March—I mean planning alone. The tentative plans have been sent to India for approval.[280]

The letter went on to give a number of practices from Inayat Khan's materials and offered suggestions from the *wazaif** for nervous people, psychics and others, with images to concentrate on. Samuel then concluded with this:

> I have not heard from the Phelps family since Nadine's marriage. I realize personality difficulties. But I have them too. I am through being blamed for things when I did nothing more than try to follow the directions that Inayat Khan gave me in the flesh in 1923 and 1926. Now, these have been all laid aside in "the interests of harmony," but I have never seen one good result from departing from his wishes.[281]

It is the first time he has alluded to the enormous challenges of his situation with Murshida Martin.

Freed from His Vows, Samuel Makes His Case

The tumult and the shouting dies,
The captain and the kings depart:
Still stands the ancient sacrifice,
A humble and a contrite heart.
Lord God of Hosts be with us yet,
Lest we forget—lest we forget!

RUDYARD KIPLING[282]

Samuel addressed the situation in great detail in his next letter to Laura, in February of 1947.

> I am not quoting poetry here. Whatever Kipling had in mind, this manuscript, for you can hardly call it a letter, is an actualization of that famous poem. Murshid said: "Neither can I be broken nor God, but the one who would break me, he is broken."
>
> After twenty years of [my] almost silent suffering, Murshid released me from some of his appointments and this gave me the right of full self-defense and vindication, which I should be permitted in the courts of the land, and which I may yet have to present more fully publicly. But as [Inayat] himself wished many things known—which were not made known—and which others should have made known, I am compelled perforce to tell it myself.[283]

* *Wazaif* is the plural of *wazifah*, the divine Names or attributes of Allah.

In this letter, Samuel addressed Rabia Martin's actions directly and those of others who joined her in ganging up on him. A new visitation from Hazrat Inayat Khan had now freed him from the constraint of his vow to protect Rabia in various ways. The letter is referred to as a document because of its length and the importance Samuel gives to its content. Extracts in this section are all drawn from this document.

Samuel began with a historic meeting:

> It began in 1923. Murshid called us into Murshida's home. Two things of importance were his group-meditation and group-concentration, and his specific subject for the meditation and concentration! He spoke to us on the building of a temple, designed for the Universal Worship and for other purposes—individually and collectively. During the years the results of this meeting were rejected . . . A specific proposal to have group concentration on the temple—rejected; to use funds accumulated for this purpose—rejected. And there was the failure of Murshida to remember either the occasion or the subject matter.
>
> This year, when Murshid came in mystical communion and released me, he also declared it was now useless for Murshida to try to build him or the Universal Worship a temple because she had both forgotten his instructions and had never defended me fully for insisting upon them.
>
> In a private interview at that time with Pir-o-Murshid Inayat Khan, I was given National Representative Brotherhood work with a hint I may have to become World leader. [I was to use] the Atlas concentration which is nothing more or less than to learn to carry all world-burdens on one's shoulders. [I was also] to write commentaries on the *Gathas.*

Sufi temple known as the Universel, envisioned by Hazrat Inayat Khan, opened July 4, 1970 in Katwijk, Netherlands.

> In 1925 Murshida sent me into seclusion and gave me instructions which are found largely in Murshid's private dictations to her. That was the only seclusion in which these instructions were followed! They were constantly altered thereafter and every effort on my part to have them become the Norm of the Sufi Movement was turned down.*
>
> In the seclusion of 1925 I had a complete physical and spiritual regeneration. When I reported it to Murshid in 1926 he wanted it made known to all *mureeds.* It is interesting that both the pro-Rabia and anti-Rabia factions paid no attention. Those against Rabia had to reject his instructions to me in 1926 that Rabia was to be his successor. Rabia and Zohra paid no attention to my appointments or to the mystical confirmations I had from Murshid . . . Excepting Mary Sorensen and Nuria Phelps in San Francisco, both the conversations and confirmations were ignored . . .
>
> In 1926 in Los Angeles Murshid not only confirmed my mystical experiences, he appointed me Defender of Murshida against the world and Intermediate between her and the problems of *mureeds* and also against the business world. I was never permitted to function.

That he says Rabia paid no attention to the mystical confirmations given him by Inayat Khan speaks volumes. She was very ready to recruit his help arguing her case as the successor, but her own personal unease regarding her relationship with Samuel, his presenting the voice of Inayat and advising her as a protector, made her disinclined to empower him in any way.

> Finally when a large sum of money was given to Murshida and I wanted it to be used for or towards the temple Murshid wanted, the Board voted against this and attacked me . . . Instead of my word being accepted—it was accepted only on the one point that Murshid told me Murshida was his successor, and I was no longer called into council . . . From then on I was only called when there was a hard difficulty.
>
> Murshid gave me some confidences. Whatever my faults are—and I won't defend them—it was always Murshid's instructions, wishes, etc. which suffered. In 1926 Murshid went over his constitutions esoteric and exoteric with me and advised me to study all reports, records, etc. I did this going back all the way to 1910 and 1911 . . .

---

*The private dictations he is referring to here are the detailed instructions for the Murshid and other classical teachings Hazrat Inayat Khan had given to Rabia.

> Every selfish person who came into the Sufi Movement [as organized in the U.S.A.] was allowed to carry on his complaints against me to Murshida when it was an issue of Murshid's actual wishes. And please note up to this point the only mystical, as against material experiences, in question, were my own of 1925.
>
> The second attempt to have me thrown out was due to this unfortunate event: I had one *mureed;* shown to me mystically, I caught her in adultery. She was off to Murshida with complaints and complaints about me. When I arose at a meeting one night, in accordance with the Brotherhood Constitution and Murshid's personal instructions to me in 1923, I was abused and the abuse led to a secret meeting in which those present condemned me—with two notable exceptions, and pledged "loyalty" to Murshida, after which they came to me separately and exposed all the others!
>
> I had to leave San Francisco. I left and Murshida took a trip around the world, failing to do what Murshid requested, although this time it was partly requests that came "from the other side." The keys to these requests are in his works:
>
> a. We should ally ourselves with different schools of Sufis. (this was largely done)
> b. We should work for Peace in Palestine, intermediating between Jew, Christian and Moslem—this was not done at all.
> c. We should look forward to a civil war in India, after which there would be a spiritual resurgence in this country.
>
> Now I lay down before God and man the specific causes for the conflicts which have been laid at my door which have nothing whatever to do with anybody's character, vices, virtues, faults, or spirituality.

Sam mentions moneys spent over his objection for plants to be put around the Rock shrine at Kaaba Allah at the request of a *mureed* in Indianapolis. Sam opposed it because it was impractical. When it failed he was among those blamed. Moneys also were collected to buy a house in Santa Barbara at the request of a non-*mureed* in opposition to the view of Khalif Connaughton. Sam reminded the Board of Murshid's instructions of 1923 and tried in vain to have the Board accept them. There was also "Plan to buy a house in San Francisco owned by I. Mehdi."*

---

* Mehdi had married Rabia's daughter.

Each *mureed* was sent for separately, excepting Harold Skinner and myself. I told Harold I was opposed to the method, not the house. When we refused to accept the building Hazel joined us and that produced an impasse. I was not forgiven for years. Please note the instructions given to me by Murshid did not permit Murshida to enter into such deals. I was following what he wanted and he had told me. It was useless and fruitless. I will not go into further details about what was done in frittering away moneys on useless business transactions that had nothing to do with Sufism or the temple for Murshid.

In 1930 Murshid initiated me into *fana-fi-Pir* [ongoing self-effacement in the Pir] with himself since which time we have mostly been in contact . . . I demonstrated this the following summer when certain clouds appeared one night in the sky and I saw the whole history of the Sufi Movement in those clouds. It showed the break up and destruction but that I, Samuel, would ultimately lead to a restoration which would bring about a larger organization than existed in Murshid's time.*

Connected with all this was a conflict between Murshida and myself on Palestine. Murshida returned from her first trip around the world very much for Jewish Zionism. I could not accept this. I was born with a consciousness that extends far, far back in time . . . I was raised in a religion that held traditionally the "messiah" would lead the children of Israel back to the Holy Land. Though I have changed my faith often it has never been necessary to change on this point. God, not man, would determine events in the Holy Land . . .

When she took her second world tour, she presented the Jewish point of view to the Muslims, but not the Islamic point of view to the Jews, which was what Murshid wanted. She always took the opportunity not only to present the Jewish point of view when I was present, but to do it in such a semi-official manner that I was unable to speak without causing breach of etiquette. Finally in 1945 she came to Detroit and instead of following the spiritual path, she fled without addressing the Muslims because they were hostile to Zionism.

When I reached New York [in 1945] I was accused of being in politics. Murshida knew this was untrue and when I said the only thing I was doing was to play my part in the war; I was told it was the same thing. Murshida fully sided with my accuser on this point, and to drive the point home openly and publicly supported the Zionist attitude at a reception the following evening. So I learned the great "truth:" being

---

* When one looks at Samuel Lewis's whole life, this prediction did ultimately come true.

neutral was being in politics, and being on a "certain side" was being out of politics . . .

Yet in the heart of this letter to Laura, Samuel returns to Murshida Martin with love:

> Murshida, thank God, after many, many years, has recovered her spiritual position, but at a price, a price which is so terrible, she does not realize it. For it had been Murshid's hope that she would become a famous woman; the chances for that today are null. Only a miracle can now bring it about. Nevertheless, her present state at this moment is just after a miracle, and in this thank God . . .
>
> In 1938 I began to have a series of experiences in which my supervisor was not Murshid, but whom the Sufis call *Kutb,* living head of the Hierarchy. I did not know who he was but he became more and more intimate . . .
>
> Murshid had me send Hazel's letter to Murshida and I said that Murshida had better put Hazel to rights, or if she agreed with Hazel they could both face me in open court. And believe me, I was ready. But Hazel got one series of shocks after another, and gradually became very friendly indeed and even veered around to my side. When I went to Washington and saw the sad letters I realized what was being done.*
>
> For two weeks Murshid stood over me day and night without stopping and then began the most forceful letters to Murshida which she has ever received . . .
>
> Murshid made me write. The first thing I said was that his Sufi was one who could see from the point of view of another, but her Sufi was one that did not have any point of view at all and had to follow the teacher while the teacher was busy collecting ideas and thoughts from others and changing them accordingly. His Sufi depended upon *hal* (mystical state), *makam* (spiritual station), dream or vision, but her Sufi was one who accepted her self-will. His Sufi spent all his time correcting his faults; her Sufi joined her in condemning the faults of others . . . I went over all the history in the early part of the letter and trapped her at every point, saying things quite opposite of what appears in the writings . . .
>
> The nexus of it has always been this: that I have opposed doing things within the Sufi Movement at the suggestion of outsiders while constantly rejecting the ideas of *mureeds.* Most things at Fairfax have been done at the suggestion of outsiders, and a few at the insistence of personal

*The sad letters referred to would have been letters scapegoating him.

self-will. Hardly anything has been done by the methods Murshid laid down, until recently.

I certainly had a heart-break at Hazel's last letter. She asked permission to do the very things which Murshid wanted from the beginning. She was a *mureed* in 1926 but not in 1923 so she did not know what occurred in 1923. I have been telling everybody that Murshid's ideas were there in the ethers for anyone to pick up, but was not believed. Now it is coming true. Also we are collecting a fine group of younger men there, to whom Hazel is a sort of mother and I am between an elder brother and father. And with God's help we shall succeed.

The other side of the picture is just as unfortunate though good. Altho Murshid wanted my mystical experiences known to *mureeds* it was never done. Rufus Mosely is regarded by many as the leading mystic of the South; he is looked up to by Stanley Jones. In a public lecture he pointed me out as a man who talked with Jesus and with God and many believe it. I am now teaching in the Methodist church at Myrtle Beach what I was never freely encouraged in in all my past: the mystical explanations of the Scriptures. It appears now I shall have more opportunities, for contacts increase.

I had to start all over here after Murshid's reappearance, but following his teachings . . . Commentaries on "Character Building" and "The Art of Personality" have been written. These papers may be mailed to you. I also hope to teach you in Occultism, etc. I will not willingly permit myself to transgress over these teachings and strive to avoid unnecessary ego-defense excepting in three cases—which are permitted—against the three women who are responsible and who have believed that scolding others was a spiritual trait, for themselves, with a special dispensation from God!

I have contacted some of Murshid's old *mureeds* and want to help bring them all together. And, while Murshida was permitting some *mureeds* to believe the Sufi Movement was disbanded or amalgamated, over in Europe another policy was followed, that it was still alive and that she was following Murshid. For several European *mureeds* want her to assume leadership, and even Murshid's son seems tractable. It is important to keep the Sufi Movement alive UNTIL AND UNLESS GOD SHOWS OTHERWISE, for "God alone was the founder of Sufism" . . .

Altho I was told that Baba does not like complaining letters, I took a cue from Nuria and investigated and sent a letter to India. I have now been asked to lay my cards on the table and have done this in part, and am ready if asked more. The things done in the name of "love" and "God" are unbelievable.

What is hard for me is that with the exception of the Zen Buddhists I do not see anybody in this country as advanced as I am—God is my witness here. I have gone through such experiences as the crucifixion, resurrection, death and elevations, also unions and no attention has been paid. These are of higher orders than dreams, visions or transmissions. They enable me to understand Scriptures. My last experiences brought blessings from Jesus and from Baba; now I have to live and disseminate those blessings. People need help, not scolding; explanations, not rebuffs.

This may not all be satisfactory and I am well aware that I give but my own side or views allied to it, so it is incomplete. But I am tired of being the butt for troubles and I am determined no longer to see, as I have seen here, persons brought down, made to go on outlandish missions and then either blamed for failure or held to public ridicule. They are publicly criticized for it. I believe the Sufic practices can help any one, and stick to them. Baba was a Sufi.

I shall ask Hazel to send you more papers, and especially on Occultism so I can help you on that subject when I go to Detroit. That is right, keep up the "Self-Protection." When I return "home" I shall go into that further, but I hope to see you in the not too distant future.

[In handscript] *Please keep this letter.*

Leaving Myrtle Beach

CN2 INTL=CD BOMBAY VIA RCA 38 29 NLT
SAM LEWIS=
BOX 487 MYRTLE BEACH (SO-CAR)=
YOU SHOULD GO TO RABIA
MARTIN AT FAIRFAX CENTRE
FOR TWO
YEARS AS YOUR WORKING
THERE WILL HELP MY WORK
STOP SHOW
THIS CABLE TO ELIZABETH
AND TAKE CARE FROM
HER=BABA

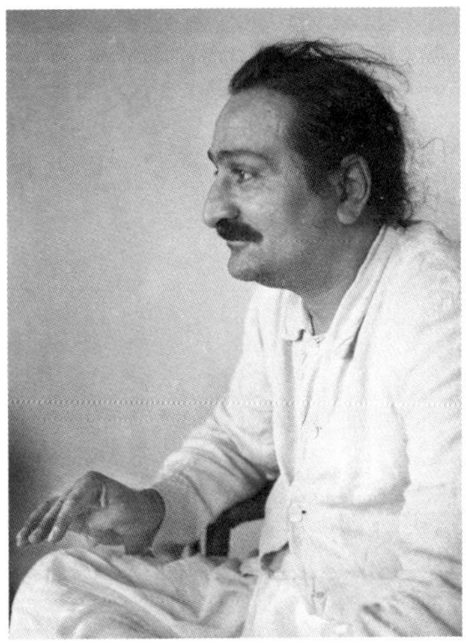

MEHER BABA[284] *

*Telegram sent from Meher Baba. He also signed for Rabia, who was unaware of it. "Care" most probably meant fare. Our date of this telegram is late March, 1947.

Samuel wrote to Rabia Martin on March 31, 1947:*

> Rev. Jones is a Methodist minister. I told him that I had to go soon. Our relations have been excellent and while I was talking to him last night he looked at me and said: "You know if those ladies had presented spiritual philosophy the way you do I would have been interested, I might even have accepted Baba in some way. But they made it impossible by denying the spiritual experiences and life of everybody who did not see just as they did."

On March 21, Samuel wrote to Laura DeLavigne.

> I am also busy on the revised commentary on the book "Moral Culture," copy of which should be sent to you when completed. (Have only done 5 of the 30 papers to date.) I have also been invited to attend a convention at Virginia Beach near Norfolk in June and want to clear up all movements before then. This means that I hope to be with you some time in May . . .
>
> Excepting for the points in the letter to Murshida all news is good and plentiful. Hoping you are all well.

It is useful to look at more details of Samuel's life at Myrtle Beach. He lived below the barn in a cellar space that was converted into living quarters. It was an old tobacco barn, brought to the center by Elizabeth Patterson. Meher Baba did all his public *darshan*† in the barn when he visited years later. Sam started a garden and was involved with clearing land and various aspects of life at the center.

He shared some of his experience in several letters to a coworker, Frank, who remained in Myrtle Beach when Sam traveled to New York. Samuel was concerned about the condition of the people in New York, speaking of Mildred and Norina needing to rest, and Nadine Tolstoi's condition not having improved.

> The strains under which Mildred and Norina live seem to be connected with their work for Baba . . . Norina has been transmitting from Baba on

---

*This section again draws extensively on the archival collection at the Meher Spiritual Center in Myrtle Beach. Quotations otherwise unattributed here are drawn from that source.

† *Darshan* is being in the presence of the teacher, a receiving of transmission through the physical presence and the gaze of both the outer and inner eyes.

> the three problems which have always been closest to my heart: Hindu, Jewish and starvation problems. All are pressing upon the world now and all are receiving the Avatar's attention. This is phenomenally associated with the strain Norina bears.

In a letter in February to Frank he wrote about the overall situation.

> Norina has been staying in her room, for her own protection. If she does not write to you, I think you will understand. Besides we have received a cable from India, to straighten out some misunderstandings here, which need never have arisen. Briefly I repeat that when I accepted Baba I was shocked by the disunity among His adherents. He is now putting his foot down, recognizing each and all in their proper places. What more can be asked? But this is just one among innumerable interruptions which keep Norina from proper repose.

The difficulties among leading members of Hazrat Inayat Khan's community resemble these difficulties among Baba's devotees. In Meherabad also, relationships were not always harmonious among the women. Baba called them together and said,

> Mend your ways or go. You leave your home, your family to dedicate all to me, yet live a life of binding. You have no freedom to go out to cinemas or theaters. In every way, you sacrifice for love. You all love me, take me to be God—and I really am God—but the one thing that is a shortcoming in you all is this complete lack of control! . . . Here, only twelve of you, and yet no harmony. You all do not love each other. You cannot tolerate each other. The slightest provocation demonstrates your weaknesses to the highest. Norina and Nadine tell the world, "We live with the greatest Master of the age!" But you do not say, "We stay with him and fight like dogs and cats!"[285]

Sam wrote: "My main instructions have been on love, to see beyond other's foibles. If they do not love, if they find excuses to be disobedient, if they live and act contrary to the Seven Principles of Baba's detailed instructions, I am to let them be, let them go ahead just as if the opposite were true, though I don't have to follow them. To help the world we have to accept Baba-in-action, not in sentiment which does not become act."

A few days later Sam continued to Frank:

> The real reason I am writing is this. Norina has been to the doctor and has been put on a diet, chiefly of fruits and sugars. I suggested to her that I write you to please get busy at once so you may have some things ready for her and Elizabeth when they come . . .
>
> Anne should be back shortly and some of the factors which led to her difficulties have been removed by Baba. He has done a little housecleaning . . . I could parody and say when Baba gives an order to six people, he has six obedient policemen who rush to see the other five obey punctiliously and literally, regardless of love. And woe if you have received a special order that the others do not know about; you have tall explaining! This is a little exaggerated but not entirely so. But I think it will be different soon. I am not innocent—do not include me out, here.

Sam wrote to Murshida Martin:

> I must call your attention to 1925 when I went into seclusion. I prepared everything as if for a great cosmic drama which was to take place and in which I was to play an uncertain part. The drama did take place in broad daylight and although exactly 22 years have passed, nothing much was done about it.
>
> Again, in both these trips to Washington, I prepared as if for dramas in which I was to play an uncertain part, and so it was. Upon my return here the faith certainly increased and the following things were done prior to the receipt of this cable, showing that I have been attuned to God, Baba and the Holy Ones, despite a host of nonsensical criticisms which have been leveled at me and which henceforth I have no time to answer. Let others do that, *inshallah.*

Samuel takes the high road in relation to the "nonsensical criticisms" that have rankled him, and instead refers to specific business: "Shabaz Best* has been writing me along a line which Murshid took with me in his first interview on Kearney Street in 1923. I could not refuse this request and promised Shabaz my full cooperation."

He reported writing to Jean Adriel (author of *Avatar: The Life Story of the Perfect Master Avatar Meher Baba,* published in 1947) assuring her of a plan to visit Meher Mount soon.

> I have also written advising Ivy that the best concentration I could do for Terry would be at Fairfax. I wrote her a not satisfactory letter which

---

* Shabaz Best was an original *mureed* of Hazrat Inayat Khan, living in Brazil.

> I shall not change now, because of the unfortunate aftermaths in every case when I have done this "telestial" without protection. Now with Baba's protection and assurance I feel absolutely free. My instructions at the moment are not to concentrate upon Terry or you until I start West.

Samuel took the telegram from Meher Baba to be one fully empowering him as a representative. Ivy Duce's husband Terry was in ill health. Telestial, here, from the context of its usage, applies to the faculty of reaching the glory of the celestial planes while in this plane. This ability of Samuel's was not one that Mrs. Duce felt comfortable with. She would readily come into an accord with Murshida Martin's trepidation about that voice.

Sam then expressed his quandary about accomplishing a number of things versus getting to San Francisco immediately. He proposed going to Detroit, Minneapolis, Eau Claire, Wisconsin, Seattle, and Portland. He spoke of writing to Hazel and added, "Previous to that I had written her regarding intensive training for her and the three men at Kaaba Allah. This is certainly confirmed by the cable. Murshid had also appeared to me at night telling me to return immediately to commentary writing. I should complete 30 of these papers before leaving and am now on the 6th." He also mentions opportunities in New Jersey, Virginia, and Ohio.

Samuel again emphasizes how he sees the merging of Inayat Khan's work and Meher Baba's: "Baba's very first words to me when he appeared in the light in November 1942 were: 'I have come! I have come to help you complete all the work which Inayat Khan gave you to do.' God is, was and ever will be my witness to that. This cable confirms what these women have ignored or rejected."

Samuel's visitation "in the light" from Baba was paramount for him. He now felt empowered to complete all the work that Inayat Khan had given him to do, and thus to write further commentaries and research the Old and New Testaments for evidence of Sufism.*

> I have also just received a letter from Don [Stevens], which is terrifically prophetic. It begins, "I hope this will reach you before you set sail again

---

*Ivy Duce had rejected Sam's experience in his meditation on Meher Baba. Meher Baba had agreed with Ivy's view, maintaining his support of her as a caretaker for his work.

from Myrtle Beach." It was in the box when I picked up the cable and here, again, there was perfect harmony.

I will not detail the other work to be done at Fairfax now but for the sake of the record these things are not to be done by me: Planning gardens, building, furniture, improvements. For exercise hikes and horseback are preferred in which I can take a *mureed* (especially Francis) and talk on spiritual things. Secondly, selecting a room for myself, or interfering with the program already instituted. Not even time for instructions is to be set by me, but I am to adjust myself.

When I first come to visit you, if you are either at Ashbury St. or Kaaba Allah, I would like Rani Begum in the place, to meditate or be with us accordingly as Murshid directs her, but no one else. You will fix the time mutually, and of course, more light will be shown later.

I am not to teach officially until atmosphere is clarified. I have no instructions to give talks on *Gathas* or *Githas* yet. All these talks will be circumferential. However, I may have to turn Baba's instructions on Meditation into the series of *Githas* on Meditation that I once worked on.

I am to work out systems of simple breathing, preferably in commentaries on Murshid's exoteric works such as the *Eastern Rose Garden.*

In his final paragraph headed BABA AND WORLD AFFAIRS he wrote:

I accept the "two years" as a cycle of patience and world-difficulties. That is why I must be near the tabernacle. I also take it that you will be healed and live despite some falsely pessimistic rumors. I shall write or wire you soon after Elizabeth arrives. May God bless you and restore your body, heart and soul.

The next day he again wrote Murshida after hearing directly from Elizabeth Patterson:

I was amazingly surprised to have Elizabeth suggest to me this morning that it may be wise for me to make a run out to the Pacific Coast. All my intuitions have been that it would be so. In my last letter to Hazel I laid down the plan for the application of healing through the gaze in particular for Theodore and herself.

It is too early at this writing to have any meditation for you or your condition. My feeling is that this will come after I am en route.

I am not too satisfied either with all these:

> a. Reports concerning Hazel are terrifically conflicting and confusing.
> b. Reports concerning yourself are not clear, and I am amazed by some strange negative suggestions concerning your present state.
> c. I have had no letter of any kind from my family and the last, from my uncle, did not indicate anything was wrong. The neighbor upon whom I was relying for information herself has been very ill.
>
> Elizabeth should be here by Easter, and I am leaving it up to her whether I should depart immediately, or wait until the work she lays out is well in order . . . Thank God I am well except for a slight case of poison oak, occasioned while land clearing.
>
> I pray for your full recovery.

On April 7, 1947, he wrote his last letter to Laura from Myrtle Beach, indicating that several recent developments would prevent his staying in Detroit; he still hoped to visit "many Muslims" en route back to California. He had plans to take up three issues of import: "the Albanian situation, the solution of the Palestinian impasse, the promotion of an anti-defamation sentiment to apply to the Prophet."

The Return to Fairfax

> *The Cayce group held an annual congress in June, and as I recall it, Sam turned up at one of these congresses. I was looking out of an upstairs window one day at a group of people on the grass below and saw a most unusual vignette. A man was balancing a broomstick on the end of his finger, and walking around the yard, looking upward at the broom, and followed like a Pied Piper by a crowd of children. Later in the day I was introduced to this charismatic character, who turned out to be Sam Lewis.*
>
> GINA CERMINARA[286]

There is no account of Samuel's actual departure from Myrtle Beach or of his arrival in Detroit. He was referenced in an article by Filis Fredericks in *Awakener,* a Meher Baba publication:

> Many left when Rabia accepted Meher Baba as Avatar but Ivy stayed "in Baba" and Lud Dimpfl, Don Stevens, and Samuel. Sam, too, lived with us in New York and was caretaker of the center in Myrtle Beach for a year. Rabia never lived to meet Baba, but appointed Ivy as her successor, a decision which turned Sam Lewis away from Baba, unfortunately.[287]

Several people at the Myrtle Beach Center spoke fondly of Sam. Judy Mangold said that Adele liked him. "He was an interesting character. An eccentric." Jeff Wolverton said, "Folks liked Sam because he was fun." [288]

He did land at the Edgar Cayce center on his way home. In his lectures in the mid-'60s, Samuel sometimes referred to his experiences there. He said their teaching was that prayer is our talking to God and meditation is God talking to us, but added that speakers would talk all through the meditations. In his brashly independent way, he asked the speakers after the meditation, "When do we get to listen to God?" He also relayed that speakers would talk about the benefit of jogging and receive applause, but none of the participants would ever jog themselves.

In his biography of Sufi poet Francis Brabazon, Ross Keating notes:

> In mid-1947 just before Murshida Martin died, she appointed Ivy Duce, who was living in Washington D.C. at the time, as her successor under Meher Baba. One of Murshida Duce's first directives was the appointment of Khalif Samuel Lewis as her representative in California. Khalif Lewis had arrived from South Carolina during Murshida Martin's sickness.[289]

When Samuel arrived at the Fairfax land he met up with Brabazon, Don Stevens, and the others living at Kaaba Allah who were busy preparing the place for Baba's visit. It was reported that "although Brabazon initially described him as a bagman in appearance, he later found him to be a genius of sorts who could converse on topics ranging from science, art, comparative religion and mysticism, as well as being a poet."[290]

Originally from Australia, Brabazon came to be at Kaaba Allah through the following set of circumstances.

> Sheikh Momin* was notified by Murshida Martin of her decision [to accept Baba], but he personally found it difficult to accept—true to his spiritual name, meaning "faithful," his loyalty remained with Inayat Khan. She sent him a copy of Meher Baba's five volume set of Discourses which he began to study along with Brabazon. Sheikh Momin

* Sheikh Momin was the Sufi name of Baron Friedrich von Frankenberg.

was impressed by what he read, but was not fully convinced of their writer's authority.[291]

Murshida Martin wrote Sheikh Momin suggesting the two of them should travel to India to meet Meher Baba. He suggested Brabazon instead, for whom he would pay all expenses. Later Mrs. Martin was advised that Baba wanted to come to America and visit the Fairfax land. As a result, Brabazon was invited to come to the U.S. first.

On his arrival Brabazon was met by Rabia. She took him to her residence and later to Fairfax. "She was a short, impressive woman of about seventy years"[292] who, according to Brabazon, radiated peace and strength. He also found her to be very down-to-earth.

The following morning Brabazon was interviewed by Murshida Martin and given specific instructions, including what she called his spiritual assignment. This entailed building a road, approximately twenty meters long, from the meditation chapel at Kaaba Allah across a steep hillside to a large outcropping of rock that Hazrat Inayat Khan had ordained to be the site for a future temple. Brabazon chose to build the road out of stone, two meters wide—and to do all the backbreaking work of carrying the huge stones up the hill by himself. It took nearly a year to complete the work. He recalled visiting Rabia while she was in considerable pain, and his lasting impression was that she was lying in bed like a lion—"just like a lion."[293]

Rabia's health continued to deteriorate and on August 30, 1947, she died. Meher Baba postponed his American visit. "Brabazon now had no real need to remain in America and yet, with Sheikh Momin's consent, he continued to stay at Kaaba Allah until March, 1948, and helped pay for his own expenses by working as a part-time gardener in the area."[294]

Mrs. Rabia Martin Rites Tomorrow

Mrs. Rabia Ada Martin, student of Eastern philosophy and founder of the Sufi movement in San Francisco, died yesterday at her home, 46 Ashbury Street. She was a native San Franciscan.

Funeral services will be held tomorrow at 3 p. m. at Sinai Memorial Chapel, Divisadero Street at Geary. Entombment will follow at the Portals of Eternity.

Newspaper clipping, source unknown

Brabazon's biographer described his relationship with Samuel Lewis:

> Both he and Brabazon were opinionated, and at times their ideas clashed. However, it was on Khalif Samuel's advice that Brabazon took up folk dancing in the local township as a form of active meditation to balance the formal and quietist meditation he practiced under Sheikh Momin. Soon Brabazon was promoting the benefits of folk dancing and became an active member of their Board.[295]

The youthful Samuel Lewis who had been morally put off by dancing was now transformed into an ardent folk dancer and a student of the dance in general. Folk dances were a source of inspiration for the possible forms to use when he launched his Dances of Universal Peace two decades later.

Brabazon later became a beloved poet in Australia and was close to Meher Baba. He and Samuel appeared together in Marin on a local radio broadcast. The host of the show, Margaret Albanese, described her contact with them:

> I [would] issue an invitation to Marin County poets to get in touch with me [for the radio show]. Sam called, we had a meeting, and I was struck immediately at that time. He seemed like a person, you can't describe it. He was completely unique, we know that. And, I thought, Wow!, I have never met a man in my whole life who had this encyclopedic knowledge, this passion for Epic Poetry! And Epic Poetry is something which almost no modern poets can recognize . . . Another time he brought his friend, Francis Brabazon, who later went back to Australia. He was really a fine poet, and they were good friends. And Francis was a very interesting, very warm sort of person. They came, and I think possibly they both read on that second program.
>
> And Francis would come with Samuel once in a while to visit me. It was really interesting over all these years, during his travels he'd write letters, sometimes I wouldn't hear from him for three months or four or five months, next thing I know, the phone would ring "This is Sam". He had this great sense of loyalty and continuity over all that time.[296]

Toward the conclusion of 1947, after Murshida Martin's passing, Murshida Duce visited San Francisco to contact the *mureeds* who were there and met Brabazon for the first time. She was sufficiently impressed by him that she decided she wanted him to become a Sheikh. She told Khalif Samuel to be his spiritual director.

Part of Brabazon's induction process included study and meditation sessions commencing at six in the morning and finishing after midnight; luckily Brabazon was able to extend his visa for an extra six months to complete his training. The final initiation ceremony was carried out in silence in a small chapel with Khalif Samuel officiating.

Brabazon dedicated a poem "Night Song" to his mentor. A verse reads:

Samuel, who befriended the Andes,
on his little five-note flute
sings:
O beloved, the flowers have closed their petals,
The moon has sunk to rest, –
But open to me your window
And the flowers will open their petals,
And the moon will rise again.[297]

This poem was prophetic. Samuel was about to enter a dark time, but things ultimately opened dramatically for him and his moon did fully rise.

Don Stevens also received instruction from Samuel. Stevens commented on him in one of his books, saying:

> Played out at the same time was a behind-the-scenes drama between Murshida Martin and Samuel Lewis, while all this was going on to restore the Fairfax property to a civilized state . . . Life never seems complete without the introduction at least once or twice of a brilliant and enigmatic character who seemed alternatively inspired by God and then the devil.[298]

Consider the situation between Samuel and Rabia at the time he returned to Fairfax. Up to this point Samuel had honored his vow to Hazrat Inayat Khan to stand by Rabia and defend her. After the spiritual visitation from Inayat at Myrtle Beach, he now felt he could freely speak and act. In the document to Laura DeLavigne he laid bare his case against Rabia's actions over the years. It is no wonder that Don saw in Sam such opposite extremes. As Samuel confirmed in his letters to Laura, he identified as someone who was strong-willed and reluctant to give in to others who might be in apparent positions of authority, saying he would frequently choose to act according to his own guidance.

Brabazon visited Rabia shortly before her death and Don Stevens visited her on her deathbed. According to Stevens, Murshida Martin took much of that time to complain about Samuel Lewis's transmissions to her. Stevens continued his account:

> Samuel had also been initiated by Inayat Khan. As time passed and Inayat Khan's travels had commenced, he suggested to Murshida Martin that, she being not at all psychic, it might be necessary at some time to confide a message for her via Samuel's marked psychic capacities. Inayat Khan was not at all an individual given to impress people by occult powers or psychic phenomena, but on the other hand he did not hesitate to use them when helpful.* Accordingly, Murshida Martin asked no clarification, only making good note of her Murshid's suggestion . . .
>
> As the years passed and finally Inayat Khan came to his early death in India, Samuel had adopted the habit periodically of acting as Inayat Khan's mouthpiece. Who knows what the truth was? Fortunately, the occasion to act as the interpreter did not occur often. But when Murshida Martin accepted Meher Baba as her spiritual guide and placed her Order under him, a circumstance of some importance did arise.
>
> Murshida Martin followed up her spiritual overture to Meher Baba by a later letter offering to place all the property of the Sufi Order in Baba's name. This meant principally the Sufi School at Fairfax. Samuel lived at the school and loved the property . . . Murshida Martin waited with great joy and expectation, for Baba's arrival.†
>
> Meanwhile she taught entirely from Meher Baba's "Divine Theme" . . . All of Inayat Khan's *Gathas, Githas,* books and other lovely offerings she unhesitatingly put aside for the rest of her life despite her adoration of Inayat Khan. [To her] this was the spiritual law. She followed it without the slightest hesitation.[299]

Rabia's view of her own actions certainly differed from Samuel's. Sam had always believed the inner purpose of the new affiliation with

---

*Inayat Khan did speak of these, and his teachings on them can be found in the *Sufi Message* books.

†This arrival did not happen.

Meher Baba would be a union that would maintain the legacy of Inayat Khan. She told Don Stevens on her deathbed that she had abided completely by Inayat Khan's suggestion to her but said, "You cannot imagine how difficult this has been. It was the instruction of my beloved master, and so I have followed it all these years since I last saw him."[300]

No doubt in her own mind Rabia felt she had always respected Inayat Khan. Samuel felt his role, as laid out by Inayat, was impossible to accomplish given Rabia's resistance to hearing any criticism of her actions. One aspect of her turning to Meher Baba was likely a relief she felt from the weight of that allegiance.

In a diary entry in 1963 Samuel said,

> There is no satisfaction in looking at what happened to "my enemies." While Rabia never intended to be classified as such there are certain outstanding facts which remain.
>
> She had a number of *mureeds* in the Orient, she established a name for herself as a Sufi, she never told anybody about them and she stubbornly refused to write her autobiography. Now this is in demand and it is impossible. I am the only one alive who had inkling of her European esotericism; the records are destroyed . . .
>
> Rabia not only did not do even simple things Pir-o-Murshid requested, in the end she assented to the displacement of his teaching methods and then was stricken, which was only natural, after one breaks the guidance.[301]

The teaching methods Samuel refers to would have included study of Inayat's writings and practices such as *zikr* and *tasawwuri* Murshid (oneness in feeling, attunement, with the teacher). They also refer to the Universal Worship service and raising funds as Inayat had requested for a temple, as well as prayers that he had given for recitation and realization.

Murshida Martin's Legacy

> *It was certainly at Pir-o-Murshid Inayat Khan's insistence that I [stuck] to Murshida Martin. This was a pretty good trial for it was evidenced that one passed her in* hal *if not in* makam *and this resulted in being estranged alike from both friends and foes of this lady. The Cause of God*

> *is nothing but the Cause of God (Allah) and the efforts of any and all persons to proclaim themselves without the Divine Grace and the proper experiences in* hal *and* makam *have led, and will continue to lead, to strange aftermaths.*
>
> SAMUEL LEWIS[302]

Don Stevens admired and accepted Murshida Martin. He had seen the rough side of her at a tea he and a close friend were invited to attend in her home. Rabia's sister had forgotten to get the tea and Mrs. Martin blamed her repeatedly and shouted at her. It embarrassed Don when his companion later told him that he thought Rabia's sister was the more spiritual.

Don's narrative about her legacy after her passing bears repeating:

> History got crossed up. In her final illness, Murshida was confined totally to her bed at home and no one but her daughter finally was allowed with her. Samuel however managed to advise her that Inayat Khan was greatly displeased by the recent course of her actions. Searching for the new master in the flesh corresponded with Sufi traditions, but making over of property was outside such custom . . .
>
> The files of the Sufis, and even the personal correspondence of Murshida Martin, were passed on to the new Murshida. In them was a letter from Murshida Martin tearfully asking for Inayat Khan's pardon for having transgressed his wishes in the new undertaking with Meher Baba. The expressions used by Murshida Martin were general and thus easily misinterpreted. The new Murshida saw them as a renunciation of Murshida Martin's acceptance of Meher Baba as the spiritual head of the new Sufi Order.[303]

Twenty years later, Don became aware of Mrs. Duce's view that Rabia had withdrawn her allegiance to Meher Baba. He and Mrs. Duce went over Rabia's letter together, and Mrs. Duce was appalled by the confusion that had occurred. She agreed it was necessary to correct the misunderstanding, but this change of view was never made known publicly. Don would later negatively address Mrs. Duce's actions in an article he wrote titled "Honesty." He indicated that she had chosen to ignore the truth and instead claim full credit for the turn to Baba.

Don summed up the aftermath of his experience regarding psychic messages relayed to Murshida Rabia: "One does not emerge from such . . . experience unmarked. I have been marked for life by it. I have a profound distrust of all manner of psychic messages. I have seen their use bring misery and threaten chaos within the orbit of even the most enlightened and sincere."[304]

Many officials in the Sufi Movement and others agreed with this dismissal of such faculties. The consequences of their belief would only harm the ones who really had such abilities, such as Samuel Lewis. Because of their attitudes, Samuel's experiences were disregarded and his character continually derided.

Although he was not at Murshida Martin's home on the day of her passing, Samuel went there shortly thereafter. Her daughter Etta did not want to let him in and offered to bring materials out to Fairfax, but he refused and insisted on finding things where they were. In two letters/diary entries to Saladin Reps he referred to what happened:

> The death of Rabia resulted from the most flagrant disobedience to the instructions of Inayat Khan. She used to tell us about those instructions over and over. When David, her husband, was ill, she gave a self-praising lecture on the point. The same was true of her daughter Etta. But when she became ill, she took exactly the opposite course and her daughter accused me, and successfully, of failing to heal her mother, when all the time the mother was doing everything the opposite of what Pir-o-Murshid had told her![305]
>
> I had to sweat blood to get in Rabia's home and Etta never let me finish. I found a complete Yoga system (or many) and another type of healing system. I had also my commentary on "Health" which includes a lot of etcetera material turned over to Rabia and never used . . . And in between more practices for developing magnetism and healing powers besides the ones I knew. I may have back memos of his original teachings. The rest was put in a book by Rabia and hidden away. Etta would not let me look and it was never found. But I can tell you that it was in accord with the Four-School Sufism of Hyderabad which in turn recognizes the six world religions of the Universal Worship.[306]

Murshida Ivy Duce

Time with Murshida Duce

The new Murshida, Ivy Duce, immediately gave Khalif Samuel responsibilities for California such as training Francis Brabazon to become a Sheikh. From the time Mrs. Duce met Sam until the time of Rabia's passing seven years later, she intermittently received Inayat Khan's teachings and historical advice from Samuel in his role of Khalif, always in a private setting. Now Samuel sent applicants Murshida Duce's way, feeling she was the right person to take on the organizational aspects of the Sufi work.

After having gotten closer to Murshida Martin, Murshida Duce was rather dismissive of Samuel, speaking secretly against him in several areas such as his peace program for the Holy Land. Still she gave him the responsibility of taking care of the files at the Fairfax Sufi School office. He lived at the school and received a stipend of $70 a month for his work. His care of the files would later become the focus for a major grievance against Samuel by Murshida Duce.

Letters from Samuel written at this time show something of the state of affairs. He wrote to Murshida Duce in February, 1948, in response to instructions from Meher Baba and referencing other issues at the Sufi School.

> As we have not received this prior to February 1, we cannot cable any plans for cooperation with Avatar. Actually point 4 [sexual continence] is continuously observed here and by most *mureeds.* Point 1., taking a meal a day might be desirable but would be difficult to work. Point 2., on silence, in part conflicts with our present program, which will be discussed further. Feeding a poor man or woman each day would please me but I have no control over the funds which would make this possible. Point 5, we virtually observe, but I shall try to "institute" [meditation] beginning tonight.
>
> Now the present program is this: failing in almost every instance to find or receive cooperation to get this office in order, I turned in despair

> to God and the answer came clearly to go out and try to receive new *mureeds,* using Baba as the head of the Sufi Order, and yourself as His chief representative of the West. And what happened? For one week we averaged a new candidate a day. Three candidates are now ready for *bayat,* two of them to receive it on February 5th, the anniversary of Murshid's passing, and one around the new moon, *inshallah.* Besides this, new contacts are being made.[307]

The points Samuel refers to at the outset would have been instructions given through Meher Baba for the Sufis to undertake in their centers. Sam's letter goes on to describe the lack of help to do a glossary, saying Dr. Ghani's work* would satisfy the cry. He speculated that the removal of Gandhi from this plane made it clear that Baba would be emerging, seen or hidden, as the one force to bring peace in India. He had plans to write to the Ambassador and would copy Mrs. Duce. Samuel also wrote on the subject of Muslims: "Following another hunch I have located the haunt of the Muslims in San Francisco, the Dewey Hotel, and may be calling there soon."

Murshida Duce must have questioned him about the instruction he was giving Francis Brabazon. He wrote "The only 'instructions' Francis has from me are: (1) sacred papers, (2) Esoteric practices, (3) Interpretations of the above given either in class or in writing." Directly addressing Mrs. Duce he said, "I have written as a person, not as a devotee, as I have 'thought' not as I have 'felt.' If I did the latter you would not get any letter, only poems and psalms of praise. This would produce much harmony but convey no news."

Meher Baba still was expected to visit and work had to be done at Fairfax to prepare. Sam wrote,

> I would like permission to submit my own inspirations on this subject which were approved by Rabia—I think even written down—then ignored. You would then be in a position to OK or reject them and submit your own plan. The house presumably reserved for Baba is occupied by Don and Pete Harling, a non-*mureed* . . . The extra room in this house which I had hoped to fix for a bedroom is being used by Hazel's nurse.[308]

---

* Dr. Ghani was an assistant to Meher Baba.

Samuel also addressed matters of concern regarding the functioning of the Movement:

> The moneys given to the Movement by *mureeds* primarily were for the receiving of lessons, teachings and literature, to help them, and for advice from the teacher. But this has never been followed too literally. At the moment a program is being followed which from my point of view is neither legal nor hierarchal. I am sending Mary Sorenson copy of the report on the status of the sacred papers. In the end it will be yourself and others who will be crying for materials that cannot easily be copied and placed in yours or anybody's hands.[309]

Sam indicated that his prospectus was "for a large movement by 1949, even without much effort. But a very cautious and careful distribution of lessons because they cannot be typed by non-*mureeds,* and available persons are not used to the full potential extent." He ended with a note that they were expecting the well-known dancer and Baba devotee Margaret Kraske, and that he might ask her to talk about Meher Baba and Spiritual Dancing.*

His ongoing relationship with Murshida Duce did not develop well, as Samuel recorded in his diaries:

> For many years I used to teach a lady in this country who was very well placed socially. And when we were studying "Light" she claimed a certain *makam* and I said, "If you have reached that [it means] you should be teaching me, not I you." And as soon as she was confirmed as a Murshida, she denounced me publicly and privately and made my life utterly miserable.[310]

In the mid-1970s, after several attempts, I was granted permission by Murshida Duce to interview her about Samuel Lewis, who had left his body in 1971. She initially said that anyone who was a disciple of his wouldn't be interested in talking to her. I persisted. Eventually I

---

*It is interesting to note that despite the many challenges of this time, Sam was also using his capacious mind to write about Kabbalah to a scholar in Jerusalem. A fascinating article was found that explored an exchange between Sam and Gershom Scholem, and showed just how well-connected Sam was with people of note of the time. Boaz Huss and Jonatan Meir, "The Light is Burning Pretty Low," in *Correspondences*, 8.2, 2020, 1-28.

quoted a saying of Hazrat Inayat Khan that a Sufi is one who can see from another's point of view as well as his or her own. She then agreed to meet with me but refused to let me tape her. She did allow me to take notes and said multiple times, "Samuel was a great disappointment to me."

She gave her version of the times as well as some information about Murshida Martin. The following is excerpted from my notes:

> In 1927 [Rabia] traveled to the Summer School at Suresnes. She never talked about this much because it was such a shock to her when it became apparent they didn't want her. They had an election and elected Maheboob Khan. Once in a private conversation with Murshida Duce, Rabia Martin said there were three reasons why she was rejected: she was a woman, an American, and a Jewess. And then she cried. She explained that she was not crying for herself but because they [had] broken the [hierarchical] chain.
>
> In 1947 [Mrs. Duce] visited Meher Baba and went to a Universal Worship service at the old metropolitan opera building in New York. Munira Non greeted her, "You must be the Murshida, you have the Buddha brow."
>
> In May of 1948 [Mrs. Duce] saw Cushing, who "told me she felt I had been a bad woman, basically because I had all those papers from Pir-o-Murshid Inayat Khan and had not done anything to copy them and get them out to people. She asked for money from me to do this, but we didn't have it to give. I believe those papers later went to Vera Zain*. I saw her around the same time and she too complimented me on my brow! But she insisted I was all wrong about Meher Baba."

Mrs. Duce said she had known Samuel since 1940, and he "turned against every woman he ever worked with. I believe he was frustrated. Never knew normal love for a woman; only love for a woman as a teacher." Murshida Vera, however, is a good example of a woman Samuel never turned against. I believe this was because she always respected him even when she disagreed with him, as she did about Rabia's turning to Meher Baba for leadership and Sam complying with her decision.

---

*Later known as Sheikha Vera and then Murshida Vera Corda.

Times of Transition and Tension

> *[On] January 7, 1949, he resigned from my Sufi order. The immediate cause was that there were two boards of directors of two corporations, the Order and the Movement. Samuel had seats on each one. After all there were only 7 or 8 old ladies. I'd developed a group in New York and Washington. I wanted them to feel a part of things, by having a representative on the board. I said, I think it would be a kind gesture if you or any others that hold two seats give it up and let someone else take it from the East. He resigned.*
>
> IVY DUCE[311]

Murshida Duce related further dissatisfaction with Samuel:

> The thing that annoyed me the most were his "transmissions" where he claimed to speak in the voice of Inayat Khan, Moses, Mohammed, or Meher Baba. In one instance when he had claimed to have a transmission from Baba standing on a balcony, I wrote to Baba about it and he denied it. I read Baba's letter before the group with Samuel there, and told him to stop it.

That denial from Meher Baba, saying he never spoke from a balcony, gave Mrs. Duce plenty of ammunition to use. Samuel Lewis responded promptly to Baba's letter, showing contrition for not recognizing his own unconscious *samskaras,** and in general fully effacing himself. He ended his letter apologizing for not having the wherewithal to travel to India. The letter concluded, "If my love be unworthy, accept my service, O Master, and if my service be unworthy, accept me as Thou wilt."[312]

Mrs. Duce mentioned how this letter had been received in India in a letter she wrote Samuel from the East Coast: "Norina told me that it was beautiful to see Baba, when he received your letter of surrender to him in India, hold the letter near His precious head and pour out love to you. Treasure the master's love, Samuel, and do all you can to deserve it. Pray that He will come to us soon."

Her account of Samuel's last days at Kaaba Allah continued:

*In Indian philosophy, *samskaras* are karmically inherited obstructive mental and emotional patterns.

> When I returned from India to Kaaba Allah, Ted [Reindollar], a newspaperman, was there.* He had some Sufi training in Algiers which had upset his Kundalini . . . He thought I would be an impostor. But felt otherwise on talking to me. He told me stories about Samuel. He said that Samuel had taken papers from the files to his home. We had been paying Samuel $70 a month to put the files in order, and they were a shambles. Ted also told me, "You know Samuel has also stolen Inayat Khan's original letters." "Why?" "Because he's going to hold them over your head to get some important post." Ted found the letters sitting in a box in the middle of the chapel and brought them to me.
>
> Samuel came in that afternoon about five and asked to speak. He called me into the chapel, raised his hands high and said: "I swear before God, Meher Baba is the Avatar, and I give my allegiance to Murshida Duce." I told him, "I'm afraid for you. What about taking these letters and papers? You're going to set yourself back." He denied it. I was annoyed by the fact that he had been supposed to organize the files and they were in a shambles. All he had been doing was continuing to write his commentaries, which I didn't want.

Mrs. Duce clearly viewed Samuel now as a nemesis and was outraged after hearing Reindollar's accusations. Samuel was fired from his job and told to leave his place of residence on December 30. Ted provided the car and drove that day and the next when Samuel moved what he could of his written materials from Kaaba Allah. Samuel recounts:

> In [1949] I was compelled to move from the house in Fairfax by a combination of concocted lies, a term I may safely use as the persons who have accepted those unsubstantiated lies have, either openly or tacitly, admitted that they should have listened to me before compelling me to leave my home. The situation was complicated because while I had no funds to support my case, it would have meant prison terms for those involved, and this would have accomplished little.
>
> Mrs. Ivy Duce either willingly or unwillingly took it into her hands not only to compel me to leave Fairfax, but having been my one and only confidante, was able to block all my plans in every direction. Without going into the nature of these plans, life—or maybe something more

*Samuel had earlier vested considerable trust in Reindollar, considering him his representative in Algeria. ("Baraka-Direct Experience," Archives.)

> than life—led to the establishment of friendships with her husband's associates one by one and this moment finds me not only on excellent terms with them but Mr. Duce himself has asked how I was getting along with projects to turn deserts into arable lands.[313]

Back in Fairfax a fire brought about major changes. The flames at the Sufi School shot forth on December 31, 1949. The headline in the *Daily Independent Journal* of San Rafael read: "4 Made Homeless by Fairfax Blaze."[314]

The paper reported that the fire, of undetermined origin, burned through the 2½-story frame structure on Hillside Drive in a blaze unnoticed until 10 p.m. According to the newspaper account, no one was in the building at the time. The building was destroyed. Long term residents Ada and Warren Willimas [*sic*] lived there with their ten-year-old daughter. Another occupant, Fred La Belle, had moved in the day of the fire. Mrs. Willimas said they arrived at the fire at the height of the blaze, just returning from a weekend holiday in Los Angeles.

Fairfax firemen stated the fire was well underway by the time the blaze was reported and there was nothing they could do but keep it under control. A fire report later cited it could have been an electrical fire caused by a new tenant who had moved in that day. The poor availability of emergency access to all the houses on Hillside was discussed and future remedies suggested in the newspaper account. The newspaper noted that for years the school had been a host to students from all over the world, and that it contained a chapel that was also destroyed.

Likewise destroyed, but not reported by the newspaper, was a tremendous spiritual library that included many of the writings of Hazrat Inayat Khan, Samuel Lewis's writings and commentaries, and still more. Sam was at the School earlier in the day to retrieve some of his writings from the office, leaving much behind as only a portion could fit into Ted's car. Neither Sam nor Ted was present at the time of the fire; they may have been at the New Year's Eve folk dance in Fairfax that evening, both being dance enthusiasts.

For Samuel Lewis the fire was a pivotal event that marked the beginning of a significant period of rejection in his life.

Remnants After the Fire

> *My Dear Samuel:*
>
> *As Don told me you were present at the fire, I would like to know from you what your impressions were at the time—psychic, intuitive, prophetic or otherwise. We apparently had to share Baba's renunciation of all His ashrams. He is at Benares. You will be interested to know that I have made a down payment on a lot of Ellsworth's at Myrtle Beach. I trust to God to be able to pay for it. The year has been a difficult one. My broken foot still suffers and my eye affliction is still most painful. I lost my father at Thanksgiving. I started this year with the heavy grippe astrology indicated. I'll be glad when Saturn gets out of Virgo.*
>
> IVY DUCE[315]

Mrs. Duce was still living on the East Coast when the Fairfax fire occurred. She wrote Samuel a relaxed and chatty personal letter with lots of questions in it and some anxieties. It is surprisingly cordial considering that Samuel had already resigned from her Order earlier in response to being displaced from the Board and had been fired from his office job and forced to leave his space at the land. Still, at this time she wanted some help from Sam.

She questioned why Rabia had no heading on her stationery except the Sufi symbol, and wondered if she had gotten into any difficulties with the Europeans. She worried about dates of incorporation and asked Sam to search through his home for letters:

> Now that you are home I wonder if you would go over your papers carefully someday and see if you can find anywhere a letter from I. Khan to Murshida. I still do not understand why there were no letters between the years 1918 and his death except the one letter written from France in 1923 after his return from America. I went through everything at Ashbury.* I am always wishing I could lay my hands on something that would prove to dissenters how he trusted her till the last . . . I would like solid ground under me when newcomers ask questions about the past. Baba has appointed me to my task, and I don't need any other appointment although I have Murshida's appointment of me.

---

*Rabia's home in San Francisco.

> I will appreciate any assistance you can give Don in teaching him how to conduct the services and things like that.[316]

Her closing paragraph references a new phase in Samuel's life. "I hope your college work is making you happy. I found myself in such disagreement with the professors most of the time that I would find it hard to take. May the New Year be most fruitful for you! In Baba, Murshida."

When Samuel was evicted from Kaaba Allah, pressure was put on his parents by Mrs. Duce and others to join a crowd who were attacking Samuel's competence and character, suggesting his admission to an asylum. For once his parents stood up for him. They felt no compunction in tearing Samuel down as they had often done, but they wouldn't countenance outsiders' attacks. His father offered to support Samuel in returning to college to complete his education in the manner he would like. Sam chose to go to City College of San Francisco and study horticulture and botany. His time at City College would help prepare him for international work years later when he was able to travel abroad.

Mrs. Duce still erroneously thought Samuel might have some of Inayat Khan's letters. She glibly smiled over his college work, while trying to torpedo him with his family. The apparent friendliness in the letter did not last long. She wrote again three weeks later. Samuel had now resigned for a second time. Here is her full letter from New York:

> Dear Samuel:
>
> I assume that a formal acknowledgement of your resignations is in order, so I hereby accept them.
>
> It would take me volumes to reply to your completely inconsistent letter of Jan. 12th and I have not the time. When you stand before the altar of God and with hands upraised swear an oath to regard Baba as your master and to be loyal to me as your Murshida, and also write out on paper in detail your attitude, I am certainly flabbergasted when you refuse to answer a question on the ground of *samskaras* and then proceed to sow them all over the place by starting another of your sniping campaigns against me by writing to Norina whom I saw again last week in Myrtle Beach, and to old *mureeds* like the Skinners in Detroit and God Knows who else, but which like everything else you do, always becomes known to me in time.

> You have been consumed with jealousy ever since I was appointed to this work. You dislike Don because I have relied on his responsibility and services despite the fact that he might not have as much esoteric learning as you have. You have fought against every woman you ever had to work with. I have protected you from far more than you will ever know; I have given you loving kindness and shared my table with you. You have betrayed me over and over in this work even when it is only by innuendo and damning with faint praise and hints of injustice and all that. I have warned you to make sure you stand before Baba with clean hands because He has appointed me to this work, as well as Murshida Rabia. What you do against me you do against Him, and against God in all of us. He has renounced three ashrams and everything in the world, but when your Murshida asks that our work on the national boards be made more national by the inclusion of other states, you cannot give up one seat even though it would have been nominally so.
>
> If you cannot await Baba's arrival for your next appointment that is up to you, but don't talk to me about *samskaras!*
>
> I would also advise you not to brag about taking the Sufi School with you when you left. I regret to say that most people do not understand the esoteric meanings you are hinting at and there is already considerable speculation in Marin County as to whether or not you had any part in this holocaust since you were there that day and no one was there that night. I must say here and now that I do not believe this at all. There was no *baraka* or *dharshana* there except the rock Murshid blest. The backbiting and fights and gossiping and performances of all sorts sent out no *baraka*. I am sure it was to free the place from just such *samskaras* that the place burned down and through its purification we have a clean slate for Baba's New Phase and the new era that is soon here.

Mrs. Duce showed two faces to Samuel. One was cordial, the other totally irate. There is no doubt that Samuel did offer faint praise and hint at her injustices. Clearly, he felt he would have been a much better prepared leader than Murshida Duce. Prepared for the role or not, he was an enduring target for abuse. There was no one ready to accept what Sam could offer.

Murshida Duce's last paragraph is the deadliest and the most revealing about her ongoing agenda. When she says that she regrets to inform him that most people did not understand the esoteric teachings Samuel shared, it is hard to believe she has any regrets at all. Although she denies believing it, she appears to gloat when she states there is already considerable speculation in Marin County about whether he had any part in the fire. Subsequent gossip gained great momentum and shadowed him thereafter. There was no evidence against him other than he was on the property during that day and that he was parting ways from Murshida Duce. He was, however, a very convenient whipping boy.

It was true, as Duce asserted, that whatever was spiritual at the Sufi School was no longer anywhere apparent. The situation had already begun to crumble some years before. What was left was the Rock, Pir Dahan, which Samuel had spent so much time working on and meditating at. It had been blessed by Inayat Khan and shared with the Zen Master Nyogen Senzaki. A temple for the Universal Worship had been imagined for there, but that was not to be.

The land did ultimately end up benefitting the Meher Baba movement when the two Sufi corporations that owned the property were consolidated into a new one called Sufism Reoriented in 1952. Its main holding was the Fairfax land, which was subsequently sold to finance the printing of Meher Baba's book *God Speaks.*

The making of the new constitution for Sufism Reoriented took some years to complete. Drafts were sent to Meher Baba for commentary and approval, leaving him to make the final decisions. Some of Samuel Lewis's work was credited in the earliest drafts.

When Mrs. Duce went to India in 1947, she had long discussions with Meher Baba about what should now happen with the corporation. Some of those discussions continued for days on topics such as levels of initiation. Baba was ultimately able to stop one persistent discussion about the various grades of initiation by saying Inayat Khan was a 5th level being while he was a 7th level. Later in his instructions to Murshida Duce and Murshida

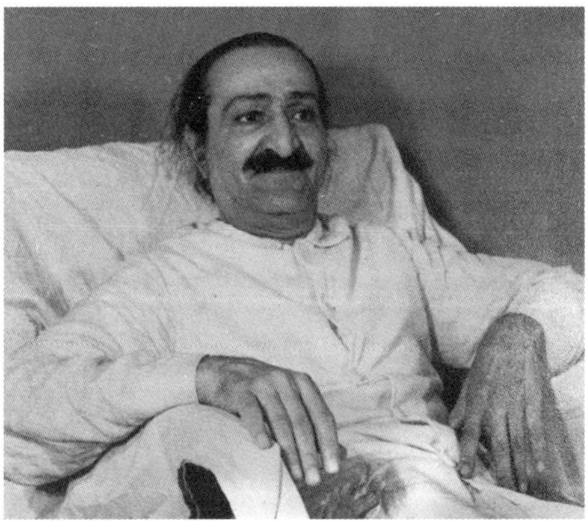

Meher Baba declared himself to be an Avatar in 1954

Martin he told them to set aside any use of the selected papers that Inayat had prepared for his students. Rabia Martin had been willing to do this immediately. Murshida Duce, perhaps because these papers were one of the few things she knew enough to teach from, begged that Baba would allow her to use them. He initially refused, but finally agreed when she asked him for a third time.

The esoteric papers would remain a major topic for Samuel Lewis. The teachings they contained had been a focus for his study and for his ongoing creative expression in effacement with Hazrat Inayat Khan through commentaries. Samuel wrote:

> One of the last letters of Hazrat Inayat Khan, on his deathbed, was to thank me for my efforts. This letter was destroyed in the fire of 1949 along with 25 years research and collections of materials on the above and related subjects.[317]
>
> [At the last meeting] Pir-o-Murshid went over everything with patience. I have since found several attempts on his part for a constitution. One was based on prowess in *zikr*, never completed. Another on advancement in *hal* and *makam*. Another on different bases. All of these records were either destroyed, lost in the fire of 1949, or came into the hands of Mrs. Ivy Duce and Meher Baba. But many of the principles are found in Volume X of the *Sufi Message* now published.[318]

At this point there were the Sufi Movement with headquarters in Europe and Sufism Reoriented with influence in the U.S., Australia, and parts of South America. Samuel Lewis was no longer functioning in either order. His loyalty to Inayat Khan and his teachings with their inclusive and universal view made it impossible for him to follow the direction being asked by Meher Baba. He was especially disturbed by the lack of love and harmony embodied in many of those who were now representing Baba in the U.S. Sam never discounted the spiritual visitation he had had from Baba in 1942, but he could see no way to continue to work with him.

Meher Baba always stood with Ivy Duce when she was criticized by *mureeds* such as Samuel Lewis and later Don Stevens. Baba had liked the fact that she admitted she lacked realization and did not feel prepared to do this job. He promised to support her, but she construed his remarks to mean he would always ensure that the leadership of Sufism Reoriented would be illuminated, a vain claim.* She later took the liberty to offer succession in Sufism Reoriented to James S.B. MacKie and make him a Murshid. When MacKie went to Baba's center in India with a group dressed in white and hanging on MacKie's words, they were met with sound disapproval. Over time, incidents like this caused Sufism Reoriented to be viewed by many as an outsider in the world of Baba lovers.

1950 found Samuel Lewis ousted from his home and without a source of income. Even with all his training, practice, experience, high idealism and boundless energy, life's circumstances were now forcing him again to return to the inner light and begin totally anew. He drew strength from his commitment to "Never surrender to anything, to anyone, to any force except God or those who represent God in the Spiritual Hierarchy." [319]

Paul Reps later had this to say:

> He blew hot and cold. Sam was kind of a prophet, a kind of a Jewish prophet, out of time, and there was no one to agree with him. His family didn't agree with him, Murshida didn't agree with him, yet he had this inner light. So he just kept changing, but always from his own inner light. It was very nice, very nice to see.[320]

Although Samuel had no established Order under which to function, he never stopped making presentations, writing commentaries, or doing his spiritual practices.

---

*For background on this and other matters related to the emergence of Sufism Reoriented, from the point of view of certain prominent Meher Baba devotees, see www.sufismreoriented.org/Sufi_Charter_Part_2_Glow_Fall_09.pdf.

Sam Lewis with his lifelong friend Paul Reps

CHAPTER 8

Key People in Samuel's Life

Elliott Lewis

From the outset, Elliott appeared to his parents to be a more promising prospect for success in society and the world they knew than Samuel, and they did all they could to support him toward this end. He did succeed in becoming very well known about town, and he moved with a celebrity crowd. Elliott liked to brag about his social connections and how clever a gambler he was. The following excerpts are from a letter he wrote to his brother Samuel shortly before Elliott had their mother confined to a mental institution. At this time, he lived alone in the house with Harriet. It provides a glimpse of Elliott's personality on his own terms:

> Ma does not know anyone any more. She is all skin and bones and must weigh less than 70 pounds. She sleeps 20 hours a day or more. She is just a vegetable. However, her heart is strong and she may go on and on . . .
>
> Four years ago I was on a party with Jimmy Durante and I began shouting "Bill Bailey Won't You Please Come Home" with him. You know I can't sing. BUT NOW, wherever I go, it is "Here's Bill Bailey" and I have to sing, I really have become a good shouter. Also I tell stories. Ted Lewis and Sophie Tucker have made me come up on stage with them . . .
>
> You know I am a life member of the Press & Union League Club. Once or twice a week I go and take the whirlpool baths there . . . Once a week I bring Lefty O'Doul and Joe DiMaggio and they take the steam baths and swim . . .
>
> Last October at the Holiday Hotel tournament in Reno, I went up a day ahead of time and Dizzy Dean was there too. Diz asked me about O'Doul's [golf] game, and I said "lousy", so when O'Doul got there I said, "Frank, I have half of your bets against Dizzy Dean." Result, O'Doul handed me $412.00 after the tournament.[321]

Unfortunately, Elliott had flaws in his nature that contributed to family difficulties. Samuel Lewis referred to this aspect of his brother's character in a letter to his cousin Marion Mann many years later in 1962:

> Elliot became angry because I did not call on him. Well, he defrauded me so many times in life it is a horrible story; but no matter what he did one or both parents supported him, excepting twice, when he stole, my father compelled restitution; i.e. twice out of innumerable times. It was no use my protesting. He has continued to steal since my father's death.
>
> He had a horrible plan which he told others, of using my mother against me and then after he got control of the major portion of the property put her away. He succeeded. He has her money and she is in an asylum. How he connived this is a filthy story.* But unfortunately every time he did anything wrong my folks talked as if I were equally guilty and I have had to face the whole life with no possibility of getting jobs or into society here in San Francisco excepting by the hard, hard way . . .
>
> [Elliott] was in the end frozen out. That's the way it went. More money was spent on his gambling debts than on my education; also on subsidizing marriages which never took place. Which is nothing to what he was able to get away with. Now [1962] he is almost friendly. [322]

As Elliott had no more money flowing from his father, he focused on his mother, joining her side of the war. From the time of her inheritance, he was able to control her money and spent it all before his death.

Professor Harry Nelson

Sam accepted his father's offer to support him to finish college. He began his studies in horticulture at San Francisco City College in the Fall semester of 1949. He received an Associate of Arts degree on June 15, 1951, earning a GPA of 3.35 out of 4.0 for 77 hours of credit in 26 courses. Professor Harry Nelson was one of his main teachers and

*Elliott apparently took her in a senile condition to a lawyer, who made changes in her will as Elliott dictated.

Harry Nelson gardening with Girl Scouts

became his foremost adviser. Sam would also go to the campus in his free time and work in the greenhouse.*

Six years later when he was able to travel abroad, Samuel used seeds and horticulture appropriate for different climes as a medium for helping countries and a vehicle of good will. He considered horticulture to be a part of his overall peace mission: through it, not only could world hunger be addressed, but nations could be brought closer together. He did not present a structured agricultural program as such but rather maintained a sensitive responsiveness to the needs of each situation.

In correspondence with Professor C. R. Cutright at the Ohio Agricultural Experimental Station, he wrote:

> I have been received in Lahore by the highest dignitaries and socially prominent and wealthy persons . . . Both these people and the executives in Agriculture that I have met tell me that I am the real "Peace Corps." . . . I am suggesting that other universities or groups thereof utilize their alumni associations to promote peace and good-will . . .
>
> The idea is also to connect people of various lands together who have common interests . . .
>
> Here the Pakistanis consider the idea of world peace & understanding through horticultural & agricultural exchange far, far better than other proposals which have received more attention than careful consideration.[323]

Later he elaborated to Professor Nelson that he had been "encouraging either free or reciprocal exchange of seeds from country to country to

*In that greenhouse Sam met other volunteer workers. With his ability to get people involved, Sam made friends and invited them to parties and events. A few would also later take initiation in Sufism.

promise peace and good-will and the increase of food and economic crops."[324]

He periodically wrote Dr. Nelson about horticultural issues in the countries he was visiting and told his adviser how he had responded. While a great deal more happened on Sam's trips abroad, horticulture was an ongoing prominent focus.

In an interview several years after Sam's passing, Dr. Nelson shared his impression of his first meeting with Sam:

> Sam was sent to study with me by Dr. Lloyd Luckmann of USF, who said he was a student of semantics. So I presumed he was from a university. He came in the early 50s. He liked horticulture. I got him a few jobs in gardening and helped him build up his clientele. He was a mediocre gardener. His main forte was to stir people up, to get them moving.[325]

Sam took numerous courses in the field of horticulture, including chemistry laboratory, soils, greenhouse maintenance, and pest control. These topics gave him a foundation for the work he would undertake during his trips abroad. He also developed an ability to find relevant published material, whether from another country or tucked away in a local library or government office. Sam made recommendations to local officials and provided them with written materials pertaining to their particular issues. His 1960 diary entries, for example, include considerations on a wide variety of horticultural topics, including types of soils, types of trees, effects of weather, soil amendments, effective ground covers, newest products in use, fertilizing and watering routines, timings for the taking of cuttings, fertilizer balances, greenhouse materials, and food production, processing and storage.

Harry Nelson had further interesting insights into Sam after meeting his mother Harriet:

> Sam didn't have much money. He always traveled in the cheapest possible way and saw the conditions of the peasants.
>
> He took quite a few courses. He was waiting for his father and brother to die so he could have a small inheritance. He took me to see his par-

> ents. The only time I ever saw Sam totally quiet. Boy how his mother could talk.
>
> He never completed anything he worked on. Start with lots of energy and then go on to the next thing. I remember one paper I asked to be written on the uses of any garden tool. He chose the hoe. What a mess that paper was. He never even mentioned what it was used for.
>
> He had a good sense of humor. Life was a fun thing with him. That was the main thing. As a student he was a swell guy . . . It was his mother's fault in my opinion for the condition he was in. Nervous energy, never settled down. Horticulture is good therapy; it keeps your hands and mind busy . . .
>
> Sam picked up organic gardening; we had a class on soils and fertilizers. Interested in mushroom cultivation, mycology.[326]

While Nelson never considered Sam to be at the level of a colleague, he did appreciate Sam's energy and acknowledged that later Sam established credibility as a horticulturalist in many settings.

> [I know that Sam] bandied my name all around the world because I got a lot of letters from various people where he had traveled. I remember one Japanese fellow sent me 25 to 50 pounds of gingko tree seeds to distribute . . . The one contact that lasted the longest was Friends of the World. I heard from this Japanese man for three or four years.[327]

Samuel did find solace in horticulture. Doing the actual work provided an outlet for his remarkable energy. When he was at the Meher Baba center in Myrtle Beach, he worked outside as a caretaker for the land. It was then he initiated a practice of reciting the sacred phrase *Allahu Akbar* 100,000 times a day for a year. The phrase can be properly translated "God's greatness is greater than one can ever imagine."

Such absorbed devotional recitation built tremendous inner and outer strength in Sam. He would need strength to face what was in front of him. The effects of his fallout with Murshida Duce and Sufism Reoriented did not fade away. He experienced continued repercussions in many arenas.

Detractors and Supporters

Hilda Galbraith, an acquaintance and travel agent of Sam's, said in an interview:

> I don't know exactly what happened [at the Sufi School], but evidently [Sam] was a disturbance to them. I had a visit from Ted Reindollar and we went out for coffee. We were talking and I told him I had quite a few visits from Samuel and he said to me, "Be careful of that man, he is a very evil man." And I said, "Well, I don't know. I don't have any fear of him." I don't know what it was, but evidently this might have been a consensus of opinion among them, because Ted was at the Sufi School also at the time of this disturbance.
>
> Hazel [Armstrong] never said anything but she was upset by this discord. Samuel could be erratic to be around and this was probably some of the difficulty . . . The capacity was there but there was something that he couldn't express as you or I would—some sort of shortcoming there. I wouldn't begin to try to analyze why, it was just what I felt. But other than that, we enjoyed him and just accepted him. He was kind of a character. Eccentric, you might say.[328]

Others who were interviewed, such as Constance Luick, were more extreme in their judgment of Sam:

> Sam sent me stacks of letters—both original and carbon copies of letters to everyone. He wrote not only full of two-faced shenanigans with regard to every spiritual leader in San Francisco who would allow him the courtesy to attend their centers, but he sent many of these copies to others. I got 4 or 5 huge letters a week for 6 or 7 years. Most were incoherent. [329]

I met Ms. Luick at a bookstore with Sam. She and Sam conversed like old friends. But the lack of acceptance that Sam had for other teachers who were better known than himself clearly affected Constance's views on him.

> I often gave Sam my first-hand objective vein of certain personal situations [when] he came to me and asked for advice; some he followed.
>
> I'm certain you'll be able to get a number of first hand views on Sam—from others—as even those he betrayed in assorted treacherous ways can still be heard to say, "Poor Sam."[330]

Constance did not explain what she meant by "treacherous ways" and simply showed that she did not appreciate or perhaps understand Sam's sometimes eccentric behavior and pranks. Ms. Luick included other negative assessments, but her final remark was the deepest and best: "PS. You'd be well to forget the biography—the whole of Sam's Spiritual Gift/Teaching lies in one area—not his writings or people's rehash of his life. If you have a recording of his 'Flute of Krishna'—that's it—without commentary."[331]

She makes an excellent point. The flute of Krishna came from inside Sam's own body; he dissolved his ego-self in the sound and brought forth impressive music from within.* Even his greatest critics were moved by this phenomenon. It was a direct transmission of his inner reality and could be experienced directly.†

As to his "incoherent" correspondence, Sam's typing was always at full speed and mistakes were common. Years later, he found secretaries among his dedicated students who could type and take dictation. Those who then received letters all said how much more coherent they were.

Teaching through direct experience would appeal to the young people of the late '60s, who would flock to him for teachings; but during the early 1950s, very few could see the depth of his being. In these years he actively released his wrath in criticism of those who held apparent authority but failed to live up to his standards of excellence or to give him recognition.

Not everyone would desert Sam during these times. Sheikha Vera knew him well. She had been with him through all his years teaching at the Sufi School in Fairfax, supporting him there and beyond.

---

*A small sample of this music is preserved in one of Murshid Sam's recorded talks: "Life and Love and Eternal Laughter, Part 2," beginning at about 18:00 into the talk. Media, "64 Talks and Lectures," Archives.

†Inayat Khan considered the flute of Krishna to be symbolic of the "abstract sound," Saut-e-Sarmad, that fills all of space and that was heard by Muhammad in the cave, Moses on Mount Sinai, Christ in the wilderness, and Shiva in his cave. "This sound is the source of all revelation to the Masters, to whom it is revealed from within; it is because of this that they know and teach one and the same truth." Inayat Khan, "Abstract Sound," in *The Sufi Message of Hazrat Inayat Khan* (Delhi: Motilal Banarsidass, 2011), vol. II, ch. 8. Available at Wahiduddin's Web, wahiduddin.net/mv2/II/II_8.htm.

Vera saw Samuel as a *madzub*. Sometimes called a *mast, madzub* refers to a human being who has an immediate and intimate relationship with the God reality, and who often is absorbed in that realm and at the same time appears strange, incoherent, eccentric, but somehow deeply invested with power. In some cultures *madzub*s are treated as sacred treasures, in others as if insane.

In her interview with me, Vera shared her view of Samuel Lewis in this regard:

> I knew nothing about "*madzub*," never heard of it. Then somebody gave me this book by Meher Baba—the great work he was doing with the *madzubs*. I read that, and I said, "Ho, Samuel's been doing this for years! He's *madzub*, and they don't even recognize it in their own midst, but they're going to India to adopt another one? He is going through the state of the avatar, and they didn't even know it." . . . When it hit me, it was the shock of my life, to realize that, yes, here is the state of the avatar . . .
>
> And the rest of my life [I] never entered a room where Samuel was present without sitting before him, humbly. And I will, within spirit, to the end of my days; because he was so head and shoulders above anything that anybody has recognized. He was working for the humanity on the plane of the avatar; and all these mad things, like feeding Asia . . . the humanity, his personal, psychic, spiritual destiny was the work for the humanity, the whole world, not us, not me individually, not you, not any of us as a small group, but the humanity.[332]

Gavin Arthur

Sam originally met Gavin Arthur at a debate where Gavin spoke on behalf of Walt Whitman. Gavin was a well-known Bohemian and the grandson of U.S. President Chester Arthur. Gavin Arthur would later say that Sam had the biggest chip on his shoulder of anybody he had ever seen. That super-sensitivity and rage was about his rejections and particularly about him not being allowed to share his knowledge and experience. When I mentioned this comment to Murshid Sam, he implicitly acknowledged the truth of it but pointed to how things had changed: "Now look what has happened since I have people who want to receive teachings from me!"

Gavin described his first meeting with Sam:

> Sam was in the audience . . . He came over to shake hands [and] he said, "I am a great friend of your friend Hugo Selig." And I said, "Oh Hugo Selig is one of my gurus." And he said, "Yes, he's one of mine too, so we're brothers," and we shook hands very firmly . . . He . . . congratulated me and said that he agreed with me very much about Whitman being the voice of the West, and couldn't he come and see me, where did I live? And I told him this slum place on . . . Henry St., which I paid $9 a week for.[333]

Photo by Mansur Johnson

Gavin Arthur at Garden of Inayat, 1971

At that time, Gavin was selling newspapers on a corner while finishing his book *The Circle of Sex.*

> I was perfectly astonished when I came back the next day from my corner. I'd found that [Sam had] moved into the room next door to me . . . He was a gardener for the city at the end of the bridge.[334]

Hugo Selig was a learned kabbalist and poet that Sam respected. He had met Selig through their mutual connections with the community of bohemians at the Oceano Dunes in Southern California.*

Some years later Gavin reflected on Samuel Lewis's astrological chart:

> I would say that it's very intellectual . . . with Virgo rising, and the Sun is in Libra, Mercury's in Libra, Mercury's very well placed in Libra, because it makes an even mind that weighs all things before making a decision. In the house of communication he has Saturn and Uranus and Venus. So Saturn prevented him from using this gift for quite a

*For a fascinating account of the history of this community (mentioning, among others, Gavin Arthur and Luther Whiteman) see www.kcet.org/shows/artbound/the-dunites-building-a-utopia-in-the-oceano-dunes.

> long time. But when he did come out of it under the influence of Venus and Uranus, the electrical planet of the unmost revealed side of subconscious, then he began to be a great speaker. But he wasn't at first because this Saturn held him back. And his Jupiter is in the house of confinement, again holding back the money for so long, but he should have had it a long time before so he could start all of these movements.
>
> He could read charts better than anybody, excepting Dr. Baker . . . They were by far the best, really without knowing how to do a chart. And one time I fooled him by saying "Here Sam, is a very interesting young fellow. I hope you'll find him very promising. I know I do. His name is Ulysses Simpson Armstrong, I think that he's going far; what do you think?" He looked at it. It was a chart done for the United States, done July 4, 1776, at 2:00 in the morning just when the Liberty Bell rang out, just like the cry of a newborn child. But he was completely oblivious of this; he read it just as if it were a young man of today, and he said, "Oh my goodness, Uranus just exactly on the horizon, he can go far, he can go far, he can go to Oak Knoll, he has Atomic Energy at his fingertips, he's too rich for his own good. Tell him that he can't buy his friends." I was having a terrible time, trying not to burst out in laughter, but luckily . . . we got it on tape . . . I told him who it was and then he said . . ."I'm pretty good, aren't I.[335]

Gavin soon recommended Dr. Blanche Baker as a perfect therapist for Sam. She became a significant friend and influence in Samuel Lewis's life.

Dr. Blanche Baker

Consider[ing] me unworthy . . . to speak on subjects . . . was a common attitude in San Francisco . . . It made one a sort of martyr . . . Doctor Baker discovered a pattern that from childhood I had something to say and was never permitted to say it, but her efforts to get people to let me speak failed. Once indeed she had a noted sociologist at her house and the place was packed. When I challenged the

> *sociologist, the whole audience was amazed and hostile that I should dare challenge him. But the speaker declared in the end that I was right, that I was far more up to date on the subject. So, he lost the audience. This was my pattern for a long time.*[336]
>
> *It is a long way from the Socratic and I repeat Socratic situation in which I was placed in San Francisco. The most ridiculous of the factors was the attack on me at the same time by Rom Landau and Rom Landau's worst enemies; by Alan Watts and his worst enemies . . . Suffice it to say they were all connected with the square of Neptune-Moon in my [chart] which set my mother against me and in turn some older women who invited me to some large city and then turned against me. This was true of San Francisco, Los Angeles, Detroit, Washington, Berkeley and other places. The "plot" was the same in every instance and after Dr. Baker and I worked this out this "old woman" complex disappeared.*[337]
>
> SAMUEL LEWIS

After his introduction to Blanche Baker through Gavin, Samuel approached her about therapy. He enjoyed telling the story from time to time in his classes: "I told her that if my case was not the worst one she had ever heard I would pay double her fee, which would be $200, but if she agreed that it was the worst, she should treat me for free. After hearing me out she agreed it was the worst and she did treat me for free."

During his work with Dr. Baker, Samuel complained about not being heard by others, so she arranged for him to speak at her home a few times. Florence Leonard remembered these events; her remarks clearly indicate that Sam didn't fully connect with some of the people there.

> At Dr. Baker's, I remember . . . he gave . . . lectures, but I can truthfully say that we got very little out of them because while [he] said a lot it was never coordinated. We used to compare afterwards . . . He knew a lot, but he couldn't give it out in a way in which other people got enough out of, except for his sincerity, and the fact that we knew that he knew a lot, but he wasn't giving it to us in a way which was usable.[338]

Margaret Albanese also spoke about Sam in her remembrance:

> He had this total rejection, total human rejection, so it's very understandable that a person should go through a long [crisis] of this kind. I

> don't recall anything he said in specific reference to working with the lady, but he did express himself very freely to us, about his feelings about all this. And there seemed to be, at times, just a real rage in him; he was reaching so hard at the time to accomplish what he always was convinced was his mission . . .
>
> He never, never lost sight of that, he never lost faith in it. And he knew, even in the fifties, he said, "These things are going to be published, I know." He said, "It may not be in my lifetime, but they will be." . . .
>
> Very strong. And that was the thing which helped me to realize that he would work out of this period in his own way, which he did, and of course, he had the saving grace of his fantastic sense of humor.[339]

Sam stayed at Henry Street until 1956. Here is Gavin's account of Sam's treatment with Blanche Baker:

> I introduced him to Dr. Baker, which as I say was really the turning point. Because before that he'd been so cantankerous . . . [I told him] "I know of no one in whom religion arouses such malevolent emotions as Samuel L. Lewis." And he took it very well, laughed, but he defended himself because he considered that he'd been treated very badly . . .
>
> He had this fearful inferiority complex, which she cured; I believe she really did, because after Sam went through her course of psychoanalysis he emerged as a very, very different person. He was no longer with a chip on his shoulder all the time . . . She had a most remarkable gift for a psychoanalyst, and also she could hypnotize.[340]

Dr. Baker referred to it as regression rather than hypnotism. Patients would remember the birth trauma and they would be taken into previous lives. She introduced psychodrama. Under her treatment Samuel was able to remember his previous relations with his family and see fairness in how karma had played out.

Gavin said,

> Sunday we would always go out to Dr. Baker's, who always had a meeting of the inner [circle] on Sunday. She . . . would have Sam soon go into the inner circle. She also had Baroness Von Stroh who was the greatest medium that I've ever known, and was part of her group. And then Dr. Baker's husband, who was part of the group and president of the Graphological Society, and I was her astrologer, and somebody else was her palmist, and so on, she had all these different

people, and we used to do each other, and find out about ourselves and know ourselves . . .

[Sam] was very unfair in many ways at that time, because he wasn't, I don't think, enlightened until after he came back from Asia . . .

You must recognize that it was inevitable that he was rejected at the time when he himself rejected everybody . . . He was so unnecessarily rude. It was uncanny, it was almost as if he was daring people. He always had this chip on his shoulder, daring people to knock it off. So, if he was rejected, it was nobody but his own fault . . . And it was Dr. Baker who'd made him see that. He owes a great deal to her . . . And because he had devoted all his time to seclusion when he felt that the world hated him, he was drawn into his shell. He made good use of the loneliness by becoming a tremendous scholar.[341]

In her response to a chastising letter from another San Francisco psychiatrist, Dr. Baker described her manner of treatment. She gladly, and somewhat sarcastically, embraced the criticism she had received for becoming close to her patients:

"Dr. B. is guilty of identifying with her patients. She believes that democratic procedures are desirable in human relations. Thus she dares to violate the code of the Mystery-Man Cult of Medicine and to practice the art of healing by being a kindly, friendly, motherly sort of doctor (or teacher) who practices brotherhood, preaches self-acceptance and even enjoys the companionship of 'dirty' homosexuals . . ." Since most people who seek my help, including homophiles, are basically hurt children who are still controlled by their emotional natures . . . I have developed the art of communicating with each individual at the various levels at which [he or she] functions. I find much non-verbal communication is required, including the warmth and affection a wise mother will give her hurt babe. A good sense of humor is valuable in bringing the shattered personality together to produce a more integrated, happy, creative and efficient human being.[342]

Samuel reflected on his time with Blanche Baker:

I have never asked to avoid mistakes but I have said that if I repeat the same mistakes I ought to be punished. Dr. Baker and I worked out my two basically detrimental karmic patterns. One was a pattern which was "inherited"—the pattern of the dominating woman which was in my

> Neptune Square Moon. After that I saw it was imperative not to have an older woman dominate me . . . [343]
>
> I once took Dr. Baker with me to an Asian conference and she never again criticized me, but I do not have many opportunities to take people to see what happens when I go forth.[344]

Blanche noted how he readily made contact with the Asian community, and she gave him her acceptance. When he departed for Japan on his first trip abroad in 1956, she arranged for a group of friends and acquaintances to lovingly send him off.

Dr. Blanche Baker is now legendary in her field. She is primarily known as the first psychiatrist to publicly take the position that homosexuality was not a disease. In the 1950s and '60s, the American Psychiatric Association listed homosexuality as a mental illness that could be cured or managed by psychotherapy treatments. While many therapists quietly dismissed this in practice, Dr. Blanche Baker put her career on the line by publicly challenging the designation. Dr. Baker spoke at ONE Inc.'s first Midwinter Institute in 1955, the first forum in North America put on by homosexuals, for homosexuals, regarding the scientific, philosophical, legal, and social questions pertaining to homosexuality. This account of her talk appeared in issue 21 of *ONE Institute Quarterly: Homophile Studies.*

> Those who heard Blanche M. Baker, M.D., Ph.D. give the address, "A Psychiatric Evaluation of Homosexuality; Causative Factors and Therapeutic Suggestions," January 1955, are not likely to forget the impact of her fearless frankness in handling such a topic. So unhackneyed were the views she expressed that, by contrast with much psychiatric thinking of the time, they sounded startling or to some, perhaps alarming. In the extended question and answer period which followed Dr. Baker patiently and wittily so disarmed the skeptical and silenced the critical that at the conclusion the entire audience rose to its feet to give her an ovation lasting several minutes. Such a response, rare as it must have been for any psychiatrist to receive, gives some indication of how remarkable a person she was.
>
> Dr. Baker consulted with ONE Inc. and their Social Services Division from 1955–1958, before beginning a column in ONE Magazine in 1958 called "Toward Understanding." Dr. Baker's advice column took on a wide

> array of issues including the causes of homosexuality, social isolation, gay marriage, gays in the military, latent homosexuality, and fetishes. The column lasted only until 1960 when Dr. Baker passed away. Although Dr. Baker's collaboration with ONE Inc. was short lived, the courage to use her status to speak out against the prejudices of her profession gave sorely needed support to ONE Inc. and its readers the world around.[345]

Dr. Baker had the capacity to be both a therapist and a friend, and became a hero of the gay community. She wrote an introduction to Gavin's book *The Circle of Sex* and was a regular contributor to a pamphlet published by the One Foundation. There she also answered frequent questions relating to homosexuality and her work with homosexuals.*

Dr. Baker liked to use an integrative quotation to spark reflection and participation when she was speaking. She sometimes chose an anonymous poem entitled "My Many Selves."

> *Within my earthly temple there's a crowd,*
> *There's one of us that's humble, one that's proud.*
> *There's one of us that loves his neighbor as himself,*
> *And one that cares for naught but fame and pelf.*
> *There's one of us that's broken-hearted for his sins,*
> *And one who, unrepentant, sits and grins.*
> *From much corroding care I should be free,*
> *If once I could determine which is me.*†

Some years after Dr. Baker's passing, Gavin said:

> I miss Blanche really, more than anybody I can think of. More than wives or mothers or any women in my life, because we used to talk in depth all the time. Every man needs a Diotima like Socrates, that priestess of the mysteries, the [Eleusinian] mysteries. If you want to be a philosopher, you have to have a woman like that. And Sam didn't have any woman like that until he met Blanche. And this I think was the turning point: meeting a woman that he could talk to, absolutely in depth, as he would to a man. [346]

---

* Gavin Arthur identified 12 gradations of sexual preference in *The Circle of Sex* (University Books, 1966).

† This poem has been attributed to Edward Sandford Martin and has appeared under various titles.

Samuel wrote in his diaries in 1963, "One thing I learned from Dr. Baker is that patterns remain until we break them and often they are so big and strong we cannot."[347] He spoke once about a session he had with her where his great antagonism for Alan Watts came up. His response to her query about it was, "I love him so much." It was a natural thing for him to give tough love to people he felt were stuck in their development. Gavin said:

> He was always fulminating against, first of all [Frederic] Spiegelberg and then Alan Watts for not allowing him to teach at the Academy* as an accredited teacher, he couldn't really do it without a degree! There was no way that they could possibly arrange it with the greatest will. And they thought that he was very eccentric, but that he was one of the most brilliant people in America . . .
>
> Sam's particular hatred was against a man that I intensely disliked too . . . [Rom] Landau was a Jew who hated being a Jew and said "I'm not a Jew, I am an Englishman," . . . and he was absolutely terrified of any kind of homosexual implications. I had a picture of a young man that I knew had very close dealings with Landau in the Alps, and this was a picture, naked, against the Alps. And he flew into the most dreadful rage at that, "I didn't know him!!!" . . .
>
> I supported Sam very much in his denouncement of Landau, because Landau was given the job of teaching Oriental religions particularly of the Western variety, which would include Sufism, and Sam who knew more about Sufism . . . it was pathetic. I agree with him that Spiegelberg and Alan Watts were wrong in putting Landau at the head of that department in the Academy of Asian Studies.[348]

People at the American Academy of Asian Studies

Florence Leonard recalled that Sam had some support from his family, and said she never thought of him as poor.

> He didn't have a lot of money, but he worked . . . He worked for people in gardening, knew a lot about plants, and he considered that his work . . . His relationship with me was mostly based on what we thought of the world, religion and all of the abstract subjects, and that was where we hit it off very well, and although we were impatient with some of his

*The American Academy of Asian Studies.

> ways, I considered him a very fine person. His understanding of what life really is and what we are here for—I think he was really one of the elect, because he had no feeling or thought for himself; he only thought about things that were wrong in the world. He was very argumentative and very unpleasant about all of it, but nevertheless—and he saw a lot that people had a way of pooh-poohing—but he was right! He knew what he was talking about.[349]

Florence Leonard spoke of her time at the Academy when she met Sam. She had classes there with Spiegelberg, Chaudhuri, Watts, Hasagawa, Agarwal, and several with Landau, who taught North African Studies, including Islam. Florence and Sam met in Alan Watts's class:

> [It was] at the Academy of Asian Studies, which was under the auspices—at that time, it was the College of the Pacific, later on it became the University of the Pacific. They were giving graduate degrees for their classes . . .
>
> Very often after class we'd walk down to Van Ness and stop in at the Hippo* . . . and chew the fat about this and that, and that was how we became more acquainted . . .
>
> We had a lot in common, and Sam liked an audience and he knew a lot. He was interesting, and he showed qualities that I admired very much. He had a very high ideal of what people should be and was constantly remonstrating about what they weren't—mostly in the professorial class, and what Americans all thought about things who were not qualified to pass judgment . . .
>
> He always met with [rebuffs], I think this was a personality problem. He had a way of telling people, and he meant it awfully well, and he knew a lot, but as one of the professors said, "Sam is like an encyclopedia that someone has torn up and thrown in the wastepaper basket." Because he had such an enormous fund of knowledge but it didn't seem to be coordinated, so that he could give it out in a way in which other people grasped.[350]

Florence had this to say about Rom Landau and Sam:

> I tell you, first of all he didn't like Sam. Landau . . . was a brilliant man, but he was a snob, and little Sam was always dressed in peculiar ways. We used to go after him and tell him to put on something else . . . He

---

* Hippopotamus Hamburger.

> was beyond that . . . but not professor Landau who was a fuddy-duddy, and who made remarks, "No one shall come to my class without . . . a tie" and so forth . . ."And my classes start at 6:30, they do no start at 6:31" . . . Nobody cared for his books . . . [351]

Sam had many quarrels with Professor Landau, Florence said, because Sam made it clear that he himself was a Sufi. "Landau said, 'There is no such thing in America; there are no Sufis in America,' and Samuel was furious."[352]

Yvonne Childs also spoke of meeting Sam at the Academy:

> I had just come to the Academy in the fall of 1955 and it was a couple of days after I had gotten settled in that I was coming downstairs; there was a lecture that night and there were a lot of people gathered around, and I saw Sam. He was just whirling around, he was just spinning on the floor! I thought he was crazy. I was absolutely taken aback, intimidated, I thought he was a total madman![353]

Papa Ramdas had been recommended to Sam by Paul Reps in a letter because "He has what you need, love and laughter." Soon after receiving the letter Sam had a vision while gardening that Ramdas would be coming.* Now Papa Ramdas had arrived at the Academy with his entourage. Yvonne's husband, Crist Lovdjieff, had more to share about this time. He stated that Frederic Spiegelberg had prepared them for Ramdas's visit by telling them:

> We would see a marvelously childlike man who was very liberated, and very, very illuminated. I was struck at the time by several details. One, that the devotees distressed me . . . I asked the assistant Swami, the secretary, what rules should I assume in preparing the food. He began to give me these elaborate restrictions on meat and meat products and so on and so on. And the old man, himself, spoke up and said, "No, whatever Brahman provides." I knew immediately the distinction between the authentic spiritual liberation and the clutcher.
>
> The other was that the woman, Sophie Ginzburg, freaked out at Ramdas's appearance . . . in the building. Her own balance, in my mind,

---

*Pir Shabda Kahn recollects Sam quoting Ramdas saying in the vision, "In one year's time by land or sea I will come to thee." (Personal communication.)

> was always dubious. The relationship between Sophie Ginzburg and Sam Lewis was one of the classics, for me, in the Academy days . . . because I think she had the hots for him. He said repeatedly to me, "She is just Kundali," referring to Kundali from Parsifal, the seductress who thinks she can liberate you by taking you on her trip."
>
> Sam Lewis enjoyed Ramdas and felt quite elated . . . with this man on our premises. And the more fidgety and nervous and upset that Sophie became, the more joyous Sam Lewis got.[354]

Here is one of Ramdas's responses to the questions at the Academy that night:

> When Ramdas says joy he means *ananda.* It is joy that spontaneously flows out of Ramdas. But to become joy yourself and to experience joy, are two different things . . . Ramdas replied to a saint in India, that he "has become like the Ganga which having reached the ocean still flows towards it." His life is united with the infinite ocean of life—God—and still he seems to be going toward the ocean, because there is joy in going towards the ocean, and in remaining separate from God, as a child, to talk to God and serve and do everything in God's name . . . Ramdas is one with the divine parent and still he is the child of Ram. As child, he is enjoying the bliss of seeing God everywhere, serving in every way and knowing that he and the entire universe are one.[355]

Samuel later would visit Ramdas in India.

Crist also mentioned another memorable time. He described it as "an evening when Sam Lewis sat perfectly still, bolt upright, in that chair in the lecture room, for such a prolonged period. The fact was that I had no notion of what this was about, or whether he could even be talked to, and in all such extremities, I always deferred to Alan Watts, who was in charge and who was in the class, and certainly seemed to know a hell of a lot more about spiritual states than any of the rest of us, and he didn't bother at all!"[356]

Knowing Samuel Lewis's capacities, it is not difficult to answer Crist's question. Sam had entered *samadhi;* it certainly wouldn't be the first time. It is easy to picture him sitting in the lecture hall and demonstrating like Bodhidharma the experiential essence at the core of what the rest of the people were speculating about.

During 1953 a famous political leader and prominent Buddhist, Dr. Malalasekera of Ceylon came to the Academy to give a talk. Yvonne and Crist remembered it.

> At that time, Theresa Moises was there. She had had a lot of problems and they all doubted that she was Ceylonese, they thought that she was just some "nigger" from Cincinnati or New York . . . and that she was just creating a big disturbance. [Dr. Malalasekera] knew her, he knew her grandfather and he brought her a little bag of rubies and that blew everybody's mind. But this other thing that happened, is that he knew Sam . . .
>
> He knew Sam and that blew their minds, too, because those were the people there that were being fucked over, royally, by everybody. Then, when Dr. Malalasekera walks in and recognizes these two people, this is the anointing.[357]

In the big picture, it was a sign of what was to come after his travels, but it was just another bump in the road at the Academy. Samuel had already been in communication with Malalasekera, who was known by Samuel's close friend, the Buddhist teacher Phra Sumangalo.

In a letter to his friend Margaret Albanese in early 1955, Samuel was happy to write about at least one favorable experience at the Academy. "My thesis for the Academy of Asian Studies, 'The Integration of the Ancient and Modern in the Solution of India's Problems,' has been accepted by the instructor, Satya Agrawal, as not only a good paper but one which could be used by the government as their future policy."[358]

Saladin Paul Reps encouraged him further in December of that year:

> Dear Samuel,
>
> It happens I am just now in Tokyo and got your letter quickly. You have been in a rut some years and digging yourself in deeper. You need (as I have told you for some years) to get out of it. The best way is take a year leave, go slowly around the world, and, it seems best to me, to go [on] one's own rather than in a group. In Japan no one talks of God. You would come most to life it seems to me in Muslim lands. My plans are undetermined but I may return shortly to USA. Have just completed 84 articles poems stories on my Japanese life and they are to be published in Japanese as a book by a big publisher here, further opportunity for reaching the people.

> The time for Delhi is winter. The time for Kashmir is Spring or Fall. The time for Japan is not winter.[359]

A response from Sam pleased him and Reps wrote two weeks later:

> Dearest Samuel,
>
> Your letter has a lot of cheer in it, some things that have happened well for you I don't know what perhaps because you're starting to move move move.
>
> I never liked the name Paul, nor do I wish to appear affected before westerners who have big doubts and questions when they bump into the name Saladin.[360]

Samuel Lewis at this time had already begun work on what would become a masterpiece on Islam, the Crusades and the inner world, a poem that he titled "Saladin." Reps would decline the dedication to himself, saying Sam better embodied Saladin than he did. In Sam's poem he took on the persona of the Saladin of history he idealized, and he also received direct inward communications from Prophet Muhammad and other realized beings as this epic poem unveiled.

In January of 1955 Sam wrote to his fellow writer Margaret Albanese about the structure of the forthcoming poem:

> Well, I am ready to start "Saladin," which will be an epic poem for Egypt and I feel it in my bones that it will become an immortal work . . . **Theme:** "The sword is mightier than the pen." . . . [361]
>
> The first book has the sections of a. "The Sword," b. "The Addresses to the Crusaders," and c. "The Addresses to the Captives, etc." . . . The second book consists in Saladin's elevation to the heavens: His appearance before Sohrawardi Maktul whom he martyred and by whom he is initiated into the mysteries of the sword, and of mercy . . . His elevation into the six heavens . . . His final elevation before the *Arsh*-Throne of God and his instructions from or concerning (I do not know yet) the great Indian teachers [Sita and Ram, Sri Krishna], Moses, Jesus, and Mohammed who appears as the Seal of the Prophets. [362]

According to Sam it was Prophet Muhammad who dictated one section of the book to its poet Samuel Lewis. Sam had been guided to Muhammad through his own retreat in 1925, an attunement that was confirmed in an interview with Hazrat Inayat Khan. Sam continued:

> I am both greatly inspired at the moment and must be profoundly humble as I am daring to follow in the footsteps of Homer and Dante on the one hand, and the great Sufis Jami and Rumi on the other, with some strong literary influences from "The Thousand and One Nights." I do not know what form it will take. It comes as a "gangue" of rhapsodic prose which may be crystallized into poetry, prose and *Gathas* or remain as it is.[363]

This epic poem evolved over the next five years. Meanwhile Samuel continued to write and to prepare for what would be his significant journey abroad.

Rev. Robert Clifton/Phra Sumangalo

Dear Samuel,

May you be blest! May you be doubly blest! How exceedingly good it is to hear from you and to know that, despite adversities, you are keeping on with keeping on and have reached that beatific state (well, anyway, an almost beatific state) of being beyond the power of joy to excite or trouble to depress unduly. Years ago I talked on "Beyond joy and sorrow" at a mid-week meeting at S.F. Buddhist Temple. "Sammy" Lewis told me afterward to look up Isaiah 30–7 when I got home.*

Robert Clifton[364]

Robert Clifton was a well-known Buddhist living in Southeast Asia whose influence spread far beyond that region.† Samuel would often say that Saladin Reps and Clifton, also known as Phra Sumangalo, were his closest friends. The meeting Clifton mentioned in the epigraph above had happened twenty years before the date of the writing. In

* "For the Egyptians shall help in vain, and to no purpose; therefore have I cried concerning this. Their strength is to sit still." Isaiah 30:7 KJV.

† Robert Clifton/Phra Sumangalo founded the Western Buddhist Order in Laos as well as the Penang Buddhist Association and Youth Circle, a concept that spread rapidly to many other regions. He was given the honorary abbotship of the Singapore Monastery Ph Em Ssu and helped start several Buddhist magazines. His goodwill tours were often carried out with Penang Buddhist Association members. *Charisma in Buddhism* (available online, www.buddhanet.net/pdf_file/charisma6.pdf) dedicates several pages to Sumangalo's life history.

1953 Samuel got Clifton's mailing address from Alan Watts and renewed their ongoing relationship. The initial meeting Clifton referred to had a profound impact.

Clifton's letter quoted in the epigraph continued:

> The next day's mail brought me a poem you had written on the inspiration of the verse indicated. I still treasure it in my bulging scrapbook:
>
> *Not to affirm—nor yet deny*
> *To seek the truth and know the why,*
> *This is "Right Meditation!"*
> *It is not on earth nor in the sky,*
> *Only in silence lives the "I"*
> *There finding liberation.*
>
> I still think that both Sammy and Isaiah "had something"—and I use the said "something" quite frequently—when samsara gets a bit too much of a muchness for a physically weak boy in his early fifties.

Clifton also spoke of the irony that Alan Watts had provided Sam with his address: "I have never had the pleasant honor of meeting Alan Watts. I have met his charming wife and children and I have known his mother-in-law for some nineteen or twenty years. In fact I visited with her just a year ago today in N.Y.C. on my way home from Europe. She is in Japan now and may decide to stay there. Anyway, I am grateful to Watts for giving you my address. Possibly it's a case of 'The Lord moves in a mysterious way His wonders to perform.'" His letter to Sam went on:

> San Francisco is mostly a blur in my memory. I clearly recall some trivia of my stay there and am dependent on my diaries for most of the rest. Individuals are mostly blotted out. I remember you and about eight or nine other individuals (and I am so glad in at least one case!). A seventeen-day bout with amnesia erased portions of my life from memory's record in 1936. Probably there was an excellent reason for the erasure. I have made no strenuous attempts to change the situation. At the moment, I might even welcome a bit more erasing.
>
> My job is not an easy one and the patience of Job and the wisdom of Solomon are requisites for the task. I have not those qualifications. So . . . I'm "pinch-hitting" until a better man comes along . . . at which time I shall so gladly turn over to him my purple robes and equally purple worries, vexations, annoyances and sorrows. In fairness I may as well

add that there are joys, too. However, as an old-timer in The Dharma-Way, I know only too well that joy and sorrow are both woven of the same staples. Nevertheless, fewer aspirins seem to be needed with joy. I'm sure you understand.

Oddly enough, in connection with your statements concerning time and space . . . last week I wrote an article of sorts for *Western Buddhist* of London. I'll probably get my ears pinned back by numerous critics. We shall see.

You speak in your letter of "the coming to an end of years of frustration . . . ," etc. Samuel, my diaries tell me of your frustration. Apparently I saw it years ago in S.F. I may as well tell you that I, too, was frustrated. At long last I came to see that the barrier in front of me was self-erected . . .

I am so glad that things are in process of shaping up to fit in with your long-cherished aims. May the Oriental journey be a source of great spiritual exaltation to you. May I assist with letters of introduction in Japan and Formosa and a few to prominent Buddhists in India . . . including the Attorney General (I believe they call it "minister of law") Ambedkar, leader of the "untouchables"—the heads of Maha Bodhi Society . . . many contacts in Ceylon and a few in Burma* and Thailand? Command me.

Samuel, my fellow-pilgrim, you have hit the hammer squarely with the nail and I am in most complete agreement with your statements concerning the morass of modern "civilization" so called. Yes, the problems seem insuperable. They are like the simplest knot in "The Boy Scout Manual!" It is hellishly hard to teach because it is so simple. It gives nothing to the mind to work on . . . nothing to "sink the teeth into!"

Basically our world-problems are simple. We insist on making them complicated. That's the trouble with Zen. Practically everyone sees it as an intellectual system. Yet it is so obvious that an ever-working mind is a real hindrance to a Zennist. Peasants and simple artisans have a better chance of hearing the sound made by one hand clapping.

In London I was asked by Christmas Humphreys, "Who in the West has the grasp of Zen sufficient to teach it?" . . . to which I could reply only with another question: "What is there particularly to grasp?" . . . and he is still mystified by my response . . . despite his book on the subject. You and I both like biblical quotations so here's one more: "Of the making of many books there is no end . . . yet wisdom increaseth not."

*Now Myanmar.

Clifton saw clearly from the Zen perspective and he acknowledged Samuel's realization. He was also very keen on helping his friend achieve success in being of benefit to the world, a goal Sam deeply desired.

Clifton continued in this letter to give Sam encouragement:

> The task appointed you by Sufi Inayat Khan will be nobly carried out. I remember you well enough to be sure of that. You have the ability. That is good but it is not enough. Dedication is the other essential factor. You have that, too. May every blessing rest upon your efforts. This reminds me . . . do you think an introduction to an American faculty member of National University of Indonesia might be of help to you? It's yours for the asking.
>
> Regarding Dr. Malalasekera. He is a learned man. Too learned. I doubt not at all that you follow this thread of my thought. He is a good and great man and a most capable and inspiring organizer and promoter. Such men are needed today. **But**, he reminds me of the story told about a Zen patriarch who, on being told: "Surely, venerable sir, Engakuji must be the nearest place to Heaven?" made this reply: "Yes, and it is also the nearest place to earth." Dr. Malalasekera's learning has vaulted into the empyrean so often that he has well-nigh forgotten the necessity of keeping his feet planted on terra firma.
>
> Just, by way of keeping my own feet firmly terra-ed, I have cultivated a very natural ability to "swear a blue streak." Very unbecoming in a *sojo** but also very effective in handling certain situations. I seem to recall that some of the Zen masters of fame were also a bit irascible . . . probably as much of a pose as my own swearing and appearing to be a stern and "difficult" person. In confidence, I have had a spot of trouble with a certain "Friends of Buddhism" society in a certain city. I've tried sweet reasoning and cajoling and all that sort of honey and treacle. It didn't work.
>
> A few weeks ago I decided to "blow my top." I'm glad to report it worked beautifully. Now all is serene in the city of . . . apparently for fear "the terrible-tempered Clifton" will let go a barrage of verbal pyrotechnics again! Even honesty can be overdone.

It is interesting that Clifton references how he blew his top and how it worked beautifully in overcoming opposition. It should be noted that Samuel Lewis ultimately had success embodying the fierce loving

---

*Bishop.

manner of Fudo.* His facility in this very area of mastery would be acknowledged when he visited Japan. Years later in the late 1960s Sam would sometimes have an outburst at a meeting he was attending accompanied by a disciple or two. Immediately after speaking forcefully he would tell his student to feel his pulse and see that it was quite peaceful.

Sumangalo revealed more to Sam of his own vast travel itinerary for the future.

> Sometime in the course of the next twelve or fourteen months I must go to Germany. We now have a flourishing mission effort there and it is growing by almost unbelievable leaps and bounds. I shall probably revisit Paris and again inflict my rusty French on the long-suffering Parisian Buddhists. Fortunately I have no German. England, too, calls again . . . likewise Hawaii and Japan. However, I have no real need to visit the last two places and so shan't go.

Clifton finishes his letter to Samuel with:

> While the *kwancho*† of Soto Zen was here he asked me some searching questions such as a working man might ask on the Zen subject. Apparently he liked my replies as he asked me to write a manual or series of essays on the subject of Zen from the workman's point of view . . . couched in simple language. I agreed. I have thought of asking Alan Watts if he might care to wade through the opus after it is done . . . I request you to thank him for his kindly act in re-introducing us. Also mention, please, this matter of the manual. In fact, show him this excuse for a letter if you so desire. He may as well have a glimpse into the alleged working of my so-called mind.
>
> May Rabbi Ben Ezra be right where you are concerned. May it surely be true that for Samuel "the best is yet to be." May All Holy Powers regard you benevolently; may you come into perfect Enlightenment.

---

*Fudo is a manifestation of one of the acknowledged Buddhas. His role is to burn through ignorance, bringing the light of Being into the Hell worlds with the possibility of moving out into the God reality. Sam saw Fudo in himself and himself in Fudo. Whenever he was going to shout at a student he would always say first, "The most important thing is don't react." If you didn't react you felt a wave of good will coming along with the words.

†Priest.

Clifton/Sumangalo did not forget Sam's mission. He wrote a letter of encouragement in June of 1954, and he gave a possible time when the two could meet.

> Dear Friend Sammy,
>
> A Buddhist missioner's work is never done. I've just got "Bodhi Leaves" ready for the printer and now I can get at some few hundreds of letters that ought to have been answered long ago . . . There just aren't enough hours in the day and enough energy left in Grandfather Clifton. Not complaining . . . just stating a fact.
>
> How goes your projected Asiatic junket? I hope all impediments are now in the past and all is clear sailing for you. I can think of no one better qualified to profit by a sojourn in the East . . . close to the seats of the Advanced Ones. It will act as a downright tonic on me if you tell me you are now able to see your way clear to making the pilgrimage you have so long wished to make. May every blessing attend your right efforts . . . and I'm sure they **are right** efforts . . .
>
> This October I shall be in California prior to taking off for the Orient. I shall be in Hawaii, Japan, Malaya, Australia, Thailand, Burma, Ceylon and India and come home by way of our various branches in Europe. If you are still "stateside" I hope to be able to have a good get-together with you then.
>
> May all the Buddhas and Bodhisattvas be the light on your path. May you attain.[365]

Sumangalo wrote again six months later from Bangkok offering some data for Sam regarding Hindu teachings on the heavenly planes that he might want to use for the paper he was writing at the Academy:

> Sammy, if only I were home I think maybe I have a mass of notes on your subject and I recall that as for the divisions of man, *narakas, pretas, rakshas* and what have you and for how much? are listed differently from locale . . . thus one thing in Tibet and another in North India and something else in exoteric Buddhism of Siam and something else in what may permissibly be called "esoteric" Buddhism of Siam . . . and still other iconographies in Angkor Wat and at Borobudur and in half-forgotten temples in Cambodian jungles. Go ahead with your paper and state your case. If you don't prove you are right at least your critics will have one Hell of a time in establishing that you are wrong . . .

> Sincerely, Robert of Banglampoo
>
> Teaching at Royal Buddhist University and 2 colleges, lecturing and radioing and studying Thai and Pali and writing. Yet I'm not overworked—?[366]

In August of 1955 Samuel was finishing his time at the Academy, writing papers for his classes, and having some fun at the expense of the authorities. His letter to Clifton at that time gives a good example of his presence there.

> Being very active in the semantic movement, some of us attended a lecture by Prof. Anatol Rapoport on "Humanism vs. Religion." Now one who has been studying the recent trends in logic, logistics and science expected much from a man who has been in the forefront. Instead he spoke very, very rapidly: "**Niebuhr is unintelligible, therefore religion is unintelligible, therefore humanism!**" This, [from] a super-intellectual????
>
> The next week I played one of my tricks. Alan Watts was speaking on "Buddhism and Semantics." I told him that I was helping to pack the hall. There is a very blind [side] in this man, of which more below. Anyhow it was necessary to bring in twice as many chairs as they had put up and it was the second largest gathering ever held at the Academy. The largest was when Malalasekera gave his farewell a few years back. In the end I asked the question which won me the audience.
>
> Well that great man Malalasekera is here. He told us the plans for a Buddhistic encyclopedia.* I am all for him but on one point—I believe that Sanskrit should be used as the basic language. The conferences in Hawaii fell down because of the multi-ordinal translations. He gave the best expositions, but alas, he used Pali. In the end this is egotism and this subtle egotism is a bar from a complete victory. Still we enjoyed him very much and he wishes to send his regards and good-will to you. [367]

Sam went on in his critique of Watts:

> My paper for Alan should be completed (revised) [today]. It is on the subject of self-surrender in the various traditions. I have dealt him two awful blows. He has had some Zen experience. He uses this experience as the basis of his lectures, teachings and philosophy. But he rejects

* Malalasekera also asked Samuel to contribute to this work.

> **your** experiences because you ain't got no college degree. Rah! Rah! *an-atta.**
>
> Point 1. The word "self" does not appear in the Hebrew Bible. I have searched the scriptures diligently to find out where it came in. It got in through the window and not through the door. Neither in the Old Testament nor in the words of Jesus Christ is there anything to suggest "self." Now for a scholar who has steeped himself in Christianity on the one hand and in Orientals on the other, he ought to have found this out himself.
>
> Point 2. I have presented a **Taoism** which he will reject and call his "Taoism" "**Wu Wei-ism**" which has never had popular appeal.

Samuel then directs his focus to engage Clifton:

> Of more importance to you, I have recorded my own inner experiences when, following a Sufic technique, Buddha was substituted for Mohammed, as the **Perfect Man**. It resulted in the visiting and cleansing out of the lower planes first, then of the higher, the complete union with all creation and a state beyond that union which is in conformance with whatsoever has been written of it. No attempt is made to show this is the highest state. One can argue forever whether it was "gradual" or "sudden." But this I can state: to those I meet there is magnetism, vitality and positive-goodwill. They may reject "me" which is all right. But I never draw on the magnetism of others and I permit them to draw on me and it does not matter. There is a world of difference between a theoretic *ji-ji-mu-ge*† and the practical feeling (**simpatico**) for those you meet.

Phra Sumangalo could well have met with Samuel Lewis in San Francisco in the fall of 1954, and he most certainly met with him in San Francisco in 1962. Like Samuel, Clifton had worldwide goals. He was very active in his efforts throughout the world to share his wisdom with governments about practical ways in which they should respond to the challenges of the times. Clifton had tried to offer solutions to the U.S. in relation to Southeast Asia, but he was ultimately stonewalled in the U.S.

---

* *Anatta* or *An-atta* is the Buddhist doctrine that there is no such thing as an ego-self.

† *Ji ji mu ge* is the Zen teaching that there is no disconnection between events; "every thing is everything."

by Secretary of State John Foster Dulles, who was uncomfortable dealing with non-Christian countries and who was not receptive to those who had converted to Buddhism. However, bodhisattva-like events were in the future of these two close Buddhist friends, whose relationship flourished and continued to be an important part of Samuel's life.

Elliott's Schemes and the Last Days of Jacob Lewis

Sam's cousin Marilou Foster recounted in an interview that Elliott had inherited his mother's money and the house, while Samuel got nothing. Quotations in this section are drawn from her remembrance. [368]

> When Uncle Jake died the will was contested. Elliott went into court and contested the will . . . I know Samuel was involved in that because my grandfather [Harry Rosenthal] came down and one of them turned him against the other brother . . . According to Elliott, Samuel had subverted my grandfather.

Sam's uncle Harry Rosenthal already had had enough of Elliott's ways. He wrote Sam that he had correspondence from Elliott that confirmed a deceitful way Elliott had gotten lawyers to change Harriet's will simply on his say-so. Harry said Elliott bragged about his scheme and said he would come down to argue the point. Samuel's lawyer John Rockwell received the letters from Harry, who insisted as a condition that if Sam got a part of the estate from Harriet, Harry would receive the $1000 he had initially been promised.[369] Rockwell also advised Sam to minimize any communication with his brother. Regardless, Elliott prevailed.

Jacob Lewis was in a deteriorating condition in 1953. During the months until his death there was still no communication between Jacob and Harriet. However, during this period Jacob had regular meetings with Samuel, whose ways he had never understood but who he could now see was an honorable man. The two were able to reconcile. Jacob apologized for his past judgments and attitudes and promised Samuel that he would give him his gold watch, honoring 65 years of service at Levi Strauss. Elliott never agreed to the legitimacy of this gift, and the watch remained an item of unresolved conflict between Elliott and Samuel.

Marilou shared more information:

> When Uncle Jake first made out . . . his own will he left nothing to his wife Harriet Lewis, and of course under the law . . . there was no way that he could do this . . . He was forced because of the community property laws to leave one half of his estate to [her] . . . and he must not have . . . gone to his grave a happy man over that . . . When Uncle Jake died the will was contested. She felt she should have received the entire estate and not the community property . . . begrudgingly left by her husband, and also I think that Elliott was trying to make sure that Samuel didn't get anything.

In Marilou's view, Aunt Harriet's senility had already begun, and she was firmly in Elliott's hands.

Marilou summed up her position with a jagged splinter of remembrance: "This was one of the court cases that they had, and evidently when . . . [Harriet] got on the stand [she] stood there and announced that she renounced . . . [Samuel] publicly . . . Oh, it had to be just really pathos."

There were other memories about the house:

> When Aunt Hatty was here in the house and Uncle Jake wasn't here it was a fun house . . . As soon as five o'clock, or whatever time Uncle Jake came in, it was horrible, it was just really horrible. There was no affection shown between anyone. None of the sons showed any affection to their parents.

By the end of his life Jacob Lewis could see both his children much more clearly. As a result, Elliott chose to reevaluate his situation, and joined his mother in opposition to his father. He strategically proceeded to fully focus on strengthening his influence over his mother Harriet.

In reply to an observation that Sam sometimes would say Elliott was always telling lies about him, Marilou responded, "Elliott could not tell the truth where a lie would serve—that sums up Elliott as best as anything."

Elliott had gone into his father's business, and it didn't work out. Marilou commented that "It was always a financial disaster whenever Elliott did anything business-wise." She continued,

> When Uncle Jake died . . . Elliott had been running the thing before then. Mother was out here between '52 and '53 and Uncle Jake was very ill at that time. He had a heart condition, he had asthma since he had been a child, but he would still go to Levi-Strauss every day, and I think there were some times he couldn't drive and Elliott would drive him . . . Because of his father's physical limitations and because of the mental state that my aunt was going through at that time, [Elliott] was pretty much in control of whatever took place in this house, except for the fact that all monies were provided by his father . . .
>
> This really tells the best story about Elliott that I can think of. When he died [in 1970] I had to take care of all the arrangements. And as far as I was concerned he was still a Jew and he was going to have a Jewish funeral. And I went over to Sinai and had the arrangements made . . . Then I had four different people say that he'd already paid for his own coffin and funeral . . . He'd gone around telling people that he'd made his own arrangements so that I wouldn't be stuck with it. Which he hadn't—this to me personified the kind of lie that Elliott would do better than anything else.

After Jacob Lewis's death on April 4, 1953, the family drama would continue to play out. Sam still had to wait for money that would allow the trip he had held in front of himself for so long.

A Preview of Papa Ramdas

During this period Sam wrote a letter to Papa Ramdas enclosing a poem on Indian teachings. He got a reply from Ramdas written July 15th, 1955:

> Beloved Friend,
>
> It is joy to read your loving letter. You have told in it a lot of news . . . What is needed is a complete elimination of the individual sense. All the forces of our being shall merge in the universal Spirit or Consciousness. God is all in all. Call Him any way you like.
>
> Ramdas is very happy to know that the younger students liked Ramdas when he was in their midst. They are so earnest, good and loving. Really Ramdas spent a delightful time in San Francisco.

Don't you know that you are He? If you do not know then know it here and now. If you know, ever revel in the bliss of the Immortal.

Yours is a fine poem. You have the talent for writing poetry. You are steeped in Indian lore. [Your] thoughts are high and your heart is aglow with faith and love.

Ramdas remembers you. You saw him at the Academy of Asian Studies. Americans are so refreshingly frank, enthusiastic, active and kindly in nature. May God bless them.

Hearty love and blessings to you all. Ever your Self, Ramdas[370]

Samuel wrote again, and again got a reply:

Ramdas had duly received your loving letter of the 24th July. You are a great student of Hindu scriptures and you are having contacts with persons of spiritual experience. As such you are flowing along the current of Divine peace, love and joy. You are a great force for disseminating a message of Divine peace, love and joy. You are a great force for disseminating a message of Divine peace and harmony by your illuminating writings and compositions.

Smile is a reality. Cat is a myth. The eternal smile is revealed itself through the cat. While the former is real and permanent, the latter is unreal and transitory. Truth alone is.[371]

Samuel's trip abroad was drawing ever nearer.

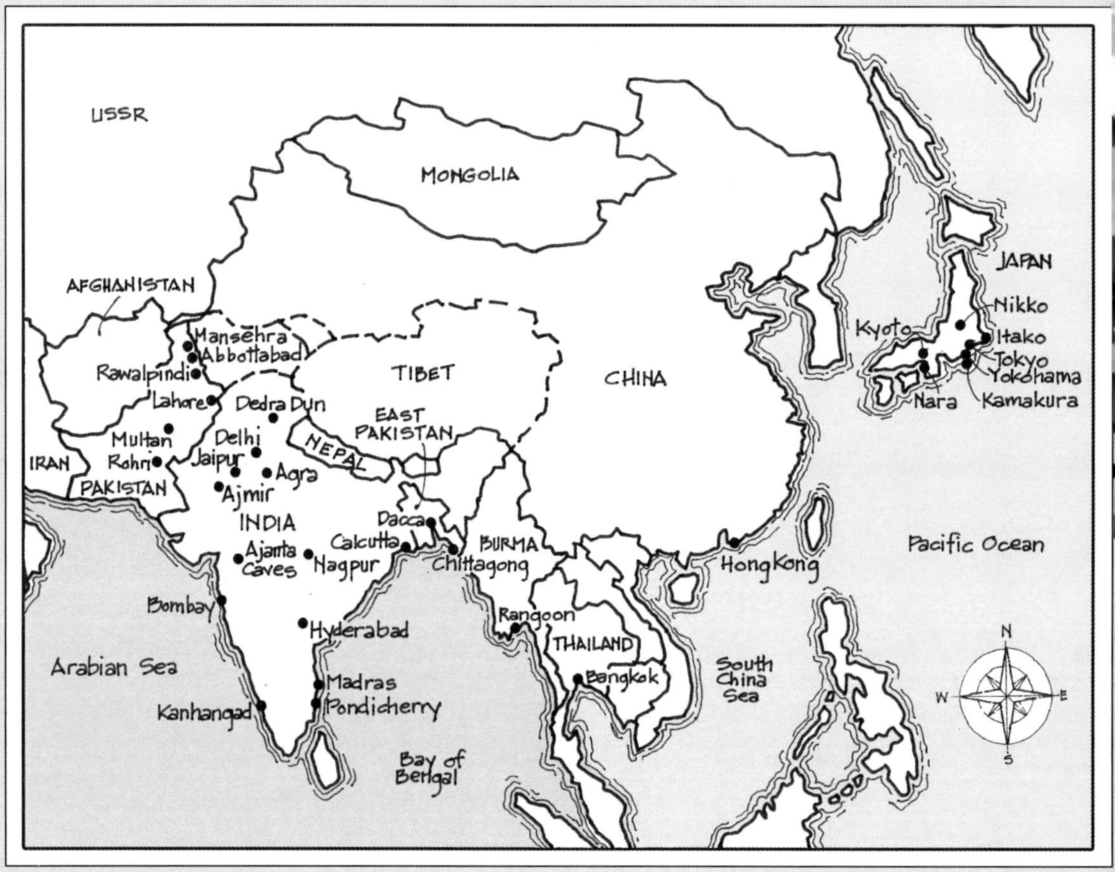

Sam's first trip abroad: May–December, 1956

CHAPTER 9

Buddhist Asia

Sam's Trip to Asia Begins

When you finally cash in on your inheritance, if you can then manage your own passage money, it is quite likely you could pick up your "keep" in Hawaii, Japan, Siam and Burma. Probably India, too, by talking to select groups and being house guest of various persons. The way of the Occidental in the Orient is not an easy one. As a monk, I am in a somewhat different situation. However, I am rapidly learning the language and that smoothes the way a lot.

ROBERT CLIFTON[372]

SAMUEL HAD DREAMED FOR YEARS OF TRAVELING ABROAD, but his financial status had prevented the journey. The 7½-month trip (May–December, 1956) would be a natural culmination of his years of study, the numerous contacts he had made stateside with visiting political and religious figures, and the encouragement he had received from close friends. Robert Clifton offered numerous contacts in Southeast Asia; Paul Reps saw Samuel flourishing in a Muslim country and had recommended Papa Ramdas to him, and Papa Ramdas himself had acknowledged Sam's broad knowledge of Hindu scriptures and his potential for spreading the Divine message.

In August of 1955 Samuel, still in San Francisco, wrote to Clifton,

> Talking about Buddhism in Korea. There is a split over the marriage of monks. It resembles the Catholic Church in the 11th Century. Practically I do not care. Malalasekera is married; Sokei-An married. My own view is that we have taken abstracted Buddhism without its Indian heritage and built upon it. This is all right, too, if we remember that we are purposely leaving something out.[373]

At the time of that writing, Sumangalo was in Thailand. Amid his busy schedule, he often saw Princess Poon Diskul. She was of the royal family and president of the World Buddhist Federation. Sam wrote his remembrance of her:

> When Princess Poon was here [in San Francisco] she argued a long time at me and then suddenly said, "What is your view?" When I started to reply she said: "That's my religion, too." No argument. Only love, compassion and good-will. I am the "Dennis-the-[menace]" to the philosophers. I look for either compassion or *prajna*.[374]

After this, Samuel got a letter, prompted by Clifton, from K. R. Patel, president of Penang Produce Company in Bangkok, who wrote, "My friend, the venerable Sumangalo, tells me nice things about you and your activities and interests. I am pleased to know of your interests in spiritual and literary matters."[375]

Sam explored ways he might develop some income to offset his travel expenses. Patel suggested Sam resell zircons in America, a product Patel's company produced. This venture never developed.

Patel offered additional guidance to Sam for his journey:

Sarvepalli Radhakrishnan

> You will do well to make contact with Prof. Radhakrishnan.* He is a genuine scholar and a truly great soul. I know him well. During the period of the provisional government of India I was a cabinet member (government in exile). At this time I came to know all those who are now in power and many who have dropped from sight or from life . . . including Bose . . . Should you ever be in Bangkok stop at 365 Siphya Road and make yourself known. I am in position to tell you who is who and to steer you clear of pitfalls that beset the friendless stranger.[376]

Shortly before his departure on what would prove to be a life-changing journey, Samuel received a letter from a Sufi representative, Viola Harris, in Cleveland. She wrote,

*Professor Sarvepalli Radhakrishnan later became Vice President and then President of India.

> I suppose [you've] heard about Vilayat.* Our small group here is very loyal. They now feel that we should have some sort of a nucleus here in the U.S.A. . . . It is time to try to get together with others who feel the same way . . .
>
> We feel that you perhaps feel as we do. We have $200 dollars in our treasury. We will send you that for your fare . . . I think it would be a good move for the Sufi Movement. You could be such a big help to all here . . . Well Samuel we will be awaiting your reply most anxiously.[377]

Samuel would address the nature of his relationship with Vilayat Khan, Inayat Khan's oldest son, years later, but at this point he was fully occupied with his immediate journey. He knew deeply that experiences from his travels would provide a fresh perspective on his spiritual work for the benefit of all.

Samuel's first destination was Japan. His ship, a freighter, arrived in Yokohama on May 15, 1956. Sam wrote that when he arrived everything seemed familiar, even though he was in a foreign country. He was immediately met by his friend Kiichi Okuda, originally from Japan, whom he knew well from Buddhist activities in San Francisco's Chinatown. Okuda accompanied Sam during many of his adventures in Japan, often as a guide.

They first traveled to Tokyo by train. The very next day, while in a bank, Sam ran into his old friend Kaoru Nakashima, who had been a vice consul in San Francisco and with whom he later spent time. In his diary he wrote that, overall, he had a feeling of being at home and of a strong Zen connection.

Sam's active energy and magnetism were enormous. Adding to that energy were his knowledge of the Japanese culture and his willingness to become involved with all types of people. His time in Japan was filled to the brim. It is easy to get lost in the numerous details in Sam's diary and other correspondence, but a partial listing of his activities—during his visit of only six weeks!—may help the reader get a feeling for the scope of his movements:

Agriculturally-related locations visited: Tokyo University of Agriculture, Chinzan-So royal garden, Imperial Gardens, Asakawa nursery,

---

*Vilayat had claimed the successorship of his father's Sufi lineage.

Chinzan-sō Garden in Tokyo, opened in 1877

Tokugawa Biological foundation, nurseries in Wayakama, gingko trees in Kamakura, Government Forest Experiment Station in Meguro, Tokyo.

Temples: Engaku-ji, Daitoku-ji temple, Kwannon Temple, Nishi-Hongwan-ji-Shinran Shonin celebration, Obaku Temple, Soji-ji, Mt. Takao Monastery, Seicho Movement, Temple of a Thousand Buddhas, the Kegon group, Hosso sect, Shingon, Shinto music and weddings, Horyu-ji.

Shrines: Tomb of Soyen Shaku, Kashima Shrine, Kasuga Shrine, Katori shrine.

Other experiences and visits: kabuki, tea ceremony, folk dances, music, mountains (e.g., Fuji), hot baths, restaurants, a hospital visit to see a friend, Friends of the World, Asia Foundation, Baron Nakashima, Pakistani Consulate, U.S. Embassy, Indian Consulate, Buddhist scholar Phillip Eidman, voluminous correspondence (including to James Michener, who had recently written about Japan), shopping for gifts for friends in the U.S., reading, singing, telling stories to and playing games with children, attending art exhibits, and exploring the possibility of sending stone lanterns to the U.S.

Connecting with the representative of Friends of the World was one of Sam's primary goals, and visiting agricultural and horticultural locations came naturally. He summed up aspects of his trip later:

> Most of the time Kiichi Okuda . . . has been with me. The rest of the time, James Kinoshita* has been with me, about which man I may have lots to say when I return—world understanding through the exchange of trees and seeds, pen-pals, etc. but always universal love and compassion. We have no weapon against love-and-compassion.[378]

Newspaper clipping; source unknown

Sam's plan involved supporting Kinoshita's approach to Harvard and connecting him with Professor Nelson. He wrote,

> This almost immediate contact followed by others seems to have no end to possibilities for the world, and for me. I also have my first two appointments with Americans today, one in the afternoon, one at night. (Time out for breakfast—been typing 2 hours already!)[379]
>
> The work with Kinoshita covers many facets and we seem to prepare to work together closely. The idea of an international tree-and-seed exchange and of building up the greenhouse, nursery, etc. at City College goes ahead. I mailed a cut-out from one of the papers on rose-growing in Japan. I also took out a membership for Harry Nelson in the "Friends of the World" for 1000Y which is slightly under $3. This will enable Harry and J.K to correspond and cooperate while I am off in other lands keeping separate contact with each.[380]

It was Kinoshita who introduced Sam to Baron Nakashima. Sam later wrote of Nakashima:

> [Horticulture] brought me in immediate contact with one Baron Nakashima, since deceased.
>
> I did not know that Nakashima was the "Pooh-Bah" of Japan, being the top *genro*†, the top lay Buddhist, the top Horticulturalist and the

---

* Kinoshita, chairman of the board of directors of Friends of the World, was Sam's main contact in Tokyo,

† Elder statesman.

> biggest political person in Japan. This was later substantiated on the visit of the former Prime Minister of Japan (Kishi) to San Francisco.
>
> This person* was tested in every respect in Japan and it might bring up a question to an anthropologist, whether there is any difference between social and mystical initiation, how far do they overlap, how far are they identical and how far are they totally different?[381]
>
> I have been received as perhaps no American has been received.[382]

Samuel had given the Baron some of his recent poetry, and the Baron in turn gave him an important document. Sam later reflected on this:

> On the last day of my visit to Japan I was honored by a great tea given by friends of the Emperor himself and a document also was placed in my hands. This document was an appeal to the Buddhist leaders of the world to unite culturally and also not to be entangled with the polities of nations who were determined to upset the economies and traditions based on spiritual philosophies.[383]

Samuel spent time in Kiichi Okuda's home village of Itako to see the countryside, visit shrines, dwell in a *ryokan* (inn) and write. He said, "If it rains, as is likely, I should be taking lessons in Japanese." [384] His account of his stay there shows again his ever-positive relationship with children and his easy familiarity with them.

> I am the only American in Itako, a village some miles to the North-east of Tokyo. It used to be known for its irises and its beautiful girls. It was the training-ground for many geisha . . . In fact, they are putting on an iris show and I shall probably air-mail a report to Harry Nelson, Greenhouse, City College . . .
>
> Today was spent with *les jeunes filles.* I was taken to the junior high school, English class, corresponding to the 9th grade. They made me honorable teacher. I heard many girls read and one boy. Then I told them to how to make money from knowing English. They liked me. While I was waiting for the VIP, I did an umbrella dance and started a take-off on George [M]. Cohan.
>
> Then I did in turn Italian, Irish, Scotch, and Spanish folk dances, topping with Russian and somewhat later adding Mexican. This broke the ice and they did for me some beautiful native folk dances.[385]

---

* Sam is referring to himself in the third person.

At the close of the class I sang for them, a song from the "Geisha," or rather the opening chorus, "Happy Japan." Good-will rush from stratosphere to ionosphere, or what have you. Everybody happy.[386]

Tomorrow I visit the Senior high.[387]

He mused about the situation of Buddhism in Japan.

When Robert [Clifton] gave me the notes of the 1934 (?) Pan-Pacific Conference I [considered Soto] my ideal at the moment although I know little of it. I see nothing to change that despite the warm welcomes elsewhere. Of course, psychologically I am close to Kegon and I think it will fulfill the needs of philosophers and scientists . . . I am a realizationist both in science and mysticism and I am being confirmed in this all the time.

I still stand opposed to metaphysics. Both Ferukawa and Uchida warned against this years ago but in the U.S. metaphysics is the fad although hiding under other names, and speculation is damned by those who do not know anything else but how to speculate. That is why both Suzuki and Takagusu have been received in Japan with a mixture of admiration, criticism and dismay.

Everywhere the Japanese bow to Kwannon but the lecturers on "Buddhism" have their own ideas which have nothing to do with history or social institutions . . . How near are they to satori? . . . The whole thing makes me want to see Robert soon, and I may push my departure date forward.[388]

However, Samuel had no problem at the personal level. He wrote:

Actually I seem to have made a hit all over although I have not been trying. A stranger is under observation. Accepting bowing, smiling, chop sticks, Japanese foods, and Japanese religion cuts down the barriers. Then when they hear me offer my explanations of ikebana and Buddhism there are no barriers at all. Besides my two closest men friends, Paul Reps and Robert Clifton, have been accepted in Japan. And so it goes.[389]

In a letter to Dean Parrish at UCLA in December, 1964, Sam reflected on his trip:

When I reached Japan I was amazed to:

(a) Be admitted immediately into Zen monasteries—no waiting, ever. (b) Satori experiences. (c) Visits to the Royal Cemetery, ashes of Lord Buddha, and Shingi Shingon esoteric temple on Mt. Takao. (d) Guest of honor at the Imperial Gardens and Imperial Botanical Gardens. On the last day in Japan I was given teas in turn by the Ambassador of Pakistan . . . the colleagues of his Imperial Majesty [and] the Japanese Travel Bureau.[390]

Some of these events in Japan deserve detailed treatment.

Meeting Rinzai Zen Master Furukawa Again

The old Roshi [Furukawa] was a "typical" Rinzai-Zen Master. He had been stern, he had been harsh, he had been cruel. Stories circulated about him. He had become the symbol of those unbending teachers of old who seemed to know how to beat and browbeat their disciples; only in the end some disciples did come up with the right answers.

Of course, the picture is not the man. I believe the Roshi was following in the line of Fudo Bosatsu, the Bodhisattva of stern but wise counsel. The true Buddhist has no ego and a description does not reveal much. We had known him in San Francisco. He had taught us much about the historical Buddha and his place in Zen.

SAMUEL LEWIS[391]

Sam's trip with Okuda-san to Kamakura turned out to be especially meaningful. He described it in his diary:

Daibutsu ("giant Buddha") in Kamakura

Kamakura . . . has been a capital of Japan; it was even more a cultural center. Today people go to visit Hachiman Shrine and the famous Daibutsu. [Apart] from this, in Kamakura our main purpose was to call at the Rinzai Engakuji Temple. This place has had an important role in history. It is even more important to Americans. The tomb of the teacher of Shaku Soyen (who first introduced real Zen to us)* is there. It also has the home of Prof. Daisetz Suzuki.

When we arrived at the gate we were asked for credentials. We told the attendant that we had once known and practiced Zen under Roshi Furukawa. "Oh, he is still alive." "Can we see him?" "It is impossible. He is nearing

*Shaku Soyen introduced Zen at the 1893 World Parliament of Religions in Chicago.

ninety and has gone into seclusion for the remainder of his life; he sees no one." "Will you take him our cards?" "Yes." Then Okuda-san and I gave the attendant our personal cards.

We did not wait long. We soon heard the clackety-clack of geta, Japanese shoes. The next thing, the gate opened and with surprise we all saw the smiling face of the venerable Roshi who beckoned us in. We do not know who was more astonished, the attendants, gardeners or ourselves—everyone stood gawking . . .

It was neither the harsh teacher nor the student of history that we met at Kamakura. Here was a boy long hospitalized, visited by a couple of playmates. Here was an old man being rejuvenated. We were children, but children of eternity. He laughed and chattered and showed nothing but joy and hospitality and love. We were honored with ceremonial tea and dainties. This was nothing like the Hindu *prasad,** except there was the spirit of togetherness.

One leaves him, reminding our friends, the general semanticists, that a map is not a territory; a picture is not a person; and perhaps the place to learn about Zen is from Zen teachers.

After that the old Roshi conducted us to another building where he introduced us to Sogen Asahina, his younger successor who now functions as Abbot at Engakuji.

If Furukawa-san represents Fudo, guiding-wisdom-love, then Asahina may be said to represent [*karuna*], universal compassion, personalized in the bodhisattvas Kwannon and Manjusri. We thus have in Zen, and in much of Mahayana, the three fundamentals of *dhyana* (meditation), *prajna* (insight) and *karuna* (compassion). Given two of them the third may come naturally.

Roshi Furukawa had been very stern on one point: no speculation. This teaching, indeed, had been offered before him and after him by Oriental gentlemen who had submitted to disciplines . . . We need, I believe, meditation, insight, and compassion though these virtues may not be confined to Buddhism.[392]

One of the abbots Sam met gave a description of Fudo, and Sam fully identified with it:

Fudo is the Bodhisattva of Compassion; he represents the masculine to counterbalance the feminine aspects which [appear] in Kwannon. Fudo

* Sacred offering of food.

> therefore leans toward Wisdom and Kwannon toward Mercy without either of them departing from love . . . [393]
>
> The speculative philosophers of the West have taken refuge in the traditional . . . stories which stem for the most part from China. It is very difficult to express certain types of experience in ordinary language . . . When I later visited a Soto Zen Teacher and he asked me about Asahina I replied: "When the peach was nearly ripe, the farmer did not have to shake the tree."[394]

Samuel spoke in a way a Zen teacher would understand. Then he remembered Nyogen Senzaki.

> Old Senzaki often quoted from Abdul Baha: "People of the world, you are as branches of the tree and leaves of the branch." This is a refreshing representation of the words of Jesus, "I am the vine and you are the branches thereof." The Whitsuntide experience, or the full communion at its highest level, brings about the realization of brotherhood and togetherness. This is for all of us; nothing and nobody may be excluded. But mostly we do not realize it.
>
> In another sense, in the presence of Asahina both my brother Okuda-san and I passed through "The Gateless Gate" with a realization that was true and lasting. Less experienced people are always dogmatic concerning that which they have not yet touched. When Buddha was alive multitudes became *arhats* just by coming into his presence. And, my friends, Truth is eternal and unconditioned.
>
> Roshi Asahina has published a little pamphlet called "Zen." It offers his suggestions for meditating: how to adopt the body to a suitable posture, and how to deal with the mind. He does not separate meditation, insight, and compassion. They are as one, to him.
>
> Americans and Europeans need to learn that meditation need not be a dry practice. It is not a quasi-muscular exercise to control something we call "mind." It is the door to grandeur; nay, it is the grandeur itself. There is a silence which is not our silence; which is not [mere] cessation of noise and emotion and run-away thoughts; which is all-pervading, illuminating, complete.
>
> Asahina has only the greatest esteem for Jesus Christ. He has not only written so, but this was particularly emphasized in our visit. To him there was no essential difference between Jesus and Buddha. Both were examples of perfection, of compassion, of wisdom. Complete surrender

> might bring this knowledge to us; anything else might hold us short of the mark . . .
>
> After our sublime communion meditation, the Roshi performed Tea Ceremony. This was a high honor. Then he had his attendant show us around the rear compound. We were told few visitors are ever permitted to enter but I am pretty sure L. Adams Beck has been there—from some descriptions in her books.
>
> The attendant told us that he was a college graduate. Most of the monks in training have already passed courses in the history of Buddhism, in art and philosophy. The two outstanding factors in their lives are meditation and hard work. You won't read much about the hard work in some books supposedly related to "Zen." If we understand "oneness" the work and the meditating coalesce.
>
> The attendant described the buildings, explained the architecture and woodcraft, and details in the habits of the monks. He then took us to a grotto which holds the tomb of the teacher of Shaku Soyen . . . Our indebtedness to this man has become overshadowed by either derivative or speculative writings.
>
> Before we left we were shown the actual entrance gate and given the details as to how applicants enter monasteries, and are tested thereupon. After the attendant bade us *sayonara* I turned to Kiichi Okuda and said: "This was an omen." "What is an omen?" "It is a sign of things that are to come, that will happen." I spoke better than I knew.[395]

Sam saw doors opening to him that were said to be closed. Not only was he granted entrance, but treated with honor and respect in recognition of his degree of realization. He deeply needed this affirmation of his realization from those who could speak directly from experience.

> Okuda-san was with me when we visited the Daibutsu Temple at Nara, and all over Kyoto and again at the Soto Temple of Tsurumi. He was not with me at the Royal Cemetery or before the Stupa for the Ashes of the Buddha; but he again was when we entered the Royal Grounds—the first humble citizens in history to be granted this honor . . .
>
> Though to the world I may be neither "Zen" nor "Buddhist" it is one thing as a matter of name, it is another as a matter of experience. In unity-totality differences do not persist.[396]

Sokei-an and Ruth Sasaki

In Kyoto Samuel had good reason to find and meet with Ruth Sasaki, wife of his Zen teacher Sokei-an. He had never reported to anyone what he had learned from Sokei-an, and his encounters with the Roshis at the temple would make this meeting all the more relevant.

Sam and Kiichi Okuda visited Ruth Sasaki. Upon their arrival, Mrs. Sasaki immediately launched into what most interested her: What had Samuel learned from Sokei-an? Samuel had waited a long time for this moment. He told her how his Zen eye had received the transmission from Sokei-an when Sokei-an had admitted to a questioner that he could see into the future. Sam said that he saw the whole rise and fall of Hitler before Hitler rose, the invasion of China by Japan, and more. After that transmission he found that all the scriptures of the world were now as open books to him, from which he could feel a stream of light flowing. Samuel documented this opening in his diaries and later in his text "Incense from Roshis."

Mrs. Sasaki's own degree of realization was recognized by Samuel's companion, Kiichi Okuda. Sam wrote, "KO places Ruth Sasaki in the same class as Abbot Asahina, which is to say, among the realized souls. I see no reason to change such a stand."[397] Samuel also later wrote, "Mrs. Sasaki is, to me and others, a true Bodhisattva."[398]

Samuel and Mr. Okuda went from Ruth's to the Temple of a Thousand Buddhas and to the Bo tree in an area closed to tourists.* He wrote, "I have within me a national epic, 'The Ascent of Mount Fuji' and several papers which may go first to Baron Nakashima . . . I now feel that 'secret' of my life is coming out."

In a diary entry to Sumangalo, Sam wrote:

---

*This tree commemorates the fig tree in India under which the Buddha sat when he attained enlightenment.

The welcome by the children has been the same and by the few peasants and peers I have met—but I have met them and had heart-to-heart talks at all levels . . .

I have seen Kwannon staring out of the eyes of millions of women. I see all the longing, hope, sadness and futility, deep passion and compassion, and these smothered by a strange combination of total exploitation and masterful spirituality which does not seem to belong to this world. The conversations with leaders have been at the highest level with requests to carry messages to other countries, or with introductions. Honganji and Zen, Kegon and Nichirin have treated me as a friend.[399]

Sam was preparing to travel and had concerns:

Unfortunately at this date, 6/14 I have heard neither from Hong Kong or Thailand and if I do not hear soon will go to Thailand Embassy for advice.

This becomes important because Baron Nakashima wants me to call on the P.M. of Thailand with his ideas; also Radhakrishnan, to whom I must write. We discussed, all rather melanged, Buddhism, Friends of the World, and Universal-Love. My later discussions with the Baron [showed in him] an anti-Christian feeling and I have proposed that instead of his Buddhist-Confucian front he work with all the Bandung nations. So far as Christianity is concerned, I defend Christ but see no room for any "God" which excludes trees, flowers, mountains, atoms and light. It is not Christianity that is to be feared but ignorance, and ignorance goes by enlightenment.[400]

Letters finally arrived from Hong Kong and Sam made his plane reservations, departing from Japan on June 30, 1956. A farewell letter to Kinoshita showed his gratitude and ever-present desire to be of benefit to others:

I have seen aspects of Japan which I have longed to see for many years. That is very fine. But what I would like to emphasize is that more Americans may also like to see some of those things, especially those Americans, and many other non-Japanese who may be interested either in the activities of the Friends of the World, or in coming to Japan.[401]

Sam had arrived in Japan on a freighter and commented to Kinoshita on the literature given to tourists upon arrival. The brochures highlighted luxury goods, steaks, cocktails and Christianity—widely available in other parts of the world and thus not a unique attraction in Japan. He observed that those who had money to spend said they would go to Hong Kong. Sam went on to provide an example of the broader interests of those with money who could ultimately benefit Japan's economy.

> I met one of them here and asked if she wanted to purchase a stone lantern. She said, "yes." I am making arrangements for her. She will buy it and ask her friends to buy them. This will build up business. She would like to have visited temples. She would have spent money at these places too, and perhaps even contributed to their upkeep.
>
> The stone lantern business can easily be established and there are other businesses which can at the same time increase good-will and bring needed dollars to Japan.[402]

Sam ended his letter to Kinoshita: "I am going to present your whole program to Harvard University and seek a tour of students of that famed institution to your land—to the real Japan, and not the luxury goods, steak, cocktail and church false front."[403]

He followed up the next day with another diary entry.

> Becoming a sort of Walt Whitman, or as I laughingly call it, Lafcadio Hearn #2* I have seen in a little over a month what many tourists do not see in two years . . . I took this nation to heart and it took me to heart.[404]

On to Hong Kong, Thailand, and Burma

> *Religion and devotion are not elaborate forms of metaphysics without beginning and end. The devotion of the heart, the expression of calm compassion, the extension of love, the actual growth of wisdom which is reflected in one's daily deeds—these matter.*
>
> SAMUEL LEWIS[405]

Samuel went to Hong Kong from Japan. It was a brief stay.

---

* Sam's encyclopedic knowledge led him to identify with Hearn, an American writer, who became a naturalized Japanese citizen.

God has been with me and my health has been astonishingly good. My plans now are to go to Thailand, Burma, (transit visa), Dacca,* and then Simla, skipping over the Indian cities until the weather is better. According to the information book June is the hottest month in India. I have also been told by friends it begins to be much nicer by the end of July.[406]

Hong Kong, 1955

Sam's playful and humorous side surfaced immediately in Hong Kong in several postcards he wrote soon after arrival to the San Francisco Chronicle humor columnist Stanton Delaplane:

June 28, 1956

Good-bye Marin, Farewell Maranouchi, git along little doggies, I'm going to Hong Kong, and hello, Mr. Calabash, wherever you are . . .

Well I've been checking upon "The Geisha" and "Happy Japan" and so far as I know it is all true.

June 30, 1956

It all started innocently enough. My host here is an in-law of close friends in marvelous Marin. The San Rafael *Journal-Independent* has been giving me publicity. So Fred decided I should be a guest of the press club here. Thus I began preparing an essay:

Hong Kong is a British Colony. It is not English—good heavens, no! It is largely Chinese. The loyal subjects of the Crown are divided into three groups: (a) Veddy; (b) Semi-veddy; (c) Right Joes—who are in the vast majority. The Veddy people are few in number and won't let anybody join them until one departs from this land by any and all means.[407]

On the agricultural front, he wrote to a Mr. Winter before leaving Japan:

---

*Now Dhaka.

When I went to the Embassy of [Pakistan] in Japan—more to test where I really stood after being so well received by the Japanese, I presented the following:

a. Introduction of trees for swamp drainage, and for arid areas.
b. Introduction of economically valuable cacti in desert regions.
c. Introduction of fertilizers which will not leach out with rains and will cooperate with micro-organisms (this may invoke enmity of certain large businesses and the good-will of others).
d. Methods of getting fresh water from the ocean at low cost.
e. Introduction of Algae as a source of low-cost protein with natural minerals and vitamins, obviating the need of medicinal expenses to supplement foods.
f. Respectful visits to shrines and holy places of any and all faiths. First, I was refused audience on the grounds I was too important (a new one for me). Then, after 1½ hours, I was asked to terminate the interview and meet the ambassador.[408]

His diary entries on horticulture to Professor Harry Nelson were numerous and detailed. Here is an example of the norm:

Visit to Tokugawa Biological Foundation

Mr. Kinoshita and I arrived at this Station at about 10:00 A.M. June 26 and stayed 1½ hours as the guests of Dr. Tamiya, the Director. He has been in the United States and speaks a good English, writes an excellent Latin—his basic writings are in Latin, not in English or Japanese—and "looks like a scientist." There was no language problem here, except the need for us to translate Latin for Mr. K.

The basic purpose of this laboratory is to study from both the scientific and economical points of view the adaptation of the Algae, Chlorella, for food. Ford Foundation put up $300,000 in 1954 and the Japanese Government an equal amount . . .

The experiments vary. There were a number of tanks using self-rotary pipe, or a series, and the water is charged with CO2. Much depends on the availability of Carbon Dioxide and sunlight . . . There are many variations in feeding . . . I called attention to the work being done on Microbiology and its value in plant feeding and questioned the use of inorganic fertilizers. They have come to the same conclusion—even for Algae, the inorganics are "dead," and are really forcing rather than feeding.[409]

At this stage of the journey Sam felt at ease with what was evolving. His approach of seeking new fields for international friendship was being consistently confirmed. While in Hong Kong he met with the U.S. Consul General, Mr. Rice, and provided him with a brief on the purpose of an all-Asian meeting, something in which the Consul expressed interest. He also called on the Burmese Consul-General and the Australian Trade representative.

About Hong Kong he wrote, "I have no troubles—none so far—in pushing my ideas. Had a nice interview with a Pakistani merchant today. There are lots of Pakistanis here, or Shia Muslims, who are largely illiterate or at least do not speak either English or Chinese. This merchant used several languages."[410]

Samuel Lewis would be just as happy and actively outgoing with the merchant as with the diplomat. While in Kowloon, he spent a "glorious afternoon" with Dr. Leung Tit Seng and had in-depth discussions on the physical body, breath, philosophy, religion, and science. Sam said that this Oriental physician was in the same class as the Buddhist Abbots he had met in Japan. An excerpt from his diary shows the depth of his feeling from this collaboration.

> **The Human Body:** He proposed two points which are entirely out of accord with present day Western teaching: a) The human body and human personality is essentially a cosmos, b) There is something more fundamental than even blood which he says roughly speaking means "[*sirr*]"* or "breath" and yet is not either . . . I found absolutely nothing which was essentially different from Kabbalah and the highest aspects of Sufism and Hindu teachings—which things have seldom or ever been given in the Western world and which I am now prepared to shout or ram down the throats of others, if it helps bring East and West together.[411]

Sam's conscientious report on his journey abroad was detailed in multiple categories over numerous pages in his diary, as were his letters from Japan to his horticultural teacher Harry Nelson and others.†

---

* *Sirr* is for Sufis the secret heart of hearts.

† Much of this voluminous and fascinating written material can be read online in the Murshid Sam Archives.

On July 2, shortly before departure from Hong Kong, Sam wrote another humorous postcard to Delaplane:

> So far there are five kinds of people I have met. The Chinese beg to grow rich and spend more money. The Hindus try to grow rich and spend less money. The Pakistanis try to grow rich. The Americans who damn the Washington giveaways rush over each other pall-mall to do their own private giveaways to help these folks out. Every counter a bargain counter. The British look on suavely and collect the rent.[412]

He also made diary entries to his friend Bryn Beorse:

> I am taking to India information about a new vegetable-protein food which can be obtained at comparatively low cost and little space with all the vitamins and minerals necessary. I have written to Radhakrishnan.[413]
>
> I stayed one day in Burma; I was not there one hour before I met a cabinet minister who wanted to send me to another cabinet minister. But I had come for another purpose. All the things of my life are clearing.[414]

On July 8th Sam went to Bangkok, Thailand. Soon he wrote to Rudolph Schaeffer at the Schaeffer School of Design:

> Here I am in the land of the "free" or Thai. I arrived after comedy of errors, but somehow or other located the house of Princess Poon. She was not at home but presiding over a big Buddhist meeting. The Vice-President greeted me and to my surprise I learn that my very dear friend, Robert Clifton—now Bhikku Sumangalo, was in a house nearby (monastery). We met and spent 2 hours together and then I was directed to my friend K. Patel at this address . . .
>
> Patel seems to know everybody in Southeast Asia and could be of greatest assistance to the United States. Actually all power is in the hands of the monks. I met the chief Abbot through him and found that he is the Chief Abbot's chief lay assistant. So I can meet anybody in Burma or Thailand.[415]

Sumangalo drove Sam to Patel's home; Patel was happy to host him and it saved Sam money. In general, Sam found the Thai people much more relaxed and less active than the Japanese or Chinese. He deeply respected Princess Poon of Thailand and wrote about their interaction in his diary.

> Yesterday I was with Princess Poon about 2½ hours . . . a good deal of this at the National Museum . . . Both there and while with the senior Monk of the Chief Abbot, while they both extended all kindness, they walked too fast for [me] . . .
>
> About everything the former king collected was saved for public conservation. The only thing official is the throne and the [Princess] showed me the different gradients of the throne—for business, pleasure, rest, and devotion.
>
> Thai painting is more chemical than esthetic and also very exact mathematically. I wonder at the patience and detail. I am still all but stunned by their ability in metals . . .
>
> When I mentioned my own criticism of certain intellectuals, like D.T. Suzuki and Takagusu in the U.S. I was all but thrown on my ear, only to hear these same people criticized in Japan. [When] I told Princess Poon I had done this she all but embraced me . . . I have met so many leaders now, wise men, realized people, and they all tend toward universality and the experience of cosmic illumination. Some are engrossed in deep translations and interpretations, and some in esthetic movements. But there is no real difference.
>
> There is a coming together of hearts which neither politicians nor Roerichs can understand. My host, K. Patel, understands, and he is one of the leaders. Neither materialistic Russia nor materialistic America will dominate the world. But the United States has to make some small simple changes, while Russia must actually change . . .
>
> **If the United States wishes to further either capitalism [or] democracy in the Orient she must stop supporting Christian missionary movements.** It is that simple.
>
> However, the U.S. is full of Professors-Suez-Canals who think they link the East and West and whose influence does not extend beyond their campus and not always there. I tell you, Rudolph, if you admire a single Buddha figure here it goes as far as if you have read all the Pali Scriptures.[416]

During this short visit to Thailand Sam visited the Mahatato Temple, which he described in a letter to friends:

What started out as a personal venture is no longer one. To run into complexities is a part of life and I am compelled to explain them in order for you and others to understand what I am trying to do. The first complexity concerns those who, because of some intelligent position, are trying to place themselves in public . . . as religions leaders and are not. They may be respected and respectful; they may know many sutras. They may be even [have] had a little—a little but not much—discipline in life. Their efforts to spread personal philosophies as "Oriental Culture" are deeply resented in the Orient. I felt this was so and it was naturally supposed to be a personal opinion. Alas, I have found the resentment extreme, [and] even terrible.

Now today I went to Mahatato Temple where people come from long distances to practice *dhyana.* It is a *samadhi-dhyana.* I don't care what books say, I don't care what professors say, I don't care what so called authorities say. I have seen it and when I attempted to express my deepest appreciation of it, the Abbot smiled and said it was not necessary . . .

I have found the temples clear and not only clear but with marble floors so it is actually a relief to take off one's shoes . . . The walls have scenes either from the life of Lord Buddha or [from] the Jatika [tales] . . . There are Chinese influences in Thai art, and here, the counter-influences of Thai art in the Chinese temples.

Bhikkus seem either to smile or scowl and my bet is that the smiling ones are the realized ones. When I saw a boy go into the *samadhi-dhyana* and the monk first explained why and how the boy was strong and I tested it, I also realized more fully the source of my own strength. There is more attention to breath than text-books suppose. I hope you will let me lecture on this subject. I have gone about 10,000 times further [than] some people who are qualified to speak—within the confines of the United States. Here it is very easy: either you know, or you do not know . . .

I shall learn tonight about the theory of Chinese Buddhism here which is very strong. But I understand it is still stronger in Singapore and Kuala Lumpur, and it has not been studied by Western investigators. I am hoping to convey your message of good-will to the Chinese here . . . They are the brains and brawn to Thailand. But it seems that the morale of the Chinese is in almost every way superior to the Thai. Their being in Buddhist country has encouraged them.

There are both artistic and cultural exchanges here. Most Thai, though Hinayana, are not [hidebound]. There are two divisions, one democratic one conservative. The latter have been in control in Burma and Ceylon. After what I have seen of the meditating, I am satisfied Hinayana and Mahayana* may come closer together. My friend, Mr. Kotani, head of the Japanese section of I.B.A., is also somewhere around . . .

Two people have assured me that Buddhism is also growing in mainland China. Christianity is not forbidden; only foreign missionaries are not allowed. The churches are well attended but the temples are increasing more. There is some feeling that Chinese traditions should be preserved. There is even greater feeling that Russia actually fears the Chinese but will goad them to action in Indo-China and Korea to play the United States and China off against each other. I am afraid this is also the view of some rather powerful politicians in the States.[417]

The next day Sam described another temple visit:

The next visit was one of the high points of my life. It was to the Annamese Temple which is called Wat Samanamboriharn . . . I was told that these people have no use for Americans and one would be unwelcome. I experienced no such difficulty . . .

On entering, I pointed to a scroll on the wall (rough outline painting). I said "That is Tamo.†" It was correct . . . There were many kinds of Buddhas there including the Burmese type . . .

I was told that the Abbot, Bao-rung, was an illuminated soul. I must say that he looked very much like Roshi Asahina in Japan . . . The chief difference is that Bao-rung gives up all his time to help humanity. He was trying to heal people. He seems to understand the nervous system and prods the vital spots with an instrument which seems pointed but did not puncture any tissues. It was like a sort of "chiropractic" on finer bodies, based on the physiology of the traditional Chinese system‡ . . .

This temple was not only used for healing, but the activity of the Abbot also helps break down the lines between Hinayana and Mahayana in practice.[418]

---

*Hinayana and Mahayana are major branches of Buddhism.

†Tamo is the Chinese name for Bodhidharma, the Indian monk credited with bringing Buddhism to China.

‡Possibly what would today be known as acupressure.

Buddhism and World Concerns in Southeast Asia

I represent the opposition of reality to realism. I represent views based on actual historical and cultural knowledge against superficialities. I represent direct observation, as in science, against indirect methods. The rise of Buddhism, Confucianism, etc. will not be reported [by the press] . . . And our confounded trust in super-power with the superficial claims to religious beliefs will cause us to be distrusted even by some of the most anti-communistic groups in the world.

SAMUEL LEWIS[419]

Sam's focus was directed to the world situation of the Buddhist countries, including the political complications. His various suggestions were in line with his witnessing of events:

> Since Stoddard wrote "The Rising Tide of Color," there has been an undercurrent in Asia of "Asia for the Asiatics." No matter what appears on the surface, it is my belief that underneath the Bandung nations* will support Japan and take every advantage of the American-Russian impasse to see that both are gradually put in their places . . .
>
> As I see it today, both Russia and the U.S. have stuck out their necks; both are imperialists; both are working in their own ways for a kind of white supremacy which both will deny, and both contain large sections of people who will be more against the Africaans (Boers) than the British or Hindus are. In other words, that strange psychology which gave us prohibition and liquor still operates.[420]

As Sam's travels progressed he developed numerous friendships, and spiritual, political, religious, horticultural, and intellectual opportunities continued to unfold. He also had time to write another of his postcards to Delaplane, in which he deftly and humorously described life based on his own direct experience:

> Here I am in the land of the Thai which means free. And if any people have gotten tangled in their alliances it is the "free." You get feudalism, capitalism, democracy, and everything all mixed up. And I don't think anybody cares. If the politicians are busy, the people are at the cinema . . .

---

*Sam refers here to the countries that participated in the first large-scale Asian-African Conference, held in Bandung, Indonesia, 1955.

Phra Pathom Chedi stupa at Nakhon Pathom

> This night life is not so lively as in Tokyo or Hong Kong. But neither is the day life. The Japanese are busy trying to imitate jet propulsion in their day-life and night-life. But if we want to win the affections of the Thai, we have only two choices: Walt Disney or a good American with lots of Mexican ancestry. I think the Thai would like Mexican food, Mexican dances, Mexican Siestas and Gordo.
>
> But there are a lot of Chinese here, and I am sorry to say the Americans don't understand these Chinese. In San Francisco, Hong Kong, and Singapore the Chinese are divided into those who want Mao, Chiang and remain neutral—and at the same time the Chinese aren't divided at all. But here the Chinese are good Buddhist which makes them friendly with the Thai and not friendly toward any politicians.
>
> Please don't blame them. Politicians mean taxpayers. The Chinese are the landlords, capitalists and workers. The Thai just stand by and say "Ho-hum"—when that is not too much exertion. Then they go to the temple, then they rest, then they go to the cinema. The land is fruitful, why not.[421]

Sam noted in his diary that the Chinese method of divination had crept over into the Thai temples. He went on to recount a visit to an important site:

> We went to Nakhon Pathom . . . where Buddhism was originally established in Thailand. It has an immense stupa and there are also ashes of the Lord's bones* there. What I liked about the place was that they are actually collecting all kinds of archeological remains and keeping them

---

*Bones of Lord Buddha.

there—especially from Ayuthia which is not close by. It is very hard to be compelled to walk quickly and not observe Indian, Chinese, Burmese and other influences. I did have an opportunity to see some local snails and can observe **double** snail influence. I do not know if anybody has written on it.

You first have the hair dressing which is supposed to represent the snails covering the Lord's head when he was in *samadhi*. But you also have a sort of conical figure, which is actually in the form of the Siamese snail. Yes, I have seen hat-figures and others, but I did not notice this before . . .

Across the river was some Buddha. How large I have no idea, but it dwarfed everything. I have seen large Daibutsus in Japan and both large standing and reclining ones here, but this was a skyscraper and all covered with gold-leaf—not gilt. And in a perfect state of repair. It was left untouched when Ayuthia was destroyed.*

The functional place of the Bodhisattva was occupied by very large figure[s] of Moggallana and Sariputra. These alone were large Buddhas. But they were plain. The disciples are always made plain. What becomes the aureole in Mahayana was made into a sort of fan, down low in front. It was elegantly enameled like the aureoles, and perhaps more so.

I found it very difficult to take notes. The atmosphere there was peaceful, really peaceful. I have tried to point out here and there the existence of meditation-Buddhism along with ecclesiastic-Buddhism. This during the Vihara or Lenten-season, which is now in vogue. Whatever the defects of Hinayana they do practice a pretty good meditation.

This also reminds me of an omission concerning Wat Samanamboriharn. The main stems of Chinese Buddhism seem to go to Chan† or Pure Land‡. I found that they especially study Lanka Sutra which, of course, is very profound, and especially valued by Chan.[422]

Sam then wrote of his departure from Thailand.

I left with the information that my flight had been OK'd on to Calcutta.§ When I got to Rangoon¶ it was not so. Then I was held up at Rangoon

---

* Ayuthia was the former capital of Thailand; it was destroyed by the Burmese in 1767.

† Chan is the Chinese Buddhist tradition that gave rise to Japanese Zen.

‡ Buddhist movement emphasizing rebirth in the Pure Land through chanting the name of Amitabha Buddha.

§ Now Kolkata.

¶ Now Yangon.

. . . [where] I found I could not book passage, then I located the Pakistani Air Lines and was told there was a plane which would take me to Chittagong* and a hotel room would be provided . . .

I called on my friend, Bill Eilers of San Francisco, who knew more about my plans than anybody else. I spent all afternoon with him, and turned over my reports to him, for his benefit. I also got some good tips from him and learned lot about Burma which is never in the papers.[423]

---

*Now Chattogram.

Story of the Coming of the Prophet and His Biography by Khwaja Hasan (Sani) Nizami, 1959. Includes Urdu translation of 10-page letter from Samuel Lewis

CHAPTER 10

Into Sufi India

Burma, East Pakistan,* and Finally India

There is a light within every soul; it only needs the clouds that overshadow it to be broken, for it to beam forth.

HAZRAT INAYAT KHAN[424]

AS 1956 CONTINUED AND SAM JOURNEYED ON INTO ASIA, he continued to record many fascinating observations and experiences in his diary.

> The Hotel Strand in Rangoon is the scene of mystery, intrigue and cloak-and-daggers. I was watched from the beginning. I began to talk softly about Buddhism and increased the amplitude so people did not have to eavesdrop. As there were execs and Chinese of doubtful backgrounds and others around, it was [just] as well. No one dares to handle a good Buddhist. But when I took a taxi I learned to be Muslim. The Hindus [overcharge], the Muslims have a fixed rate, when I greeted them they shaved this down. I won't worry over East Pakistan, but may relax until I reach Calcutta; then we shall see.[425]
>
> When I arrived in Chittagong, I had no local currency. It has been a legal holiday in Burma, it was also one in Pakistan and neither country honors Thai money. Hotels do not receive travelers' cheques there. Why, I don't know. This hotel has already given me rupees for dollar . . .
>
> They sent me to the U.S. Consul who turned out not to be the U.S. Consul at all, but Mr. Sparr, head of the Forestry Department organization on some deep diplomatic exchanges. And meeting him more than compensated for all the trouble. In [no] time I found information on the library shelves that would have taken me months to fathom out and he told me the best place in the world for further information and it appears to be not far from Simla . . .

* Now Bangladesh.

> I got off to Dacca bright and early . . . to find that my host-friend had first moved, then left Dacca for Chittagong. He left a message with a friend, who was out. Hard luck? Hardly. I was in the hands of one Jemal Ghandhuri, a nuclear physics grad at the University . . . He sent me to USIS* and then to this hotel which is much cheaper than others because meals are thrown in as in Japan.
>
> I hardly signed the blotter when I found myself talking to a UC student from Berkeley who knew the first references I gave him and also knows Muin Khan who invited me here in the first place. Well, it was Muin's cousin, Ahmad Farid who was supposed to be my host. I . . . went out to look for their aunt, Suphia Kamal, who is the leading poetess of East Pak. By the time I caught my breath I was eating and meeting one number of the family after another and the dates began to pile up . . .
>
> One thing I cannot overestimate is the kindness and hospitality already received. It is the finest [yet] . . . I met the Japanese as if we loved each other but [here] I meet people as if we were part of one family, very close indeed.[426]
>
> Before the day was over I met many friends of my friend Muin Khan who is now in Indonesia. And with the coming of evening I was in the midst of a Sufi group led by Pir Maulana Abdul Ghafoor . . . The first to greet me was a disciple of my own teacher Pir-o-Murshid Inayat Khan. I submitted to tests, I listened and I spoke and now my program is very full indeed . . .
>
> No names are mentioned but the fact that an Islamic Society is organized in San Francisco, independent of other societies, influenced strongly by non-Muslims and newly converted people who know very little does not meet approval. The introduction of politics, especially in the name of "no politics" actually provokes a horror.
>
> When you meet real saints, real *khawwalis,*† real sages and real Sufis, and feel the marvelous spirit about the educated, you can ask for no more. But neither can you surrender to the less. It is all but forbidden to me now to follow the ignorant and self-willed, no matter now "nice" they are.[427]

Sam went on to describe an intellectual argument where he had taken a global stand in relation to Islam.

---

*United States Information Service, later known as United States Information Agency.

†Spiritual singers.

> I was strongly challenged last night but reached this agreement: either Islam or a universal religion. Either Islam proves its superiority, or it must join with other religions as one of several ways. It will not bow down to other religions, but it must either take its place alongside of them or [present] its prowess. It does not prove [its] prowess by argument and force, still less by rage and anger.
>
> I admitted it was possible for sages of other faiths to reach the higher stages and perhaps even the highest. But I had to add I have not yet myself met any non-Muslim superior to my own teacher [Inayat Khan] and I have met the greatest men in Buddhism and Christianity. The real test will be with the Hindus. If they have love and insight I shall have to admit it. But while I bow with all humility to their sacred books and philosophies, I must confess I do not understand their religions at all. I find little connection between their sacred literature and common practices. In humility I shall try to learn. It is not revulsion against idolatry that prompts me, but revulsion against ignorance and superstition.
>
> Therefore I am not against Nehru as some people are. I talk here of his philosophy. My stand on Kashmir is that if we surrender to God, this will straighten out the problem. But the Muslims are going to lose Kashmir because they have made the thought about Kashmir a partner to the thought about God and sometimes they think much more about Kashmir. This is not Islam and can only have the same results as happened in other lands. Seek wealth, property and empire and you will lose both them and God. Seek Allah and you may gain wealth, property and empire. At least this is my stand now.[428]

The Forestry representative had told Sam of resources to examine in Simla. He mused about his situation:

> I can hardly keep up my diary. I have been going to Pir Maulana Abdul Ghafoor . . . whenever possible. Yesterday I was the luncheon guest of Capt. Sadik who is also a devotee. Today I shall be with the Brigadier. I was with the Swami Maharaja in the evening. My day report at the university will follow. I have been called a *Khalandar** and a *Jalali*† and even more. It is hard to realize. The Pir has loaned me *Futuh-al-Ghaib*‡

* A *Khalandar* is a person with the gift of insight who has achieved Oneness with all that is.

† A *Jalali* is one who has mastered power/strength for the benefit of all.

‡ *Revelations of the Unseen.*

Samuel Lewis, 1956 passport photo

of Hazrat Shaikh Muhyuddin Abdul Qadir Jilani* . . . At 11 I am supposed to meet a venerable Sufi. Tomorrow to a shrine.[429]

He wrote further to Abdul Rahman in West Pakistan:

Yesterday was a very trying day. I went to the Pakistani Observer office and spent all morning waiting for the editor who did not show up. I then went to the radio station. I was introduced to the staff and preliminaries were made for recording my voice, finding the records of my teacher, Sufi Inayat Khan, and obtaining introductory letters to Husein [Sani] Nizami† of Delhi, son of Hasan Nizami.‡

However I was compelled to cut the visit short in order to retrieve the watch held by customs. They had kept me four hours at Chittagong, and then, all efforts to get information about it had failed. Major X, however saved me and took me to the airport.

I had had so many estimates of duty, and when the final figure was given me I refused to pay it. Fortunately a compromise was quickly reached and though there was a delay the amazing thing was the Major knows the relatives of Abdul Rahman in [West Pakistan]! Then, to add to our amazement, we were late to get back to the radio station only to find the whole staff with Mr. Nasari in front of my hotel! This sequence of dilemmas and surprises is now a daily occurrence.

It started when I failed to find my host Ahmed Farid, to land in the midst of a Sufi group headed by Pir Maulana Abdul Ghafoor. I must now state once and for all that this nonsense in San Francisco about there being no Sufis or that they are unimportant must stop . . . I may have to write a book on my experiences here. The Pir Maulana is the most perfect **ordinary** man I have ever heard about, but his father was extraordinary . . . Through him I have met leader after leader here—

*Sam looked upon Hazrat Shaikh Muhyuddin as one of the greatest members of the ongoing Spiritual Hierarchy, who manifested Islam at every step.

†Husein's given name, like his father's, was Hasan. The name Husein, an affectionate diminutive, was used by family and intimates in part to differentiate the son. Hasan Sani Nizami (Urdu for Hasan Nizami the 2nd) is the name by which he is known throughout the world.

‡Hasan Nizami is known as a prominent writer in the history of Urdu literature.

civil, military, professional, educational. There is hardly an important man in East P. that I have not met or who has not sought me [out]—mostly the last.

I did not have a chance to rest when my friends look me to the tomb of Pir Shah Ali. Dervishes came to East Bengal around 856 A.H.* and began converting the peasants and established the first mosque in a wooded country. A century later the Pir came and really established Islam, this long before the Mogul conquest . . .

I chanted *zikr* there and believe me there is also going to be no more nonsense about my not chanting *zikr.* If Dr. [Chaudhuri] does not permit me full sway, superior to that of politicians taking over in the "non-political" society, well and good, I'll speak on Castro St., but even more likely in more important places.†

Last night I went to an Islamic wedding. The place was packed, but for everyone who accosted the groom, ten went to Pir Maulana. The Kadari Pir was also there. I have met many holy and wise [men]; I have met more good [men] in every broad sense. The good-will was the most perfect I have experienced. If I remained here another week, I would be a famous man, but my job is to do Allah's will.[430]

Samuel was advised to visit the tomb of Pir Maulana Ghafoor's father.

Typical Moghul architecture in Dacca

The last night in Dacca will always stand out. I was feasted and had the most loving embrace from a large number of men, some saintly, many officials and intellectuals, but all loving. I was advised to visit the tomb of the Pir Maulana's father . . . popularly known as **The Murshid**. I hope to

*That is, about 1478 CE. A.H. represents the year count in the traditional Muslim calendar; it stands for After Hijra (or Hegira).

†In fact, in 1969 Samuel Lewis did end up speaking in the Haight Ashbury district at a small café run by a Christian group, the Holy Order of Mans, which honored him as an educator.

> have his life story when I return as it is now being published in English.[431]

Sam's flight was from Dacca, East Pakistan, to Calcutta, India. The head of the East Pakistani army and his aide, Captain Sadiq, took him to the airport and he found fellow Sufis on the plane. He went directly to a host's house there. After a short supper they went to The Murshid's shrine.

> I started to chant *zikr* but it was soon that the Murshid was using my body to chant through me. He then told me that I need not wait to go to Ajmir, he confirmed my musical gift and said I was to use it immediately. He also gave me the blessing of the crescent and star at the top of my forehead above where Murshid Inayat Khan had made his [sign]. He said he would guide my footsteps in India, and certainly till I went to Delhi and visited the *dargahs.**
>
> I have had a letter of introduction from Ansar Nasari, director of radio at Dacca. He is also a Sufi. My voice will be broadcast shortly. During the actual broadcast I seemed to receive divine guidance . . . It is going to be very hard for all but my closest friends to realize that I, Samuel, now known as Ahmed Murad and as Sufi Ahmed Murad, the initials of which are S.A.M, which is also my name, have been nominated as a candidate for the *waliyat.*†
>
> In any event the grapevine is very strong in my favor, as strong as it was weak before. Those like Hugo Selig and Paul Reps and Corinne were very very right. The events prove it. It is beautiful to see others touch the feet and hands of holy men, but it becomes awkward when one finds himself a subject of veneration . . .
>
> This whole trip has been stupendous but the Pir Maulana said it will be more so, and he has confirmed every experience that I thought was spiritual. All this has forced me to use the whip on Alan Watts and by indirection on Rom Landau. I am not to use the whip on Mrs. Duce, who is liable to become Mrs. Dupe. She may need care and help. The death of Rabia, the hospitalization of Norina, the injuries to Elizabeth Patterson, the demoralization of Jean Adriold, the dramatic demise of Malcolm Schloss all show a definite pattern from which I have been rescued, but which experience I must have needed for my own evolution and development.[432]

---

* Saints' tombs.

† Sainthood.

Based on his history of being rejected unfairly by certain kinds of academics, Sam naturally felt the impulse to counter such people. His aim was to efface his self—not build up his ego—burning through his own particularized sense of separated self-identity so that the real light could shine forth. On this present journey he received tremendous confirmation of his realization and experienced broad acceptance, which strengthened his being. The whip he mentions is Fudo's way of action, forceful and wise to burn through ignorance. Sam now had much less hesitation in following through with a strong course of action. In his diary he went on to show his challenges in Pakistan and India:

> But things are utterly out of my hands. "Food for India" and "Water for Pakistan" still stand out. I am liable to do a little shouting . . . I can get all the introduction . . . necessary for West Pakistan, but must take one thing at a time. Pir Maulana says, "This breath is the one that counts." At the same time there is an all abiding all-pervading Divine Breath.[433]

Sam left the following night for Calcutta.

Calcutta and Delhi

> Sri Ramakrishna:
> *If neither mind nor matter [nor] self persist,*
> *Then did you live? Or living pass to finality?*
> Nagarjuna:
> *What is this mind and matter and existence?*
> *What is this birth and death, living and extinction?*
> *Are all our efforts to describe the sky, the sky?*
> *What is the hamsa-bird? The simurg? The garuda?*
> *Rising above limitation, how can we portray*
> *That which is boundless in terms of limitations?*
> *My terms of limitation more limited than their sphere?*
> *If X be a function of Y, can Y be a function of X?*
> *Is the unknown in the terms of the known really "unknown"**
>
> SAMUEL LEWIS[434]

---

*This extract is from a long poem Sam wrote in which he rendered realized Hindu and Buddhist teachers including Krishna, Ramakrishna, Maitreya and others. He sent the poem to the Mother at Pondicherry.

Temple Dakshineswar, Calcutta

Samuel's visit to Dakshineswar became the occasion for further profound experience. Writing to Rudolph Schaeffer, he shared his rich observations, reflections, and intentions.

My dear Rudolph: I have just returned from Dakshineswar, the temple compound famous for its association with Ramakrishna, Vivekananda and the Tagore . . . My report may be disappointing to some people while it may refresh others. I am not to be taken as an authority. I can only see according to my own light and training. I differed somewhat from the Hindus on the subject of awe. I differ from them very very strongly upon returning from the temple.

I entered the place with more interest in architecture than in religion or sculpture. I left with the same feeling. There is a distinct flavour of the buildings which is akin to frozen music. I may not go so far as I did in Thailand and say that the greatest devotees were the builders, not the monks. But I did not see any beauty in the idols or symbols. They are like plastic dolls compared with beautiful girls, with respect to their nature in contrast to the forms in Thailand, Japan and Southeast Asia . . .

I even wonder whether some contemporary trends in American architecture are not leading the way to something greater. At this writing I have great hopes in the architecture and music, next in house-interiors, and far less for painting and poetry—at the moment. But the spirit is there, and I am wondering if I find it here.

The relief of famine is an example. These people do not relieve—it is not a question of whether they can—they don't. They pray when they should work, and they beg when they should pray.

Samuel then spoke of the profound gifts he was able to share:

I visited shrines and I was blessed, but at Dakshineswar it was I who did the blessing. I gave out the calls of Krishna's flute myself. They cannot do this, Samuel can—never mind how. That will come out later. In Dacca I was recognized. You may judge for yourself what this means.

> Only a few people [ever] really saw me, and they saw me much better than I could judge myself. I play a new role. East Pakistan more than confirmed Japan.[435]
>
> I go to Simla and there shall write to the Aurobindo Ashram—I have something for them. It seems that I am to **give** to the Hindus and **get** from the Sufis. This needs no commentary. I must lecture when I return, but I should prefer to arrange things with you—and with the World Affairs Council (Russell Smith) before others. Today, thank God, I am fully alive. [436]

Shortly after, he wrote:

> I spent two days in Calcutta, chiefly in the company of . . . disciples of Maulana Ghafoor. We visited the shrine of the Maulana's father twice, each time with blessing . . . We went also to the tomb of a Syed saint and I felt the atmosphere very strongly. I then sought some healing power to help my friends . . . The visit to the hdqrs. at Wellington Square to buy pictures brought a fine response from the monks. There is a strong reaction today against idolatry, supporting the Arya, Brahmo and Vedanta movements. The Sufis, while in some respects very strongly anti-Hindu, favor these movements and say if idolatry is wiped out they have no objection to Avataris, interpreting [Avatar], as I have done, the same as *Rassoul*.[437]

In other words, Krishna and Sita and Ram can be regarded as ones who are equal to the state of a *Rassoul*. As he liked to do, Sam invented the word "Avataris."

He later reflected in a letter to Quantz Crawford:

> The Muslim situation is delicate at home and complicated abroad . . .
>
> I ran into one of the Muslim leaders . . . He gave me Lahore and Karachi contacts but these people have so mixed their spirituality and politics that they don't know whether they are coming or going. I seem to be doing little things which will make me a sort of saint in some places.
>
> I have rather fallen down in following the Ayurvedic people but with all that I am carrying it may be too much—now.[438]

What Sufi Ahmed Murad was carrying included horticulture contacts in the field and in government, many detailed agricultural reports to Nelson, meetings with numerous religious groups and leaders,

Lama Anagarika Govinda ca.1941–1945

goodwill contacts with Buddhists, visiting shrines of Sufis, Hindus, and others, and receiving and sometimes giving spiritual instruction during such visits. He had interactions with people at every level, lectured at universities, met with gifted Asian doctors and Ayurvedic practitioners, sought out and found folk dances. Sufi Ahmed Murad Chisti was already carrying the world on his shoulders in his inner and outer life. His focus now was on benefitting Pakistan and India.

Sam wrote a diary entry/letter to Professor Sorokin at Harvard on August 27. He had received from Professor Chatterji of Calcutta the names of several people on the staff at Harvard, whom Chatterji hoped Sam would meet when he went there as planned. In the letter Sam emphasized several of his pet peeves. In his offhand way, he referred to a group he called S-C, which was short for Suez-Canal. He had ongoing complaints about the group, an obstacle that thwarted his assignment from Hazrat Inayat Khan to clearly bring the mystical knowledge to academia.

Sam wrote this about S-C:

> [It] covers a number of intellectuals who regard themselves as authorities in explaining everything "Eastern" to the West and everything "Western" to [the] East. They have highly commended themselves to themselves, and to each other. Unfortunately they are placed where they can and do grant high scholastic degrees and even place their graduates in lucrative positions in the State Department. Situated at scattered points in the Nation, they can easily recommend each other's books and do. They do not come out so well when they attend or send papers to conferences at the University of Hawaii and elsewhere. They brush off criticism with disdain and go ahead making the same mistakes. **Actually 90% of the actual Suez controversy of the day is due to the influence of such men in all parts of the world.**
>
> The Professors S-C would have [no] time for any reports I have to make. Neither do they place any validity on the masses of devotees, even though these number into the hundreds of millions in certain faiths. Nor are the monks or priest who head these faiths allowed to do

so. Nor are the English writings of these devotees or their prelates given much record.

Of course the Professors S-C are among the most stirring champions of the **Anti-Personality Cult**. And I can assure you, professor Sorokin, that if I have an introduction from the members of the Indian Cabinet or the Swami Maharaja or the Rama Krishna Mission [or] Vice-President Radhakrishnan, with all of whom I have had very friendly and very lengthy discourses, these same Professors S-C would reverse themselves and want my papers. They would especially accept papers on Buddhism and Sufism, which high philosophies are not those of the persons mentioned or referred to. All of which prevents valid and concrete examples and explanations of these movements becoming known to the American Public—not while the Professors S-C can help it.

I have before me *2500 Years of Buddhism* by P. V. Bapat with an introduction [by] Vice-President Radhakrishnan. Much of this book is not written by Buddhists at all. But there is one Anagarika Govinda, a German, who has become an Oriental devotee who strikes out boldly and unequivocally against the S-C type and shows point by point where a certain authority is wrong, and not only wrong but has spread confusion through the world. At least I can support this gentleman by my own visits to leading Buddhist monasteries in Japan which gives one valid objective data, all of which would be in support of Anargarika Govinda, but not necessarily thereby acceptable to the professor S-C type.[439]

Sam was able to go directly to Delhi, where he met with Khwaja Hasan Sani Nizami. Shortly after, Sam wrote to Vilayat Khan, offering some guidance from the Khwaja on contemporary matters. Sam also emphasized his own relationship with Vilayat's father.

Samuel Lewis at the *dargah* of Hazrat Inayat Khan

Signs and portents continued when I arrived in Delhi. The taxi stopped dead right in front of your blessed father's tomb. I went in and had a good cry neither of grief nor sorrow, but knowing I inherit an unseen cloak which nobody can take from me. I had very long talks with Husein Nizami, the exoteric Sufi leader in India, especially of and for the Chishti Order.

This concerns many things and directly or indirectly you are connected with these many things and for that reason I write to you.

Hussein Nizami wishes to see publication in English on Sufism spread around the world. I know there are signs both with you and with our associates in Los Angeles to start such things. I am not enthusiastic over articles which overemphasize personalities and do not awaken the hearts of the living. Most of these ultimately fail financially, and then start begging. This shows the absence of Divine Will and Divine Guidance . . .

The next thing is to form an international Sufic alliance which would include all groups which could continue to function therein as separate elements if they so desired. Nizami-Sahib does not look with favor on the efforts of various peoples to start or continue mushroom movements, holding back papers and teachings, and ignoring each other. He went further than I did in expressing a sort of goodwill toward you personally.

You must remember that I said . . . that your father selected me for certain missions because I might remain longer in the flesh than certain other [people]. The same is true about you, that whatever be the impulses of people in Geneva and Holland, they are not surrendering to any ultimate-will-of-God. Good hearts, even, are not awakened souls.

There is a total ignorance on the part of most of them of the real nature of Sufism. In 1926 your blessed father gave me the gift of his experiences which literally took my breath away. He gave me a look which he has apparently not given to anybody else. They saw the saint; I saw the master and the prophet. No one can take this from me.[440]

Tomb of Sufi saint Hazrat Nizamuddin Auliya

The strength Samuel had absorbed from Inayat Khan in that moment stayed with him his whole life.

Hasan Sani Nizami, whom Sam met there for the first time, was now an outer representative of Sufism in India. His father, whom he succeeded, had been a

The largest sundial in the world. Jantar Mantar, Jaipur

head of the Chishti Nizami Order. Hazrat Inayat Khan died in Tilak Lodge in Delhi, and Pir Hasan Nizami performed all the necessary rituals, washed Inayat's body, performed the burial, and supervised the area the body inhabited near the *dargah* of Nizamuddin Auliya.

Writing to Quantz Crawford, Sam expressed confidence that he and Hasan Sani Nizami would meet again. He continued:

> Visited tomb of Nizami-ud-din Auliya and Princess Jayonara.* Greatly impressed and chanted *zikr.*
>
> Went to Airlines Hotel. Sought Guide. One Mr. Kabalee come up and offered his services. He is a *bhakti* Yogin, yet the pioneer of aviation in India and a great engineer. He took me to Jantar Mantar, the 18th century astronomical observatory. I asked about astrology and was told there were few astrologers in India—but one was coming the next day. I met him and gave him my horoscope. I shall either hear from him or visit him in Jaipur.
>
> We saw the Kutb Minar and Asoka's pillar. Then to Birla Dharamsala, a group of new Hindu Temples. Got nothing out of them but went later to the temple of Krishna, and chanted Krishna's flute to the astonishments of the audiences. [Kabalee] then invited me to visit him at Bombay† and meet his brother who is a great Bhakti and also a great musician.[441]

Sam presented the sound of Krishna's sacred flute throughout India and Pakistan. His expression of it always brought a response of awe and respect from those who were present.

Sam's analysis of national and cultural issues was always sharp and clear. Writing to the World Affairs Council, he referred to two types of evil:

---

*Sam here refers to Jahanara Begum, eldest child of Emperor Shah Jahan. Jahanara was also elder sister to Dara Shikoh, about whom more later.

†Now Mumbai. To preserve contemporaneity of expression in this case, we have retained the spelling Bombay when referring to Sam's experiences.

> The first is the evil of semi-official support in any foreign land for the sectarian missionaries . . .
>
> The second evil is the surrealism of a portion of the United States concerned with publicity—movies and the press. In the case of the latter it is much worse because long commentaries are written on present-day events without any consideration as to what has happened before, or as to actual feelings of actual people. My own suggestion to combat this surrealism is not to interfere in the slightest but to flood this country with agricultural journals, particularly from those parts of the United States which have similar conditions, or similar crops. Then Asia could learn from a real America instead of from a surreal cover.[442]

Sam had traveled to Simla and Dehra Dun* and returned to Delhi. His interests in the horticultural appear strongly again:

> This point must be considered in all seriousness. When I visited Dr. Deshmukh, Minister of Food and Agriculture, and his top experts, every one of my suggestions was belittled or outright rejected. This despite the fact that some of them had been highly evaluated at the Forest Research Station, Dehra Dun, by India's greatest botanical scientists.
>
> This rejection was followed by a long conversation on the deeper philosophies of India. When these high officials in Dehra Dun recognized the seriousness of my approach and the introduction of modern scientific methods and actual agricultural operations in harmony with the spiritual traditions of India, there was a complete reversal. This matter had already been taken up in California with experts and university professors . . . Some . . . are outright skeptical. But I doubt whether these men ever interested themselves in Indian philosophy, psychology or religion.[443]

He was invited to return to the Forestry station in Simla to give a speech.

Interview with Hasan Sani Nizami

The influence of Sam's experience with Nizami extended for many decades, well beyond their meeting in 1956. In 2007, more than five decades after Sufi Ahmed Murad's visit, Pir Shabda Kahn was in Delhi to

---

*Now Dehradun.

cohost the annual *urs** celebration of Hazrat Inayat Khan. Pir Shabda was then (as now) head of the Sufi Ruhaniat International, the Order ultimately founded by Sufi Ahmed Murad Chisti.

Hasan Sani Nizami, 2007

During the time Pir Shabda was in Delhi he recorded several long interviews with Hasan Sani Nizami.[444] They provide an important historical record, and his memories throw much light on Sam's life story and accomplishments, as well as Chishti Sufism.

Khwaja Hasan Sani Nizami's interview describes his ongoing relationship with Sufi Ahmed Murad Chisti. He mentions encounters with other Westerners he met years after Sam's visit, as well as with those who were connected to Hazrat Inayat Khan in some form. In later years Murshid Sam would mention experiences from his travels but would often add that it would be much better if one could have a report from someone else who was there rather than himself. Fortunately, this interview contains just such a report.†

Khwaja Hasan first asked about what had evolved in Sam's life. He then spoke about a great debate of 800 years before when the King asked Hazrat Nizamuddin Auliya to give evidence that music is allowed in Islam. The great Sufi master quoted a *Hadith* of the Prophet Muhammad, but the *Ulamas*‡ present thought his citation should come from a different source, perhaps more Sunni than Shia. He answered, "You are asking me to find the preaching of a follower of the Prophet. I am quoting the Prophet."

When asked, "What did they say to Nizamuddin then?" the Khwaja laughed.

> They took out their daggers, so the king admonished them, saying "Why are you taking out your daggers?" It was because nobody was able to try to debate Nizamuddin because they knew they could not compete with

---

* Anniversary of the death of a Sufi saint; literally "wedding."

† The interview has been edited for easier understanding by English readers.

‡ Scholars of Islamic law and theology.

him in the knowledge of Islam. He was a master of Islam and they were only court people. From the very beginning of our Chishti orders, Sufis put a ban on all persons who are in government service; they cannot preach and they should not be appointed preachers, because if that happened the Sufis might become a political weapon."

The Khwaja continued,

> After that Hazrat Nizamuddin Aulia ordered one of his greatest scholars to write a small book on the civility of music in Islam. He wrote a book on the basics of Sufi music. And the first sentence of that book essentially means, "A Sufi is a person who keeps open all his options." The way of life is the road. There are many roads toward God, so one should not limit the options. To create a new Sufi order, if it is linked by earlier orders, then there is not harm in it.

Pir Shabda replied "*Subhan Allah*"* and the Khwaja repeated, "No harm in it. But if he invented a thing, that is not good. And if you have no connection with earlier Sufi orders. You should have some kind of link [or lineage]." Nizami went on to speak.

> As your Murshid was a *mureed* of Sufi-Sahib [Hazrat Inayat Khan] . . . Here is a link. Sufi Ahmed Murad was a Sheikh of Chishti Nizami Order. Valid with all authentic connections. So, if he gave a vision to one of his *mureeds* to initiate people, then he is fully authorized. First, he should not deviate from the main road. He should not go now here, now there. So he should follow a certain road. So if your Mr. Lewis, Ahmed Murad, established a new branch of the Sufi-sahib's order, nothing is wrong with it.

Sam was a kind of spiritual uncle to Khwaja Nizami. He wrote long letters to the Khwaja in response to the Khwaja's questions. When Pir Shabda remarked, "He was such a wonderful Murshid," the Khwaja replied:

> Fantastic. Yes, he was! And one thing which I published was a [10-page] letter he wrote to me, and I translated it into Urdu myself. He mentioned that I was always worried that all religions ended up in worship of images. The religion started with worship of one God and ended in the

---

* Sufi expression of praise and surrender, literally "Glory be to God."

worship of images. Why, in Islam, was that not happening? And, in Islam, in many sects of Islam, the most vulnerable sect who were supposed to worship idols was the Sufis, because they have human masters. And they were supposed to worship those. And people think they were actually worshiping.

Pir Shaba responded: "Confusing worship with *fana*." Khwaja Nizami agreed.

Yes, yes, yes, that's the thing. He mentioned when he went to Pondicherry* and met the Mother there, he was much impressed by that personality. And he said she is a very extraordinary human being. That is why she was appointed there. She came out of her hiding place once a week to give *darshan* to her followers. And all those people who were there at the time of the *darshan* were much impressed by her personality. So when Ahmed Murad came to the *khanqah* he asked me to take him to the *khanqah* of Nizamuddin Aulia.

Any guide can take you there, but he chose me because I was a representative of a Pir, or a father, who was very close to Sam's master. He took me with him in that way. And I showed the things which nobody can see or can be shown to you. He was much impressed, and he spent a lot of time there. I was sitting with him, and I am telling him the stories of that place. One story I am going to tell you.

Hazrat Nizamuddin Aulia was living in the third story of his *khanqah*, he lived there, the last story. And all the five times of prayer he used to come down even in his very old age to perform the *namaz*.† Once when he came down he went inside his reading room, the library. On the way there he reached the open space outside the room. He saw in the courtyard a big banyan tree. A young man was standing there, so Hazrat Nizamuddin Aulia sat down on the threshold and asked somebody to call that young man. And asked, "Why have you come here?"

The young man told him that he came from Ayodhya‡, the Bliss. "And my father is a trader of silk and clothes. I heard so much about you, and I came here to become your *mureed*," which happened. Another gentleman, the grandson of a historian, was leaving the place at that time, but Hazrat Nizamuddin Aulia called him, "Sahib, come here sit here."

---

* Now Puducherry.

† Muslim prayers.

‡ Birthplace of Rama.

And he started teaching, a very nice sermon; I have a copy of it. So I repeated that sermon to Sufi Ahmed Murad. And all of those happenings in that *khanqah* which I knew, I repeated. And he got in a certain condition—I cannot explain that condition—but he was in *that,* and he was very happy, and he was not ready to come back! He was sitting, sitting, sitting. And I was also sitting there. I also felt much comfort there at that time.

That same night he saw Hazrat Nizamuddin Aulia in his dreams. And Hazrat Nizamuddin Aulia said, "You are wanting to see my *khanqah.* I'll show you! I'll show you." And he took him in all the rooms and to the dervishes who were sitting there. Yes, Hazrat Nizamuddin Aulia did this. And when I asked him to write an article to be presented in a seminar he said, "I am not going to tell the story of the dream, because people won't believe it. I don't tell that. But I will mention all the authentic historical evidence, besides the things which I saw in the dream."

So, I said there will be no seminar or symposium, only one lengthy article from you. He gave that lecture, a long lecture, and it is about more than 100 pages. And after that it was published not from India, but from Pakistan. So many editions, so many editions!

When asked about the grave of Dara Shikoh, a great Sufi with whom Sufi Ahmed Murad deeply identified, the Khwaja said the grave was in the precinct of Humayun's tomb and nobody had known its location except his father. He proceeded to explain why:

In 1904 or '05, Lord Curzon was the Viceroy of India. He started the protection of old monuments. He brought in two Indian scholars. The first scholar did the first Urdu text. The second scholar was my father. And Curzon was so interested he often showed up. He asked my father, "There is a very beautiful door inside of the stone," and would say "This is the tomb of Babur, Humayun."

My father corrected him. It was not built for Babur but for his beloved slave Fahim . . . I thought, "Why did my father know that thing which nobody at that time knew?" Suddenly, I remembered when the last Moghul king, Bahadur Shah, came out of that fort, he met the maternal grandfather of my father. He met him, and he gave him a small box in which there were some relics of the Prophet, and some other things. My maternal grandfather's family were actually the managers and caretakers.

When he established a Sufi order in the first decade of the 20th century, he formed an organization using the name Nizamu. And the founders of that organization were great persons. The first meeting, which consisted of only five persons, was held at the grave of Dara Shikoh!

Humayun's Tomb complex, Delhi, presumed burial place of Dara Shikoh, eldest son of Shah Jahan.

All the Moghul kings who came after Aurangzeb tried hard to conceal the grave of Dara Shikoh, because they were afraid that people would come here and worship it. So, it was kept secret. My father knew that, and that's why he had that meeting there. Such a vision! Yes, yes, that's why [Dara Shikoh] was so close to Sufi Ahmed Murad. Both were thinking in the same way!

I got that letter, Sufi Ahmed mentioned in it why there is no image worship in Islam, in Muslims, and also why it was not in Sufis. So, suddenly, when I was sitting in the *khanqah* meditating, it was revealed to me that the devotion should not become stagnant. If you see a really great spiritual master, his personality is so impressive, that you see only him and nothing else. And if you can't go beyond him, then that is the basis of image worship.

Khwaja Hasan then related a fascinating episode that took place among Khwaja Moinuddin, Moinuddin's disciple Qutbuddin Bakhtiyar, and Bakhtiyar's disciple Baba Farid. This event shows Baba Farid's deep respect for the *silsila.*

This happened even to Baba Farid. Khwaja Moinuddin . . . asked Farid to stand between the two of them, and [the Pir] also stood and made many gestures to Baba Farid. After some time Bhaktiyar asked his disciple Fariduddin to touch the feet of his *dada* Pir, Moinuddin Chishti, but Farid didn't do that, he touched Bhaktiyar. Twice Bhaktiyar said it, and each time he was touched.

On the third time when Bhaktiyar said that, Khwaja Moinuddin Chishti stopped and said it was fully successful—"Now he knows only one existence. For him the existence is One. Nothing else." For Baba Farid that existence is of his Pir, his master. Moinuddin then took Bhaktiyar to Ajmer against the protests of all the people who came out to plea for Bhaktiyar not to go. So Baba Farid is representative of Moinuddin Chishti and Bhaktiyar at the same time.

From the Nizami pamphlet. Urdu caption reads "Samuel L. Lewis Chishti at the tomb of Khwaja Saheb (Please read his letter in subsequent pages)." Khwaja Saheb refers to Hasan Nizami, father of Hasan Sani Nizami.

> At the Pondicherry ashram Mr. Lewis said that nothing existed behind that lady.* Where is the *silsila?* All the devotees who were seeing the lady, they could have seen also the person behind her, and the person behind that person, and behind the next one. This chain is called a *silsila* chain. Chain means one single being, and then the next one, and the next one, and the next one. The devotion neither goes here or there, nor is it stagnant on a certain person. It is always traveling. Devotion is traveling. There is no image worship. He wrote all this to me. Ahmed Murad is a very extraordinary person. Very extraordinary.

Pir Shabda replied that Murshid Sam's work now is in over 50 countries, spreading quickly there from 150 *mureeds.*

The Khwaja's interview fully confirmed the spiritual station of Sufi Ahmed Murad Chisti in great detail. His description of Sam sitting in a state of complete absorption, and the fact that he was carried into that state himself, contrast greatly with the way Sam's inner gifts had been scorned by others.

---

*Sam was referring to the Mother.

Pir Shabda's interview with Khwaja Hasan continued with more direct recollections of Sam's visit.

> Samuel first came to the door of the *dargah* of Hazrat Nizamuddin Aulia on the head side of the grave. He came there and he asked about the house of Khwaja Hasan Nizami. People told him that Khwaja Hasan Nizami is no more, he died. It was the 31st of July 1955 that he had died. The servants thought that Sam was a *madzub*. Sam responded to the questions saying God is very much here. And he said, "Where is the grave of Khwaja Hasan Nizami? Guide me to that grave. I will meet him there at his grave. I will meet him there." So he came without meeting me. I don't know how much time he was sitting there. Somebody came and said a white man is sitting at the grave of your father, so I went there. He met me like I knew him or he knew me for a very long time. He hugged me and expressed much happiness.

Pir Shabda mentioned the difficult, painful organizational politics that arose around Murshida Rabia Martin, and Khwaja Nizami remembered her visits to India. He said, "I was very young when she came here, that was the '30s. She came so many times here, many times. Once when she came, my father gave a great reception to her. And all the VIPs were invited, and then after that function there was a big group photograph."

That was likely the time when Rabia received the certificate in Urdu from Pir Hasan Nizami. His son then turned his attention to speaking to Pir Shabda about a practice he recommended that would serve Sufi Ahmed Murad Chisti, to whom he here refers as Sufi-sahib.

He told a story and gave a suggestion to Pir Shabda and the others there:

> I don't know whether this thing is going on in the U.S. or stopped. I don't know, but, if you can do this it will be very serviceful to Sufi-sahib. I was the manager at Ajmeer for three terms of five years each. I was a member of the *dargah* committee in Ajmeer. So, in the last period, the official administrator was a person who came from the military, and he had the rank of Brigadier. When the time came, I asked the Brigadier, can you arrange this to happen. He said that the jail rules will not allow you to serve private food in the jail, but if you can use your personal

> influence and the jailers agree to accept the food supplied by you, then you make a proposal before the jailer—the *dargah* people would like to send the food for the breaking of the fast. We will send *langar* from the *dargah,* and that food will be better than the food you serve to the prisoners.
>
> When it was proposed to the jailer, he said that it is not allowed. But they gave me so much respect they said, "If you take personal responsibility in writing, I will accept it." So I did, and he accepted. And, within a few days, a report came from the jail: the whole atmosphere of jail had changed. Every Muslim prisoner started fasting and became pious, worshiping all the time. And, when the Hindu prisoners saw that, they also started fasting, and having their *puja.*
>
> The jailer was very happy. Many of his problems were solved, so he could see that there were nice things we have done, and the Hindu prisoners were also very calm, quiet and praying. So, he said that for them we also sent for *bharat* (they called it "*bharat,*" the vegetarian food), and that was very nice. When I went to America, so many used to come to me. Perhaps they heard that I did that and that it is very fine. So, they started teaching Sufism, which I advised. They started Sufism in a jail! That was a good idea, to work in those areas where nobody works.

It has become a practice in the United States that Sufis go into prisons to offer Sufi teachings, including the Dances of Universal Peace.

Khwaja Nizami spoke further, mentioning examples of how the Chishti *silsilas* had spread around the world with the blessing of Hazrat Nizamuddin Auliya. Pir Shabda responded, "This must mean that we're in your *tariqa,* because I am a *mureed* of Sufi Inayat Khan." The Khwaja laughed and said, "No, no, no. You are not in my *tariqa.* You are in *tariqa* of Sufi-sahib, and you are in *tariqa* of my father. Not mine. You are my brother in faith. And actually speaking, I think—I don't know—but, I think all the Jews, all the Christians, and all the Muslims are my brothers and sisters in faith. Because fountainhead is one."

Pir Shabda spoke of his own Sufi musical training and sang for Khwaja in his home. This inspired the teacher to speak further:

> Hazrat Nizamuddin Aulia taught, God says in Qur'an that God created first of all, souls, not bodies. Bodies were created later on. But the souls,

> spirits were created first. And, God asked those spirits, those souls, "Am I not your creator and Lord? Am I not?" So, all the souls replied, "Yes, my God, you are."* Hazrat Nizamuddin Aulia interpreted that order by saying that the voice of God was so melodious that all the spirits started dancing. And, they heard that voice—every soul heard that voice of God—in a new *raag,*† not the same *raag.* So there are as many *raags* as there are souls. You can't even count them with the help of a computer! And Hazrat Nizamuddin Aulia said, "I heard that voice of God."

Pir Shabda then sang a passage in Rag Todi that mentioned Hazrat Nizmuddin Auliya. Khwaja Hasan replied, "Very nice, very nice," and then said:

> There was a general tendency in those days to learn about music, and there were those people who thought that it was a wrong thing or something else. Amir Khusro not only allowed Hazrat Nizamuddin Aulia to practice Sufism, but he also gave permission to the son of his benefactor at that *khanqah,* my great grandfather, to learn music. So, Hazrat Nizamuddin Aulia learned, but he was not performing in public places. Once, near Old Fort—called Hadriya Tulsi—there was an earlier Pir. Hazrat Nizamuddin Auliya used to participate in the *Urs* held at Hadriya Tulsi. Once he was there attending the *Urs,* but the listeners there were not in a state of ecstasy when they were listening to him. Hazrat Nizamuddin Aulia was with such close friends that he intervened in the management of the *Urs* and ordered them to stop. He then asked Amir Khusro to sing. That was, I think, the first and last public performance of Amir Khusro . . . And when Hazrat Nizamuddin Aulia felt that Amir Khusro needed an accompanist, he accompanied him, so they both sang.
>
> There are so many Sufis who used to go West. Sufi Inayat Khan sahib is most important. The most important persons are those who went to the West and who took use of music for spreading the message. He is the first person, and he was the capital of that because he was a great music master. So Inayat was a great man. His grandfather [Maula Bakhsh] was a renowned Chishti Sufi. I think there are so many who espouse orthodoxy, and I don't think any such person should be allowed to use music for religion. In that sense, it is not good, rather harmful. But it also gives

* Qur'an 7:172

† Raga.

> you an opportunity. Do you know what that opportunity is? Think and tell me.

Pir Shabda responded, "No conflict. Universal language." The Khwaja replied, "I am telling you about India. So many fundamentalists and communal persons. I don't think they will disagree as far as the music is concerned. Nobody will disagree. And, all over the world, the same thing. You can win or you can lose religious battles, but not musical battles."

Pir Shabda then mentioned a recollection from Sufi Ahmed Murad's diaries, that Sam thought he was with the Khwaja when he received a certain robe in a vision. Khwaja Nizami responded, "There was more than one *khirka,* more than one robe. The robes were given to him from Khalifa, my father, and one I gave him myself."

He was then asked to say more about his relationship with Murshid Sam.

> That morning,* it was quite late. I had my breakfast by that time. Why I thought of breakfast, I don't know. I can't explain it. But, I asked him, if he had taken breakfast? He said, "No. I will take it with you." I told him that I will give you company, but I have already taken my breakfast. So, he came here with me and he had breakfast. I don't know whether the breakfast was to Western standards or his choice, but whatever thing I presented him, he ate it as though he was enjoying it. And then, he started spending time with me, for days on end.
>
> So, after that, when he was going to South India, I gave him introductions of many of the Khalifas of my father who were living there . . . One of them, actually at least, was an international figure, Mr. Fayazuddin. Actually, he was the chief town planner and chief architect of Hyderabad state during the time of Hyderabad state.

Meeting Vice President Radhakrishna and Swami Maharaj in Delhi

Arriving in Delhi for the second time, Sam was affirmed in his recognition that "when hearts are attuned all suggestions are welcomed." [445] He wrote a letter to his friends at the World Affairs Council in which he

* After Sam's journey to the tomb of Hasan Nizami.

demonstrated his overall approach and engagement. Several excerpts are given below.

Sam described an introduction to Dr. Syed Mahmud, Minister of State for Foreign Affairs, showing their affinity:

> The conversation with Dr. Mahmud was on a level which is little understood in the United States and not understood by the press at all. These people are everywhere interested in religion and man's relation to eternity, whether they accept God—as they do in India—or not, as in Thailand and Burma. The case of the Chinese and Japanese falls between these but is closer to the Indian and Muslim points of view than is popularly supposed—practically all the books to the contrary notwithstanding . . .
>
> The very close spiritual sympathy between Dr. Mahmud and myself made the conversation as if between long-time friends.

Having a meeting with the Indian vice-president was a major moment for Sufi Ahmed Murad Chisti. Many of his critics in the West would never believe he actually met with Dr. Radhakrishnan. Sam was very accustomed to criticism of himself, and indicated that his critics could read the letter and believe it or not. He wrote:

> Later in the day I spent some time with Dr. Radhakrishnan. This was a very easy interview because I have read practically all of Dr. Radhakrishnan's books, enjoyed them all, probably agree with him on everything, and, no matter how abstruse, believe I understand them. The claim to the understanding of India's most complex philosophies may seem hyperbolic, but I can assure you, they soon find out. And it did not take Vice-President Radhakrishnan long to find it out!
>
> In a certain sense I find Vice-President Radhakrishnan has a blending of Thomas Jefferson, Walt Whitman and Will Rogers. He has the [same] universal outlook which is now becoming prevalent in some of our large Universities and is excellently expressed in the works of Professor Oliver Reiser of Pittsburgh. But it is almost out of [place] to verbalize encomiums on a man with whom you agree entirely.

Sam's universal outlook took him into further contact with the Sikh religion:

> The next day was spent at a memorial given to Master Tara Singh, head of the Akali movement. I do not know what this movement stands for

> except that it is one of the two large divisions of the Sikhs. I do not believe our press, or even our missionaries, could understand that the meeting was started by the leading direct descendent of Nizam-ud-din Auliya, the greatest Muslim saint of this area. Many of the speakers were Muslims and Indians and all came out wholeheartedly for nationalism and brotherhood. Again and again America was cited as an exemplary land of complete religious tolerance and confraternity.
>
> Not only did Muslims and Hindus speak, but the leader of the opposition group of the Sikhs also paid tribute. It was exactly as if Mr. Truman had been invited to come to the Republican Convention and say nice things about "Ike." . . .
>
> One element of surprise was a vociferous speech by a Kashmiri (Muslim) asking to speak for Kashmir. That is not the fashion in most parts of the world. Great nations claiming to be in the vanguard of "democratic" movements of all sorts, have been pre-determining the fate of Kashmir without any regard to the peoples' opinions. Here no one objected to letting a Kashmirian present his views on the subject.
>
> In conclusion, it cannot be stressed too much that there is practically no pro-Russian feeling here . . . Far from being internationalists the so-called Communists here are supporting the most reactionary and federalist movements; and supporting them by riots and bloodshed. Even if they succeed in one or all of those ventures, it would not add a single item of benefit or relief for any of the downtrodden. No wonder India is looking to America.

The next day, Sam added, "When the event was nearly over Nehru came in and he was the only one who did not speak like a politician."[446]

Sufi Ahmed Murad briefly mentioned his visit to Khwaja Hasan Sani Nizami in his diary of this day:

> We . . . visited the ruin *khankah* of Nizam-ud-din Auliya. Very much impressed. Wish to meditate where he did, to spread out a carpet and also give spiritual help to humanity therefrom. Hope this is possible on my next visit. At the Singh dinner I was introduced as an American Sufi. "What does Sufism mean?" "God alone exists." "That is the same as Vedanta." "Yes."[447]

In a September 3rd diary letter, Sam wrote about meeting a woman in terms that suggested he was seeing a possible romance. This proved to be the beginning of a significant part of his life story over the next several years. Various sages had prognosticated about his future, many predicting great success and marriage. Sam had his eyes open for the right woman to come along, someone whom he could see himself marrying. Now he thought such a one had appeared in his life, and while he made light of it in his letter, he took the encounter quite seriously.

Here is the diary account he gave of the meeting.

> I am at the Imperial Hotel [New Delhi] and when I got here there was one guest, a woman. She had to leave to be hostess to the Warrens. But she introduced me to a temporary guest—ah! young, beautiful, and costumes. Well I have given pictures and two addresses . . . She not only does all the ancient Indian [dance] but is said to be the best rumba artist in the country. You can see it in the rhumba costume (!!). She is divorced, but don't get any ideas because there are several girls back home who have. Anyhow, I am going south and she north. Think nothing of it. But we are both going around in circles . . .
>
> When the women were away there was only an Englishman here, and he told me the problems of a poor girl.* It was a poor girl like in the movies. She was doing some Buddhist research and needed help. I, although not a Charles Boyer, offered help. Then I learned that her father is one of the richest Sikhs and her brothers have a library worth untold dollars, rupees, and everything else . . . Why must it be me that is always asked to help the damsel in distress?[448]

Sam wrote others about the beautiful dancer he had met and sent pictures of her in costume. More will be told of this story.

To Jaipur, Agra, Ajanta Caves, Bombay, Nasik, Hyderabad

> *The vast difference between making God one's adventure and writing about it is tremendous. My whole career has been that fools do rush in where angels fear to tread, and one Swami Maharaj told me he hoped America [would] produce more fools like myself.*
>
> SAMUEL LEWIS[449]

In making God his adventure, Samuel made the most of his time as he traveled on through India. He wrote:

---

*This was not the dancer, but another woman.

I went to Jaipur on August 31 because it is a "must." Everything is a "must" here. You "must" visit please which the other fellow hasn't seen . . . The Maharajah of Jaipur is still functioning and when I was in his palace they were getting out the red carpet for Earl Warren.* I mean they were getting out the red carpet for Earl Warren and no figure of speech; also the blue, Greek and a lot of other huge Persian carpets. Because nowadays Maharajahs cannot buy slave girls, only carpets.[450]

To Fred Reinhold he wrote in his diary:

I went to Jaipur to meet an astrologer which proved to be a frost. I also ran right into the Austrian doctor whom Atmananda wanted me to meet.[451]

After a brief stay in Jaipur, Sam departed for Agra.

I did not write complete notes on Agra. I told my guide, Mohammed Shafiq, that I was a most unusual person. Thus, I asked him where Shah Jehan was imprisoned, where Akbar played chess and where Tansen lived. I am the first Occidental to have performed the pilgrimage to Sheikh Selim Chishti's tomb, chanted *zikr* there and had a certain portion of my future revealed. I learned that the Chishti family has continued on as guardians of Fatehpur Sikri and they must be in possession of important historical records. I have been invited to stay with them should I come this way again and I think it is so written.

I visited the famous mosques of Agra and there met with the Sufi Imam who gave me a book which corroborates some of my, let us say, deeper wisdom. The Arabic words *ma'arif* and *ilm* have no exact translation and they are used in very confusing manners by Arabists and Ph.Ds. who monopolize—up to this time—the scholarship on what they called "Sufism" which has no relation to Sufism. Thus I was again, for the third time, called upon to explain Ibnu l-Arabi, and I assure you, Fred, anything I have said publicly would be rejected in almost

Tomb of Sheikh Selim Chishti at Fatehpur Sikri

* Warren was at that time the Chief Justice of the U.S. Supreme Court.

> all the "leading" schools of the Occident, and has won unanimous approval so far, in the Islamic world.[452]

One very important element of Ahmed Murad Chisti's future was revealed at the tomb of Selim Chishti at Fatehpur Sikri. It was a vision of a Dance of Universal Peace, based on the rituals of the four major religions, that could bring peace and harmony to multitudes of people, and included a perspective of how it all might unfold. In the course of time Sam learned that he had drawn this Dance out of the ethers where it had been placed 30 years earlier by the renowned dancers Ruth St. Denis and Ted Shawn. From this vision Sam later developed the Dances of Universal Peace, which spread around the world.

As Sam journeyed on from Agra, he had a surprising encounter and interesting conversation with a friend who was a Buddhist and who had a spiritual background similar to his own:

> I took the express train from Agra to Nagpur which is the central point of India for all practical purposes, and there, like a thief in the night came Rahul. He must have gotten off at Sanchi, for after he gave me all the help he could, I promised to help him in the morning and in the morning he was gone.
>
> We discussed at some length the condition of Oriental studies in the U.S., a subject to which he has given some attention. His opinion of Yale is the same as mine and in accord with what Prof. Chatterjee said in Delhi. We both were strong for Harvard and Pennsylvania (Browne) and he criticized Columbia . . . [as well as] any person who, because he has Ph.Ds. from universities in the U.S. and abroad [can] grant [Doctor of Divinity] or similar degrees in religious organizations to which they do not belong, except by verbal claim. No Pacific School of Religion could grant to anybody the right to become a priest and preacher in a Catholic Church. And the same holds for Buddhism. In fact, Rahul, who is ready to go to Kathmandu said I could not go, but since I have actual written authorizations from both Soto and Rinzai Zen as well as Sini Shingon I am one of these fools who can rush in where certain professors will fear to tread—and if they did, they would be thrown out . . .
>
> The Professors Northrup, whether they are in Yale or San Francisco, who arrogate to themselves certain knowledges and certain credentials are abhorred here far more than your Billy Grahams and Richard Nixons who are certainly not popular . . .

My future was told by one sage who said that the very persons who stood in my way in the past would want to jump on my band wagon and pull for me the hardest. Years of my life were devoted to Akbar and the Moguls in general. When I complete my journey, I am going around to purchase pertinent books which are practically unattainable elsewhere and cost very, very little here.[453]

Horticultural issues filled a great deal of his time and he continued to share his findings:

I have been kept very busy here with persons and also visiting gardens and farms. Pests are the main problem here although there is a supposed nitrogen deficiency in the soil . . . I leave tonight for Ajanta Caves if my reservation goes through, otherwise to Bombay.[454]

The reservation did come through, and as Sam arrived at the Ajanta Caves, he once again wrote to Rudolph Schaeffer:

A single visit to this place does not convey too much, or maybe it does convey so much that one cannot speak . . . It looks as if certain monks must have spent their whole lives on a single panel, or at least many years.

There is a certain uniformity of perfection in the carving but not in the painting. Roughly speaking, painting is of two classes. The one, mostly on walls, comes from the Jataka or Birth-stories, or else from the life of the lord. In these there is a certain finesse and finish and it is usually "civilized." As art it is supreme, but it does not always convey the awe and holiness of the "gate" and "stupa" carvings I saw at Calcutta. The wheel and the lotus either disappear or take on actual rather than symbolic representation. Much more seems to be done to hair and head-dress than anything else. The pictures give everyday life of a clearly developed community.[455]

Carved Image of the Buddha, Ajanta (Cave IX)

On September 13 while still at the Ajanta Caves, Sam wrote a diary entry to Chris, a student of Dr. Chaudhuri in San Francisco. It emphasized Sam's position on various religious teachers:

Exterior view of the Ajanta Caves

I could easily confute most of the articles in "Twenty-five Hundred Years of Buddhism." Not only that, I could do this successfully at Kathmandu. I had a long session with a leading Buddhist over credentials and he finally reversed himself and wants me to go there, but this is too much.

One person who will most certainly not be invited to Kathmandu, even as a listener, is Mr. C. [Christmas] Humphreys (excuse his first name). Like a lot of other highly degreed and pedigreed intellectuals he puts out books which have nothing to do with Asian Buddhism in operation and which may never have been in operation. But he is an authority. These authorities are, in part, becoming the laughing-stock of Asians, and where they are not laughing-stock, they are totally ignored.

There is nothing so ridiculous as a champion of *an-atta* boosting himself, and having mutual boosting admiration societies with others.

On the other hand, I owe a certain indebtedness to Haridas [Chaudhuri]. Please tell him I spent an evening with a Mahdva Acharya* here in Bombay . . . Despite the fact that he holds an actual exalted position . . . and has no doubt had *samadhic* attainment . . . , he treated me as a brother human being. His explanations of God were new to me but very acceptable and quite different from anything I had ever heard excepting from Ramdas and [he] was especially cordial when I said Ramdas was my guru.[456]

From the Ajanta Caves Sam went to Bombay for three days, a familiar city to him now. Soon he was off to the massive Kumbh Mela pilgrimage in Nasik.

Sunday I went to Nasik, to join a pilgrimage of over 100,000—maybe many, many more. It is a 12-year cycle . . .

I had a hard time finding the hotel because it had changed names and owners. The present owner is a Farsi . . . and a devotee of Meher Baba. Baba lived in Nasik, has a center there and many followers—which didn't include the rest of his family . . .

---

* Acharya was a teacher of Chaudhuri's lineage in Bombay.

Just as I was about to give up hope, my host appeared, delayed also by the change of name and ownership—he comes just once every 12 years. He took me into the crowds, and they were crowds. **The army and boy scouts had been called out and they were needed, much needed.** I had my baptism in the Godavari, and except for place etc. it was not very different from Christian methods. Then we went through very crowded streets. A rich widow was distributing bread to the poor who were lined up against the wall, but some intrepid people, mostly young men, began to follow and mob her so she quit cold. I don't blame her. The Indians are the finest and least considerate people on earth and you can't make head or tail of it.

My friend-guide Kabali then took me to his guru who is known as the Fruit-Swami. Mrs. K. collects funds to buy fruit. The Swami then cuts it up into salads, put on small banana-leaf plates, blesses it and distributes it. He lives entirely on milk and curds himself and has a vigorous body. Without waiting he began a profound discourse on God and self, meaning my-self. When Kabali told him about Ramdas he then explained how Ramdas was helping me by the cat-method, well known in India, and the advantage of the cat-method over the monkey-method.* He gave me curds and fruit—which I ate later.

The Swami impressed me with a vigorous body and mind, and clear eyes and heart. He made no attempt to go farther except to say that Ramdas would help me. I later went back to the hotel. I was having trouble getting a taxi when the officer in charge put me in with several Indians and I got to the station. Then, although I had a first-class ticket, I could not get on the train—it seems that the first-class compartment had been invaded by holders of other tickets and they were not examined until we got a mile from the station.

But while in the taxi I explained why I had come to Nasik and my own views of Indian philosophy. This surprised and awed my companions. So although the train was full, one of them signaled me and I got into the concession car, which was not crowded and had more seats than the first-class compartments. All of this seems miraculous so I want to have it on record. It is also strange how many times I have been asked to visit the Aurobindo ashram. Well I have also been twice to the Indian School of Music and Dancing here in Hyderabad. I have chanted for

---

*In the cat method, the guru as elder cat takes responsibility to ensure the younger arrives at the desired goal. In the monkey method, it is the responsibility of the younger to hold on to the elder.

them, discussed the deeper aspects of their philosophy and last night it came out that the percussion player is also a disciple of Swami Ramdas who has many followers in these parts.[457]

Sam then returned to Bombay.

Exploring Bombay; Horticulture; Meeting Fayummudin in Hyderabad

> *A man's methods of observation and conclusion may not have universal validity, but at least they offer a form of first-hand knowledge of sorts. The type of information will no doubt be at variance with much of what appears in the press. My own cayennic* opinions indicate that the true historian will not depend too much upon the daily news although in theory it ought to offer the best source material. I have found, with few exceptions, that pure objectivity is unwanted. Even those who write keenly about "semantics" tend to use it as a weapon against others.*
>
> SAMUEL LEWIS[458]

It is apparent that Ahmed Murad Chisti readily interacted with groups wherever he went and was actively involved in influencing politics and criticizing existing U.S. government policies. His overall grasp of world issues is evident and was central to his global purposes. The diary letter quoted above continues:

> I am still hoping to meet some Indian communists myself. But I have met innumerable Indians who have told me that they were strongly questioned in the U.S. where there are feelings that communism is very strong here. Yes, Senator Unowho [McCarthy] is resented everywhere . . .
>
> The arrival of American farmers here is, in my opinion, going to do more good than 1,000 newspaper men or orators, excepting a few like Chief Justice Warren who have heads, hearts as well as tongues. The resignation of Ambassador Cooper is coupled with the policies of Mr. Dulles on Suez. Dulles is now the target for all the [Bandung] nations. Russia is seldom mentioned and there is a strong feeling here that that country is going through difficulties . . .
>
> In going through this country I find remarkable objectivity among the scientists and cultural people generally, coupled with a [reverence] for

* Perhaps Sam's way of saying "peppery."

their older philosophies and often a much better understanding of them and of life generally than one gets from books or attractive lectures on the subjects. Any real Emersonian American can have a capital time here . . .

I hope, after posting this, to visit the St. Xavier College, and if not now, later. They do respect the philosophies of India without touching the religions. You can read Upanishads a thousand times without ever feeling like going to the temple or turning from the church; the Catholics know this; the Protestants will not even look. You can draw your own conclusions . . .

Even on the sacred pilgrimages yesterday, for every single person who asked me what I thought about them, five asked me about Suez Canal! When I say that Katharine Mayo, Gandhi, Gardner Murphy, Toynbee, Bowles and Mitchell ("India without Fable") were all right, it may sound crazy and it is probably crazy. But that's the world in which I am living.[459]

Sam was persistent in his work to meet world needs through horticulture. He wrote of this to his teacher Harry Nelson.

I ran into some other problems. One is bat control, especially fruit bats. They say that Oregon has this problem and they want literature. I see that I am going to be very busy. It is evident that my idea of flooding this country with farm literature is meeting a fine response. It is all the more important because many Indian magazines and also stores lean heavily toward Russia. Russia is well able to give them cyclotrons and tractors but not simple machines that go out into the fields. It is impossible to take any but the lightest two-man equipment into the paddy fields . . .

I then went to the City Park which has fine Islamic style gates, which are the best garden gates I have seen outside of Japan, or maybe even including that land. They are all kept bright and clean.

Zinnias are among the most common plants here but in the private gardens they have molds, the same as at home. The park ones are taller and cleaner . . . Salvias are all over and doing fine. I saw many types of Casuarinas, and met the Superintendent. I complimented him because it really is the first park I have seen which is operated in the way I think a park ought to be operated.

They are doing here what I have been belly-aching all over India about. The trees are pruned, and well pruned. The leaves are taken off and put in composts and they have large compost piles. The wood is divided into twigs and fagots, and heavy wood, which is used for fuel. No wastage.

Although I told the Supt. that the trouble with India was lack of coordination, he denied this. Then I asked him about the lawn and he was lugubrious in his praise of *C. dactylon.* I just finished the standard work on Indian Agriculture. The writer skips all the evils of insects and diseases and puts in pages damning *C. dactylon.* You takes your choice and this is called "coordination."[460]

From Bombay, Sam traveled on to Hyderabad, where he was moved by the great skills of his host, a disciple of Pir Hasan Nizami. To Gavin Arthur Sam wrote:

> I spent some hours before I located Fayyum-ud-din; my host. I found that he is not only Chief Town Planner, close personal friend of Nehru, yet possessing the good will of the Pakistanis **and is the actual exoteric head of the branch of Sufis into which I was originally initiated**.
>
> He says he has ten thousand followers in this district alone and gave me a little of the connection between himself, his father, Husein Nizami (the friend of the Gradys') and my own teacher, Sufi Inayat Khan. He introduced me to his staff. I also learned he is a close friend of the Superintendent of Parks here with whom I had been spending much time, and, I guess, does understand the combination of my love for plant-life and spiritual development produced a marvelous harmony. I am putting all this in my diary which will also be of use when I enter the actual Harvard arena against the methods used by Yale which latter methods have **authorization** in the U.S. but cause consternation in the Orient.
>
> I run into the same thing here. Fayyum-ud-din said he would introduce me to Ameer Ali, chief soil man of the Deccan. He had already met Mr. Engel, chief American farm adviser for all India. I met Engel too when I had had an introduction. He was not in Delhi when I was there. Engel claims he is a great authority on fertilizers and no doubt is, but he is thoroughly "civilized." He does not understand Oriental philosophies at all, and has overlooked the whole Japanese approach. This I have thoroughly explained and this is what the Indians want. And while Engel would undoubtedly be an authority over me, a rank amateur . . . when I tried to tell Engel about Calspray's (S.F.) policy in Thailand, he waved me off. This is why the U.S. Govt. doesn't get to where it should and why I get to all kinds of plans and peoples.[461]

Continuing in his diary to his friend Rudolph Schaeffer, Sam indicated that the Minister of Information in Hyderabad needed reorientation to tourism there:

> [In Hyderabad] they send out booklets which presume one is an Orthodox Christian interested in obscure points in Indian temple building; one who desires to retain luxurious living and travel in an ox cart; one who must come by air and then use a flimsy bus to get to his destination; demand, deserve and sleep in dark bungalows. Not only are these things incongruous, they are fallacious. The Americans here and southward are nearly all interested in farming and education, and the tourists mainly in Kashmir.[462]

Papa Ramdas and Mother Krishnabai

CHAPTER 11

Completing the First Asia Trip

Ahmed Murad Chisti Offers Shams-i-Tabriz to Pirzade Vilayat Khan

My dear Vilayat:

Perhaps the most wonderful thing in life would be if you would let me play to you the role Shams-i-Tabriz played to Maulana Roum. Shams was a wild sort of fellow who had been a friend of Jelal-ud-din's father, and when the Mevlevi Order was started he came to Konia to help the cause of God. You can read all about this in Efleki's Lives of the Adepts *which I once read, in French, at a time when I was still well acquainted with that language. To me, your reading it should be a must. But I also realize the futility of imposing any will of anybody by anybody in the cause of God.*

Samuel Lewis[463]

During his travels in India Sam wrote to Vilayat Khan, Inayat Khan's oldest son, the Pirzade.* Sam had never met Vilayat in person to demonstrate the authority Sam's spiritual experiences provided.

Sam's letter to Vilayat begins with the paragraph quoted above. It continues:

> *Inshallah* is not so much my motive and motto but my way and it has been a very successful way. I no sooner wrote to you than I began a series of very strange but also very true adventures, the nature of which is entirely in harmony with the episodes in Efleki, but which have been rejected almost in toto by people who called themselves "*mureeds*" excepting the Connaughtons in Santa Barbara and Saladin Paul Reps and Aramdarya Luise Berrenberg in Los Angeles, and one other person long since deceased. That was enough, for your blessed father told each

* *Pirzade* means son of a Pir.

of these people very little of what he told me—the denouement of which instructions has already come to pass.

Hostless, I wandered through Dacca to find myself in the midst of Sufis and sitting next to a man who was engaged in translating Hazrat Inayat Khan's writings into Bengali. I was "in." All my spiritual experiences of whatsoever nature on whatsoever plane were corroborated, and what is more magnified in such a way that I knew and I know that every little, as well as every big word your father spoke to me is, was and will be true, *inshallah*. I don't remember if I wrote to you much from there, and I shall not recount the stories because there is too much to say now.

I was sent to the tomb of the Ghaus, the father of Pir Maulana Abdul Gafoor, at Calcutta and there received my next spiritual instructions in the manner and by the way in which true Sufis work. The inner eye, opened by your blessed father, exactly three years to a date after his passing, again functions in a more abstruse manner, but it functions. My work in the field of music, following the proposal of the blessed Syed Mohammed [Madani], "By the power of thy music unite East and West" goes on. The demonstrations which I have given both at tombs of saints and in Hindu temples goes as accepted evidence in the East.

My first meeting in the flesh, of your blessed father, should have been accepted—and it was not—as a sign of the depositing of the Sufi Message in the Western world. Not words, not writings, not philosophy, but of living experience, heart-to-heart and soul-to-soul. My next interview, though not phenomenal, was long, and today's events prove in every and any manner the importance of it. He gave others short interviews, then me a long one, which established seeds of Jealousy which were only overcome when people died.

Tomb of Mohammed Ghaus, Calcutta

I knew then (in 1923) that I would [be] either the last or the next to the last of the disciples of Sufi Pir-o-Murshid Inayat Khan to remain on earth. I have not seen any sign to the contrary. Years have not weighed upon me and I do not appear as an old man. Not only that, but both inward and outward indications have been that if I keep to my trust, methods will be shown to preserve or increase vitality. I seek no magic or phenomena, but the Cause of God, or *tasawwuf,* requires surrender even of surrender . . . I must go to London, but not to Paris, later in the year, and if you can come to London and meet me there, I would appreciate it. Not only that, I might even lecture for you about my adventures. You will have to think this over . . .

The stages in Sufism are *fana-fi-Sheikh* [(1)] *fana-fi-Rassoul* (2) *fana-fi-Lillah* (3) and *fana-i-baqa* (4), with a possibility of *fana-fi-Pir* between the first and second. All disciples of Sufi Inayat Khan, and I know as yet no exception, have not accepted even *tasawwuri-Murshid.* I say this and do not care who or what personalities were and are included, living on the earth or in the unseen.

Not only is God my witness but myself have been trained in *fana-fi-Pir* and more so in *fana-fi-Rassoul,* and having had that thoroughly corroborated within and without, I can at least say that until disciples are willing to go on the tremendous adventures of the Inner Path they cannot spread the Message of God. I am no novice. I have lived now 36 years as a disciple of *tasawwuf,* maybe longer.

My music [the flute of Krishna] has already been given out and no man can stop it, so long as the breath is in my body. I need no metaphysics. Yet also your blessed father asked me to train myself as an intellectual, even as a super-intellectual. The people here have remarked not only of my vitality, but of my competency to take part in discussions on every subject. That was part of my spiritual training. It begins but does not end there . . .

I have long stood almost alone on your father's dictum that "It is the *mureeds* who make the Murshid." How long people are going to worship the Master and ignore his teachings, I do not know. Buddha said, "After me the dharma," and instead he is worshipped sanctimoniously, formally and hypocritically in many lands. I reject this utterly. Passion is not love, infatuation is not love, true love is a strength and a surrender . . .

In company last night I challenged the whole of India in favor of *sanatana dhama,* or eternal truth, and everybody accepted it before I left because of the ring in my voice. What is the use of praising a book like *The Mysticism of Sound* if we do not understand the rings in others' voices? Your father left many papers which are either hidden or not understood. He also said, "What I give to [you,] you must give to others." Instead, just as he prophesied, his teachings have been treated as if given to monkeys.

I am sorry if I have played here the role of teacher to you. If you question this in your inner being you will learn that I have both authority and inner knowledge. If you meet Saladin Reps he will corroborate this. But work of the Message goes on, for God, with God and in God and I cannot turn back, *inshallah.*

Faithfully,

Samuel L. Lewis, Sufi Ahmed Murad[464]

Sam would never turn back on the work given him by Hazrat Inayat Khan. It should be remembered that he was now beginning to outwardly function with his strength and power. What might sound like braggadocio to many people was just Samuel Lewis reporting in. The manifestation of Fudo that was recognized in Japan was active.

This was how Sam manifested. He had suggested to Vilayat that he could be to him like Shams-i-Tabriz was to Rumi. Shams, through his great magnetism and awakened realization, brought the brilliant teacher and philosopher Mevlana Jelaluddin Rumi to a deeper direct experience of the God reality. He was the effective turning point in Mevlana's life. Sam could draw from his own experience of Khidr's manifestation and blessing from his retreat in 1925. He was willing and able to give Vilayat a strong dose of that same energy.

Samuel didn't receive a response to his letter, which was written shortly before Vilayat's announcement claiming the Pirship of the Sufi Order. After Samuel returned to America he nevertheless responded to the invitation to teach that he had received from Sufi representatives in Cleveland. These long-term *mureeds* were supporting Vilayat in the organizational struggle roiling the Sufi Movement.

Pirzade Vilayat's Letter to the Sufi Movement and Ahmed Murad Chisti's Response

Pirzade Vilayat's letter of August 11, 1956, was sent from the family home in Suresnes, France. In this letter he claimed leadership of the Sufi Movement esoteric school, known as the Sufi Order.

Pirzade Vilayat Khan, 1952, Paris

Dear Fellow *Mureeds* . . .

The day has come for me to speak to you with the utmost sincerity. It grieves me to witness the deepening during the last thirty years of the division amongst the *Mureeds* in a movement that is meant to stand for unity.

Thirty years have now passed since our beloved master was last walking amongst us in his physical shroud, and should we be able to see Him now, as we did then, we would witness His distress to see how sadly His last wishes have been mishandled, or simply ignored.

For many years, I have kept silent, hoping that what is right would speak for itself, hoping to serve harmony by my silence. Today I find that my silence, if continued prolongs a feeling of uncertainty that is not conducive to harmony.

In 1917, a few months after I was born, and again in 1924 and in 1926, thirty years ago, Hazrat Pir-o-Murshid Inayat Khan, my Father, designated me as His successor in the chain of the Chichti [*sic*] Sufis, and as Head of the Sufi Order which He founded. I was in 1927 ten years old, a minor. My uncle Shaikh ul Mashaikh Maheboob Khan, who was my legal tutor, shouldered the responsibility of leadership saying to me, as he confirmed again even a few days before he passed away that he was only keeping my rightful heritage until I was ready, but wished to give me more and more esoteric and administrative responsibility.

At the time of Shaikh ul Mashaikh's passing I considered it yet premature to assume this sacred position, and in an official letter to the Esoteric Council of the Sufi Order, which was read before the meeting of *Jamiat* in October 1948, gave mandate to Murshid Ali Khan to assume the function of spiritual head of the Sufi Order for the time being.

From that moment, I was systematically opposed in my activities in spreading the Message in lectures as my Father had asked me in my last conversation with Him. The handicaps thrown in my way were all in the name and under cover of officialdom. The chief accusation was always: "Vilayat has no authority to do this," and this from the very one whose own authority was based upon my mandate . . .

The esoteric constitution drawn up by Hazrat Pir-o-Murshid Inayat Khan does not allow for the spiritual head to be elected; this function

> can only be entered by nomination of one's predecessor. Such is also the custom prevailing amongst the Sufis of the East.
>
> It is necessary to clearly state here that Pir-o-Murshid Inayat Khan was the successor in a chain of Sufis each of whom designated his own successor, descending from the very origin of Sufism. The Sufi Order which He founded in the West is a continuation but reshaping of the Chichtia [*sic*] Order . . .
>
> Please search your conscience whether you feel with conviction that Murshid would approve that Vilayat whom he nominated openly Head of the Confraternity on September 13th, 1926 has been refused on July 27th, 1956, by express instructions of Murshid Ali Khan to enter the hall of the Summer School in the Hague to hold the prayers as he has done in the past, thus preventing him from carrying out the task that Murshid entrusted him to the knowledge of all. And why? Could it be because Vilayat considered it his sacred task to maintain his friendship with all the *Mureeds* irrespective of parties, and overbridging distinctions and differences; and in particular because, in the recent events, Vilayat has not prevented *Mureeds* who have for years spared no effort in the spreading of the Message, and the protection of the sacred land, to justify themselves? . . .
>
> Therefore there remains for me today no alternative but to claim this sacred heritage.
>
> Today I solemnly declare before all the *Mureeds* to withdraw the mandate that I handed to Murshid Ali Khan in 1948, because he has failed to respect and preserve the integrity of the Order entrusted to him.
>
> Nevertheless, I thank him for his efforts, because I still try to believe that he meant well.[465]

When Samuel Lewis received this announcement in India, he waited until he was in Bombay to reply. He took exception to Pir Vilayat's deification of his father through the use of capitalized pronouns. Sam had seen enough misuse of this in the followers of Meher Baba who could not recognize anyone other than their own teacher as a realized being and did not treat other teachers and spiritual organizations with respect.

On September 17, 1956, Samuel Lewis strongly endeavored to advise Pir Vilayat on what he viewed as mistakes in his statement, and at the same time to show support.

To Pirzade Vilayat Inayat Khan:

I have your long circular and am answering it immediately because air mail from Bombay will reach you quickly and tonight I go to out of the way places which would greatly delay your receiving anything. I have been going over your statements very carefully and give you my immediate views. Perhaps due to time-pressure they may not always be in the purest form, and are naturally subject to human weaknesses and even bias.

I must commend you from start to finish in upholding a thesis which your father proposed and which, incidentally, he went over in detail with me. I have always felt and I feel today even more that one reason that he did this was because from the very beginning he knew I would outlive in the flesh most of the *mureeds.* The second reason concerns that most important and almost extra-legal subject, initiation.

I am first going over our differences. These may be small but as you may be involved in legal complications I shall none-the-less point them out. Whenever and wherever I go and am asked to define Sufi, I answer: "Nothing exists but God." . . . I am not meeting obstacles. I am meeting friendships, cordiality, hospitality and spiritual accord. I have been to Sufi holy men and holy places and Indian holy [men] and holy places, and Buddhist holy men and holy places. I have had my experiences inner and out from superficial companionship and guidance to things which should concern you, but which do not concern law-courts.

The last paragraph of the brochure of August 11th reads, "It is necessary to clearly state here that Pir-o-Murshid Inayat Khan was the successor in a chain of Sufis each of whom designated his own successor, descending from the very origin of Sufism. The Sufi Order which He founded . . ."*

Sam launched his argument.

Now I have to ask you clearly plainly and open-hearted, in surrender to whose will was the capital introduced? If only God exists and if we say, "Praise be to Thee . . . the Only Being," who is it that ordains or has the right or had the light to ordain capitalization of pronouns? If you are going to start off by demanding that others adhere to pure teachings and you yourself permit departures there from, where is your strength? your guidance? your worship?

---

* Sam erred in referring to this as the last paragraph.

India is full of teachers who permit this. They divide humanity. They delude their followers. There are universal brotherhoods all over this globe, some very exclusive indeed, but they call themselves "universal brotherhoods." What is that? You ask me to believe that your sainted father gave you an appointment; did he give you authorization to capitalize his name? If somebody gave you that authorization that person must be superior to your father and it is that person who should have his name capitalized, not your father. Of course, if you have any inner or outer evidence I shall accept it. But will the law-court?

Sufism is either a trade-name or an authentic name. If it is an authentic name then it covers certain principles. I have met several Sufis, including heads of three groups of Chistis and a representative of at least a fourth. None of them would stand for this making partnership with God. Even those who have had God-realization do not do that. A clever attorney will seize upon this point at once and you will have no support on earth, or I believe from heaven, I do not think it appears in either the Esoteric or Exoteric Constitutions to which you appeal. Why not stick to them? Why add anything at all? You have spoiled a perfect case when there is no need to spoil it. I cannot make you take my warning or [advice]; I am used to giving warnings and advice and see the failures follow because it is unheeded. That is the past history of my life.

Today people are listening to me. I try to help them in ways they want or need help and I listen to the holy men and beautiful saintly Sufis. I am not dwelling in any world of my fancied imagination or personal beliefs or ideas or thoughts. Neither am I endangered by legal complications.

Now let us turn to other things. Unfortunately, all my papers have either been destroyed by fire or seized by Mrs. Duce. To give you an idea of what I had to go through, one person challenged me for 20 years to produce my credentials.* When her daughter died—I found them, in her own personal safety box in a bank. That gives you something of who I had to go through.

I had to go through it because your father had to go through it. I still remember in detail all his instructions and suggestions. He told me and this I will swear in any law court, that even among those who thought he trusted them the most and who were [sure] (each one of them) that they loved him the most, only Sakina Furnee, E. D. Cruzatt Zanetti, and perhaps Miss Dowland were fully worthy. I don't know anything directly

* Sam is here referring to Rabia Martin.

of these people but I remember what Sufi Inayat Khan said, and I am still here. And I am spreading the music which is helping unite the East and West as blessed Syed Mohammed [Madani] said: "By the power of thy music, unite East and West."

I read all the early reports and especially those which distinctly stated that *Shifayats* and *Khifayats* could not be Murshids.* Each has his line. I have a distinctly different line. I am entitled to be on *Jamiat Aam.* I can give detailed explanations and commentaries of all the *Gathas* and *Githas* as is definitely stated in the Esoteric Constitution and should I ever have access to esoteric papers again could continue this work.

In the earlier papers and studies there is distinct reference to *fana-fi-Sheikh, fana-fi-Rassoul, fana-fi-Lillah.* My work under *fana-fi-Rassoul* is newly finished . . .

You are entirely correct on each point about the "election" of teachers. I made this point in the 1927–1930 era. The same about other elements, on which points first M. E. de Cruzatt Zanetti supported me and then reneged.

You are entirely correct on all the explanations you give from that point on. I do not see how, in a law court, anybody would dare to flout the esoteric and exoteric constitutions. They would make a laughing stock of the word "Sufi." Both Europe and America are derided in much of the East and rightly derided. The West takes the most holy things and to use your father's expression, makes monkey's toys out of them.

I am in a very strong position to help you coordinate with many, many people in the Orient. But I have to travel incessantly. I am now accomplishing the work of universal brotherhood. It is up to you whether you wish me to continue in friendly alliance or absolute affiliation. I have, [by] God's Grace the strongest weapons in my hands. Nobody else wants them, so I have them.

These weapons are hierarchy and initiation. Although it is distinctly stated in *The Unity of Religious Ideals* that hierarchy is more real than the earth itself. Who believes it? We start out throwing away the teachings of a messenger and think we make up for it by capitalizing his pronouns. This method has been one of universal failure, not universal brotherhood. Among the Sufis here I have had both evidence and instruction on this point of hierarchy. The Western "Sufis" may throw it out; let them.

---

* *Shifayats* are those recognized to lead healing circles. *Khifayats* would be called Khalifs and Khalifas today.

> Then they will fail. All that is written in the *Gathekas* and in this book will have to receive the proper, and to me, supreme evaluation.[466]

Pir Vilayat's letter enumerated a number of measures to take to promote his assumption of leadership of the Sufi Order, including calling for a *Jamiat Aam.* There were indeed legal issues raised against him, barring him from functioning, and many difficulties for Pir Vilayat to go through. His father had warned him and others that would happen.

Pir Vilayat and Samuel did not meet in person for another 12 years. As for what Sam felt at this time, he wished Pir Vilayat well. The future would tell. It was important to him not to gloss over the history of the Sufi Order and the distortions of purpose that Pir Vilayat described on the part of Ali Khan and others. Of equal import to Sam was emphasizing the central significance of Prophet Muhammad, especially to those Board members of the Sufi Movement who had strong reservations about that.

Samuel's poem "Sand and Glass" holds up the life of the Prophet Muhammad as a model for humanity.

> *A man was born in these wastes,*
> *A spiritual son of solitude and emptiness*
> *Who lost his father even before he appeared,*
> *Who lost his mother while yet a little child,*
> *Who never lost the endless Grace of Allah,*
> *The Grace which embraced his vivid emberant heart;*
> *For whosoever walks a single step toward Allah*
> *Will find Allah taking a dozen steps toward himself.*
> *There was a meeting place of the heart-of-man and the Heart-of-God,*
> *There was the removal of a single drop of blood of the young Ahmed*
> *And Qur'an was revealed, revealed upon a solitary peak,*
> *Revealed where the eye sees only far stretching wastes,*
> *Revealed among the ignorant of the ignorant*
> *Who, despite their state, dwelt within the confines of Divine Mercy,*
> *Who, despite their state, became transmitters of the Message of Allah.*
> *So Mohammed, the orphaned Hashimite, became the Messenger of Allah;*
> *So Mohammed, the exiled Meccan, became the spokesman for Allah;*
> *So Mohammed, whose purity of heart excited even his enemies*
> *Became an exemplar for the human race.*[467]

At the Aurobindo Ashram and Anandamayee Ashram

We should be careful to take away from ourselves any thorns that prick us in the personality of others.

Hazrat Inayat Khan[468]

The heart contains all notes, consequently it can harmonize with any other heart. When there is disharmony, it is a head condition; no matter how justified that disharmony, still it is related to nufs. *God in the Supreme Essence contains all goodness and badness or none; that is to say God is the Perfection of quality, never its extension—no matter how great the extension be. God is not multitudes, or largeness, but infinite, and this infinite qualification escapes comprehension of finite mind.*

If the spiritual aspirant keeps the breath in fikr, *if the* talib* *holds the heart in* ishk,† *it is impossible to be unfavorably affected by others. One is either united with all souls or not so united. This does not mean condescension to others. It means either change yourself to become harmonious to that person, or else—with all the force at your command—to drive the evil spirit out of the other and make them whole. The use of this power is not contrary to* ishk *if it heals another."*

Samuel Lewis[469]

Samuel's travels and life-changing experiences in India continued during and after his correspondence with Pirzade Vilayat. He first went to Madras‡ from Hyderabad, then on to Adyar before coming to Pondicherry and the Sri Aurobindo Ashram, where he had been asked to visit several times.

As seen in his descriptions of Sri Aurobindo Ashram and Anandamayee Ashram, Sufi Ahmed Murad uses both the method of becoming harmonious with all as well as the power to drive out ignorance in the course of healing. First he reflected on his experience at Sri Aurobindo Ashram:

> It is indeed a strange experience to find oneself in a realized "Shangrila" or "Shambhala," to find, in fact, what has appeared in book or legend . . .

---

* Seeker of knowledge, student.

† Divine love.

‡ Now Chennai.

Sri Aurobindo Ashram with the Symbol of the Mother above the entrance.

The Roerichs wrote long tales of fancy and fantasy and considered the "truth" of them more important than the facts of life. One stands constantly between the surrealists who vainly consider themselves realists and in no case will examine the world as it is, and those metaphysical people who are only interested in hyperboles which they also call "truth."

The Sri Aurobindo Ashram belongs in all three classes—it is a fact, yet is full of fancies and most of the people here want to be realists with regard to their own accomplishments and skeptics or downright scoffers with regard to others. The worship is directed to Sri Aurobindo and the Mother, which obviates a good deal of prejudice, sectarianism and nonsense, but equally veils the Cosmic God so that He becomes a sort of backstage hand who obeys orders. This is a terrible indictment of what is undoubtedly one of the most curious and also marvelous places in the world.[470]

I was well able to "gauge" the spirituality of the ashram, to compare the India *darshan* with the Sufic *tawwajeh*;* their concentration with the Sufic *murakkabah*† and their *prasad* with Sufic methods. The main difference is the unhallowed method of Indians to claim spirituality in all they do and deny it to others. My Persian Sufi friends reached exactly the same conclusions independently.

This leaves me for a moment in a strange position. In my anti-Billy Graham attitude, I want to tell the world that Shangrila does exist and is neither Buddhist (as the Roerichs dogmatically insisted) nor Christian (?) derived from Milton, but Indian. I would like to tell America that India can tell us a good deal about God. Unfortunately, while the Ashram peo-

---

* *Darshan* is a Hindi word and *tawajjeh* an Arabic one. Here they both refer to the soul-to-soul transmission via the glance from one person (typically a teacher) to another.

† *Murakkabah* is the practice of developing the faculty of concentration and becoming at one with what the student is concentrating on.

Sri Aurobindo

ple also hold to this view, they immediately follow it up by ignoring Christ and Mohammed, compare Aurobindo to Buddha, make Nirvana into a concept—and not a very high or noble concept at that—and call their system "Prana Yoga" which is neither *prana* nor yoga. It is exactly the Indian counterpart of the Japanese *tariki* (other power) as opposed to *jiriki* (self power) . . .

India marches on and the Ashram has much to teach real India, but it could teach a lot more if it would learn, and I am afraid, excepting for the wonderful devotees, it will not. Unfortunately, the devotees, though many, are wrapped up in devotion and leave the noise-making to others.[471]

Sam went to the grave of Margaret Woodrow Wilson near the Sri Aurobindo Ashram and found it to be in poor condition. Eldest daughter of the former U.S. president, she had turned to Indian spirituality toward the end of a life of service. Sam left a contribution and expressed the feeling that the gravesite would someday be a place of pilgrimage. He respected women pioneers and felt they would be more and more included in the times that were coming.

His visit to the Anandamayee Ashram was "short and most important." Anandamayee was described by one swami as "the most perfect flower the Indian soil has produced." Sam met Anandamayee at her Ashram and had much to say:

I definitely felt her instructions, which were like this:

All these Swamis, true and false, establish *sangas* and in turn these *sangas* tend to perpetuate the names of their Founders. This has the two questionable results of establishing rival *sangas,* which is ridiculous; and producing mental idolatry in place of the physical ones at the temple. In either case, instead of finding God you find something or someone else.

Real instruction comes from self to self. Mother [Anandamayee] does not use *manas* [mind], and there is no need for her to. *Manas* is for science, art and culture, not for God-realization. In writing letters or talking to scientists, *manas* is necessary. *Manas* is finite, not infinite. Mother

> uses *Vijnanamayakosh* when she has to speak.* This produces strong result and strange effect, but it does not establish hindrances to spiritual development.
>
> The commentaries of her followers, other than their spiritual experiences, are useless and confusing. Their experiences are valid and their love is valid. The most is nothing but egotism asserting itself. It would be better for them to repeat *La Ellaha El Il Allah.*† Now, despite her efforts, her followers remain in ignorance. But her love prevents her from scolding them often and her love would be the best means to elevate them, not her words. And if she avoids all the rival schools her followers will establish another and rival school too.
>
> What is worse, her followers call her Avatar, Saraswati, Kali or higher one moment and even in the [same] article compare her to Kant, Carpenter and Krishnamurti, etc. This is the stigma on all spiritual movements.
>
> Fortunately Atmananda has not fallen into this trap and I hope to visit her and [that] ashram later.[472]

Upon his departure, Samuel headed not to the Atmananda ashram but rather to the ashram that held the highest magnetism for him, Anandashram in Kanhangad, where he traveled by train after a few days' stopover in Madras. Responding to an invitation to visit there, he was elated at the prospect of meeting up with Papa Ramdas again in person.

Papa Ramdas Loves Everybody

> *Papa loves everybody. From one point of view, being a Sufi, I am a Muslim; from another point of view one could call me a Buddhist, for the whole life has been commingled with the intellectual and spiritual pursuit of the Buddha-Dharma. With Papa, I was his child.*
>
> SAMUEL LEWIS[473]

Papa Ramdas had earlier recognized Samuel in several letters, praising his knowledge of Indian teachings, and remembered him from his visit

---

* *Vijnanamaya kosha* is a Sanskrit term referring to intuition, intellect—that aspect of our consciousness that is not entangled in what we are doing or thinking, but rather, is acutely aware of what we are doing and thinking.

† This is Samuel's typical rendering of the Arabic phrase more commonly seen as "La ilaha illa'llah" (There is no God but God), which also may be understood as "Everything is transient except for God, the one and only being."

to America. Sam was determined to reunite with this teacher. He saw in Ramdas an illuminated embodiment of God realization through the heart, a true *bhakti* yogi, and he wished to learn everything he could from this extraordinary man. Happily, Sam was able to travel south and spend a week at the ashram.

Later he would write about Anandashram in "The Lotus and the Universe."

> Go down the Malabar coast, and not far from the town of Kasaragod, there is a little railway station called Kanhangad. A taxi or a man may be sent to take you to Anandashram, the "Abode of Bliss." It is like stepping into a Marie Corelli novel—someone will shortly appear and whatever has been your thought or wish will be provided. This is due to the living Grace operating through Krishnabai, the Mataji or Mother . . .
>
> Anandashram is Sanskrit for *Gan Eden,* which we translated as "Garden of Eden." Both mean "The Abode of Bliss." All religions proclaim the primordial and the ultimate bliss; some insist that bliss and everyday life are not separate. This is the teaching of scriptures, unfortunately not the teaching of men, for men proclaim . . . what they themselves have not experienced. Bliss is operational, God can be and is known . . .
>
> Swami Ramdas, whom many of us called "Papa," was what he preached . . . He has been both a man of the world and a *sadhu* (recluse). He has known both society and solitude, pain and pleasure . . . He lived in God, for God, with God . . . [474]

One need not write at length on Swami Ramdas; one can obtain his books.* Samuel Lewis did become Papa's child. Years later among his students in San Francisco he often talked of his time at Anandashram with Papa Ramdas and Mother Krishnabai. He was wide open to receive from them. In particular he loved telling the tale of how Papa helped him in his meditation. In the morning there were classes and opportunity for *bhajan* (devotional call-and-response chanting). Papa was available in the afternoon to those who were visiting the ashram.

Sam was there as a student, not a tourist like most, and he wanted time with his teacher. Papa found Sam in the afternoon sitting in the

---

*Ramdas's brilliant, transparent autobiography in two volumes, *In Quest of God* and *In the Vision of God,* is available. For downloadable ebooks, see anandashram.org/media/ebooks/e-books-in-english/.

Entrance to Anandashram

meditation room, quite obviously intent on sitting in full lotus posture. He said Sam was too stiff and to stop sitting in that posture and drop the tension. He then piled up pillows, and then more and more pillows, insisting that Sam should sit on them all. It allowed full relaxation into the reality of heart.

The mantra *Om Sri Ram Jai Ram Jai Jai Ram* was a constant in the ashram. Meditation required the breath and the heart to focus on the continuous internal repetition of the mantra with each breath. Of course, the radiant presence of Ramdas's bliss and his devotion to the God Reality in each and every being was its own elixir. Once Ramdas was asked to describe his state of realization. His answer was magnificent. He said, "Like the sacred river Ganges that has flowed from the source and become one with the Ocean, I continue to flow toward the ocean."

Sam echoed this in "The Lotus and the Universe."

> In a truly scientific and yet noble spirit [Ramdas] sought and, even after finding, continued to seek, as if the living God were a mine of ceaseless treasures, a fountain of truly living waters.
>
> That God is the Reality, the Life, the Love, the Bliss, is neither new nor original . . . Papa was not the first, nor will he be the last of such a stream . . .
>
> The lover of God is the lover of humanity. He does not have to hide in forsaken caves and monasteries. Jesus has told us, "Let your light shine before men." This can be a reality even here, even now, and not just a symbol . . .
>
> India has many problems, complicated by the predicament that Indians know everything; they know everything and do next to nothing.

There is no difficulty in convincing these people: whatever one affirms is in their traditions . . .

If Papa had met Friedrich [Engels], they would have probably gotten along fine . . . Papa concentrated on feeding the poor and not on treatises on the subject.

At Anandashram, Papa's community, we find poverty is faced not by dialectic, not by ethereal planning, but by substantial effort. While the Congress and the Communist Party people stand glaring at each other, the expanding Ashram has been caring for more and more of the poor of the region.[475]

Sam described the ashram, which lies at the foot of a mountain.

The barn is kept scrupulously clean and the washings gravitate into a surrounding foss. All available animal droppings are also thrown into the foss, along with vegetable wastes. In other words, we have an organic gardening farm . . .

Springs have been found . . . and so a complete irrigation system has been provided . . . There is continuous harvesting of protein crops. Besides the coconut, one finds cashews, peanuts and other legumes . . .

The Ashram also has its hospital and clinic . . . The "garden" is dominated by a kind of cotton bush which functions horticulturally like an ornamental rose. It supplies bolls continuously and keeps one man busy full-time through the year attending them, harvesting, spinning and weaving.

Mother Krishnabai [has been called] a living miracle . . . Her heart and being comprehend everything and everyone . . .

Mother Krishnabai

Mother Krishnabai supervises every facet down to the slightest detail, and she does this naturally . . . My first meeting with Mataji Krishnabai came in San Francisco . . .

In San Francisco, Mataji helped prepare a dinner for Swami Ramdas and one could observe her manners. It was as if she were preparing for a communion service. Later I saw her both supervise in the kitchen at Anandashram and prepare the meals. She is the heart-blood

> of the *sangha* (brotherhood)* which brings all vitality and takes away all poisons.[476]

Both of these beings had a tremendous impact on Sam's life. When he was ready to leave the ashram, he was totally absorbed in the reality of Ramdas's presence. Sam told of this departure on many occasions. He related that when he woke up the last two mornings at the end of his visit, he believed he was Papa Ramdas. So, he found himself experiencing the world as Papa did. On the day of his departure he said to Papa, "Papa, it's time to go," and Papa responded, laughingly saying, "Yes, but who stays and who goes?!"

Sam had fully met Papa's soul. It was a true soul-to-soul transmission, and it brought the joyful realization of Ram (God) in every aspect of being. This transmission had a beautiful positive effect on Sam's life. It was the final touch deeply needed by him to move joyfully toward completeness in his growing work as teacher. When he gave the Walk of Papa Ramdas to his advanced Saturday night class, it was full of realization. To his students it looked like the walk of Murshid Samuel Lewis that was quite visible every day.

Sam was impressed with Anandamayee's realization and her constant love, yet he felt she maintained a distance from the students rather in the manner of a hermit. In this way she starkly contrasted with Mother Krishnabai, who had no such withdrawal. Sam accepted Mother Krishnabai fully in every way. In the mid to late '60s when he had large classes in San Francisco and in Marin County, Murshid Sam would at times say that Mother Krishnabai was the most realized person living on the planet. She ran the ashram after Papa Ramdas left his body only a few years after Sam's visit. Krishnabai, too, was a fully realized presence of her teacher.

---

*Today this term would more typically be translated "spiritual family" or "spiritual community."

The Evolution of a Name; Ajmir, New Delhi, and on to Lahore

Moineddin Chishti

As he recounted in "Vision and Ritual in Sufism,"[477] prior to 1946 Samuel had always considered Hazrat Inayat Khan his "guardian spirit." After that time, having lost the same tooth that Muhammad lost and seeing a laughing Inayat in vision, he understood that Inayat had turned him over to Muhammad. From then on, it was either Muhammad or Jesus Christ who appeared as his guardian spirit. Muhammad gave him the initial and name A. Murad,[478] a *murad* being one graced by the Divine Spirit. When Sam was in Dacca earlier in his current journey, Maulana Ghafoor of the Chishtia Order gave him the more complete name Ahmed Murad.

After his week at Anandashram, Sam traveled by train straight to Bombay, a city he now was accustomed to, visiting folk dancing events and familiar places. From there he went to Ajmir where he visited the *dargah* of Moineddin Chishti many times, "the most celebrated Islamic shrine this side of Iraq." Samuel had long foreseen Ajmir to be the culmination of his visit in India, his Mecca.

> There had been no letter or communication but when I arrived at the [Ajmir] station it was filled with people. The whole crowd followed me to my rooms and told me they were waiting for me at the *dargah*.
>
> I was taken to the tomb of the saint, but in a ritual and with one or two exceptions this was the only place where there was a formal ritual. I was the guest at lunch and then they took me back to the tomb when my guide said, "Close your eyes. What do you see?"
>
> Closing my eyes I felt the presence of a man who gave me a robe (it has always been the same robe), but this vision was different from any before and since. For when I closed my eyes it appeared the same, and it was like a solid vision, and I tried opening and closing my eyes many times. Always the same. Then my guide asked me my name and I told

Dargah of Moineddin Chishti

him "Ahmed Murad." He said, "From now on it is Ahmed Murad Chisti." I am to represent the Chistis in all non-Islamic countries.*

The next day there was a big feast and a great ritual. But on the evening between there was the musical performance . . . I have never heard such uplifting music. There is nothing like it in the whole West. There is some "uplift" from Eastern rites and also from the Sufi ceremonies in the Near East,† but they did not have the tremendous effect on the heart and consciousness. It is like being bathed in an infinite ocean of love.[479]

It is beyond belief what happens to the human voice actually in love with an actual God.[480]

In Ajmir, Samuel also twice visited the shrine of Moineddin Chishti's successor in Delhi, Pir Qutbuddin Bakhtiar Kaki. He wrote:

> As soon as one sat down to [meditate], the whole place walls, floor and ceiling began to echo and reecho loud and in English, "**What Do You Want**!"
>
> Your Murshid was not such a hero and ran out of the place.
>
> At the end of second day . . . one came back and then asked the Saints [for] blessing and guidance and the answer came clear, and again in English and loud: "**The Request Is Granted**."[481]
>
> The next time I received a supernal instruction in the love and compassion side of Islam.[482]
>
> I had an inner initiation from Moin-ud-din Chisti and an outer initiation from Syed Faruq Hussein Chisti. Similar things happened in vision and in outer form.[483]

Once more Sam went to New Delhi.

---

*Research has not uncovered corroboration of this assignment. Possibly Sam here refers to a foretelling in vision; as he later notes, events sometimes occurred both "in vision and in outer form."

†Today this region is generally referred to as the Middle East.

> The final touch . . . came when I visited the Egyptian Embassy for two hours. Just to show you how God works—Murshid manifested and foretold me exactly what would happen—the man I was going to see in Egypt is here in India now acting as cultural advisor. I was with him a long time and we discussed what I have never been able to talk about to or with anybody. The meeting with the Asst. Consul was even more cordial. He welcomed me as a Sufi and no nonsense.
>
> The Pakistani Commission at Bombay thinks I am already a saint. The meeting was over my head, but the following three—American Consulate, Ajmir, and Egyptian Embassy—shall make me quite considerate.
>
> I visited Murshid's tomb as if for the last time. He told me he was everywhere, and as he had already manifested elsewhere, it was not necessary to [give] my spatial obeisance.[484]

Sam arrived in Delhi on the 25th of October, 1956. He would only spend three days there but was quite happy with the experience. He reflected on his trip in a letter to a friend, persevering in keeping his diaries up to date despite his seemingly endless activities:

> I think my 3-months trip cost me about $600, or $200 a month. The expenses have been some air travel, and for a while, mailing, which, together with gift purchases accounts for a good $100 of this $600. Naturally, city expenses are high. In Calcutta, a hotel runs over $6 a day, this one a little over $4, but at Bombay, it costs about $3. Taxis have been high, but that is because of the need to save time, and the extreme success I have had in making contacts . . . A small item has been gifts, added by the fact that I wish to assist in some of the present flood relief.
>
> I gave 20 Rups. to my guide, 20 more to the caretaker of my Murshid's shrine, and 50 Rups. to the Ramakrishna Mission—which amounts, with taxi fare, to over $20, and may give more before I leave. Indians are, as a whole, spiritual, without being humanitarian. I have to excuse the Ramakrishna Mission from the last. There are, no doubt, men in India who are more advanced than the Ramakrishna Vedantists, but that advancement is one-sided . . . They have not the consciousness of the whole of humanity . . .
>
> This balanced inner and outer development I have found among the Ramakrishna people.[485]

Sam was very grateful for the presence of Papa Ramdas in his life. He was happy to report being embraced by the depth of love, joy and devotion that he attained because of his special relationship with this Guru.

> Remember God brought me to Papa. I needed an element of *bhakti* for my own development. I feel personally attached to Anandashram and believe I shall so feel till the end of my days. I do not feel any personal attachment to the Ramakrishna Mission at all. But they said I had kept my inner and outer eyes open when I gave my report today to the two Swamis Maharaj (of Calcutta and Delhi). These men have asked nothing from me. They have explained their work. I have seen a good deal of their work which they have not explained, but I have seen it. It is both humanitarian and humanistic, and so, is not a lopsided spirituality.
>
> Propaganda is not truth and noise does not make a *mantram.* I told the Swamis that, en masse, the Indian people were, to me, the most spiritual people in the world, but en masse, the Brahmins, priests, *pundits, sadhus,* and *sannyasin* were even behind the spiritual leaders elsewhere. They thought that that was a very observant conclusion. It is my own. I made it. I happen to agree with them. I gave though they asked me for nothing. I did not give much at Ajmir where I had the most wonderful social and spiritual experiences. Those people do not sense the suffering of flood-victims. My Sufi colleague even refused a contribution from me. He thinks even flood sufferers should work and not beg, but he permitted me to give to the *dargah*-custodian referred to above and I shall give again.
>
> Charity is a racket in India, but not like the U.S. At the top, there are many who lovingly give, and at the bottom there are many who selfishly take. The Vedanta Mission is doing such a colossal work without trumpets and in time of greatest need among the people. The Orthodox spend their money on gaudery and piffle decoration.
>
> The swamis also agreed with my criticism of Indian art. The Southern ornate massive-idol buildings are not to God. They are super-expressions of the deification of man's emotional nature and sometimes his ego. They have nothing to do with Truth or Ultimates. India has not yet discovered Ramakrishna. It may put his name side-by-side with others.[486]

Samuel Lewis always had before himself a vision of the whole of humanity and had no hesitation in reaching out to others as well as learning from them. From New Delhi he wrote to Professor E. T. Bell at the California Institute of Technology in Pasadena, commenting on Professor Bell's book, *Men of Mathematics.* He had picked up the book in Bombay to counterbalance the emotional-metaphysical milieu he had been operating in. Sam titled his letter "New Opportunities for Mathematics" and went on to discuss in detail his views on General Semantics, logic, architecture, infinity and cosmic consciousness. He ended his letter with, "Finally, the Orient needs the kind of sincere, straightforward thinking you have given in your books, plus the delightful coloring of wit and humor, to carry it along. I am sure there are many ways East and West can get together, and I am sure Professor Radhakrishnan would be among the first to welcome this."[487]

The October letter to Nuria also revealed Sam's concern about whether his letters had been taken seriously, then provided reflections on his last days in India:

> I have failed, for the most part, in getting replies from people in the S.F. Bay area, excepting my attorney, who has been very prompt . . . I can only conclude either that mail has not gone through (this I know has happened in some instances) or that my reports have not been taken seriously. In the case of my attorney, I stressed over and over that my position in the Orient was about 10 times as high as presumed, but my guess was indeed much lower than resulting events have shown.
>
> I leave this Saturday for Lahore. I have failed in my astrological and Ayurvedic efforts. The former has little promise; the latter became too big, plus the fact that my hosts were compelled to change their posts without notice . . . I must come this way again.
>
> From Lahore, I go into the Northwest. Changes now require my traveling by rail in Pakistan. This will slow the journey, yet enable me to visit places otherwise off schedule. I had expected to be in Egypt by December 1, and in the States by Christmas. Unless advised otherwise by my attorney, it will take another month to reach S.F.: Boston, New York, Washington, St. Louis, Dallas, (Houston?), Albuquerque, then a long stay around L.A. Most of these are "heavies" too. And I do not know where I shall settle. I should be studying languages and it may mean re-entering college, but I come at the wrong season for languages, so we shall see.

> The importance of Yoga here has been much exaggerated. Sufism has 10 times as much to give as Indian philosophy, with the very possible exception of Vedanta . . . Yet there are many great thinkers here, especially around the universities, and many great scientists whose fame is abroad but not at home. The Northerners and Punjabis seem to have the best "stuff" in them. I no longer know how to be both honest and diplomatic . . .
>
> I shall later write to Vilayat Inayat Khan. I like him in general, but told him I would never accept the capitalization of his father's name—utterly uncalled for.* I can assure you that the Arabs and Egyptians who are versed in Sufism would be appalled. Swami Ramdas told me Sufism is sweeping Europe, but it stems from Morocco, and I bet it is not mixed up with personalism.[488]

Departure from Pakistan, and a Sought-After Poem

> *It is also time for those who think they can explain samsara to take a calm, dispassionate view of all the drama on earth. And for those who give superfluous lectures on* lila *to stop emoting when the newspapers clamor. This is not only the history of the earth; it is the super-history of samsara. Fortunately, there is another force on earth above, beyond and inside all this noise, which is Providence. God. Allah. It is beyond the understanding of those who use the phrase "beyond understanding" and keep on talking. It may be quite within the comprehension of those who never say that—children and Ramdases, and real sages.*
>
> Samuel Lewis[489]

Ahmed Murad Chisti left India and arrived in Lahore, West Pakistan, on October 28. His stay was short, but he was recognized and invited to speak several times, and he connected with professors at both the University of the Punjab and Islamic University there. Lahore would become a major focus for him and his Sufi work, and he would return there when he traveled to Asia one more time.

Sam wrote of a few highlights of his time in Lahore:

---

*Sam refers here to the capitalization not of the name, but of pronouns referring to Hazrat Inayat Khan in Pir Vilayat's letter.

> Went to . . . the Shahi Mosque of Shah Jehan, where we climbed to the top of a minaret. There are four, and they are smaller than Kutb but open to public for 2 annas. There is a fine view from the top. Lahore is pleasant at this time and there are many trees including some Eucs.* The mosque has not been kept up but the local govt. is doing some repair work . . .
>
> I was too [tired] for Shalimar, and did not get my rest; I knew I would be unwell and am, slightly. For I had to visit the young men at Ahmadiyya for dinner. We had [Pakistani] chicken and rice, which I had before, sweet, grapes and apples. I do not care for the sweet but the rest is OK. But the Muslims do not have enough vegetables for me and the food at this hotel is very good and balanced.[490]

During dinner with the Ahmadiyyas, an Islamic revival sect, he discussed areas where they differed from Sunnis:

> a. Death, etc. of Jesus . . .
> b. Selection of a reformer
> c. Modernization of customs
> d. Liberal versus rigid interpretation of Qur'an.[491]

Sam found rigidity and suspicion of each other among other Muslim sects: Sunni and Shia (strongly) and Ismaili (to a lesser degree). He concluded,

> I shall try to follow this up. I am as yet un-satisfied with the way they write their books, using whitewash instead of ink.[492]

Sam left Lahore on October 30. In a diary entry he wrote of his activities in the cities of Rawalpindi, Abbotabad and Mansehra, which he visited from October 31st to November 14th.

> Had a fine meeting at the Consulate, with introductions, such as Wilson at the YMCA, who is interested in Square-Dancing. Bought cards for 8 Rupees from the Civil Military Gazette who treated me wonderfully.
>
> Saw Rock Edict of Asoka . . . Went to dinner on November 3rd to meet a lot of VIP's. Spoke a few moments and when I said I would introduce Sufism to Harvard, was given an ovation, followed by questions and discussion with a few . . .

---

*Eucalypti.

I have since spoken on "the Influence of the Prophet on Human Destiny," and November 6th,* at the Forestry Exp.† Station on "Forests I have Dwelt in and Visited." Well attended and I met some fine scientists. Chief, Dr. Khalil.

I wrote to Kinoshita . . . I gave him a list of people he might contact . . . I have a strong feeling something will come of it . . . The training school and exp. station go to Peshawar next year. I am awaiting tree lists from both the Conservationist and Director of the Forestry Exp. at this writing.[493]

On November 6 from Abbottabad, true to one of his primary missions on this trip, Sam again wrote to Professor Nelson in San Francisco:

In an exaggerated sense, it may be said, that I have laid aside hoe and Levis' for cloak-and-dagger. It is not that, but I did run into a nest of Commies and later met a bunch of Hruskies.‡ Then I had a long run of hosts getting ill or being transferred during a political upheaval . . .

The other day, I was taken northward about 20 miles, to a friend of my friends and he proved to be the largest landowner in this region and the most enterprising Pakistani I have yet met. He has a very diversified farm—something I have not yet seen in all Asia. He does not only grow Rice, Jute, Wheat and Sugarcane crops, but all kinds of truck and garden vegetables. These are all familiar: Radish, Cauliflower, Spinach, Onion, Potatoes, etc.

The fruit trees especially interested me because he uses the method which I always claim is natural. There are wild Apricots, Pears and Olives on his land, so he grafts onto them. He has introduced six kinds of Japanese Plum to the Apricots. *P. persica*, Orange, Lemon, Walnuts (native varieties, as yet no grafting.) In other words, I was in California.

He has also introduced Eucalyptus and Ash. This brings me to that controversial subject, the Euc. All over India I ran into: "They might grow them in that Province, but they will not grow here," only to find more in the next Province. Politics and linguistic feuds result in ironic and stubborn ignorance . . .

---

*Sam often began a diary entry on one date (here November 4) and completed it on a later date.

†Experimental.

‡Russians.

> Late in the afternoon yesterday I visited the Exp. Station and college. He (the Director) has promised to give me a list of seeds and trees available for sale and exchange. I told him a little of my Japanese experiences and gave him a brief on California in general and you in particular. (There is a job open here if you want it—instruction is all in English.) They use a mixture of International and English names for plants, not always sticking to either the common or scientific usages, but that makes it rather easy for identification.[494]

The last thing Professor Nelson might have been interested in would be getting a job in the Far East. However, he was good-natured and he put up with how Sam had mentioned him to every person and in every place he visited related to horticulture. Nelson had said Sam's greatest ability was inspiring other people to do things. This trip was certainly an example of that. There are more than 30 letters that he wrote Nelson, often filled with potential contacts for him. Sam ended this last letter to him from Asia:

> The Forestry Department has done a lot of work on Medicinal Trees and Shrubs which is out of my line and a little, too little from my point of view, on Mycology. The above leaves a lot of room for follow-up. They have worked out an Ecological Map based on Acacias for West Pakistan. I once worked out the same thing for Oaks in South Carolina. End of official report.[495]

On November 12 Sam was in Rawalpindi and found a poem he had long been looking to find again, in the book *Great Men of India*. In it was an article on Aurangzeb, a 15th century Mughal emperor, by Elizabeth D'Oyley. Sam quoted her as writing, "Less wise than Akbar his great-grandfather, he could not see that no power on earth can make men think alike, and that God is to be reached by many ways."[496] Sam had found the poem meaningful to him personally. It aligned with his great interest in the Mughals, particularly Emperor Akbar. The poem reads:

> *O God (wrote Abul-Fazl, friend of Akbar) in every temple I see people that see thee, and in every language I hear spoken, people praise thee.*
> *Polytheism and Islam feel after thee.*
> *Each religion says, "Thou art one, without equal."*

If it be a mosque, people murmur the holy prayer; and if it be a Christian Church,
people ring the bell from love of thee.
Sometimes I frequent the Christian cloister, sometimes the mosque.
But it is thou whom I seek from temple to temple.
Thy elect have no dealings with heresy or with orthodoxy; for neither of them
stands behind the screen of truth.
Heresy to the heretic, and religion to the orthodox.
But the dust of the rose-petal belongs to the heart of the perfume seller.[497]

In his heart Samuel Lewis recognized himself in this beloved poem. He was certainly a gifted perfume seller. Sam returned to the school in Rawalpindi and gave two talks, "The Teaching of Islam in the West" and "Spiritual Aspects of Islam." From there he wrote:

> May join the Royal Asiatic Society of Great Britain when I get to London—if London Bridge does not fall down. Sorry, in a sense, not to be able to go to Egypt. Otherwise, my trip has been very, very successful and I am wondering whether I shall have to go back to work. My income has been greater than my expenses—one forgets when one calculates in all different coins and the Rupee has been going down. At Lahore I expect to make large book purchases, and here and there I have been buying Pakistani shoes.[498]

Back in Lahore, Sam wrote on November 18:

> The weather here is lovely and there are moonlit nights. I generally walk before breakfast—for exercise; and at dusk, to the book stalls. Newspapers are hard to get. The *Pakistan Times* is the most bigoted paper I have ever read and as dishonest as the Communist press, although possibly subsidized by them. I say they have lost Kashmir on account of it. When the paper is not criticizing a foreign power—U.S. more than France—it is attacking the government. I have said I did not know God made so many mistakes until I came to Pakistan. Yet strange to say there are more saintly people here also. Thank God they generally do not read English.[499]

He then wrote to Gavin Arthur about Munshi Bashir Ahmed, an astrologer he had met:

> If what the astrologer told me is true—and it does not go contrary to my intuitions or occult experiences—my next mission will be big. These

> experiences are all along the lines of Sufic tradition, and they can neither be invoked nor prevented. They form a definite pattern and some of them have been confirmed so soon after that one cannot lay them aside. My manner of getting money, as told by the Munshi, also was in strict accord with Sufic tradition.
>
> I kept on repeating this. I have written a final letter to the Islamic Society of S.C. Either I am one of them or not. No fence sitting. If they want to follow [Landau], God bless them; they will need it . . .
>
> The occult-mystical tradition behind Islam is tremendous and effective. I may do some intellectual work on it, either in New York, or in many places, again according to advice.
>
> Remember I expect at least one big meeting at Rudolph Schaeffer. If this Munshi thing goes over, I do not wish to make it public. I want to work [in] a semi-secret quiet manner with [one] Myra Kingsley and with [one] Gavin Arthur—if he can stick to it—as if God were money. This because the broadcasting of it will render it entirely ineffectual. This is either a great find, or a great hoax.[500]

Sam was interested in bringing this astrologer to the U.S., if the Munshi was as good as he thought he might be. He added that he expected to be in London about December 8.

On November 27 he wrote Quantz Crawford again:

> I have been positively successful in all my ventures, but this very success, or stream of successes has tired me . . . They may seem fantastic and some of these will seem fantastic . . .
>
> I have asked Gavin and Chris Lowejieff . . . to intercede to try to make peace with the Asian Academy* on Broadway. I want either peace or war; there will be no cold war. The whole continent of Asia is now in no room for nonsense. I cannot make little people big nor can they make me little. God has ordained a place for me, it was clearly expressed in Murshid's very early American lectures (1911–1912 period) and by his instructions. I am not rolling them out carefully. The West does not know Sufism and the West cannot stop the message of God, whether through one person or others. I have written strongly to Vilayat. I am stronger now and have many interviews coming up.[501]

---

*Sam refers here to the American Academy of Asian Studies.

Sam reported that he had gained confidence. All his experiences abroad supported that new strength and he was now turning his attention back home. However, the Asian Academy did not respond to Sam's efforts to bridge the gap, no matter how hard he tried.

On December 3, he found time to write two more diary letters to friends.

> I have to get to the right men at the embassy. When I get to the Americans, as in U.S.I.S., there is nothing to it . . .
>
> I next have coming up an interview with the Auditor General of Pakistan. I went to the Egyptian Embassy the other day and my mission to that country was completed even without visiting it. You can see how fed up I am concerning that nonsense there are no Sufis! Why my interviewer understood me better in 10 minutes than some people have in ten years. And this morning I was closeted with my newspaper vendor who belongs to the Kadiri order of Dervishes . . .
>
> **Anyone who lectures on Sufism is a liar, a thief and an idolater.** This is one of the basic premises of Sufism! One talks of God, about God, how to find God, how God helps man and the knowledge and [attributes] and wisdom of God, etc. That is the only Sufism.
>
> You may add to that, if you will, the methods used by Sufis to attain to spiritual understanding. But a description of those methods feeds you like a cookbook or menu writer feeds you . . .
>
> College super-graduates to the contrary, even Moineddin Ibn l'Arabi, can be understood by one who has performed Sufic practices and attained to grades and stations in accordance to these practices. In life we use soap without knowing its chemical formula, though I doubt if we could make good soap today without knowing organic chemistry.
>
> There is the moral side of Sufis and the esoteric side. The one you learn by following precepts and practices of others; the second, though you are given the directions, you must perform yourself. The moral emphasis is much greater than in Hinduism; the esoteric certainly less than [in] Tantra. But Sufis never give long discourses on the wonders of wisdom. Discourses on the wonders of wisdom are only veils over the truth. They often do not even awaken the intuitive qualities in us. [502]
>
> **I Am Not Fooling in the Least.**
>
> In my relatively short journey I have met either the cabinet ministers or the real rulers of every country. I have been at the tops socially but what is more, I have been with the top leaders of the "religious" world

who wield [far] more power than the Pope. It is hard to understand this. Sam Lewis is hardly a small frog in a small pond at home but **No One Refuses Anything to Ahmed Murad Chisti,** who is yours truly.[503]

In the midst of everything Sam often looked for humor.

From Abbottabad to England and Back to the U.S.A.

Sufi Ahmed Murad Chisti made his way via train to Karachi, which he thoroughly enjoyed. From there he took a flight to England, where his stay was brief.

Sam found little genuine Buddhist activity in England, as Robert Clifton/Phra Sumangalo had written to him would be the case. He visited such landmarks as Kew Gardens, where an attendant apologized for there being very few plants in bloom. Sam's response was that he could already see them as they would turn out to be. He made a connection with a Buddhist teacher there, Jack Austin, whom Sumangalo had mentioned and with whom Sam would continue to sporadically communicate.

He wrote to Gavin Arthur in his diary of December 13:

> I have been way behind. The last days in Karachi were very successful . . . I left again on a Saturday, my bête noire which always means one cannot get cash readily. I had to buy more rupees than I wanted . . . Got stranded in Vienna . . .
>
> On top of that I met two of my hosts immediately and had tea with Prof. Gilbert Brookes (S.G.B.) who taught English and Literature at Peshawar. He lives in the home of Michael Faraday.* He says Faraday wired the house himself and many things have not been changed. Then met Jack Austin and we had a Chinese dinner which cost a little over $3 for two, which he considered expensive—but they had a chicken liver curry which was excellent . . .
>
> Have tickets for *The Gondoliers* and Sadler's Wells Ballet. Have done a lot of walking, always interesting . . . Have also gone to Downing St. and spent some time trying to locate my old friend Joe Wood at the foreign office. It took two hours to locate him and then to learn he has a roving job (just as he always had). I later talked to his Father-in-law. If we meet, we can do a lot about the world problems. This seems braggadocio and will to those who know nothing of operative Sufism.[504]

---

*An English scientist, Faraday made significant contributions to electromagnetic theory.

Samuel Lewis saw himself as an example of operative Sufism. He was always focused on the universal good. He could only make claims for himself because he had surrendered his sense of self to the One and Only Being and was dedicated to acting as an instrument of that reality.

In England his ever-energetic activities continued. He wrote to Gavin:

> Spent some time locating the Royal Asiatic Society which I have joined . . . I failed to find the Society for the promotion of the Study of Religions, whose letter I have carried . . . But when Jack Austin asked me to go to Younghusband's house I met Miss Sharples with whom I used to correspond years ago. When I announced I owed them money, everybody was happy. I was embraced after the meeting by a lady, the Princess Poon of England, who is a daughter of the late Lord Curzon. Do I get in and how? I don't know myself. I shall see the secretary Monday. Have to go to Kew today. Met the Asst. Supt. yesterday and when he learned I was actually interested in his actual research—the grasses of India—had a lovely time.[505]

Sam spent two days at the Kew Gardens, and wrote a critique about the grasses of England and more to Professor Harry Nelson:

> Kew is over 300 acres and even now is not bad. I was not impressed with the greenhouse collections. The houses themselves are being remodeled, with trouble. They are making them with corrugated plastic. The last experiment was the use of Aluminum instead of iron or steel and the coefficients of expansion of the Al. and glass were so different

Greenhouses, Kew Gardens, England

that there have been drafts in winter and inability to open the vents in the summer. Some of the houses are very old, and despite what I have read in books and magazines on mechanized farming I should say the frames and houses are behind the times. There are far less pipes than I have seen in the U.S. or Japan, and there is not great heat although I did not visit the orchid houses nor ferneries. And where I did go there were few or no attendants—evidently when it is not too cold or rainy they work outside.[506]

He wrote from London to Robert Clifton on December 17.

Well, old dear, my trip nears its end and it has been most successful and enlightening. I do not know whether you have written to me or not. I do know I do not receive mail and I also know my mail is not received . . .

I did meet Jack [Austin] because I sent a cable and he sent me to the World Congress of Faiths, a group which I used to belong to and we lost all track of each other. I am rejoining them . . .

Well I mentioned some of my researches, the usual British answer: "Oh, but all the research has been done on that by experts." So I asked for a certain book. "Never heard of it." Well they had it and when it was opened, the usual flourish of apologies. Good old British reactions . . .

Jack spoke last night. I pity him. Try to explain Zen to a mixed audience of [Theravadins] and Tories and make Zen clear to each in their very different outlooks. His talk was clear enough, his manner OK and his answers excellent. But whether they reached the cortices of his hearers I do not know. Anyhow I am going to try to link him with some others in the States and I certainly want to give him at least limited cooperation . . .

I also have re-contacted my best friend here. It is another of those fairy book experiences. What I told him years ago still holds and now we are both in positions to do something about world affairs, not just talkie-talky.[507]

He went on to criticize aspects of England:

Despite "Joy to the world," despite "Nirvana," despite "Islam" there is almost universal gloom here and I am running around calling myself "Puck of Pukhtunistan" and laughing. Jon says I [look] younger than 12 years ago which may be true. I am Alice at the finish of the two books, finding all those great characters to be mere [pawns] or words.[508]

Throughout his trip Sam would often mischievously present himself in the guise of the character he called Puck of Pukhtunistan. Years before, when he worked with Dr. Baker, he shared the idea of putting on the Puck persona for fun. When he got to travel in Afghanistan and Egypt he created "Pukhtunistan" for additional delight.

Puck was Sam's alter ego. At times he let Puck have full charge and even wrote letters and articles from Puck's point of view. That voice allowed Sam to be serious and comical at the same time.

Sam had a great ability to adapt to different identities based on his inner capacities and his ongoing desire for spiritual freedom in the midst of life. He freely and without fear danced into many cultural circumstances, often with great acceptance. His unusual capacity to become what the situation called for was ultimately a major aspect of his function in the Spiritual Hierarchy.

Sam concluded his trip to Asia with several concerns. He had earlier written to his friends that when he was in South India he found himself in a nest of Commies and reported it at once. In Bombay the Consul insisted he expose every non-American in any university in the U.S. who stood in his way on Asian subjects and said further that the U.S. intelligence service would back him. As he had told Joe and Margaret, "Personally I prefer some constructive methods especially in the international exchange of musicians and folk dancers. I am going to Washington to try to get active help."[509]

Sam arrived in New York City with his trip abroad behind him and yet absolutely with him. Great changes were on the horizon.

Edna Bellefontaine, dancer and painter—known as the Mata Hari of Kashmir

CHAPTER 12

Between Travels

Samuel Lewis's Romantic Connection with Edna the Dancer

I have always had a "song," I [have] always been looking for a "dancer."

SAMUEL LEWIS[510]

THE BEAUTIFUL AND TALENTED DANCER SAM HAD MET in India was prominent in his mind. His proposed union with Edna Bellefontaine and her unusual life story deserve attention. Sages in India and Pakistan had seen marriage in his future along with great success. However, marriage was quite out of tune with the Sam many people knew. For example, Sam's friend Sumangalo had written saying a known acquaintance of theirs had begun to deal with his chronic sexual impulses and had become a Mahayana monk. Sam responded:

> It is strange and I never could understand it, or Freud, that just so much of the mental apparatus is given to sex. I have refused ever to call sex behavior or misbehavior "right" or "wrong" and I have refused to stuff the whole cranium down into a portion of the cerebellum where it obviously is not. People say you have not lived until . . . but there are a lot more gray cells than that.[511]

Back in the Bay Area in 1957, Sam was enthralled with Edna and often shared his feelings with friends. In a 1958 letter to his confidant Leonora Ponti he wrote about his prior history:

> And this brings me down to the last point, the husband-complex. I have been turned down again and again and again. And never despaired. My life is that of a Billikin* that is always knocked down to bounce back . . .

* A monkey-like doll said to bring luck.

> I lived for years under a "Beauty and the Beast" complex. I always felt intuitively that if any woman anywhere gave me a symbolic or psychic kiss, it would bring great changes in my character and career and outlook. Well, Leonore, it has happened.
>
> I have been attracted to certain women here and there, and mostly to my own trouble later. I have followed the roles of a Lochinvar and other story-book characters.* It did no good. So then I became more like Vanderdecken, The Flying Dutchman, who only had a chance [every] so many years. But when he met his Senta, it relieved him from the curse. Only with me it was "Beauty and the Beast" and no curse. And a real beauty has given me the "kiss"—it is true it has been at long distance, but it is true. And I feel both very sure and reassured that it is so. Time and place separate us, but not in the heart.[512]

Leonora was receptive to his state. But his Uncle Harry Rosenthal wrote to Sam, "I am surprised to think that you fall for what fortune tellers tell you. Fortune tellers of all types is a lot of bunk. Besides if you want my opinion, I think you would be foolish to get married, especially when you cannot provide a good home for your wife. But, of course, that is all up to you."

When Gavin Arthur was interviewed, he chimed in on the subject:

> He would have these spiritual love affairs, like that dancer in India, whatever happened to her? Does anybody know? When he came back from India he had her picture on his bureau and he was talking about her all the time, and then he seemed to transfer his affection to Ruth St. Denis. I think he idealized women. I'm sure he never had any physical contact with them.[513]

Sam was convinced that Edna had accepted him as a husband-to-be. His enthusiasm was great and he was making plans. His friends' responses were encouraging but often filled with disbelief, especially since his only women partners in life had been folkdance partners. Over time their mutual correspondence disappeared. None of Edna's letters remain, but there is a partial copy of one of Sam's responses to her, written from Marin County in November of 1957:

---

*Lochinvar, a fictional knight hero in the poem of the same name by Sir Walter Scott, was known as a romantic figure.

My dear Edna:

This is the letter of a man who leads three lives, and for the last days was so tired that he slept almost 36 hours to wake up refreshed at last, and the events which took place locally tie in so much with what you have written that it would seem a drama is going on synchronously on two sides of the earth.

There is a humorous side of me called "Mr. Puck of Pukhtunistan," the largest, real imaginary country in the world—you will not find it on the map, but you will find it in the encyclopedia. He has said: "The heart is the shortest distance between two points." Now I have to answer you from the heart, but first I have to answer you as if I were an advanced Vedantist, which it may be.

There are three levels: the levels of the discursive mind, the level of intuitive, integrative mind and the level of heart which extend beyond the realm of earth. The way you have written can only be explained that you know me not at all, or that **you know me very, very well**.

What you have written can only be taken most seriously and would require some deep meditation and consideration. Yes, the outward errands will be performed. The lady whom I expected would help me has failed, but in meditation I am reminded that one can order dresses very easily at Montgomery Ward which is just one block away and they would package them accordingly.

The mental level is direct and often unbeautiful. For while I feel and fall in with all you have said—which follows—physically I am already in my sixties. Ah! But then I am a Yogi, and you have touched very deeply some things. Years of my life have been extended, whether by Divine Grace or design or my own efforts I know not, but extended they have been and my journeys through India and Pakistan brought out a great deal of the hidden side of life. It has not been meant for me to be alone either. But while I have had romance and love-affairs, it has been almost impossible to get the ladies concerned to look into heart, and there one is stuck.

I came to the Orient to seek, or complete my legends and these legends found me. Have you ever read *Mr. Isaacs* of Marion Crawford? Although this is regarded as fiction, it is based on fact and although I have always said I was Mr. Isaacs, nobody believed it and yet my journey was nothing but a repetition of all that appears in that book—except on one point—it was not completed with romance.

But there was another legend also, and when I met you I was so awe-struck I could not say anything. To me you were, and in a sense are Mumtaz Begum returned.* What does this mean? Ah, my dear, I would suggest you visit the Durgah Nizam-ud-din Auliya which is not far from the tomb of Humayun, and ask to visit the tomb of Pir-o-Murshid Sufi Inayat Khan; also to meet Khwaja Husein Nizami. He has my full confidence in all things.

The day before I left New Delhi for Jaipur and Agra I went to the tomb of Humayun but did not go around. When I found there that Dara Shikoh was buried I walked 7 times around his grave and said, "Let us go." He understood. So few Americans—indeed only the late Flora Annie Steel seemed to have fathomed the hearts of Akbar and his great-grandson Dara Shikoh who loved both Hindus and Muslims with a kind of love so akin to that we ascribe to Jesus Christ, as yet so little comprehended in this world, but which is the heart-love of the Sufis, and also of my guru, the saintly Ramdas in South India.

Husein Nizami also showed me the tomb of Jayanara, the eldest daughter of Shah Jehan and Mumtaz Begum, who also lies buried in the compound of Nizam-ud-din Auliya. He also took me to the *khankah* of Nizam-ud-din Auliya and there my whole future was revealed; it began to be revealed in Calcutta when I visited the tomb of the late saintly Dadajan and was completed in Lahore. I am to visit these places again, but not yet, not yet for several years as God wills.

Your letter was most aptly timed for it came just before the session of UNESCO in San Francisco with the theme: "Asia and the United States: What the American Citizen Can Do to Promote Mutual Understanding and Cooperation." And there I constantly ran into your counterpart, my dear friend Emil Fairchild. His problem is exactly the symmetrically opposite of yours: to go to India to teach and learn dancing. I may be able to learn the details of what went on there from friends, but my own time was spent with the session purportedly devoted to religion and philosophy. Most of the panel sessions failed by far to touch the real heart of communication.

I am now rapidly reading Ambassador Bowles's writings. I was able to say farewell to him: "What you have said I expect to do."

---

*Mumtaz Begum was the wife of Shah Jahan, who built the Taj Mahal as her tomb.

> What did I "see" at Taj, and Fatehpur Sikri? At the Imperial Hotel they were amazed. Or when you reach San Francisco I can introduce you to Mr. Singh at the Indian Travel Bureau: "You have seen what no other American has seen."
>
> I would also like you to visit a very different sort of friend, Mr. E. A. Srinavasan, who is now in charge of the department of Press and Public Relations, Ministry of Foreign Affairs. He was long stationed in San Francisco [and] his picture of me is very real. But he may be able to give you suggestions and introductions.
>
> You have given me just the strength and inspiration to put the final touch on my "Shiva! Shiva!" purporting to be a national poem for India. Edna, do you know what I did in India? Do you know what I dared to do? Again and again and again: "Do you want to hear the flute of Krishna? I am not talking poetry—do you want to hear the flute of Krishna?" And I chanted the flute of Krishna at the Krishna temples in Delhi and New Delhi, and before the great Swamis, and at the Krishna temple near Amravati and in the house of Tansen at Fatehpur Sikri and wherever I went, and was heard and understood, and no door was ever closed: Christian or Hindu or Muslim or Buddhist. I have always had a "song," I [have] always been looking for a "dancer."

Sufi Ahmed Murad may or may not have known much about Edna's life in India. What became of her, Gavin had asked. Fortunately, research turned up an answer in a 1970 UPI newspaper article from Trenton, NJ, entitled "Royal Life in Kashmir Ends When Police Oust Dancer."

The article recounts that Miss Edna Bellefontaine was born in England and moved to India at the age of 10, her father being a Belgian civil engineer working for the maharajah of Mysore. It was there she became interested in Indian art and particularly Indian dancing. She spent her student days in Bangalore,* then lived for a time on a houseboat in Kashmir, hiked through the Himalayas, and painted as well as danced. The "petite blonde artist" went on to become known for her dancing as the Mata Hari of Kashmir, performing before maharajahs and gaining significant notoriety. According to the article, she was even in the

* Now Bengaluru.

"Pounding Rice," 1949 by Edna Bellefontaine

gardens of the presidential palace in Karachi with Pakistani President Mohammed Ayub Khan and President Iskander Mirza just hours before Mirza was banished to England.

On August 7, 1953, Miss Bellefontaine was ordered out of Kashmir at gunpoint by Indian police. She was accused of plotting to secure the province's independence with then prime minister Sheikh Abdullah, who was arrested and jailed. Her later autobiography was reportedly titled "Externed from Paradise."

Miss Bellefontaine accumulated numerous costumes, which included rich clothing and ornamental jewelry. The article reports her as saying, "The dances are physically exhilarating, but the legends and myths of India inspire such peace of mind. And these days, we can all use that."

Edna became Mrs. Bailey, marrying a man in public relations; they had lived in Trenton for four years at the time the article was written. Their apartment was described as exotic and richly decorated with "Indian carpets, ornaments, weapons, bells, long-necked musical instruments, and ornate lamp shades." It is reported that she continued to dance for "soldiers, the wealthy, and women's groups" in the area. [514]

Edna's adventurous life appears to harmonize well with the adventurous character of Samuel Lewis, but there was the matter of his age and lack of funds. Research has not disclosed precisely when he learned she had made other plans than being with him. He held on to a belief that something would happen right up to his departure from the U.S. in 1960. Gavin had noted that Sam began to turn his attention to the famous dancer Ruth St. Denis, whom he frequently saw when he commuted to Los Angeles. Both Edna and Ruth inspired Sam in his poetry.

Sam's Poetry Speaks

Sam's hope for marriage with Edna, and the distinct possibility that she would make a different choice, did not change what she had already influenced in him. His epic poem for India "Siva! Siva!" tells Shiva's* story and introduces the many different forms of Yoga. Toward the end it speaks directly to marriage. Sam, drawing strength from his relationship with Edna and that "kiss," had now become emboldened to write of the union of partners with full confidence as one who had experienced marriage in its highest terms.

In the poem he tells the tale of Shiva's love for his consort Parvati. In part it reads:

What a wonderful beginning for new adventures,
For in loving Parvati I came to love the world,
And I found in her that self-same wonder
That I had learned in the vastness of the jungles.
To me the wife was more than miracle.
To me the wife became more than an imagined divinity,
To me the wife was more than all my faculties,
That before our marriage I had known only half-life,
Now there was fulfillment of every part of personality.
Man needs God to become complete, and woman also;
But the male may discover divinity in the female,
And the female may encounter completion in the male.
Then indeed does marriage become a communion,
Then is every interaction sacred . . .
Parvati and I became as one . . .

For the vibrating cosmos is its Lord in delight . . .
Where power joins with beauty in supporting the cosmos. [515]

Gavin Arthur and Ivy Duce both said in interviews that Sam idealized women, but never had the experience of being physically together with one and was never able to be committed to one through marriage. Sam did have women friends such as Sheikha Vera, Vocha Fiske, Ruth

---

* Siva derives from the Indian spelling Ṣiva; this name is more commonly spelled Shiva in the West.

St. Denis and others, yet no doubt there is truth in Gavin's assessment. It should be remembered that one of the major problems he took to his therapist, Dr. Blanche Baker, was his pattern of being repetitively under the power of domineering women. One could easily put his mother, Rabia Martin, and Ivy Duce in that category. He received healing advice from Dr. Baker on this subject, which helped him move forward with strength and confidence. Blanche could not solve issues such as how to court a woman, yet through the faculties of his inner world Sam found an ideal partner.

The poem ends with Sam's rendering of the Dance of Shiva:

Thus God awoke and in the dance did substantiate
The universe and its multitude of facets,
Took of itself the grosser parts to make the earth,
The subtle parts to create the unseen,
Sustained them by God's breath and perfect love
So that harmony may reign supreme on every plane,
Yet gave to man a will to be independent
Both of the Lord and of that karma
Which carries all imperfection in its grasp.
All the laws of the many sciences are derived
From these incessant cosmic harmonies,
Impressed as such upon the mind and consciousness
But realized when, as in the dance, man portrays God –
So meditation, concentration and Yoga
Are conjoined with art and beauty and skillfulness,
That the divine in man approach the divine in the universe
Until one is merged in the other, self and not-self together –
The culmination of the love of Siva and Shakti.

The Watcher is the Prayerful Devotee,
But the Dancer Becomes Divine.[516]

This poem expresses Sam's deepest intentions and goals. He brings love, harmony, and beauty, particularly music, dance, and the arts forward as necessary aspects in a person's awakening.

Sam completed the poem "Siva! Siva!" after returning from his first trip and began writing the poem "Crescent and Heart." In this latter series of poems Sam describes his own realization of the God reality in the voice of Khwaja Moineddin Chishti, who brought Sufism to India. The last poem in this collection concludes:

Published 1980

In the Name of Allah Who Is Mercy and Compassion
Says the Khwaja:
I am singing to you. I am singing to you of Love,
I am singing to you the only song which is in my heart,
But that song contains all songs;
It is the praise of Allah, the Beneficent, the Merciful . . .
I am the zero where two lines cross,
The line of nothingness where two planes meet . . .
If Truth is different from Love and Knowledge
What can be said to exist? . . .
I lost my tongue in the land of silence,
And my silence ended when I entered the heart;
I beheld the Holy of Holies and fell in a swoon,
And since then has Khwaja been lost.
[How] can I say where I am?
Go, stare five minutes at the noon-day sun,
And walk straight to your destination.
What is your destination, blind in darkness and blind in light?
I thought I was the seeker and found I was the sought,
I thought I was the fowler and in love's snare was caught.
I thought I was an entity and found that I was naught,
And in Love's ecstasy I ceased from thinking thought.
From my-ness and from I-ness was I snatched and made a slave,
And in my slavery I found escape from karmic grave,
What happiness in slavery when freedom does deprave,
And a song of glory is the essence of the soul! [517]

Poetry had become an essential form of expression for Sam since his life-changing retreat of 1925. In 1957 more poems were in process, with more to come. Three of these poems highlight the major religions of the West: "What Christ? What Peace?" (Christianity), "The Day of the Lord Cometh" (Judaism), and "Saladin" (Islam). They were later published together under the title *The Jerusalem Trilogy: Song of the Prophets.*

In 1957 the epic "Saladin" was expressing itself afresh in Sam's inner life. It tells a story of the crusades in which captured European troops had

Published 1975

been taken into custody by the Emperor Saladin. Saladin lectured them about their own religion in ways they had never heard before, and shared teachings of Islam, allowing all who were interested to become Muslims. When he received a ransom for these troops to return home, he gave them the option to remain in the Levant.

"Saladin" is a highly perceptive and creative piece filled with wisdom. It culminates with Saladin's journey through the heaven realms guided by Moses and Jesus. Murshid Samuel Lewis often affirmed that this immense journey was directly dictated to him in the inner world by Prophet Muhammad. Some excerpts are offered here.[518]

VIII

. . .

Guiding my footsteps over that narrow blade,
Guiding where it seemed impossible to proceed,
Where all around was a vast inexhaustible abyss . . .
Only to find myself moving onward, onward, onward,
Moving under guidance and not as if self-propelled,
Moving with unerring swiftness toward the Arsh-*Throne . . .*

Where every personality is all personality,
Where every one is every other thing-being;
Only for the purposes of assisting the creation,
For the sake of aiding humanity they appear as different
With tremendous outbursts of aureoles and auroras,
With endless all-compelling illumination,
Lights reflecting lights, lights refracting lights,
And with them all, through all a voice of wondrous sweetness:

"I am the Seal, the Seal of all the Prophets,
Whose testimony is my testimony and I their testimony,
Who are all Muslims, accommodations of Divine Will,

Empty egos, filled with eternal spirit,
Operating as nafs alima, *the self-empty-universally-filled . . .*
The Messengers of God whose hearts are altars
Expressing under varying conditions the sempiternal Message,
Attuned to the ever-beating heart of Compassion and Beneficence,
The undertone of the very essence of Being . . .

"Honour those whom I honour and you honour me,
Belittle other Messengers and the appeal is vain . . .
Learning is not enough, wisdom must be added,
Nor is it necessary to apprehend a multitude of forms,
Nor to be concerned with constant repetitions,
Nor to close oneself from the habit of repetition,
For simplicity of heart is quite sufficient;
Self-surrender is enough . . .

"Ya Allah, in love, in reverence and humility
I surrender to Thee and Thee alone
And thou dost raise me spiritually." . . .

"Allah is Al-Hayy, *the living Eternal,*
Whose many attributes are latticed into personalities,
Effects of a unitary cause . . .

The sudden disappearance as of a vision,
The transformation of person into essence
Within or without, I could not tell. I did not know,
But immediately I heard another voice:

IX
"I am the voice of a once perfect King,
Coupled in eternity with an equally perfect Queen . . .
Ram was, Ram is, Ram-Sita for ever.

"Even as the systole and diastole of the heart are as one,
The blood rushing to aid the suffering tissues,
The blood returning as if compelled back to the heart –
Thus the operation of the lovers of humanity,
Thus was Sita, the seeker of my being,
Thus the role of love beyond name and form . . .

"God, the All-all, created men and women in His Image:
Religion is therefore for both men and women.
Spiritual liberation is for both.

The false have declared the male to be superior,
The false have declared one caste to be superior,
The false have proclaimed a racial superiority . . .
"All Prophets in all ages presented Islam,
All Messengers have emphasized surrender . . .

The real teaching of India is sanatana-dharma,
Nothing to do with exclusive sects and cults . . .
So symbols must be restored to their proper setting,
And the veils over meanings be lifted . . ."

Then by the transcendental process of all-being,
Becoming one with Ram, becoming one with Sita . . .
In the ultimate synthetic unity we call soul,
Absorbing full wisdom with conscious immediacy,
I knew the various meanings of the Ramayana,
The spiritual folk-lore epic of the Aryans . . .

In Allah one finds the perfection of all qualities
Which sustain the universe from its Fountain-head,
So true religion is Islam and sanatana-dharma . . .
Realized in the Light-Light where Allah is serene.

Next Saladin is introduced to Shiva, who performs the cosmic dance of the universe. Shiva tells Saladin:

"Ishvara, Osiris, Asar, Asher,
Variations of the One Holy Name,
Taught to Moses by Khidr in the form:
Ehyeh asher ehyeh*—*I am Ishvara who was, is, will be,*
That One Who is the Only-Only-Only,
Forevereverevermore, and on and on,
Represented through a name-veil offered by man."

Then he meets the cosmic flute player known as Narayana Krishna:

"Love, love, love, stupendous love . . .
Joy, joy, joy in the extreme . . .
"So I sing the universe unbounded
And electrify the universe which is bound,
In song and dance and ecstasy of being."

---

*This Hebrew expression is commonly translated "I Am That I Am.

Sakyamuni Buddha then speaks to Saladin, saying:

"I am the spirit of the universal bliss,
Which is to say the happiness of beings . . .

"Let me inform you, beloved Saladin,
That I was one among innumerable Buddhas,
Identical with the Messengers of God,
With no other purpose or mission . . .

"The doctrine of absolute oneness
Was transmitted onward by me to my disciples,
Handed down by those we now call patriarchs
Until this day. But it is not different from
LA ILLAHA EL IL ALLAHU"

"There is a universal salvation or there is none,
For where can there be limitation to Compassion?
To Mercy? To Beauty? To Grandeur, to Wisdom?
Buddhas, Avatars and Messengers are as One." . . .

Then I saw a flickering in the Light,
The procession of a glorious multitude,
All the Messengers and Prophets of Allah
Passing and repassing upon the cosmic stage,
Angels and archangels and choirs of celestial beings
Singing and chanting in supreme jubilation
To the dancing of galaxies of galaxies.

Saladin's words conclude this section of the poem:

I was the pain and joy of every one,
I was the life and death of every thing,
I was totality in my nothingness,
Effaced in the Sheikh, the Prophet and in Allah,
Sharing in the primordial Nuri Mohammed*
That which was and is and ever shall become,
Ever-was, ever-is, ever-shall-be, world without end,
And I awoke,
As from a dream.

---

* Primal light; the first creation.

Connecting with Professor Siddiqui

A very dear friend arrived from Penang, Malaya. He is in this country to collect funds to be devoted to a real Institute of Oriental Studies. He reports that Russia is doing just that with a Buddhist teaching Buddhism, and an Arab teaching Islam—something which is very seldom done in this country. He is quite pessimistic about bringing misunderstandings and he has some authority having devoted his life to that cause. I am now awaiting his return.

SAMUEL LEWIS[519]

Ahmed Murad Chisti showed the depth of his knowledge of Islam's situation in the world in his letter to Professor A. A. Siddiqui at the University of Punjab in Lahore, excerpted above. His close friend Saladin Paul Reps remembered him as a Jewish Prophet who was ahead of his time, and who was able to meet rejection by revitalizing himself from the great inner light he carried. Sam's letter to Professor Siddiqui continues:

> More recently I have written to President Rafiuddin of Ikbal University in Karachi. I am wondering how well you know him. He is seeking cooperation in bringing Islam and modern science together. Well, I have proven this in the laboratory and also by analogy covering a large portion of Islam studies. I did mention one thing to the Botanical Department when I visited your university and that is on the relation of *jelal-jemal* in vegetation in the dichotomy between woody and herbaceous growths.
>
> Actually this *jelal-jemal* polarity is found everywhere in nature, such as the crystalline versus non-crystalline forms of matter, the skeleton versus the flesh parts in animals, etc. Indeed those principles which I have learned such as *urouj, nasoul, zaval, kemal, jelal* and *jemal* I have tried to apply to known scientific knowledge.*
>
> I think Prof. Rafiuddin has made an initial but not important error. There is no such thing as Islam but there is a study of Allah and the revelation and wisdom from Allah constitute Islam; and there is nature and the wisdom we derive from nature may be called Science. But what is Nature but the body of Allah? Consequently, there is only One Truth, and whatever we find or know comes from that one body of Truth . . .

---

* *Urouj* is the rising energy of the inhalation, *nasoul* the offering of the exhalation. *Zaval* is the ceasing of activity, as at the end of exhalation. *Kemal* is the perfection or emptiness of absolute stillness, as between inbreath and outbreath or outbreath and inbreath. *Jelal* is strength or power like the Sun, *jemal* is empathy or beauty like the moon.

The local Governor-General of Indonesia showed me a release from his Central Government and it said: "*Shariat* is the boat, *Tarikat* is the diving equipment and *Hakikat* presents the pearls from the Ocean-of-Truth."* He said he could not give me an extra copy and I asked: "Do you think five men in this country would understand and accept that?"

That is to say, as I see it, despite much pessimism Islam is progressing in many directions but the rather "exiled" communities, not keeping in touch with contemporary currents and tendencies tend to crystallize in a deadly conservatism which they confuse with orthodoxy. It is natural. But I found the Imam at Washington of another type. To begin with when he heard that I had come from Ajmir and Lahore he opened the grounds to me although they were not yet in readiness at the time, the public being barred. And he was equally well aware that in the United States Islam could be presented in a modern fashion, i.e., in accord with accepted scientific teachings.[520]

The success of Sam's first trip abroad in 1956 left him with a deep sense that there was more he could contribute to the Middle East and more that awaited him there. In early 1959 he was busy with meetings, letters, and preparing for his next trip abroad. He had met with Rudolph Schaeffer, discussed spiritual ways of seeing art, and offered to secure items for Schaeffer on his upcoming trip. Sam had a great deal to muse about.

Dance was also taught in Rudolph Schaeffer's Design School

I may be lecturing and doing research work in Cleveland. Doors are opening rapidly for me even here in San Francisco now, perhaps for the first time in my life. I am making excellent contacts of all kinds. And also getting more introductions for a lengthy journey abroad.

One thing I do not wish is going away parties. Anybody that can buy an extra bottle or get me a present can do much better by contributing

---

* *Shariat* offers the accepted forms within the religion, *Tarikat* is the inner teachings of the Sufi path, and *Hakikat* is the realization of the omnipresent God reality.

> to charity abroad. It is very hard to understand the great poverty I have seen and what I expect to see further of in other lands."[521]

Meeting with Phra Sumangalo

Sam deeply wanted to be with his closest friend and fellow bodhisattva Sumangalo; he and Sam stood for the same essential reality throughout the world. Sam knew that Sumangalo had much to say to the U.S. government: there was much the latter should hear from one who was very knowledgeable about the world, and who was widely embraced by heads of state and religious leaders.

Sumangalo, however, had not been well received in DC. He and Sam met in the Bay Area in mid-1959, following Sumangalo's DC visit. Sumangalo arrived feeling rejected and dejected. He had tried to warn Washington about coming difficulties in Southeast Asia, but to no avail.

One story that Murshid Sam periodically told at his meetings in the late 1960s was about this meeting. Sumangalo in his disappointment said to Sam, "We don't have it!" Sam then jumped up from his chair and shouted, "Yes we do have it!!" When he related this he would actually jump up from his chair, filling the room with energy as he shouted it out. He communicated to his students that Sumangalo had taken heart from this Fudo-like outburst.

In letters to friends and acquaintances over the years Sam reported on his experiences with Sumangalo/Clifton and their meeting. In January of 1961 Sam wrote to his friend Willie Wise:

> You must bear in mind, Willie, that my friend M. T. Kirby for years kept writing me of an imminent Japanese attack on Hawaii; and then my friend Robert Clifton told me the same about Laos. He came to Washington and had the door shut in his face by Dulles. And not one editor would interview him. He went back to Southeast Asia, gave up his citizenship, and after the fighting there, Mr. Dulles pursued him all over. So, I am proposing and seriously proposing that we listen carefully to Americans who go abroad and especially who live abroad who have something to say.[522]

Sumangalo continued to work throughout Asia until his death in 1963. In a 1965 letter to UC Berkeley professor Morris Hirsch, Sam wrote:

> Since 1947 I was made acquainted with the affairs and events in the region involved by one Robert Clifton, also known as Phra Sumangalo . . . Clifton himself worked in every country of SE Asia, was well known to king and prime minister and to all the leading Buddhists of all schools. But two visits to this country did not get him a single meeting with any member of the Foreign Service, nor with the press (excepting Mrs. Meyer in Washington), nor with the radio-TV, until it was discovered he was a third cousin of Senator Fulbright by marriage. Then all the doors opened to him but instead of accepting the welcomes he gave up his citizenship and vowed never to return. He died of a broken heart.[523]

In 1966 Sumangalo was still on his mind:

> Years ago in this very chair I said: "Robert, you and I are mere nobodies. Neither of us can get an audience, both have been rejected by the press and State Department but I doubt if there is a King, Prime Minister, Cabinet Member, Holy Man, saint, professor, or even peasant from one end of Asia to the other whom either you or I or perhaps both of us can meet if we haven't met them already but who will believe it?" "Very true, Samuel, very true." Now my friend is dead. We are having the Vietnam war because he wasn't believed and already monuments are going up in his name all over Southeast Asia![524]
>
> Sumangalo . . . and I spent long hours in discussion in this room* and recently I had the chairs repainted. Now these are going to be called "sacred chairs" and some day they will be left to some Buddhist teacher or *sangha* here in San Francisco.[525]

At the time of that writing, Samuel Lewis had just begun to attract students. He would always teach sitting in one of those two green-painted chairs he had shared with Sumangalo.

One of the chairs was later given to Jiyu-Kennett Roshi, who was a graduate of the Soto Buddhist school into which Sam had been accepted. Sam had developed a deep spiritual friendship with Kennett Roshi; that green chair was preserved at her new *zendo* in Northern

---

* A small apartment in downtown San Francisco.

Jiyu-Kennett founded the Zen Mission Society in San Francisco in 1969, and Shasta Abbey in Mount Shasta in 1970

California until after her death, when it was returned to Sam's successors. One episode that stands out was a day Sam returned to his office (where I worked as his secretary) from a visit with Kennett Roshi in the city. When he entered the room he was totally ecstatic, exuding joy and exclaimed, "I just lost a debate with Kennett Roshi, and you know how she defeated me? She quoted Gilbert and Sullivan."

Teaching in the Cleveland Area

After meeting with Sumangalo in 1959, Sam traveled east to Cleveland and followed up on the invitation he had received several times from Viola Harris, a supporter of Pir Vilayat's. She had written to Sam,

> You see when Vilayat was here, he said he would send us papers. Apparently he doesn't have the earlier papers of his father, but I understand he had a lot that Ali Khan did not have. We have received 2 papers since. He doesn't answer letters of any one not even Claire. I feel as you do that if these papers can't be published or mimeographed in Europe they could be sent here and taken care of, not even for us but for the future. I feel Samuel that there are not too many people left who have the good of the message at heart.
>
> There are only five really interested people here . . . I feel Samuel that the time for passivity is past and the time for action is now. Now this feeling that I have is not one of rushing into things for I have been passive for many years and never felt the urge as I do now. Unfortunately, I know so little.[526]

Referring to *The Practice of Zen* by Chang Chen-Chi, which he had read before leaving San Francisco, Sam wove its message into his activities in Cleveland:

> The Chinese and Burmese do not indulge in double-talk, niceties and diplomatic nonsense, which gives us poisonous soothing syrup instead of friendship. But so many Americans just "love" poisonous soothing

> syrup and prefer "The Ugly American" to truth, and a pleasant speaker to an informative one . . .
>
> I gave a talk Sunday on "The Gospel of St. Thomas" with some covert criticism of Billy Graham and attention to the passage, "The Father is an activity and a repose," calling attention to its Mahayana aspects. Well it seems that the organizers of the Center were present. They had arranged a seminar for Alan Watts; now, they want to know something of the techniques of Zen and Sufism.[527]

Sam had been invited to speak at The Center in Cleveland, a place that was open to all religions. His host, Viola, told Sam later that their group was no longer using The Center for their programs because attendance was low. Nevertheless, Sam made numerous connections wherever he went and received more speaking invitations.

> Dr. Baker will remember how I behaved during the UNESCO a few years back. The same thing is happening here. I went to register for a forthcoming institute on "Giants of Asia" and opened my [mouth] to the man just [ahead] of me in line for tickets. His name is Reynolds, he is a Cal. Agricultural Expert and has just come back from India. We had much to say and should be meeting this weekend.
>
> Went with Viola Harris to the first colloquium. The main speaker was a Dr. B. S. Gilani who spoke as a representative of India. After the question period I asked: "Didn't you come from Iraq?" "Yes." "Then you are a member of the great family?" "Yes." He is a descendent of the Grand Sheikh* and a cousin of the man who was my host in Washington years ago when I started out on plans for the Near East. I shall write him shortly . . . [528]
>
> The main problem that I felt would appear and has appeared is a sort of pressure connected with success. My chief hostess here has been troubled about my meeting one professor Saha. Well, I met the Professor in the ordinary course of events without turning a hair. My timing has been perfect. The World Affairs Council has had lectures and an institute on India and China. I met the representative from the Embassy and made a date for April 27. I have already met another professor from a Sufi family.
>
> Tomorrow I give my Easter lecture. This partly because my hostess leaves soon and partly because I shall be in Columbus and give this talk,

---

* Abdul Qadir Jilani (also spelled Gilani).

> presumably, for the T.S.* The subject will be "The Body of Light." While I shall use N.T.† texts I shall interpret it also in terms of Sufism and Vedanta. I expect a fairly large and sympathetic audience . . .
>
> I go to Wooster on Monday, April 11, to speak to the T.S. presumably on "Real Saints, Real Masters, Real Shrines."[529]

The University of Michigan was on vacation, as was the professor Sam wished to see. True to his own character, Sam contacted several local Pakistani students, including a Soil Major who invited him to the Eid festival where other Muslims were to join. Sam wrote:

> It was noteworthy that the Pakistanis were in large abundance and the Turks, surprisingly, far outnumbered the Arabs. Today we hear about the Turks abandoning religion and the Arabs often using Islam as a façade. There I learned that there is now a complete American Islamic Movement headed by [one] Mr. Khalid of Dearborn, who is in close touch with both Al-Azhar and Cairo . . . This will be of value to me when I reach UAR.‡
>
> On my return I found a large envelope from Jonathan Garst, brother of the man who was Khruschev's host in Iowa. This is a fertilizer program for India. I am going to share it with Professor Saha and then perhaps take it on to Washington . . .
>
> Somehow or other I am always keeping busy and am becoming self-assured. But sometimes the best way to success is to listen and take suggestions—then do something. I am hoping to call on Chester Bowles when I reach Washington in regard to some of the above.[530]

Sam's Article in *The Western Buddhist*

> *The Dharma-tradition is not a Dharma-transmission. That is to say, it cannot be limited to doctrines . . .*
>
> *Here we have something more than philosophical truth. We have living truth. Buddha-transmission goes from enlightened person to enlightened person and this has been from the time of Sakya Muni to now. This is also called "transmission of Dharma."*

---

*Theosophical Society.

†New Testament.

‡The United Arab Republic, which at the time included what is now Egypt, Gaza, and Syria.

> *And what does the experience of enlightenment bring? Not some philosophical explanation of ten kingdoms which may exist in theory or in actuality, but the conscious realization of them both within one's "self" and in the universe. Then there is no difference between self and self, between self and totality. We are everything we comprehend or apprehend. What we understand is, or becomes us; separations are in words and illusions.*
>
> *Thus there is much more in universal Buddhism than in becoming a Buddhist. One becomes Bosatsu, the Bodhisattva who sees all beings, enlightened and ignorant, with the same compassion. He does not frown upon the multitudes who do not know the Dharma or who have incomplete notions of Dharma. He treats all from the standpoint that nothing is true except enlightenment and yet this enlightenment belongs to all. Thus he is able to help others though he does not consider his actions as help-to-others. In other words, the supreme end of Buddhism is that everyone is a Bodhisattva and comes to realize that he or she has always been a Bodhisattva—or Buddha.*
>
> SAMUEL LEWIS[531]

This epigraph is taken from a paper "How to be a Buddhist? How to be a Buddha?" that Sam wrote for Roshi Taizen Saito of Soji-ji, Tsurumi, Japan. First printed in *The Western Buddhist,* Autumn, 1959, the paper gives a full view of the Buddhist path.

In a diary letter to a friend Charles Siegferth written soon afterward, Sam addressed the theme of this paper:

> You chant Prajna-Paramita, you read it in translation, but that does not always mean that the Prajna-Paramita Hridaya is understood. I met one of Senzaki's pupils. I told her she looked like old Man-Mountain himself and I had a great secret to tell her. Then I whispered to her "*hridaya*" and said she would understand, and she understood, and there was nothing more to say for that word contains everything old Fat Stomach gave me.*
>
> You have studied Vedanta and in the *Taittiriya* Upanishad it says we have five bodies: flesh, breath, mind, intelligence and bliss. The pre-Buddha Dharma said that and the post-Buddha Dharma is still Dharma; there is no second Dharma. It is the same as you find in the Christian Bible where it is called "Logos." Logos is the same as Dharma,

---

* *Hridaya* means heart. *Prajna Paramita Hridaya* is translated Heart of Perfect Wisdom.

there is no difference although you can have a thousand lectures and be thoroughly confused.

What language did Saito-san use to me, with me, on me and me? Being Dharma, he tackled all five avenues together, flesh, breath, mind, intelligence and bliss. Then he added the Charlotte Russe* on top which we call *prajna;* only in the five avenues there is communication and in *prajna* there is no one to communicate or to communicate to. I knew everything he said or meant long before it was translated. Bingo! . . .

Sure, Roshi Taizen explained the Buddha-transmission, the *Sangha*-Transmission, the Dharma-transmission; and despite all the noise pounded out by intellectuals one had telepathy and super telepathy and blending of egos and more on top of that, all at once. The Roshi did not just talk; when he did you realized—all five levels, flesh, breath, mind, intelligence and bliss. From the intelligence we get the Buddhist term *alaya-vijnana.* From the bliss we get the seed of the realization when Kasyapa shouted "*Ananda*" to Buddha's cousin.

Thus, one can say there is no difference between a samsara and Nirvana, or one can deny it and the sameness and difference have no meaning and all meaning.

The failure in the grasping of Buddhism, or Dharma, is that we try to grasp it with the ego. That is where Theravada fails. Shaku Soyen used to say: "There is nothing to receive and no one to receive you." This is the reception and it does not look logical.[532]

Further University Connections

Sam wrote to Professor Walter Fischel at UC Berkeley:

As a free roving Ambassador for the University of California, perhaps I should have visited you before embarking on a projected journey which may take me across Asia from one end to the other. As I am going entirely on my own and have at least three huge projects in mind, I found it impossible to visit all the presumably interested departments on the Campus. One never knows exactly what type of reaction will be obtained—if satisfactory one has to spend more time than one has in reserve (this happened this year); if unsatisfactory one can only depart in chagrin (this happened previously but the negative personalities have since been disciplined for quite different reasons. . . .)

* A classic dessert.

The three projects I had in mind were:

a. Exchange of crop data, especially to carry information to lands with surfeits of deserts and salt-encrusted soils.
b. To engage in real cultural exchanges with two-way traffic; indirectly to combat the somewhat unwholesome of effects or defects of Mortimer Adler's.
c. To further programs already instituted for peace efforts through the arts with some emphasis on Islamic Arts, to fill a big gap . . .

My immediate reason for writing, no doubt, is that I obtained a copy of *The Muqaddimah* in Los Angeles and have been reading it assiduously. The criticism I make of this work is the same as I must make of the grand white Memorial Library here in Cleveland, that there are hosts of books in the library, listed on classifications which simply do not hold. *Ikhwan-Issafa* is listed with Indian literature because the issue on hand was published in that country. The best Urdu and Sindi books are so listed, too.

In 1930 I called on your former colleague, the late Professor Popper. He was then enthusiastically studying Al-Ghazzali. He could not understand how a person could know Sufism without studying the great philosopher. But the Iranian says; "*Tasawwuf* consists of experiences and not definitions." If wisdom consists of experiences and not definitions, it cannot be obtained through philosophical books—a point on which I stand far apart from many of your colleagues in this country and in Europe . . .

Or you can test this yourself by going to the Ferry Building and talking to the staff of the Indonesian Consulate. Just inquire if disciples in Sufism partake in politics or not.[533]

Arabic edition of *The Muqaddimah*

The Muqaddimah, a philosophy of history written by Ibn Khaldun in 1377, had been translated into English by Franz Rosenthal of the Dept. of Semitic Languages at Yale. Sam wrote to Dr. Rosenthal:

There may be a temptation, off hand, to compare *The Muqaddimah* with *Ain-I-Akbari.** Both works are

* *Ain-I-Akbari* was a 16th-century document recording the administration of the Mughal Empire under Emperor Akbar, written by Akbar's historian Abu'l Fazl.

> encyclopedic, both envision the larger area possible of the time, both were written by men associated with high government positions, and the authors—despite your colleagues in Chicago—were profound students and disciples of Sufism.
>
> This last point must be re-emphasized because one of my goals is to go to Aligarh University where they have already accepted my theme for a thesis of "The Reconciliation of Oriental Wisdom with Contemporary Science." This will be done first with Sufism and then I may move to other arenas and areas.
>
> In January of this year I received my appointment as American (and international) representative of the Chishti order whose headquarters are in Ajmir and I am also closely associated with the Nizami Chishtis of Hyderabad, New Delhi and elsewhere. Their acceptance and nominations comes from knowledge, as Al-Ghazzali would say, of experiences, or of "states" and "stages." Consequently, I shall be in position to lecture on *The Muqaddimah* and to write reviews—which will be favorable—but do not wish to do this without some acknowledgement from your good-self.
>
> I arrive in New York about May 1, and within a [week] must go to Harvard University to meet several professors in different departments there. I do not know whether it would be feasible to stop off at New Haven on my return (I must get there as soon as possible), whether you would be in that region (because of vacation), or whether a personal meeting would be in any way profitable to either or both.
>
> Despite all I have written, despite Mortimer Adler and his competing "great books limited to Europe prior to 1910," I want to see universal knowledge and universal cultural exchange and I believe sir you have made a marvelous contribution in this field.[534]

Sam never forgot the mission given him by Hazrat Inayat Khan to be a bridge of understanding to the academic world on mysticism, and to promote the hiring of faculty who had direct experience in the religions taught. He already had allies such as Professor Sorokin at Harvard and Professor Moore at the University of Chicago, and had now gotten in touch with Dr. Rosenthal. Sam continued corresponding with them and other teachers. Sorokin invited Sam to come meet with him at Harvard, and Moore invited Sam's explanations for problems he faced in his own writings.

Sam also never abandoned his wish to bring art and dance into the fragmented world to offer a fresh approach to collaboration between different cultures. There was some interest. Professor Charles Morris, of the University of Chicago, for one, had asked Sam to tell him more about the Emperor Akbar. Sam responded:

> There is no question in my mind—and this conclusion has been reached by all those who have studied Akbar—that he was equally accomplished in physical-material, intellectual-artistic, and spiritual-ascetic aspects of life. But his physical, his material, his intellectual, his artistic, his spiritual and his ascetic accomplishments are reached very high toward the degrees of human perfection. Here is a man surrounded by wealth and with many women in his harem. Here is a man who knew how to overcome sleep and spend long hours in deep meditation. Here is a man who established workshops and laboratories way ahead of his time. Here is a man who did more to promote the arts of the sub-continent than anyone else, ever. Place him among the ascetics, he is high; place him among the gourmets, he is high; place him alongside any of the rulers of the Renaissance period in the encouragement of arts, he will top them. So, I can go on, and on.[535]

In April of 1960 Sam also wrote from Columbus, Ohio, to Professor Harry Nelson, mentioning that he had spent a profitable 1½ days at the Agricultural Experimental Station at Wooster. He also mentioned that Dr. Blanche Baker, a former Ohio State biology instructor, had provided him with introductions to Dr. Clifford Cutright, Chief Entomologist at Wooster, and to Dr. Mayers, head of the Botany Dept. at Columbus.

Sam left Columbus for Washington DC and wrote for his diary:

> This hotel is badly located for my personal business, being far away from Embassy Row. On the other hand it is just across the street from the House Office Building so I went at once to the offices of Congressman Shelley and Miller . . . I spent a long time at the Indian Embassy today . . .
>
> I can't remember all details. Monday I called on my friend, Mr. Huq, at the Pakistani Embassy—it was most fortunate and propitious. For tonight I have been invited to attend a special meeting designed to form an Iqbal Society. I want to be a charter member. After all, Iqbal was my

mentor in poetry* and the reception of my own writings at the Mosque, etc. is going to push things fine for me.

After leaving Mr. Huq I spent some time with Mr. Heinlein at the American Friends of the Near East; I must return again tomorrow to find if Mr. Minor has returned. This meeting gave me everything that I might have wanted from the State Department. I also visited World Neighbors and must return. I do not know whether I shall join the group or not; it depends on details but not principles. We are in entire agreement. I am very happy to find myself finding Americans with whom I can associate.[536]

The Period Before Sam's Second Trip Abroad

Although away from the Bay Area for some time before departing abroad, Samuel Lewis nevertheless made efforts to come to grips with the situation at hand there. He had differences with the recognized academics and others who minimized and rejected him and his knowledge, including his claims of being a Sufi. He chose to avoid direct conflict with these individuals and instead was inspired to make a major effort to connect with the University of California. In a letter to Hugo Selig he wrote:

> There is now a flurry of literature by Japanese and Chinese to the effect that Watts, Benoit and Humphreys don't know what they are talking about when they write on Zen. But Humphreys agreed and asked for advice. So I sent him advice and he accepted the advice. I don't ask for people to accept my advice; I ask to be heard. Watts was a champion at not letting me be heard but many of the Academicians were not too far behind. If I am heard, and then my stuff is rejected, all right. But the point, Hugo, is that when it is heard it is generally accepted. There were other profs. at the Academy who let me submit papers and they accepted them.
>
> Now the University of California is filled with profs. of similar points of view. When I went to one man the other day he said: "I suppose you are a Yogi." "Yes." "Well, my pupil here is a Yogi, too." I extended my arms and said I could hold them indefinitely. The Hindu student said: "*Pranayama*." "Of course." So, we had a valid conversation on the real stuff—something that seldom goes on here, but it has gone on at last.

*Sam refers to Sir Muhammad Iqbal (1877-1938), recognized as the national poet of Pakistan. Iqbal, a fervent supporter of Islamic civilization, wrote in Urdu and Persian.

> Indeed, I was surprised to find general acceptance all over the campus . . . The secretary of the South Asian department knows me and with that one person on "my side" the rest was easy. To hell with the metaphysicians from now on. Being nice is one thing, being honest and informed is another.
>
> But the whole tenor of things is the same. Monday I am to have my third long interview with the new cultural attaché at the Indian Consulate. And so on.[537]

Sam's connection with other professors and religious leaders was very active. He wrote a letter to a well-known philosopher, Oliver Reiser, about the book Reiser had just published. Reiser responded in a letter written at the end of 1958:

> Thank you most cordially for your stimulating letter. I have received a number of comments on the new book, but yours are surely among the most helpful. The problem of integration—cultural as well as intellectual—is indeed varied and complex and your suggestions will prove valuable to me in this most difficult task. Your knowledge of Oriental cultures balances my own Western-oriented training, and I hope someday to do more along the lines you have sketched out.[538]

Sam's contact with Reiser would continue for years.

Mary Farkas in New York, a disciple of Sokei-an Sasaki and the Zen Master's representative at the institute he had founded, had an ongoing correspondence with Samuel Lewis. Here are a few excerpts from her letters:

Mary Farkas of the First Zen Institute of America

> I was much interested in the report of the translation of the Sixth Patriarch Sutra by Drs. George and Paul Fung and would be delighted if you would order a copy for the Institute or give me their address so I can do so. Sokei-an's translation, on which I am working, is wonderful but rough and from the Japanese view. I have a very good one by a Chinese, but am always looking for more, as the two views are not identical, but complement each other. Do you know which text they used?[539]

> The Sufi group here—they occasionally purchase incense from us—are slowly ending their activities with advancing age, to which no new blood is added.
>
> Your description of your Senzaki "transformation" at the meeting in San Francisco was delightful. Some of his followers wrote me very enthusiastically, in prospect of Soyen Nakagawa's visit. Too bad their *Zendo* is dismantled. I wonder if the group will have the heart to continue.[540]
>
> Thank you for your letter of September 11. I am always fascinated to hear about Sokatsu, Senzaki and Sokei-an. Whatever became of Senzaki's biography of Soyen, by the way? It would be such a pity for it to be lost.[541]

While Sam fostered his relationships with academics and spiritual organizations, Edna still figured largely in his mind. Toward the end of 1959 he heard from a friend Gwyn wishing him luck on his writing and saying that she hoped he would be seeing Edna soon, finding her an inspiring person.[542]

In a letter to the Royal Asiatic Society Sam wrote that he was planning to leave the U.S. and spoke of marrying a lady of English nationality who lived in India and had been recording native music and studying Indian dance. He was still optimistic about the proposed wedding. The rest of the letter outlined his plans for his trip in 1960, for which he spent a great deal of time making arrangements and setting up contacts. Around that time he also wrote to Professor Siddiqui in Pakistan and enclosed a photograph of Edna.

Once he arrived in Washington DC, Sam continued to plan for his journey.

> I visited the Sudanese Embassy, got some information (don't know whether I shall go to that country or not); went to the UAR consular offices for my visa, and had them half laughing while I was filling out the forms, but have to bring my pictures—anyhow I go back in that region at least twice more. Then a very long interview at the Indian Embassy where the main persons were away but I evidently made friends. The doorman, an Englishman, wants me to write to him and I suspect I shall.

Later on I went to the Arab Information Office; the director was away but the girl knows Mr. Mehdi in S.F. (she also comes from Bagdad) and gave me a most important introduction in New York. I also have the right introduction to the Al-Azhar University . . .

These letters will be mailed before going to the Iqbal meeting. I understand that either the Iranian Ambassador or someone near to him will be chief speaker and I shall meet people from the Near and Middle East.

I still have to visit some Congressmen, Senator [Engle] (out of courtesy), at least the Burmese and Ceylon Embassies, perhaps Lebanon also. If any time will go to art galleries, but I have to be out anyhow because rooms are needed.[543]

During this time in DC Sam wrote to Murshida Ivy Duce. For a long time she had opposed him in every way. Now he wrote her a cordial letter in which he was pleased to establish his own viewpoint through reporting on his Washington activities as well as his worldwide goals.

Henceforth you may be hearing from me anywhere, any time or not at all. In the Cause of God one . . . serves in reverence, love and humility and sometimes also with a blare of trumpets.

The ways of man are negative, the ways of God are positive as I have written:

The strong say "Yes" to God,
The weak say "No" to man –
This has been the habit
Since the world began.

Whenever I see a negative given, I know it comes from the tongue and mind of those who fear, those who are really weak, those who do not overlook their own virtues and overlook their short-comings. But no matter how determinate man is, he cannot hold against the flow of time any more than King Canute did against the waves.

The last interview today was with Mr. Minor, who is a friend of Terry* and yourself. I made it clear that I was a cultural representative of Sufism and though empowered to give spiritual instructions my work was in the cultural field, and yours presumably in the teaching field. I said no more. Pir-o-Murshid, God, then my present Pir-o-Murshid, then the Sufi Brotherhoods have asked me to conduct this work. The Sufi

---

*Ivy's husband.

Brotherhoods are recognized even politically. The dervish can enter where others do not or cannot, and he does, and he receives welcomes.

Washington has been nothing but a series of welcomes, some of them the warmest received outside of Asia, and these warm welcomes come from both Asians and Americans (and you can throw in a few Africans, too.) The warm heart is never outside. Plans that were thwarted by human will are only thwarted in time; in the world of principle, they are not stopped. And so ultimately, they come from the world of principle into manifestation.

I keep no list of autographs nor record of the Prime Ministers and Ambassadors I have met. Tomorrow I must return to the Mosque for some long consultations. If they follow the pattern of my interviews the last few days, they will become very important. I become now the recognized traveling dervish. Man, indeed no man can stop this; only in the Name of Allah can it be stopped, and when one travels in the Name of Allah, who will stop?

Plans to build up friendships, honest friendships will, to my mind, do more than anything else to stop the dehumanization of mankind proposed by several kinds of governments today. Living in friendship one is welcome but one carries others' banners. One does not give up insight, or experience . . .

I came to Cleveland to be welcomed by five Sufis. While I was there six other former members took the pledge of *bayat* and two new *mureeds.* But I told them I was not the Teacher, and while the Movement seems to be in four groups—none of whom share the teachings and all who demand "authority." I waived all objection to anybody they would accept esoterically. But my esoteric position is clear and cannot be touched, not in the least, by man, any man or men.

My scientific mission has, if anything, been more successful than the literary and spiritual one. If, in the course of time, I meet again with Dr. Shawarbi, we have great things to do, really great things to do. Little people would not let me; big people are very open hearted in this. I meet the world's leading horticulturists all over and am greeted by them at the top levels. But I keep my findings "esoteric," sharing them with one man in San Francisco who has the know-how and who himself has been spurned so many times . . .

I cannot find out if it is expensive to live here because I have to go at the end of four days; as usual, praise be to Allah, I have had long series of successful interviews and conferences. Those who are willing to accept,

> let them accept. I have had against me a lot of Europeans known as "Orientalists" including some of Baba's worst enemies, too. They are, on a whole, doing much harm in preventing straightforward American-Asian relations. You saw that with the Czech Prof. here, but that has been wide-spread. The new generation of American professors in the Oriental field are different and they are my friends; my address book is overloaded.
>
> I say nothing more of the courses you have taken. What you do positively is your own affair. But what Allah does positively becomes the affair of His devotees. I was not stopped all over Asia; I don't know whether I shall be or not, but no human being, acting in the name of Allah without having the Grace of Allah, will stop the Cause of Allah. All the people here are looking to my publishing memoirs. I think this will be done before long.
>
> Then I expect to write, "I meet the Sufis." Not now, but later. It is about time that the mystics begin to speak for mysticism.[544]

Sam was ready to travel, but was the world ready for him? He was waiting in New York City for his ship to leave, but there was a major obstacle in his path that was beyond his capacity to overcome. He wrote about it to his friend Dorothy.

> I am just back from Gloucester and am in a sort of quandary, nothing bad, but much determinate. Visited Harvard and while I was there telephoned Adolph.* To my surprise and delight he called on me the next day and took me to his home. It was one of those things—on the right side. I apologized and said I had brought them no present but had my work clothes with me. That was just what they wanted! Instead of being in the food business they run a greenhouse and nursery and I kept pretty busy around the place—from putting in a rock garden, to potting and now arranging their stock.
>
> I found the place entirely to my delight and the weather also. I met a lot of their friends and some of Eva's relatives. I liked the relatives, but it was not so easy with the Boston Jews who have a much more limited geography and so outlook. I did meet a beautiful nurse who is interested in India and did not get any plaudits from the men because I "stole" her right under their noses. I met some poets and they want to see my work.

---

* A cousin on Sam's father's side.

> Now the quandary is this: I have had no confirmation as to my sailing date and my travel agent . . . owes me money too. This throws me in the lap of uncertainty. On the other hand I can leave here and go to work up there and stay as long as I want to. This means taking my typewriter, etc. up there with me. In any case there is no loss.
>
> Had a series of interviews at Harvard. In the case of the Far Eastern section it was very good, but the professors in International Relations and the Near East were away. I may meet the professor who has been working on the Dead Sea scrolls because I have something for him. Such a meeting would be very valuable.[545]

It was important to Samuel Lewis to follow through on his connections at Harvard and also to relate to members of his family tree. He wrote of this in his diary:

> It was most important that I go into Massachusetts on three major errands. One of these, to contact Prof. Staley of Harvard, who is opening up a new school to teach all religions, has not come off yet. A second, to meet Prof. Sorokin to whom I am dedicating my books, did happen with not only expected pleasantries but surprises.
>
> It was Sorokin who held that Love controlled the whole universe, and my previous journey, and evidently the forthcoming one, has evidence of it. But he is also a man of love with supreme intellect. Several people I met think he is crazy and to use the radio comment, "and thou likewise" only I don't think Sorokin is crazy. He is not only a man full of love, but one full of information, of widest outlook, spiritual and has the finest Azalea garden I have ever seen; and believe me I have seen some Azaleas in life.
>
> Adolph Matz is my cousin on my father's side. I have the strangest sort of relatives around Boston. Independently of one another, we seem to have been attracted toward the Orient and spirituality. In politics, art, religion and all major subjects we think and emote similarly . . .
>
> On top of that I have been introduced to a poet I like; and to a poetry editor who wants to see some of my things, so I am taking my poems and also my manuscripts with me. It will be much easier to work there than in New York . . .
>
> I have been somewhat emotionally concerned about inability to establish a time program and this means more recourse to meditation. One morning, after such a session, I went suddenly to the Iraqi Consulate. Now I have had no intention of going into that country which is

presumably on bad terms both with the UAR and us. But as Holy Murshid* was guiding me there was nothing else to do.

To my amazement I received a wonderful welcome. I had asked for the Cultural Attaché. This was easy because the Visa Secretary was not in. I met the Visa Secretary later and he looked like a man who likes to say "no!" and he was not too happy that he could not say **no** to this **hombre**.

I had to fill out a form and I put down that the reason I wished to go to Bagdad was to visit holy places. He said: "Tomb of Abdul Kadir-i-Jilani." I replied, "Absolutely." "Why?" "I am a Dervish, one of the few American Dervishes, and my name is Ahmed Murad Chisti; also I was initiated into the Naqshibandi Order." He was surprised and delighted and we had a wonderful conversation.

So I filled out the forms but on account of the international situation I shall have to go from Lebanon to Bagdad, not from Damascus, unless the international atmosphere is clarified. However, there is no question about it.[546]

In a diary letter to Charles Siegferth, Sam reported further:

In 1957 I predicted trouble in Iraq when UNESCO imported a non-American, non-Muslim to speak as the "expert" on that religion, and Professor Moore, in the chair, refused to let the Iraqi have the floor. He walked out and wrote a strong letter which was read and confined to the waste-basket.

My experience is still to have my proposals treated lightly "lest we offend the Asians" and every Asian I meet is in favor of them. On the impersonal side I want to see Asians and Americans direct all studies in our mutual relations. In the Far Eastern Section of Harvard, the director is an American, Prof. Reischauer, who is highly respected by the Orientals and who has a very clear picture of what Buddhism is, including Zen. His chief assistant is a Japanese, who is thoroughly skilled in all branches of Buddhist culture. We spent an hour with him and he showed us the huge library of Chinese and Japanese classics. This is what it should be.

The Near East Studies are directed by a Briton and a Hungarian. It is just like SEATO,† designed to "defend" South East Asia, and ignored by Burma, Malay, Laos, Cambodia and Indonesia. We won't let the Asians alone.[547]

---

* Hazrat Inayat Khan.

† South East Asia Treaty Organization.

Sam continued to visit relatives in Cambridge and Gloucester. He was happy that he now had friends throughout the members of his family tree in the New England area. Given his difficult relationship with his parents and brother, relating well to other members of his family was very important to him.

The wait for his ship was long, with no certainty in sight. In July, 1960, while still waiting to begin his upcoming journey, Sam became aware of unexpected recognition, which inspired further expression of his vast knowledge and insight. He concluded a long letter to Rudolph Schaeffer about art and what was happening in San Francisco: "At the time the so-called anti-American riots were taking place in Japan, I received another copy of a magazine honoring me. It has led to my writing an independent article which may be submitted to certain publications. The strange fact, Rudolph, is that Paul Reps and I have been accepted in Japan as few or no other Americans have."[548]

Last Days Before Departure

> *The Columbia contact was perhaps easy because my grand teacher in both Mathematics and Philosophy was the late Prof. Cassius Keyser . . . There was a strong meeting of minds in the combination of the Integral and Pragmatic outlooks and against any and all dialectics.*
>
> *All the professors I have contacted are sympathetic with the approach of advertising the United States and not referring to Russia at all. I have a grand portfolio with excerpts from many of the New England poets which I hope to read abroad. And with that also present the names, at least, of some of our philosophers, mostly from Harvard and some contemporaries who are not so well known and should be known abroad.*
>
> SAMUEL LEWIS[549]

Samuel Lewis wrote in his diary about his last days in the U.S. before departure. In a lengthy letter to Mr. and Mrs. Smith, high-ranking officials at the Bank of America for whom he had worked as a gardener in Marin County, he wrote on many topics.[550]

> It looks as if, at long last, I shall leave the country. There has been a strange enigma about my departure, that the line on which I was origi-

nally to sail changed the date of departure three times, twice without notifying me. Instead I am going on a freighter at much less cost and in somewhat more rapid time. This enigma seems to support the existence of a Spirit of Guidance or Divine Wisdom, for certainly I depart without much of the equipment originally intended, and with much more intensified in other directions . . .

Bank of America. I have left my affairs in their hands. I purposely went down to the office which was formerly on Wall St. and now on Broad St. The ease with which I obtained transfer of funds is so wonderful that perhaps I may now write a pamphlet.

He wrote about his visit to Harvard and how he was pleased about his developing contacts with the universities.

I am leaving the country with extreme satisfaction. Ford Foundation has selected, in particular, those universities which seem to me to be outstanding in so many respects, viz.: Harvard, Columbia and U.C. I go away carrying two projects for Harvard and one for Columbia. One Harvard project concerns archeological research in that part of the world—Indus Valley and Hindu Kush where, other things being equal, I may be staying the longest.

The second is in the field of religious study on an honest objective ground—which is not yet true for most of this country. I have been in this field all my life, although not always openly. Correspondence with Bishop Pike has resulted in his request to see me on my return with two projects:

a. Opening a branch of World Congress of Faiths in California.
b. Battle against the exceedingly off-beat "morality" of our movies and fiction on sale abroad . . .

This last week I again ran into another strange piece of luck. Went down to the New York Horticultural Society to look up the possibility of a perennial Tomato, especially for India. I have been offered acreage there; and in addition to work on flowers I have just had a good drilling in actual greenhouse and field work on this crop.

With regard to his travel to the Near East he wrote,

I only carry a Lebanon visa along with that of the UAR at the moment. But the last weeks have brought much encouragement on a project to

> introduce *C. libani,* the Cedar of Lebanon, into this country for both experimental purposes and as a contribution to every town in the United States with the name of "Lebanon" to further better international relations.
>
> Massachusetts seems to have more cultured people than elsewhere. There are not only many universities but the total enrollment is stupendous. My family and social contacts did bring me into the orbit of people who have been pretty close to both Kennedy and Lodge, so I learned many intimacies. However, leaving the country, only the positive elements will be presented to foreigners. I discountenance the opposition to Kennedy on the ground of age. We forget how young both the elder and younger Pitt were when they began Prime Ministers; but otherwise I am leaving politics behind.

He continued with regard to Asia:

> I was also fortunate in meeting, while at my cousin's, a Youth Hostel leader who comes from Ceylon and has offered to be my guide and interpreter. Much of the rest of life has been of the same order.
>
> Publication. This has been my difficulty and I am not going into it. Newspaper interviews have so often brought a rejection of the true yet unusual. These things go on and Asians in general cannot understand, or will not accept, a strange subjectivity—in a Nation really dedicated to the practical and pragmatic.

Sam also wrote an extensive letter to his friends Fred and Corinne, who were at that time in Cairo where Sam was headed. Several excerpts from that letter[551] are presented here. Sam touched on a broad range of subjects, as he so often did. Among other things, he showed how important it was for him to have deep contacts with members of his extended family:

> I had my favorite cousin out last night and was pleased to find far more agreement than I dared let her know at the moment. Her father was related to both my parents. He was at least 90% Jewish, a rover, adventurous, free in his outlooks and conventions and the older boy follows him in much of this. The mother was a German Lutheran and one daughter follows her to the extent that she married a friend of [Chiang Kai-shek]. These strange polar inconsistencies are found all over in my kin and lead to a spirit of unsettledness. An equilibrated

state between them, however desirable, seems hard to find . . .

Repose is our great lack and I believe that repose itself is the depository of a corrective wisdom. Here again Providence has intervened. In the last few years I have taken on the role of god-father, even fairy god-father. It has not, on the whole, been successful. But is has brought to New York some of my "children" and in their cases not only extreme good-will and affection but latent yearnings of the exact same kind I have had—and perhaps you have had—for Oriental and "spiritual" teachings. This is extremely satisfying . . .

Social anthropologist Bronisław Malinowski, "father of field research"

I have been reading Malinowski whom I find rather subjective, but differing from Marx and Freud in that this subjectivity is needed to bring balance and objectivity. It must have been done purposely. The discovery of Radium shows that the odd provides the norm. I think this is true everywhere and the "odd" (to us) in Malinowski has provided some norms which are slowly but surely penetrating the mass mind.

The noisy problems of the present, like the election campaign, Congo, U-2 and Cuba, have such tremendous psychological factors that I am unable to view them other than indifferently politically. As a nation we have come to accept and love noise and we're trying to impose noise on others without considering that they may react differently to it than we do. Forces are born in the midst of it, grow up with it and it has become our second nature. Other people are not so imbued with noise, activity, hard work, gadgeteering and de-naturalism, and many strong reactions and rebellions arise from the unconscious . . .

I am purposefully going into other lands with other customs and outlooks, differing from Malinowski in that all of them are presumed to have reached high cultural levels. They will be and are unanimously critical of the U.S. and if left alone, could be still more critical of the U.S.S.R., but we can't leave them alone . . .

In the case of Harvard, the last effort was in regard to a new school dedicated to this subject wherein the teachers will not be persons who derived their knowledge from books, lectures from opinions, but who have had both experiences and non-academic credentials stemming from the parent-group of whatever the subject matter is. This will be most marked in the case of Sufism . . .

I only wish to call to your attention that statistically there are now and there have always been more Sufis than Zen Buddhists, Yogis,

> mystics and esotericists of all other schools combined; and, despite opinionated professors to the contrary . . . they convey positions of trust in many governments, particularly new ones. The omission here of a large portion of humanity in psychological and religious study is stupidity or nonsense . . .
>
> The Vedanta Society [in Boston] was financed in the beginning by kinfolk, and I visited Boston, but not to satisfaction. One day the secretary telephoned me, at a time I had hours to spare, poured her grief and gripes on me and made an appointment. The grief and gripes covered the same subjects and some of the same persons as my own. Her name is Mrs. Worcester and I hope to meet her some date.
>
> I met Swami Akhilananda, and it is quite obvious that the Vedantics in this country are divided into the poetic-philosophers and the psychologists, of which Swamiji is leader . . . The purpose of [his] book is to relate psychological types to Indian types . . .
>
> Lecture Abroad. So many doors have opened in and for India and Pakistan we can wait until I go through actual experience . . .
>
> UAR granted me a Courtesy Visa and I finally won over the Lebanese people with a couple of projects down their [alley] . . .
>
> I failed to meet Mrs. Coomaraswami and I did meet Dr. Rifsdahl, a woman who is one of the world's leading Egyptologists so I guess there is something in the wind. But this is opening the door for the Hollywood artists, and yourselves, in case I send objects.

Sam felt his conversation with the highly regarded Egyptologist was a good omen, since he planned to spend much time in Egypt (the UAR). In his positive and optimistic manner he often looked to find ways to financially support himself as well as benefit friends at home. He wrote, "If I am fortunate with my big projects, I would accept in return pieces of things not well known, which could be displayed—and in some cases sold."

Sam also wrote that his financial situation was like that of "many old Sufis":

> It has been impossible to relate income and expense. I am thrown here and can't get away . . . Instead of hurting me, it balanced or benefitted me. For between working for cousins and sharing expenses with a friend here there has been no great hardship. The last thing was to draw money from S.F. and apparently drained my checking account and in two days an unexpected check arrived filling the void.

My room and board in UAR will be less than $100 a month; and if I get lecture assignments, or research work, that may come out even better. I am making every effort to do everything on my own, hoping for adjustments after return to this country.

And concerning his good health:

> My working for my cousins in Massachusetts during this interim has again caused me to feel and look well and strong. I am constantly running into criticism socially and otherwise, following by apologies when people find my age and how I look. I do not understand it myself. I have taken no vitamins but have some for abroad. There is a sort of purging-of-mind which seems to facilitate bodily functions.

Sam wrote further about his last-minute thoughts before departure. Edna's separation from him seemed more than probable and he revealed other challenges he faced.

> I have rather run out of gas. The romantic element is absent just now and I can't evaluate that. I have some professional rather than personal matters to consider with you both . . .
>
> My contract with Columbia is resulting in strong emphasis on integrating and unitary flows. The question is how much one can hold oneself together and control both thought and habits . . . Institutions and symbols, yes, but perhaps there is over-compensation here.
>
> My next letter should come from Cairo.

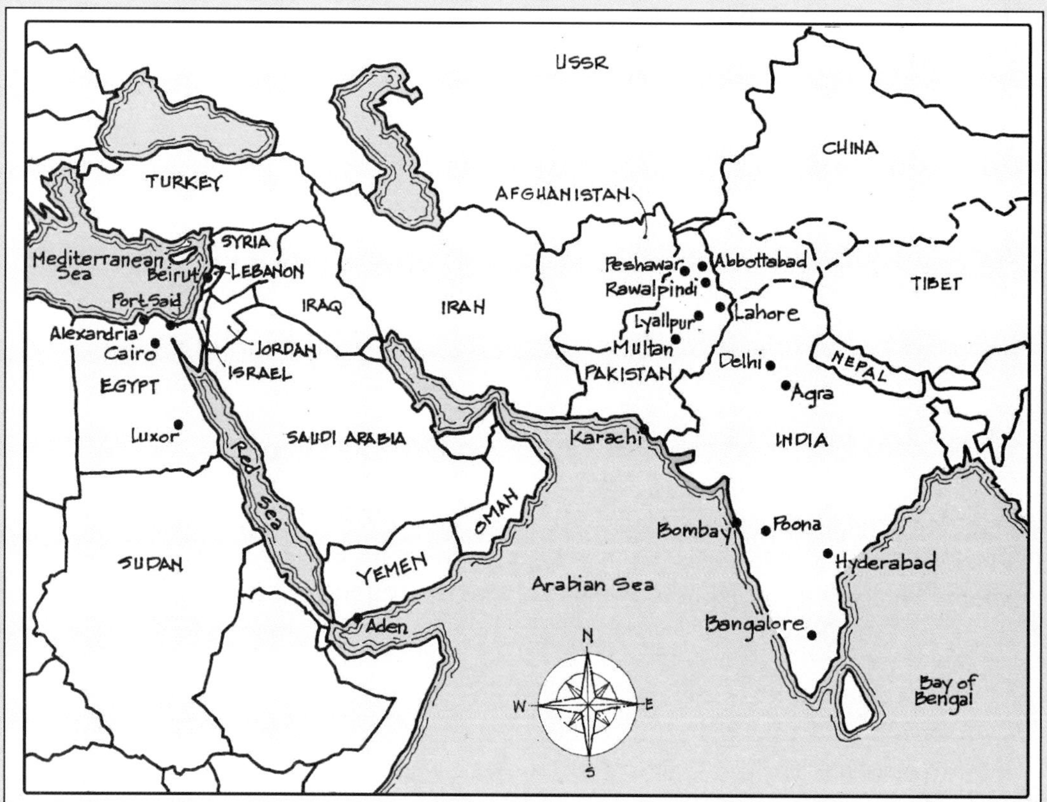

Sam's second trip abroad: August 1960–August 1962

CHAPTER 13

Egypt

Atlantic Crossing

Pir-o-Murshid said that Spirit-Of-Guidance was the same as Bodhisattva which means "Buddha in essence" and that is what we all are. Only we don't know it. The forest is made up of many kinds of trees as well as shrubs, flowers, herbs and grass. We can see the perfection in each and also the variety. But we do not see the perfection in "the forest of humanity." Nor is it easy. But it is so.

I am remaining in a kind of unknown, and strange to say, in my own country. I don't know what wisdom is behind it and am troubled by impatience but by nothing else.

God bless you all.

SAMUEL LEWIS[552]

SAM'S FIRST DESTINATION ON HIS SECOND TRIP ABROAD was Egypt. He was finally able to arrange passage to cross the Atlantic by freighter in August, 1960. After a few days on board, he wrote a diary letter to Bill Hathaway.

> This is really a long diary and I am not sure of continuity . . . There are only 4 men passenger[s], the rest women, and the men are either harmonious, alike or tamed—this include[s] myself. The women not so.
>
> Sam is not having too good a time. The weather is very stormy and there is almost a continuous headache, but not so far, thank goodness, any trouble with the stomach. This makes for listlessness and I am taking refuge at the typewriter and there is no eagerness. I did a few moments calligraphy this a.m. and have my language books out, but no campaign figured as yet. At the moment there is no chance of any hostilities with Miss Missionary. Madame Puerto not only came on board, but took over. She is stout, extroverted, loud, fond of men and wine, an entertainer, very talkative, very active and it is not so much nervousness as being her actual nature. There does not seem, for the moment, any middle ground between her and the missionary. The latter is retired and

almost sullen. Courtesy and consideration do not bring out smiles in her, and the loud kindnesses of Mrs. P.R. are misunderstood.

Last night I was asked to move my table to sit opposite Mrs. P.R. so the ladies could sit together, Miss Missionary with them. But to my amazement, at lunchtime, the latter also moved and to an empty table and would not—I mean would not and did not—sit with the women I thought she knew. The result has been considerable confusion socially and otherwise and I do not know where it will end.

On my Pacific trip the Captain took over socially and everyone became adjusted. But this Captain has a sour disposition. He is agin' the government and I rather sympathize with him. He is a Southerner, which we did not [expect], though his name "Lang" might mean something else in ancestry. Although he disclaims book learning, I have seen no evidence of this and he has strong opinions, based either on study or experience.

At first it was a little hard to get at him because he attacked persons, ideas and institutions at me and through me when in fact I also might be expected to attack the same person ideas and institutions. It took him a little while to find I was not a real antagonist, but I don't know what will happen when he becomes more familiar with other passengers whom I suspect will not always agree with him . . .

I think Miss Missionary is also rebuffed—by herself, of course—because nearly all the passengers like cards and games and probably liquor also. She is treated as if a Protestant nun and I don't think she wants to be treated as a Protestant nun. . . .

I have had no dreams and can't think, ideate or get in any mood, creative, literary or otherwise—at this moment, 14:10 o'clock watch time which is neither authentic, official or anything but quasi- or crazy-New York time.[553]

Sam wrote a diary letter to Leonora Ponti on the 27th while aboard the freighter.

In crossing the Pacific my stomach was bad and my head good; in crossing the Atlantic my stomach was good and my head bad. Still I prefer the latter. We ran into hurricanes and billows until we neared the Azores. After that things calmed down, my head got better and I have been feeling fine since.

I feel slightly like a veteran along with the companions. Most of them are taking a world tour, which does not cost much but does not give them much time inland. They are planning all sorts of things which I would not dare to [plan] so you can't catch planes like trains and when you have to change at airports to lines of different nationalities you can get stuck . . .

There is a lady on board going to Pakistan and we may get off at Beirut together and visit the American University. At the moment I have no other [plans].

I found that many of the officers seem to like folk-music. One man specializes in Polish dances on American things which we use in square-dancing. I enjoy those records.

Purchased a small transistor* from Japan just before I left New York. Got it at an inside price . . .

Around the Azores we began picking up Portuguese stations and more and more of them and then Moorish stations. We had a near collision last night and the whistles woke me up—just in time. For we were passing Gibraltar and I thought the whistles were signals therefore. I found nearly everybody was up—the crew at stations, the passengers to see the light on either side.

We sighted Portugal long before and today we have been sighting the Spanish Coast. I was not successful in picking up any Spanish station until today, with one [exception]. That exception was putting on a tango program. So were a lot of other stations. Tangos have their place but not off the coast of Andalusia. Well bless you this a.m. it was deef-fir-ent (pronounce French way).

Have I had a castanet session! Have I? Don't ask! Boy, was it great. We had flamenco and all kinds of la musicas and I got excited and came back and finished my writing so I could record this. I may be out on deck more so I can try out the stations and castanets and all. I am hoping by the time we dim out for Spain I can pick up Italy.

Have written a few other letters but again don't know where I shall post them. We do not land until Beirut which means a quick trip, but after that? Only I get off at [Alexandria]. They will be stuck in the Red [Sea], I think at Mocha. Some may fly immediately to India and others will not get off until Karachi, and think they can "see" India in a few days picking up the boat at Bombay. I am afraid there will be sad awakenings for them.

---

*Small is relative. A single transistor today is about 425,000 times smaller than in 1960. Sam refers here, of course, to a transistor radio.

My writing is on "Saladin," the guy that gave the Crusaders the good ol' one-two. Feel fairly confident that it will be received.

August 27. 10 o'clock or so. I guess.[554]

That night Sam had a prophetic dream about the passing of his therapist and friend Dr. Blanche Baker. The next day he wrote about it to Gavin Arthur, who had been devoted to her. Given what is known about Sam's faculties it should not come as a surprise that his vision would prove to be accurate.

> This morning I woke up after some complicated dreams in which you were the chief character. I arrived back in S.F. to find you in a very strange state of mind. You told me you were in a horrible fix as Dr. Baker had just died and you could not get any more horoscopes, but through the series of episodes, in one after another, you had no time to sit down with me as you had a sudden appointment to go out and arrange a chart. So you were in and out constantly and I could make no head or tail of your affairs because it appeared you were earning more money than ever.
>
> You were not happy but your astrology work was taking you further afield. You not only had more clients but they were spread out and evidently informing others. So, with the disappearance of Blanche you were not only on your own but making good.
>
> I could learn nothing more in the dreams from you either about yourself or anybody. You looked somewhat better than when I had last seen you but carried a look of dismay.[555]

Early photo of Blanche Baker, M.D., Ph.D.

Dr. Baker would die that December and Gavin would feverishly miss her. She meant more to him than any one person in his life. Sam's vision of Gavin's success as an astrologer on a large scale also ultimately proved accurate.

Further on in the diary letter of August 28 Sam wrote about meeting the difficulties that had arisen for him in California with the American Academy of Asian Studies and others:

> Turning to Bertrand Russell today I am strengthening myself in just those matters of logic and thinking upon which doors were closed in California and opened on the East Coast.

American University of Beirut

What that means at the moment I do not know, but I am carrying Oliver Reiser and Pitirim Sorokin around and may be introducing them into the Orient.

I have three complete avenues in Egypt: The American University, the mixed ones and those which are obviously Arabic. I am planning first to call at the American University at Beirut. Most on board want to go to the Holy Land—there will not be much time, but they will go so I may be the only passenger the last few days. We passed near Tunis today.[556]

A few days later Sam chose to describe his ship arriving in Beirut, Lebanon in the voice of Puck of Pukhtunistan.

It is with extreme delicacy that the diary entry for today should be written in the name of Puck or no other than Samuel. We reached Beirut on the night of September 1st and the Captain summoned us to his quarters to meet three Lebanese doctors and all that. "*As-salaam aleikum.* I am dar-veesh." The Captain then challenged and we gave a lot of answers that he could not understand and when the customs man came around, "You have nothing to declare, no contraband," holding their heads in the opposite direction and saying, "Glad to meet you Ahmed Murad." Which adds another chapter to innocents abroad, or something.*

By six o'clock in the a.m. we were alongside and a grand rush of men came up the gang plank. Were they customs men? Money-changers? Merchants? Travel agents? Boy, how wrong can you be. They were barbers and they followed everybody around and made all business on board impossible. We could not organize, we could not eat, the cargo was not being unloaded and they could go in and out of a crowd like nobody. Then they went around and knocked on everybody's doors, waking up those who had just come off watch and sleep was impossible. Fortunately we had gone to bed early, had a wonderful night's sleep and we were delightful.

---

* *The Innocents Abroad* was Mark Twain's account of his 1867 travels in Europe and the Holy Land.

Most of the folks went to Damascus. This includes Julia who is not talking to us and eight people who are not talking to Julia. The last we heard was that they were fighting. Then the barbers surrounded us and I said: "I have plenty of business." "What kind of business?" "I am Ahmed Murad and I am a dar-veeeesh." Barber No. 2 looked at me, dropping his jaw, dropping his tools, dropping his head and looking about as astonished as it is possible to look astonished. "I am Ahmed Murad and I am a dar-veeesh!" "Come! I give you fresh hair-cut!" . . .

Well, we visited the American University and had a fine time, only it is summer session and the place is empty of Syrians, Lebanese and Americans. This was fine for Puck who ran into Pakistanis about every three inches and finally settled on two from Dacca. "You know Shantin-angar St?" "Of course, of course." "You know Maulana Abdul Ghafoor?" "Of course, of course. He is my murshid, I am darveesh." More jaw-dropping, etc. They also know Sophia Khan the poet and all that. They introduced me to a man from Iran. "Where you come from?" "Shi-raz." "O city, of beautiful poetry. O land of Hafiz, and *bulbul* and *gul* and running streams and holy places . . ." The Iranian began to drop his jaw more than the Pakistanis. Anyhow we gave them all choco-laat and distributed choco-laat all over the campus, even to the profs . . .

Went into Mosque. It was Friday but early. Everybody was studying Holy Qur'an, really. Nobody paid attention, no spies, no suspicions! Imagine, a Mosque and men praying to Allah and not eyeing the foreigner. So we did three *rakats* and got up and put our shoes on and gave £1-Lebanese to the door-keeper who knew I was a holy man and then I said "*Subhan Allah*" and he was sure of it, but Puck does not know whether he is a scoundrel or a hypocrite or the real thing, whatever that is.

The passengers had visited down town the night before, but we took a different look. We visited the Lebanese museum. To get "in" with the Lebanese all you have to do is say: "I think you are the descendent of the Phoenicians." That makes them happy.

Anyhow the museum was closed. "Too bad, and I am so interested in the Phoenicians!" "What you say?" "I am so interested in the Phoenicians." "Come inside so I can hear?" "I am so interested in the Phoenicians." "Oh, you look around." So Puck looked around and saw plenty. "I am so interested in the Phoenicians!" . . .

I asked the cabbie, what religion. "Maronite." "What language you use in church?" "Silly question, Arabic, of course." Last night I asked the steamer agent. What religion? "Maronite." "What language?" "Silly question, Latin of course." Then I asked the guide, what religion? "Maronite." 'What language?' "Old Syrian, of course, foolish question."

Sam then left the museum.

We saw the rich section, then to our surprise, a very large and prosperous Jewish section, all looking well-to-do and smiling. It was almost unbelievable, but there it was and Hebrew writing staring me in the face.

We then called at the Indian Embassy. My friend Bannerji has been promoted to under-secretary of Foreign Affairs and is back in New Delhi . . . This will help when we get there . . .

Next Day. The tourists came back and saw the haircut. "How much?" "Nothing." The next: "*No questa nada.*" "But you must have paid something?" Next person: "Didn't you have to pay anything?" "*Rien du tout.*" By this time Puck's stock hit a bear market. They began looking at each other. In walked the Second Mate. "So you got a haircut, how about the price?" "Who said anything about price. I got a haircut. No price." "But what did it cost?" "A thousand ciphers!" By that time Puck's stock had recovered: it went up and up, even out of the bull-market range. Puck scratched his head—he should have invested in himself. "O ye men of little faith." Then Puck gave a lecture and they listened: "When in Lebanon if you meet a Muslim praise the prophet; if you meet a Christian, praise the Phoenicians." The opposition melted, the tourists became so meek that they might even inherit the earth.[557]

Alexandria and Cairo; Early Explorations

Sam's diary continued aboard the *Flying Clipper.*

Sighted Sicily, Tunis and Cyprus. The Mediterranean was blue, calm and delightful. I should say it was about as delightful as any journey I have made so far and certainly recommend it.

Although we left New York about 5 days late, we have picked up a little time—it does not matter much, I guess. Yesterday was spent at Beirut where I visited the University, the air-port, one mosque, the Indian Embassy and had a fine lunch on my Diners' Club Credit card—strictly Lebanese food, some new to me . . .

Most of the folks went to Damascus and Baalbek. Here I must say that the Isbrandtsen line is very cooperative and informative and I am

> hoping to have a little of the same at Alexandria. It is possible that I may return to Beirut later on, en route to either Damascus or Bagdad. This depends on the unforeseen . . .
>
> This is a good line to take my trip to Karachi, pending ability to get a room. I had the stateroom alone due to cancellations, and there were no uppers—plenty of space and a nice closet. Sometime, when I am home, I hope to take the Captain and the Stewart to "The Captain's Galley" in San Francisco, on Chestnut St. But this is ahead of schedule.
>
> Since entering the Mediterranean I have slept wonderfully, even with all the noise at the dock . . . We arrive [in Alexandria] early on the Morning of September 4, after leaving N.Y. August 17th—which I consider good time.[558]

Around the same time Sam described interacting with different cultures in Puck style, with the usual comical touch:

> The Spaniards and the Commies danced to avoid each other. Puck met the delegate from Lemnos, and the Consul from Cocos Island and New Falklands and a lot of other places. The trouble is that he has to go home and look at Atlases. The Ambassador kept the cultural attaché close by and always asked him—in Hindi, of course—"Where the h—l is Sputnikistan, or something." "Oh, I just love your country. I think the New Zealanders are the best people. . . ." "But I come from New South Wales." "Isn't that a part of New Guinea?" Puck prefers to discuss food and does not get into geographical messes; he has his own kind of messes.
>
> The Soviet delegate did not come. He talks about the masses and gets into the messes. Puck talks about the messes and gets into the masses. There were no servants, only one or two caterers and they had to hop, skip and jump. You can tell the rank—those who go after the drinks and avoid food are always the rankest. They don't bother about the guest of the evening. It was the same—nobody knew the Ambassador and nobody cared much, but everyone noticed he has a pretty wife. The only trouble is that saris make all women look beautiful; still they did not compete with her, they just out-competed the Europeans. The French women looked awful. The Indonesian women also looked beautiful, the Spanish . . . the Indonesian were also beautiful . . . the Americans . . . don't bother Puck. He was speaking to the Indonesian women and telling them he would like to visit their country. He really would. The Ambassador from Indonesia looks as if he were half-Chinese.

Despite what you read, the Indonesians greeted all the Chinese and not many others, of course Puck.[559]

Cairo University, the second largest university in Africa after Al-Azhar University

On September 4, 1960, Sam arrived in Alexandria. On the 5th he was in Cairo. He visited Al-Azhar, the Egyptian University in Cairo, but wasn't able to establish a relationship with them at that time.

Two days later he wrote Harry Nelson after visiting Cairo University and their Dept. of Agriculture, the Reclamation-Irrigation Service, and more. Some excerpts follow:

> My dear Harry:
>
> I feel like a person who has asked [for] permission to visit a playground and while he is waiting has been given free tickets to the World Series. When I visited the Soils Section of Cairo University I was told I had to see one Mr. Salah who is a big shot in the Agricultural Department and he told Mr. Dewsouki that a new government regulation had gone into effect requiring permits for visits. This was undoubtedly true for I was fortunate enough even to get into the high echelon offices and most of the time was spent trying to get through crowds who were being held back. It was not that way before.
>
> Mr. Paul Keim, U.C. '23, of ERIS, which is the Reclamation-Irrigation Service cooperative between the UAR and the U.S. has given me a stack of names and I can't visit them all—in fact I have not gotten very far down the list and am busy every day. He sent me to Dr. Turki, who is the head of the National Research Bureau. This is a coordinating **functional** department of all the top scientists of this region. It is divided into five sections: Chemical, Physical, Agricultural, Medicinal and Coordinating-Publications.
>
> Dr. Turki turned me [over] to one Dr. Kabash and the big parade is on for me. First I visited section No. 5 and in a sense will be dealing with them on and off. They are very much delighted with the plans we worked out—indeed everybody is here. The only thing is that I am on the spot and am given personal credit, but I think I'll bring up your name more beginning today.

The Library and Publications section have [scientific] books from all over the world . . .

They have a large and active photography department, microfilm department and all the latest equipment—assuming I know what I am talking about after visiting Berkeley, Japan, Ohio State, etc. . . .

I was particularly interested in the Soil Science because I have been argued down by brand names people **not** in Horticulture on this point and equally cornered by brand names **in** Horticulture for the same thing. Yesterday when I was waiting I came upon a copy of "Soviet Soil Science" . . . but I saw nothing to indicate good chemical knowledge and techniques . . .

Of course there was a good geological and fase-soil analysis. But here in UAR the whole problem is the adaptation of crops, etc. . . .

The big problem is the Cotton Worm. It is a different species but the same Genus as the one in the States. However it eats anything and escapes from one host to another. Like in India they have all the right spraying equipment and the chemicals but they do not understand the heat and wind factors and spraying has often been done at too high temperatures. So they often resort to handpicking. This has had the result of the worm leaving the cotton fields and going on to food plants . . .

I dropped the typewriter to go to the Embassy where I am not only spending much time but given every consideration. The years I have given to Oriental studies has been recognized and the difficulties I ran into in so many institutions in the United States because the instructors in so-called "Asiatics" were Europeans is recognized; I am given full sympathy. Both the Americans and Hindus are giving full cooperation for a future lecture program. This will cover many branches of American Culture: art, philosophy, religion and science. All my past inhibitions have been overcome and it is even possible that I shall be programmed at the Embassy.

On top of that the new Ambassador from India is an old friend who long lived in San Francisco and who was my host in New Delhi. It is possible that I shall help arranging a joint social affair here in this regard.

After mailing this I visit both the Research Center and the vegetable Experimental Station . . . One of the managers here and I may tour the bazaars. And next week I hope to be at the disposal of Dr. Hasan. In other words, Harry, I am going on all cylinders but watching my step . . .

There have been dangled before me trips to distant areas. I hope this is possible. The integration of agricultural, social and archeological research is one of my local themes. There are great Christian ruins in places now called deserts where there used to be much water. What happened is a mystery and though I am reading one of the few books available on that period, it throws no light on the subject . . .

I do not know how they can introduce organics here other than the present green manure cropping. The nearest Forestry college is at Alexandria, though I may get introductions from Syria. Few of the trees here are extremely drought resistant. But this one cannot face all problems at one time . . .

PS. Another bit of luck. Don Smith of the USIS arrived here today. He was my host at Karachi, and I already have the whole Embassy working for and with me now.[560]

Two days later Sam wrote Harry Nelson again. He spoke of what he had found in Lebanon at the American University, but mostly was focused on his relationship with Dr. Paul Keim.

[I am] in and how! Here is a man, coming from the campus which authored "The Ugly American" and doing everything the opposite and with official sanction. But no publicity, [no] nonsense, no press releases. New villages, new building programs and the Egyptian substitute for forty acres and a mule; only they are given a choice between a cow and a buffalo . . .

My presumable host, Dr. Shawarbi, the chief Agricultural Chemist, is in the States, but I have plenty of instructions Anyhow. My other endeavors may move slowly as college does not open until October 3rd. The Chief American authority on art is a friend of owner of this pension. And already I have the problem [of] more interviews, contracts and anecdotes than I feel like writing . . .

There are no signs of Russians; the city is typically commercial, the banks seem thriving (one [big] shot, whom I met is also away), and the anti-ugly-American work is gaining many friends. Neither Mr. Keim nor I are "optimistic" about the Russians being able to build Assouan* dam. Not only that I have my material on salt-water conversion [from Shamcher Beorse] and the Americans are making the badly needed hydrological survey. I think by Sunday I shall have enough material to submit an article for publication either to the *C.S. Monitor* or San Rafael *Independent.*[561]

---

*Today spelled Aswan.

Sam felt the success or failure at Aswan would likely be a matter of engineering, and he speculated that water would be brought to the land from several sources before the dam was completed, were that to happen at all. The land, historically rich with underground water, was now vast tracts of desert. Still, he observed that there were areas such as the Red Sea with enough temperature differentiation between the surface water and the deeper waters to allow the production of electricity and the conversion of salt water into potable water. The water research was continuing, and Sam was a part of it.

As described in a September 8th diary entry, Sam was a guest of the Government Agricultural Department and was pleased to see Americans working with Egyptians at the same level and pace. There were many University of California graduates in positions of importance both in the American group and the UAR government itself. He saw a land running on essentially capitalistic bases, modified by monetary power, but he also saw humanism. One factor held against the U.S. was our failure to have real racial integration.

Sam had promoted the planting of Eucalyptus trees in India with no response, but here he found the trees thriving, "fast growing trees, giving fire wood and enabling the peasant to return dung to the soil."[562] Sam also observed, "This is really becoming a land of small farmers. There are many improvements over traditional methods and every worker is learning to use hand-pump spray equipment."[563]

Adventures in the UAR

To be successful here one should have two of those three credentials (a) Know something about Egypt or Islam; (b) know something about plant materials, especially food crops; (c) know something about the Berkeley Campus. The latter is most important and copy of Hilgardia* *which I happen to have smuggled in was nearly as good as my passport.*

SAMUEL LEWIS[564]

---

*A respected journal of agricultural, environmental, and nutritional sciences published by the University of California.

Ahmed Murad had remarkable success at making important connections wherever he went. His confidence and energy helped. He also focused on horticultural plans he and Harry Nelson had originally outlined.

> The plan worked out by Harry Nelson and myself is succeeding. I was given all kinds of problems on Cotton, Sugar Cane, Soy Beans and Tomatoes and consulted my bulletins. Oh, Yes, Peanuts. The latter matter material I found in the Florida and Georgia bulletins and Louisiana supplied the Sugar Cane answers . . .
>
> There are big hydrological surveys on and as water is discovered or uncovered, the marshlands, the depressions and oases are being utilized. Saturday I am "being taken for a ride" to a distant province—in the North West. I am trying to see Keim Friday because that is the Islamic Sabbath. I have had no day of rest—Saturday and Sundays at the U. I also expect to call on the Japanese embassy Friday, which is between the sections of the American [Embassy] . . .
>
> I have far more introductions than I can use as offices close either at 1 or 2 and that is it for the day excepting that the American library and Tourist offices re-open at 5. Between them you can eat, sleep or play—unless you are a mad man or Englishman and go out in the noon-day sun . . .
>
> They invented the coffee break here, and sometimes you have one after another with occasional work in between. Maybe someday I'll get technical and [tell] you about the work. Yes, I have seen the latest in grass cutters. But yesterday I saw a book on plants growing in the Sinai desert. And what is foremost; *C. dactylon!** Even the mosquitoes draw the line somewhere.
>
> Cheerio[565]

Sam continued to describe his time in the UAR in a diary letter to his confidant and close friend, Florie Leonard.

> This is my diary entry for today and I am sending a copy to a small group of Muslims in Cleveland . . . There has been a drop in temperature and, of course, I am becoming used to the weather. It is warm and dry, not nearly so enervating as our Eastern seaboard or India and [points] east, but still too hot to warrant much walking.

*Bermuda grass—considered a scourge in Egypt, but a valuable forage crop in India.

If you travel by taxi, they drive fast and you hardly see anything. If you take the bus or car, you are crowded, and in any case, you do not see much. So I essayed a walk which I presume is about four miles each way, going by one set of streets and returning by another.

Without saying I love Cairo, I prefer it to our Eastern cities and to some in India. I would like it better than Los Angeles if it were not so flat. Like Portland, Oregon, it is divided by a river and I have not found any city limits yet. I have not tried to see any historical [monuments]. Nearly all my time has been spent at Cairo University or with different branches of the Government.

Many factors are working for me here. The two outstanding are my interest in Islam and my being a life-member of the University of California Alumni Association. Not only is the top American from Berkeley but more graduates from there are in important Government offices than from any other American University, or, so far as I can see, from all the Iron Curtain countries put together. Every interview is torn by the situation of a grand welcome and a need for me to be touring the States and telling people what I see . . .

The first situation I explained was the rivalry between no less than six Pakistani groups to "convert" English-speaking people. They all ignore each other, and mostly print in poor English. The majority assume Islamic teachings and then try to **prove** them. Four of these groups are more or less Sunni and two are Ahmadiyya. I placed the Ahmadiyya Prayer book in the Director's hands for review. I shall return in three or four days for his decision and possibly my instructions in *Salat* and *Nimaz*,* etc. . . .

Al-Azhar Mosque and University

I took a note over to Al-Azhar Mosque but the attendant speaks English and welcomed me. This made me feel very happy. There are in a sense two Mosques, one being a grand courtyard, surrounded by alcoves. There were many classes in these alcoves and, so far as I could see, they have co-education with the boys and girls not particularly different than in our country. I think they are using it largely as a kindergarten or pre-school place . . .

*Arabic and Urdu terms, respectively, for the Muslim ritual prayer, performed five times daily.

> The inner Mosque is, I presume, the famous one. There were a few classes on, entirely of older people. The adults were of all ages, but generally young [men] or those who have reached the period of retirement. The place was not a congregation of beggars and "bums" which one finds in India and Pakistan. Some of the staff do not like what they saw there, especially around the shrines. As I belong to the Chisti, they told me some of their objections to what they saw. I admit ceremonially and outwardly there is "saint worship" but inwardly there is something else and there are only two ways to convey that "something else." One is by a visit and the other is by disciplinary instruction.[566]

On September 20 he wrote Harry Nelson again in great detail. Here are a few excerpts from the letter. It focuses on the Aswan Dam and certain problems with the Nile River.

> The subject is the problem of the Nile. Now I am not so vain as to presume I can offer a "solution" to a large problem . . .
>
> Turning to the Nile, I have been opposed to the Assouan Dam for many reasons. One is I think the cost is too much for the Nation and the same money, used in Salt Water conversion plants and in a more complete hydrological survey including chemical analyses of soil and water would be more effective.[567]

Shamcher Bryn Beorse with an Ocean Thermal Energy Conversion model

This type of saltwater conversion was a program supported by Sam's good friend and fellow disciple of Inayat Khan, Shamcher Bryn Beorse. Sam went on to say:

> In one respect the Nile resembles the Indus. India and Pakistan have just signed an agreement with regard to the waters. On the other hand, it resembles the Colorado where a number of States have entered into a pact almost like an international agreement. But there is no such pact concerning the Nile. And it is always possible that Ethiopia may indulge in engineering projects like Colorado, carrying water over a shed into another region where feasible, to open up large tracts. Ethiopia is a

> land of extreme contrasts between wet and dry regions and she may do something about it . . .
>
> [Louis] Bromfield shows the difference between the handling of the Missouri—which he considers was done badly—and the Ohio, which he admires. The Missouri again, is much like the Nile, going through warm dry country in the summer. Bromfield advocates up-stream control and that is the only thing I see. Despite the "Arab Bloc," the Nations have not learned to cooperate and have mutual exchange.[568]

In a letter to Professor Cutright of the Ohio State Agricultural Experiment Station in Weedstar, Sam wrote about his time at the Central Vegetable Experimental Station. He was taken around by Mr. Azad, who conducted sweet potato experiments.

> One of the things, perhaps the [thing] I want most is international Horticultural exchange. I was glad to get the main gripe I hold and that is, instead of sending newspaper men out, we should even subsidize retired farmers and have them visit the Asian countries. I omit Africa on account of the weather, not because of the race problem. In "The Ugly American" the lament is for linguistic communication. I believe "down to earth" communication is a thousand times better.[569]

In a diary letter to Rudy, a friend and travel agent, Sam spoke of what was unfolding for him in Cairo:

> The American Embassy has been very cooperative with me. I also take books from their library, mostly on Horticulture. About half my mornings are spent with the technicians in this field. I spent some time with George Scanlon at the American University. He is the contact man on Islamic culture, especially Art. But by agreement I am to wait for one Dr. George Creswell, who is considered by all hands to be the . . . expert. I then called on the head of the University Library, one Mahmud Shenecti.
>
> I told Scanlon I differed from the "experts" on Sufism because despite their statements, and often arrogant statements, I had met Sufis in high places. He conceded that this might be true of further parts of Asia but was not true here. But when I was talking with Shenecti, he brought up the name of Abdul Kadir-i-Gilani and we found ourselves in complete agreement . . .

> Actually the politicians seem to be cool toward Sufism, the scientists quite warm.
>
> Monday I picked up my Visa for Pakistan. It is multiple entry good for four years and subject to renewal. The clerk was rather haughty . . . I simply wrote a letter to the Consul General in San Francisco, sent a copy to the Ambassador with a note, setting forth some of my credentials—which I can assure you are top-notch. I received an emergency call from our own Embassy and the clerk stood at attention and saluted when he gave me the Visa. I told the hotel owner I did not know whether to get angry or laugh, and in a sense still do not. When I have been meek, officials have often been haughty and when I show credentials, they are liable to go to the other extreme, which is not much better.[570]

Sam wrote about a deep side of Sufism and what as an experienced Sufi he would recommend in the way of psychic research:

> There is a side of Sufism, which is deeper than Psychic Research. Mrs. Garret and the Cayce Foundation have both rejected tentative papers on the subject. That is why I am for a more serious and impersonal research group which will go into phenomena, not personalities. I have been asked again and again to go to some holy places here and it is quite possible that there will be "emanations of *baraka*" there, to which I am sensitive.[571]

In Cairo with Sufis and the Government

Sam trusted his friend Florie Leonard with all his deepest experiences. In a diary letter of September 25, 1960, he wrote of the many important contacts he was making.

> Yesterday I visited the Embassy again and also strolled to the Japanese Embassy to see the cultural attaché. My relations with the Americans are very cordial although I have run into one off-key note. At the University they defended Von Grünebaum whom I accused because he said the downfall of Islam was due to the refusal of Sufis to take part in the government. I pointed out the large number I had met elsewhere. They answered, "Yes, elsewhere." The hotel owner reaffirmed this position.
>
> But the other day my temporary host, Fouad Fisk said, "I have a grand surprise for you, another member of *tarik*," which is to say, the esoteric path. He is Mohammed M. Billah and a member of the

> Shadilya Order.* Today we discussed Sufism both at length and deeply because Ali Ezed who is supposed to be conducting me around was called out of the office constantly. Meanwhile the grapevine is working for me and tomorrow evening I have my first invitation to an Egyptian home from one Dr. Mustapha Kemal Ahmed. He has been to the States for Horticulture training and is listed in the phone book as one of the top advisors in this field. But he also wants to see me because of my interest in Islam . . .
>
> Today Mohammed M. Billah told me that there are lots of Sufis around, chiefly Shadilyas whom I want to meet and Rifa'i. The latter are the "howling Dervishes" and they perform all those phenomena which we attach to the term fakir and which have wrongly been thrown at the Hindus who are not so adept I believe in either mysticism or magic, though they get the name for it. I do not wish to devaluate the Hindus. I wish to elevate the Muslims, both esoteric . . . and exoteric, and think I can do it now, with the backing and authorization I am receiving. The end of the Academy and the temporary tragedy of the Islamic Center will clear the path for proper instruction. I do not have to look down or at those persons who would not permit me to speak, or who gave excuses for strange politics.[572]

The next day Sam again wrote to Florie for his diary. He had gone to the Agricultural section of the Embassy, where he received positive feedback. He said, "They understand thoroughly here what I am doing." Later in the morning he went to the Chamber of Commerce and met a man who launched into politics and was "so long and vehement about it we never did get down to business." The diary entry continues:

> A reporter came in from "Akhbar" or "Akhbar el-Yawm," which means Daily News or something like that and attention was turned to me. We had an interview and later on the reporter will call at my hotel and give me a long interview and take my picture for an article. I shall then get the article and send it to Mr. Mehdy in San Francisco and Mr. Schwell in New York and a few extras for the Bay Region . . .
>
> This afternoon went to the Tourist Information Office. It was a regular Puck visit. "How can I go to Syria?" "You can get the information

---

*As Sam described this meeting in his October 2 letter to Abdul Sattar, "It was love at first sight and has been ever since."

> across the street." "How can I visit Karnak?" "You can get the information across the street." That is about all I got . . .
>
> So I went across the street. They can arrange my plane flight; and also my train trip south but not any hotel. The travel bureaus I like tell you about hotels . . . They had all the dope. It is available, but the girl at the Information Office gave me nothing but negatives. Anyhow if I go to Damascus I must book long ahead. But if I visit the temples 24 hours' notice is enough.
>
> In a few moments I shall have the radio broadcast in English of Nasser's address. Then I shall start some very heavy writing.[573]

On September 27 Sam wrote again in his diary, this time to Jack. He was ecstatic about the acceptance he had received in the horticultural field.

> Today I got [a] direct picture [of] myself at the top level. Doors are being opened here for research scientists and they are not iron curtain country people . . .
>
> I started off this morning by visiting the Embassy and the Vegetable Research Center. I am doing top technical research work mostly in literature. Or course if I had to demonstrate with equipment, I could probably do that too. I have found that my work is being appreciated by both the Americans and Egyptians. This is after a long hard struggle, Jack, but I have just received an acknowledgement from the Alumni Association of the University of California thanking me for my last report; so far as I can tell the next one will be a humdinger, or if kept quiet until I return, I may even be given a banquet . . .
>
> What I have found out confirms what I have been saying. I cannot compel a metaphysical world to accept faster . . .
>
> There is an open display of magazines on a table, where they are left for two weeks prior to filing. The ones I saw from Russia were all on Physics. In checking on Organic Chemistry the United States was ahead [but] Russia, India and Italy also had plenty. I did not count . . .
>
> In the section devoted to yarns, etc., Germany decidedly led, followed by the United States, and a number of other nations also contributed, the Japanese among them but far behind. I am not going to write anything on the leadership in science and technology, but this "neutral" observation point with materials from all parts of the earth is an excellent one.[574]

Inside the Amr ibn al-As Mosque

On September 28, Sam sent his diary entry for the day jointly to Willie Wise and William Gaskin.

This day I saw much of Cairo on feet. I was taken by a hotel clerk who likes to walk so we walked. I have now been in this city the better part of the month and have not gone out of its environs . . .

We walked the whole length of the town, excepting for a short trolley ride to the oldest Mosque here, that of Amr ibn al-As. It was probably built on a Christian Church. I had already been to Al-Azhar and noticed what I humorously [call] the "pillars of Islam" which are Corinthian and more than five, no matter what the theologians say. The Mosque of Amr ibn al-As covers a large courtyard—now deserted—and inner courts which were being used by women in the morning. Most of the pillars are Corinthian but some are Ionic and a few a modified type showing distinctly Egyptian influences. This, of course, was before the rise of distinctly Islam art.

Old Cairo contains the poorest part of town but it is surprisingly small in comparison with other districts . . . What interested me here were the kilns . . .

We next went to the Asultana Hasan Mosque which shows an advanced Islamic art and was very busy with devotees. The same principle held for the Zayyaid* Hussein [mosque] where the bones of the grandson of the Prophet are buried. There is a constant movement of pilgrims going on and both Qur'an reading and study. There is no worship hour between early morning and after 2 in the afternoon.

What I have seen in the Mosque so far include a high degree of lattice work, non-objective formations, excellent work on inner doors and vaults—the higher up the finer the art and it is wonderful because these men must have worked on ladders and scaffolds . . . [There was] only lighting when necessary, so it was hard for students to read. I noticed here that one devotee did not even go in but chanted in the doorway where it was light. I found the chanting very beautiful.[575]

---

*Variously spelled Zayyaid, Syedna, Sayiddna.

On October 2 Sam wrote to Abdul Sattar at Pakistani House in San Francisco, focusing on issues concerning Pakistan:

> I am now not only busy looking into the agricultural and scientific problems of this region, I am receiving full cooperation . . . Both Egyptians and [Americans] highly [commend] my study of this region in order to obtain information and ideas which may be applied in the Indus Valley. The parallels are many.
>
> When it comes to water supply, I think your country has been very wise and the Egyptians would be well to cooperate with Sudan, a presumably friendly country which they have tended to ignore, while both the Indian officials and your esteemed President have had engineering if not political foresight . . .
>
> I am making copious notes and reports which I shall have in my diary and to place before Mr. A. A. Cheema of the Central Agricultural Bureau if he be still in Karachi when I get there, or to take to 'pindi* which can so easily be reached from Abbottabad.
>
> Aside from general soil and crop problems I have been given some Sugar problems and whether the answers are forthcoming or not, they will benefit Pakistan. Not only that, I shall certainly urge missions to come here and some students to visit this region.
>
> I have benefited tremendously in the scientific and agricultural ventures because of my interests in Islam and because of my connection with the University of California. This has added to zeal on both sides and utmost cordiality. The result is that I am actually functioning at a higher level than ever before . . .
>
> Actually it is very difficult to delineate between "orthodoxy" and "Sufism" in the lives, not of the poor, ignorant and superstitious, but in the lives of the most educated and enlightened people here. I meet with them occasionally socially, often professionally.
>
> Yesterday Mr. Billah said that he would like me to accompany him on the birthday of the original Syed Hussein, the Prophet's grandson. His tomb is here in a Mosque which I have visited. There will be a gathering of dervishes from all over the Near East. And, praise be to Allah, our birthdays fall on the same date. I am looking forward to this occasion like a child to a great party . . .
>
> Inasmuch as I should be speaking in many universities I cannot gauge the time and I want to visit the farm of Mr. Jamshyd Khan at Mardan

* Rawalpindi.

> and we shall have lots to discuss, too. Today I feel much more self-assured and even capable of performance.
>
> Dr. Cromwell should be here any day now. He is the authority on Islamic Art. This is another venture I am undertaking in joint cooperation with friends in San Francisco and with [the University of the Punjab]. I write fairly regularly to my friend, Mrs. Florie Leonard, which is about all I can do.[576]

He wrote Florie again on October 4th, detailing some of his memorable contacts.

> I have failed, in the midst of other activities, to keep up a diary. Things happen which are of no record, or are of import. Yesterday I had a big disappointment and then the opposite.
>
> The disappointment is that after being here one month I have gotten absolutely nothing out of Al-Azhar. I do not like to complain. I went there the first place, the first day. I have been given hospitality and the best coffee imaginable. Excellent tea, fine feeling, but on the intellectual plane absolutely nothing. I do not understand this but I find it is partly true of others too. How can we bring teachings to the U.S. if nothing is done? Everybody cries to heaven, or hell, that we the Americans are unfair and then when we want to be fair, or to take their side, what happens? . . .
>
> I have turned down several people who wanted to help me, because I wish to work with authorities. Or again, I have had the vision of a Murshid and reported it and it may be that he is the one who is going to give me exoteric as well as esoteric instructions.
>
> I left Al-Azhar at 10:15 yesterday morning and then things happened the other way. I met Mr. Pande, cultural attaché at the Indian Consulate. He invited me to meet Prof. Chandrasekhar who spoke last night. Dr. Chandrasekhar is perhaps the best demographer on earth and he specializes in population problems and **their solution** . . . He gave one of the most rousing talks I have ever heard and was well received by the intellectual elite. The people here are willing to learn and this is a man to teach them.
>
> He was very pleased that I remembered his talk in Berkeley. But he is one of the men on earth that I definitely respect and in a sense follow. If you have time or occasion can you telephone the Moraines (Lloyd or Mary) and tell them that Sam Lewis has met Dr. Chandrasekhar in Cairo. Do not say much. I have known Lloyd since his early boyhood,

he was originally a protégé of Vocha Fiske who is, perhaps, my closest confidante . . .

Next I have been permitted to take on books from their library which is excellent and am reading *Outlines of Islamic Culture* by A.M.A. Shustery which is the best work philosophically and theologically I have ever seen but filled with very bad and very inconsequential history, particularly in the foot-notes . . .

I am reading the sections on Sufism, which are informative . . .

It has long sections on Hujwiri, Ibn l'Arabi and others, and full of meat. In fact the book is meaty all the way through. It has by far the best material on the relation between Sufism and Vedanta I have ever seen, and constant and mostly excellent parallels between Indian scriptures and Islamic teachings . . .

[More] important perhaps was the news that the next Ambassador from India is Mr. Hussein who was Consul-General of India in San Francisco years ago. He used to go to Minte's on Castro St. and Asara and others know him [well]. As we have exchanged confidences in the past, his coming here is a strong [indication] of great fortune, or blessing. His father was Sufi and he is one of the few men on earth who knows what I am doing.[577]

More Reflections from Sam

When the heart is open and there is no adherence to self, there are no strangers anywhere.

SAMUEL LEWIS[578]

While still in Egypt, Sam wrote to Quazi Mehay Allum in Narayanganj, East Pakistan.

As-salaam aleikhum.

I am greeting you for a very special reason and ask that you share this letter with our wonderful teacher [Maulana] A. Ghafour and all the brethren. I am writing to you for this purpose for within two weeks I should be sending in a long and important report to Ghulam M. Ahmed at Chittagong. The report I make to him will be for publication but this is what we call a "preview."

I am by Grace of Allah having the most wonderful time in this city. It is very hard for me to complain. Ever since arrival here I have had nothing but utmost cooperation from both Americans and citizens of the

UAR. My whole life is now concentrated on how to bring these peoples closer together, in part of a broader purpose to bring many peoples together.

At the lowest level you may not understand how little Islamic teachings are offered in the United States. Ninety-Percent of the teaching is done by foreigners who are neither Muslims, nor, of course, Americans. Many of them are Jewish and while not all of the Jewish people are Zionists, the non-Jewish people, whether Christian or unbelievers are often more Zionist than the Jews. Strange to say the best among them are often missionaries who have some regard for the Prophet though they do not accept his faith.

Then there is little study of the history of Islam and still less of the history of this region. The result is a complete lack of understanding of points of view accepted here. One does not have to agree with President Nasser but one cannot even honestly disagree if he has not the facts.

The next thing is the untouched field of bringing the peoples together through common exchanges of arts and literature. Here there is a more friendly feeling. Part of this is due to the fact that here Americans, not Europeans, are the teachers. They are more open-hearted and open-minded. Besides there is a great movement in the United States in what is called "non-objective art," which is quite close in feeling and spirit to much of Islamic art . . .

As I work mostly with the scientists I hope to tell about what they are doing when I arrive in Pakistan, beginning at Karachi. I also hope to give some talks on what is going on here and especially study the changes in Nile economics so that the Indus may benefit. This is a long and complicated story.

[Three] weeks ago I met Mohammed Murtaz Billah, who is a follower of the Shadhili *tarik.* We understood each other from the first glance and I feel he is my dearest friend here. There will be a gathering of many *tariks* in a short while. I hope to meet and greet them and report in full to Chittagong.

While I have not seen anything of ancient Egypt I have taken long walks here and visited some of the most ancient and also the most holy Mosques. I am studying them first for artistic reason, and second for atmosphere. I have heard some very spiritual music, second only to what I have heard at Ajmir . . .

I have also been blessed with a vision which seems to indicate I shall meet a teacher of the Rifa'i Order. They have a mosque which I have

> not visited. At least once a week I walk all across this city from Al-Azhar. This has been a most interesting place on account of its historical significance. And now I have begun an intense study of the art of this region. This is partly so I can report to and speak at Lahore. I am gathering materials just for Lahore and California as I have no funds to do more than that, although at the moment Allah, to whom be all Praise, seems to be providing for my wants in every direction.[579]

The following day, Sam again wrote to Rudolph Schaeffer, this time speaking of gold purchases in the Bazaar in the Eastern part of Cairo near the Al-Azhar and Syedna Hussein mosques. These included a scarab bracelet in honor of his friend Dr. Baker, who had given him the money, and he was considering a copper piece for his friend Mrs. Magana Baptiste.

Sam felt his life had struck a high note with all his efforts in various fields of endeavor being supported by the Embassy and the UAR government. He noted that the United States Cultural Center had presented a series on Modern Art and soon would begin the first readings on Contemporary Drama. He even had managed to have Schaeffer's school added to the Information Bureau's mailing list.[580]

Sam finally had his visa, but travel to West Pakistan was still up in the air, with his schedule heavily packed with horticulturally- and spiritually-oriented meetings. On October 12 he wrote his good friend Florie, "I do not see how anybody can explain what is happening to me unless he accepts the existence of a wise and benign deity."[581] Although not feeling too well physically—perhaps due to the unusually warm weather, which often had a spread of 40 degrees or more during the day—Sam was grateful to feel in "tip-top shape" psychically and emotionally.

Sam addressed the problem of food increase through nitrifying algae with directors of the National Research Center, after which he was sent to the Dairy, Nutritional, and Microbiology laboratories.

> I have written to Stanlay Diamond of the Agricultural Division in the Ferry Building [in San Francisco]; he would get a report from me, but I warned him it was a serious matter. Stanlay is connected with the General Semanticists who have refused not only all my papers, but even my

> request for membership. The ridiculousness of it is that every one of my rejected ideas has been accepted here and at levels these people could hardly approach. But when I got to the Dairy Section, praise to Allah, I met another University of California Graduate, Ibrahim Rifaat. Well you can bet I had the time of my life.
>
> Visiting these research Laboratories is becoming a delight. For we not only exchange scientific information but I have never had such willing ears in my explanations of Islamic philosophy. It is beginning to look as if I may be called on in some higher quarters to give a full address . . .
>
> There is a lot of unnecessary tension here concerning Jordan but though I disagree with the tension I have no use for playboy "kings" and want to see the Empire of Saladin restored. Naturally I have gotten sympathy here.
>
> Yesterday we went to the bazaar. I bought my first present, which is for Dr. Baker . . . Most of the purchases will be for the Rudolph Schaeffer School but I want to get a lot of prayer beads for presents in Pakistan.[582]

Sam shared more evidence of his busy schedule with Harry Nelson in a letter dated October 16: "I still have a number of unsettled matters in the Agricultural Sections of the Centre. I have still to see the labs concerned with Aromatic Plants, Genetics, and Seed Investigations about which I shall report to you . . . before I visit the Vegetable Experimental Sections again."[583]

Two days later he continued his international networking, writing to Professor Clifford Cutright of Ohio State. Sam indicated that his trip to Suez had been cancelled, and instead M. M. Billah had taken him around the facility in Dokki. That day Sam was given objective data to substantiate what he had previously heard, that pigeon manure made an excellent fertilizer in that area. He informed Cutright that Kinoshita in Japan was obtaining another variety of soybeans that were easier to cook.

Sam's letter to Cutright continued:

> The plans worked out by Mr. Harry Nelson and myself have brought about excellent response. The other day two Federal Government experts looked up my work and have commended it, so much so it will be much easier when I get to Pakistan. Then, today I was questioned closely about agricultural information. Mr. Nelson collected bulletins

> from all over the country for me and I shall take them and have them reviewed first at the Vegetable Experimental station and then perhaps elsewhere. Mr. George Kenyon Jr., who has an office in New York and who may be the largest magazine distributor in the country, said he would cooperate fully in the plan to distribute all agricultural literature to Asian countries. All he wanted is depots, and there are certainly a number of willing depots here, if the press would only face the fact that the people of the world are much more interested in food [than] sex (from our point of view), we would be gaining friends instead of losing them in the U.N.[584]

Being a Sufi in Egypt

At this time in his journey Samuel had experienced many encounters with Sufis. He wrote about some of them in another diary letter to Florie:

> Yesterday was my birthday, but here it was the birthday of Husein, the grandson of Prophet Mohammed, who is said to have obtained the divine wisdom and to have died a martyr. Although the people are not Shias, the day was a holy-holiday and the night time was the climax of a festival which began Monday and may continue on . . .
>
> I do not know whether the American public has been shocked by the closeness of the vote on admitting China to the U.N. . . . But "we" continue to harbor huge areas of blind spots about the cultures, religions, outlooks of Asians and are either cynical or look to these damned European "experts" for what simply is not, or else throw out the term "fanatic." Any and all these courses are turning Nations against us . . .
>
> My immediate introduction has been through Mohammed Murtaz Billah who is usually called Murtaz. I do not know whether he was converted to Sufism or not, but if so it was by his wife. And who is his wife? She is a top graduate, who is now training for her Ph.D. by doing research on Ice Cream. We have probably already met because she told her husband an American came into her laboratory last week and I was in that lab last week. So we begin with an intelligent and intellectual woman, whom I expect to meet soon . . .
>
> I not only have had conversations with Billah on the intellectual level, but with many others and I have flocks of introductions all over

the place, made more difficult by my being often stopped in the street either for tea or arguments. Even at Al-Azhar I have found a favorable attitude toward Sufism although the gossipers who don't go near Al-Azhar tell me differently . . .

The Khan-i-Khalili is a bazaar district near Al-Azhar. It is full of narrow streets and lanes and has many small mosques and still more *khankahs* where Sufis meet. One needs a guide at night unless one has a compass.

It was something like a mixture of Chinese New Year's and Summer Fair at the same time. Tremendous crowds surged down alleys, lanes, and what not, made difficult by boys using a sort of football formation to surge forward, endangering the blind. There was considerable lack of human consideration. There were many women in the more open places, but the narrow slots had only men, or the women connected with the stalls. There are woman dervishes who meet separately. So far only the Chistis have had the men and women do *zikr* together . . . I saw just two veils and when there were women they mingled with each other, or men, not noticeably different from other peoples.

It took us quite a while to find the Shadhili *khankah.* Each group meets separately in the same building. My friend's Sheikh is no more, but two or three Khalifa led the ceremonies. There were some readings of the Qur'an and chanting. Then the *zikrs* in which I could join, singing the name of Allah.

The first thing noticeable is that these groups perform functions like both antiphonal and choir singing in the Christian churches, but to me, with a rather purer sound. Later on there were melodious songs—beautiful arias and not just chants, in which others, including the younger men, repeated a phrase of *zikr* in rhythm-background. Then we held hands and performed *zikr* standing close together and later on in a sort of jump movement and some swung their backs; this was heightened in speed and loudness for a while and touched the depths of my being.

Then they varied the *zikr* phrasing—I notice all Sufi schools do this somewhat, passing from the intelligible to the semi-intelligible or non-intelligible **intellectually**. On this point Alan Watts has been entirely correct. I find when one says **Eleh** instead of **Allah** it is much easier to sing and feel. I noticed also that these men tended to pronounce the name of God, i.e. Allah, as I have been used to do and as I have been corrected in parts of India but stubbornly refused to withdraw. Whatever impetus I have had for my pronunciation, it accorded with the Shadhili chanting and must have made me more welcome.

After the ceremony which was long and involved we had some discussion, food, more discussion and finally tea. The one thing I objected to was the insistence I must learn Arabic. And so far as Sufism is concerned, the "mantric" modification of words makes their argument seem weaker than ever.

On the other hand, in the conversation with those who speak English, I found surprisingly great agreement. Orthodoxy is needed for the beginners. It is best to be trained in some form of ceremony, law, custom, but that is introduction only. The men explained "spiritual liberty" exactly the same as my first Pir-o-Murshid Inayat Khan did, and they had the same attitude toward religion and religious. The educated ones were far from dogmatic and were all universal. There was agreement that Mohammed was the **Seal of the Prophet[s]** which meant recognition of all prophets and their teachings. This was far from the Arabism of one of them.

As a side note, I went to Cairo U. yesterday . . . and the Chief Superintendent rather surprised me by asking me to come again so he could take me around. I do not know how such friendships are established; they are a constant source of wonder, but this will lead me to the scholastic side of Islamic mysticism.

Around ten o'clock we went to the Syedna Hussein Mosque where three groups of dervishes were holding forth, but the place was crowded. Then we visited some *khankahs.* And so on until the groups were completing their sessions. Most of these were "wild," but the largest one seemed to be made of intellectuals who were sober and far more numerous.

The Rifa'is were more ecstatic than the Shadhilis, but there were some very wild and the large sober group I did not find about, nor did I meet the Naqshibandis. The first and most obvious impression is **the fact** that there are many thousands of Sufis here. They fall very roughly into three types—the parasites, the young and the mature. The parasitic type is shushed and I think they are a dying cult. I am told the Mevlevi or Whirling Dervishes belong here. Despite their wonderful beginning, the substitution of "family" for spiritual attainment as the way to leadership has undoubtedly caused this. Wherever family steps in, God steps out—although we do not learn this lesson easily. The Shadhilis lean over the other way to see that leadership does not come through inheritance.

I find that not only do these sessions take the place of hymn and other singing, there is undoubtedly a lot of blowing off of steam and even transmutation of sexual and lower faculties. This is obvious when one sees so many hundreds of young men, and also the presence of Negroes who are prone to ecstasy anyhow.* We have not looked into the psychological advantages of the . . . processes and I do not intend to do so now. But there is also a moral advantage and more. A single experience on almost any level is worth thousands of lectures.

I do wonder what the introduction of jazz will do here but I am inclined to believe it will strengthen Sufism at the expense of orthodoxy rather than otherwise. This has already happened in West Africa. Hundreds of thousands of people are becoming Muslims, but all either through the Ahmadiyyas or through the Sufism . . .

I met one Peter Ross who has lived in Los Angeles and New York and who accepted Islam yesterday. We were given the prayer instruction which I know fairly well, but in going over it I found deeper meaning . . .

In the office afterwards I met a young colored boy from New York who is going through training here. I regard him as a sort of ally and when I leave here will correspond with him . . . I am only hoping that young [men] like this Peter Ross, in their enthusiasm for a new religion, do not overlook the endless possibilities in brotherhood. Yet perhaps my stand here is partly due to my zest for brotherhood above all things.

I also met a Pakistani from Peshawar who was very effusive. He is here to study European Languages and to major in English so he can go to the States . . . I can see he is a lonely man, a sort of double exile. So all my heart goes out to him, but I am going to be slightly slow in expressing it. I did leave him two of my published articles to read. He is also a lover of [Iqbal]. But it is this type of man to whom I feel so close in heart, and I know he feels that too.

I have just returned from an invitational opening of the Indian Art Exhibit. This is an honor for there were present otherwise only dignitaries and artists of the highest type. Not even the U.S. Embassy was represented. I find the paintings vigorous and excellent, integrating the best of modern movements with certain traditional techniques and outlooks.

---

*Sam found Negroes to be more inclined to having open hearts and to freely expressing themselves.

> It appears to me—but I may be too much of an enthusiast here—that India is fixating itself in art.
>
> Although I saw the Buddha Jayanti exhibit I saw such trash in connection with religion that I did not see much hope. Not only that, too many Indians tend to defend the total absence of devotional feeling in Circean-like posters for their religious festivals. If one says anything they ascribe it to Islamic prejudice. But art without feeling is bad enough and in religion it is worse than idolatry. The Hindus present all seemed to be of higher caliber and the art showed the one thing that India needs—positive strength. So I see great possibilities . . .
>
> I also was in the Bazaar section today . . . I called on Isaac* and gave him a good kabbalistic interpretation of parts of Genesis based on the Sufi approach and also on "Nathan the Wise." It is the Germans who have been showing "Nathan the Wise" here—I think this is marvelous. In his speech yesterday Nasser used the word "Jew" just once and I am not sure of the translation. He only speaks against Zionism and does not even use the term "Israel."[585]

In another diary letter that same day,[586] Sam wrote about current events spanning a wide range of topics. These included national happenings, Indian art, dervishes, his upcoming trip to Pakistan, personal experiences, and more.

At the Indian Art Exhibit mentioned above and later reported on to the Rudolph Schaeffer School, Sam renewed his connection with Mr. Pande, the cultural attaché. Pande had been studying Sam's two Indian reports and was taking time to give them due consideration.

Sam noted that the dervishes were generally more aligned with the occult than the mystical side, and that clairvoyant experiences were especially honored. He reflected that mystical experiences come from Divine Grace. Likewise, Sam questioned the books on Sufism he found, noting that Sufism did not develop in Persia even though the mystical poets had lived there. He related that the atmosphere of Egypt was thousands upon thousands of years old, and he found it electrified and magnified in the esoteric realm.

Sam told the story of a young Christian whom he had criticized severely for the boy's ignorance of his own religion's mystical roots, until

---

* A Jewish merchant in the Khalili bazaar that Sam frequented.

the boy was pale. Then Sam said, "Wait, I am only half done. Now I am going to answer every one of my objections." The boy knew nothing of Gnosticism or the early Christian Yogis who lived in Egypt or even of the Gospel of St. Thomas. Sam sent him back to his church.

On a final topic, Sam wrote that it was fortunate the engineers cleared land in the deserts, dug for water and combined this with archeological digging. He was confident that this work would bring light to most of the Christian Gnosticism and the path of the spiritual hermits whose scriptures had been hidden under the sands. He added that this was more interesting to him than what was in ancient Egypt.

Sam's Time in Egypt Continues

> *I can only say here briefly that I entered this country as a VIP, my treatment here has been as a VIP but my "success" has been far out of line with any portion of my earlier career. For not only have all my proposals been accepted by Egyptians or Arabs but the government has commended me and the whole force of the American Embassy is behind me. Not only that, but at this writing the San Rafael* Independent *and Chet Huntley have asked for news. I have known Chet at two different periods in Hollywood, the first when he was a nobody, the second when he was becoming somebody, and now, of course, when he is tops. I have also had articles in the daily press, in Arabic.*
>
> SAMUEL LEWIS[587]

In a letter to his friend Peg Allmond in San Francisco, Samuel Lewis gave a wonderful overview of the breadth of his activities and observations during his first months in Egypt.

> I have been in this far-away land for over three months and will probably be here two months more . . .
>
> Primarily I came to this country with a number of missions. Most of these missions were snubbed in the United States, where I could hardly get an interview. But my experiences in Oriental countries had been so totally different one could not help wondering whether the Arabs would greet me as had the Japanese, Thai, Burmese, Pakistanis and Indians, or greet me as the Americans, or as the Europeans who not only snub but sneer . . .

Khan-i-Khalili Bazaar, built in the 14th century – considered the largest in Africa

Cairo is a wonderful city to me for two quite different orders of reasons. The one, of course, has been the gratification of the treatment received at all levels. At times this is hard to take, and I will not write further on it here. Only it becomes a question as to what degree of "fame" is achieved here, which may be effective when I return. I have no intention to bother with other persons for it would seem I am "growing" in effectiveness and that is important to me and may also be a deciding factor in where I live afterwards.

The second series of reasons why Cairo is wonderful is that you find it a series of cities of all periods from 960 to 1960 both inclusive. It is very hard to get an over-all . . . [of] lives of intermediary periods. So that when one walks about, which I do a good deal, one enters into different centuries, so to speak. This type of adventure is far from exhausted.

The most interesting part of the city, outside my profession, is the Khan-i-Khalili Bazaar. There all kinds of folk arts are preserved. I have sent and may send a few things to Gump's and to the Rudolph Schaeffer School of Design. I have also sent essences of perfumes to the [Faverman] Drug Co. on Larkin & Turk. I am unable to do more as all moneys for all purposes come out of my own pocket (and actually I am accomplishing what some rather vociferous corporations are crying for money for and not doing at all).

The bazaar regions are of two types. In the one type you see the segregated [professions] as cloth merchants, goldsmiths, silversmiths, leather workers, ironworkers, etc. occupying whole streets or even districts. In the other arrangement, there is more general merchandising. I ran into both of them today.

I am in need of shoes. There are at least four types of footwear here: modern shoes, mosque shoes, folk-shoes and slippers or sandals, which do not have leather bottoms. As Pakistan has both better heavy shoes and folk shoes than this country, I want to get the mosque shoe type. This can be slipped on and off easily and as the mosques represent the best type of historical edifices, everybody visits some of them whether one is a Muslim or not . . .

I have also done my first sampling of Arab clothing for myself, which again, is part of folk-art effort. The man's gowns may be picturesque, they make good lounging robes, but hardly are adopted to dancing.

I am now glad I did not bring my record player here. This country is not ready for folk dancing, yet. You have to take it on faith that I have met thousands of people and I find that the serious young are more interested in having dancing introduced than the mass. I have received a letter from one Bette Reeve of Mill Valley whose mother was my first dancing partner, that there is a move to introduce folk dancing as a counter-effort to subversive espionage. I am all in favor of it, but you can't do it en masse here through any YMCA. This would attract a limited clientele.

The Whirling Dervishes here are of a low order, other dervishes, whom we entirely ignore, are great in number and contain very high-class members, including large segments of the leading scientists and apprentices in engineering and scientific research. TV is just beginning . . .

I have seen several dervish ceremonies. They have unusual forms of singing, none of which I have ever heard recorded and I am inclined to believe there is a strong Christian influence utterly ignored by book-writers. They also have movements in their ceremonies which are like letters of a dance alphabet and sometimes movements without moving from place. The few Negroes I have . . . seen among them are the most skillful in this and also in the singing, but I think some of the dark-skinned are Sudanese and not true Negroes. I do know that I can tape-record all kinds of things others are not permitted or do not care to see.

Yet it is among the younger of these types that I have found the most cordiality. Recently I did see a large group of un-chaperoned young people trying to have their own folk-dancing in a park. There were no elders around. They may have been Christians for this seems to me unusual for Muslims. But there are plenty of Christians, too, here—I mean among the Egyptians.

For my part the best type of dancing to start off with would be the line and circle dances found from Yugoslavia to this region. There is also some interest in "Latin-American" dancing.

Before Squares could be introduced the shyness of body-touching would have to be overcome, plus the suitable arrangements of calls. Of course our calls themselves are a sort of lingua franca. This subject I

> shall look into again in Lahore, Pakistan, where there had been a beginning when I was there four years ago . . .
>
> There is now some infiltration of Syrian influence. The Syrians, though Muslims, do have some folk dances but I have not visited that region and it does not look as if I can with limited finances and tremendous numbers of projects to keep me busy all the time.[588]

In January, Sam again made observations about introducing dance to this part of the world.[589] He spoke about undeveloped dervish dances that, if developed, would be without partners. He saw much more opportunity for unpartnered than for partnered dances, but he felt changes could take place, especially with the fast rate at which music was developing. He then turned to his travel plans.

> I shall have been in this country about 5½ months and I expect to stay at least an equal time in both Pakistan and India, though I do not know how much will be in traveling or how much in one place. My life here is full of adventures, mostly recorded; and on the whole very much better than I had expected . . .
>
> Of course I have all sorts of materials for books and have been off the beaten path, but the unusual is not always welcome and there is plenty of the unusual here.[590]

Sam's Edifying Year in the UAR Begins to Wrap Up

> *This morning I thought of the worst criticism of Christianity: "There was no room for him in the inn," but the inn has taken over the religion, especially Christmas. I am getting more and more antagonistic to Christmas.*[591]
>
> *I am closing a most edifying year. Everything has turned around and I think every upset of almost every earlier part of my life has been reversed . . . I am satisfied that both the American Friends of the Middle East and the World Affairs Council are taking me seriously.*[592]
>
> SAMUEL LEWIS

Sam attended the Islamic Congress and reviewed the condition of Islam in America for participants. Neither the Pakistanis nor the Arabs there were satisfied with how Islam was being taught. They felt that the U.S. had warped views on the personality of the Prophet Muhammad and on polygamy. Additionally, the Pakistanis thought too much politics was involved. Sam was pleased to be respectfully heard. He offered to entertain any suggestions they had, adjusting his full schedule as needed to give their input full consideration.[593]

Sam's schedule can be sampled from the accounts he wrote to his friend Florie. For example, he frequently attended the mosques in Cairo as he felt their atmosphere was nourishing. He found loving and lovable people there more numerous than one might meet in other parts of the world. The Information Bureau urged him to visit the Social Sciences sections of the National Research Center. He said, "I am not refusing but I am so busy. Actually I get tired, but one hates to let up in the 'middle of a harvest' as I have projects or visits every day."[594] During his visit to the Pakistani Embassy, conversation spanned topics from travel to religion to horticulture to art.

On January 4, 1961, Sam wrote a diary entry to his friend Ruth, relating that on the previous day he had visited a mosque and *dargah* that very few Americans saw. He saw more and more dervishes, and in the mosque where the dervishes met a sign read, "God is Love" (in Arabic, *mahbood lillah*).

He wrote, "I have not yet met any of the teachers to whom I was promised introductions but go as often as possible to Sheikh Abu Salem Amria of the Rifa'i school. I had experiences in accordance with this School before I met the Sheikh so was quite ready when they appointed me . . . their representative for America."[595] Sam remarked further on Islamic teachings in the U.S. and showed concern about what he was seeing:

> What is wrong here is that in religion we are supposed to becalm the *nufs* or ego, and the spirit of agitation is the very thing that stands in the way of God-realization. I am trying to avoid any form of correction, but when one sees vibrations rise and fall, and agitation and disturbance, that cannot be the **right path**.
>
> My paper referred to, which was given to Dr. Hussein, concerns "Surrender-Consciousness" and "Identity Consciousness." This may be long and involved, but it is a very important teaching. My purpose, *inshallah,* is to draw heavily on the books at the Library when I return and try to "push" those who can be pushed, and to guide the others at a suitable rate. However I am still cautious about any kind of division.[596]

At this point it seemed to Sam that he would remain in Asia all of 1961, God willing. His plan for India was to visit the many Sufi Centers and shrines he had not yet seen, and to revisit several other places. He hoped to end the year in Penang, Malaya,* where his best friend Robert Clifton Sumangalo lived.

In a January 5 letter to Florie, Sam commented that many people overlooked his age because he had a certain élan and exuberance. And the shoeshine boys who used to charge him a good deal of money for a shine now fought for the privilege to shine his shoes for free because of the *baraka* they perceived coming from him. This supposition about his spiritual state spread beyond the shoeshine boys:

> I received a call from one of the leading newspapers here. We finally arranged an interview which lasted about an hour and a half. They took at least six pictures with discussion of my scientific work, Sufism, Yoga, etc. It was so long and involved. It came out of the reaction to my poem "Saladin" and my paper on "Surrender Consciousness and Unifying Consciousness." This received the highest commendation from the savants here and as soon as the present pressure dies down I shall write to Aligarh University in this regard.[597]

As he retired for the night, Sam received an hour-long call from the Islamic Congress. Not only had they accepted his full report on Islam in the U.S., but they were also planning to meet and establish a program for him when he returned. They also asked him to write a paper on "How I Became a Muslim" and "An American's Reaction to Ben Gurion." Sam indicated that the latter would be an unusual paper because he would attack Ben Gurion in part on universal grounds and in part on his departure from traditional Judaism. The Congress was in Sam's corner when he complained that the greatest name in Islam (Muhammad) was hardly mentioned in any courses in the West and that real Islamic Philosophy had been smothered by Europeans. He affirmed this view was shared by Indians, Pakistanis, Indonesians, Malayans, Burmese, Thai and the Japanese.

---

*Now Malaysia.

Mosque of Sultan Hassan, Cairo; lithograph of Louis Haghe, 1838

In a January 8 letter to Florie, Sam described his second visit to Sultan Hassan Mosque, this time with a group, mostly Americans, under the leadership of Dr. Scanlon of the American University in Cairo. Scanlon claimed the Sultan Hassan Mosque was the best in Cairo, but listening to the talk, Sam described getting aesthetic fatigue. The mosque was so large and detailed that despite his keen interest in its history and construction, his eyes grew tired. He left with an overall feeling of awe and austerity.

Sam had written papers for the Islamic Congress and planned to outline others when he returned to the States. He tried to enlighten Washington, remarking that U.S. politics and economics were fine, but that we lacked any moral or psychological approach to our relationships abroad.

Sam had given carbon copies of his articles to the scientist and dervish Attia, who was also a businessman. Consequently, he once again found himself involved not only in scientific and personal affairs, but needed to "meet a Sheikh and then prepare to meet more Sheikhs and Allah knows what dignitaries."[598] He was following with full faith his Murshid's instructions, saying there was nothing secret in them, but everything was sacred about them.

Sam attended a packed talk given by Sheikh Amria, where Sheikh Mohammed was also in attendance.

> I cannot explain this man. There is such tremendous love between us that is real and the manifestation of it astounded even the *Ulema** and many of the devotees. And it is Sheikh Mohammed who is taking me out today . . .

---

*Body of Muslim scholars.

This is a holy week. It is in honor of Zeinab, the grand-daughter of the Prophet. "Women have no souls in Islam" but can you point to a single woman-saint in Judaism or Protestantism? This very subject was touched and I can name several woman saints in Islam.

The first question that Sheikh Amria asked me was, "Have you visited Syedna Zeinab?" Well I had made a special visit to that shrine just before and you can believe or not . . . that there is no telepathy or super-telepathy, but why this question as a greeting? I have had many such experiences.

Some day there may be in American schools for religious studies, schools for Islamic studies. [Last] night there were studies—only from Holy Qur'an, many from *Hadith* and many from the lives of the Kaliphs. This is exactly what I wanted but evidently my Allah whom I hope I worship is not the same as the "Islam" which some people have substituted for Allah and then filled with any selfish content they desire. Allah grants wishes. This god named Islam apparently does not. This god named Islam is just like the old Hebraic deity, a private one in whose name one can do anything and everything. I'll have none of it and neither will the world, but we all say "*Alhamdu Lillah*" and that ends the communication.[599]

Sam reached out to his teacher Harry Nelson in a long letter on January 13, mentioning a young man working in Egypt who wished to come to the U.S. and take Nelson's course of training. Much of his letter describes Sa'ad Kemal, Chief Geneticist at En-Shams University, formerly a professor of horticulture but now handling statistics at the University. Sa'ad served as Sam's guide and included a trip to a cotton research locale. Sam ended their visit by again recommending sending farmers as good-will ambassadors and horticultural advisors.

Always thinking of his friends back home, Sam wrote frequently and purchased gifts when he could. A fine Nefertiti robe with green shoes to match was secured for Magana and Walt Baptiste, yoga teachers in San Francisco with whom he had studied. Magana was also a dancer and loved music, so his letter of January 16 to them focused on their skills and knowledge.

The work being done by scientists here has amazed and delighted me. I am now concerned with cultural and related exchanges. The arts are not so well developed here. Painting is catching up, but dancing not so . . . I even heard square dance calls in Arabic. You may be glad to learn that some of the Hindus I meet have heard about you and there is no doubt that you could draw many people if you came here. But the State Dept. and ANTA* are still too much concerned with brand names and a visit of [Louis] Armstrong is going to delight the Americans and the American press; but I doubt much whether there will be any valid communication or "meeting the people." That is something which is not going on at a proper rate.[600]

Preparing to Leave the UAR

The heart of every person, both good and bad, is the abode of God, and care should be taken never to wound anyone by word or act.

Hazrat Inayat Khan[601]

If there were not some good in the human heart, life in the physical body would be impossible because the blood would be carrying poison to every cell and muscle and gland . . . Every harsh thought of man immediately affects two fluids: the vital fluid or energy called prana *which flows in and out with the breath, and the Universal Life-Love Essence which holds the very earth together, which is the heart energy. The harsh thought through* prana *affects chiefly the mind of another, for it is directed toward such a one; but such also is the nature of* prana, *so also does the exhalation of the breath operate that it touches the mental body of each person in its course and whatsoever it gives to another it gives to oneself.*

But the effect upon the heart-energy, which may be considered as the Universal Life-Force, is to strike every human being upon earth, even to affect others upon earth and those in the unseen. The proper use of this heart-energy is called ishk *by the Sufis,* karuna *by the Buddhists, and* agape *in the New Testament, which can be translated as "selfless love." . . . Thoughts affect chiefly the thinker and the thing or person concerned in the thought, whereas the feeling affects the whole cosmic body of Adam, the Universal Man. In this, by our feelings and attitudes, we either raise or lower the whole humanity. So when Jesus Christ said, "Love ye one another," when Mohammed taught in Koran that Allah created us from clots of blood, it was in reference to the fact—the great truth of existence—of the Universal Love-Energy.*

---

*Likely the American National Theatre and Academy.

> *The Master, the Saint, the Bodhisattva place their consciousness in this great stream, in this ocean of love, and by sending forth their thoughts of loving-kindness they benefit the whole humanity. When these thoughts are individualized they reach a few; otherwise they reach many. This is the reason for silence on the part of sages.*
>
> SAMUEL LEWIS[602]

In reflecting on his life in Egypt, Samuel harkened back to predictions made about him. When he was an infant, three fortune tellers had predicted he would die famous. A few years before the current trip, a reading of his coffee grounds indicated he would be honored for his work with the U.S. Government. Despite his predicted eminence being well documented, it was not universally accepted. Sam commented, "Every time I open my jaw to say what has happened there is a roar of opposition."[603]

In the UAR, however, top scientists, including a number of Sufis, were his dear friends with whom he met frequently. One scientist Sam mentioned in a January 18, 1961, diary letter was Dr. Mohammed Kemal Hussein. Sam spent time at his home and spoke on Islamics and later horticulture. Hussein's review of Sam's epic poem "Saladin" placed it in the top ranks of all poetry. The new director of the American Friends of the Middle East, Colonel Evenson, likewise lauded the poem—even to Ivy Duce's husband Terry.

Scientific endeavors only occupied a third of Sam's time. The week of the above diary letter Sam met Sheikh Sharabassi of the Rifa'i dervishes and was honored by him at a public meeting. Sam noted that this type of honoring was becoming commonplace and that most people were calling Sam Sheikh. Sheikh Sharabassi invited Sam back, along with his new friend Atila to interpret.

Sam wrote that he was now no longer controlling his affairs but was only a witness to their unfolding. One example he gave occurred while he was at Khan-i-Khalili bazaar. There Sam was taken by the hand to the downstairs part of "The Garden of Allah," one of the shops, where he met an old blind man, also a sheikh. "We sat silently and I gave him my beads: 'Naqshibandi!' He glowed all over—he is the Naqshibandi teacher here. We embraced and then one experiences *baraka,* not just blessing, but the warm fire of love and magnetism and joy penetrating all through one's personality. It was a tender moment of happiness. There are things beyond words and language."[604]

Sam's plan was to leave the UAR on February 16th for Port Said and to arrive in Karachi, Pakistan, on February 26. He expected to find Pakistan easier to navigate based on his previous experience of more English-speaking people and more openness, plus he had the added benefit of coordinating his travels with Abdul Rahman in Abbottabad.

His initial address was care of the consulate in Karachi, then care of Jamshyd Khan, the most successful modern farmer in Pakistan, who lived in Mardan, NW Pakistan. The sons of Hasan Nizami had a coal company near this farm and Sam hoped to be able to ask them about his teacher Inayat Khan's last days.

Sam mingled with people everywhere and was universally accepted. His knowledge and gregariousness made him well known in many circles. He planned to advise Al-Azhar University's new radio station on how to best reach the English-speaking world, but he did not shrink from criticizing the U.S. for raising funds that never reached their intended recipients. "Only the A.F.M.E. mentioned above, the YMCA, and CARE do anything here—and for that matter wherever else I have been."[605]

Sam had a long interview in the Ambassadorial section of the U.S. Embassy. He stayed for a conference for the first time, the outcome of which he described:

> They want a full report from me, my ventures, contacts, suggestions especially. The day is over when whatever knowledge I have collected or experiences I have had are going to be by-passed. I am quite unconcerned with rejections. The bigger the people the less the rejections. I have long since broken down the dividing lines between the races and social groups. I have done this in every country and I do not think there is anybody I cannot meet anywhere. No, I have not met President Nasser yet, but I only recently asked to see him. I have my epic poem for him which has been very highly praised . . . As I went along I found my writings evaluated higher and higher by Asians of all arts and now by Americans in the Foreign Service. I have studied more about certain phases of Asian culture than any man I know and have so been received here as I have been in each Asian land I have visited.

The magazines want my material, one a local one, but one, thank God, American, due to my work on food problems. And the Agricultural Department has long since accepted my works; they are much easier to meet than the State Department which in turn, is much easier to meet than the press . . .

The United States both as a government and as a compendium of human beings has made a severe error in international affairs by . . . not meeting peoples of the world directly. No doubt one needs someone here who can speak both Arabic and English, and in Japan or Indonesia bilingualism or multilingualism is important. But art and heart are also important.

The Rudolph Schaeffer School has had some excellent art-and-heart interpreters and there does not seem to be any pretense that such instructors know or knew many languages. A man knowing Arabic, Hindi or Japanese does not necessarily know how to interpret the paintings, architecture or music of those countries and it is doubtful whether linguists, as such, have contributed much to learning outside of language itself—where their contributions must not be under-estimated either . . .

The President has been blamed for our low prestige abroad, the politics and what not, but I can assure you that the low prestige abroad is quite apart from our politics. It comes in the strange, almost national behavior, in not meeting peoples face-to-face, mind-to-mind, heart to heart . . .

I can assure you, . . . this American is welcome, has been welcome all over Asia . . . And other Americans, all Americans can do this without knowing languages or even religions if they just take other human beings directly as our own Declaration of Independence holds.

It is not easy to live a dual life, to have to transform oneself constantly every day in going back and forth between social groups. That has made my work hard and tiring, but it may make it easier for those who come hereafter.[606]

Next Sam visited an old Sephardic synagogue, noting that Jews were present there before Turkish times. He also visited a Franciscan monastery, which impressed him.

Studies are made in early Christianity, not only the Church Fathers but all aspects. There is still a big gap between the very early Christianity and the literary periods, however developed before the time of the

> Islamic conquest. I am not interested in theological differences and schismatic quarrels. I am interested in liturgies, music, ceremonies, monastic disciplines and spiritual experiences.
>
> Although I have been accepted and apparently will be accepted more and more both as a Muslim and a Dervish, I do not criticize Christianity—excepting indirectly for the modernism which has refused to face the facts of filthy literature . . . I consider these Fathers clear and clean and while I do not wish to use the term "saint," in the earlier Hebrew sense of "holy ones" or pure ones (Chassidim, etc.) it would fit very well. The meetings were very cheerful, wholesome, cordial.
>
> I am told there is a place where the Holy Family rested. I am not interested in testing the historicity of it. I am interested in the feeling behind it . . . I am trying to study this country as it is, not as I or anybody else would desire it. This may not be easy, but it is worth trying. Certainly with all its faults this country has made such gigantic strides that not even the apologists can keep up with them. Only, like in India, I hope this can be done without the expense of dispensing with so much of the old. In the next few days I expect to attend more dervish gatherings and to hell with Prof. von Plotz! The U.S. Government is now accepting all my reports on this matter. We need to know the religion of this region and we do not.[607]

Prof. von Plotz is Sam's made-up name for a professor exemplifying those in the West who said there were no *khankahs*, no dervishes, no living Sufis, and no inner dialogue with the mysteries.

Tying up Loose Ends; Criticism and Plans

> *At the moment with my interest in dervishes I may seem over-enthusiastic. Religions are like trees and when we try to describe them in seed-form we are projecting and differentiating and not describing. Islam, even more than the Catholic Church, includes all sorts of phases and institutions. To regard them as "wrong" is like regarding the oak as a "wrong" Rose-bush or "wrong" Pine tree, there is no "right" or "wrong" about the so-called accretions. They are there, [they] are part of life. We can study and even come to understand them, but to give them moral or personal judgments is totally nonsensical. It prevents communication and lack of real communication prevents understanding and peace.*
>
> SAMUEL LEWIS[608]

Never one to sit still, Sam attended Al-Azhar University for special training in the Qur'an and visited several mosques, especially those of the Rifa'i Dervishes. He frequented the tombs of the Mameluks to meet the Sufis there and noticed that they celebrated saints' days more than he had seen in India and Pakistan. "They have *moulads,* which means festivals like Mardi Gras and includes everything."[609] He described a circus with side shows, lion-taming—portrayed as a combination vaudeville and animal show—native dancing, and candy for sale which was said to contain *baraka.* Not wanting to leave any Sufis aside, Sam hoped to get to Tanta as well, to sample the Bedawi dervishes' candy—which was held to be particularly sacred.

At another level, Sam was writing candid reports for the American Embassy with his unfiltered opinions of those in positions of authority who he felt knew little to nothing about Asia. This long-held viewpoint had only been strengthened during his travels.

His therapist and friend Dr. Blanche Baker had died the previous month and Sam mused about her life. "No doubt Blanche took on too much karma. She did not know how to rest."[610] Others could have said the same of Sam, questioning whether he too did or did not know how to rest amidst his many projects and goals. Whether he also was taking on too much karma was a legitimate question. Of himself Sam said that he was very much alive and getting very strong.

On January 30, 1961, Sam wrote a diary letter addressed to Beloved Ones of God and began with the Sufi invocation given by Hazrat Inayat Khan: "Toward the One, the Perfection of Love, Harmony and Beauty, the Only Being, United with all the Illuminated Souls who form the Embodiment of the Master, the Spirit of Guidance." Sam went on to describe more of Inayat's approach and compared it with that of Orthodox Muslims.

> One cannot compel the surrender of any ego but despite all the words in all the scriptures on "surrender" it is not usually a living function.
>
> In Pir-o-Murshid's original teaching there were two paths distinctly marked out: a) the path of progression in *zikr;* b) the path of progression in *fana,* which comes in three stages, *fana-fi-Sheikh, fana-fi-Rassoul, fana-fi-Lillah.* In practice there has not been too much understanding of

these ways of progression and I can only refer to them here as part of one man's biography, regardless.

In *Moral Culture* [by Hazrat Inayat Khan] we have reference to the Law of Reciprocity, Law of Beneficence and Law of Renunciation. Reciprocity is the Moral Law for ordinary persons. Call it karma or not, it operates, and, in the teachings, one should take advantage of all the suggestions. Beneficence comes from the Spiritual Path or *tarikat,* and in Holy Qur'an we find *Bismillah er-Rahman er-Rahim* which indicates the identity of surrender (*fana*) with beneficence. But people identify these qualities with God and do not usually try to live *akhlak Allah* which is to say, in the manner of God, or, in the presence of God.

I find myself at a distance from Orthodox Muslims who place all the virtues in a Deity and do not try to develop these in themselves. No doubt it is a first step to see them in God, but it is not a last step and it is not a Path or Progression. Whatever way you place religion, it universally teaches "Guide us on the Right Path" but it is not the prayer, nor the words; it is the adaptation of the life within oneself. This is the greater Jihad.

Paul had to correct the people of his time [who paid] too much attention to *fana-fi-Sheikh* and he tried to universalize *fana-fi-Rassoul,* whether people were ready for it or not. In bringing the Message to the West, people became enamored with *fana-fi-Sheikh* and they did not rise to *fana-fi-Rassoul.* The words of [prayers] become empty. They remain just words. If a man wishes to change these words into truths he will be misunderstood, but if a man desires to change these words into truths he will gain understanding, and perhaps wisdom.

Here there is a great deal of difference between any invocation of "United with all the Illuminated Souls Who form the Embodiment of the Master" and the direct understanding thereof. It has been insisted by many that there is a living *Kutub* in this area. I cannot argue, though I have not met him yet. But I have met many Sheikhs and from them received so much love and Baraka that I can never thank Allah enough . . .

I have received *baraka* both from human beings, usually Sheikhs and Khalifs; but also in the Mosques, especially the Rifa'i Mosques. But there is another form of *baraka* which comes in *fana-fi-Rassoul.*

Pir-o-Murshid gave us a long list of Messengers ending with Mohammed. I have experienced the *fana-fi-Rassoul* in and with Mohammed, but immediately after that with Jesus; and in the course of time with Buddha and Siva and then under the guidance of Mohammed with all the

> prophets of God in all religions. In theory, this completed the path of *fana-fi-Rassoul.* But when one regards God as the only being, one does not, maybe one cannot of himself distinguish between *fana-fi-Sheikh, fana-fi-Rassoul* and *fana-fi-Lillah;* nor does one care, for as Pir-o-Murshid said: "Thy light is in all forms, Thy love in all beings . . . in an inspiring teacher."[611]

Following the literary method of the Zoroastrian religion, Sam chose to paraphrase for his own records the teachings in *fana-fi-Rassoul* received that very day in which Muhammad seemed to play the part with him that the Angel Gabriel did with Muhammad.

He expressed that if one accepts the Fatherhood/Motherhood of Allah, that essence is everywhere in everything. He went on to say that if one also accepts the spirit of Brotherhood/Sisterhood in humans, there should be *kibla,* prayer in the direction of Mecca. He criticized Kabir, saying that, in breaking down certain Islamic institutions, there was a dissolution of that spirit of Brotherhood. Also, he said that the Sikhs carried the "logical" argument to the extreme, and analytically were right, but instead of any kind of Brotherhood, nothing but strife followed. So he advised the observation of *kibla.*

In answer to the question of the difference between Jerusalem and Mecca as a *kibla,* Sam chose to have The Spirit of Wisdom answer:

> Jesus spoke of Jerusalem as being the city that stoned its prophets. Despite the Hebrew claim that only Jeremiah was persecuted, we have no record of any prophet of God actually being welcomed in Jerusalem. Indeed the career of Jesus there ended in failure.
>
> On the other hand Mecca has been the *kibla* of success, both with Abraham, the Friend of God, and Muhammad, the Messenger of God. One does not like to put forth the argument that Jerusalem has been the *kibla* of failure and Mecca of success, but you can still see the Christians fighting each other there and the Zionists are all divided as to religion.[612]

Sam continued to write in the voice of the Spirit of Wisdom:

> Qur'an distinctly says that there are no distinctions between the Messengers of God. And though it is said that prayers are not made to me,

there is psychological intercession. The psychological intercession falters if it becomes merely theological, which it usually does; and it benefits when people learn to pray **with** the Seal of the Prophets, and not mention his name at all.

This is very difficult but the errors in religion usually come from too much zeal and zeal alone is not bad but it becomes a substitute for morality and selflessness. There is too much praise for literature called Holy Qur'an and *Hadith* and too little concern with the contents thereof. The same is true with most scriptures.[613]

Sam added that the initial stage in *fana-fi-Lillah*

. . . follows the same pattern as took place with Pir-o-Murshid [Inayat Khan] in his 1911 career. Then he was using mostly music and concentration. He sometimes broke into ecstasy and sang loudly in praise of Mohammed. This probably did not go over big. But I have found there are three sorts of praise of Mohammed and they all look the same, but are different:

a. The initial stage is that one praises Mohammed and it may even be that he has inherited this phase of religion . . . Actually, it is no better or worse than the praise of Jesus or Buddha or Krishna nor anybody, but neither is there any gain by dispensing with it.
b. The second stage is that one praises Muhammad because that is the experience; he is really talking about himself and he is not talking about himself. The change from *fana-fi-Sheikh* to *fana-fi-Rassoul* in one's life is revolutionary. One is no longer restricted in vision or in faculties and he finds a tremendous universe . . . Time and place and stage and condition become small things. He cannot prove this nor is he doing this by himself.

   In his first sessions on Sufism Pir-o-Murshid placed Mohammed as the Perfect Man of all times . . . I think the Sufis in Islam generally work from this position.
c. The third stage seems impossible, that while one is being immersed in God the praises of Mohammed become grander. Dante had it of Jesus, but I don't think Dante reached the highest stages. He held on to selfhood. Even the mystics of Christianity excepting a few like John Tauler* never got above the selfhood or to the Unitarian realization . . .

---

*A disciple of Meister Eckhart, Tauler was one of the influential mystics of the 14th century.

There are two aspects of Allah, the silent and the creative although neither of these words is exact. The silent praise is discussed in *The Mysticism of Sound* both in the chapter called "The Silent Life" and in the final chapter which is partially a dissertation on *zikr.**

The Bible says that God created Adam in His image, but Adam is usually associated with "sin." There had to be a perfect man for redemption. Now, there are all kinds of correct men and as perfect men I do not wish to raise any distinctions or differences between them. But the Buddhist does not live like Buddha, nor the Christian like Christ nor the Hindu like Ram or Krishna. We wish to live in an operative world, to raise families and go into business and study and do all those things which we consider human. It is on this point that Mohammed excels. He does not excel in being nearer to God, the Creator, but he does excel in being nearer to man, the created.

Anybody has a perfect right to differ from him here, but the point is not argument, but demonstration. He does not see people demonstrate what Jesus did, or Buddha did; we do see people demonstrate what Mohammed did . . . The idea of Adam, derived from *dam,* earth, is that the Light of Allah had to come through the earthly forms. But how did it come? In *Masnavi*† the cosmic evolution is taught ending in man; and the cosmic evolution continues until the perfect man, or as I see it, the perfect-perfect-man.

Buddha was a perfect man who showed the way to Nirvana and in the Southern Buddhism this teaching is kept. But it is a limited Nirvana and not the perfection. But the layman has received perfection and so the later Buddhists said, no, that creation and Nirvana were identical. Only this means that the common man could attain perfection. But what common man has attained to perfection? One cannot call Rama common because he was a king and Krishna also had a special place in society and Jesus and Buddha became monks. There was only one ordinary man who represented both Adam and perfection and when an ordinary man reached perfection, this closed the revelation. So, with Mohammed the revelation was sealed, which does not take away from any Scripture or teaching.[614]

What Sam was speaking about was his own experience.

---

*This foundational collection of the writings of Hazrat Inayat Khan is available today under the title *The Mysticism of Sound and Music,* (Boulder, CO: Shambhala, revised edition 1996).

†The epic poem in six volumes of Jelaluddin Rumi.

As Al-Ghazali said: "Sufism consists in experiences and not premises." Only previously I have told my experiences and there is a personality reaction. So I have clothed what I am experiencing in philosophy which is a veil over it and is not **it** . . .

Pir-o-Murshid Hazrat Inayat Khan and Pir-o-Murshid Maulana Abdul Ghafoor have given me the whole world to work in and with the intellectual people. So I transfer my experiences into philosophy. But some day when people want truth and will accept from the simple man he will give the simplicity. As the simplicity is rejected he gives the philosophy.

Jesus taught that one must be like a little child to receive the kingdom of heaven. One can always be open to blessings. One can always listen to the "Voice which constantly cometh from within" . . . but if we keep on using the mouthpiece we can't hear what is coming over the receiver.

I am sometimes destined like Pir-o-Murshid wrote, about the career of the dog who took 2 days to go from Basra to Baghdad instead of twelve. "I owe it to the kindness of my fellow dogs. Whenever I stopped to rest they came and barked at me." So the more humanity barks the faster the progression. Every time a rejection or a seeming failure, Allah comes and brings me blessings and success and this will probably be my career until I am called hence. I, Samuel, have nothing to do with it.

There has been a school of Sufis called "[M]alamatiyya" which depended upon public blame; only they sought it. I do not seek [it] . . . Every rebuff is followed by meditation and/or prayer and in turn, something pleasant follows, usually much more pleasant than conjectured. So one comes back to the first lesson: *Subhan Allah, Alhamdu Lillah, Allaho Akbar.*"

Letter to Ghafoor; Further Cairo Contacts

Near the end of January, 1961, Ahmed Murad wrote to his beloved teacher Pir-o-Murshid Maulana Abdul Ghafoor in Dacca, East Pakistan, one of the last letters he sent from Cairo. Portions of it are presented in the extracts that follow:[615]

Beloved Teacher:

Allahumdulillah Rab-ba alamin, er-Rachman, er-Rahim . . .

I have come to this land with many purposes and little external assistance. Nevertheless Allah is Great and though a man walk alone, whether through strife or ease, it is possible that heavy burdens or light

> may come to successful fulfillments. This is not due to his person so much as to the fulfillment of righteous duties laid before him.

Sam felt that, God willing, reports he submitted to the U.S. State Department and to Sheikh Absalem Amria of the Cairo Rifa'i Order of Dervishes each marked a culmination of his external reasons for being in the UAR. Previously closed doors were opened wide; there was a reversal in others' attitudes and responses to him, and unforeseen opportunities now stretched out before him.

Samuel's inner and outer life was rich. He interacted with numerous Sufis as well as horticulturalists while continuing to be blessed with visitations of Saints and *Rassoul-lillah.** Murtaz Billah of the Shadhili Order, a horticulturalist, shared similar private interests with Ahmed Murad. Yusuf Ali, another horticulturalist who claimed to be a disciple of all the living *ktub,* gave Sam reports on operative Sufism that were quite in harmony with what Sam had been taught and had experienced. He attended many *zikrs,* chiefly of the Shadhilis and Rifa'is, and ever expanded his deep and warm Rifa'i connections. At this juncture Sheikh Muhammad Dessougi and Dr. Sharabasi figured among those close contacts. From the moment Samuel entered the UAR, he felt all indications were pointing to his induction into the Rifa'i Order.

He wrote:

> I must record here one incident. I entered the Sidi Shirani Shrine one night on the occasion of this saint's birthday celebration. There were thousands of people present. As soon as I took off my shoes and crossed the threshold, two arms seized me. I thought: "Now your presumption has caught up with you; you have dared so many times to enter holy places without permission." Instead I was immediately conducted to the microphone and found myself guest speaker of the evening! One does not know how these things occur, so thousands heard my voice on a single occasion . . .
>
> Also I have had many interviews for the newspapers but so far few articles published. This is always likely to occur . . .
>
> My health, beloved Murshid, has been remarkably good and my strength has been preserved through the years. This story . . . has already

* *Rassoul-lillah,* Prophet of Allah, is an appellation of Muhammad.

> been published at Aligarh University and will probably be known to the world. And last night Sheikh Amria gave incidents also of the appearance of **Khidr** to living persons.

Khwaja Khidr had appeared to Sam several times during his spiritual retreat in 1925, and the confirmation that Khidr was not simply a legend was important to him. Sam stated the same in his poem "Saladin" and carried a carbon copy of the poem with him. This allowed him to share sections that dealt with the loftier aspects of experiences in *fana-fi-Rassoul* if needed.

With less than two weeks remaining in his stay in Egypt before heading to West Pakistan, Sam worked to tie up loose ends. He made another trip to the Islamic Museum, where he purchased postcards and pictures for his friends. He spoke with the curator at the museum about art books, but they were out of Sam's financial reach and were mostly in French. He wrote a long letter to Rudolph Schaeffer[616] in which he reflected on his intent to travel to Southern California to give a talk on Islamic Art and Modern Cairo, advising Schaeffer that he hoped to discuss the art books with him at a future date.

Sam was suddenly called to Alexandria as a guest of EARIS, the Egyptian American Rural Improvement Society, an institution for American cooperation or aid, which he felt was a grand social and scientific experiment. After the EARIS meeting he called at the Tourist and Information Bureaus in Alexandria and had one of his most delightful experiences in the UAR—a place where he had already had many such. He wrote in his diary:

Islamic Museum, Cairo

Ceramic tile, 17th century, Islamic Museum, Cairo

> The woman in charge of the Tourist Information desk is one of the most beautiful women I have ever met. This is important not because she is beautiful so much that she attracted all kinds of persons and there was a continual parade mostly of men, not interested in tourism at all, and by this means I met quite a few notables, which will enhance my enjoyment when I should visit Alexandria again. As it was raining torrents, I remained in those offices all afternoon.
>
> I had hardly had a chance to call to this woman when a man, the manager came in and said, "Ah, there you are. I have been waiting for you." Shades of Paul Brunton. He had eyes exactly like those which appear in the last part of *A Search in Secret Egypt* and he could read my mind like a book. He claimed to have the faculties of telepathy and clairvoyance and it was obvious that he has them both from the statements and questions he regaled me with. Like myself he is a dervish . . . [617]
>
> I did not get it at the Valley of the Kings, but at the Tourist Information Office, Alexandria. He told me I was travelling to escape, that there was a woman in my life and I could not think who it could be. When I got back to the hotel (Leroy) I do remember one such woman with whom I have had a sort of aeonic romance, but she had long gone out of my memory. I had forgotten all about her; but whether it is she or another I don't know.[618]

That the woman he had originally planned to marry on this trip abroad was now described as forgotten is well worth noting. Sam's fortune had been told five times, but he perceived them all the same—Sufi Sheikhs, card readers—and they all stressed romance. Perhaps somewhat sobered by memories of Edna, Sam remained neutral about any potential romantic future.

> At seven o'clock my host, Mr. Fuad Laithi, the district attorney of Cairo, and another man went with me to a studio. The artist's name is "Seif Wanli" or something like that. They said he ranks among the great artists of the world and has won prizes all over. I do not place him with anybody but Picasso. He started out in the orthodox styles attempting for the element of integration, bringing [Arabian] and African materials together with the European; then he worked impressionistically, then went into

surrealism and now creates in the modern "geometrical" manners. One could see the great parallels with Picasso, although at times he deliberately patterned himself after one or another of the French masters.

The trouble was that I remained there only one hour as my hosts had other engagements. I told them that that hour was worth the whole trip to [Alexandria], and I am sure I enjoyed it more than I would have to the Greco-Roman museum. Perhaps this came as an aftermath to the visit of the Modern Art Museum which is right close by (so not visited until recently) . . . All this keeps one busy and whenever I go to Alex. again I want to visit with these people and the studio—in addition to whatever else is in store.[619]

Yesterday was a theoretical "Sufi" celebration being the anniversary of the death of Pir-o-Murshid Inayat Khan. I had one of the dreams of my life fulfilled—riding an Arab horse. Went from the Pyramids to Sahara city and back. I originally took up horseback riding because I said that someday I would go to Arabia and I might as well learn. I had forgotten all about the incident. But the reason I went was quite different.

I had gone to Mona Village (near the pyramids) at the invitation of two close friends and they introduced me to a Sufi Sheikh. He earns his living by renting horses. So, on account of this I hired him. On our way back we had a "crazy" time chanting sacred phrases. I don't think any Egyptian ever before had such a client. He then took me to lunch but while waiting I danced for his children. I also left a good gift for the children, giving me an idea which I shall discuss forthwith. I was pretty tired when I left.[620]

That fatigue didn't slow Sam down. He went home, took a "real hot bath," had hot chocolate, then was off to the Rifa'i dervishes, where he stayed 2½ hours and came home again only to meet a delegation of Kadiris from Iraq. "They want me to visit their country for spiritual reasons. I have neither the time nor money now, but will visit them and then take it up with the U.S. Embassy."[621]

Sam hoped that some benefactors would arise to support his many projects. As he put it,

I am working all alone as in a terrific vineyard with an unlimited harvest and nobody else there . . .

You can see from my reports—as well as from conclusions reached through many other sources—that there are levels of consciousness and activity. Our conscious sense of assumed superiority is a great bar to international understanding. We are trying to reach friendship on the political level.[622]

Sam's conviction remained strong that true friendship could never be attained on a political level but required person-to-person diplomacy.

Leaving the UAR

During his last days in Egypt, Sam sent Rudolph Schaeffer this list:

> Projects Incomplete for the Future:
>
> 1. Recording Sufi and Coptic and any other unusual music.
> 2. Getting certain basic scientific index-works for the national Research Center.
> 3. Cooperating in getting proper literature in the universities and institutions of culture.
> 4. Possibly introducing folk- or popular-dancing on the common level, providing same does not [intrude] on the folk mores.
> 5. Arrange trip through Syria, possibly from Latakia down and stay according as to needs of any and all kinds.
> 6. Arrange visit to Bagdad, etc., at suitable season. This especially to see the tomb of Abdul Kadiri-Galani, and other sacred places.[623]

Due to his busy schedule Sam was unable to visit the semi-holy city of Tanta. He reported having "entire psychological satisfaction from this trip" and planned to write in detail for the San Rafael *Journal-Independent*.

Sam then described the work he was doing with his own feelings of resentment.

> I have to learn to have as little resentment for what has happened to me, but I am making a special division between:
>
> a. Personal resentment which intruded on my ego and does not affect the international situation.
>
> b. [That] which does.
>
> I have no time to argue with all and sundry of the first class. I certainly have no intention to lecture for Fritzi Armstrong* at any level

*Fritzi Armstrong owned an occult bookshop in San Francisco.

> without an apology and certainly do intend to lecture for the Baptistes at any level on any terms they may lay down.
>
> As to the second class. I have already seen the redemptive karma on Mrs. Duce. But I do not like to see these European intruders in the Asian field who misinform our public and control avenues of education and communication. So long as they are "in" I shall not be satisfied, and I know foreign governments will be unhappy whether they tell us or not.[624]

On the whole, Sam was very happy. He called at Cory Brothers, the agents for the steamship line that operated the SS *Cilicia.* The ship was scheduled to sail from Port Said on February 20th and arrive at Karachi on March 3rd, but Sam took a bus to this port city on the 15th, considering the possibility of an early departure.

In a diary letter to Abdul Rahman in Pakistan Sam mused about his plans.

> Today I spent a whole hour at the Iraqi Ministry. I do not know when I can go to that country. I have neither the money nor the time now to visit everyone. If I can get funds, this may change plans. Anyhow what I learned was most important. That the Ambassador from Iraq to Pakistan is another Abdul Kadiri Ghailani and I should call on him. I am told he is a very spiritual man and honored in your country. I have reasons, both private and public for wishing to visit him and I am hoping we can go together.[625]

Sam had some not-so-good news to share as well.

> My visit at the Islamic Congress was long and involved. There has been a complete change of administration and the former secretaries went off with my papers. I have no time to write them again. It took me hours upon hours and that looks as if wasted.[626]

He then went on to reflect on how things would be when he returned to San Francisco.

> I had to go over the program for San Francisco and for the United States. They spend more time crying because the Zionists are strong than in doing anything. The Zionists are strong because Muslims just sit back and cry. They don't send anybody to present their side.[627]

Sam continued this letter saying that in the U.S.A., and in particular in San Francisco, there were a number of Jewish leaders who did not respect him and his views. In addressing them about the formation of the Jewish state of Israel, Sam expected to face a hostile audience of people who he considered had hypnotized themselves in various forms of Zionism based on emotion, sentiment, ego-wishing, and ignorance. He saw these Zionists, both in the U.S. and abroad, as trying to define and control Islamic society. This to him did not mean that the Arabs who protested Jewish rule were entirely right so much as that their critics might be entirely wrong. He felt that all peoples inhabiting the land that was now Israel needed to be accorded equal respect, and that sites considered sacred by them, be they Muslims, Christians, or Jews, must be universally honored and made accessible—something that was not part of the current plan.

Sam saw no need to attack the synagogue as an institution and would resent such attacks, excepting on the level of superficiality in religion. He was equally against superficiality in Islam, having experienced deeper levels of Islam where he found great meaning. His intention was to take up these issues further with the mosque in Washington DC, where he had received cooperation earlier.

He further shared his opinion on this problem:

> One of the great troubles is that everybody says Islam has Five Pillars, and when it comes to practice one finds everything but those Five Pillars. Instead of *shahud** and *salat,*† I find zeal for Arabism, converting everybody else to go to Mecca without going oneself, more insistence on others performing [prayers] than prayer and devotion, and a whole lot of crying about Congo. In this, Allah is lost . . .
>
> They told me they had started a new school in Somali. They were using the native language and not Arabic. That I like to hear. I told them that all over Africa there were people using Swahili, Hausa, and many other languages and I don't think those people wanted to learn so much about Arabic, they wanted to learn the religion.[628]

---

*The practice that embodies the quality which expresses God's witnessing all things without limitation. Also direct or deep sight.

†Real attention to prayer.

Regarding his travel plans, Sam wrote,

> Fortunately, again, there is an Islamic League in Karachi under the direction of one Abu El-Allah El Madudi,* and they want me to call on him.
>
> I could say that this may be one of the first orders of business for me while I am in that city. I also wish to call on the Mardan Coal Co., see about my mail and money and then get out, *inshallah,* assuming that we shall stop in Sind on the way north.[629]

On February 9th, Sam wrote about his visit to the Islamic Congress.

> We did agree, and they admitted I was right, on two very important matters: One was that the world needed a lot more of Islam; and second that it had to be taught in all languages . . . We then discussed the religion and culture. In Somali-land they are teaching the religion and culture together. In San Francisco they don't study either, they just cry for money and they want money and they want an Imam, but they want to tell the Imam, not listen to him . . .
>
> The Islamic Congress is very broad. They are trying to have all Muslims work together. They don't go into distinctions as to sects, and dividing up and the Pakistani method of having a lot of rival missions wasting their money and all doing the same things. They are not even against the Kadianis.† It is certain that the Kadianis are making a lot of converts today especially in West Africa. The Sunnis are not doing much. They wait for the Sufis or Kadianis or Ahmaddiyas to do something and then go out and correct . . .
>
> The Congress is also willing to give money and books but I don't want any money to go to S.F. and have it wasted. They want social life and I think Americans have too much social life. At the Congress they asked me if Americans did not have a great void and I told them, yes, and that that void should and could be filled. This was a very good visit. But I told them that there had been lots of money in San Francisco and a few people did not like the Ahmadiyyas and would not accept their Mosque . . .

---

*Abul A'la Maudidi was a well-known conservative Muslim philosopher, activist, and scholar.

†The Kadianis (today commonly spelled Qadianis) are a sect who follow the Ahmaddiya form of Islam, a movement the Pakistani government has considered non-Muslim.

> Now I told them I would open a big school for all religions if necessary, and get Islam in that way. I would see that the other faiths had their teachers and I would see that Islam was presented. You may be glad to know that the U.S. Embassy has accepted all my ideas, many of them . . . It means that everything has turned out wonderfully here whether I see President Nasser or not, and I must return to this place whenever Allah directs.[630]

On the 13th Sam wrote Dr. Nelson again, summarizing details of his horticultural activities and travel plans. The following day he said his goodbyes at Cairo University and at some of the Ministry of Agriculture's experimental stations. His schedule remained uncertain, due in part to the prospect of opening another "home" in Pakistan. Sam finished his letter with an objective evaluation of his condition: "I am tired."[631]

On the 17th Sam wrote a diary letter to Jack Betts about Port Said:

> The weather here is moderate all the year around. It is cool, but not so cold as Cairo which at this season is not so cold as Luxor which is always hot in the summer. This is the season and it is full of Americans. It did not stop a mob from attacking the Embassy and breaking all the windows. The mob was made up of school kids, some left out purposely. They first set fire to the Belgian Embassy and then attacked us. I think they also attacked the U.N. headquarters. The police did nothing. Even a Sam Lewis is worth ten police and I am afraid what a Jack Betts would do to them if they got funny . . .
>
> I was given a farewell tea by a Sheikh and his friends. Next morning I made a final plea to the American Embassy, for God's sake have Arabs teach about their country and don't subsidize English, Germans, Hungarians and Irish Jews. I made my point but too late for the mob. I had warned USIA long ago that they would remember my words when they were mobbed, but the man I had warned was away.
>
> I think they are fairly well convinced now we don't need European [outcasts] to tell us about Asia. Anyhow some of the Embassy staff was in the restaurant when I was having my farewell dinner and I was warmly greeted. I have been given so many warm greetings you can understand why I want to come back . . .
>
> I can have a job, too, teaching at the National Research Center. This is going to be pretty hard on Lloyd Morain, who [as a proponent of general semantics] never gave me a chance.[632]

Sam spent much of the rest of his time in Port Said picking up gifts for his friends and acquaintances in San Francisco: silver work for Ching-wah Lee in Chinatown; a charm bracelet with ancient Egyptian figurines; hand cymbals for himself and for a dancer in Pakistan whom he expected to visit in Multan. By coincidence Sam encountered Claude Dahlenberg, who had managed the East-West House in San Francisco on California Street on which Gavin Arthur had modeled his "Global House." Bumping into Claude on a sidewalk in Cairo far from home was Zen according to Sam.

Once again Sam acknowledged that he was tired. He had only had three free days in more than 5 months in the UAR.

In closing, Sam dismissed the contents of the letter as nonsense, and said the rest of his mind was pretty much a blank. He suggested that Jack, the recipient of the diary entry, should feed the letter to his dog Cha-cha.

On February 20th Sam wrote a diary letter to Rudy from on board the SS *Cilicia*. He delighted in his first-class air-conditioned room with bedding, and even though he found the room quite small, there was space for his nine pieces of luggage. He likened travel aboard this vessel to steam-boating on a lake, grateful not to be experiencing physical ailments he'd had on previous voyages. The next morning brought the sight of the Sinai Peninsula, and a rested body to the weary traveler.

Sam dined with Sindhis on board, who were Hindus by faith.

> They lacked the depth of the "Indian" Hindus but we enjoyed the same food. The "Indian" Hindus are about the same as others: philosophical, broad-minded, deep, but not always pragmatic . . . Most of the Muslims showed more heart, if not head, and you could feel it. On the whole the Muslims in this region are more heart-centered and less mental than the Hindus, but I am delighted with the universal views expressed by many of them. This is due, no doubt, to Sufism and the Moghul influences.[633]

In a diary entry on February 25th, Sam described his stopover in Aden.[634] When his ship landed Sam did not want to spend money, yet his friend Abdul Rahman from Karachi wanted a camera, and he wished to find one for him. His group was taken to a shop where none of them bought anything. In the next shop he noticed a man with prayer beads and Ahmed Murad mentioned that he was a dervish. Then he learned the storeowner was the local Rifa'i Sheikh. They immediately embraced and the Sheikh started dropping prices.

The unexplained magnetism that connected Sam to and with dervishes had multiplied and it left him wondering why that attraction was so strong. He had felt a similar strength of attraction when he met Claude Dahlenberg on a street in Cairo. Aboard ship the Pathans had sought him out, acting as his friends and protectors. He also got along well with most of the Asians on board, which he felt might be explained by reincarnation or perhaps by factors such as in the case of Nilla Cram Cook.* All of these attractions were similarly mysterious. Sam mused that the next thing psychologists might consider about this type of attraction would be a broadened sense of the word "we." What draws any two entities into the same environs and unites them with a shared bond?

---

*Nilla Cram Cook was an American writer and linguist who converted to Hinduism and later to Islam.

Samuel Lewis in Pakistan, 1961

CHAPTER 14

On to Pakistan and India

En Route to Karachi

In February, 1961, on board the SS *Cilicia* "somewhere in the Red Sea" Ahmed Murad was able to easily engage with a large cross-section of Asians. He wrote to Gavin Arthur, "We can and do discuss the philosophies and religions of their respective countries. What is more, they look up to me." [635] Samuel Lewis was one of the rare examples of a person with true cross-cultural understanding. He had a clear view of the strength and breadth of his connections with people, exemplified by his experiences in the UAR. "I meet people; I commune with them. I was as welcomed by the top scientists as by the lowest artisan as by the professors and by the common people—but nowhere more than in my own profession, and in this by Americans and Arabs alike." [636]

Sam was not naïve in his interactions. "I am, it is true, carrying some of Whitman's poetry but I am more concerned with Whitman's ability to mingle with human beings and love them and be loved. This is not mere social intercourse, keeping the latch open for every lout or schemer who comes one's way. It requires some vision and circumspection." [637]

He also felt vindicated through his relationship with Harvard *vis-a-vis* other institutions of higher learning. They had said to Samuel, "We want to learn from you everything you know that we do not." [638]

About a week later, Sam wrote a lengthy and scientifically based letter to a science-minded friend John. Here the inquiring mind of Samuel Lewis appears in a space where chemistry, physics, biology, and cosmology meet, assailing the limitations he perceived in conventional scientific thinking. As with so many of Sam's writings, the interested reader is commended here to the full text of this diary entry in the Archives.

I am writing on board, en route to Karachi where I shall soon land. This trip has been most important in resting my mind and body and I am so mentally relaxed at the moment that I feel like writing my thoughts on paper. I am writing them to you first to see if they contain any ideas which may be of help directly or indirectly to you and those who have been protesting against "space" experiments. Then, if these ideas are serious enough, to let Paul see or have them . . .

[Two] completely different approaches have brought me now to the same point. The first is western and involves Haeckel and Reiser; the second is Oriental and revolves around Dr. Radhakrishnan. Haeckel, for some un-reason or other has gone out of fashion . . . The experiments I have witnessed in the UAR would have delighted such a man. His monism of matter-and-energy seems to have been substantiated a great deal by modern advances in Physics.

If we turn to the Carbon-cycle and the Nitrogen-cycle we find ourselves in a world of embolism and operation, strangely identical with Indian doctrines down to the smallest iota. In these cycles it is obvious that both C and N have functions in- and out- of living bodies. So long as there are no radioactive transformations, there is the operation of cyclic law which can to some extent be examined and understood and perhaps even controlled.

Turning from Biology to Physics, we admit that electrical energy in its largest sense also operates within and without bodies. The great doctrines of Conservation of Energy and Matter seem, today, to be unified, justifying the monisms both of India and Haeckel. But when it comes to Life we are facing, or rather refusing to face a certain enigma.

Is life energy? Well energy exists within and without bodies. We have the electrical discharges in "space" . . . These charges may or may not be limited or unlimited to ionosphere, stratosphere, etc. etc. Are there fields of force around us? And are these fields of force living or dead?

We immediately get into complexities. Our present pseudo-conceptions of life restrict it materially to a Carbon-Oxygen complex both within and without bodies, with chlorophyll or protoplasm. But there is no fundamental reason why life-energy must be any more (or less) involved in chlorophyll or protoplasm than magnetism must be involved in Iron and related metals . . .

Is life inherent in space? Is space living? . . . I am placing this question here because all nuclear experiments have assumed the contrary which is metaphysics and not science. The blind assumption can be disturbing . . .

I am inclined to think that life-energy is scattered in the universe and that the manifestation of life through the Carbon- and Nitrogen-cycles is a peculiarity of earth itself. The life-energy may manifest through other cycles elsewhere and even the beings of other planets may have delivered developed "minds" or "spirits" based on different chemistries than ours . . .

I am therefore at the moment at the conclusion that Space may be as varied as earth-matter; that just as the unit-electron manifests by vibrational attunements, rings, etc. into the chemical or atomic elements, so space may be as varied **energetically** as earth is atomically and chemically. We are assuming uniformities based on non-experience and this is a dangerous precedent for science, if it is to be science at all . . .

I think the field-theories of Einstein and the corresponding discoveries of mathematicians [have] been treated as too specialized to affect common logistics and logic. But Professor Oliver Reiser, with his Integrational Philosophy, begins, not ends, there. And if we apply these to our thinking, or assumptions, or practice, we shall have to change our attitude toward space and begin to differentiate as was done by the ancient Hindus, between the space as the Grand Totality and "space" concerned with a specialized or limited phenomena . . .

The uncovering of "non-matter" may ultimately prove to be more revolutionary than we have any idea about. I cannot overlook these things if one tries to grasp a picture and not just a symbol of the universe. At the same time the Upanishads have given me working models and each year I find the integration of Western Science comes closer and closer to these models. What it means in the end, I do not know. But I see a Universe quite diverse in each of its aspects, areas, arenas, yet; and I have always believed, since a little boy, that actual "space-travel" would show how "wrong" **we** have been—meaning mostly the humanity and literary traditions, when they dare to hold conclusions as conclusions and continue with their continuum of theological psychologizing outside the field of religion.

At least these are my momentary conclusions. I do not know how clear they are. Clarity is here more important than truth . . .

One does not know how valuable or important this is. But I am scheduled soon to speak on the relation between Oriental Philosophy and Modern Science and . . . have not run into any objection to my momentary conclusions. Every person I have spoken to or with—mostly scientists but more recently diplomats, businessmen and philosophers (all Asian) agree. The scientists were about 50–50 Western and Near Eastern. All seemed to be looking toward integrational approaches and welcome them.[639]

First Days in Karachi

Ahmed Murad arrived in Karachi on March 3. He did not waste any time getting involved.

In Karachi I got rid of clothes purposely, as *zakat** and tips, so I could buy local things for myself. I was very satisfied with what I bought before, from every angle. The sari is used here, too, more sombre colors than in India and also they hide the dirt more, but preserve beauty and dignity. Of course as one gets into the Pathan country the clothes will be different and in Punjab they are different. Here too one often sees the women in pantaloons of some kind and the men without pants.† There are many kinds of costumes in Multan, which is a crossroad of several types of culture. The architecture is predominantly Persian.

There are American engineers here building houses at great speed for the people. Karachi has been marvelously cleaned up by Ayub Khan and the country is so different from what it was before. I have also found much more English than I expected . . .

I have to write a letter to City Hall, because I met a niece of Don Cleary here. She was born in S.F. and educated in L.A. The Americans here act like Americans and not like a "foreign colony" which was true of those I have met in Hong Kong, Karachi and Cairo. This made "infiltration" natural and easy.

Karachi in the 1960s

This city is noted for dust, flies, heat, beggars, dirt and tombs. I visited the tombs before and the dust and flies kept away then. The weather, strange to say, or *alhamdu lillah*, is perfect at the moment! . . .

---

*Charitable donations.

†Traditional dress for men in that region was a skirt-like wraparound garment.

The people who live next door have enormous albums of records and Bill [one of Sam's hosts] has tape-recorded these and they are one of the chief forms of amusement . . . There is also a demanding kitten here so I have right off-hand two forms of amusement. There are also free American movies at the cantonment nearby. Saw an Orson Welles production the other night—so sweetly saccharine . . .

The main problem [here] is with *bakshish-wallahas.** (The tombs have boxes for offerings and I gave to them and nothing to the beggars. I simply refuse and if they argue I yell I am a dervish and they should be giving to me.) The point is that I always prove my point. In accordance with my friend Reps they find I know more of the depths of their religion than they do which leaves them aghast. Then instead of wanting *bakshish* they want *baraka* (magnetic blessings). Those I give freely and thus I am liable to leave this world a "saint" or "mysterious" character. This is to some extent true and is another reason for writing to you in such detail. I am not concerned with reactions in the U.S.[640]

He closed with love and *karuna*† and *ishk.*

On March 4th Sam wrote the World Affairs Council of Northern California.

My dear friends:

I have now been in Pakistan four days and have had a very rapid start . . .

I . . . went to the Embassy where I had three long and successful interviews . . . There was also there a letter of my close friend, Robert Clifton and between us, in a sense, we cover the whole Asian continent; have been uniformly successful with Asians, and unusually unsuccessful with the press.

Excepting *Marriage Ceremonies in Morocco* by Westermarck I do not know any books which detail the Islamic religion as it is practiced. I can refer you to a book in the S.F. Public Library on Chinese funeral customs and you will look in vain in them for connections to and with the stuffs peddled out as "Confucianism," "Taoism" and "Buddhism" by various worthy graduates of European universities. They take you into the higher echelons of wonderful metaphysical speculation but tell nothing about people as they are.

---

*Beggars.

†Compassion.

The political attaché in Cairo finally assented that we have failed to establish contact with the public and public mores in the Near East. The political attaché here [in Karachi] knows it and is doing something about it. The attaché in Cairo has now asked that I report in detail actual communistic doings which I run upon and the attaché here had me tell him in detail how I turned the mob on the commies in India—the life I saved happened to be my own. I am forced to pun, that the un-usual in Asia is too often the un-news-ual, and this is a cold war.

Actually the commies have started an Anti-American movement here which, as with most such movements, are financed and supported by Americans! There have been reports of conversions to Christianity in Pakistan . . . Feelings have run high and commies are undergrounding it that the Americans are behind these efforts to make conversions. Unfortunately some of our staff in Foreign Service are very pro-Christian and make no bones about it. This was not true in Cairo; I met nobody there who permitted feelings to enter into this subject . . .

Fortunately, there are people in Washington who are engaged in objective studies of the culture of the Near East . . . The selection of Prof. Reischauer as Ambassador to Japan is exactly what I have been advocating for years. We do have Americans who know something about Asia and are admired in Asia . . .

I once proposed that you invite Dr. Kingsley Davis of South Hall on the Berkeley Campus to speak before you. I have been estimating him very highly, but his estimation here both among the Pakistanis and Embassy is of the very highest. It is this sort of man who should be addressing audiences and giving them information . . .

Much of my time has been spent with Dr. Farooq, assistant to the Agricultural Attaché, who is at present in Washington. He was very enthusiastic about the program outlined and happens to be a close friend of Mr. M. A. Cheema of the Ministry of Agriculture who was my previous contact . . . I have still to find an agriculturalist, or perhaps even a scientist, who is not entirely objective and impersonal, and purportedly practical.

I have already spoken at a Junior College where they train young men to be Agricultural Inspectors and Advisors. The failure of our Point IV program has been that between the colonels and generals on top and the privates (peasants) there were too few intermediaries. Now we shall have corps of sergeants, so to speak, well trained in science, English and accounting methods.

My other contacts overlapped and include both Islamic teachers and Sufis. I am particularly anxious to have some Islamic teachers in the United States at the Universities, or even at centers. I am concerned with information, not "conversions." . . . With the large number of Islamic nations in the [UN] it is time we at least learned about their religion and folk-ways. My own opinion at the moment is that the best presentations of Islam are made at the Seminaries in Hartford and Berkeley. Missionaries are trained in the actual details of the actual religions which they are to face . . .

I had, again, my farewell from the Indonesian Embassy in Cairo, and those people have again and again invited me to their land to try to bridge the misunderstandings between our countries. I must repeat, it is they who have extended the invitations. For my own part I am pleased to report our Foreign Service is fully in favor of it, but my resources are limited and my successful ventures are increasing . . .

You do not have to believe it, but there is a kind [of] conscious and also a kind of unconscious telepathy or empathy which brings us together. In Alexandria my contact (who has a high position in the U.A.R. government) had the conscious faculty. In Port Said unconsciously my contact was a Sufi teacher. In Aden, where I stopped to make some purchase, my contact was another one. And here I met the Sufis very rapidly and shall meet more . . .

Monday I hope to visit the American Friends of the Middle East. They have done much to try to establish "semantic" relations between Christians and Muslims and the effort therefore is the success. Getting people to sit down together is to me, the recognition. Agreement is not so important.

The next underground step is concerning India. The selection of Chester Bowles enables the underground-grapevine to say we, the U.S. are pro-Indian. When I was here before I saw the rather successful efforts of the commies to "prove" to the Pakistanis that we were pro-Indian in Kashmir; and to the Indians that we were pro-Pakistani. Our USIA programs, with their noble and lofty overtones, do not reach the masses. Our art and musical shows are nothing but boondoggling for those who need no such support. [641]

Sam was an early observer of the discrediting by Muslims of Western mores. He continued:

Off hand, here, as in UAR, I hope to emphasize agricultural cooperation as the basis for friendliness. Here the whole thing becomes complicated

> and unified. I have been urging more agricultural literature and less "true immortality" pulps. The Islamic distrust of Christianity here has nothing to do with the missions. The Protestant Churches are blamed for the lurid literature and surrealistic movies, and they themselves protest against them, but not loud enough . . .
>
> I met a large number of Asians on the ship, giving me more contacts. In general they hold that both Great Britain and the United States are offering the scientific and cultural training needed in Asia. It is only when sensitivities are concerned we fall down. The staff at the Embassy here assents to my contention that it is a myth and a very bad myth that we do not discuss religion abroad. We are held to be materialists. This was the unanimous opinion of Hindus, Pakistanis, Pushtuns and Persian-Afghans, however else they differed. I do not know how long we shall continue to be limited by our myths. We have others.
>
> These people, however they differ, live in psychological longevity. Metaphysically it makes them our superiors and more; but physically it tends to have them adhere to principles rather than actions. The two need to be brought closer together.
>
> I shall be with Americans in Multan and learn what they are doing there; then go to Lahore to plan an ambitious series of programs. Then to Rawalpindi where my friend Ahmed Bashir Minto, once of San Francisco, lives, and where the government is moving, then to Abbottabad, my "home." From Abbottabad I must move in all directions.[642]

Sam went on to affirm his view of his immediate future. He had started off energetically in Karachi with positive results and expected to leave as soon as all his business was completed at the Embassy. He did not wish to become too involved there, however, since friends were waiting for him in other cities. About his activities in Karachi Sam wrote to Rudolph Schaeffer:

> I met Mr. Farooq at the Agricultural section in the Embassy and we hit it right off. We have had three conferences with at least one more coming up. He had me speak at a school where they are training young men to become Agricultural inspectors. The Political Attaché took extended notes and gave me the name of a man in the State Department who is interested in Sufism. After all the tripe they teach in the U.S. it is no wonder that Asians resent us . . .

In the afternoon my friend Abdul Rahman (a longtime resident of S.F.) found me and we went to a friend whom I also found to be a Sufi and have met several Sufis among the people contacted here. We have now purchased our tickets, he going to Lahore, but I'll stop off at Multan where I have personal friends. Then I must go in turn to Lahore, Rawalpindi and Abbottabad.

Ghor Valley, Jordan, where AFME was bringing agricultural training

I had a short but most important meeting with Mr. M.A. Cheema, who is now Secretary-General of the Ministry of Food and Agriculture. He had been my contact before. He is now the chief permanent servant of the department and gave me advice which I shall follow. It means most of my time should be spent at Lyallpur, Lahore and Peshawar, all in the North.

But it also means my departure by sea again. I do not know whether I shall be going all the way to Chittagong by sea and then visit India later on or stop at Bombay. If business requires my going to East Pakistan first I'll do that, for after all my present Murshid is in Decca, too.

It is not yet hot here—it gets up to 90 but cools at night and this is even more so at Multan and Lahore just now. In fact some districts are unequally cold at night but Spring and I shall be keeping company. I expect to stay in the North for many months and may go to unusual places.[643]

Addressing the American Friends of the Middle East

In early March, 1961, while in Karachi Sam wrote a letter to the American Friends of the Middle East (AFME) in San Francisco. It was addressed to Admiral Evenson and Friends:

> Most important to me here is your library. I have been [protesting] and howling, and I shall continue to protest and howl over these points:
>
> a. The wide-spread market for lurid American literature.

> b. The almost esoteric attitude toward good trade, technical and scientific magazines.*
> c. The failure to recognize that most people have been attached to the land.†
> d. The strange acceptance of European authorities on Asia—men who are little regarded in Asia.
> e. The strange down-grading of American authorities on Asia—[men] who are highly regarded in Asia.
> f. The refusal to look at the religion, folklore and habits of people as they are . . .
>
> I grant the right of every man to differ, but first we should have the facts. As a nation we simply do not know what these people believe and practice.
>
> The Indian papers are editorializing about Pakistan's trend toward neutralism. It is a trend into which they have been pushed. They want Islamic culture and we do not face it. They want certain kinds of foreign aid, and we want to give certain kinds of aid, and we have not sat down and talked everything over as [we] should.[644]

Sam reported that in the UAR he had found "tremendous anti-Russian and anti-Chinese sentiments," and he opined that perhaps it was even more so in East Pakistan. However, he explained,

> It is based on different premises, premises which we as a Nation should face. We are the strange country with a fundamental Declaration of Independence which we do not always appreciate. It was all right for our Forefathers to talk about God, but we are so afraid of stepping on other people's toes. We keep silent.[645]

Sam wasn't silent and he was intent on relaying his experiences in this area.

> The effects of the AFME to have Christians and Muslims sit down together is very much appreciated—abroad. Today a tremendous [number] of

* Sam's use of "esoteric attitude" in this context refers to the stance of people who feel they are superior to whatever has been published, and who therefore ignore it.

† This reinforces Sam's position on the need to get to know people as they actually live their lives, not as concepts.

> Nations are either Catholic or Muslim—something our press and public does not seem to realize. It is not only to stem communism (and with it mass-starvation and barbarism) but the progressive development of mankind which is in the offing.
>
> I have had nothing but delightful interviews here; with the police; with the Ministry of Food & Agriculture (Mr. Cheema); with our Embassy; with both orthodox and heterodox Muslims and with citizens. There is a plan on foot to have me speak at Karachi University when I return. But I have so many plans for Lahore. I was told your office in Pakistan is there so I shall see them and keep them informed.
>
> My itinerary is very complicated socially but not geographically (in India it will be the opposite). I expect to go even into Afghanistan, *inshallah*. But I am of those who would rather do [than] just talk.[646]

Sam received tomato seeds from Ohio State and passed them on to Mr. Cheema, but he saw that his main horticultural work would occur later in the North. His sights were set on Lahore, where there was a campaign to speed up the agricultural universities' research, and a world gathering of lay Muslims would soon take place. En route he planned to stop at Multan to visit a Christian mission and perhaps do a little work there.

Before leaving Karachi, Sam had a deeply moving experience. His friend Abdul Rahman took him to a mosque where they met a series of Sufi friends, then went to one friend's home. Sam was shown a picture there by yet another Sufi that reminded him of one depicted in a certain occult work, possibly *Brother of the Third Degree*.* As Abdul's father explained the picture to Sam, Sam felt he was also explaining Sam's life mission. Shortly before leaving, Sam told Abdul Rahman, "Not one moment here was wasted. Your father thought he was explaining a picture to me; actually he was reading out of the '*akasha* records' my duties." [647] Sam then left Karachi.

---

*The opening of the summary of this intriguing volume, from Google Books: "Set in the near future (early twentieth century), this 1894 occult novel is a tale of eternal love, albeit chaste."

On to Multan

It was only four days later, on March 12th, that Sam was in Multan, Pakistan, writing a summary of his experiences to Dr. Cutright.[648] Several excerpts follow.

> I have been in Pakistan some nine days now and I hope you do not mind some reports. I have disposed of the rest of the Tomato Seeds given me but shall not ask for more until I know definitely the best place to send them.
>
> Sometimes a life story unfolds like a piece or pieces of fiction. My visit to the UAR resulted in [a] series of rather favorable reactions. One of my last ventures was to boldly request a position in the National Research Centre to instruct the librarians in how to utilize the vast collection of materials they have in practical research. The experimental scientists and their staffs do not know how to utilize literatures. The collections tend to be vast because in part, due to cold war rivalries more and more books are contributed, if not purchased by the UAR government.
>
> I have to use here cold-war rivalries. We think off-hand of the competition between the U.S. and Russia. But there are also competitions between India and Pakistan, between the Arabs and Israelis, etc., etc. all of which stimulate both research and book-writing and this has been of benefit to the document section of the Research Center.
>
> **Multan** is known as the city of flies. When I was here before, the Chief Engineer begged me to do something to help eradicate the fly-nuisance here. I spent some time with DuPont people who told me they had agents in Pakistan. I asked them if we had to wait until the Russians had a fly-swatter or spray before we would rid this region of flies. In an earlier age we did wonderful work in Panama, the Philippines and Cuba in eradicating insect menaces. No politics were involved.
>
> On shipboard a Pathan became particularly friendly with me. He learned that I shall have to come to Peshawar some time and we agreed. Then I asked him his profession. **He is the manager of a** D.D.T. factory!* But I have learned that today some work is being done with spraying and the army engineers are also active in the region. In any event when I do get to Peshawar I expect to visit the place and send in a detailed report.

---

*In that period, before DDT's environmental consequences were well understood, DDT had been hailed for its miracle results in controlling insect populations.

Sam also learned that there was a large fertilizer factory some eight or nine miles from Multan, which he was interested in visiting. He witnessed several severe problems in the area, chief of which were high salinity and a high water-table. He wrote, "There is not the rainfall even of the Alexandria region. The soil is either very, very friable or [clayey]. This city is noted for shrines and today I found that the hill-tops where these shrines are located have been landscaped. The hill-tops, of course, are above the water table and there is no saline problem then."

Lahore was Sam's next stop, followed by Abbottabad and then supposedly Mardan, where the largest successful farmer using modern means had been expecting him. But he learned that one Judge Rabbani was also awaiting him. Rabbani had the largest successful farm using traditional methods, the hand labor of peasants rather than modern equipment.

Judge Rabbani was also one of the leaders in reforestation, and a project was currently underway at Quetta in Balochistan. Sam noted that the soil in this part of Pakistan was friable and dusty, so it was conducive to seed planting. Because of this, Sam thought the desert problems would be quite different from those of the UAR, and in particular the salt problem would be worse. He went on to write this about the area:

> West Pakistan is largely the Indus Valley. The Punjab—literally "Five Rivers" means mostly branches of the Indus. The Kabul River is on the other side and I hope to visit that valley, going up the Khyber Pass to Kabul itself on this journey. I am told that that region resembles California in many of its aspects. This includes Abbottabad where I shall "live" and have been before.
>
> The garden flowers in general that I have seen are those of California but in Karachi I saw the largest Petunias yet and also the largest Lantana grown as a big shrub. But this is a country where *buxus** is a **tree**, not a shrub. I have not the secret of that—yet.
>
> So far I have just touched the soil and crop problem and wish to unload my literature on these things first. Then I shall go into pests, etc. Outside of flies this immediate region is rather free at the moment but I

*Boxwood.

think this is due in part to the regular DDT spraying. "American" grasses are used on the lawns, and not the ubiquitous *C. dactylon.*

This is sheep and goat country. Milk, etc. come from both the buffalo and cow but in this household they get their dairy products which are air-borne from the States.

Food processing is even more important here and no doubt I shall be collecting notes which may interest your colleagues in Columbus.

Sam ended his letter to Professor Cutright,

> I do not know when I shall be writing again. The possibilities of extending horticultural exchange whether of persons or knowledge are endless. I met a group of farm boys in Karachi en route back to the U.S. It seems that the Kansan Universities made the exchanges here. Of course, I may meet some of your own students on the Indian side, but that is far off, in time.

A Surprising Meeting

It was exhilarating to Sam to find a changed Multan. His Pathan companion on the ship was addressing the fly problem there and bringing it under control. Still, Sam envisioned one more project: to bring in vacuum cleaners to missionary hospitals and mosques in Multan, even though it might have to wait for his next visit.

In Multan, Sam encountered a woman he referred to as "Beatrice." The meeting was a great surprise for him, for he already knew her—she was the Edna he had hoped to marry. Earlier on the trip, in response to a Sufi giving him a reading about his life, Sam reflected that he had "forgotten" about this very woman.

Sam wrote to his friend, the dancer Magana Bapiste:

> I had originally planned to stop at Multan and visit Dr. Girardeau who operates a mission hospital here. But in the meanwhile "Beatrice" had moved here and she and her husband, Bill, kept on writing constantly to come here and here I am. Beatrice's actual name has the [same] meaning, but is in another language. I have written tremendous poetry for her and even about her. But now comes the most fictional-like facts that makes one wonder.

> Beatrice has lived most of her life in India. She is the only non-Indian who has been trained in all sorts of Indian dancing. She is a friend of Asoka whom she says is now in Hollywood . . . She married Bill [Bailey], who is an American, and who works for the engineers here. I had never met Bill and don't know what she told him—but he is the spiritual one. He believes in Yoga and occultism. Our views on politics, international affairs and esoteric matters are so closely akin there are times when it is like looking at a soul-mirror-image. He has also lived much in India. I have not his story yet, but he is certainly another one of us reincarnates from India [in] Western bodies, for whatsoever purposes the Wisdom of the Universe wishes. So it is with him and to him I have been drawn. This has produced some strange complications. For these complications are nothing like triangles but follow almost weird patterns.
>
> Yesterday Beatrice and I visited the tombs of saints here . . . Beatrice, who was with [me] and is a skeptic, received an earful. Bill, who was not with me, accepted everything. It is extremely difficult for me to write and yet I have to keep my diary . . . It is a continuing fulfillment of my friend Paul Reps, who writes Zen material (the real thing). "Sam, you have to go to Asia to teach the Buddhists dharma, the Hindus their religion and Sufism to the Muslims."[649]

He had more to say about Beatrice:

> I must tell you . . . She wanted to come to U.S. and continue with her career as a dancer. I was trying to help. Now she has given this up.* It does not matter perhaps because she has a husband and is both a professional photographer and painter and her work in either of these two professions is proficient enough for her to make a success in the U.S. I did not mind her giving up her profession—that is a private matter. But she got rid of many of her costumes and that whacked me and is the main reason for my writing to you now . . . I don't want her to give up many of her costumes from this point on.[650]

Sam begged Edna not to give up any more costumes of any kind, asking that she either hold them until she reached the U.S. or to let Sam send them to Magana in San Francisco, despite not having Magana's

---

*Sam's view of her plans notwithstanding, as was recounted in Chapter 12 Edna did bring her dancing to New Jersey in the late '60s.

permission yet. He addressed Magana as Queen Nefertiti and said this was one of those cases where the Queen of Hearts would shout, "Off with his head" and "If the subject had not the perspicacity and perspicuity and pertinacity and persiflage, then it ought to come off."[651]

Sam also shared with Magana about Claude Dahlenberg, the man he had run into on the streets in Cairo, and whom they both knew from San Francisco. Sam described how Claude had been with him walking through Cairo and "saw the people tumble out of shops and bazaars" to honor Sam the moment he arrived in the neighborhood. Sam was delighted about this event. He needed such recognition in the face of all those in San Francisco who wanted to write him off as someone who made things up. Now he had an eyewitness that they would have to acknowledge.

Sam Writes from Lahore

Six days later Sam wrote from Lahore to his trusted friend Florie Leonard:

> I am on the train in the station here ready to go to Rawalpindi . . . So many, many things have happened that I must record them . . . It must be made clear to you and everybody else that I am no longer the person that left home, and the prowess and also power within me has been given full scope. This scope has increased, for the numbers of my friends, allies and associates is increasing and at a rapid rate.
>
> I arrived in Karachi on 3rd March. Shortly after that Abdul Rahman met me and took me to a Mosque. There I met the missionary Ibrahim who has been at the Center in San Francisco. Instead of listening to my story he regarded me as an individual and as a possible missionary . . . I met a missionary from Ceylon . . . I have met two in Cairo. They are much better adapted to influence the Western mind; they all dress clean and seem to have high moral outlooks. In other words, everything one wants to expect—in others.
>
> My hosts, who were friends of Abdul Rahman, were also Sufis . . . There is an underground ill-feeling between Christians and Muslims owing to the high degree of conversions to Christianity. In this I find that the missionaries today are highly educated and moral and transfer some of their virtues. The old mullahs simply have not these virtues.

> But it is not the part of any Federal government official to side in this conflict. The funniest thing is that although the chief of the Cultural Center in Karachi leans toward the Christians, the Chief at Lahore leans the other way . . . On the other hand in Lahore I have been asked by the cultural staff of USIA to give them talks on Sufism and Islamic philosophy. This is a great diplomatic and personal victory . . .
>
> This auspicious beginning has been followed at a great rate. I met the *Wali* of the *Dirgah* Shams-i-Tabriz and astounded him and his associates by going deeply into *tasawwuf* right off-hand. Before we left all three of our pictures were taken together which made him feel very happy.[652]

Sam later reported that all rose and embraced him after giving his teachings. This acceptance made him hopeful that he might also be acknowledged when he returned to the U.S.[653] His letter to Florie went on to say that the biggest thing he had accomplished in Karachi was meeting Dr. Farooq of the American Agricultural Section. Dr. Farooq heartily endorsed all his ideas.

In a letter to his friends at the Pakistan House in San Francisco, Sam described his visit to Lahore's University of the Punjab, which became very important in his life.*

> I first went to [the department of Islamic Philosophy] and Prof. A. A. Siddiqui was delighted to see me. I had spoken twice with him before. He gave me a tremendous build-up and made arrangements so I [could] meet his colleagues and other worthies the next day when the [Ramadan] fast ends. This delays my trip to Rawalpindi . . . But this build-up is very important. Dr. Siddiqui is very much against the phony experts who lecture in California about something they call "Islam" and who are believed and followed. He speaks excellent English and is the sort of

University of the Punjab in Lahore

*In his diary, Sam incorrectly refers to this as Punjabi University, which is a different institution in India. The University of the Punjab in Lahore, established in 1882, is the oldest public university in Pakistan.

> man who should be sent for when the Federal Government finances studies in Asiatics.[654]

Sam had been writing to the Department of Fine Arts at the University of the Punjab with plans to share recent creations from the UAR through slides and purchased wares. These were timed for arrival when Sam was scheduled to be lecturing in this region. After the lectures, the artifacts would go to the museum across the street from the university and the slides would become the property of the Fine Arts Department. The slides ended up being sent to Abbottabad, which Sam hardly felt was a mistake. He showed the slides there and arranged to show them in Lahore on his return trip in May.

His letter to Florie continued and showed he was still under the influence of love:

> The new head of the Fine Arts Department [Mrs. Ahmed] is just the sort of woman I might liked to have fallen in love with. She was born a Jewess, in England. She left the synagogue because it was too narrow and became a Christian and left that religion for the same reason. She has married a Muslim and has risen socially and intellectually. Besides this her views on modern art and art in general are about the same as my own.[655]

Their friendship became a lasting one.

Sam visited the Botany Department, where he had an interview on technical subjects and then contributed some of his printed materials. Staff encouraged Sam to retain the major portion of his books for his time in Lyallpur, where it was probable he would give at least one talk after going to Peshawar. There were "revolutions" in teaching, research and reorganization at both Peshawar and Lyallpur so his visit would be well timed.

At the Tourist Bureau a long article was requested from Sam on Tourism, which would go to one Mohammed Idrees. Sam typed the article that night and Idrees had Sam's picture taken the next day for the *Pakistan Times*.

Next was the *Civil & Military Gazette*, Kipling's old newspaper, where Sam was given a hearty welcome by Mr. Makhzan, his previous host there. He introduced Sam to the editor, and Sam promised that as soon as he reached Abbottabad he would start a series of articles on Pakistan and his reasons for revisiting it. Sam wrote:

> I learned that Mr. Marghrab Siddiqui who originally invited me to Lahore was back and head of the department of Journalism at the [Punjab] University. I visited him the next day. He was a friend of my friend Surindar Suri, and he also visited the Islamic Center and A.A.A.S.* on Broadway where I first met him by appointment. We had a long and cordial visit.[656]

In his update to Pakistan House Sam noted that the *Pakistan Times* had fallen under anti-American influences and was perpetually anti-government without having a constructive program of its own to offer. This had changed, but the need for readjustment of policies had stimulated the *Civil and Military Gazette* and elevated its prestige to the plane that Sam felt it deserved. Both newspapers asked Sam to write about his scientific mission there, as well as his studies and knowledge of Sufism and Islamic philosophy.[657]

Lahore the Beautiful

While in Lahore Sam also wrote his friend Harry Nelson:

> I cannot escape it. It is inevitable. I follow the old E. Phillips Oppenheim dictum "Fools for Luck." I could not get accommodations when I arrived at Lahore and I was shunted to the Imperial Hotel, which is an old group of buildings made into a new hotel. They may be charging me a lot or a little but for the moment it does not matter. For I wander around alleys—they are not dark in this section of the city—and the first thing I see is a building: "Agricultural Department" so I nosey in and send my card and in about two minutes I meet Mohammed Ali Bokhary.
>
> I tell him about my missions and that is what he is interested in. I tell him about deserts and desert reclamation and that is what he is interested in. I tell him about salt-water from the ocean and that is what he is interested in. I tell him about reclamation of saline soils and that is what he is interested in. I even tell him my private ventures and that is what he is interested in . . .

*Likely the American Academy of Asian Studies.

> At the moment Lahore is very beautiful and I am not far from the Zoological Gardens where I met or rather was contacted by A. A. Shah on my previous visit. The whole city is in flower. But what do you get? Daffodils? Pansies? Violets? Jonquils? Well you find Dahlias in full bloom and Hollyhocks seeking salvation in Heaven and Cosmos all over the place. This is Springtime, *n'est-ce pas?* You also do see Pansies but no lilaceous or orchidaceous plants. The Roses are here but not in profusion. There are Gaillardias and Marguerites and Coreopsis and Sweet William. The most profuse flower is of the same order in structure but looks like a Bougainvillea in color; I don't know its name. There are several flowers which I cannot name . . . There is still much to be done both on the actual plants of Pakistan and the plants that may be grown here . . .
>
> In Multan American aid is very active until 4 P.M., building, feeding, instructing, helping—and after 4 P.M. all the Americans go down and teach the Pakistanis a game called baseball. In Lahore they must be different Americans for I have seen many a baseball field and hardly a cricket field, but baskets all over the place. Only it is Ramadan and as you are not supposed to drink during the day time at the moment they are not in use. But I never have seen so many basket-ball courts . . .
>
> Anyhow I have arranged sundry lectures on everything from Islamic Philosophy to research in Genetics and how to get around in modern Cairo. I have so many people in the American Consulate wishing to hear me that I have arranged for private talks.[658]

Secretary-General Cheema of the Food and Agriculture Ministry had made the outline for Sam's trip. As he made his way through the country, Sam was introduced to the Siddiqui family by Abdul Rahman and learned that they were interested in Sufism. From the political attaché in Karachi he learned that there was a research scholar in Washington with the same interest. Connections such as these happened over and over in Ahmed Murad's travels as door after door was opened to him.

Following are several excerpts from Sam's March 18 letter to his friends at Pakistan House in San Francisco. He recounted one of many readings he had from clairvoyants during his travels:

> One does not have to accept the statements of clairvoyant Munshi Bashir Ahmed. He was waiting . . . and called my name out from a dis-

> tance. Later he told my future, using two or three of his several methods. He is positive that I shall live long, gain fame or influence or both and in general succeed in life. He bade me take things very seriously, and I am doing just that whether his predictions turn out correct or not.[659]

Sam experienced his previous visit to Lahore as though it were "a compilation from the works of Marion Crawford, Rudyard Kipling and Talbot Mundy," giving him what he called the happiest hours of his whole life. And now the same was happening all over again.

While at the University's Fine Arts Department Mrs. Ahmed gave Sam a number of books, which he planned to either keep or send to the Rudolph Schaeffer School. Sam believed that Rudy had received warped impressions of the art of the India-Pakistan subcontinent that omitted Moghul and other Islamic influences, an omission he hoped to someday rectify.

Sam wrote further about the spirit of the art found at the Department of Fine Arts:

> The class work and the exhibitions show a remarkable freedom of spirit. There are traditions but they are not necessarily from one direction, being Islamic, Indian, British or French—not much Persian here . . . Few of the artists went through periods of "civilization" but seem to have passed quickly from childish art to the newer methods. I gave the class a short talk on my views of spirituality in art and found they had all come to the same conclusion.

Following Mr. Cheema's guidance, Sam's travels would take him away from Lahore for almost two months. He decided that upon his return he would share with Mahmood Ali Bokhary of the Agricultural Department everything he was able to accumulate. This plan dovetailed well with Lyallpur University's opening session of April 3rd and would give Sam ample time to make the return trip from Rawalpindi if necessary. He wrote,

> I understand that the network of bus lines has been increased. These lines as well as rail and air have both been quite efficient. My main proposal has been to have an international airport either at Lahore or

> Islamabad; and, if the one at Karachi is retained, to arrange tours to Thatta and Mahenjo Daro for Karachi has little to offer. Its hotels are fine but the best amusement are the movies.

On the other hand, Lahore had so much—not only Shalimar Gardens and Badakhshi Mosque, but modern gardens and bazaars. Sam didn't have time to go to the old city but did visit the *dargah* of Mian Mir, where he had previously received guidance from the Sufi Sheikh buried there. His plans to visit either mosques or *anjumans* or *jamias** were constrained by an expected telephone call from the American Friends of the Middle East that he didn't want to miss.

Abdul Rahman had gone ahead with part of Sam's luggage, including gift perfume oils Sam had purchased for Rahman's nephew. Sam was going to remain in West Pakistan for several months at least, and was also scheduled to go to Swat, an area that intrigued him because of the Buddhist art that remained there. He wrote of these plans:

> Whenever I do go to Mardan I shall follow this with a visit to Peshawar, perhaps [arrange] for lectures and then go through the pass to Kabul. I do not wish to remain in Afghanistan but I do wish to see the American Agricultural Attaché there. I also wish to relocate Mr. Spahr, our forestry expert, who may be roaming in either the Peshawar or Quetta areas. There are now large reforestation projects going on in those regions . . .
>
> I am delightfully amazed at the number of friends I have here and the bright hopes for several of my many missions.

Sam also stated his intention to arrange lectures and reports to the American Friends of the Middle East, the South Asian Studies Dept. of the University of California, and perhaps to the World Affairs Council. He closed his letter to the Pakistan House with the words *As-salaam aleikhum,* and his names Samuel L. Lewis and Ahmed Murad Chisti.

---

*Persian and Arabic words, respectively, for gatherings, often educational.

Sam's Letter to the AFME in San Francisco

Ahmed Murad left Lahore on March 18th. Over the next seven weeks he traveled back and forth between Rawalpindi and Abbottabad, considering Abbottabad his "home." True to form, his life was filled with meetings with government officials and spiritual leaders, giving talks, making recommendations to both foreign and domestic organizations, and even some mountain climbing. To get a real taste of the breadth of his activities it is helpful to delve into more details of this period.

In a letter of March 23rd to the AFME, from which several excerpts are presented, Sam wrote:

> The political attachés have been most helpful and perceptive, but the cultural attaché not so. They are either self-satisfied or in Karachi [pro]-Christian and any attitude other than strictly pro-American is dangerous . . .
>
> When I visited your library, or **any** library in Karachi I almost fell over. Here was a library full of authentic books, with **every American authority on Asia listed**. These things don't exist elsewhere. They don't exist in many of our schools or departments for Near East studies in the U.S. (some very important notable exceptions) and they certainly didn't exist in the otherwise fine library in Cairo. The library had an excellent selection and assortment of books but the Near East section was not only small, it contained some very questionable books. The AFME library in Karachi, ought, in my judgment, become the model for all libraries on the near East and Islamics . . .
>
> The library avoids the two evils of not having enough books, or of having the shelves filled with over-advertised works by Europeans which do not explain the Near East at all. *Alhamdu Lillah,* I am very satisfied, perhaps in some sense, for the first time in my life.[660]

Considering many of the previous events and people who had scorned him, it is fascinating to see how well this strongly driven and brilliant man was being accepted throughout Asia and in the Middle East. Sam hoped to introduce a deep approach to religious practice in San Francisco so that "real explanations can be given of living . . . religions by people who know them, and not imaginary descriptions, defenses or criticisms of beliefs of centuries back," which he felt had nothing to do with the world of today.

> I have one slight fear which may be imaginary. When I visited Asia before, the work of Asia Foundation and the AFME did not overlap. Now they are both in Lahore. Perhaps their fields of endeavor are separate. I can report with excellent authority that in S.E. Asia there is competition between American societies organized to promote . . . relations with the Orient and the upshot is that people react just as they did to rival Christian missions. And in Lahore there is a strong reaction to rival Christian missions which seem more keen on rivalry than on Christianity.

Poetry was the most popular art form in that part of the world and had been so for thousands of years. Not only was Sam writing epic poems to great acclaim, he was inspired to start writing short verses as well, which were being sought after for publication in New York.

> Tomorrow is Pakistani Day and I am on the Program. The morning and afternoon will be devoted to parades and sports; the evening to intellectual matters. I have spoken in Abbottabad before and many remember me. This time I shall read from "Saladin" and also perhaps one short Islamic poem. Some of "Saladin" may be translated into Urdu and it is possible that all of it will before I leave the country, *inshallah.*

As an ambassador of goodwill Sam was hoping to get some recognition and assistance, for he could not manage all that was before him. He had rushed into a vacuum in the UAR, and now rushed into opportune times. Although he had been granted the right of residence for a full year, he expected to leave the region in September.

On March 27 Sam wrote of a visitor who he hoped would turn out to be a help for him financially. Having sufficient financial resources was often an issue for Sam. His many activities rarely were focused on serving himself, but rather on serving his ongoing experience of the God reality. Occasionally opportunities appeared such as the one he describes here:

> The other day a Mr. Qureshi came to my rooms. He is descended from an Arab Family which became custodian of the Moghul Court Jewels.*

*Custodian on behalf of Aurangzeb, referred to as the last great Moghul.

> [The jewels] are supposed to have disappeared. I have seen them. He has been negotiating with a Los Angeles firm and it was agreed that transactions could be handled through the Habib-Bank of America hook up. I have written to Conlon Associates on Clay St. about them. I saw by far the largest and purest Rubies in my life and some very ancient specimens too from this region.
>
> It is possible that some business will result though it may take time. The immediate transactions will run up to six figures, and he calculates his heirlooms easily run into seven figures. If God wills and I get even a small commission here, it may change my financial status. This may be slow but my former trip was helped by a similar deal through the sale of Thai Zircons . . .
>
> Qureshi Sahib also has a lot of uncut stones. This is his own possession, as against the heirlooms. He has told me there are many gems in this region and I hope to see some of the mines. But I have been tipped off too to other possibilities. While this would involve far less money, to me it is much more exciting and interesting.[661]

Sam later shared that the authenticity of Mr. Qureshi's stones had been verified: "Every stone has been weighed, tested for 'water'—that is light behavior, chemical formula and age. Not only that, these tests have been recorded and notarized."[662]

Sam eventually began work as part-time secretary to Mr. Qureshi, the more exciting and interesting work referred to above.[663]

Qureshi unveiled to Sam a man Sam initially referred to as Chisti Sahib. This Sufi had been mobbed because he denied the efficacy of political prayers. Sam entered in his diary an item from his fictional *Pukhtunistan News* ("All the News that gives Fits to the Printer"),*

> Chisti Sahib here is very unpopular. He denounced the Mullahs and the Mullahs denounced him and tried to mob him. There were only a hundred people in the mob and Chisti Sahib said the odds were too great—on his side. Unless they got a thousand people to mob him he refused to be mobbed. It was admitted they would not get a thousand people for all Muslims being brothers absolutely, there are so many sects here of people who don't pray together that you can't get a thousand people on

---

*A play on the *New York Times* slogan "All the News That's Fit to Print."

> any side. The mob got so angry at this they refused to martyr Chisti Sahib.[664]

Sam had been told that this Sufi was very poor. But "I called on him and took one look at his eyes—full of love."[665] The Sufi spoke only Urdu and Persian, but Qureshi knew both those languages and English. As a result they all had a very rewarding time together. Most of the time this Sufi, whom Sam now referred to as Khwaja Sahib, explained Moin-ed-din Chisti and Jelal-ud-din Rumi, both of whom used music in their spiritual training. He went on at some length and Sam was inspired to offer to this Sufi the flute chant, which came to him through his whole body. Doing so demonstrated Sam's understanding of Rumi, and Khwaja Sahib said afterward, "Yes, the real flute is in ourselves."[666]

Sam went on to write:

> From the occult point of view the Chisti stories were the most interesting. Khwaja Sahib had many powers and he was able to control the water supply at Ajmir. I told him I had been at the very place and it is mysterious to find a lake high up in the mountains above a desert. I often wondered about it and have talked about it many times.
>
> The essence of Sufism comes in the *auliya,* saint or hierarchal development and a master learns to have control over the elements. This is not nonsense. I am pretty sure that Chisti Sahib has both power and wisdom.* He also told part of my future which corroborated in every detail what the Munshi [Bashir Ahmed] said but added more. Most important is that [Khwaja Sahib] feels I should establish myself . . . still more marvelous is that he came into the room at this point and gave me his blessing! I hope to see him soon and often.
>
> We did a little talking through an interpreter. Both he and another man here are really "disguised saints" operating as very poor men.[667]

The Khwaja Sahib's instruction to Ahmed Murad that he establish himself was itself a prophecy, a prophecy that would more than be fulfilled in the years following Sam's return to the United States. Ahmed

---

*The power Ahmed Murad is referring to is actual power over the elements, the reality of which was in harmony with Sam's life experiences.

Murad would become established in a way that others most likely did not expect, and perhaps not even as he himself imagined.

Visiting the North-West Frontier

While fully engaging himself in this large region, Sam also invited his correspondents to educate themselves on the political situation, of which he felt most people in the U.S. to be sadly ignorant. He wrote:

> There is always another Laos or Czecho-Slovakia or VietMinh in the making. American reports have been turned aside by the press who then criticize the State Department. My records have been accepted by the Foreign Service here. I have met many Pathans and everyone is from Pakistan. The universities are crowded with Pathan students; many of the Urdu-speaking youths go to Europe or Great Britain or the United States for instruction.
>
> The Pushtun leaders have been subsidized by Afghanistan. They have not been very successful and one, the leader, has gone to Soviet Russia. The Russians are encouraging a very reactionary region in Afghanistan, but you can be pretty sure when it is overthrown it will be by a "Castro-Junta" to our dismay.* We have treaties with Pakistan in S.E. Asia and here. We have treaties. The people have in many instances asked me whether it would not be better to "trust" Russia whom they can honestly mistrust than the United States which never seems to be with them in crises.[668]

Sam also wrote about the emergence of local democracy. "[In Abbottabad] I have been the guest of Judge Mohammad Rabbani Khan whom I visited before and who has been in San Francisco. At that time he was operating the largest successful farm in this area. But at the moment there is a movement called 'guided democracy' and I went to meetings."[669] This was a movement toward a distinctive Asian type of democracy. Begum Khan, the widow of the first consul general from Pakistan to San Francisco, whom Sam visited in Abbottabad, had taken leadership with the women to instill a political consciousness in them.

---

* Again Sam foresaw serious disruption down the road.

> Rabbani took me many miles north. We passed a village called "Khaki" and I was told that that is where we got the English word. We arrived at a village called Khwaja [Gan], and I saw what they are doing in what they call B. D. or Basic Democracy. It is sort of cross between the ancient Indian Panchayat and the New England town meeting. It is self-determination with a vengeance. I told a few of them, that it was not my business to comment but that what I thought they needed was tree-planting. I got it right back. At their first meeting I was told that all the simple villagers who, strange to say, were allowed to talk, came out for tree-planting. It was carried with enthusiasm.[670]

Khwaja Gan was also the junction of territories where Pathan was spoken in one direction, Swati in another, Punjabi in a third and Urdu in the fourth. According to Sam, they were learning a common national patriotism and they were delighted with it.

Rabbani Khan also took Sam to Mansehra. Sam detailed the subjects of their first conference as follows:

> 1. Agriculture and reforestation in this region.
> 2. Establishment of the World Congress of Faiths in California.* [Rabbani] was long on the Board of Directors. Bishop Pike may become the leader there. The idea is to present the actual living religions as they are, by their own followers and not by carefully selected Europeans or others who have become the "authorities" and simply gotten by—while our USIA libraries are mobbed by people who are not permitted to present their living culture to us.
> 3. Semitic Archaeology. There is evidence that the Lost Tribes of Israel came to this region. I have the green light from Harvard (Prof. Cross of the *Dead Sea Scrolls*) to ask for a permit for the Dept. of Semitic Archaeology to work here. I am going further into this tomorrow.

Delegation of the Northern Kingdom of Israel, ca. 840 BCE, British Museum

*This Congress originated as the Parliament of World Religions at the World's Columbian Exposition in Chicago in 1893.

4. A serious program of actual cultural exchange between this region and the U.S. without any more intervention of European and sometimes Hindu obscurantists.[671]

Sam's reputation spread not only among the students at the local college but he was acknowledged and honored at multiple institutions of higher learning.

> Before seeing Rabbani I was closeted with the Principal of the local college. There I am now scheduled to give a series of talks on the [relation] of Islamic philosophy to modern science.[672]
>
> I have in mind the four subjects of Logic, Psychology, Physics and Botany.[673]
>
> Ultimately [they] were to be given at Aligarh U. in India but now first to the . . . [Punjab] U. in Lahore. They may also be given to the Islamia U. in Lahore for I recently met a U. C. grad, Dr. Barker. I know very well that some of my past seems very paranoic, but the fact is . . . Dr. Barker had the same difficulties with the same foreigners to whom we have given over the instruction on Near East Culture in the S.F. Bay region—Cal., Stanford, Pacific, and the radio and TV networks, to say the least.[674]

Likewise in Abbottabad, Sam found a kindred spirit in Professor Connaught from San Francisco and Stanford, who taught English at the local college. Sam respected him for mingling with the people and learning from experience, and he felt Connaught and Barker were the best peace ambassadors he knew. Unknown in their hometowns, they were well received and respected in Pakistan.

Sam was a champion of the equality of women in all walks of life. After meeting with Begum Khan he remembered his visit to a sect in Karachi that also supported women's place in their midst. He wrote,

> I have omitted my visit to the Ismailia Sect in Karachi. I went there because I dared not be intolerant, and my personal rejection of Aga Khanism is contrary to my general outlook. I found the staff all highly educated and they are giving an examination to missionaries. These missionaries must be equipped to explain religion in at least two languages one of which must be Arabic or Urdu. College graduates are preferred. They are also keen on the moral outlook . . .

> The biggest thing about this sect, and the most important to me, is their recognition of women. Women are supposed to pray and study religion and are encouraged in it.[675]

On April 1st Sam traveled to Rawalpindi, where he became the guest of his old friend and fellow Sufi Ansar Nasri, the director of Radio Pakistan. He had met Mr. Nasri on his previous trip to the area in 1956 and was delighted to see him promoted to Joint Commissioner of Radio and Communications in Karachi during this stay, even though it cut short their time together. Mr. Nasri was friends with Secretary Shahab ("the real Mr. Big behind the scenes"[676]), who was also a Sufi and secretary to the President of Pakistan, General Ayub Khan. Sam wrote of the outcome of their association:

> I have been having doors open for me all over but at Rawalpindi they opened faster.[677]
>
> Secretary Shahab accepted every single one of my projects and then, with General Ayub's approval added one more. The most personal of these was my poetry and that was demanded on the spot, in his home. I had to copy one section immediately for translation into Urdu. It is being published piece-meal in East Pakistan, but I have discovered an extra copy which will be taken to Rawalpindi by me on my next visit. **I am accepted at the top level as a successor to Iqbal.** Fortunately for me, Admiral Evenson of the American Friends of the Middle East "discovered me" through my poetry; I know it will live.[678]

Sam rarely shared the very human side of his increasing acceptance, but in a letter to his friend Jack Betts he wrote:

> My belonging to the Chishti Order of Sufis has been of great social and material assistance to me although that was not in mind. The strange and immediate acceptance of my poetry plus the OK given on all my projects at the highest level has undoubtedly somewhat un-nerved me. If you struggle and struggle and get a sudden release it is not always easy to adjust.[679]

Sam was delighted to have the opportunity to share local folk dancing in Rawalpindi.

> I have tried to learn Pathan dancing. I have had many promises but most of the students are too busy preparing for examinations. Their common name for Folk Dancing is "Kathak" which is also common to India and there are common elements. But I was told Swati dances were different and Greek.
>
> Well I showed some of the boys some elements of Greek dancing and the riot began—they all proclaimed that the Swati dances are the same! This got me excited and the more I performed the more excited they became.[680]

After returning to Abbottabad from Rawalpindi in late April Sam lived in a hostel near the college, where he spoke to the Junior Science Club.

Samuel Leonard Lewis's character was epitomized by an insatiable desire to learn. He went hill climbing with Arif Khan, and upon hearing that his family was starting both a soap factory and a ceramic factory, he commented, "I shall learn everything I can."[681] Arif took him past the Forestry College. Not surprisingly, Sam wandered in. There he encountered Dr. Abdul Hamid Khan, UC Berkley, 1948. The two of them had an immediate understanding. They shared a mutual friendship with Secretary of Agriculture Cheema, and Sam would later act as the go-between who introduced U.S. State Dept. agricultural adviser Ted Thatcher to Dr. Khan. By October he was listing Dr. Hamid Khan as one of his hosts in Lahore.

Sam later paid a visit to the assistant botanist and the Chief Ecologist at the Forestry College.

> We were together about one hour and a half, and it is agreed that I am to copy the tree list from "California Desert Agriculture" and also look through the bulletins on trees of the Southwest (needed for West Pakistan) and Swamp areas (needed mostly for East Pakistan). There is no question that the problem of water-logging is next after dry climates.[682]

In addition to the plans Sam already had for lectures and conferences in Lahore, he was given leads on where to offer his literature on these subjects, places that might indicate what was needed next in the country. In multiple ways Lahore would remain central in Sam's trip, and he looked forward to reuniting with his deeply respected friend, Major Sadiq, in whose home Sam would be staying.

Ahmed Murad with Major Sadiq and Others in the Punjab

> *I am in Pakistan, in the Punjab which has been the site of innumerable cultures and wars. [Westerners] do not know about these cultures or wars and we know even less about the hearts of peoples. Wesley, there are sciences of the heart as well as the mind and body . . . The medical sciences are not exact. The laws of cause-and-effect do not hold as they do in branches of true sciences. There are too many factors at loose ends.*
>
> SAMUEL LEWIS[683]

Sam had met Muhammad Sadiq during his previous trip to Pakistan when Sadiq was a captain in the East Pakistan army. The connection was immediate and deep, and Sam considered him his spiritual brother. They had sworn "eternal friendship" but had lost track of one another when Sam's address book was stolen. When Sam located him during this journey, Major Sadiq immediately wired to advise that he was living in Lahore. Sam returned to Lahore at the beginning of May and became a guest of Major Sadiq. He said they saw in each other a person who had advanced much in the last five years.

> I am living in the home of Major Muhammad Sadiq . . . We have both had the [same] teacher. A marvelous man whose fame is just spreading now. His name is Maulana Abdul Ghafoor. From him I have learned to treat the world as a whole single body and to learn to appreciate the hearts and minds of other peoples; so I do not travel as a stranger. In San Francisco I sat in audiences or I was shut out of audiences. If I had any ideas, I was seldom permitted to express them. In the Orient, it was totally different. I was admitted into the company immediately of the top sages, and later on of the top industrialists. Here it is no different, nor has it been different in Asia.
>
> The Major has the gift of healing. There is a constant procession of people. Many of his patients have gone to Lourdes and he has even [effected] cures of some who have been there. He does this by the touch, by manipulation, by magnetizing water and by magnetizing bodies. These things are not as [simple] as they [seem]. He has two faculties

which are not recognized in the West. They are called "Spiritual" and no doubt they are spiritual, but this does not make them non-material. The means are not [too] mental. He has a sense of feeling and a sort of sight or insight which enables him to locate and heal; and another faculty which enables him to diagnose when that is necessary. Usually he does not diagnose, but when he is not successful, he checks on the diagnoses of physicians.[684]

The Major was known throughout Pakistan.

He used to live in the city of Jhelum and people came from all over Pakistan. He thinks he has treated about a million people. I saw some cures in my own presence. He also works with hospitals and doctors and I went with him to one hospital on a cancer case and to another on a T.B. case. He works every morning with the army and rests a while in the afternoon. After 5 o'clock he treats people until it is dark, then he goes to hospitals sometimes.[685]

The general basis of his faculty, which we both hold is a grace and not a possession, coincides with the "theories" of Pir-o-Murshid Inayat Khan and some of the details of the applications are the same. Yet because my studies with Pir-o-Murshid have been fairly thorough, I have been able to make a few suggestions.

If we begin with the theory of Jesus Christ that the body is the temple of the holy spirit and [continue] on to include some of the teachings of a Pir who recently died here, we can apply to a complete method of "cure" and sanctification which is entirely in line with the original idea of "savior" which has little to do with divinity or theology, but meant, in a sense, a metaphysical or superphysical healer.

At this point please include all your interests also in psychic phenomena. There is no question that there is a clairtactic power and it seems also to both of us that the higher psychism, as against mediumship, is clearly related to the opening of centres, particularly those which we identify more or less with the Pineal and Pituitary glands. We are going today to *zikr* meetings of the Naqshibandi school of Sufis which set great store on the opening and development of these and other centres.[686]

Sam also mentioned the four schools of medicine he found in Pakistan: Allopathic, Homeopathic, Greek, and Indian. He categorized them as follows: "The last two are traditional from ancient times. The last three all use herb medicines, the Homeopathies being systematic; the Greek approach being based on the 'humors,' the Indian or Ayurvedic, I do not know at all. Between them they seem to [effect] a lot of cures."[687]

On May 9th in a diary entry to his friend Wesley, Sam wrote about his contribution to a difficult case involving Major Sadiq:

> I was thrown immediately into a cancer problem. The Major works with medical doctors and there was a case where he and the doctor had "lost face." The patient was a brother of the doctor and this was not an ordinary doctor but the head of a big hospital. So the loss of face was very serious. Besides, the Major seldom loses cases. He took me to the patient. I said that the man was holding a secret, either a loss or worry or there was somebody or something he hated or feared, or there was an event in his earlier life where in he felt he had [committed] a sin—a sin and not a wrong. But a "sin" is a mark on one's conscience for having done something against a code and is a mental more than an ethical tort. But whether mental or ethical it established a focus of infection and that focus could not be destroyed unless the patient stopped blaming himself. As the semanticists say, "God may forgive your sin but your subconscious own mind will not."
>
> The patient denied this entirely and said he had [a clear conscience].
>
> His case did not improve. The major went again, the patient was adamant, but his pain became terrible. Then the Major [demanded] a showdown and the patient broke down and as soon as he broke down, the Major's methods were effective and in the last days there has been a great improvement.[688]

The Major did not take money for healing although people on occasion spent considerable sums to visit him. In the U.S. Sam was aware that this might need to be handled differently, but funds would come in large part from Pakistan. They were planning a joint venture in California to bring in genuine Oriental philosophy and mysticism, and Sam tried to make arrangements through friends. He reassured his friends that there was no desire to establish a cult, and that in fact it would be a great danger to do so.

Ahmed Murad spoke further about his life in Lahore, starting with his time living in Major Sadiq's house.

> While I was with him there was feast every night. This was hard because it was very warm in the daytime, sometimes the thermometer going to 105°. And I could not walk in the heat and besides everybody treated me like a great person. Not only did the servants wait on me but all kinds of people and it is hard to believe that even some of the richest and holiest men in Pakistan waited on me. It was like living in a dream. Sometimes I went to mansions for feasts and the other times army officials and doctors and generals and ex-generals and top people in all walks of life came to see me.[689]

Sam also wrote on this theme to his friend Wesley:

> Last night I was to dinner [with] an industrialist who is striving to expand the cement industry here. We had a very good number of talks. Generally the people present looked to me—on all subjects. It is very nice but so totally different from California it is hard to adjust to. I am treated with tremendous respect. When one goes into a room and not only ordinary people, but high government officials, army officers, bankers, industrialists and especially college professors stand when I come in, do not sit down until I sit down and listen attentively to everything I say it is hard to picture we are in the same universe.[690]

He wrote to his friends Fred and Corinne, saying, "I have long foreseen intuitively that this period would be the most dramatic or the most important in my life. If I had not foreseen it I should not have been able to adjust to it . . . Lahore has now on each visit given me the most blessings of any place in the world."[691]

To his friend Lemanda Sam wrote:

> You see . . . this is my home and these are my people. In this life I had to be born in a Western body so I could bring Oriental teachings to America. But this is new and hard for me. It is easy to live with the Punjabis either on this side or on the Indian side. I feel at home with that. I also feel at home with the Pathans.[692]

Sam had by now already addressed thousands in Lahore and was to speak on his experience of "Islamic Art in Cairo." He continued to reflect on America:

> People have, of course, every right to reject Sufism, but in a world of international relations we should at least know something of its

> operations and its personnel. I have failed, and perhaps it is my own fault, to reach the Near East Department [at UC Berkeley] (which relies on European humbugs too). I have a list of untouched subjects for research ranging from Aramaic archaeology to the music of the dervishes, and from the natural resources of Pakistan to the continuance of the caste-system in South Asia. Sometimes I long to return to the campus, but today every door is opening here in every direction because the people want to love Americans and to be loved, to know about us and to have us know about them.[693]

He ended his reflections on the world situation with these words,

> There can be no peace without friendship. Otherwise it is just status quo or armistice. Getting rid of arms without getting rid of hatreds is wasteful and useless. We talk about "education" but half the time we mean propaganda rather than information.[694]

Ahmed Murad and Sufi Figures of Pakistan

> *I am today to learn about Abdullah and Ahmed. Those who proclaim* Mohammedar-Rassoul-lillah *let them prove it by radiating love, peace, justice, tranquility and every sort of healing. I am still in the stage of learning. I was never told I should be or become a Murshid. I even like my spiritual duties and do not seek any others until it is so ordered by Pir-o-Murshid or* Rassoul *or Allah.*
>
> SAMUEL LEWIS[695]

While in Lahore, Ahmed Murad met Khawar Khan and members of her family. She later became his goddaughter, devoted student, and Khalifa; he gave her the spiritual name Saadia.

In a documentary filmed in the year 2000,[696] Saadia shared her recollections of meeting Ahmed Murad during the period 1961–62. Saadia's mother had passed, and Saadia was living with her grandparents and her aunt, Bibijan. Bibijan had become a mother figure for her and though she was a very godly woman, she could not answer questions that sprang from Khawar's heart, thirsting to know God. Khawar was teaching at a local college, having already earned two Masters degrees, and had just come home when her aunt rushed in saying, "Hurry. Hurry. There is an American Sufi here I think you need to hear." Khawar doubted that this

American could teach her anything since Americans came to Pakistan in search of a spiritual master, but she knew she must obey her elder.

After entering Major Sadiq's home with her aunt and waiting 30 minutes, Khawar asked to use the restroom. She started out in the direction indicated, then involuntarily turned in a different direction and opened a curtain. "Here was this saintly man. A luminous face. I was just wonderstruck and stood there motionless. He was in deep *murakkabah.** I kept looking at the face—just full of Divine Light which we call Nur. I had never seen a face like that before in my life. Although I had met people from all different religions, never that face." After an indeterminate amount of time, Ahmed Murad looked up, motioned Khawar to enter, and said, "Come in, my daughter." He placed his hand on her head, which in Pakistani culture signifies "you are my daughter." Khawar said her feelings were indescribable. "The only thing I remember is I thought I was transported to another world; it wasn't that room; it wasn't a friend's house."

She wanted to invite Sam to their home for dinner. However, her grandfather was a scientist and could not abide religious people. When Sam was described to her grandfather as an American visiting Pakistan on an agricultural mission, an invitation was immediately extended. Sam came and spoke with the grandfather over dinner exclusively about agricultural matters. Since God was never mentioned, Khawar came to understand that Sam's "heart speaks to everybody: his heart tells him what to say where and to whom. That comes intuitively only to men of God who are God realized, and he was God realized."

Khawar's aunt became very fond of Sam, so she and Khawar would follow him around wherever he went, introducing him to family and friends at large. One day Sam announced to Khawar, "Khawar, you are my goddaughter." She couldn't imagine herself being any happier. She was in her 20s at the time and knew nothing of Sufism. In fact, she had only a basic understanding of Islam since she had attended a school where Bible studies were compulsory rather than Qur'anic studies.

Her initiation likewise came as a surprise. The college where she taught closed early one day in June due to excessive heat and humidity.

---

*Spiritual concentration on the name of Allah.

She came home for lunch and was surprised when Sam rang the doorbell. He had her follow him outside, perform ablutions, then enter the family's attached prayer room. After two rounds of prayer, which Khawar followed along in performing, Sam took her hand, said the *Fatiha,** recited the *silsila,* gave her the name Saadia and initiated her into the Chishti lineage. "Allah has witnessed this initiation. Do you accept the initiation?" "What could I say? I said Yes. But I didn't know what initiation meant—which of course he taught me later."

Sam took Saadia to several *dargahs,* where he provided her with teachings. At many of them he would circumambulate singing the Three Wedding Gifts.† People would drop what they were doing and join him. "He was like a magnet. There was a charisma about him, indescribable in words."

One of Sam's teachings to Saadia was to open the eyes and ears of her heart. "Then you'll think you're in a paradise." Saadia was to witness the realization of this very teaching.

Renowned Islamic professor Seyyed Hossein Nasr spent time with Saadia, and later wrote to Sam:

> Honorable Sufi Ahmed Murad Chisti,
>
> It was a real spiritual pleasure and happiness for me to meet Khawar Khan in my last trip to Lahore and through her to learn something about you. Thank you also for your kind letter. The fraternity of Islam to which that of *faqr*‡ or *tasawwuf* is added travels over the greatest distances embracing all of those who follow the path toward Allah or who have reached the goal in a single community. I hope, *inshallah,* to have the honor of seeing you some time whether it be here in the East or in America . . .
>
> During this last visit to Lahore with Khawar Khan we visited the tomb of Hujwiri§ with whom you are so close. The great saint whose

*The *Fatiha* is the first chapter (*surah*) of the Qur'an.

†*Hadith* tells that when Muhammad's daughter Fatima requested a servant, Muhammad taught instead that these three *wazaif* would serve her for life: *Subhanallah* (glory be to God), *Alhamdulillah* (praise and gratitude to God), *Allahu Akbar* (God is the most great).

‡Choosing a path of "poverty" to attain mystical knowledge and intimacy with Allah. One who chooses such a path is referred to as a *faqir* or *fakir*.

§Sayyid Ali al-Hujwiri, Medieval Sufi intellectual and theoretician, who sought to establish balance among all dimensions of Islamic thought and practice, with Sufism as the

> Persian [book] *Kashf al-Mahjub* has always been so close to my heart penetrated my heart at that time in another way and much grace was received through the visit.
>
> I usually reside in Tehran (being a professor at the Faculty of Letters of Tehran University) and would be happy to meet any of your friends who come by. Meanwhile I pray Allah's benediction and peace be upon you and ask for your prayers as well. May you prosper in your task.[697]

When Sam later left Pakistan to return to the U.S., he asked Saadia to rely on the protection of Sufi Barkat Ali of Salarwala, Pakistan. Sufi Barkat Ali was a sheikh whom Sam and Major Sadiq had met on the sheikh's land and with whom Ahmed Murad had connected very deeply. Saadia took Seyyed Nasr to visit Barkat Ali, whose land contained only mud huts as living quarters. It is evident that the eyes and ears of the professor's heart were open, for upon leaving, Saadia quoted Nasr as commenting to Barkat Ali, "You live in a paradise."

Sufi Barkat Ali became a key figure in Samuel Lewis's life and a living Pir-o-Murshid for him. Although the details of their meeting in 1961 are not known, Sam included an overview in "Vision and Ritual in Sufism." At that time he indicated that his activities centered around Major Mohammed Sadiq.

Sufi Barkat Ali (1979)

> Major Sadiq was pursued and transferred at the behest of a "counter-intelligence" and wherever he was sent there was a saint waiting for him. This is a long story but ultimately he met Sufi Barkat Ali, the former factotum of Field Marshal Auchinlek, head of the British Army during the war.
>
> My meeting with Sufi Barkat Ali exactly duplicated that with the American Christian Mystic, Rufus Moseley.* I became [Barkat Ali's] disciple.

---

animating spirit of the whole.

* Sam had encountered Moseley and, in Sam's words, it was "love at first sight." See "The Relevance of Eastern Religions to Western Youth," ca. 1967, Archives.

Murshid Samuel Lewis, now designated Sufi Ahmed Murad Chisti

Sam later described his encounter with Sufi Barkat Ali as one of "instant recognition." He stated that the Pir more fully manifested *fana* and *baqa** than all the "holy men and saints of all faiths" that he had met. And it was Sam who encouraged Barkat Ali to secure a typewriter and start writing letters, something the latter embraced wholeheartedly. They maintained an active correspondence for the rest of Sam's life.

Early in 1962 Samuel Lewis was appointed by Pir Sufi Barkat Ali as a full Sufi Murshid of the combined Chishti, Qadiri and Sabri Orders† and was "given precedence over the other Khalifs or successors to the Pir."[698] Samuel Lewis then received the full designation Sufi Ahmed Murad Chisti in a ceremony attended by approximately 500 people.

The robe that Sam had seen in vision during his 1925 retreat reappeared during his time in Asia, first in New Delhi in 1956 at the *dargah* of the great Urdu poet Amir Khusro.‡ When Khusro appeared in vision to Sam and presented him with the robe, he said, "I initiate you into the school of Jelal-ud-din Rumi as the successor to the late great poet, Mohammed Iqbal." [699] Samuel had already started writing poetry that was reaching acclaim in the Near East. Then the robe was again given in vision to Samuel at the *dargah* of Moineddin Chishti as described in

---

*After emptying/annihilation of the self (*fana*), *baqa* is the state of living as a purer, truer manifestation of God: with, through, in, and for God.

†Sam explained, "Pir Barkat Ali combines the *tasawwuf* of the Chisti, Kadiri, and Sabri Schools. The Chisti use music, mainly, and there have been some excellent *kawwals* (songs of devotion) presented there by individuals and groups. The Kadiri teaching takes into consideration the use of repetition of spiritual phrases, mostly from Holy Qur'an and all in Arabic. The Sabri School has a moral training, not too different from that offered in the Indian Bhagavad Gita, so that one can practice a sort of 'indifference' under all circumstances." From "The Lotus and the Universe," undated, Archives.

‡It would be difficult to overstate the stature of mystic, poet, singer, musician, and scholar Amir Khusro, known variously as the father of *qawwali*, the father of Urdu literature, and the "voice of India."

Chapter 11. Finally, the robe seen in vision three times previously was physically bestowed upon Samuel by Sufi Barkat Ali.

Sam later wrote about his meeting with two important figures, *Khalandar* Ali Mastana and Pir Golra Shereef.

> The *Khalandar* Ali Mastana . . . saw my full person and mission—it has turned out that way anyhow. Then, after denouncing Golra Shereef he took me [to see him].* It was strange because that night I had had a visit with this Pir and when we went there everything happened as in the vision. The Pir dismissed everybody and gave a prediction which has proved to be absolutely correct, correct [down] to details.[700]

The prediction directly related to what would turn out to be Ahmed Murad's future life in America. Later, Sam described what had happened to him overall: "I have met, I am told, more holy men, saints, and spiritual teachers than any foreign visitor to date. My last was to Golra Shereef; very, very satisfactory."[701]

Ahmed Murad later wrote Barkat Ali about the *Khalandar.* Several excerpts from the letter follow:[702]

> [The *Khalandar*] wishes, or is guided, to bring the message of spiritualism to my country and to other countries. He has given me many evidences of his powers and what he calls *kashf,* but what he calls *kashf* is not the same as what I call *kashf.* Which does not mean that I am right and he is wrong. Only his *kashf* seems to be concerned with seeing and an ability to escape from the body, to function in "heavens," to meet saints, and to have grand faculties . . .
>
> Now I am receiving instruction from the *Khalandar* and he believes he is one of the most powerful men in the world, and maybe he is one of the most powerful men in the world. He knows much about sacred phrases, he undoubtedly goes into heavens and he may have miraculous faculties. Maybe he is one of the few who has them and maybe many have them. He says he has 38,000 followers and they will help him to travel. I have no follower. I am going over the globe a second time. I have crossed the United States many times. I crossed the United States without having 50 rupees at any time and yet lived in fine homes

---

*The *Khalandar's* views on Shereef were complicated.

> and hotels as well as in poor places. I had nobody but Allah and He showed me. This was a different kind of *kashf.*
>
> The *Khalandar* asked me to ask Mohammed where he belonged in the assemblage. I am only in the rear rank of the assemblage. I have not been allowed to see many there, only Isa (Jesus). But I told him I could not ask Mohammed because I had already asked Allah. He did not seem to realize that if I could ask Allah this might be higher than asking Mohammed.
>
> I told him he was greater than I in all but [one] thing—I could be a greater pupil than he. I could learn from him, I could listen to him but he could not listen and learn from me and although in *rubuyyat** and *kashf* and *shuyukhuyat*† he was far above me, I was a greater *mureed.* This rather surprised him . . .
>
> When I left the *Khalandar* yesterday convinced of his great power, a flock of little boys followed me. I danced for them and finally bought each one a sweet. I have been showing little boy's games. I am nearly 65 but when I function [as] *Abdullah*‡ I do not feel any age. Indeed I was surprised in looking into the mirror the other day that I am looking younger. This has happened before. I have died before death§ and my vigor and looks are the best answer I have to that devil-show-off¶ or whatever he is called at 'pindi . . .
>
> The success of my poetry ends [the *Khalandar*'s] claims and his false school forever because they demonstrate nothing, only claim. I claim nothing, only demonstrate, *inshallah.*
>
> I have asked the *Khalandar* to answer me two questions:
>
> a. Why is there starvation in West Pakistan?
>
> b. Why is there unhappiness in West Pakistan?

Ahmed Murad records no responses from this man who claimed so many powers. Sam continued:

---

* *Rubuyyat* or *rubaiyat* refers to poetry.

† The life path to be undertaken by a Sheikh.

‡ An *Abdullah* has the life path of one who effaces all ego claims and works tirelessly as a satisfied servant of God.

§ To "die before you die," a practice recommended by Muhammad, means to release all attachment to identity.

¶ This is a joking nickname for Sheikh Dewwal Shereef, who will be introduced in the next section.

He claims Abdul Kadiri-Gilani is the greatest of the great. I claim nothing. He knows *mushahida** and disclaims *murakkabah.*† I try to practice *murakkabah* in the way you showed me in the writings of Abdul Kadiri-Gilani. I keep on succeeding even when I have no faculty for success . . .

Today I have to meet the *Khalandar* again. He sees in all three worlds, so to speak. I have not even got good sight in this world.‡ But seeing in all worlds and functioning with full mind and full heart are different.

There are those places in this universe above assemblages, even above in faculties, which are the well-springs of all blessings. I may be just sipping through one little straw from these well-springs but if I sip truly then I may be fulfilling the purpose of my life. It is exceedingly difficult to be compelled or impelled to take teachings about Mohammed from others and have these different from and often contrary to *Hadith.* I am not concerned with titles, I am concerned with functions.

Sufi Ahmed Murad's influence in Pakistan spread and it has endured. In 2014, Sheikh Asim Maharvi Chishti of Pakistan was interviewed at *Khankah* SAM in San Francisco. Quotations that follow are from that interview.[703]

Sheikh Asim's family had much knowledge of Hazrat Inayat Khan, Ahmed Murad Chisti, and Sufi Barkat Ali. As representatives of the Chishti Nizami lineage, the father, grandfather, great grandfather, and more had been active in these men's life stories. As he moved into adulthood, Asim embraced the Sufi path and received permission to teach.

Asim opened the conversation.

I have to admit one thing. I knew of Murshid Sam Lewis, but not this name Sam Lewis. I never knew that because back there in Pakistan where he was in the late '50s and early '60s he was always known as Ahmed Murad . . . [Back then] not many people knew Urdu. There

---

* *Mushahida* is a practice of contemplation in which a devotee who has cleared away all impressions is able to be God's representative to humanity within the realm of what he cares about. Murshid Sam would often quote Edna St. Vincent Millay's poem "Renascence" about dying and rebirth: "The world stands out on either side no wider than the heart is wide."

† *Murakkabah* is developing the faculty of concentration and becoming at one with what you are concentrating on.

‡ Sam was three times rejected because of poor eyesight when he applied to be a soldier in World War I.

were few people with whom actually he was talking English; they were in company with him. But with others, they were having his good company and the spiritual transformation, but that level of communication was not in English!"

Asim went on to describe what he knew from his family about Sufi Ahmed Murad and about Sufi Barkat Ali:

Now Sufi Barkat Ali Sahib migrated from India. He was not a resident of Pakistan. When the separation [from India] happened in 1947, he moved from Ludhiana Punjab India to the Punjab in Pakistan. My great, great grandfather's *dargah* was the main Chishti Nizami *dargah* there . . . [Barkat Ali] and . . . my maternal grandfather became friends and they studied together for a couple of times and then they traveled . . . and my grand grandfather had a few pieces of land in the area where later Sufi Barkat Ali got all his *khankah:* Lyallpur . . .

It was my grandfather's property but it was of no [agricultural] use, and Barkat Ali was his dear friend trying to settle at some place, so he gave that land to him . . . We had our *khankah* at Pakpattan Sharif also, so Sufi Barkat Ali used to prepare at Pakpattan Sharif at the shrine of Sheikh Baba Fariduddin Ganjshakar, but he never really lived close to there or to my family.

We use this word *gora.* Gora means "white." The elders used to say that a *gora* was here, a white man was here, and that was referring to Sufi Ahmed Murad. I was very rebellious at the beginning of all this tradition, even though I was born into it and Sufism was in the air I breathed. So they used to give me [lectures] saying you who were born here, you are not following the tradition or anything, and this man from so many thousands of miles traveled to learn this. But you know as a youth you just listen and then you ignore.

There were so many stories of how Ahmed Murad was searching for spirituality and how he conveyed it to people shows what he meant to them. He was the sort of person such that he would go into the fields and work with the farmers.

I agreed: "Sam had no sense of class distinction. He would go shopping wherever, even 'bent can' stores, and would treat everyone the same, just as if he was talking to the Dalai Lama. Yet he would be talking to the man at the checkout counter." I told Sheikh Asim of having been with Sam at such a store. "The checkout man barely listened to Murshid

Sam, who said, 'I am going to a grand conference of religions in Geneva, but I am not going to tell them to love one another. They can't do it. But I will tell them to respect each other.' Different kinds of people didn't matter to him. It was the same. Sam's effacement was in Allah."

Asim came to the States in 1995 to study. He had been told by his grandfather to try to find his old friend Sufi Ahmed Murad Chisti, but had been unsuccessful. He had no way of knowing that Sam had passed on by then. Sheikh Asim began his 2014 journey from the East Coast to the West Coast taking Route 66, a famous historic highway. His *mureed* and companion Brother Wasif said, "We are on a route to see the life and things, so we should search for some other things."

In Ohio Asim met Sheikha Munira Reed, who was from Murshid Sam's lineage. She told him about Lama Foundation and Murshid Sam's *dargah* being there, but she didn't mention the name Sufi Ahmed Murad Chisti. Taking the approach of "seeing other things," Asim ended up at Lama and discovered it housed the *dargah* of the man he had been sent to find. He stayed for a few days and an inspiration in Sam's voice came to him: go to San Francisco. He was encouraged by Lama residents to follow that advice and to meet me. Sheikh Asim wanted to experience how Murshid Sam's *khankah* felt, and he felt very much at home when he stayed here.

I gave him a copy of *Siva! Siva!/Crescent and Heart,* poems Murshid Sam wrote. *Crescent and Heart* was written in attunement with Khwaja Moineddin Chishti. Sam felt he was in a similar position as Moineddin Chishti, a messenger in a strange culture, trying to bring forth the Chishti teachings. Likewise, he identified with the story of Lord Shiva with his consort and his knowledge of all the Yoga systems.

I continued:

> Every section begins with, "Says the Khwaja . . .", so he's in that feeling but he's also in his own sense of being here in America. The first part of the book is his work on Shiva in which he goes into all the different yoga systems that Shiva represented, because Murshid Sam was trained in everything. He was very much a universalist. He was ordained already to be a Buddhist teacher, Sufi teacher, and Hebrew teacher. Also Hindu because he had that ability to be in the moment . . . He would go into a Krishna shrine in India and he had this gift of producing the flute of

Emperor Akbar, early universalist

Krishna from inside of himself. He would just walk in, do his *pranams,* sit on the altar and then he would release this flute of Krishna. He showed "I am Krishna. I am Shiva. I am a prophet." It was in that sense of the One Teacher, the One Teacher of all Who takes many forms.

And he presented his students the Qur'an in that context, and made it clear it accepts all the messengers. Yet not one [of his students] who came to him was a Muslim. Everybody that came was from some other background or had no religious background or they'd given up religion for good. People were drawn by the experiences they were having, and they were looking for someone to be able to throw some light on it. Sam hadn't really decided until 1966 that he would teach these young people and teach Sufism. He decided to proceed that way, but he very much loved the legacy of Emperor Akbar and of Dara Shikoh. He felt very, very close to that.

Emperor Akbar was a universalist like Samuel Lewis, and among the wise things he did was to establish in Fatehpur Sikri the world's first meeting place for a continuing debate, inviting all the world's religions to come. Sam also felt very close to Dara Shikoh, the elder son of Shah Jahan, because he was a brilliant Sufi practitioner who was loved by the people. Dara's teacher was Mian Mir. Ahmed Murad had meditated at Mian Mir's tomb in Lahore and he, like few others, received many teachings through the saint's ability to continue communicating after leaving the body. Dara Shikoh was assassinated by his younger brother Aurangzeb, who wanted to claim all the power. Many scholars have called this event the beginning of the fall of the Moghul dynasty.

Sheikh Asim continued:

> Inayat spent most of his time here in the West but he visited Pakistan also. When he was on his travels [in western India], he visited the Punjab, present day Pakistan. There was one bureaucrat who wrote a book, and in one of its chapters he mentioned Hazrat Inayat Khan's visit to Pakistan and his meeting different people there. Probably at that time

> he was not known. Maybe since Sufi Ahmed Murad went there, probably that was the time when our people came to know more about Hazrat Inayat Khan.

That seemed right to me. "I know Murshid Sam said as much. He felt he had the obligation to present Hazrat Inayat Khan back to the people there because they didn't know who he was or what he'd done or what he had brought to the West."

Sheikh Asim agreed. "Yes. Probably this reintroduction was done by Murshid Sam over there. By the time when I was growing up, what I was listening about Inayat Khan was already known to people over there."

Again, I was in complete agreement. "I'm sure you are right about it, because Murshid Sam went to all the places and he was not someone who would be a tourist. He would go right to the heart. He would find the Sheikh."

Sheikh Asim continued:

> That's probably the time when he liked the role of Dara Shikoh, because Dara Shikoh was a disciple of Hazrat Mian Mir. And every Sufi, all the Wali Allah, after attaining the Unity, still has faculties that function, *azmizad* as we call it. He spent his life mostly secluded away from people. There are not many people who go to him now. Today, if you go to his *mazar,** you will find that peace is there. There are not many visitors or pilgrims visiting his place, but Mian Mir had this aesthetic sense in his life, and after his physical life that *mazar* of his became a courtyard of peace as such. And in a sense he doesn't allow many people to come there. Those who truly come and visit there get the peace.

I added that when Ahmed Murad had been there on retreat, he had walked from Khawar Khan's home through the extremely hot weather to the *mazar* every day for several weeks. The Saint then had spoken to him saying among other things that the real meaning of *Allahu Akbar* is "peace is power."

I asked, "Did you know Sufi Barkat Ali?"

---

*Mausoleum.

Sheikh Asim replied:

Yes, I saw him as a child. He didn't have any sons, but the daughters and his son-in-law sometimes came to our center. Now they have made an organization by the name of *Daar-ul-ehsaan* and they have opened some kitchens to feed people. Sufi Barkat Ali had this project of *Qur'an Mahal.* That is where they are storing all the Qur'ans they have and those that were given to them. He was a person who was busy doing *zikr* most of the time, offering *zikr.* Those were his two attributes which always dominated his personality and the humbleness he had, but he was very firm and he would crack jokes and sometimes hit the *mureeds* also. "What are you doing here? Just go away!" And you know the *mureeds* are like your family: your son or daughter, so sometimes out of your love, you become louder unto them. He would cook and do *zikr* all the time. *Zikr* was dominant for him. And I once had a chance to sleep in his garden. I myself heard the *zikr* going on, although he was not there physically, and I was simply in it sleeping on. So that's how he was. And he had enormous love for the Chishti *sharifs,* especially Hazrat Baba Fariduddin Ganjshakar . . .

I had this urge that probably my Sheikh will ask me to read, all night some *zikr* or do some meditation. I mean, just like any person who has this yearning and this quest and who is just willing to do something. But what happened interestingly with me was that whenever I visited my Sheikh, he sent me out for hunting. And for 4 months I was being sent for hunting. I was hunting all the time, although I never had any interest in hunting! I was a person who loved to read and would love poetry or nature or sitting and meeting people probably. But I was never a hunter. After 3 months, this frustration within me got to that boiling point when I literally cried before him. He said that you will understand one day why I am making you learn to be a hunter. And before he passed away, he was in the hospital bed and I was standing beside him just doing massage on his shoulders, and he said, "Do you remember when you came here you cried, and you were not happy with what I was doing with you? And now you understand what are the qualities which a hunter gets. First of all, it is patience. He is very patient. Then he knows how to hide himself. Then his senses are attentive, and then he has stillness, and all his senses are watching on the target when that is coming up. You have stillness, you have patience, and you sit for hours and hours waiting for the goat or the deer to come. And then you only need to press the trigger once." And then he gave me the examples

> of the clerics and of the sheikhs at the time—that they are not the hunters! "So hunt! Everything goes away because the clerics are standing in the limelight. In the time and day where you are entering, probably the Sufis should be more like the samurais and the hunters. You should be focused on the work and not get into the limelight. Hide yourself. Your work is more important."

I commented that Murshid Sam, too, brought people into an experience. They could appreciate the religion because of the experience, for without it, there was no value. Sheikh Asim said, "Having no experience to me is simply like reading the menu and not tasting the dish."

I said: "The youth are looking everywhere. I know we have a tremendous opportunity here."

Sheikh Asim answered,

> And I am of this belief, as Hazrat Hasan Nizami said in the *ijazat* of Rabia Martin, that spirituality will spring forth from here in the West, not from the East. And the reason why I say that is that people in the East, they are still running for the material things. They are all over-occupied with that. And they have been infused with this fear of hunger and with this fear of insecurity and everything and they are shown that material things will bring them security, so they are running after that. But here, in contradiction, people have almost all the facilities and now they are looking beyond the material. Because the material is just material. Here people are more outwardly engaged, and they will engage in real study, even if it takes some 40, 50 years or something like that.

Sufi Ahmed Murad Chisti and Pir Dewwal Shereef

Among the many relationships Ahmed Murad established in Pakistan, one was with a powerful Sheikh, Pir Abdul Majid Khizri, commonly known as Pir Sahib Dewwal (or Deval) Shereef. Sam had been aware of the Pir since his first trip to Pakistan.

> When I had been with Major (then Captain) Sadiq in Dacca in 1956, we had been invited to dinner by his chief, Brigadier Ghulam Mohammed Khan. The "general" (in our terms) was very careful not to throw rank at us in spiritual matters, but told us that sooner or later we would both come to recognize his spiritual teacher. Having then entered into bonds

Pir Dewwal Shereef

with Maulana Abdul Ghaffoor and later with Pir Barkat Ali, we believed we had come to that place wherein we could and would progress without any further "aid." But it was not to be. Pir Abdul Majid Khizri . . . had his *khankah* or headquarters at Islamabad, just north of Rawalpindi. The Brigadier, now retired, had his home nearby.[704]

Ahmed Murad's first encounter with Dewwal Shereef was in the company of Major Sadiq. They had hoped to show the flaws of the Pir, exposing his exaggerated claims. "Hazrat Pir Dewwal Shereef claimed to have received his spiritual illumination through Khizr, that semi-legendary figure who, with Elijah, remain as the 'two guardian spirits' of this world and the next. Those to whom Khizr appears are supposed to be specially blessed."[705] Upon meeting Dewwal Shereef, however, to each of the first six questions Ahmed Murad was asked by the Pir, he responded, "Yes." The Pir then commented, "Before I ask you the seventh question, have you noticed that you've said only 'Yes'? Where do we differ and why won't you become my disciple?"[706] And so it was.

Dewwal Shereef had migrated to Rawalpindi in the 1950s and established a shrine with the support of former President of Pakistan, General Ayub Khan. Ahmed Murad described his relationship with this Sheikh in 1961:

> I was taken to a most important Sufi, Pir Dewwal Shereef. He at once offered everything to me and I am to be his representative in America. He wants me to introduce [Sufis to] spiritual philosophy and healing. He has . . . been most successful in collecting funds for Islamabad University and I have already written Berkeley for reciprocal relations. This is a story by itself.
>
> He is also the Pir of none other than Ayub Khan and visited him twice last week . . . I don't know what people can say when I return to represent the same Sufi teacher as President Ayub has.[707]
>
> I was . . . appointed as field representative of the projected Islamabad University . . . Dr. Kirk of Princeton is the cultural attaché here and we are certainly "brothers under the skin" in so far as non-American,

non-Asian Professors of Oriental subjects are concerned and then some. We had a complete understanding. This work is not so much out of my hands as beyond me—I am only a single person. The American Friends of the Middle East may take over.

Along with this I have been confirmed as the Chief Sufi Teacher for the United States of America—and along with that been [confirmed] as a healer. I have tried nine times to heal people and have been successful nine times. But now I have not only been given increased knowledge as to Sufi and spiritual healing but the whole door of Deaf-therapy has been opened to me, and this will require some research. I am ready both here and there.

Along with my future this was told by Pir Dewwal Shereef exactly the same as Pir Barkat Ali exactly the same as Munshi Bashir exactly the same as Shah Sahib exactly the same as the Sufis at the tomb of Data Ganj Baksh exactly the same as the *Khalandar* exactly the same as the Sikh in Delhi, etc. I am going to write this to Prof. Joseph Rhine* at Duke . . . Anyhow—and this is all conjecture, without exception they say I shall become famous, rich and successful and also married. I am not counting on such fortune but if it comes, I may have to take you and Bob Stice under my wing directly without depending on anybody else.[708]

Sam expounded on his time with the Pir.

When I was living in Rawalpindi, Pakistan, His Holiness, Pir Dewwal Shereef, President of the University of Islamabad, asked me to contact groups in America engaged in what they call "spiritualism" (actually *ruhaniat* which is somewhat broader); that they wanted cultural exchange; that they had already provided a considerable sum for that purpose, allocated and not to be used otherwise.[709]

Hazrat Pir Sahib Dewwal Shereef was called on to superintend the construction of Islamabad University on the site of the new capital of Pakistan . . . The university plans to coordinate the ancient and the modern, to preserve religious and spiritual traditions, to incorporate all aspects of modern knowledge and methodologies, but in particular those arts and crafts which require some use of the hands.

Pir Sahib realizes the weakness of Pakistanis: their unconscious Indian heritages of class and caste, their low regard for certain types of

---

*Founder of the study of parapsychology as a branch of psychology.

> labor and endeavor, and their complete ignorance of the personal habits of Mohammed and his immediate successors.[710]

Ahmed Murad also related experiences he had while in Murree, on a western spur of the Himalayas in Pakistan.

> I spent some days with the Pir at Murree, his Himalayan retreat. As with Paul Brunton, it was not necessary for me to use words or the ordinary means of communication; and, as the heart becomes more alive, this method becomes facile and effective. Our bodies may occupy different portions of "material" space; but in the heart-world there is a totally different sort of arrangement. Attunement is of prime importance.[711]

Ahmed Murad related an encounter between the Pir and one Syed Mahdoodi.

> Syed Mahdoodi, regarded as one of the cultured champions of Islamic conservatism, had come to visit the Pir . . . Dewwal Shereef. This man may be known as *Naqib,* one who acts as an external spokesman for the mystical brotherhoods. The two men had held profoundly different opinions and each seemed rather adamant.
>
> Each had a large following, and there was some uneasiness in Pakistan as to the exact nature of "Islam."
>
> They debated for two hours. At the end of that time, the barrister [Mahdoodi] came from the class-room and sat down on a bench with me (we had not met before): "My whole life is ruined. I have been wrong in everything. All my writings are wrong. All my teachings and contentions are wrong. I have been mistaken in everything. I am ruined." He burst into tears—this from a once proud and self-reliant man.[712]

An answer was given by Ahmed Murad:

> Nothing is wrong, nobody has been ruined. Allah is the Most Merciful and Compassionate, and All-Wise and All-Loving. You have been calling yourself a "Muslim," but you did not know how to surrender in anything. You demanded, you did not concede, you did not surrender. Until this moment you have not had the slightest idea of what peace is or means. Now you have surrendered for the first time and yourself become a submissive one and, being a submissive one, you have become a Muslim, *Alhamdu lillah.*[713]

Sam went on with his report of a visit to the Pir by another Sufi leader:

> The Grand Sheikh of the *khalandars* visited [Dewwal Shereef] while I was at Murree, and it was a strange sight. The old man, then a hundred and fifteen (115) years of age, acted more like a youth in love.
>
> Except for his wrinkled skin, he showed no sign of age. And it was even more remarkable to find the spiritual leader of one School paying much obeisance to the Pir of another Order.[714]

Sam was hopeful about a visit by Pir Dewwal Shereef to the U.S.

> My host for the moment, Malik Hamid, is still determined to liquidate and come to the U.S., and if he will unbend—and he may have to, a door will open. Then Pir Dewwal Shereef and his treasurer, S. Noon, are planning to come to America. They have money and have been successful in raising money. He (the Pir) is a great spiritual healer, etc. and will need services after arrival.[715]

He also previously had high hopes for Major Sadiq's visit, but doubt was creeping in.

> Next the story of Major Sadiq is so complicated, so full of pathos, success—and frustration that I cannot say anything. He has been stationed at Kohat unwillingly and is most[ly] not there. There has been an invasion by Pathans who come for his spiritual healing on such a grand scale the General of his sector wants to remove him. And the Pir . . . also wants [Sadiq] to come to America for his healing; and he, the Major, wishes to come to put through a very large commercial deal. However, he was in an auto accident (only the car, not the riders) and so he missed me at both Lahore and Rawalpindi and his wife has been elsewhere, the house is locked up with my possessions and communication bizarre to say the least, i.e. Snafu.[716]

Sam had hoped for official recognition of either Major Sadiq or himself, especially given his relationship with Pir Dewwal Shereef and by association with President Ayub Khan. Even with all his faculties and his successes abroad, such recognition would be long in coming for Sam in America.

Leaving Lahore and Continuing to India

Sufi Ahmed Murad Chisti had stayed on in Lahore well beyond what he had expected. He had planned to go immediately into India and function as he had before, but frequent appeals to secure a visa for India fell on deaf ears and tested his stamina. He finally received the required documents, but he could no longer include travel to Southeast Asia to see his good friend Phra Sumangalo in his plans. Additionally, Sumangalo was not entirely healthy and had gone on a private retreat in the wilderness.

While no details of Sam's departure from Pakistan are available, he did write from New Delhi in late January, 1962, a letter filled with details of a once-again packed schedule.

A letter dated mid-January came to Sam from Kanhangad, South India. The letter was from Swami Satchidananda, who was a very close disciple of Papa Ramdas. It read:

> Beloved Ram,
>
> We got your long and loving letter of the 9th instant only yesterday. We are glad to know that you are planning to come to Anandashram.
>
> Swami Ramdas' health has not been very good in these days. He is having some liver trouble and is advised to take complete rest.
>
> You may plan your visit as to be here by the 3rd week of February as there are a large number of visitors at present and we have an acute shortage of accommodation. Kindly write . . . again when you are coming here.
>
> Swami Ramdas sends you his hearty love and blessings.
>
> Ever your Self,
>
> Satchidananda[717]

Sam may have briefly visited Anandashram, although he wrote no notes on it at the time. He did write to Swami Akhilananda at the Ramakrishna Mission:

> I came to India with added spiritual missions and began visiting holy places. Perhaps it was dramatic, but more perhaps it was real that going to the tomb of the martyred [Sufi] Surmad I whispered into the attendant's ear: "Dara Shikoh." He almost fainted and then warmly embraced me and gave me the covering over the tomb. For it is certain that in this

life I continue the work of the Moghul Prince, and . . . there is no nonsense about it.[718]

Ahmed Murad indeed walked in the footsteps of Dara Shikoh, who likewise sought to bring the different religions into harmony.

Meanwhile my immediate host, one Mithal, also took me to Rehana, a Muslim born lady who seems to favor the Indians. They say that the top people, the President, Vice-President and Prime Minister all favor [her]. On a re-visit I also met a great Pundit. Unlike the Europeans and Americans who "teach" Indian Philosophy, he asked me for my discourse on Gita. I became naught. All I remember was saying:

The Gita Is the Flute of Krishna Turned Into Poetry.

Who took over, I do not know, but the wisdom poured out from the lips. Much of the *sanatana dharma* is to be restored, but by what means I do not always know.

I was fortunate, despite Independence Day, to have half an hour with Dr. Radhakrishnan, terminated by me, not him. Steps have been taken to bring the philosophers of integral outlook of East and West together—and not the apologists for integration or praise of *Vijnana, Prajna* and *Ananda* who cannot and do not function.

Sam in another letter commented, "My job with Dr. Radhakrishnan is to bring the Integralists of the East and West together."[719] Sunday evening my host and I parted, he to go to Krishnamurti and I to the Vedanta Temple.

I was in Lyallpur. The erstwhile host was too busy to care for me and almost locked me in a room which happened to [contain] his Indian Library. There were the works of all the recent "liberators" and there was a chance to compare them. There was no comparison. One had empty words. One had empty claims. One was so full of intellectualisms that even the gods would get tired of [reading] him. Another was full of self and nothing else. Another was empty of self and nothing else.

Then I picked up a book of Swami Vivekananda. The words became living flames and danced all around me. They were flames of pink-love. I could not read, only meditate and adore. Half a page proved to be too much but the experience did not prove to be too much.

Of course claims like these mean nothing to many people but this is exactly what happened. I type it here also because your Brother, Swami Maharaj Ranganathananda receives a copy and I did not relate this to him.

Tea in India

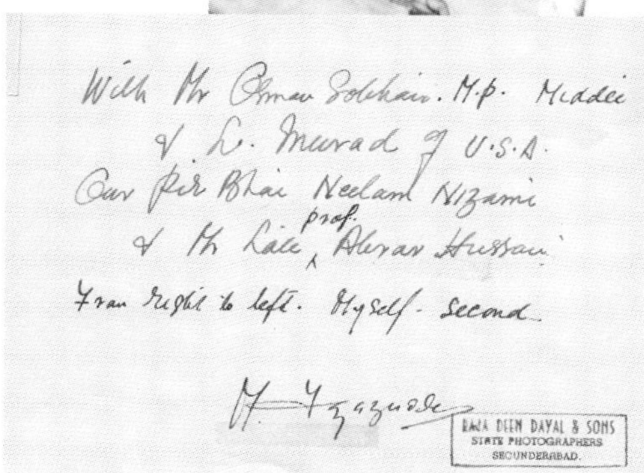

On Sunday night last [I] visited the Ramakrishna Mission. The buildings, not started when I was there before, are completed. The lecture hall was filled by a large audience of high caliber. The talk was to the point—words and symbols can confuse and mislead; spiritual experience does not. The whole stress was on experience. It was the proof-of-proofs.

My own discourses always include: "I am a scientist. What I know of nature comes from study, investigation, research and hard work—all experience. There are no speculations and no emotional adoration of great scientists; only the knowledge that comes as knowledge comes, out of life itself. Spiritual knowledge is not different in this excepting that the knowledge is of a different order."

This Sunday night the meeting was in open air and all talks but one in English with a loudspeaker. There was also a very large audience. In the morning I had gone to the Dilip Kumar Roy Ashram, an audience of about 200, clean-clothes, intellectual appearances, etc. But this was a much larger audience and I should say 2,000. But the same about clothes and appearances. There is no question that Vedanta is growing . . .

I gave one poem direct to Swamiji in New Delhi and left another in his absence. I expect to edit a third and give it to him on my return there. My external researches into Vedanta are restricted now, but I expect to return here in 1965. The "internals" go on.[720]

Last Days in India

Toward the end of January, 1962, Sam wrote to his friend Willie Wise.

> I did not try to see the Ambassador—anyhow he was just coming as [I] was leaving, but got a blurb on him which went to U.C. But if I accomplish what I have started to do I think he might see me. I saw the Chief of Protocol afterwards, anyhow. And yestereve had tea with my good friend, Dr. Radhakrishnan . . .
>
> Much of the rest of the short communion between the Vice-President and myself was of the same order as my again meeting Swami Maharaj Ranganathananda of the Ramakrishna Mission here. I brought him one of the poems dedicated to him and heard him speak. He is in such contrast to Krishnamurti who is also visiting New Delhi and gives essence of sugar as cosmic philosophy. Swamiji is very solid. I brought him another poem later but he was not in and anyhow I should prefer to visit him after he has read them. I am not worried. This is not America; this is where Indian-Indian philosophy is understood and appreciated . . .
>
> I have not revisited the usual tourist haunts, unless one calls the tomb of Nizam-ud-din Auliya such, and even that visit was the most unusual. But have visited other saints' tombs and what is remarkable is the art-work and care in preservation. Much of it is in marble too, and the preservation of a high degree of Mogul art other than in pictures . . .
>
> Delhi has grown; it is like a combination of Los Angeles and Washington. Like Washington it has the governmental buildings, embassies and circles with radiating streets and avenues. Like L.A. it sprawls without definite planning, but with pretty good bus, taxi and ricksha (motor driven) conveyances.
>
> There is no question that New Delhi looks brighter today . . .
>
> I was fortunate in meeting Prof. Montgomery of Kansas State who passed by . . . He is stationed at Poona* where I expect to be shortly. There I may also contact the musician Dilip Koomar Ray, who was for a short while in San Francisco and operates an ashram. In South India I expect to meet both agricultural and spiritual leaders.[721]

*Now Pune.

Sam shared a typical exchange from his travels that illustrated the divine flow in which he operated.

> "Taxi Taxi!" I told the driver to stop the car. "Pardon me, will you do me a favor?" "What?" "Take me to the Ramakrishna Mission." "Yes, if you will do me a favor?" "What?" "Take me to the Ramakrishna Mission." This happened yesterday on Vivekananda's birthday."[722]

On February 20th Sam wrote to his friends Grace and Nick:

> Your letter of the 8th found me in a Yoga Ashram. It is not what the average American calls "Yoga" which consists mostly of "making it like a fish, making it like a crocodile, making it like a stork, making it like a tree, but like a human, not making it." I leave the postures to my good friends the Baptistes, and they are my good friends. There are three basic types of Yoga—work, love and calming the mind. I do not wish to go into that now. But this gives me a place to be quiet.
>
> For two years now I have been moving incessantly and generally successfully. Indeed this year has been so successful so far that not only Asians have welcomed me (they always do), but also the Americans . . .
>
> Visited the oldest Jewish congregation on earth at Cochin. The synagogue is not so old and like all good anti-protocolians (of which I am one) they have a floor made out of wonderful blue-and-white Cantonese tiles of which there are no better on earth. (Ask Chingwah Lee haven't I been studying Chinese art for generations!) If they ever had to mortgage the place, they could reap in simeleons by the thousand! But think nothing of it—the tourists are coming, hurroo, hurray. I picked Friday p.m. for a visit which was the best time as the Rabbi was in. It was a delightful visit, somewhat technical, of course . . .
>
> As usual, every folk-dance festival I have expected to attend **has been called off by rain**. And it is now raining around my next destination: Bangalore![723]

At the beginning of March, a month before his return from India to Pakistan, Sam wrote a diary entry to Harry Nelson while waiting in Bangalore. Sam saw himself as equal parts scientist and mystic, and his interest in seeing an agricultural exchange with Asia never waned. His letter detailed time spent with Dr. H.R. Arakiri, Deputy Director of Agriculture of Mysore State, as well as with Dr. N.P. Patil, farm management researcher in Bangalore. The chief concern of the latter—lack of knowledge of exact water requirements of trees and crops—just "happened" to be a chief item on Sam's agenda. Sam went on to detail his findings and recommendations regarding farm advisors, saying the very knowledgeable local advisors needed additional staff. Sam envisioned the staff even could come from young 4-H club members as well as the previously mentioned southern farmers. Ever a proponent of doing, Sam wished to bridge the gap between research and actual farming.[724]

By the end of the month he was preparing to leave India and again wrote Willie Wise:

> I have been having a rush-rush all over India and am so tired I cannot even take the trouble of proper farewells. I would reach a city with three introductions and all three people would outline a complete program for me. This is delightful as hospitality but hard on the psyche and stomach.[725]

In April Sam returned to Pakistan for a four-month stay and kept up his usual full schedule of meeting scientists, mystics, educators, and governmental officials. From Lahore he wrote to his self-appointed godson Norman McGhee:

> The news is fast and furious. In a few days I hope to be visiting Rawalpindi with my friend and host, Major Sadiq. We have at least three big projects which will bring us to California, presumably in the next two months. The nature of these projects may not concern you, although at least one will—but our present plans are these:
>
> If anything (not everything but anything) goes right, we will fly to San Francisco which may be our temporary headquarters. We plan to rent or purchase a car and will need a driver. I have recommended Norman for many reasons and some of them have been contained in the correspondence between us. While our main trips will be between California and Texas we shall sooner or later have to go east, in particular to Cleveland. So we are going to stress every means possible to have enough funds for those two purposes—a car and driver.[726]

Sam continued to share his plans for the future.

> **Trip to the Orient**. If we are at all successful I might remain in the U.S. and Norman might get an opportunity to come to Asia . . .

> **India**. Even if Norman reneges or refuses and wants to go to India, I have a big open door for him—he would have to pay his way no doubt, but I can help him if he is willing to help some others. Purchases of things would be made in San Francisco by me. One of these would lead to top level people in Bombay. The other to top level people in Hyderabad . . .
>
> **East-West Relations.** Among other things we are bringing [more] real spirituality and spiritualism. My own position among the Sufis is very, very high today. I also have some material on the relation between Zen and Hinduism which has never been given out. My visits to ruins have convinced me that Zen was the central theme in Buddhistic practice long before Bodhidharma.[727]

A few days later he wrote to his friend Willie Wise:

> [Pakistan] is a country of many cultures, most not presented in the U.S. lest we hurt somebody else's feelings. This is a country based on religion and we do not like to discuss religion. This is a country with a strong undertone of serious philosophy; it is in the papers all the time. Not only have my outlines on philosophy been accepted by each university I have appealed to, but the President himself has asked for outlines from me . . .
>
> This is a country whose spiritual father (Iqbal) was a poet. Poetry gatherings are like dance gatherings with us. I have read in public and gained many well-wishes. I have read in private with Secretary Shahab with a select gathering—which I found out later was more select [than] I dreamed, and immediately [there were] requests to copy for translation into Urdu and be published—I could not get to bat in America, [but] just wait.
>
> I have met agricultural experts, authorities, . . . the deputy of Soil Conservation, and the top Floriculturist in Pakistan—more will come out of this . . .
>
> So you see, Willie, my knowledge of Art, Poetry, Flowers, Botanical and non-Botanical Sciences, Philosophy, History and Religion have all done me good.[728]

Ahmed Murad Chisti left marked changes behind in the wake of his travels in India and Pakistan, including new folk dance work in Karachi. Years later in his classes with students he would occasionally, and humorously, tell a story about how people would come up to him and say they were happy a Saint would be speaking. He would reply, "I Yain't a Saint." He then would say that a sign had been put up that read "I Yain't, the Saint, is speaking."

To Leonora he wrote, "It will be good to get home and be anonymous, or will it and do I want it?"[729] He closed another letter to Willie Wise saying "I was very tired coming back from India—exhausted. My career there was like a series of dreams, nearly all pleasant. It was like some kind of super-telepathy was at work and maybe it was. Now I feel sprightly but nostalgic."[730]

Murshid Sam leading Dances in Central Park, NYC, 1970

CHAPTER 15

Back in the U.S.A.

Coming Home to California

Author's note: During the period covered by the remaining chapters, I met Samuel Lewis, became his mureed *and esoteric secretary, transcribed his dictated letters, diary entries, and spiritual papers daily, and lived with him for several years. I took part in many of the events recounted here. Where my personal observations and discussions are reported in the following chapters, I use the first person.*

MURSHID WALI ALI MELVIN MEYER

SAM RETURNED TO THE U.S. IN AUGUST OF 1962. October found him in San Francisco at the art exhibition of his friend Gordon.

> Last Sunday I visited your exhibition in the De Young Museum and lest there be anything that looks like flattery, I am giving you a sincere and somewhat detailed report. It is easy enough to be influenced by, or to respond emotionally to a friend. But looking at it from a distant view I found such enjoyment I could not look at other pictures and had to go into the Chinese room "to cool off." What is it that evoked such responses? I left with one question: "Are you depicting the present age? or predicting the next?"
>
> Leaving the Museum I glanced down at the Terrazzo and saw the sympathy between your work and "nature" . . .
>
> I myself am at the bottom of the ladder, taking up drawing at the Rudolph Schaeffer School. There is a long story here bringing together the two facets of my trip abroad—the scientific one concerned with the food problems; the [esoteric] one concerned with occultism and mysticism . . .

Fortunately, the scientific people do not operate as do [newsmen] and metaphysicians, so the way has been entirely edifying; everywhere. The same is true with saints and mystics; often they see full at a glance or even without looking.

The two phases, scientific and mystical, were synthesized by one Sufi teacher [Dewwal Shereef] . . . I have been assigned the subject of "Leaves." This is basically a book of scientific research . . . Unlike Audubon I am a Yogi . . . That is to say, I know both the plant physiology and vital life force in trees and shrubs, and this will undoubtedly affect the ultimate style . . .

This would bring one to the point: what is the reality in the plant? Or leaf? Instead of answering this technologically, I hope to find it through life's experience. I have already discussed this at the Schaeffer School and there is agreement on the value of synthesizing science and art.

I am not now prone to discuss my trip. The few persons who have been my confidants are more than satisfied. The need for writing books with a purpose overshadows any effort at autobiographical sketches. Yet memoirs are needed. Paul Brunton is now walking in my path whereas before I walked in his. I know the holy men of each land and I know the uselessness of trying to make this known, or rather this was true until recently. Last year at long last the actual Zen Buddhists in America got together and published an anthology of Zen. The American Vedantists have done the same thing. Nobody has touched Sufism though there are many times more Sufi disciples [than] all other schools combined. But this departure is encouraging and will be included in my [book] *The Lotus and the Universe* in answer to *The Lotus and the Robot.**

My Main Work, "How California can help Asia"† is all absorbing and has brought nothing but favorable responses everywhere. Again, I am rather careful to whom I divulge plans. It will probably take two years to write, but I have or can get the material. In this area I have received more encouragement in the last two months than in the previous almost sixty-six years of life.

Among my minor assignments has been that of locating an architect for the new Islamabad University to be built in the projected capital of Pakistan. The possibility of "winning the cold war" by showing the superiority of American art and technology had not been tried. The "cold war" would have been over almost from the start if the editors could

*Arthur Koestler's exploration of eastern mysticism.

†Available in the Archives under the title "How California Can Help the Orient."

> stay out of the way; they can't and won't and they really miss everything.[731]

Back on his native soil, Sufi Ahmed Murad actively fostered many of the contacts he had made abroad. His ongoing exchange with his goddaughter and *mureed,* Saadia Khawar Khan, is especially noteworthy. His letters gave Saadia a complete picture of Sufism, just as his Pir Hazrat Inayat Khan's letters to Murshida Martin had prepared Murshida Martin for the Sufi path.

According to Saadia, Sam wrote to her on average a letter a week. She said each word was a learning experience and transported her to a different world. Whatever questions or concerns she had, the letters would answer without her having expressed them. She shared the letters with her aunt Bibijan, who disclosed to Saadia a desire to take *bayat* with Sam. Despite Saadia's encouragement, Bibijan did not write to ask for that. Then a letter arrived from Sam stating, "I feel strongly I should give a *bayat* to your aunt."[732]

In September, 1962, Sam responded affirmatively to Saadia's request to send dollars to friends of hers in the UK; in exchange, Saadia would send saris to friends of Sam's. He added details of his life since returning to the U.S.:

> The strange thing I do not comprehend and I have not meditated on it is that predictions concerning myself seem to be coming true, almost like a rehearsal turning into a drama, but with my friends this is not so. This is especially true of fellow *mureeds* and I have no time to pray or meditate.
>
> I am busy writing two books and this takes nearly all my time. In this I have been most fortunate or rather Allah has blessed me. So I now have a fairly complete program for salinity and will soon be writing to the *Civil & Military [Gazette]* and to *Food and Agriculture* at Karachi. But people expect more from one than he can give.
>
> I meet very few happy people, and many of [my] friends are unwell too. On top of that, the Islamic Center here is in a terrible mess. The leaders never would permit a lecture or report from me and now they are busy fighting each other. I wrote them saying that a Muslim was one who was either (a) peaceful or (b) capable of surrendering. I also told them I was more interested in an Imam than in a Mosque. They began with many Imams and mistreated them all. I have further advised I was

> interested in (a) religion (b) informing the American public about Mohammed (on whom be peace) and his mission. They are interested in entertainment, social affairs and praising not Allah, but their ancestors.
>
> I am going to Sacramento to meet my former *mureed* who strayed far from the Path and has been in endless difficulties. I am not concerned with past mistakes or even sins. When there is *taubah** one can change or be changed in a twinkling of an eye. My re-studying of *Kashf-ul-Mahjub* has strengthened me inwardly very much.
>
> My next attention is to those who are in difficulties. I spent considerable time warning [this *mureed*] that it is not my goodness, but my religion that impels me to this. I know she is emotionally unstable now, which is quite natural. She and another lady, who have been classmates, both lost their husbands and fortunately are very good friends. As my dancing partner married a man of mixed-blood and was socially ostracized, I have cut myself off from all companions who favored such ostracism. But the time spent at this typewriter (and my other one which is being fixed) seems endless. Only Allah restricts me to ten letters a day, though I may do creative writing and have interviews . . .
>
> Please give my *salaams* to your family. I have been well but have not heard from Major Sadiq.† On the other hand, Pir Sufi Barkat Ali and his *mureeds* write regularly. Only they expect me to be back soon. I expect it will take four years to accomplish what was laid before me, but then again Allah knows best.‡ God bless you.[733]

Ahmed Murad appends to his letter an offering of practices from the 99 Names of Allah for Saadia. The remarks he makes on each point to aspects of Saadia's life. His final statement sums it all up:

> May Allah's love be with you forever, Saadia; these are from the *Asma-ul* cards.
>
> Al-Ghaffar (The Forgiver); Supreme Crown, covers your soul.
>
> Al-Mushi (The Accountant); Wisdom crosses you influence.
>
> Al-Kuddus (The Holy One); Understanding, crowns your obstacles.

---

*Turning, especially toward loving forgiveness.

†It was a significant disappointment to Ahmed Murad that the Major did not in the end come to the States, for reasons of health.

‡What was laid before Sam was an opportunity in the future to function as a leader there.

Al-Ghani (The All-Sufficing); Love, beneath rising from your feet.

Al-Shakir (The Thankful); Power, behind you.

Al-Wajid (The All-Perceiving); Beauty, before you.

Al-Hadil (The Equitable); Endurance, you.

Al-Kabiz (The Closer); Majesty, your house.

Allah; Foundation, hopes and fear.

Al-Hakk (The Truth); Kingdom, outcome.

Allah is within you; you are His instrument and through you He expresses Himself to the external world. The man filled with the knowledge of names and forms has no capacity for the knowledge of Truth.[734]

Sam had this further report for Saadia:

Most of my work has been collecting materials for "How California Can Help Asia." But some has been for the Islamabad University and in general this has been most successful and the people contacted are most interested. So far I have not met the Consuls General of India, Pakistan and Egypt and have avoided Iran on account of the catastrophes there of a totally different nature.

The other day I went to Sacramento to the State Fair and everything there was so lovely; I shall have to make several tours while collecting materials. Then I telephoned the woman who had been my *mureed,* who had betrayed me at every opportunity and has been false in everything and to everybody. I simply called her up and said: "This is your Murshid." The reaction was so loving and lovely. I may see her as soon as possible and this is the sign I was waiting for, the beginning of my spiritual work in this country. The astonishing thing was it was exactly as the Pirs foretold. But while I felt reassured in other things, this was a test and *Alhamdulillah,* successful[735]

Ted Reich was president of the Theosophical Society in the 1920s and also spent a good deal of time with Nyogen Senzaki. Over the years Ted's path and Sam's crossed frequently. Their friendship deepened gradually, and in the 1960s they maintained almost daily contact. In an interview years later, Ted countered the claim that Sam's work for Islamabad University had been "most successful." He had observed that virtually all the people Sam approached had not wanted to get involved with giving money to anything Muslim happening in Asia.[736]

Connections and Challenges

In a January, 1963, diary entry, Sam related not only the synchronicity of events transpiring in his life, but also how he was being sought out by practitioners of diverse Eastern and Western religions in the area.

> After [Saladin Reps and I] talked about other things, I suggested sending for the poem "Saladin" and I would take care of it as soon as I returned. And as soon as I returned, in the next mail there was a letter from Khawar—suggesting the return of the manuscript—right to the dot. And two days later, right to the dot, a letter from Saladin. And in it, also the name of his local publisher.
>
> I have already made some preliminary steps to get [a] day in typing.
>
> **The Ted Reich Story.** Ted has been telling me about an awakened interest in spiritual Judaism, and at the same time, he has been deeply involved in Theosophy and Buddhism. Yesterday, January 8, I spoke for one hour at the Rudolph Schaeffer School of Design on "The Interaction of the East and the West in the Arts." The lecture—entirely under inspiration—began with a free translation of the opening of Genesis: "**At first in principle he—the Gods thinked the essence of spatialities and the essence of form**."
>
> The lecture went on, mostly dealing with the symmetrically opposite approaches of the Mediterranean and Chinese people; and interludes of the circularism of India.
>
> After the talk, I was surprised to be besieged by several Jewish women who had been in the audience, and they begged me for more. They wanted to know (a la Ted) about both Judaism and Buddhism. So their names were recorded, but when I arrived home, there was an invitation from the Buddhist-Taoist Assn. (Iru Price), so I am holding off decision.[737]

What later developed for Sam in San Francisco was a collaborative group of Buddhist teachers who worked together in the city and in the world in general. "Meanwhile, saw Ted to tell him about the above incidents. And in turn, he told me about some of the psychic research people here who wish to know about Sufi Inayat Khan. So an arrangement has been made for tomorrow night."[738] The feeling of adventure in new directions was in the air.

Sam and Ted often continued to do things together, but Sam was short on money. He wrote:

Edward Connaughton sent me a scroll to be sold and I looked up Ching-wah Lee—and met him in the street. If this can be sold it would give me some money for a part-time secretary or other purposes.

Ted also gave me Carlton Kendall's address, and [also] Lottie Fernandez. It would seem in general a lot of my very old friends are coming back into my life.[739]

A few days later Sam detailed his activities with Ted Reich and various religious groups, acknowledging his mutable acceptance in the Bay Area.

Most of the things that have followed are connected with Ted Reich. Lottie Fernandez has come out of her hole and appears at the TS [Theosophical Society] on Tuesdays. I hope to see her and arrange a meeting with Della Goertz. One does not know if there is any advantage in bringing the Rinzai and Soto people together. Tomorrow afternoon, I go to the Buddhist-Taoist Assn., which is Chinese and Americans, but contains more mature people, and some I knew at an earlier period. The Chinese Buddhists are as divided as the Japanese, but the Japanese differences are based in part by analytical selection, and the Chinese by synthetic selection (like the Brahmo Semaj*).

Last night was spent at the home of Mrs. Charlotte White . . . It was complicated because she, her friend Pelle, and her closest associate, all wanted to learn both about Sufism and psychism, and it took about two hours to integrate them. However, these are functional people whose psychism depends neither on mediums nor trances . . .

Ted loaned me a copy of *Atomic Suicide* by the Russells. I had met Walter [one of the authors] two or three times in 1946, very long sessions. He is a sort of mystic, and certainly has a cosmic vision. He was very anti-[M]atchabelli. Besides, his work is remarkably impersonal. A single reading does not impress, and the authors distinctly ask readers to read at least three times . . .

Ted has also located Paul Reps' publisher, and has prepared the way for my visit . . .

Life shows at the moment the rejection of reports by a lot of people I thought would receive them, but a much larger acceptance by people I did not know before. Between the blank walls met by psychic researchers, people with streams of unhappiness and inhibitions, and the

* Brahmo Samaj (or Semaj) is a monotheistic reformist movement within Hinduism.

> searches for God and spiritual freedom, the outlook is favorable at the moment.[740]

Despite having received confirmation of his realization during his travels, Sam continued to document his lack of recognition by local groups and even by people he considered friends. Thankfully there were notable exceptions, and he never gave up trying to share what he knew in his soul. Inner conviction carried him forward and he was supported by regular correspondence from abroad. Too, Sam was gregarious and always ready to engage with people.

Sam's diary entries continued.

> The best laid plans of mice and men often come up with other answers. The most ridiculous situation is that two efforts to see old friends in the T.S. have resulted only in their preaching to me and not listening to where I have been. I look over the names such as Alice Bailey, Krishnamurti, and Manly Hall, none of whom has done anything but surfeit us with words and cause confusions. The worst thing is to mention "Jesus Christ." It is a shame and an annoyance, the way they wince. After two such experiences, I almost regret the need to go there again and see Lottie Fernandez, who was for so long my sister in Zen . . .
>
> Then there is Fritzi. I went to see her, and instead of putting me on for a lecture, she has offered me the whole place—just like that. I was not ready for it, but the way she expressed herself, I cannot refuse. One does not know whether this is because she has been convinced I have a message—or she has been given occult guidance—or she wants to put it over on La Duce—it is probably all three. The old Hindu "The enemy of your enemy is your friend" sometimes works ironically. There is almost complete slate-cleaning here now from the days I was accused of suffering from paranoia . . .
>
> In the meanwhile is that peculiar general situation of the difficulty of presenting to anybody I know well about my trips abroad, or even the journey to L.A. I ran into Walt Baptiste. "I have a Pearl of Great Price." "May I see it?" **It is the question of salvation** . . . One can come and have all the healing in the world. It becomes a secret, not because it is a secret, but because people won't listen or accept. So Walt got in five minutes what, with the exception of Sheikha and Ted, I have not been able to give away, show, or demonstrate since I returned. The result can

only be laughter. The challenge is a blessing, and by being challenged, I gave to Walt and blessed him.

[Rudolph Schaeffer] was not present when I spoke [at his school], but the wonderful response of the audience is the turning point in my San Francisco story. There is only one way to go . . . and that is up.

Three big situations discussed with Admiral Evenson, most dramatic of which is the possible open forum of Bishop Pike on Palestine. We may start in as *amicus curiae.** This is on the agenda.[741]

The other night a Swami was telling the audience that you can judge people by the glint in their eyes. And I looked around the room and saw solemnity and seriousness and that rapture which comes when a speaker ecstatizes the audience—but no glints—not a glint in that room. Excepting, of course, in the swami himself.

When I was with Swami Ramdas I ran out of the lecture room to play with the children outside. This sort of thing would scandalize the "old ladies" who go to "spiritual" lectures; but the Swami knew what I was doing and said that when one can play with children as their equal, he must be spiritual. I can see the audiences ogle and applaud anybody who says that to play with children is a sign of spirituality, but I can't see the audience running out and playing with the children. I know a few who do and of course they are marked down immediately.

The next thing that is noticeable is the number of excellent letters I get from abroad. Every time somebody says "nix" to me here I can be sure I'll be getting a letter from some faraway place lauding me to the skies.[742]

Rifts continued in the local Buddhist community, but the possibility of future friendly meetings is reflected in Sam's correspondence with Eugene Wagner, a Buddhist student who had been ordained by Sam's friend Phra Sumangalo.

Dear Bodhisattva Sam,

It was good seeing you few days ago, and I want to express my thanks for giving me the opportunity to be the witness to your acceptance as UBF† representative. I also want to assure you that I shall keep in confidence all you've told me . . .

---

* *Amicus curiae* translates from the Latin as "friend of the court." It refers to a knowledgeable party who assists the court by making an impartial contribution to a legal or other discovery proceeding.

† United Buddhist Foundation.

[I wrote] to Mr. Priebe in regard to the anonymous memorandum I received and correcting the inaccurate intimations it contained . . .

It is disheartening to see so many so-called Buddhist groups constantly at one another's throats. But in spite of all the fears and distrust, I feel that there will be soon some concrete beginnings to a [greater] harmony among the various branches of the *Sangha.* At any rate, I intend to do all I can to help bring this to fruition . . .

Iru* called tonight to tell me he had just written his resignation as V.P. to the UBF and his membership there-in as well.[743]

Later that year Rev. Wagner wrote Sam again:

Sam, you have far, far more wisdom and experience to draw upon than I do. What is the answer to the apparently deliberate persistence in the separatism exhibited by the priesthood? Unless I've missed more lessons than I think, we are all members of the same *Sangha* and presumably conducting ourselves towards the same conclusion. I can understand an occasional lapse in several areas, especially since levels of awareness vary so, but I cannot comprehend what appears to be premeditated spitefulness if not actual hatred. I know there is an answer here, but I do not know what it is.

Outside of Iru's place I know of no other Buddhist gathering place where Buddhist priests are not welcomed either with indifference or hostility. As you know, both Iru and I have some basic differences, but we regard each other with respect and warmth. I must say the Chinese Bdst. Assoc. is this way also.

There is nothing I should like better to see than a burying of the hatchets and a courteous respect for one another. I must confess I know not how to begin. Is it better to antagonize by going to places where one's presence may in time break down some of the hostility? Or is it more beneficial to all concerned to do what must be done while working more or less alone? Or will this constitute a calculated separativeness again? Again, I do not know, yet I must find at least a partial answer to this. I need not enumerate to you the groups and individuals who each, individually, possess the total answer to all facets of the experience.

To my knowledge you are currently the only one in this area who is not encumbered by a job and who is "free" to devote full time to the problem. It is gratifying to see that you are now able to do just this with

*Iru Price was one of the Buddhists in the area with whom Rev. Wagner wanted Sam to work.

the most tangible results, although the process most assuredly won't coincide with the popular version of effectiveness. But I consider this *prajna* in action, and the popularity can go hang.

Today's *Chronicle* carried an article on the editorial page suggesting that perhaps the American answer in Vietnam might not work and that an Asian answer might be the only effective one. This from a newspaper reporter in San Francisco nearly floored me. I'll enclose the clipping. Perhaps the seed will grow, in time . . . [744]

The State of Buddhism

In a diary letter in January, 1965, Sam discussed the problem of the state of Buddhism at home and abroad.

The difference between the Enlightenment-experience of Lord Buddha and his numerous dharma-transmissions, and the derivative, analytical schools is today so vast that it is very difficult to overcome them. My meeting with the Roshi at Nara—where again I have been one of the few Americans to "pass"—was based on the acceptance of Universal Buddhism and Buddha-Mind. This is reflected in the World Buddhist Federation also . . .

Sam in Buddhist robes in front of the Mentorgarten

Photo by Mansur Johnson

From the Sufi background I was able to see clearly the type of meditation or contemplation that would clarify the miasma there [in Southeast Asia]. These practices are not easy, but they are as effective as difficult.

You may know that in the twenties there was a rage for Tibetan Buddhism and there are still a few of my old cronies around. There was come here one Dr. Warwick, who was initiated in the Red Hat School and who knows the difference between initiation and ceremonial ordination . . .

Dr. Warwick, the sadly rejected Red Hat Monk, has interested one of my *mureeds* in Tibetan Buddhism and this *mureed* showed me a recent book on Tantric Yoga . . . I was struck

> by the innumerable resemblances between the Actual Sufi methods and those of the schools involved . . .
>
> I brought back from India a pretty complete amount of Tantric materials which I shared with one old crony . . . I turned these over to a professor at the University of California who not only has "recognized" this person but gotten others to.
>
> The most important of these items in Tantric Yoga was what I found is called the *Mahamudra* Meditation. I was amazed to find that this was what this person has done many times and which to him has the key to the clarification of the whole South Vietnam and Cambodian pseudo-complex. If ten Buddhists would study the teachings of Lord Buddha and put a few of them into practice there would soon be peace there, but I know that in America yet you could not get ten Buddhists to study the teachings of Lord Buddha, perform either the *jhana* meditations or the *Mahamudra,* or if taking up Zen, reach the stages of the "Higher Ko-ans" which have become mythological."[745]

In an attempt to overcome the ongoing divisiveness, Sam's good friend Rev. Eugene Wagner made a bold proposal that February. He called on Bay Area Buddhist leaders, including Sam, Neville Warwick, Iru Price, and others, to unite in planning a commemorative service to honor the date recognized as the Buddha's birthday. In September Rev. Wagner wrote to Sam on the theme of cooperation and its difficulties among the distinct groups.

> This person wishes to thank you for lending him the booklet from the WFB* and the book on Indian background for Hindu/Buddhist thought . . .
>
> The WFB pamphlet is pretty simple and very basic, especially for beginners in Buddhism. Perhaps the most noteworthy part of it is in its making a distinction between Buddhists and those "interested" in Buddhism. People in this country are commonly prone to lump the two categories together in an unsatisfactory arrangement. However, the booklet says what we in Hawaii, and the P.B.A. in Malaya, taught our Dharma Class (Sunday School) kids for years as a platform for the more developed Mahayana schools of thinking . . .

---

* World Fellowship of Buddhists.

> It was interesting to note the UBF's contribution . . . in light of its actual attitudes and activities. It is signed as having come from Ojai, which presumably means Priebe. Inasmuch as no one from the UBF has ever bothered to make any contact with this person, with the single exception of Priebe's unsigned memorandum to me . . . his claim of choosing to "assist in promoting cooperation and unity among all faiths so as to prevent misunderstanding and assure that the moral and social development, stability, security, and progress of all will be achieved," smacks to this person as rank hypocrisy. So does his following statement in which he claims his stand of Buddhist co-operation.
>
> I am afraid that until such time as the WFB and the UBF show some sign of responsibility to their fellow men instead of prating sanctimonious mouthing, this person's vows, which require individual action, cannot permit support of those whose position enables them to "do," but who will not. When Sumangalo and I extensively discussed this point, he was in complete agreement with it.[746]

Mansur Johnson recounts an episode that took place several years later when Sam chaired a meeting of Buddhists in the Bay Area.[747] Johnson relates that Iru Price claimed for himself the role of chief local representative of Lama Govinda, a move that both Murshid Sam and Price's initiator Neville Warwick considered extremely inappropriate. But Sam also considered Warwick's responding attack on Price to be off the mark. Sam asked Warwick, "Where is Compassion?"[748]

Sam considered that one of Price's serious failures was to not appropriately "recognize his fellow initiates." Sam's letter continued, "Iru would be compelled to affirm or deny the initiations of another person. If he does not affirm I shall tell the Lama that the American people are not going to accept any egocentric as his representative, no matter how many ceremonial ordinations: that the dharma is not based on ordinations but on attainment."[749]

Sam also recognized certain parallels between Warwick's situation with Iru Price and his own with Alan Watts. "I cannot be a hypocrite and demand or even request you act differently toward Iru than I have toward Alan, but I see today all possibilities of Alan some day, somehow, reaching the door to humility (not humiliation) and becoming a devotee."[750]

Correspondence with Barkat Ali

In late 1963, Sufi Ahmed Murad was also continuing his correspondence with his teacher Sufi Barkat Ali:

> Beloved Pir-o-Murshid:
>
> It is with all Praise to Allah that greetings are sent. For your *mureed* has now a completed copy of such of the teachings for Murshid's that came from Pir-o-Murshid Hazrat Inayat Khan and are in his hands in the regular order. The teachings out of the regular order will take some time to compile for they come also from many notes left by Hazrat Inayat Khan, and also from *Irfan,* which was the source of inspiration for Major Sadiq and from the teachings of Waris of Lucknow and from other inner and outer sources.
>
> These teachings . . . are connected with other writings which are presumed to be known and with experiences also which are presumed to be known. Originally the constitution of the Sufi Order called for twelve grades based on Initiation and this was shown by the progress in *zikr.* But then it was changed to accord with *hal* and *makam* by methods other than *zikr.*
>
> These were divided between some left in San Francisco with the late Murshida Rabia Ada Martin and those left in Europe. Each of these were in turn divided and the divisions continued so that the whole body of literature not only did not come into one hand, but each secreted what papers he had.
>
> In the West the teachings left with Rabia Martin were in part lost because secreted away; in part destroyed in a fire and in part left in several hands. In the European groups, also some papers were destroyed in the war and the rest divided into four places which have not been on mutual terms. And although the lesser teachings have been and are being published in England, the amount of writings left by Hazrat Inayat Khan are voluminous . . .
>
> Americans insisted I wished to be a Murshid. Neither Allah nor *Rassoul-lillah* nor Hazrat Inayat Khan has ever said that I ought to be a Murshid. And it [was] only in Lahore, that I was challenged by little old Abdul Latif, who is to be the Voice of Allah in the most unlikely form.[751]
>
> When Abdul Latif challenged me for not being a Murshid I, finally exhausted, gave in and said, "All right, I am a Murshid and you are my first *mureed.*" I gave him instructions and within a few hours this

> 70-year-old man had the spiritual realization and came back dancing: "I have a real Murshid! I have a real Murshid!"[752]

Sam was a firm believer in the inner initiation: "People who [come] along and want titles or leadership without the divine sanction may win popular acclaim but in the unseen it is not so. In the unseen it is as it was, but it is in accord with Hierarchy."[753]

Sufi Barkat Ali gave warm and strong recognition of Ahmed Murad's spiritual achievement:

> Your letter . . . breathes of the spirit that Allah placed in Adam so that man can know Him. Praise be to Allah that you are proving His existence by deeds and not mere words; and not only by deeds, but by experiences. A Sufi is he who tries to manifest the qualities which reached their perfection in our Holy Prophet. He succeeds best who surrenders the most—surrenders body, mind and soul. Hard it is to bring the body under the sway of the mind and make both subservient to the spirit. But our *tarikat* calls for it, and you have achieved it—*alhamdu lillah.* By the power of *zikr* these three act as one because they all have the same single aim—to sing only the praises of Allah. Whether you walk, or talk, or pray, you are perpetually worshipping Him. And are we not born only to worship Him?
>
> You live in a difficult land at a difficult time—so strong and yet powerless—so wealthy and yet so friendless—so advanced and yet ignorant. In such hard soil you are sowing divine seeds, and in some cases, a harvest is being already reaped. *Inshallah* the Light that was flashed on in Arabia more than 13 centuries ago will prevail in the New World also, and Sufis like you are in the vanguard of this momentous struggle. Can any battle compare with this tussle? With the sacrifices so gladly made, the loneliness self-imposed, love countering hate, the Kalama triumphant when presented with faith and inspiration. The greatest jihad is the battle for souls, and only a chosen few can wage and win it!
>
> At Salarwala here, the Will of Allah rules, and my constant prayer is that all those who come within its orbit should receive the *baraka*—that invisible shield of protection that Allah bestows when His lieutenants beseech Him. This proud world thinks that name and form and mind is all that exists, and that all progress is solely a product of the intellect. Little do they know that it is the ceaseless chanting of Allah's *Kalams*

every minute of every day by purified souls that causes the Creator to nourish His creation. When this spiritual symphony ceases, the Day of Judgment will have dawned. Intellect will then avail them naught, and those who worshipped at its shrine will be aghast.

This body knows little rest, but with the heart resigned to His Will, and the *nufs* rendered ineffective by *zikr,* no tiredness is felt. Eighteen years of effort have culminated in the completion of the *Tarthib Sharif,* a compilation and commentary on the *Hadith.** It will run into 1100 pages and will be distributed free. Printing has begun in Lahore and copies should be out after two months. Thus it will have fulfilled the task entrusted by Sabri Sahib† of Kalyar Sharif.

I write to you with joy and abundance of good-will. The details you have given are a precious record of mystic achievement. The experiences are valid and conform to the highest tradition of our glorious heritage—it is the life blood of Sufi realization, unseen but vital, subtle but real, spiritual and everlasting. Its fragrance takes one to Him and through Him we are linked in this happy bond. On this note I end with love and every good thought.[754]

Perhaps a year later Sufi Ahmed Murad Chisti wrote to Sufi Barkat Ali.

As-salaam-aleikhum. One writes not knowing whether one is reporting or seeking advice. One writes because there is a sort of "psychic" climax which may or may not be important. One writes knowing the extreme difference which may be between actual surrender to Al-Hayy [the Ever-Living] and something private called "Islam," which may or may not have meaning . . .

It is now some time since my return from Pakistan and the total fruit of effort in relations between that country and the personal self has not been very much . . .

Now suddenly or gradually personality relations with large segments of this earth have changed. When one is on the path of the *auliya,*‡ life may go in one of several directions. One direction is to be more concerned than ever with religion, its edifices, its rituals, its teaching. Another is to be concerned with an area as if Allah has entrusted you

*Much of Sufi Barkat Ali's work can be found at darulehsanpublications.com/index.htm.

†Hazrat Alauddin Sabri, 13th century Chishti lineage holder.

‡The saints, walis, and leaders who serve as protectors of the *mureeds.*

with the guardianship of an area. Another may be to become *mast.** Another is to pioneer in awakening mankind where man has been asleep, and this has to do with the evolution of the whole race. Or one may be sent out with a particular message, a sort of *rassoul* without being in any way a *nabi* . . .

This person has been entrusted with two general duties in life, one concerned with the sciences and food production; the other with the awakening of hearts. Both of these will come to a climax this year in California.[755]

The Berkeley Psychedelic Conference

The following year, Sam participated in the Psychedelic Conference that was held June 13–18, 1966, at UC Berkeley. His history and outlook suited him well for work with the youth involved in the '60s drug culture. Sam wrote about the Conference in a letter to Gavin Arthur:

> Having the knowledge of the Stages of Consciousness both by book and dharma-transmission, as well as by conscious experience, one is in a much better position to deal with problems (much exaggerated) from the taking of drugs . . .
>
> There were several things which came out of the Psychedelic Conference.
>
> a. The close relation with Allen Ginsberg—this works both ways and I laugh about each.
>
> b. The agreement of all the participants to accept Dr. Huston Smith as the wisest. This man is a real [initiate] into mysticism. He has lived in the real Orient and learned from real Masters. And it is notable and noticeable that in consciousness we were on the same plane and I could think his answers to exact words.
>
> This is something beyond the stage reached by drugs and certainly beyond the stage of most popular lecturers.
>
> c. I was not only permitted to speak—something disdained by cultists and metaphysicians, but every point was accepted.
>
> This leads to the next step, if there is to be a next step—the conscious awakening of awareness without any resort to anything artificial.

---

*A God-intoxicated being, who may have the appearance of madness. Also referred to as *madzub*. Sam had no problem communicating with such people.

Richard Alpert, later known as Ram Dass

> At the same time in my real scientific research I have gone ahead some in the search for *soma* and *amrita,** a point now accepted by Dr. Lal, the science editor of the Hearst papers.
>
> The theme, "Joy without Drugs" will catch on sooner or later, whether I personally am involved or not. It was conferred by Papa Ramdas whose spirit I had received long before he came on the scene. At the moment I am beginning to look like a Pied Piper, rather than a Messiah and perhaps this is better so. It fits in with some of my missions.
>
> The karmic law, the principles of justice, retribution and balance are certainly coming into operation. I am preparing to appear as a Sufi in "good society" because of some events on the horizon.[756]

Sam did put forth the theme of Joy without Drugs, but he was open-minded about people's psychedelic experiences and he came to see positive results there as well.

One thing Sam always included when he spoke of the Psychedelic Conference was his response to Richard Alpert, Timothy Leary and others who said that what they were experiencing on LSD and other psychedelics could not be described. Sam at that time asserted that there was not a single thing they had experienced for which there was not a word in Sanskrit. He then was delighted when Alpert went to India and found his Guru, Neem Karoli Baba. Sam, of course, had also found his guru, Papa Ramdas, in India, which led to a beautiful strength of love that all could feel. Both Sam and Alpert would end up in deep relationship with the Lama Foundation commune.

Remembrances from Early Disciples

The changes happening now in Sam's life were dynamic. He had already begun to draw more and more young people, who often became his ini-

---

* *Soma* is a sacred intoxicating drink used in Vedic ritual. *Amrita,* literally "immortality," is also referred to as a nectar.

tiates. Between 1964 and 1966 some found their way to Sam at his small apartment on Clementina Street.

Remembrances such as those of Ralph and Nancy Silver show examples of the effect Sam was having on those drawn to him, how he nourished them in their lives. Ralph said:

> '65, '66 was when I met him . . . [I had gotten] a reading of my chart from Gavin Arthur and I was at loose ends in myself . . . People whom I'd been doing some work with—spiritual work—told me that there is this eccentric Sufi living over in the Mission and you should get over to see him. They mentioned his name to me and they mentioned it always in a way that was never phony—there was always a ring of reality about it, but it was always non-verbal, that ring of reality . . . And I was always rather attracted to find out who this man was . . . And then I had this reading with Gavin Arthur and Gavin Arthur was, of course, a very close friend with Sam Lewis, which I didn't know. And he looked at my chart and . . . he said, "I've got just the man to help you." And he called him up and he said, "Sam, I've got a man here who needs help and he deserves it and I'm going to send him over to see you." So he packs me up with my chart, gives me the address and says, "Go see Sam Lewis." So I said, "Okay," and went over there to Clementina . . .
>
> He opens the door and there he is, Sam Lewis . . . He was kind of disheveled; his shirt was hanging out, baggy pants and his sock was half off. The kitchen sink looked like it had never been cleaned, and he had cards all over the table . . . there were books all over the floor, and manuscripts all over the desk, and the bed was unmade. I said, "My God, what the hell is this?" . . . But somehow I . . . had to stay because there was something kind of authentic about the way he was . . . Then he did something very peculiar. He sat down on the bed and he started playing the flute that he plays; but it wasn't a flute—that imaginary thing he plays. I just said, "God, what is this?" But he did it with himself; did it with who he is. When he was doing this, you had the feeling that he was expressing his inner being. And it came to me—I was able to recognize the truth of what he was trying—although I'd never seen anything like that before—but there was this inner ring to it which corresponded in him, and, to make a long story short, from that time on I related to him as a man who knew.[757]

Meeting a Moroccan *Sidi*

In 1966 a major event occurred in Sam's life. His friend Ted Reich reported that 1965 had been a very traumatic period for Sam.* However, Sam met with a Moroccan *sidi* (saint) in late 1966, and Ted saw Sam's connection with the *sidi* as a key turning point in bringing future disciples to him.

In November Ted drove Sam and himself to the home of Rev. Neville Warwick, whom Sam described as having life-long training in esoteric schools. He also said of Warwick, "Like . . . myself he is not 'nice,' he is not suave, he does not put on a front, and when you prick his skin you find pure gold."[758] The head of the philosophy department at Temple University, Dr. Phillips, had arranged a meeting with a Moroccan Sufi named *Sidi* Abusalem Al-Alawi at Rev. Warwick's home. Ted described the Sufi as being one-eyed, and Sam was known to refer to him as "the *Sidi*."

The night of the meeting with the *Sidi*, Sam was wearing a hat Ted had bought in Aden earlier that year and given to Sam on his return. Ted described it as a square white *yarmulke* with red and gold on top.

Ted recounted this meeting when I interviewed him in 1971.[759]

> When [Sam] met the [*Sidi*]† . . . the funny thing about it was the minute he came in, the Sufi looked at the hat, and went like this, at Sam, and Sam [made a similar motion], and whether it was the Sufi hat or not I don't know . . . I think Sam and the *Sidi* recognized each other . . . They really gave each other the high sign . . .
>
> **Wali Ali:** "Murshid said one time that the [*Sidi*] spoke in Arabic, and that someone translated from Arabic to French, and from French into English . . . Murshid said that towards the end of the evening he got so high that he was translating directly from Arabic and he didn't even know it." . . .
>
> **Ted:** "It was quite a big room, and we were all sitting around . . . I think the [*Sidi*] and his two interpreters were sitting in the middle, and Sam

---

* Sam was still meeting closed doors and repeated rejection in the Bay Area.

† Mistranscribed in the Archives as "Siddhi," which is a Sanskrit word that refers to spiritual perfection or miraculous power.

was sitting in the middle of a couch . . . and he was having a terrific time."

WALI ALI: "Let me ask you something and see if you remember it about that night. Murshid said that evening there were a lot of people in the audience who were interested in having, say, a [*Sidi*] establish a center in the area. [Al-Alawi] was asked a question, 'Will you establish a center?' and the [*Sidi*] replied, 'It's not necessary—there is a man in the audience who has *baraka*.' This is what Sam told many times . . . Do you remember this remark, made by the [*Sidi*]?"

TED: "He could have, I don't know. . . . As I say . . . it must have happened, because one of the major impetuses of [Sam's] whole life was that."

WALI ALI: "He said after that time all his efforts flowered."

TED: "He was evidently touched. He had a whole new impetus."

Murshid Sam shared his own experience of this meeting in letters to a variety of his friends, including his goddaughter Saadia. Not only did he experience foreknowledge of how to approach the encounter, but he also found direct parallels with the teachings of Hazrat Inayat Khan.

> There is the faculty of Insight which we as a people reject and even so-called Buddhists and Sufis which stress it theoretically reject it practically. Last Sunday a Buddhist friend told me he was to be host for a great teacher from Morocco. I knew exactly what to do.[760]
>
> I was asked to bring credentials and came in a Sufi robe, chanted Sufi style and then showed the Saint a picture of his own sainted teacher. I think this was enough *kashf=prajna* which seems to be a forbidden subject. Indeed one result is that I am now teaching with some zeal those portions of "Sutra of the Sixth Patriarch" which are ignored by the schools that revere verbally or ritually that Teacher.[761] *
>
> And do you know what Abusalem Al-Alawi told us? You can read it all in *The Sufi Message of Spiritual Liberty.* It was no different and although I do not understand Arabic intellectually, in the heart it was easy to follow. Sometimes he used whole phrases exactly the same as Pir-o-Murshid

---

*Sokei-an Sasaki, from whom Sam received the Buddha Dharma transmission, wrote a book translating the "Sutra of the Sixth Patriarch" into English from Japanese and presenting how the teachings pointed to the essence of Buddhism in a very clear way. He and Murshid Sam had the same approach to transmitting the teachings: heart-to-heart, soul-to-soul direct communication.

> did [and] during the question period, the answers were the same all the way through.[762]
>
> Sidi Abusalem Al-Alawi came here and spoke on the need for a spiritual guide and then on Sufism—exactly the same as Hazrat Inayat Khan throughout. And later, I heard, he told people that this one [Ahmed Murad] was fully qualified to be a spiritual teacher, in everything.[763]

Sam also described an effect of the meeting with the *Sidi* that manifested within Sam's own family:

> Since the saint (*sidi*) from Morocco came here and left his blessing (*baraka*) everything in life has reversed, and sometimes with remarkable changes. On the surface the most important has been the complete reversal of my brother. He has lost two fortunes trying to prevent me from getting one and now he insists we join forces to unload a very large amount of money which has been piling up in my father's estate from which neither of us benefits.[764]
>
> All kinds of holy men came [to see me] and sometimes they do not call on other Americans. There is a sort of insight and sight and recognition and there is no way to put this into words.[765]

Nancy Silver, another follower of Sam's and a very busy actress in Los Angeles, also reaped the benefits of the *Sidi*'s effects on Sam. She said:

> [His apartment was] kind of shoddy and run down. We go into this room, and he sits down on the bed and says I should sit down in a chair. . . . He looked at me and I looked at him . . . All I know is that I went off somewhere; I went on a flight. I had no idea where I went, but I know I was with him, and I knew it was nothing I could interpret. There were no images or residue experiences. When I came back, I realized that I'd gone off somewhere, and I looked at him and he was no longer this man, this sixtyish man in the car. He was someone with whom I had an incredible bond, just because we had gone away. I could never name it, I just knew. No words were said, and nothing was laid down. We were friends; there was this connection made . . .
>
> This is the bare bones of it . . . And Ralph . . . Sam's kind of acting in this . . . capacity of an advisor, a helper, a teacher. Ralph has told me that Sam had always saved his life and had always kept him going. When he was down and desperate, he could always speak to Sam and Sam would always give him hope.[766]

In the ensuing years, Sam would sometimes call Ralph up in the middle of the night several times a week and without prologue shout into the phone, "More love! You need more love!" and then hang up. Sam's Fudo was speaking then.

Nancy went on with her interview about this remarkable man who changed her life.

> All I knew when I went to Sam's place was that it was very, very empty, it had an empty quality . . . It had a Buddhist feeling to it, I don't know why. There was no talk of Sufis. There was no talk of anything. There were no books brought out, there was nothing handed around . . .
>
> [In April, 1967,] Murshid gets sick, I don't remember what happened . . . He goes to the hospital and I go up and see him with Ralph. There is nobody in his room. There are very few people around him at the time. He's basically unknown. He said, "God has manifested to me, and He has told me I am to be the leader of the hippies, to be the leader of the young people." I think this is when he told me, "I'm to take you, I'm to take you as my god-daughter." It was . . . in the hospital, and this was the first hit that I'd had of his being a teacher or anything . . .
>
> Nobody ever talked to me that way before except my father . . . but it made complete sense to me when he said this to me . . . It came right into me, just as if we had talked that way before, it was part of our language and he knew that I would understand. There was no space between us. There was this tremendous intimacy, and it made all the sense in the world. And when he went home, he said he found his doorsteps flooded with young people. Then he moved . . . from Clementina to Precita, and we all helped him move . . . He had 1½ things, and the rest was all papers . . .
>
> I knew that he was involved in writing letters all over the world, about ecology and politics and nobody could ever agree on anything. I knew he was a genius and was involved in all those things. But in terms of anything esoteric, I had absolutely no idea.

I asked Nancy, "Did he ever actually initiate you or did he just assume that you were initiated? . . . 'All disciples stand up.'" Nancy replied:

> "All disciples stand up," and I'm still sitting down. I'm noticing that Murshid is getting annoyed, but I'm not quite sure why, and he is getting very impatient. He said, "I said, all disciples stand up, please," and he is looking glowering at me. I said, "Murshid, I'm not." I couldn't even

get the words out. "Up, up!" Then, when I questioned him later about it, he said, "You are a disciple. I asked a question only a disciple could answer and you answered it." . . .

I know that in this period that there is a tremendous love that was between us, and it was always there. The funny thing about it is that I can't interpret it. In one way, it was a selfish love on my part, because I was never aware of the burdens that he carried as a spiritual teacher. I was like a child who does not realize what a parent has to go through in order to service its needs. I had no understanding of the burdens that were on his back . . . but I did have a real love for him, and I think that's probably the seed of the first conscious love I would ever experience in my life, the beginning, the planted seed.

Wali Ali: "I think it was one of his first experiences, too, with people. Certainly among the first where I think the love that he got from the young people that he came in contact with made him free to be what he was." . . .

Nancy: "It's very interesting how he changed . . . I had said, 'Murshid, I want to give a party for you for Christmas. You just invite all your disciples and I just want you to do whatever you want to do. I want you to have a wonderful Christmas.'"

This was Christmas, 1967, and Sam was described as being so happy there, he was in *samadhi*.

Getting to Know Murshid Sam in San Francisco

In early 1968, at age 71, Sam responded to a survey conducted by one Chris Fueloep-Miller entitled "The Relevance of Eastern Religions to Western Youth." It is illuminating, even delightful, to see how Sam reported his eclectic influences and views. The survey and Sam's responses are presented in full in the Archives.[767] Selections are offered here.

1. d) Occupation
   Retired Gardener, Horticulturalist. Now writer and teacher of Oriental philosophies . . .
1. e) Number of years interest in Eastern religions:
   Since 1915. Began reading Max Muller and "Sacred Books of the East" in 1916.

3. a) Which specific Eastern religion are you interested in and why did you choose it?
All religions. Influence by the late Cassius Keyser of Columbia to a universal outlook. Later also by Lord Russell to universality, and of course, Emerson and Jefferson, later Whitman.
4. In the religions content, would you comment on Kipling's phrase: "East is East, and West is West, and never the twain shall meet."
You are quoting a single line from a poem which says otherwise at the end. Read the whole thing. (Was last person to be given a tea-of-honor in Kipling's old workshop in Lahore.)
7. a) Give any information you wish about your social and religions background.
Tried four kinds of Judaism, then six kinds of Christianity. But with rare [exceptions] direct experience not accepted—until one also met Christian and Jewish mystics—and these, not until long after one met Oriental mystics.
13. Was your original scale of values (i.e. before you came to Eastern religion) enhanced or changed by your contact with Eastern thought and religion?
The Divine Experience (neither "East" nor "West" and yet both) transforms all values.
14. Sum up as best you can what the relevance of Eastern religious thought and practice is to you.
Having attained to Spiritual Majority, confirmed by Sufi Pirs, my own Gurus (Paul Brunton and Swami Ram Das) and several **Asian** *Buddhist Masters, the best evidence has been the manifestation of untrammeled vitality in a body over 70. Also ability to help others toward self-realization, at least to Love, Joy and Peace; and in some cases by having disciples who have had self-realization . . .*
Samuel L. Lewis
S.A.M. (the Yogi)
Sufi Ahmed Murad-Chisti (the Sufi)
He Kwang, Zen-Shi (the Buddhist)

Turning back to remembrances of early followers of Sam, Moineddin and Fatima Jablonski also shared how they came to know that he was to be their spiritual leader. The interview began with "Did you know right away that he was going to be your Murshid?"[768]

Sam with future Pir Moineddin Jablonski

MOINEDDIN: "I guess I had a feeling, but it certainly didn't present itself like that. I didn't know anything about discipleship or anything. I just knew I wanted to meet a Zen master."
FATIMA: "We knew right away that we were going to study with him, because we were going to [Subud]* where we had to sit outside for 3 months and listen to them inside. So we went and sat outside for 3 months and we were just about to go in, and then we met Murshid, and we never [went] back to [Subud], I remember that."
MOINEDDIN: "Yeah, yeah, we gave up [Subud] instantly as soon as we met Murshid."

He continued:

Anyhow, after this first meeting at the Cosmic Messiah's house,† we started going to public meetings [at Sam's] . . . The address was 772 Clementina St. and it was the apartment formerly occupied by Gavin Arthur . . . You could look up at the dingy ceiling and see where some astrological symbols had been fixed, like little labels, and taken off . . .

---

*Subud is an international spiritual movement that began in Indonesia in the 1920s, founded by Muhammad Subuh Sumohadiwidjojo (1901-1987). The name Subud is formed from the first letters of the words *susila, budhi,* and *dharma,* together symbolizing the possibility for one to live a right life according to the will of God.
†The house of one Alan Noonan, said to be an "11th density being from the planet Jupiter." Recall that this was San Francisco in 1967.

> Anyhow . . . that little room was permeated with the kind of atmosphere that I'd never experienced before. Even the type of incense that he burned at the time, Murshida Vera burns the same kind. It was a Japanese incense, purple stick I think. It always reminds me of Clementina St., because the atmosphere was so potent it could just transform your being just by walking into it, even if Murshid was there or not . . .
>
> Mansur [Johnson] was actually my first guru because I said I was kind of on an atheist trip and Mansur, no matter what he said, always said that God was real. And that he connected or identified God with the experience of eternity, which we got glimpses of on our drug experiences or psychedelic experiences. It was really Mansur that gave me the glimpse that God was and could be a real being . . . So, we were writing to the Johnsons and ultimately they did come out the following fall of 1967 . . .
>
> I wrote to Mansur and told him I'd found a Zen Master, who turns out to be a Sufi teacher, which I don't know what I can tell you about, you just have to come out and experience it for yourself. That was an interesting thing because we'd invite our friends to come meet Murshid . . . who we called Sam at the time . . . We'd never heard the word Murshid. So, they'd say, "What's he like?" And we'd start saying, "He's like this," and we'd get halfway through our description of what he was like and realized there's every possibility that he's not like that at all! If they went to see him, he'd manifest any way he wanted to manifest . . . He'd be very sweet, or he'd be very nasty—anything could happen. Actually though, I must say, those were the days he was all sweetness, primarily . . . He never showed his rough side or his Fudo side until he moved to the Mentorgarten.

At Sam's meetings in the Mentorgarten, he usually began the class asking if anyone there had cold feet or an empty stomach. When someone would say yes, he would massage their feet or take them back into the kitchen to get something to eat.

Sam with Rev. Blighton

Moineddin continued his story.

> We went to meeting twice a week on Clementina St., and at one of these meetings a fellow who was later to play a certain role in Murshid's life . . . Father Earl Blighton, who before he died last year sometime [1974] was the head of the Holy Order of Mans,

> a Christian mystical organization—came to one or two of Murshid's meetings on Clementina St., as well as some of his disciples . . .
>
> [In] those first days on Clementina St., there were roughly 5 or 6 people who used to come and listen to Murshid's talks . . . He sat on the side of his little single bed there and spoke to us . . . Akbar was the first young person in our group or in the SF area to be initiated by Murshid. Murshid had . . . initiated quite a few people when he was living at the Kaaba Allah *khankah* in Fairfax. At this time in his life he had a few older *mureeds,* at least in their late 30s or early 40s. All men . . . We were really a new wave type of people who were seeking spiritual teachings and *baraka* and so forth. So we came and more and more people started coming and it started building very gradually.

In April of 1967 Sam fell ill while traveling.[769] Moineddin's recollection continues:

> After Murshid's return from Ojai, we heard he was in the hospital . . .
>
> We went in and I couldn't believe it . . . He just sort of looked ashen gray and . . . supremely subdued . . . It was as though he were hardly even alive . . . And as he later said, he'd [gotten] ptomaine poisoning, and I said Wow! What a bout you must have had with ptomaine to put you out that much! . . . That's where we met Joe and Guin Miller* for the first time. Joe and Guin were there and Joe was being his usual self—mostly serious this time. He was actually exhorting him to live . . . As I recall, he was saying "You know Sam, this world is waiting for you to give what you got to give them." And sure enough Murshid did rally back from the experience, which we later found out from his old friend Bill Hathaway, he said, "Don't tell the kids this, but I really had a heart attack." . . .

The attending physician confirmed the heart attack to Ted Reich and a few others.

> It was during this time in the hospital that [Sam] had a very profound vision. He said, "Yes, I saw a mountain, and at the top of the mountain was this little tiny trickle of water, and as it went down the mountain, other little trickles of water started gathering into it, and then a little farther down the mountain pretty soon streams began to run into it and

---

*Important friends and spiritual companions of Sam's, Joe and Guin Miller were later to play a significant role in support of Sam's followers.

then rivers . . . By the time it was down to the base of the mountain it was this tremendous wide expansive water that kept going and going." And later he realized what this was, which was the vision which was indicating to him that [this] stage of his mission [was] as a teacher. He said that the first trickle was the first disciples, and gradually as the message began to come down from the mountain top, more and more disciples were to come, and the message was to become broader and broader until finally . . . it went in 3 stages. The 1st stage went from 5 to 30 disciples, the 2nd stage was from 30–60 disciples, and the other stage was from 60–100 disciples.

And he was waiting for more than that I'm sure. He told me once, "God tells me that I may have to stay in the body till I'm 119!" And I could believe every word of it, because when he was vigorous, he was absolutely vigorous! . . . Shortly after this hospital trip which Murshid used to characterize by saying, "I'm a pretty feisty guy; sometimes even outright nasty, but, when I was in the hospital flat on my back, that's the time Allah chose to come and speak to me, so I couldn't talk back. I was flat on my back, I was just told what to do, so, and I couldn't talk at all." And he said that was the time God came and said, "I make you spiritual teacher of the hippies!"

That sort of concludes the Clementina St. chapter. Shortly after that Murshid . . . found a place over in the Mission District, which turned out to be 410 Precita Avenue, which is now known as the Mentorgarten . . . It was June of '67 he moved to Mentorgarten and set up house there.

Moineddin went on to describe his discovery of the great strength Sam carried, in addition to the sweetness he had always experienced. Moineddin had been experiencing difficulties with a house guest.

We . . . went to a meeting and I think Murshid picked up something through the ethers, and he just said to me after the meeting, "You're gonna have to tell that man to get out of your house." . . . Up to this time Murshid had shown the "sweet" side of his nature, and when he asked me to kick a man out of my house, I realized all of a sudden there was a certain strength in his being which I simply hadn't realized. I think he knew that it was going to be a problem for me to do it but he asked me to do it, so I said I would and I went home and I did. I kicked him out and I said, "You're simply not right for us at this point, so please leave." And he left . . .

> [In] my first meeting with Murshid as my Fudo, or Fudo-sama, who is the bodhisattva of dharma protection who manifests his fiery nature or his powerful nature more often than not . . . Murshid said if you're really Fudo, you have to have Quan Yin or all mercy behind your actions just as if you're Quan Yin you have to have the strength ultimately to back up your gentleness.

Moineddin also related his experience of Sam as a reincarnation of Marpa, teacher of the famous Tibetan yogi Milarepa.

> Murshid was leading us on [a particular form of walking, and] at this point on our walk, we were coming down the hill real fast, my mind doing what you might call a real fast water walk. And it was so fast, my mind started delighting in the step we were taking down the hill, and we were actually way ahead of Murshid and I looked back and said, "Hey Murshid, Clark said that you were Marpa in your past life." And I looked in front of me so I could see where I was going, and I heard this voice yelling, "Yeah, what of it?" It was Murshid's voice. I said "Yeah!" and he said, "So what'd you think?" And I felt this attraction to look backwards again . . . and there was Murshid and all of a sudden it was just Murshid leading us on a walk. He was full of this incredible, as Wali Ali would say, this radioactive power which was just exuding or flaming out of every pore, and at the same time he was just this compact fiery being just like an atom bomb, mini-sized. I realized later that this was the first manifestation of Fudo, in his own way, in Tibet, many centuries ago. The effect it had on Marpa was to produce cosmic awakening, which was the whole point.

Samuel Lewis had begun to fully devote himself to taking in *mureeds*, mostly hippies, and teaching them, among other things, how to walk.

An Unusual *Mureed:* How She Lived and How She Met Murshid Sam

Another poignant account of what could mystically happen when meeting Murshid Sam comes from Deborah Churney Lewis, to whom he later gave the name Devi. She showed up after his heart attack at only 15 years of age, having left her difficult home situation. Her father was absent, her mother disconnected from her, and she needed a safe place to live. She was invited to live in the apartment of Brian, a young British *mureed* of Sam's, which she did. She met Sam not long after.

I interviewed Devi in 1976, five years after Murshid Sam had left his body. The following excerpts are from her remembrance.[770]

Devi described how she first met Murshid Sam:

> I remember . . . we came and picked [Murshid] up here [at the Mentorgarten]; Murshid sat in the front seat and I sat in the back seat. Brian drove the car and there was no one else there, and I was really in awe of [Sam] for some reason. I had just heard about him . . . He turned around and he said "Hello." He just said "Hello, what's your name?"

Decades later Devi reported that Murshid Sam had played the flute of Krishna for her during that car ride. It affected her deeply and is a living memory for her.

> I don't think that he said anything else, but as soon as he got out of the car I started crying for no reason—I don't know why, I just couldn't stop crying. I just cried for about an hour . . .
>
> I loved him, I really loved him the first time I met him, but I was always afraid of him a little bit . . . the whole time that I knew him . . .
>
> The one thing that always really upset me, as I remember, I asked after I'd been to I don't know how many meetings, and maybe I'd been with Murshid for a month or so and I asked him if I could become a disciple of his, and all he said was, "Sure," and he never initiated me. He just said, "Sure," and there it was, and I never got initiated and I never asked him about it afterwards.

I commented on that remark: "But then he always considered you a disciple and he had you come to disciples' meetings and stand up when he asked his disciples to stand up and all that . . . There were a whole number of people, especially in that first period before things became somewhat more formal that he didn't formally initiate but he just took them on in his heart."

Devi replied:

> Yeah, I always felt that in action but I always felt that because he had me present for initiations for other people after that—not too soon after that—I would be in the room and he would initiate people, and I would

always say, "Shouldn't I be?"—and I thought, "Oh well, I'm not going to say anything because he never said anything to me" . . .

I loved the dancing, and I remember the first class that he had. He had a women's dance class . . . There were 3 or 4 ladies and it was upstairs here at the Mentorgarten on Friday afternoons, and I always used to get out of high school early—they let me out so I could come to it. I don't know how I talked them into it but they let me out—so I used to come to that, and we would just work on the planetary walks, in the very beginning, and then it turned into men coming too to the class. That's how that Saturday night dance class began.

Devi related that most of the time was spent working on "the astrological things," and there was a lot of walking. Sam would have them do walks through the Haight-Ashbury. Often they would eat dinner at a vegetarian restaurant, the Brother Juniper Café, which was owned by the Holy Order of Mans. Later Murshid would occasionally offer teachings there while sitting at one of the tables.

Devi shared that her first dream was to pursue dance. "I was really dreaming of that, but I was only studying Indian dance with that lady Janicki . . . a few times a week, and I wasn't studying anything else in the other forms of dance." Murshid had plans of his own to support that:

Murshid said that I should go to India and that he would send me, or that is the impression that I got anyway—but I was only 16 at the time, and so there was some doubt as to who would go with me, because I couldn't legally go out of the country at that age, but he wrote all these introductions; he wrote one to the President [Hussain] of India . . . He took me to Air India and to the Consulate and to a travel agent and—I didn't know exactly what was happening, because I obviously didn't have the money to do it . . .

To clarify, I asked if he had said he was going to find the money for her to go. Devi responded, "That is the impression I had. I never, of course, would approach him."

I commented:

But see, it's [an] interesting thing to bring up, because I know about [him and] money, that he had a funny attitude in the sense that he would never like to put a negative out in terms of something that was

> possibly going to happen. He always felt like if he kept doors open in a positive direction something might come, and he always had a great intention to want to help people materially, which occasionally would backfire on him and he would get uptight and complain to me or to some other person that was close to him about people that were taking advantage of him monetarily . . . it was an on-going thing, because after [one *mureed*] moved in here, then shortly after that he started having these operations and he didn't have the money to pay his rent and so on, but Murshid would oscillate between being very generous materially and drawing out of his own income and then finding that he was short in terms of money.

Sam managed to get the *mureed* a place at the Holy Order of Mans, where he could stay without monetary problems. To Devi I added:

> [Sam's] attitude towards money, I think, is interesting because he scrimped and saved most of his life and had to live on virtually nothing and then he said that he'd gotten a sign to be generous and not to worry about money. The last years of his life, he got himself into some funny situations about it. I know he often indicated or hinted that there might be money coming to this or that, to underwrite a program or scholarship or . . . event, and he was kind of hoping that if he put it out and concentrated on it that it might manifest, [if] not through him exactly.

Devi continued:

> I thought of him as the prophet in a certain sense. I thought of him as . . . his being makes me cry when I think of it, and it always did—I respected no one more than I respected him, and I didn't not respect people, but I didn't listen to what people said when they were older than me just because—I was very rebellious in a certain way—and I would do anything that he wanted me to do, although he never told me anything to do.

Except, of course, for practices.

How I Arrived on Sam's Doorstep

> *Our limited self is a wall separating us from the self of God.*
>
> HAZRAT INAYAT KHAN[771]

> *All spiritual training and discipline has no other purpose than this, to escape from this thought of self, to rise above the mind-mesh, to become*

> *free from limitation. It is our own thought of self which confines us to limitation. Laying this aside, we lay all burdens aside. Do not cease to think of self; think of God and let that thought draw all other thoughts. This is the way to liberation.*
>
> Samuel Lewis[772]

Knowledge of Sufi Sam's existence and teachings was growing in 1968, and his meetings at the Mentorgarten were well attended. I arrived at Murshid's home through a most unusual and spiritual set of circumstances. I was one of those hippies the voice of God had drawn to Sam.

As an undergraduate at the University of Alabama I had become editor of the school newspaper, and later I got a fellowship to Vanderbilt in Philosophy. It protected me from being drafted to go to Vietnam and gave adequate income for me to go to school and rent an apartment. After several years I passed all the tests that were necessary toward receiving a Ph.D. My dissertation was to be on "Cosmic Laughter, the Laughter of God." I had gotten the inspiration for it on an LSD trip with a close friend on a mountain in Maine. The point of it was all human beings are intrinsically filled with the God reality and still most of us go around complaining and being our own worst enemy. I wanted an experience and not just recognition. When I looked in the eyes of my professors, I could see that they hoped I knew something, and I hoped they knew something. I was ready to leave. I picked up a Master's degree in passing and headed for San Francisco to connect with a community that had been publicized as the Summer of Love. It was early in 1968 when I arrived and I was hoping to find some LSD. I finally got the psychedelic, and after taking it began to roam around in Golden Gate Park. Suddenly I came upon a rally supporting, of all people, George Wallace for President of the United States.

Naturally, I turned around and went in the other direction.* A group of youthful people chanting Hare Krishna saw me and invited me to come

---

*Somehow I have to give George Wallace thanks for unconsciously helping me on my journey. When I was editor of the newspaper, we published an article in strong support of integration. George Wallace's response was to call the university president and demand, "Get that damn Jew off this campus!" The University responded by hiring private detectives to follow me and my friends and fellow workers at the school newspaper. These men they hired had been policemen in Birmingham, where the Black freedom riders had

to their center nearby, where they were having practices of recitation and worship. I walked there with them and after sitting in their midst, floating around above it all, I was moved to talk with a man about my age. He had a nice red beard, and I liked his face. I approached him and said the first thing that came into my mind. "I'm writing my dissertation on the laughter of God and I wonder if you could be of any help." (I had no interest in actually writing it.) He made his living playing guitar on Haight Street, leaving the case open for donations. He answered me immediately and said, "I know somebody who has that quality, but I doubt if he would be interested in helping you with your dissertation. He would be much more inclined to help in your spiritual development." It took me all of a few seconds to say yes. The bearded man's name was Daniel Lomax and he proceeded to write down for me Sufi Samuel Lewis's name and address on Precita Avenue. There was a meeting that night. He drew me a map of how to get there, and also gave me the name of a Buddhist teacher in Chinatown with an address up three flights of stairs.

I took off for the Sufi teacher's place, got lost along the way, picked up a taxicab, and arrived somewhat late for the meeting. Once inside I walked upstairs to his front room. It was beautifully filled with about 20 young people. I sat down in the doorway to the room and Sam shouted at me, "Don't block the doorway!" I awkwardly found a place inside.

During his talk that night he spoke of his training in Zen Buddhism, where he had received all the different forms of laughter from the monk Nyogen Senzaki. He also expressed his dislike for professors who just had concepts and were not fit to teach. At that moment I decided not to share my own history with him any time soon. I was completely attracted to him. His voice was filled with wisdom and confidence and you could look right in his eyes and see something. I immediately decided to keep coming back to classes there.

The next day I found my way to the Buddhist temple Daniel had written about. There was an awesome atmosphere there as well. The teacher in charge was in a period where he was inviting a number of

---

been attacked with cattle prods. The president at the University of Alabama ultimately rejected Governor Wallace's demand. After that I went to Vanderbilt and from there came to San Francisco.

guest teachers, and that day Joe Miller, one of Sam's closest friends, was the speaker. He was loud and also full of mirth like Sam, but I knew of no connection between the two. Joe would sometimes address Sam as Marpa, and Sam would reply calling him Milarepa. It was all full of happiness, and beneath that, a layer of great wisdom.

I continued to concentrate on being with Sam, going over to help him with his work almost every day if need be. I was asked to do some basic functions like washing the dishes and filing documents, taking out garbage. I never missed a class. Sam spoke at those classes and often said that he had no room for any new disciples at this time. In the course of the classes he also sang *La ilaha El Allahu* as best he could in the melody originally given by Hazrat Inayat Khan. This practice would directly lead to my initiation.

My apartment was out by the ocean and I still had one more dose of LSD in my possession. I took it and walked over to the beach. I noticed that I had a kazoo in my pocket for some reason I was unaware of. I found a seat looking out over the Pacific Ocean and began to try to sing the *zikr* I had heard from Sam. I was trying to sing it using the kazoo and felt very absorbed in it, unaware of other circumstances. After about half an hour in this state I came to my senses, stood up and moved to walk onto the beach. Now I noticed that I had been surrounded by at least a dozen people. They were all shouting to me, "You can't leave us in this state!" I ignored them, played my kazoo and walked on.

Now I could really hear the *zikr,* and it had become the voice of the whole universe! All of it was coming forth from the kazoo in the most beautiful of melodies, and I was happy beyond belief. Suddenly I realized that while I could draw out the sound of the kazoo beautifully, I had totally forgotten how to talk! I could not speak a single word, much less a sentence. Inwardly I was guided to look for Samuel Lewis. Then I felt his presence and heard his voice saying, "What got you this far will take you further on. It has taken you up and it will take you down to earth."

About a week later I was granted an interview with Murshid. I was concerned because I had heard him say in two previous classes that he had no room for more *mureeds.* I told him of my experience at the beach and he replied, "That itself was an initiation. Come to the class for *mureeds* on Thursday night and I will initiate you," and he did.

After becoming absorbed in singing Hazrat Inayat Khan's *zikr* and hearing Sufi Sam's voice of encouragement, I immediately moved from the beach to a house on Cole Street near the panhandle of Golden Gate Park. Only one of the people who lived in the house, Rashid, had a job, which was with the U.S. Post Office. He paid the whole bill every month and the large size of the apartments created the space to welcome others. The young people living there were all connected with Samuel Lewis through his classes and his reputation as a powerful mystical teacher. Daniel Lomax lived there as well. A few weeks later an old bus showed up with a family inside, who were also welcomed into the apartment. Daniel's wife-to-be was on that bus. The way this community house formed was in tune with the times.

Photo by Mansur Johnson

Sam with Wali Ali

I still commuted frequently to Sam's house on Precita Avenue to help give my teacher the support he needed. I could be seen as a bit of a misfit in the community house on Cole Street, in that I had gotten a job at the synagogue in Marin, where for $100 a week I taught the confirmation class using *Tales of the Hasidim* by Martin Buber. It was a very popular class, but I was informed not to come one week because an Israeli group would be in charge of addressing the students. I told the head of education there that to balance things I would bring in some Palestinians the following week, who could then express their different point of view. After that I was called in to a meeting with the Rabbi and was fired from my job.

Other communes and community gathering places were arising throughout the Bay Area and Marin County, including the *khankah* in Novato called The Garden of Inayat. In addition to the walking practices that Sam was already giving to groups, there were weekly classes at the Garden of Inayat, the Mentorgarten, and the Garden of Allah community in Corte Madera. Some classes were in a few *mureeds'* homes such as at Sheyla's in Marin. Olompali Ranch, an unusual commune near Novato already forming on a large scale, became a place from which

Sam dictating to Wali Ali

some people were drawn to Sam.* Paul Reps and Murshid Sam dreamed of creating a school based on the vision of Hazrat Inayat Khan, and considered Olompali Ranch a possible site for it.

Toward the end of 1968, Murshid instructed David Hoffmaster to invite me to come live at the Mentorgarten with Murshid and David, commencing on the first of the new year of 1969. I relinquished my apartment and moved. There was no charge—I had free room and board. When Sam saw that I was an excellent typist, he gave me a great deal of work copying his commentaries and poems and taking dictation from him when he composed letters. It all was part of the ongoing journey in my life, a blessing that I have never regretted, and often laughed at.

Saadia Visits the U.S.

> *Your suggestion about coming here is most wonderful. I would think it over carefully and pray for guidance because here I might be wishing. The spiritual love is not the divine love. In the divine love we see Allah and only Allah and in the spiritual love we see His Attributes rather than His Essence. The most important attribute is* **rahm**, *which is the root of* rahman *and* rahim, *which is in everybody's prayers and only in the hearts of Dervishes, not ordinary people.*
>
> SAMUEL LEWIS[773]

Turning back to Sam's goddaughter in Pakistan, Saadia Khawar Khan reenters the story during this time, finally able to make her long-planned trip to study in the U.S. in 1968. As early as 1963 Sam had been making plans for her arrival and envisioning what she would be able to offer as well as study. "The letter from Khawar indicates she would be coming

---

*Mansur Johnson, in his book *Murshid* (Seattle: PeaceWorks Publications, 2006, 74), relates that the ranch was a place "where the Grateful Dead play, people swim nude, several of Murshid's disciples live, and he visited from time to time."

after the next semester and as she wants to get a PhD in Islamics I have recommended either the Middle East Institute Washington or UCLA. She has films of the holy cities (Mecca and Medina) and there is already a sponsor for their showing plus a big conference in March."[774]

Sam later wrote Saadia about what was happening in San Francisco:

> There are a large number of young people called **Hippies** and they have been coming here and receiving spiritual instructions, in particular *zikr* and now, *inshallah,* I am ready to open a *khankah* and teach the *zikrs* on a large scale. My closest spiritual brother has urged me to go the authorities, which I shall and place everything on the table. For there seems to be nobody who can handle these wild young people but a single Christian minister, who is an outcast and a very good friend, and myself. They resound to love and blessing just as earnestly and eagerly as others do not. I am limited to the number of [12 *mureeds*] at this time . . . Therefore I shall not go to Pakistan unless there is a Divine Command, an *amr,* or *kashf* or especially *shahud* [direct or deep sight]; the last has been very strong lately.[775]

He was torn between the idea of returning to Lahore to use a place Saadia owned as a center, and remaining in California with the hippies who looked up to him. He had described part of the backstory earlier:

> I'll skip to the most remarkable of series of events. Although direct romance always irony-izes—and the door isn't closed . . . I met Khawar Khan in society and we were drawn to each other by a superlative force as if we were part of each other. Within two months I became two things we do not have here [in the US.]:
>
> a. Her god-father. When a person, especially a woman, is an orphan, she finds a god-father or a god-brother, etc. and these persons become her legal and even moral confidants.
>
> b. Her spiritual teacher. This is something I cannot explain because we have nothing exactly like it in this country . . .
>
> Inasmuch as there are restrictions on women this meant gossip but step by step the whole thing has now reversed. Khawar was the youngest whole professor in Pakistan who is a woman, one at 26. In addition to that she had gone to Mecca which made her prestige rise . . .
>
> Then I found she was very wealthy although I did not know this. She also owns the property which was Gandhi's before partition, and this may be very important.[776]

> It is mine for use whenever I want it.[777]
>
> Now she has won first prize at an all-Asian conference of Psychologists and because of this my own prestige has gone up and up.[778]
>
> Since she won the award . . . she has been offered more jobs and has so much money she is willing to support me for the rest of my life—five sources of income and no dependents.[779]

Saadia had graduated from the American University in Beirut. She had a Professorship at University of the Punjab in Lahore and had also taught at the College of Domestic Arts and Sciences. She was recognized throughout Pakistan as a professor whose writings on Islamic matters were respected by all, including the President of the country, psychologists and philosophers. Sam had written of her increasing renown earlier, "[We] collaborated on a paper to be presented at an international gathering of philosophers (I don't have 'credentials' sez who). It won first prize! She was acclaimed, the paper was sent to [President] Ayub and is being published."[780]

Saadia went on to complete her doctorate and to serve as a member of the Higher Education Commission of Pakistan, as an advisor to the Government of Azad Kashmir for Curriculum Development from the point of view of Islam, and as a contributor to the book *Islam and Ecology: A Bestowed Trust*.[781]

Sam also wrote,

> Helping [Khawar], she was boosted as being Public Philosophy #1 and now she reports she was acclaimed as Public Psychologist #1, given long publicity in Pakistan (she sent me extensive clippings) and has been invited to Iran, too. Now the people who do not realize or accept that it is the *mureeds* who make the Murshid cannot realize what this means to my face and career abroad. For, every virtue and success of hers is ascribed to my *baraka* and not to her personal wisdom.[782]

Part of Ahmed Murad's role as godfather had been to find a suitable husband for Saadia. About his attempts he wrote:

> My adopted son [Anwar], who is also the brother by adoption of [Major Sadiq's] wife, has met my Khalifa Khawar and fallen in love. I should have wished this, but Khawar did not want a divorcee. Each of these

> persons has offered me a home—Khawar in Lahore, and the Major Anwar in Islamabad. For me, personally, this would be the greatest blessing possible, but we shall see.[783]
>
> On top of that she has received another proposal, this time from Iqbal's son. We had discussed this before and I told her I could not be disinterested because such a marriage would immediately push my poetry forward; for letters from him would help me greatly toward publications. Since my god-son, Anwar, has also proposed, this puts me in a strange position for while I have given him a blessing, I have given them both suitable *wazifas* which will reach their hearts and lead them aright.[784]

However, the various persons brought up for consideration were not accepted. Quite unannounced and to the surprise of many, Saadia appeared at Cornell University in Ithaca, New York, in 1968, where she matriculated and where she met the man who would become her husband. The groom was chosen by Saadia's family, and Bibijan, who had joined Saadia in Ithaca, wrote Sam about it, seeking his blessing. Sam looked forward to meeting this man in Ithaca when he traveled East.

Sam's First Meeting with Pir Vilayat

Hazrat Inayat Khan's son Vilayat and Sam had communicated previously although they had never met. Now, thanks in part to the encouragement given by Shamcher Beorse to both of them, Pir Vilayat and Sam met in June of 1968 at the Mentorgarten, where Pir Vilayat had been invited to speak to a goodly number of Sam's students.

Because Vilayat was not recognized as Pir by the Sufi Movement, he organized on his own under the title of the Sufi Order. When he came into Sam's home prepared to give a speech, he was wrapped in a large black robe and was noticeably nervous, sweating profusely. I was there among many others in the upstairs room.

Pir Vilayat spoke at length of his experience with the Sufis in Konya, the realm of the dances, and how he was requested to join in. He also told stories about the amazing qualities of different dervishes he met on his travels. At the conclusion of his talk he welcomed questions from those present. One of our number raised his hand and said in a beautifully naïve way, "Where can you meet one of these dervishes?" Pir Vilayat immediately pointed to Sam, who was sitting in his robe at the front of the room, and responded, "You've got one right here!" Sam often described his meeting with Pir Vilayat by saying, "I had only one breath to decide whether I would accept him or not, and do you know why I chose to accept him? Because I am a romantic." Sam also observed, "This was not personality agreement. We live and move and have our being in God . . . Hearts may be at ease, you may be at ease. My work is intensive in time and space and Vilayat's extensive. The soul of Hazrat Inayat Khan may now rest in peace."[785]

Sam was certainly in part a romantic, but when Pir Vilayat pointed Sam out as one of these mystical dervishes that he had been speaking of, it would have made every difference to Sam, who had always wanted to be recognized as truly authentic by the family tree of Hazrat Inayat Khan. The effect of this moment was much like Sam's response to the acknowledgement by the *Sidi* from Morocco.

About five days later, a regular meeting of Murshid Sam's students was held at his home in the city, filling the front room. A few minutes into the meeting Murshid said to us all, referring to Pir Vilayat's previous talk, "You all are interested in Dervishes. I have danced with Dervishes all over the world. We will do what he talks about!" This remark was not meant to be offensive. Sam was a doer, and he wanted to bring alive the Dances and more. As was his way, he also praised Pir Vilayat, saying that his talk about the Dervish dancing had made Pir Vilayat the father of the Dances. With that remark he led us downstairs to the garage, where there was an oil stain from David's pickup truck and where we would practice many times before it got dressed up as a meeting room. It was here that the Saturday night Dance and Walk class was held. Male students were allowed to join after passing one of the Astrological Walks that Murshid taught.

After Pir Vilayat's visit to the Bay Area he made a trip to Los Angeles to meet with his chief secretary. Likewise, a new Mentorgarten resident named Zeynab made the trip with three other *mureeds* to tape some of Pir Vilayat's lectures. She responded to Sam's indication that he needed financial help to succeed with his work by securing $1000 from her bank account and sending it back to Sam. She had been in a very difficult mental state when she met Murshid Sam and felt that he had changed her life. "I had no need of a $1000—I needed my sanity."[786] She continued to live at the Mentorgarten for a year and a half.

It was a year later that Sam traveled to LA to join Pir Vilayat in a business meeting after Vilayat had stopped for a short visit in the Bay Area. Sam's traveling companions were of three of his *mureeds*: Moineddin, Zeynab, and Mansur.

On the trip down they stopped in Camarillo at the land of Sheikha Bhakti Engel, whose husband had been a leader in the Sufi Movement in New York and Cleveland. Despite a heated conversation between Murshid Sam and Bhakti about the propriety of charging for Sufi teachings, the group would stop there again on the return trip. Sam wrote,

> We went first to Camarillo where some spiritual colleagues live—five children and a whole orchard of Avocados (yum-yum). Then we called on [Papa] Ramdas's grandson in Hollywood and "then the fun began." We went to so many places and generally ran into friends of Gwen (Zeynab) our housekeeper. It was just like a series of stories. We also met at least one Bengali musician and friends, etc., etc. His name is Alla Raka.* In all places we danced our *Subhan-Allah, Alhamdu Lillah, Allaho Akbar.*
>
> We did an awful lot of jumping. Now the story of "love" is out. I learned my name has been given over the air as a sort of mysterious [San Franciscan] who is using a "love-cure" for Hippies. Anyhow one feels more assured and more tender.[787]

Walking and Dancing with Ruth St. Denis and Murshid Sam

> *We are now the "children of God," and in the exact measure of our understanding of this spiritual fact will our interpretation of the human body and all its movements assume a different picture to our minds and deeper assurance to our hearts. We shall see that we are looking at the total person! We are looking at a child of God; a ray of the Divine Light; an idea of the One Mind!*[788]

---

* Alla Rakha was the father and guru of illustrious tabla virtuoso Zakir Hussein.

The dance of the future will no longer be concerned with meaningless dexterities of the body but will move in harmony with the compassionate and joyous rhythms of love, and will obey in strength and balance the vital laws of truth. Here upon the eternal lotus pattern of love and truth the Divine Dance treads the measures of eternity in praise! [789]

RUTH ST. DENIS

Ruth St. Denis was the renowned dancer who had hired Inayat Khan and his relatives to give the musical openings to her dance performances. At that time she was focused on what she pictured as Indian dance. Her packed audiences were not impressed by the classical Indian music Inayat and his kin opened with. This ensemble had even been applauded after tuning up their instruments by an audience that couldn't distinguish Indian music from tuning. Ruth deepened in her understanding of India as time went on. Her relationship with Sam, whom she saw occasionally over the years, was positive. He looked to her as someone he could fully trust in the area of creative dance.

Sam had brewing within him visions of how he would revolutionize the world. He was strongly drawn to share these visions with Ruth St. Denis and often later related to his students the story of a memorable exchange in 1964. He recounted that when he came into her room he shouted, "Mataji, I'm going to change the world." "What are you going to do?" she said. "I'm going to teach little children how to walk." She then jumped up from her chair and shouted back, "You've got it! You've got it!" Such support was very important for Sam.

Ruth St. Denis

Although this seemingly simple original inspiration was focused on teaching little children in Pakistan, it was based on Sam's belief that through Walking practices, one could gain direct wisdom through their own inner knowing.

He desired for people to move from a "world of sayings" to embodied experience, and the Walks provided a tool for just that. They developed groundedness and self-assurance as each person discovered their own natural rhythms. Concurrently practitioners developed mastery of various rhythms to aid in the formation of a more complete picture of their being. Several approaches were employed to this end: Centering Walks (focused on the several body centers), Elemental Walks (focused on study and development of the elements earth, water, fire, air, and ether), Planetary Walks or Astrological Yoga (using the qualities of the planets), *Wazifah* Walks (embodying the Divine qualities) and *Tasawwuri* Walks (walks of effacement in or attunement to the great teachers of humankind). When engaged in depth, the Walks offered a full course in spiritual development: concentration, breath practice, centering, self-effacement, attunement, and devotion. Through inner discovery and intention, people could learn more about themselves and actualize their divine natures.

Beyond the inspiration of Walking, the vision of the Dance of Universal Peace Sam experienced at the tomb of the Sufi Sheikh Salim Chishti in Fatehpur Sikri was unfaded. He shared this vision with Ruth, who, Sam reported, told him she and Ted Shawn had placed it into the *Akasha** and went on to teach him how to draw dances from that source.[790]

The Walks and Dances were a central teaching focus for Sam on his return from LA. In *Spiritual Dancing* (written in the 1930s) he had already brought forward an approach well compatible with that espoused by Ruth St. Denis (as illustrated in the epigraph above):†

---

*A Sanskrit term adapted in usage by Theosophy, *Akasha* here refers to a universal etheric field storing a record of all events, thoughts, and emotions.

†Research has not established the timeline of Sam's earliest meeting with Ruth. However, this passage in *Spiritual Dancing* could easily be referring to her, possibly based on direct encounter: "In and around Hollywood there is at least one teacher whose methods are based upon cardiac mechanics and heart-concentration. Its pupils learn, more or less consciously, to invoke psychic forces. They imbibe philosophy from the dance itself. Their spiritual faculties unfold without anything being said of them. At the same time, they emphasize interpretative rather than program dancing. To them, the right interpretive dance offers full scope to the will of the performer and gives her every opportunity for self-expression."

> Indeed, we look for a universal spiritual-aesthetic revival. The cultivation of ecstasy and attainment of superconsciousness are steps on the way. We are here to complete our humanity, not to avoid it. Therefore, we must hold before ourselves the idea of the holiness of man and the sacredness of the body. Institutions, themes, forms and ideas are inferior to man, for man was created by God, and these things made by man. As man grows in understanding, in consideration and in compassion, spiritual art will unfold itself accordingly. Man's heart-awakening must come first.[791]

Sam had long been delving into the transformational aspects of the Walks and had prescribed them to Saadia Khawar Khan in Lahore.

> My brother Saladin [Paul Reps] was here and the first steps were taken to show somebody the spirituality of how to walk, how to breathe and how to use the names (or attributes) of Allah. This is really the gist of *tasawwuf,* with or without books, and lectures and sermons.[792]
>
> Now your Murshid has a whole compendium of *tasawwuf* inside, as well as the writings, to show even little children how to walk with the *zikr* and *kalama* from earliest childhood. Only this must be illustrated. And when it is taught and done, there will be no boundary to either Islam or *tasawwuf* or anything and even a child will have direct wisdom from his own capacity.[793]
>
> Now I have learned the Walks, and there are the Walks under karma, and there are the Walks under salvation. These two stand distinct. The Walks under karma can be analyzed and learned and mastered, or they can master us. The Walks under salvation can be learned and mastered but not analyzed. When you were in love, could you analyze the walks you took to your beloved, or the walks your child took to you?[794]

In 1966 Sam wrote again to Saadia about the Walks and indicated his own progression with their application.

> Now as for walking. Till this time I have walked as devotee, to feel the presence or the *sifat* of Murshids and Saints and Allah Himself (*Akhlak* Allah) and now your Murshid must walk as a Murshid to attune to and help the *mureeds* in so far as Allah permits and blesses. This has never been tried but now His Blessed Majesty of Mecca Shereef [Prophet Muhammad] gives this as instruction, and it shall be tried either after this letter is completed, or if it be long, then during the writing.[795]

In the spring of 1967, some Walks classes for early *mureeds* began. Sam later wrote in his diary:

> This gadfly jogs and listens to God-Allah, and the young believe and they ask how they can learn. The first thing was to teach them how to walk . . . And while the old ladies snicker one taught them how to walk, and to breathe and pretty soon miracles began to happen.[796]
>
> I only have room for twenty here [at the Mentorgarten] and if the groups get larger, will break them up. Saturday morning is based on walking. We have the "Walking Yoga" and it has been effective not only in awakening the inner consciousness but in helping the devotees to walk a long time without fatigue and also to climb hills. The subject of *tassawuri* was not introduced [by Inayat] until [a *mureed*'s] sixth year, I believe. But I am unable to follow the complete *Gatha-Githa* method because I do not have all the papers and will not ask anymore.[797]

Pir Vilayat had asked Sam to form a center of the Sufi Order in San Francisco. At that point Sam informed him that Ivy Duce had taken his own commentary writings as well as various teaching papers of Pir-o-Murshid Inayat Khan. Over the ensuing years, Sam's commentaries and many of the other papers were returned to him through the help of Pir Vilayat's brother, Pir Hidayat Khan, who had become the head of the Sufi Movement, and later through the help of Pir Vilayat as well. Sam had obtained teachings of Inayat Khan among Rabia Martin's things and had delivered them to both the Sufi Order and the Sufi Movement, a gift appreciated by both parties.

Sam spoke about Pir Vilayat to Shamcher Beorse:

> I can only accept him as a Murshid, or even a Pir-o-Murshid, and am setting about doing just what is in his mind. We had already taken the first steps to restore the ancient mysteries of the Dance. We are in agreement in accepting Miss Ruth St. Denis and it was a joy to hear somebody show the relation between Pythagoreanism and the Mevlevis and explain what is behind the Astrological mysteries. . . .
>
> If there was any [theme] with Vilayat it was that Knowledge is born of Love, and the fact that this impressed all these young people is most important. He has a good knowledge of cosmic philosophy growing out

of his assimilation of all faiths on a much higher plane than the local "universal religion" people, who have not worshipped in churches, temples, pagodas, mosques all over the world . . .

One of our next jobs will be to remove some of his pain. This seems to be innately and intuitively a common project.* People who receive enthusiasms and applause do not reach depths. Here the depths were reached. These are not the Old Age emotionalists who seize vocabularies. These are the New Age people, generally with Indian "souls" back to earth to continue their [aeonic] mission and growth . . .

We are not only in the New Age, Shamcher. **We are the New Age.** Older people will not accept it and younger people will not reject it.[798]

Sam used to say, "Focus on inner space and inner feeling happens first. Vision comes by grace, not in response to an audience." The first public Dervish Dances began on June 24, 1968. Sam wrote more about developments with the Dances and Walks:

Dancing gives more than Walking and especially when accompanied by the proper instruments. Several young people have learned the tabla and they are well qualified to work with dancers . . . Just as real Sufis of other ages have found benefits from singing and dancing, so Sam . . . is doing the same . . .

I have open house on Thursday and Sunday nights and restricted classes in dancing by invitation only. What is written can be demonstrated; the cults do not demonstrate, that is the difference.[799]

Early dancers

Sam's *zikr* class was overflowing and his *fikr*-Walking group was also growing. Ahmed Murad, a Saint in his Pakistani Khalifa's book, had given Walks to both Saadia Khawar Khan and her aunt Bibijan to perform after their prayers. He was continuously writing as a teacher to Saadia and her aunt. In March of 1968

*Hazrat Inayat Khan had quietly mentioned to a few *mureeds* that his son Vilayat would have significant problems in his life.

Ahmed Murad told us, "The Sufi Dance will not be on different principles from the Walk so far as the inner practice is concerned, but **instead of space taking us in, we will take space in**. And that is the difference between the dance and the pilgrimage." The Dances work from inside out, not outside in.

Ahmed Murad's Teaching Centers Expand

Pir Vilayat responded to an invitation to visit the Olompali land in November, 1968, just a few months after his appearance at the Mentorgarten and his recognition of Samuel Lewis as a Murshid in the Sufi Order. Finely attired as always, he moved among the people there. His coat bore a button that said "I am you." The pool was open and many of those present disrobed and went for a swim in full view of all.

Pir Vilayat had told his secretary that he would later dedicate an International Meditation Center during a camp gathering in Colorado. However, given the importance of the moment and the many happy faces around him, he chose to make the declaration at Olompali during his talk. His approach fit in perfectly with Murshid Sam's view of establishing a universal school there.

It was only the month before, on October 20, that the Garden of Inayat had been formally opened with a large outside celebration that included the Dances. Murshid Sam decided to present the Murshid's Blessing Dance. In this Dance every person in attendance was individually called into the center of the circle to be face to face with Sam, hands extended, turning in step with him and saying powerfully *El Allah Hu.* It was a transmission Dance. I had been in the Dance, and while saying the *zikr* with Murshid I had felt a strong collision outside of my body, like two trains colliding. I said nothing of it at the time. Three days later Murshid and I were having dinner together in San Francisco. Out of nowhere he said to me, "That was some collision, wasn't it?" It was a surprising thing to hear, but then Murshid was quite at home in that arena. It was brand new for me.

Sam described the day of the opening of the Garden of Inayat *khankah* in Novato.

In the kitchen at the Garden of Inayat

From *Sunseed*

In the first place, it takes considerable time and attention to be a murshid to over 50 *mureeds.* It takes more time and energy to lecture to the general public and to help prepare others for *bayat.* On Sunday October 20 we opened our *khankah* in the city of Novato in Marin County, some 30 miles to the north. This is only 2 miles from where the Pir dedicated his International Meditation Center. We had about a 100 people attend . . . the program which consisted mostly of dervish and yoga dancing.[800]

The event was full of life and joy. After the *khankah* opened, Sam had two offices: Novato and the Mentorgarten. He spent three days a week in Novato and four in San Francisco. He also held daytime classes at the Holy Order of Mans that included talks on Saint Paul and on The Gospel of St. Thomas.*

> I am addressing about a hundred young people every week but the signs are of breaking out. My colleague [at the Holy Order of Mans], Rev. Earl Blighton who went through the Valley of the Shadow of Death with me, or I with him, has also jumped from three to a hundred disciples in a very short time and has three centers, three outposts and cannot handle it. As the psychotherapist said, the young seek love and peace, and all their elders give them is "excitement."[801]

Murshid Sam also had a weekly daytime class at the commune on Cole Street. He gave talks inside the house, then took those present to the Panhandle park and led the Dances, especially the *Ramnam* and *Hari Krishna* Dances. Anyone could approach and join in. Sam's schedule involved six or more classes a week. It was in his Thursday class at the Garden of Inayat where he offered the *Gathas* and *Githas* of Inayat, hav-

---

*The latter, a brilliant lecture, sadly was not recorded. Audio recordings of the former are available in the Archives under the title "Ten Lectures Inspired by St Paul's 'First Epistle to the Corinthians.'" The ten lectures were edited by Walter Bowart and published under the title *This is the New Age In Person* (Tucson: Omen Press, 1972). The complete text of the book is also available under that title in the Archives.

ing finally secured these papers. A secretary, often me, would transcribe his commentaries and make copies of them. Sam also worked in Novato in the garden, conducted interviews, and wrote letters to people around the world.

Photo by Mansur Johnson

Horticulturist Sam at work in the Garden of Inayat, ca. 1970

At the Mentorgarten Sam woke up early every day around 6:00 AM and did his daily practices in the front room, loudly enough to wake me up. Then he would take Saul's large dog Wuta, waiting eagerly at the front door, and scurry through Precita Park collecting and discarding loose paper. He and Wuta would end up at the bakery, where Sam picked up, among other things and unbeknownst to Saul, doughnut holes for Wuta.

Sam's morning world always included writing letters to people like Art Hoppe, a daily newspaper columnist who wrote with humor and usually replied to Sam. The two enjoyed bantering with each other. Herb Caen, another humorous San Francisco columnist, was also on Sam's list.

Dance gatherings and teachers of the day including Murshid Sam, Pir Vilayat Khan, Reb Shlomo Carlebach, and others were being filmed religiously. Sam can be seen in *Sunseed,* the movie on the spiritual movements of this period, giving the Islamic call to prayer atop Bernal Hill with motorcyclists revving by. During the filming, an interviewer asked him, "What do you want to do before you die?" He laughingly answered, "That is a funny question to ask a person who has the experience of immortality direct."

Sam and Shlomo, a charismatic rabbi with a community in town, developed a very close heart connection. Sam was present when Shlomo and friends led a large circle in songs and movements while holding hands. Just as he had generously shown his respect for Pir Vilayat and called him the father of the Dances, Sam expressed his deep respect for Shlomo, honoring the way he had brought to everyone an experience of joy. Sam told Shlomo that the Baal Shem Tov* had won, and his joyful approach to Judaism had been reactivated. Sam likewise called Shlomo a founder of the Dances of Universal Peace, bringer of joy to the world. Shlomo had clearly modeled himself on the example of the Baal Shem Tov, and he sang beautifully for his students as well as gave interpretations of the Torah and various Rabbis' opinions.

The Garden of Allah in Corte Madera became an important center for Sam's teachings. He presented Dances and Walks there, while guests such as Neville Warwick and Frida Waterhouse often were invited to teach. Several days after Sam and Warwick danced together at the Garden of Allah, Warwick was criticized by a colleague. Sam defended him saying that although their view on Warwick might be right, he had communed with Warwick's inner self when they danced together and found it in good shape.

Frida was a spiritually oriented therapist in San Francisco to whom Sam had given permission to counsel any of his students in need. She saw and influenced many. Numerous women came to her door to address episodes of abuse, mostly by men. Frida also had a wise and comforting voice for those in the gay community. Her usual approach was to ask participants to find their inner voices and isolated places of self. Moineddin loved to visit her home and use her approach. Under his leadership, this approach became known as Soul-Work; it was further developed and continued by many who drank from Frida's cup.

Frida Waterhouse

The San Francisco Theological Seminary in San Anselmo was a major meeting place for the Dances. Sam wrote in May of 1969: "The Marin meeting last night had an audience of about 70 of whom 40 are *mureeds*. The San Francisco meetings though smaller are several

*The Baal Shem Tov (Rabbi Israel ben Eliezer) was an 18th-century Jewish mystic and charismatic leader from Poland. "Baal Shem Tov" means "Master of the Good Name." He is considered the founder of Hasidic Judaism.

and separate."[802] The large meetings in San Anselmo lasted many months, then moved to the Sausalito Art Center, a spacious facility that drew people from San Francisco as well as Marin County.

San Francisco Thelological Seminary, San Anselmo

Regarding the developments in his Dance and Walk program, Murshid Sam wrote in his diary,

> It is time for man to exhibit those attributes which he ascribes to a Deity. I am teaching the Divine Epithets now through the dance. I had hoped to do it through sound and voice and this is still possible, but it is being done through the Dance and one does not care anymore whether one is accepted or not. The rise in mystical consciousness of those who participate is sufficient evidence. The Dance Class is entirely esoteric and we give out Kundalini and other Yoga practices. Hazrat Inayat Khan had them and a lot of other things—nothing has been lost. But there are public gatherings, too, and the increment of Joy (as opposed to euphoria) is evident.[803]

The Saturday night Dance class in the Mentorgarten garage was decidedly esoteric. Among other practices, Sam used astrology as a tool for concentration. After looking at a person's chart he would note the aspects that could be combined to prescribe a karma walk, something that provided a rhythm for everyday life. The chart would also reveal to Sam what concentration the person needed to master; that in turn would lead to a dharma walk. He limited the dharma Walks to planets that were farther from the Sun—Pluto, Uranus, Neptune, and others that might be combined with them. For Neptune Murshid had people attune to their crown chakra with their breath as they walked. Uranus movements were outside the box, full of changes, and for this Sam had his students focus on the third eye in the center of the forehead.*

Many Walks given were in the realm of *tasawwuri.* For example, to do the walk of Hazrat Inayat Khan Sam had everyone slow their breath

---

*Murshid said many times that Moineddin would be his successor because Sam had immediately and clearly seen the Sufi Symbol upon his forehead.

Murshid Sam leading a Dance at the Garden of Inayat

Photo courtesy of Mansur Johnson

and walk holding the *vina,* the musical instrument Inayat played and which represented his gift to the Western world. Students were learning how to manifest the steady majestic rhythm of Inayat. They were learning to absorb and transmit divine qualities through their breath and to bring these qualities into their lives. New Dances were often formed from Murshid Sam's dreams during the night. He would stay awake thinking about them, then present them in the next class.

The time had come for Murshid Sam and Pir Vilayat to consider the relationship of Sam's activities to the Sufi Order. In late February, 1969, Sam wrote to Pir Vilayat offering a trove of detail about current developments.

> *Asalam-aleikhum!* The other day I wrote a long letter to one Shamseddin Ahmed, the last of your Blessed father's New Delhi disciples . . . When you were here and asked if I would be your San Francisco representative, I saw an arc about 100 miles in diameter. I have neither chosen nor been asked to move beyond this limitation, nor do I so wish at this time. The plain fact is that I have been invited to speak in Sonoma County in the north and Monterey in the south. This will keep one very busy, very intent and very inspired.
>
> There were two seemingly different factors which prompt this letter. One arises from the suggestions or inspirations of Paul Reps. He realizes in full the significance of the walk and Dance inspirations which are now being presented to young Americans, first in the form of dervish dancing; second as yoga and mantra dances; third as mystery and ceremonial dances. These are being presented in cosmic vision and personal inspiration far more rapidly than they can be recorded . . .
>
> The second need to write is the obvious awakening of at least two men who may be called the *Jelal Kalif* and the *Jemal Kalif,* the former is

Akbar Simmons whom you well know. He is referred to but not by name in the current article in *Playboy* on "Cultsville U.S.A." . . .

At times I feel like Junaid in his relation to Shibli, that the teacher receives from God, so to speak, full awareness of the mystical elevation of his leading, or even of all his disciples. In any event, I have started Akbar on *shagal*. This may be only the beginning, because not only have I a compendium of your sacred father's material on *shagal* but am receiving from the inner side enough knowledge to write a full esoteric book, "*Shagaliat*."

Awakening has also come to the presumable *Jemal Kalif*, Moineddin Jablonski. As I only got the report yesterday outwardly—inwardly it had long been shown—I have not yet put him on *shagal*. In a sense, it might be proper to wait for a public ordination in the case of these two men and others . . .

Besides these two men, there are three women all here in Novato who have given evidence of further awakenings. At times, I feel humble and abashed, but such humility can also be a form of egotism. It is necessary for me to function variously as Murshid, Father, Grandfather and Hierarch. Add to this the exemplification of *salat*. . . .

Don McCoy of Olompali Ranch and Timothy Leary have been performing "Love-in Dances." These dances are primarily material (*jagat*). The magnetism is a mixture of sex and youth; when it is worn out, the participants are fatigued. The Chassids performed dances similar in form with chanting a divine name. The Dances now on my program compel the participants to be aware of the subtle as well as the physical. But tonight I am instituting dances that also impel, not to say compel, the participants to be aware of the causal or spiritual body. In other words, these are three vehicle dances, even though in form they have elements resembling the others.

The termination of this, of course, is *darshan*. Even the cynical writer of the article in *Playboy* very well described one's transformation in *darshan*. So much for a report on walking and dancing . . .

The staff of the Indian consulate in San Francisco . . . have been going around saying, "Do you know Mr. Lewis, he knows more of India than any other American." "Do you know Mr. Lewis? He is the reincarnation of the Moghul Prince Dara Shikoh."

Whether this be true or not, several of the staff members of the University of California witnessed the greeting and meeting between the Vedantic Swami Ranganathananda and Sufi Ahmed Murad Chisti. That

> was enough evidence for them, although there was also a large number of young people to witness.[804]

One of the witnesses asked the Swami if his meditations were beyond the ordinary and his response was that all meditation was beyond that. Asked later about the Dances Murshid Sam was teaching, the Swami recommended that these teachings be shared in places such as Indonesia; he felt the people there would be in tune with them.

Sam wrote:

> While this is going on, I am assiduously working on the tasks assigned me by your Blessed father. The commentary on *The Inner Life* has been completed. The commentaries on *Gathas* I, 7 papers, is nearly done. The quantities of *ryazat* and esoteric practices I now have from many sources is voluminous. Besides that, God is always speaking to me as concerns the Walk and Dance above. In addition to that, now after many years, my oracular work is being accepted.
>
> The local magazine, the *Oracle,* will now publish one of my early prognostications in this form . . . The simple fact is that the young people want this . . ."The Rejected Avatar" has been published. "What Christ? What Peace?" has been read to a fair-sized number of young people who were deeply impressed. The probability is now that the Christian San Francisco Theological Seminary will want to hear it. Etc. Etc. Etc. . . .
>
> Fortunately, Allah has come to my aid here and something more may come of it, *inshallah* . . . I have at least 4 expectant mothers whom I am giving in turn the Avalokita Walk, the Kwan Yin Walk and now, the Saint Mary Walk. This has cemented some beautiful bonds, but it cannot be repeated too often, "It is the *mureeds* that make the Murshid." At times I break down and weep; your father never had such a following.[805]

Pir Vilayat wrote to Samuel Lewis in May from Fazal Manzil, the family home of Inayat Khan in Suresnes, France, following up on organizational plans.

> My dear Murad,
>
> In a rush on my way in the course of a hectic program, I just want to confirm that I rejoice in the work you are doing especially for the young people and there seem to be ideas in the air which both of us pick up and which answer a need of our time.

I wish to confirm that I shall be coming to the States presently and I have scheduled a visit to your center on July the 2nd. I have also been requested by the Asian Institute to give a lecture there and have allocated for that purpose, the date of June 12th . . .

I am sending you therefore herewith my official recognition of your position as leader. For the good order of things, it would be desirable for you to send us an application for a Center. We have forms for this purpose and I am asking the General Secretary to send you the necessary papers to avoid you a lot of unnecessary trouble. We will then send you a "Charter" establishing your center on the authority of the Board of Trustees of the Sufi Order in the United States. Again for the purpose of facilitating the work, we would like to request you kindly to send us the name and addresses of *mureeds* for our files and we shall send them membership cards (regular Members).

It is probably not necessary for you to register your branch in your State, unless you wish to do so or unless the State requires such registration by any group meeting regularly. However the simplest solution would be if you would accept my appointing you as leader and consequently President of the Cleveland Branch. I would furthermore suggest you send a letter to whomsoever you choose, appointing him or her as a vice-President to assist you in the work or replace you in your absence. It is our policy to cumulate the functions of Secretary General and Treasurer General in one person, as the Secretary General generally knows better what expenses are needed and how to raise funds . . .

For the sake of helping us in keeping in order with the official side of our Sufi Order, which we have registered in California, we would like to ask you kindly to give power of attorney to any of our Californian members to represent you at the meeting of the Sufi Order which is scheduled for June 16th. You will be receiving from my secretariat official papers.[806]

Murshid Sam did appoint Moineddin to have his power of attorney in such meetings as Pir Vilayat described.

Sam responded to Pir Vilayat's letter:

As-salaam aleikhum! Before answering your letter of 16 May it is notable that when you spoke to me last I had visions, and the affairs of the last year have borne out these visions almost exactly. I am now in the cycle of 60–100 disciples. I do not know how many applicants there are but recent visits to the various colleges have all brought fruit, howsoever small. And because of the vision, perhaps cosmic vision, coming out so exactly one hesitates to put up any kind of negative.

We shall therefore be ready to greet you around June 12 . . . I must say at this writing that I am now on excellent terms with a number of the Asian Departments of the better-known educational institutions. In fact last week the Dean of Studies at UCLA telephoned me personally.

I have placed in the hands of Moineddin Jablonski the material from Secretary D'Mitrieff. I am hoping that we may both go to Hollywood for that meeting. Secretary Mansur Johnson will soon be off to the state of New Mexico, and in August I shall personally follow up whatsoever he may have accomplished. The *Oracle* is now out. I do not know how it is selling but there are articles in it by Shamcher Bryn Beorse, Paul Reps, and myself and several of the disciples. It has almost become a Sufi organ.

The total audiences of each week this year have been larger than the previous one. An increase for every single week from January 1 to May 18. While I do not know whether this will continue—it is in the hands of God—there is no question that if the sales of the *Oracle* mount so shall the audience. It will be no effort to get you 100; we had 150 adults at our Wesak celebration.

I do not think I have any more contacts direct in Cleveland . . . But I shall be pleased to serve you in any capacity because this may be written in the Sphere (*inshallah*) . . . I have full authority from both the combined Chisti-Kadri-Sabri Orders in Pakistan and the Islammiya Ruhaniat Society of Islamabad to select and ordain Khalifs but should prefer to work in unison . . .

The fire of 1949 destroyed all the official papers I had from your blessed father and also all the appointments received from Geneva prior to 1927. I am having your letter read also by others and will have at least one meeting soon to cover these points . . .

Fortunately my health has maintained itself wonderfully and the financial outlook is quite favorable praise to Allah. You are quite right in pointing out the need for some kind of organization and coordination . . . This is the last week when I shall have to have 9 classes. Some of them may be turned over to assistants and associates.[807]

In June, Sam reflected further on organizational arrangements before Pir Vilayat's return to the Bay Area from his Colorado camp:

Vilayat does favor Mansur and Daniel having official positions, and Moineddin will be vice-president and my proxy. Both he and Akbar

> shall be promoted when Vilayat returns . . . But Daniel now has two outside jobs and Mansur one and we have not yet proper help. Sponsored by me as my representative, Melvin who is now Wali Ali leaves Thursday for Colorado to join Vilayat in his summer camp. Jemila, Shirin, and James are going and possibly Ruth (Parisa) and Barbara (Ayesha) too. And Barbara is supposed to be taking Daniel's place excepting for the financial job. Both Vilayat and Murshid want him for that, and I think [Daniel] wants it also.[808]

Those of us who attended Pir Vilayat's camp in the mountains of Colorado were happy to see upon our arrival a large number of people roughly our age from a religious group in Kansas City, who had come at Pir Vilayat's suggestion. Murshid Sam had told me that I was to represent him at the camp and lead the Dances, which were very well received. There were people present from Texas who had some training in the Dances and they, too, periodically led. The group from Kansas City had prayers to sing, which we put our hearts into while standing in the circle.

As part of the camp activities Pir Vilayat called forward a series of individuals who would be silently observed by the group. Those present were then asked to share what they saw in the person standing before them. At other times meditative practices were given by Pir Vilayat, talking us through them and often pointing to the heavenly realms.

Sam continued his correspondence with Pir Vilayat in July:

> Last Sunday an Indian guru suddenly showed up and we showed . . . the *Ramnam, Ram-Sita,* and *Shiva* . . . dances. But we have also started the "mystery" dances although we already have the Sun dance (men also); the Moon dance (mostly women); and the Wheel dance (sexes equal). Now we are working on the Bacchic ceremonial; and the first Egyptian ritual . . .
>
> This year will mark the 50th anniversary of the studies in *tasawwuf.* Then we had no books or papers but did have the first edition of *A Sufi Message of Spiritual Liberty.* I am not sure whether this was republished exactly, and call attention to this quotation:
>
> "The Sufic method of realization—study of *shariat, tareekat, hakeekat* and *marefat,* also the practice of *zikr, fikr, kasab, shagal* and *amal* is claimed to be the easiest, shortest and most interesting for spiritual accomplishment." . . .

> I know at least three supremely esoteric sciences: *irfan* (for which I have literature); *mushahida* (which is often mentioned but is not being explained); *mujahida* (which is seldom mentioned without being explained). I have been invited to join the Muslim students of this land in their annual conference and if so will speak on *mujahida*. In any case my Goddaughter, Miss Saadia Khawar, intends to go and she will have my paper if I cannot attend.
>
> I am continuing the instructions of your blessed father which keeps one busy all the time . . . But there is now seriously enthusiasm and a desire [for] "May the Message of God reach far and wide."[809]

Pir Vilayat returned in time to attend a July meeting in San Anselmo. At that time Murshid Sam gave Moineddin and Akbar public initiations as Khalifs, bestowing upon them orange robes. Pir Vilayat did not react, even though his position was that he was the only one in the Sufi Order who could offer higher initiations.

People fell in love at the camps that summer, including Pir Vilayat and Jemila. Sam later revealed his perspective, saying "There have also been numerous problems arising out of the Summer Camps, but I think many of them were tests for me, personally, and on the whole they have

Photo courtesy of Mansur Johnson

Front row: Wali Ali Meyer, Mary Sue Sitton, Parisa, Murshid Sam, Pir Vilayat, Jemila Johnson, two guests of Pir Vilayat. Back row: David Hoffmaster, Mansur Johnson.

resulted (with a little drama) in the spiritual elevation of several of the persons concerned."[810]

Incorporation

Murshid Sam now decided, in dealing with all the paperwork connected with the Sufi Order, that he was being encouraged to incorporate on his own. Already established as a center by the Sufi Order, he wasn't required to register with the state, and he had a historic connection with the early constitutions of Inayat Khan. He also had an ongoing relationship with Inayat as his inner guide.

Yet given Sam's broad approach, there was something of a question. Hassan Herz, a *mureed* of Sam's at the time, offered some perspective on this:

> When a Buddhist would come visit, come to the area, and we would see them, Sam Lewis would embrace him as a Buddhist. If a Swami came that he knew or liked, we would do Hindu practices, so there truly was the sense of there are multiple avenues to realization . . . When he gave practices to *mureeds* it . . . wouldn't be only Sufi practices, there would be a multitude of practices.[811]

Hassan, who soon joined the Board of Directors of what would be the new organization, expanded on this.

> So . . . the question was . . . who are we going to be when we incorporate? We would do . . . practices of Papa Ramdas, we did . . . Buddhist practices, Inayat practices . . . And . . . Murshid said, let's do Sufism because it accepts the most, it's the broadest, it accepts the most other religions.[812]

In making this choice about incorporation, Murshid Sam called together some of his *mureeds* to participate. Sam proposed the name Islamia Ruhaniat Society, which he had been given from Pir Dewwal Shereef, the Sheikh of Pakistani President Ayub. The *mureeds* present preferred to include the word Sufi. Sam was hesitant to do so because of his history with various groups calling themselves Sufis who had rejected him. However, he acquiesced, and the organization came into being as the Sufi Islamia Ruhaniat Society (SIRS).

Murshid Sam's instructions to me had been to read the work of Seyyed Hossein Nasr on the establishment of Sufi orders and to write up what was important in it. Sam's first goal was to write an esoteric constitution that avoided the mistakes made by the Sufi Movement Board of Trustees that had broken Inayat Khan's heart at the time. Nasr's instructions on topics such as the Pir's role as well as the respect to be accorded the Pir and Prophet Muhammad were entirely consistent with Murshid Sam's point of view. The document that resulted from this research and deliberation exists to this day as the esoteric constitution of what is now called the Sufi Ruhaniat International.

Connecting with the Academic World

In the midst of his burgeoning following and attendant responsibilities, Murshid Sam never faltered in pursuing his lifelong thirst for knowledge. He attended classes at UC Berkeley Extension as well as at San Francisco State, sometimes taking a *mureed* with him or sponsoring *mureeds* to attend other classes. His mystical experiences were finally given credence in the academic world and his approach to learning was lauded by his professors.

In January, 1968, Sam wrote:

> After attending the first class in Buddhist studies yesterday I felt it important to write a paper on "The Union of Hearts."* This is an expression I have both seen and witnessed. The first was my blending with Inayat Khan on the night before he arrived in San Francisco in 1923 . . . Years later I had the same with Senzaki.[813]

Formerly ostracized by the university community, Sam now found acceptance and even esteem. In February, 1968, he wrote to Shamcher:

> Just as in a previous generation one could not get a word in edgewise at the university, now it is the opposite and great caution is needed because everything is accepted. In the philosophy class [of Dr. Jacob Needleman] a man was criticizing the Mathematical Infinity from what he called a "Zen standpoint." It did not agree with Zen books he had read. I told the teacher that having had the direct experiences of **Infinity** in Zen, in

* Sam later referred to this paper as "The Blending of Hearts."

> Cantor's Transfinite and in Edna St. Vincent's Millay's "Renascence," I failed to find any differences between these various "infinities." Not only was the point taken but I demonstrated how to produce harmonies out of seemingly conflicting views.[814]

Following Inayat Khan's directive to bring mysticism into academia, Sam pointed Jacob Needleman (professor, philosopher, author, and religious scholar) to reputable Sufi writers such as Titus Burckhardt. Needleman developed much respect for Sam and his knowledge. This quote from Needleman appears on the back of Mansur's memoirs of Murshid: "I have no fonder memory of the 60s than the appearance of this strange-looking man, who said things that made me laugh, then later pause in appreciation of a spiritual original, a pioneer."[815] In July, Sam wrote to Paul Reps:

> I am studying Titus Burkhart's *Alchemy,* this being a book by a modern Sufi. I intend to work it into the dance [and] also into the transcendental psychology used to place people into harmony with their own selves.[816]

Sam had by now made valuable contacts at UC Berkeley. He studied with Dr. William Brinner and colleagues in the Near East Languages Department, became familiar with their views, and began a scholarship for their department to which he contributed monthly. In a 1976 interview[817] Brinner shared his relationship to Sam and Sam's relationship to the work being done in their department.

> As I remember, he started writing to whoever was chairman of the Department around 1960 . . . and indicated that he had an interest in both Islam and the actual physical development of the Near East. He was very interested in water problems and things of that sort, so that he [had] contacts with people on this campus in Engineering and Agriculture, as well as Near Eastern studies . . .
>
> We invited him to attend public lectures that were sponsored by our Near Eastern Studies Department and he began to do that. I remember meeting him for that first time at one of those lectures where he was sitting holding his rosary beads, and he told me later that he did that very deliberately so that people would ask him why he was doing that, and that would lead to a conversation, and that was precisely what happened in our case. And from that time on we used to occasionally . . .

talk and then he sent me a number of letters—sometimes very, very long letters . . . some six or seven pages closely typed having to do with a number of things: both his interest in Islamabad and the university there, and also the whole question of Middle Eastern peace which was something that was very much of concern. What he wanted primarily of us was to get our students interested in that aspect, and to find every way possible of locating students who would be interested in taking both Hebrew and Arabic, and sort of doing cross-culture things so that they would be open to both sides of Middle East conflict . . .

He told me at one time that he was very impressed with the fact that there were Jews and Arabs on our staff and that we all spoke to each other, and he felt that that might be a good sign for possibilities in the Middle East. And then, of course, he recommended various students to us, students with whom he was very friendly . . .

I was very impressed with one thing about his stories of the trips. He would always stress his complete belief in Divine Protection and Intervention, and he would keep telling me about . . . all sorts of incidents that took place on those trips where people were not expecting him, and at least he had not notified them in advance of his coming, and yet they knew that he was coming and would come to meet him, or things would be prepared for him that again he had not indicated that he was interested in them—but he was deeply interested in—and had been hoping to get. So these were the types of things that he often would talk about when he discussed his trips to Islamabad and so forth.

Wali Ali: "Did he participate in any colloquia here? Do you recall any areas of particular interest, or any discussion on –"
Dr. Brinner: "No, that was one of the things that always sort of surprised me. He came to many of them but sat very silently."
Wali Ali: "That is quite different from his behavior in quite a number of other settings. It shows he had a great respect for what you were doing."

Dr. Brinner agreed.

He would sit, he would smile occasionally to indicate approval—that was very clear—and as I said, he would always have his beads with him, but during the meetings themselves, he would not speak up. He was full of comments, and not always in agreement, but for some reason or other—maybe it was that he had respect for the people that were involved or simply . . . didn't want to speak up at that kind of gathering . . .

> We had a . . . very easy relationship, very unusual because we never knew in advance when he was going to appear. He'd come . . . [and leave] a handwritten note . . . for me if I wasn't around on the day that he came. He would simply drop a note into my box indicating that he had been here, and indicate what he had in mind at the time.

I commented that Sam had of course been ahead of his time in terms of interest in the Far East and the Near East, and had had to live through a number of "experts" on the subject who were afraid of having their veneer pierced because their knowledge wasn't particularly deep. He was so overjoyed to see a new generation of American professors who weren't threatened by non-academic knowledge on the subject. He was particularly delighted with what was going on in Berkeley. I think he felt his participation was on a larger scale even if it was on a smaller scale outwardly. He wanted to support people that he felt were really bringing light into the study of these things. That, as much as anything, as I understand it, explains his great love for what was going on here and his wish to start a fund, even though his own means were quite limited.

Dr. Brinner agreed. "So I understood, yes, but as you see from the letters he was quite sure that he was going to get the inheritance, therefore he was beginning to make the contributions, and eventually he hoped to do it on a larger scale."

Asked to describe his impressions of Sam as a person, Dr. Brinner described his own response to Sam's presence:

> He impressed me, and one of the reasons that I was interested in him was that I always had a feeling of his radiating joy whenever he came here . . . He was a very unusual individual in that sense; we don't always get people who come to us from the outside who have that type of aura about them . . .
>
> In any of the conversations that we had, it was obvious that he had read a great deal, and he understood what he read. He very often would interpret those things differently than the standard interpretation, but he certainly knew what he was doing.
>
> Wali Ali: "When you say 'differently from the standard interpretation,' what do you mean?"
>
> Dr. Brinner: "Very often when we would talk about Islam, I would say that there are certain ways in which scholars who are not necessarily

within the Islamic tradition will interpret various things. Lewis considered himself to be within the tradition, in a sense, and would accept—or at least give an interpretation that was, I would say, closer to what one would expect of an orthodox Muslim."

Back to School

A 1968 diary entry indicated that Sam was enrolled in two classes in Anthropology. Early in 1969 he wrote about a class entitled "Influences of Ancient Asian Religions on Contemporary Society," saying that reforms in Asia were discussed and every one of the instructors accepted contributions of experience, a new and uplifting occurrence for Sam. The class used Huston Smith's book *The World's Religions;* Murshid mentioned that Mansur had been close to Smith as a student in college. Professor Smith later told members of Sam's lineage that his meeting with Murshid Sam and Mansur had been memorable, and that Sam was the most joyful person he had ever met.

Sam ran into a class called "Is God Dead," which he despised and wrote critically about in his diary in April of 1969. However, he spoke highly of a seminar on mystical experiences. More than twice the number of expected enrollees showed up. Sam wrote that although the class was divided between supporters of Buddhism and supporters of Buddha, the majority held that churches were passé and it was spiritual leadership that was needed. "The upshot on this point was that the instructor, Professor Needleman of San Francisco State (Dept. of Philosophy) wants to meet Rev. Dr. Warwick as early as possible, so I am sending [Warwick] a copy of this letter."[818]

The autumn brought Sam to a class on the Islamic Art of Asia, where he planned to present Titus Burckhardt to the class. In October he was in another of Professor Needleman's classes and was asked by Needleman to explain the *alaya vijnana* doctrine,* "the first time, I believe, this has ever been done."[819] He took poetry and philosophy classes and a class on "Problems of Southeast Asia." He felt the professor

---

* *Alaya vijnana* can be understood as "fundamental storehouse consciousness." For an interesting article on this Buddhist concept, see "Cleaning Out the Storehouse" in *Tricycle,* Fall 2016.

of this last class was actually carrying on the work Sam had outlined in "How California Can Help the Orient." Sam felt that personalities and cults were finally being exposed for what they were, and that true philosophy and spirituality were at long last being discussed.

Sam also took several courses in Ancient Egyptian History with a professor who thought he was magnificent. Dr. Becker-Colonna wrote, granting an honorific and referring to a Ph.D. that of course Sam had not earned in the typical sense:

> Dr. Lewis came to one of my courses at U.C. Extension in S.F. ca. 1955 or 1956 and after that time he continued to attend my courses, almost all of them, until the unfortunate time when he prematurely passed away. My subject matter being mainly Mediterranean Archeology and Religions he was especially interested in both. At the beginning I thought of him as one of the majority of my students, an adult, retired gentleman who wanted to find refuge in the studies of the Ancient Civilizations as an escape from our too hectic and troubled way of living. As I vividly still see him in my mind, he was a quiet, unassuming gentleman, with kind manners, a sweet smile and a very intelligent face. He began asking questions always to the point, sensible, which sometimes led the two of us to very interesting, constructive discussions which I thought . . . very constructive and stimulating also for the rest of the class. At times in my evening courses I had an attendance of ca. 50–70 students, which for an Extension class is a considerable figure. But Dr. Lewis stood [out] from [the] rest of the audience because of his interesting personality. At first I was puzzled as he showed [himself] to be not an ordinary man but someone who was very learned in a field which was related to the one I was teaching. In fact when [we] became better acquainted I found out that he held a Ph.D. and his field was in the Eastern Religion. One of Dr. Lewis qualities was his humility which was as profound as his knowledge and wisdom.
>
> Actually the real great scholars are very modest as they know quite well that the more one knows the more one is aware that he does not know anything. Dr. Lewis recalled to my mind, in [our]Western knowledge, Socrates, the Greek Philosopher who was just as simple, as humble and as modest (according to our tradition) as Dr. Lewis. He sent me one of his beautiful poems on "Saladin" which I cherish and admire. He sent me occasionally some of his publications and soon quite a good friendship was formed between us as we discovered that we both were

looking for that truth, which for me and my Egyptian studies is Maat, while for him it was the same basic truth which is the cosmic order and is reflected in the Moral Order in men.

During the period he was attending my courses, he organized for me a very interesting program with his students. I remember what a pleasant evening it was at U.C. Extensions with his handsome, well-behaving young people who played beautiful music, danced, recited poetry. Because another good quality of Dr. Lewis was that he loved young people whom he tried to lead on the right path of life. He was a "guru" in the true good, honest way (not as so many that today go around exploiting the inexperience of life of young people and deceive them). When he passed away I felt that we have lost a great, good man who could have contributed so much to the good of our world . . .

I must state once again that Dr. Samuel Lewis was one of the most outstanding, remarkable man for his knowledge and wisdom and one of the kindest, unselfish, humble persons I ever met . . .

Please convey my best greetings to all his disciples with my congratulations for all the good work they have been doing. The world should have more young people like you, to go back to a better shape![820]

Continuing Developments

The South Korean Zen teacher Dr. Kyung-Bo Seo was now in the Bay Area. He recognized Samuel Lewis as a Zen Master, which entitled him to function as a Buddhist teacher, and gave him the name He Kwang.[821] Soon after that Joe Miller also was recognized. Rev. Seo at this time was teaching at Temple University in Philadelphia, and he also appeared for a time at the UCLA campus. Sam felt that Grand Master Seo's Buddhism was more inclusive than most although he also carried on the Lin Chi-Rinzai methods.

Dr. Kyung-Bo Seo

Sam wrote, "I am also involved again in the Vietnam complex at the request of the Vietnamese."[822] Sam brought Vietnamese monk Thich Thien to the Mentorgarten to speak; when the monk was asked about the war in Viet Nam, he said the important thing

Left: "Reverend He Kwang," meaning blessing of light or full light. Buddhist name given to Samuel Lewis by his Korean teacher, Kyung-Bo Seo. Calligraphy by Master Seo.
Right: Letter of recommendation issued for Sam by Master Seo. "People come and cross the bridge. Under the bridge the water is flowing or not flowing."

was to see the Buddha nature inside every person. When Rev. He Kwang (Sam) was asked how to stop the war, he looked at everyone in the room and said, "Stop pulling the triggers."* With Master Seo and Thich Thien the whole emphasis was on being or becoming what you teach or venerate.

---

*This was a reference to Sam's frequent theme of gaining control over our reactive, unenlightened traits. Expressing these, he taught, was to add to the "war" energy in the world.

From *Sunseed*

Jemila and Sam as Radha and Krishna

The Dances continued to progress in many places in the Bay Area. [*Ed. note:* For a detailed recollection giving more of the flavor of Murshid Sam's life during this period, see Appendix: Wali Ali's Diary of Life with Murshid Sam.] During larger meetings Murshid Sam would sometimes feature certain groups he worked with, often presenting the women's dance class and the men's dance class. What he loved to present with his women's class was the dance of Sri Krishna with the Gopis. There were about eight women in the circle with Murshid and each was recognized by him in the role of Sri Krishna. Then the time would come when Murshid would take Jemila by the hands to do the dance of Radha and Krishna at a moderate distance from the remaining circle. This dance would last a relatively long time and would always work beautifully. On a number of occasions Murshid would explain to other *mureeds* that he chose Jemila because she had the faculty and ability to rise into higher states.

Murshid Sam confided that of all the things inner guidance prompted him to do as a spiritual teacher, taking on the role of Krishna was the hardest. He had written about the requirements of this Dance in *Spiritual Dancing:*

> When Krishna and Radha render *ras lila,** the eyes of the body also perceive perfection. In it man and woman harmonize, and in the highest sense. They give and receive all that they regard as holy. They complement one another, so that two seemingly imperfect beings constitute the nexus of perfection.
>
> *Ras lila* is for lovers, sweethearts, wedded couples, else it must be performed only in the highest devotional spirit. The currents should be directed upward as to God, never to the partner. Thus, this dance

*Dance of divine love.

> belongs to **Tao**, the Supreme, and not to Yin or Yang. *Kemal*, perfection, holds forth here, rather than *jelal*, majesty, or *jemal*, beauty.[823]

Murshid was deeply affected when Jemila left to be with Pir Vilayat. Besides being the primary *mureed* to represent Radha to his Krishna in the Dances, Jemila was one of the original *mureeds* of his Novato *khankah*. There was also Jemila's husband Mansur, who was Murshid Sam's esoteric secretary. Mansur was bereft at Jemila's departure and later gave a revealing description of his state of mind at the time:

> When Jemila and I were living in Bolinas I was occupied all the time watching my breath. I grew very detached from the earth plane, so that when my wife would speak to me, her words and thoughts would appear ridiculous . . . Sometimes I would dismiss them as too ridiculous to waste any time trying to figure out . . . My love was expressed in the nonverbal fact that I lived contentedly with Jemila and entertained no thought of any other woman as my wife. (Wrong.).[824]

Some of the *mureeds* living at the Garden of Inayat were highly judgmental and awaited Murshid's reaction. Sam appeared to be in a bind. He wanted to protect all his *mureeds*, but also wanted to show respect toward Pir Vilayat. Sam's choices appeared to be condemnation or acceptance. Murshid Sam, however, refused to be defined by concepts or the expectations of others. In his memoir of Sam Lewis, Mansur quoted an illuminating remark Murshid Sam made about how he approached the situation:

> This may give you a glimmer or a glimpse of my almost compulsory silence of what I have seen concerning Jemila, her purpose in life, her immediate and not so immediate future. It is not in accord with my personal views. It is not in accord with any traditional or personal or other ethical standards. But it is in accord with vision and with cosmic karma, and purpose in life. Each one of us has his purpose, his own fulfillment, and in our Sufi Thoughts there is a phrase, "Constantly leads his followers toward the Light." Whatever has happened to Jemila, there has been a marked increase of light.[825]

Much to Sam's delight, Saadia came to the West Coast in June of 1969, stopping briefly in San Francisco on the way to LA, where she met Seyyed Hossein Nasr again. She returned to the Bay Area in August, where she remained for the month, staying at the Mentorgarten. She

Saadia Khawar Khan

was taken to both centers in Marin County and commented about the Garden of Inayat *khankah* in Novato, "It was like living in Allah, through Allah and for Allah. Everything seemed to resound 'Allah Allah Allah.' The echo was always there." Saadia also said, "I thought Murshid was Ecstasy himself. This heavenly light would surround him when he was alone with his Beloved, Allah. We would get glimpses of his being in union with our Creator, our Cherisher and our Sustainer."[826]

During her stay Saadia gave classes at the Garden of Inayat on the *Hadiths* of Prophet Muhammad, using the book by Sufi Barkat Ali. She also spoke at the Holy Order of Mans and other religious settings on the Christian treatment of Mary and the Qur'an's treatment of Mary at Jesus's birth.

At one Dance meeting where Saadia was present, a Swami from India made a presentation to the group. She felt that the Swami was looking at her in a disrespectful way and left the meeting. She first took refuge in Nancy Silver's home, crying intensely about this insulting situation, then traveled on to the Garden of Inayat *khankah*. There Murshid comforted her and addressed her needs by having her recite *zikr* for an extended period.

Later that summer Murshid Sam served as a teacher for the Lama Foundation commune. Asha Greer, one of the founders of Lama, wrote a remembrance of how Murshid Sam arrived there and more:

> A couple arrived at the Lama Foundation from San Francisco and thought that we might be interested in hosting Murshid Sam for one of our retreats. They spoke highly of him as a person who was intelligent and interested in the unity of all spiritual ways and that he seemed to be gathering as students people who would be interested in coming to the Lama Foundation. We wrote to invite him and he sent us an emissary that summer to "check us out." His name was Mansur Johnson and he arrived by himself. There were four of us in residence at the time, plus 3 young children.

Mansur stayed a few days and led us in a "Sufi dance" each morning after our morning meditation in a forty-foot octagon meeting room that we were in the process of building. The sun shone through the roof framing onto the floor and walls through the diamond shapes of the framing. It was totally strange, new, exciting, magical, and both fun and funny. Part one was to chant El Allah Hu standing in a circle moving our heads to the left, the middle and the right. It felt odd . . . and fun. The next part was Allah Hu in step chanting to a simple rhythm with our right hand on the left shoulder of the person in front of us and stepping forward. The last part was chanting Hu Hu Hu Hu rapidly with gusto in step, with one of us turning in the middle intoning HUUUUUUUUUU. It was our first introduction to Sufis and to Arabic. We agreed in our consensus meeting to make it part of our regular practice.

Mansur gave a good report to Sam who agreed to come in a few weeks.* When the time came, two of us drove to the Albuquerque airport with no clue as to what Sam Lewis looked like nor the airline. When we arrived and I got out of the VW bus we were in and walked in

Photo courtesy of Mansur Johnson

Front row: Fatima Jablonski, Murshid Sam, Saadia Khawar Khan, Jayanara Herz.
Back Row: Moineddin Jablonski, Wali Ali Meyer, Mansur Johnson.

---

*Sam arrived August 7th.

the door, within no more than ten feet was what looked to me like a tiny gremlin, like a smiling man in a brown suit carrying a big paper bag and hoisting a small suitcase. He had a beard and longish curly gray hair and was very smiley, funny and energetic, executing a huge atmosphere in full motion, walking straight toward me, speaking directly to me and saying something like: "IamSamLewisandIknoweverythingaboutthe-CosmosandthemusicofthespheresandIhavecontactwiththeHoliestof-holypeople . . ." and we walked out the door to the vehicle.*

He continued this amazing talk all the way to Lama. We did stop in Santa Fe so he could purchase gallons of ice cream for the Lama residents. A rare delight indeed at Lama. We arrived at Lama and the nightly meeting was going on and, having children to attend, I got reports the next morning that he had people rolling on the floor with his stories. The community, this time more than 25 people, perked up, and the first thing he did that morning was to take the contents of the bag he carried out of the airport down to the garden and pour fish emulsion on the entire vegetable garden.

That got our attention. He explained that he had gone to India and seen much starving there and he determined to put his energy into food rather than flowers which he really loved. He played games with the children, by this time there were 12 or more, and would lead them up to the kitchen in a snake dance chanting Allah. He was beloved by everyone and stayed a few days in which we hiked (he was faster than anyone else), listened to him tell stories, and got advice from him about having a community and dances which he had put together. When he departed, he left some of his magic in us! The dances were of course a wonderful gift and gave the structure of the dome and its shape many hours of love and joy over the fifty years of its existence. He also understood what we

Some of Sam's playmates at Lama

*When Asha later told me this story, she said he went through everything he had done in his spiritual life, but it wasn't bragging; he was just reporting in for duty.

were trying to do there and was extremely supportive of what we were already doing. He promised to come back.[827]

Asha's depth of character impressed Murshid Sam so much that he asked her to serve as his secretary when he met with individuals to be given *darshan,* the glance of transmission. My remembrance of her description of these meetings is that Murshid had her seated near him with a sheet of paper. Following Sam's instructions, she recorded the zodiac sign for each person and let Sam see it. He also had her make columns for C, R, and M. After he had given *darshan* to each person, he would give Asha one of these letters to use for the record: C was for Christ, R was for Ram, and M was for Muhammad. Asha also noted that Sam would give each participant something from the garden, even a rotting cabbage.

Murshid Sam was invited to teach at Lama Foundation again in June of the next year, 1970, and he agreed. After leaving, he made valuable contacts at the University of New Mexico, which led to two philosophy professors indicating future plans to visit Lama to study with him. Then he was off to San Francisco, where he was warmly greeted on August 21, 1969. Murshid returned to his packed schedule of classes and meetings, writing up Dance manuals, counselling disciples about their personal lives, and hosting Saadia, who had remained in the area while Sam was at Lama.

Murshid's stress at the time, along with his interest in having some time away from all his responsibilities, led to him asking Mansur and Saul to drive him to points north on September 10, 1969. Saul's dog Wuta sat on Sam's lap the entire 10-day trip, undoubtedly providing some much-needed comfort. They ended up in Vancouver, Canada, visiting Sam's last and oldest relative, Uncle Harry Rosenthal. (According to Saul, Uncle Harry once stole a train from Pancho Villa and sold it in Texas.)

Before Murshid Sam's trip, he had taken Akbar and me under his wing at the Mentorgarten to receive a transmission on mastery and the spiritual hierarchy. He gave us the walk of Abdul Qadir Jilani, often seen as the permanent head of the spiritual hierarchy. We recited *Ya Zal Jalali wal 'Ikram** while doing the walk in which Murshid, who embodied the

*This *wazifah* evokes the divine essential qualities of strength and generosity.

Saint, strode from planet to planet and throughout the Universe bringing forth his divine good will to all.

Then, during Murshid's absence, I was approached by Jemila, who informed me that Pir Vilayat was sick and in need of special treatments. Jemila, Amina, and I met at the home of a *mureed* of Sam's in Marin County. With Abdul Qadir Jilani in mind, I began the recitation and had Jemila walk with me. She opened up and drew this great master's blessings from the experience. Even Amina's dog became peaceful and quiet after the walk. In contrast, when I talked to Murshid about it after his return on September 20th, he was gruff. He felt Vilayat personally needed to dive more deeply into the teachings of this amazing Saint (Jilani), who showed in his discourses and in his atmosphere the inner heart and strength and wisdom of Allah and Islam.

Events Around the Bay

Allaudin Mathieu was a well-known and respected musician in the Bay Area. He was teaching at Mills College and the San Francisco Conservatory of Music and was a maestro at the piano and a musical genius. He, too, was drawn into the vortex of the spiritual revolution of Murshid Sam and Pir Vilayat, and his talents were quickly recognized. He ended up bringing together people in the Sufi community to form the Sufi Choir, for which he wrote all the music. Murshid Sam first wrote about Allaudin: "Another thing that is going on, absolutely successful, has been the work of Bill Mathieu (now known as Alla-u-din). This choral group is more than something; it is so marvelous. We are going to have programs next Sunday, and then for Christmas, and then for Vilayat Khan."[828]

Allaudin Mathieu

Years later the Sufi Choir was selected by Jerry Brown to perform at the celebration of his first election as Governor of California, and Allaudin was invited by Gov. Brown to sit on the State Committee on the Arts. The dancer Zuleikha, not yet an international performer,

Sufi Choir at Masonic Auditorium

came to the forefront in 1971 dancing to the music of the Sufi Choir at large gatherings.

Pir Vilayat Khan came to San Francisco in January of 1970. It was a day-long meeting during which he lectured and guided people in meditation practices. As usual, he drew a large group. He had devoted followers in the Bay Area and there was now an ongoing conversation about starting a house on a hill in San Anselmo where the Pir and others could have a center; it was given the name Hurkalya.*

There was a large celebration that coincided with Gavin Arthur's March birthday, hosted by a group that invited many of the known teachers in the Bay Area. A few days before the event, I was riding with Murshid's *mureed* Shirin in the family pickup truck when she gave me a warning: the organizers of the event were going to put LSD in the punch bowl without telling anyone. When I told Murshid what she had said, he chose not to go. For Gavin it turned out to be a breakthrough and a nightmare. As he later reported, after drinking the punch he began to go through the experience of dying and being embraced in the next world. He shone in this state, but the nightmare came when he was required to come back to this world. He had to limp

*In Sufi tradition, Hurkalya is the archetypal realm underlying all forms observed on earth; it carries the connotation that what we witness is to remind us of the Source of all, taking us back to the form's purest manifestation.

Sam with Gavin Arthur and community at 1970 Spring Festival

back from the other dimension filled with fear. Soon after that Murshid Sam invited Gavin to the Spring Festival, where Sam had him sit up front in a chair next to his and held his hand, providing grounding and support. From there they could observe the joyful practices such as the Astrological Walks and spins and the Dances.

This Spring Festival, held at the 1970 equinox at Nicasio Reservoir in Marin, was a huge event. People came from all over the area and the crew of *Sunseed* filmed the gathering. Murshid Sam was able to present many aspects of his work for all to see and many to participate in. The walk of Quan Yin is a good example of his focus, and his explanation of how to do the walk was cosmic. Several of Murshid's women *mureeds* had young children and he instructed them to hold their child to their heart as they walked, seeing that child as all of humanity. Both mothers and fathers participated.

The wedding of Murshid's two students Michael and Banefsha that opens this book was held at the Spring Festival. Embracing Murshid Sam's wholehearted welcome of all religions, it was a Jewish wedding officiated by Buddhist Rev. Eugene Wagner.

Banefsha's activity in the community brought in mostly women *mureeds*, who performed several of Murshid Sam's poems through dance and recitation in pageant form. The first women's performance is said to have occurred at this wedding. Additionally, both Banefsha and Michael were involved in causes Murshid was interested in seeing developed. One was to serve the cause of Middle East peace by bringing Jews, Christians and Muslims together, along with members of other faiths, to share food and conversation.

Murshid had previously selected several people to form a group for this purpose; they called themselves Hallelujah! The Three Rings, following Sam's lead in choosing a name inspired by Gotthold Lessing's play *Nathan the Wise*. The group was able to engage, not only with local people, but with people from Palestine and Israel who wanted to step across religious and national boundaries to deeply communicate with each other.

Murshid envisioned this as a worldwide effort and he drafted an entire plan for peace in the Near East to be used by Hallelujah! The Three Rings. Building on his lifelong experience, the plan emphasized the need for clarity in language and logic; recognition and respect for all the religions, cultures, and peoples of the region; ecological and water issues; and mutuality of give-and-take. The complete "Integrative Program for Peace in the Near East" is available in the Archives.[829]

Connections with Judaism

Connection with rabbis and with Judaism was part of the development of Hallelujah! The Three Rings. It reached from Haight Street to Jerusalem. Aryae Coopersmith was a 22-year-old student in 1960s San Francisco who, along with his wife, decided to start a community for Shlomo Carlebach, the charismatic Rabbi who sang and danced with those who came to be with him. Before long they found their house (later named the House of Love and Prayer) to be at the center of the San Francisco spiritual revolution: thousands of young people—Jews, Christians, Buddhists, Sufis, and followers of gurus—flooded in through their doors.

The House of Love and Prayer was founded in 1968. Carlebach was joined in its leadership for some years by Rabbi Zalman Schachter-Shalomi. Both Shlomo and Zalman were good friends of the Sufis, and both were a part of what they named the Jewish Renewal. Members of Hallelujah! The Three Rings were often at Shlomo's meetings, listening to him sing and interpret the Talmud. Along with Murshid Sam, through music and dance and study, these leaders were contributing to a new age of religious practice.*

Plans were made for activities in the Near East. Providentially, there were groups in that area who were open for dialogue. Most of the work of Hallelujah! The Three Rings took place after Murshid's death, but directly received its inspiration from his life.

---

*Aryae wrote a profound memoir of his time with Reb Shlomo, *Holy Beggars.* It is full of courage and love.

Murshid Sam in Pakistani robe presenting the flute of Krishna

Photo courtesy of Mansur Johnson

CHAPTER 16

Growing Renown

It is wise to see all things, and yet to turn our eyes from all that should be overlooked.

HAZRAT INAYAT KHAN[830]

It is the soul which sees, the heart which understands. Mind of itself is nothing, but mind properly trained and controlled gains the whole world without losing one's soul. In this condition one sees because God sees through one; one does not have to see for the sake of sight or for the sake of self, but for the sake of God one has to see. Now if we reflect upon what we have seen, if we give much thought to what we have seen, this is sight for the sake of self; it is not sight for the sake of God and our saying so does not make it so.

*That sight which is insight (*kashf*) sees the attributes and essence together and has no need to analyze persons or situations. It sees the complete unity [with] all its parts, and yet does not attribute moral valuation to any condition or thing. This is having Right Views, where the fruits of sensation are left to God.*

SAMUEL LEWIS[831]

Geneva Peace Convention

UN Peace Palace in Geneva

In April of 1970 Murshid Sam took Mansur, in his role as one of Murshid's secretaries, with him to Geneva, Switzerland, for the Temple of Understanding Spiritual Summit Conference. Its theme was "Practical Measures for World Peace." Sam was virtually unknown there, although some of the Asian leaders he had met on his

Lama Foundation, New Mexico

previous trips abroad were present. He came away from the conference calling it a turning point in his life. His Sufi robe and beard drew outer attention, but Sam's inner wisdom and heart were given the acknowledgement and respect he had yearned for. While at the conference, Sam would occasionally get up to briefly speak, and later would joke that he had the reputation of writing the longest letters and making the shortest speeches.

Sam's brother Elliott died while Sam was away. Grudges between the two had already been left behind. Pragmatically, Elliott's death released more capital from their father's will to go to Sam. This helped Sam fund the scholarship he had instituted at UC Berkeley.

After returning from Geneva, Murshid Sam turned to Lama, where he taught for the month of June. This time frame roughly coincided with Pir Vilayat's camp held in Paradise, Arizona, for several weeks. Pir Vilayat had returned to the Bay Area for the Holy Men's Jamboree, which took place in June at the Family Dog (a concert venue near the beach) while Murshid was at Lama. I led the Dance program at the Jamboree at Murshid Sam's request. From Lama, Murshid Sam wrote about the event: "After I left San Francisco to come here, there was a so-called 'Holy Men's Jamboree' of, I am told, 1,500 or more young Americans and they were entirely won over by my colleague Pir Vilayat Khan (oldest son of my original teacher Hazrat Inayat Khan) and my representative, my esoteric secretary, Wali Ali Meyer."[832]

Returning to Lama

There was plenty for Murshid to deal with while at Lama, starting with events that happened on his drive there with Mansur. On June 3, 1970, Sam wrote a letter to the *khankah* in Novato giving them a picture of what was happening.

> The Message is manifesting in so many directions one has to adjust to opening and widening doors . . .
>
> Now as to initiations. It is alright to take them theoretically. When Jemila left I knew this was Mansur's initiation. I saw everything that was to have happened, and the book was closed when we returned from Boston. Then [Mansur's] car broke down, and I knew this was another initiation. But this time his foresight has been awakened. It came very clearly to me what Pir-o-Murshid [Inayat] said, "Pleasure blocks but pain opens the door to inspiration." But this time it was like two doors, one for him and one for me.
>
> My door is seen in the increased dance inspirations, in the absolute harmony with the diverse plans of young people in this state and in the ease I am getting transmissions.
>
> [Mansur's] thing is so clear to me and his plans for New York and I presume Boston seem to me to be [so] totally in accord with the spirit of the Message that I am delighted.* While every pain and sorrow is not an initiation, those that come upon us suddenly and where there is apparently no moral sin involved, the initiate is paying a karmic debt and removing [*samskaras*]. This means an elevation on the spiritual path and in and toward hierarchical functions.
>
> I am not courting suffering, but as a Murshid I have to be aware at all times of the awakening of the disciples, whether by the positive experiences of Fatima and Akbar or the negative ones of Mansur. These may

Dances led by Mansur at Lama Foundation

Photo courtesy of Mansur Johnson

*Pir Vilayat would give Mansur a suburban center near Boston for the Sufi Order in that area.

> or may not happen at any time as it is said, "in the hour ye think least the son of man cometh."[833]

At Lama Murshid Sam presented practices first thing every morning. Asha reported that they were outstanding and that all the Lama community uncharacteristically showed up for them every day.

Asha was also Murshid's guide to two nearby communes. She approached Sam in her only skirt, which Sam found to be too short, so she went back to where old clothes were stored and found something more appropriate. When they arrived at the first commune, they saw two very pregnant women sitting on a bench at the entrance totally undressed. Sam said nothing. Asha announced his presence, but they were ignored. She then looked at Sam and asked if they should leave. He nodded and said, "It's dense here." Asha then took him to another commune, one that she knew would embrace him, and they did. There he shared his Dances along with his love of and genuine interest in true seekers.

In early June, Murshid wrote to his friends at Anandashram:

> Sam received a surprise as soon as he entered this state [New Mexico]. There are tremendous numbers of young people who wish universality, universal universality, and not special leadership. You can get them to chant *mantrams* more easily than inviting them to a meal. Already Sam has been sent for in two parts of this state. While he foresaw this by *prajna,* still he was surprised. The young have no response to the ego pseudo-leadership of seniors. Yes, they may even accept not me power wealth God, but God power wealth me, which is something most of the pretending world and universal groups will not accept. They will refuse to relinquish leadership, and they are crying for moral resurrection without showing any signs of being willing to relinquish leadership . . .
>
> Before he leaves [Lama] Sam expects to institute the *mahamudra** contemplation. He has used this himself a little. To restore the Dharma means to restore the dharma. In teaching spiritual dancing Sam has said, "It is absolutely necessary to adhere to the *mantram;* it is not so necessary to adhere to the techniques of singing and dancing but never change the divine words." Everywhere the young love this. And if there does not

*Literally "great seal," a meditation practice of mystical union originating in Tibetan (Vajrayana or Tantric) Buddhism.

At Lama

> arise a leader who will lead in the name of God and not for his ego Sam may be compelled to play a larger part in world affairs. There are already legends going on, especially in the last few years . . .
>
> From four different sources, all mystical, in the past two weeks have come signs to restore certain elements of Christian mysticism which have either been discarded or forgotten though not entirely. We hope to have a universal, all-inclusive cosmic approach. When Sam was asked what his position was, he said, "The highest point on a ball." The young all recognize this and laugh. As to others one leaves them to their own devices. You should see and hear how these people praise God and work hard in love and mutual respect.[834]

Sam also wrote from Lama in early June to Finley Dunne at the Temple of Understanding, referring to the filming of *Sunseed:*

> There have been films taken of the work chiefly of my dancing classes, of my disciples, of the Vajrayana Buddhists, and the Hasidic Jews. One critic has said, and I think rightly, that there is no amalgam. What I had proposed from the very beginning was to use this film to support **The Temple of Understanding**. It would synthesize and syncretize. It is also peculiar that in the room where I was personally interviewed in Novato, your emblem was on the wall . . . I think we can all work to and for a common purpose in supporting **The Temple of Understanding**.
>
> I am introducing here and developing the Dances of Universal Peace. Sunday the doors will be thrown open to young people from Santa Fe and Albuquerque and later we (Mansur and I) should appear in those cities before returning to California.[835]

Ralph Silver had become the producer for *Sunseed* and promoted the film. However, Murshid did not want the crew from *Sunseed* to film events at Lama and disrupt what was taking place. (There were voices in the Lama community that disagreed with his position on the filming.) Sam also objected to including Tassajara Zen Mountain Center in the film.

Regarding Tassajara, it should be noted that Murshid Sam's background in Buddhism was fully developed, and he had been in harmony with the earliest Zen teachers who succeeded in America. These included

Nyogen Senzaki and Sokei-an Sasaki; Sam's confirmation came from both of these great teachers. However, the head of the San Francisco Zen Center, Suzuki Roshi, was from a different Zen lineage and had not been receptive to Sam's presence or interested in those Sam had worked with.

For Murshid Sam the issue with Tassajara was both personal and impersonal. He had a longstanding relationship with Ralph, and it was arranged for them to meet in nearby Taos. Ralph, when I later interviewed him,[836] shared that he ultimately realized Sam's position wasn't about filming Tassajara, but rather was a spiritual lesson for someone involved.

I commented to Ralph that Sam "was under the impression that you had surrendered to him at Lama . . . that you'd agreed to do it his way. He thought that was the most wonderful thing."

Ralph said:

> We had agreed about something, but I'm not quite sure what we had agreed to . . . I went and there wasn't any problem at all. [Jonathan]* was sitting there, watching the whole thing . . . He said, "You two were putting your arms around one another." It wasn't quite like that, but he wanted to demonstrate a straight spiritual power to me at the level of awareness that has the authority. He wanted me to understand that that level is what you give yourself to. You need a certain preparation to do that. Obviously, I wasn't . . . able to do it, but I was able to agree with him that that was right . . .
>
> I want to say one thing about . . . Sam Lewis . . . He expressed the heart . . . Through the whole mind, real mind. That's what he really did with people and that's why people found that they could move, they could change, because he lived it. He was able to live that. It wasn't little heart; it was the whole man . . . This is not a fragmentation with Sam. Most of us are just a fragmentation, we get it in bits and pieces. Heart, a bit here, a bit there . . . But he had heart and he had the whole thing. How he got it I don't know.

I answered, "Grace! He said it was Grace."

The filming at Lama never proceeded. Ralph received Murshid's energy and understood its purpose.

---

*An early financial supporter of Lama Foundation.

Despite the many issues in getting *Sunseed* out to the public, in many ways the film was instrumental in Murshid Sam's becoming more widely known. When Silver showed the film to Oscar Ichazo, founder of the Arica Institute,* Ichazo's response when he saw Sam Lewis appear was, "That's it, that's what you work for." Of all the people in the film, he said, "That's the example of it, but you don't get it for nothing, you pay a price for it. That man paid a very big price for what he got."[837]

When I heard this account, I replied,

> He did pay a big price and part of the price he paid was reflected in the recurring theme about the rejections he had received in life . . . Behind this tremendous exterior of power and presence that he built up . . . if one digs deep, one finds a real, vulnerable, innocent type of man who trusted . . . who . . . really took some things so to heart that he just couldn't bear that pressure inside of not accomplishing something.[838]

Different versions of *Sunseed* were screened, and the ones that included scenes from the Zen Center were the most successful. Ralph felt that these scenes helped to balance out the rest of the *bhakti*-flavored film. He added, "The Sam Lewis sequences and the Zen Center sequences are the best sequences in the whole film. It's very interesting, you know, that which caused the most conflict came out the best."[839]

Sam wrote during this period:

> In my poem "Saladin" the Messenger of God appeared in all capacities up to the most profound; but we also chant . . ."Ya Mohammed Abdul la" which is to say, Mohammed is a perfect karma Yogin—I mean example by working, not by writing books about it; example, by being one among humanity, not one so superior and even separate from the rest of humanity.[840]

As exemplars of a being who is one among humanity and does not separate himself out, Murshid Sam and the great teacher Grandpa Joe Gomez step to the foreground. Murshid Sam presented Dances every

---

*Ichazo pioneered the modern study of the Enneagram of Personality in the context of his approach to spiritual development. Notable students of Ichazo's include Claudio Naranjo and Hameed Ali.

Murshid Sam giving *darshan* to Saul Barodofsky at Lama, 1970

morning at Lama. Looking across the circle of people one morning, his eyes met with this great man and he felt an ongoing oneness with him. Murshid frequently spoke about his relationship with Grandpa Joe as experienced through that glance and in the Dance, holding him always in the highest regard. Here is Asha's remembrance about this hero:

> Grandpa Joe Gomez was an Elder at the Taos Pueblo and a leader in the Native American Church. He lost 7 of his 8 sons in the Second World War and taught me how to fish. He was an inspiration of sweetness and his major teaching was his Being. One thing that stands out was that when he wanted to know how you were, he would ask "OK?" and often mentioned that OK is good enough. He remains one of Lama's great heroes. His singing in the peyote circles at Native American Church Socials was transcendent.[841]

Murshid Sam felt at home at the Lama Foundation. On June 27, 1970, he wrote a short note to his Uncle Harry: "This is now a permanent summer home for me if I wish it, and soon I may have 'homes' in so many places."[842] When he spoke of other homes, he would likely have been thinking about the space Saadia had set aside for him in Lahore.

Other teachers were also invited to Lama, including Ram Dass, various Vajrayana Rinpoches, and Rabbi Zalman Schachter-Shalomi. Zalman was always ready to listen to others and to make connections with other cultures. The strong connection between Lama and the Indian community in Taos was a continuous blessing from its inception to today. Zalman was invited to a Peyote meeting and he went attired in nice boots and wearing a *yarmulke* prayer cap. In preparation for the ceremony, Zalman had taken off his boots and left on his *yarmulke*—but the Indian perspective was that one did not wear a hat inside the teepee and should always wear their boots. His hosts embraced him in their prayer ceremony—after making sure he had put on his boots and removed his hat.

Zalman was a true Sufi at heart and saw God in the hearts of all. His work with Jewish Renewal opened for women the right to study to be rabbis and to be accepted and counted along with men to make the traditional minimum of 10 for a *minyan.**

Asha's brother Siddiq (Hans Von Briesen) was present at Lama during a time when a Peyote meeting was held on behalf of Moineddin, who was sick. At the end of the ceremony, one of the Indian guides said something to Siddiq that he said always makes him cry when he thinks of it. The guide said, "Someday we will not need this medicine because it will all be in our heart."

Mureed Saul Barodofsky and Sam traveled back from Lama together, stopping at Sheikha Bhakti Engel's in Camarillo on the return trip. There it came to light that the person Saul had studied with at Mt. Shasta, Mary Mae Maier (commonly known as Mother Mary) was friends with Sheikha Bhakti. Sheikha Bhakti had introduced Mother Mary to the teachings of Inayat Khan and it was Mother Mary who pointed Saul in Sam's direction as the spiritual guide he was in need of. Undoubtedly, this connection aided Saul at a later date when he asked Sheikha Bhakti to share the transmission of the Healing Ceremony of Inayat Khan with him. Up to that point he had been basing his healing rituals on Murshid Sam's commentaries, not having access to Inayat Khan's original papers. Sheikha Bhakti insisted that Saul make an oath to never change a word of Inayat Khan's in the prayers or elsewhere. Saul did his best to keep that promise and was later designated by Sam as the *Hakim*† for the healing circle.

First Arizona Sufi Camp, 1970

Meanwhile, Pir Vilayat's Sufi camp in Paradise, Arizona, was taking shape. When driving to the camp, a group of us had spent the night in Tucson at the home of Walter and Peggy Bowart. The Bowarts were

---

* Prayer gathering.

† Literally, wise leader.

An early Dance circle

freely offering their unused land in Paradise to the Sufis. Peggy was from a very wealthy family and Walter aspired to be a publisher. After hearing stories of Murshid Sam, Walter became dedicated to publishing Sam's written work. He was already printing a magazine and their center in Tucson attracted people interested in Sufism. Daniel Lomax, whom Murshid Sam had earlier initiated as a Sheikh along with me, accepted an invitation to go to Tucson with his wife and young child to be a representative of the Sufi Order. Walter, months later, asked Murshid Sam to come live there to write his autobiography. Although interested, events of the times delayed Murshid's visit.

The camp in Paradise quickly began to fill up with interested young people. Over the course of the camp a crew from *Sunseed* came to film. Some early camp attendees found time to play in the wooden water troughs on the land, taking off their clothes to do so, and naively attracting the crew to film them. The atmosphere of the camp at this stage centered on Pir Vilayat. He gave yoga practices framing the sun in the morning. Some of those present, yogis among them, also took off their clothes. This place was beginning to have the scent of Olompali Ranch. Peggy Bowart had phoned the police several times to let them know that the camp was taking place. A few days into the camp two policemen came to look around. Their interest entirely landed on the young women there, especially those who chose to be topless. The policemen stood around like statues. At this point in the drama, one of the cameramen from the movie asked the policemen, "What do you think about this?" Their reply was, "This is a really nice group of people." They never got in the way after that. The camp went on—music, Dance, Walks, meditations, group processing, initiations, and many new friendships.

Shahabuddin David Less (still going by Lonnie at that time) and his friends Iqbal Jonathan Lewis and Sitara Tessler were strongly moved by the camp. It was all new to Lonnie as well as to other people who came from the East Coast, including a number of excellent musicians. He wrote:

> I went to the Sufi camp in Arizona, the first camp there, knowing very little about what's called spirituality. I was blissfully and blessedly naive to the whole inner world and most of the outer world as well. At the end of this camp in Arizona, I realized that my whole life had changed. My two closest friends were Iqbal and Sitara and they said that they were going to go out West to meet this man named Murshid, and I was in the middle of an election campaign and I had to go running back to the East coast.[843]

Shabda also chose to return to New York from the camp to be of service to his father who had just had a hip replacement. He was well placed in that locale to serve Murshid Sam's needs when Sam traveled East in the fall. Shabda quickly connected with Lonnie in New York City.

Growing Recognition of Murshid Sam

Sam returned to San Francisco on July 3rd, 1970. There were already about 40 people arriving from the Paradise Camp who had come to make a connection with this mystical teacher they had heard so much about.

I had led almost all of the Dances in Paradise, and although Murshid liked to lead Dances in Precita Park, which faced the Mentorgarten, he told me to lead Dances that day. I started the Dances and people enthusiastically joined in. Being familiar with the various Dances, I kept them moving to everyone's delight. Well, not quite everyone. About 45 minutes into the Dance program, one of Murshid's *mureeds*, Abraham Sussman, came out of the Mentorgarten and approached me in the Dance circle. He brought a message: "Murshid wants to see you." I left immediately for the house. It was the only time that Murshid Sam ever shouted at me after I became his *mureed!* Whenever Murshid was about to shout at anyone, he always preceded that by saying, "The most important thing is don't react, don't react." Then he lit into me and roughly said, "You think you are helping me by getting everyone up in the air. Now I have to take a lot of time getting people to come down to earth, to a rhythm that works for them in everyday life." To me the most magical aspect of this was when he started shouting. I remembered what he said about not reacting. I didn't react, and what I felt was, instead of judgment on his part, a continuous feeling of good will.

I didn't try to defend myself at all. I sat down in my room and chanted *Om Sri Ram Jai Ram Jai Jai Ram* for at least an hour. That seemed to please Murshid very much.

While life went on as usual in the Bay Area—Murshid leading many classes, people from the Arizona camp moving to the area including into the Cole Street house, Iqbal finding a place in Marin for himself and his two dogs—a major concern for Murshid was that his named successor, Khalif Moineddin Jablonski, was flat on his back in a hospital in San Francisco with kidney difficulties. He would spend nearly six months in hospitals that year during the summer and fall. With Murshid Sam's trip to the East Coast scheduled for late September, Sam felt he had to act. One morning I sat down next to Murshid in his office and he spoke to me with a great deal of emotion. As well as I can remember he said, "Today I have to do the hardest thing I have every done in my life. I have to go to the hospital where there is this man that I love and give him hell." He went to Moineddin's room at the hospital and gave Moineddin hell. Murshid shouted at him saying that he was lazy and if he wanted to sleep his life away, he could find a job in a mattress factory. "You think you are going to heaven? You are going straight to hell! You have a family and a mission. Get out of this bed!" He didn't let Moineddin say a word but just left. It turned out to be Fudo at his finest because afterwards Moineddin's condition would get noticeably better for a while. When Murshid came home later that day, he took me aside and told me what he wanted me to do. "You go there too, but you don't need to give him hell. Tell him about every great thing that is happening in this community. Don't let him say a word, and then just leave." I was able to do that, and Moineddin's health did improve. A decade later he got treatment from Stanford with what was then a new type of kidney transplant.

Murshid Sam's name was also getting wider recognition through the *Oracle* newspaper, and even his oldest and best friend Mrs. Vocha

Fiske was moved by the brotherhood and cooperation she witnessed among the disciples. The *Oracle* had been taken over by one of Murshid's disciples, Philip (Vasheest) Davenport, who was able to attract interviews with Timothy Leary, among others. The May 5th issue had a cover by Fatima, pictures of Murshid leading Sufi Dances, an article by Murshid entitled "Toward Spiritual Brotherhood," another by Shamcher entitled "Obsessed" and also one by Paul Reps. As Murshid wrote to his respected friend, the philosopher Professor Oliver Reiser, "The distribution of this paper could make one better known, or notorious." Still, Sam challenged the *Oracle,* asking why it wasn't an oracle. Sam's oracle might well have been the Bowl of Saki with his commentaries, the deep mystical teachings that have helped many *mureeds.*

Murshid Sam also shared his recent successes in a letter to Anandashram describing innovations happening in California.

> Everything is coming out wonderfully. It is not only our joint Israeli-Arab dinners. It is the reports of our cultural exchange missions to Asia. These have been successful far beyond their dreams. They have had the most wonderful welcomes . . . Sam has long said, "Unless the Lord buildeth a house, they labor in vain who build." Both Rabbis and Arabs are accepting Sufi Love, Love in operation not in theory. The attendance at all our meetings is increasing. The young are hungry for love and peace. Really they are hungry for God. All our Dances are based on repetitions of the Divine Name. The young, first by 10s, then by 100s, now by 1000s, are accepting this.[844]

When he spoke of thousands accepting these Dances using the Divine Name in various forms, he was not exaggerating. Shortly before flying East, Sam was invited to an event in Golden Gate Park sponsored by the Sikhs who studied under Guru Yogi Bhajan. Baba Burt was Yogi Bhajan's chief representative and organizer there. More than 1000 young people joined Murshid Sam in the Dervish and *Ram Nam* Dances. Murshid had invited me to come to this event with him and we set up comfortable chairs for later. People were playing drums for a while, then Yogi Bhajan arrived with dozens of students dressed in white. From a distance Murshid Sam noticed this and he sent me with a message. "Go over and invite Yogi Bhajan to come and meet me; I am older than him."

When I approached the group of people surrounding Yogi Bhajan there was one man who, like a very focused bulldog, was continuously criticizing the Yogi, claiming to point out all his weaknesses. For example, he said, "Your teachings are limited," and Yogi responded, "Limited is perfection." But the bulldog would not stop. I spoke up inviting Yogi Bhajan to meet Murshid Samuel Lewis. He gladly agreed and followed me over to the other part of the meadow where Sam was sitting. The bulldog followed and never dropped his concentration, all the time attacking Yogi Bhajan. Sam could not get in a word, which was unusual. After the bulldog said something bad about Yogi, Sam would say to the Yogi, "I didn't know you were so great." This would repeat itself and Sam would now say, "You are so great, I feel like I need to bow at your feet." He got down and bowed several times. Finally, the bulldog lost his concentration and addressed Sam directly with a lot of emotion, "You are an ass." Sam's response to that was to say "Hee Haw" numerous times, moving his limbs up and down. The bulldog was silenced and walked away.

Later that year something similar occurred. Murshid Sam's open class at the Mentorgarten was filled with a dozen hippies who had arrived earlier. An intoxicated-looking young man appeared and, as he walked into the classroom, yelled at Murshid Sam, "God has appointed me to be your spiritual teacher!" As soon as he heard that, Sam, who was sitting in his robe at the front of the room, jumped up and said, "I accept that on one condition." The young man shouted, "Which is what?!" Sam immediately said, "Show me one person in this room that God has not appointed to be my spiritual teacher!" A cloak of quietness came over the young man; he was silent for the rest of the class and then walked out silently. We never saw him again.

More than forty years later Baba Burt, continuing to function as a Sikh leader, came to an *Urs* celebration commemorating the day of Murshid Sam's passing. When I reminded him of what had happened at the park he said something very surprising: "That night when Yogi Bhajan returned to the ashram he told us all, 'I have always believed that I would never meet an illuminated person in America, but today I met one!'" Sam that day had easily handled the moment as a realized Zen monk who had just answered a koan.

Saadia's Marriage Arrangements

Before initiating his journey to the East Coast, Murshid Sam wrote to Saadia indicating the developing states of realization he was experiencing. "This person has had more experience in *hal* and *makam* in his recent period than in any other time in life . . . The same is true of several disciples."[845] Previously he had gotten a letter from Saadia's aunt Bibijan concerning the decision about who would be Saadia's husband. Now he would be able visit them all. Bibijan's letter read:

> My most reverend Pir-o-Murshid,
>
> *As salaam aleikhum* . . . Saadia has been receiving all your letters but has not replied to them, which is due to several reasons. May Allah be with her always. *Amin!*
>
> We called you and Zeynab received the call and told us that you left for Europe a few hours ago. We are overjoyed to hear that you are coming to visit us in the near future. I am impatiently waiting to get this opportunity after about nine years and get your blessings. I have been doing the *wazifas* regularly and felt as if I was under your search light. Praise be to Allah Who has given us a Murshid who is a real saint. *Alhamdu lillah.*
>
> Murshid, I know that your affection for Saadia is deeper than a father for his daughter. She is your spiritual daughter and whatever you decide for her will be the best for her. I am picking up courage to say something only because you wrote in one of your letters that you will bring one of your favorite disciples as a proposal. You had mentioned that you will leave it to me for the final decision, if you had said that you had already made a decision and were bringing him along with you for an engagement ceremony. I would have accepted him as the best match for Saadia without giving a second thought; but since you have left it to me, let me tell you that a very strange thing has happened here contrary to my wish and expectation. *Kashf* has operated and while I was awake a voice clearly said "Give Khawar's hand in marriage to George." After that there were many signs approving the marriage. So when George came to me and asked for Khawar's hand I agreed without consulting anybody. I would have called you to seek your advice. But you were away in Europe and I did not know your address. As things stand now, I think it would be better if your disciple Mansur does not come along with you here and is not given any assurance, but I would request you to come here whenever you

find it convenient so that you as a spiritual father may put the engagement rings on Saadia and Atta's fingers; for as you know according to Islamic law a girl and a boy do not touch each other until they are pronounced as husband and wife in the name of Allah.

I have mentioned the name Attaullah. This is the spiritual name of George as it came out in the Holy Qur'an. The name means gift of God. I will tell you the details of all the signs and Atta's intense desire to marry Saadia on meeting you.

I must also tell you that the proposal in Pakistan of the C.S.P. man is now refused through my sister.

Before I close I must request you to consider Atta as your spiritual son just as you consider Saadia as your spiritual daughter.[846]

Murshid Sam replied:

One accepts wholeheartedly the name Attaullah. It seems that the disciples here have been adopting Qur'anic names right and left, especially for their newborn children, and often without consulting Murshid. This is acceptable and accepted because *kashf* is more real than personality.

In the name of Allah the Merciful the Compassionate, as Murshid in the Chisti-Sabria and as Khalif in the Chisti-Khidri and Kadri Schools, I declare that Attaullah is now and henceforth my spiritual son. This does not bind him to become my *mureed,* but it does impose the obligation of ultimately having *bayat* in some spiritual order through his own awakening and from his own vision and faith.[847]

Sam flew to Ithaca, New York, on September 25, 1970. After three days he would move on to New York City and Boston. He described his Ithaca visit in letters to Shamcher and Gavin.

This is one of those rare times when there are a couple of hours in which there is nothing on the program. I arrived in Ithaca totally worn out; a half-day off in September and very few nights' sleep. These nights were filled with visions of dances, and most of these dances have now been presented to the young people . . .

I ran into extreme hostility here to what is called "Semantics." Lloyd Morain and Don Hayakawa are regarded by most philosophers as they probably should be regarded—superficial pretenders.[848]

I have an appointment with a top Jesuit. It seems that all the "good," "fair-minded" groups have refused to permit me to say anything on Pal-

> estine. Received so many apologies this year; they are still coming in, and our joint Arab-Israel-Christian dinners are succeeding. The youth of the world are joining—each other . . .
>
> Despite all that is said above, there is not only no resentment, there is a Puckian appreciation for all those personalities and groups adhering to "liberty, democracy, humanity, and peasants, shut up!" They have made me what might become a national hero to the succeeding generations . . .
>
> I begin tomorrow night with a crowded schedule in New York. At least I have the satisfaction that I shall be permitted to speak and will be judged afterwards, not beforehand.[849]

More was revealed when Sam wrote to W.D. Begg in India, who was writing a book on the life of Moineddin Chishti.

> My last efforts before leaving San Francisco were in three directions: a) to open up *zikr* as science and art for the spiritual development of the young, b) to extend Dervish dancing. On the day before I left San Francisco I had about a thousand young people dancing and chanting Allah, something that has never been done in this land before. It is due to Divine Grace and the grand transmission of *baraka* stemming from our saint, Moineddin Chisti, c) Our efforts to bring Muslims and Israelis—not Jews, but Israelis—to dine together has been most successful. It is exceedingly easy to get young people of Jewish ancestry to repeat *Kalama*. Even the synagogues are becoming uneasy because they do not retain their young. I have not had the slightest opposition in presenting Mohammed (from whom be peace) to the young people . . . At Cornell University I spoke on the relation of the *Miraj* to Khalif Omar's entry into Jerusalem.[850]

Sam mused on his followers and those of Vilayat Khan in a letter to Shamcher:

> I have felt that my immediate followers were far greater than those personalities who surrounded Hazrat Inayat Khan. Now I find that the audience awaiting Vilayat is far far superior to any large group I have ever encountered . . . He is certainly far ahead of me in attracting older people, and I am quite willing to let it go at that. Besides, I am here mostly to promote peace and understanding.[851]

"The Black Christ"

During his stay on the East Coast, Murshid Sam once again met with Karmu, a man introduced to him in Cambridge on his return trip from Geneva in April. He wrote of him at that time, indicating that Karmu was both clairvoyant and well versed in herbs and massage. His apartment was near Harvard Square and Sam saw in him the ability to read the future. He concluded that Karmu acted like a real Bodhisattva, "adjusting bodies and minds wonderfully." The poem *The Black Christ*, excerpted here, was a result of the meeting.

B.
I have been to churches (they would not let me in)
Although the sign upon them says: "No one is free from sin,
Come pray and be for given,
Forgiveness is for the whole world,
Forgiveness leads to heaven."

But there's another temple
Where they don't ask you for your rank,
Your feelings or your ancestry,
Your social status or anything
No it's called: ***The Blood Bank****.*

C.
"Gimme, gimme, gimme, O Lord."
In after-life they shall have their reward:
A bill.
Use me, use me, use me, O Lord,
I do not seek any other award
Than to do Thy will.

D.
I don't own my Savior,
I hope my Savior owns me,
Yet for my heart's dear Savior
I'd be nailed to the tree,
For on the tree I'd feel no pain,
Who crucifies, crucifies in vain,
The love of God is a mighty kiss
That keeps the lover forever in bliss.

E.

. . .

I won't wait for Judgment Day to see will God's will be done.
I shall follow the Scriptures to the letter,
To aid the oppressed and the debtor,
My house shall have only an open door
For the sick and sad and crowds of poor.
I'm going back to Africa, and it won't be for fun,
I'm going back to Africa to see God's will be done.

F.

Here you have loss and you have gain,
Here you have gladness and you have pain,
But after? There's nothing but laughter.
Here you have sorrows and you have woes,
Here you have friends and you have foes,
But after? There's nothing but laughter.

G.

Come, my love, and fly with me
Off into eternity,
Eternity is found my love,
Wherever the heart is full of love.
If you have love and a sunny disposition here,
You will have love and a sunny disposition there,
And that's all I care.

H.

I've got no hard sermons for the sinners,
I've lullabies for the beginners,
I've explanations for the curious
And self-responses for the spurious.

God don't want your dollars, dimes, and cents,
God wants your heart's free recompense,
God blesses and heals and gladly forgives,
Rejoice, my friends, for thus He lives.

I.

Why did Christ come down to bless me?
I only wish I knew.
He found me laughing beneath a tree
And said "You'll do, you'll do."

I did not know it was the Lord,
It was not like a vision,
But He calmly said "I want your word,
Please come to a decision."

But before my mind made up its mind,
My heart opened its heart.
"I'm ready Lord, to help mankind,
I'm ready now to start." . . .

K.

. . .
O Mr. Bill Graham, did the Lord send you down,
Just to save the white man, and not the black or brown?
Mr. Billy Graham, I'm going to send you a bill –
For disguising a part of the Scriptures as the total of God's Will.

There's a "Church of the Open Door," just go in my tawny friend,
And partake of their communion and wait until I send
A messenger to the minister, telling him to rejoice,
And come and visit me in my church, the church of "The Still Small Voice."

I'm come to save you all my friends,
Salvation blots out all sin.[852]

Sam now knew Karmu as a healer who never charged and never failed. Murshid enthusiastically recommended Karmu to Pir Vilayat as someone he should have a session with. When it took place, Pir Vilayat was very disappointed because his physique was not as powerful as Sam's and he found the massage to be very painful.

Karmu spoke often of Murshid Sam with great respect, calling him Sufi Sam. He felt that he had a responsibility to help Sam's students after Sam passed, and he came to San Francisco a few years later to bring his many gifts to the Bay Area community.

Carrying the Message to the East Coast

When Murshid Sam came to Cambridge in 1970 with Mansur, he was received by Azimat Shreiber-Cohn (a *mureed* of Pir Vilayat) and Patricia Walden (Murshid's *mureed* who went on to become a world famous Iyengar Yoga teacher). The Dances in Cambridge at that time were being led by several local residents. Murshid, along with Shabda and Sitara, led Dances set up by Ron White at the Episcopal Church, and also presented at a Dance Free meeting.

The story of Murshid's experience in New York City can be said to begin with his invitation to speak at Columbia, where he was received with openness. Lonnie Less became his host in October of 1970 and was given the name Shahabuddin by Murshid Sam at that time. Here are selections from a 1976 interview with Shahabuddin that give a taste for the events of that period:[853]

> In those days, the only holyman I had ever met was Pir Vilayat and I could safely say that [he] was in his formal British stage . . . I should also say that just to show how little I knew at the time . . . I thought Murshid was his first name and Samuel was his second name . . .
>
> The day finally arrived in N.Y. when Sitara and Murshid were supposed to come . . . They had just flown in from Ithaca where they had seen Saadia, and I was waiting patiently for their arrival . . . About noontime the buzzer in my apartment rang and my heart started to jump and the adrenalin was flowing and I tried to keep myself together, and I walked to the door and I opened it and it was Shabda. He said, "Ha, ha, I bet you thought it was Murshid." I tried to be cool, and I said, "Yes I did," and we went back inside and waited for them. And I guess it was about an hour and a half, and I was debating whether to hide all my ashtrays or not, because one doesn't smoke in the presence of a being like this. So I decided to brave it . . . and I left them out, and we looked out the window, and sure enough the car came down the street, and miraculously there was a parking spot right across the street from the house . . . We both went downstairs and opened the door of the car and out walks this man wearing a plaid sport's shirt and a plaid jacket, baggy pants, straggly beard, unkempt hair, and shoes that obviously didn't fit, and were causing him tremendous pain to wear, and the backs were broken to boot. And he shuffled out and he gave Shabda a big hug, and then he turned and he looked at me and he shook my hand and he said, "How do you do?" I said, "Uh, I do alright," and he starts running across the streets around the apartment . . . From the first moment that I saw him I felt this incredible, indelible love, and it was like I knew that whatever craziness or extraordinariness was coming out of this being, it all didn't matter. And from that moment I was committed, even though there were times when I had the thought that one of the two of us should be committed . . .

> Then we got upstairs . . . Murshid looked around for a few minutes, turned to me and he said, "I have nothing against tobacco," and just this sigh of relief went out . . . Then he faced me squarely and he hit me with the first mystical question, he said, "Do you have any string?" I said, "I'll get some string," and I was frantically looking through my drawers and I had no string. And I figured, you know, this is a test . . . I took a strings mop that I had and I cut off about six or seven strands and I tied them together very carefully and I went up to him and said, "Will this do?" And he said, "Yes, very good." And he took the string and he put his hands behind his back while holding the string, and he started to walk around the room while bouncing the string ever so often. Now I had four cats, and all four cats came running out and started to follow him, jumping after the string, and he did this while I was talking to Sitara and Shabda, and the string kept bouncing and the cats kept playing and he turned around to me and he said, "Now that I've made their acquaintance, I'll make yours."

While walking around the room, Sam noticed a Bible, which he picked up and took to Shahabuddin. He said, "You should go through this whole Bible and everywhere that you see the name of God, you should scratch it out and write in 'Breath.'"

Earlier Shahabuddin had shared with Iqbal that he didn't know how to behave around a spiritual being and had asked for guidance. When asked about that during the interview, Shahabuddin said:

> The only thing Iqbal had told me was—he said (not a quote) there's a phenomenal lesson that I've learned . . . and I said, "What is it?" And he said, "I can't tell you." And that was it . . .
>
> Murshid put his robes away, took over my closet which [was] what we had arranged for in advance . . . and the second great question came, and he said, "Do you have the Yellow Pages?" * . . . I gave him the Yellow Pages, and he went into the bedroom and he sat on the bed and then after about five minutes he said, "Could you come in here?" . . . He had the Yellow Pages opened to . . . the Restaurant Guide . . . He was going over almost every restaurant there, and said, "I picked out this one, and this one, and this one," and I used to go to a lot of restaurants in N.Y. so I

---

*At that time, telephone companies in cities around the country would print and freely distribute directories of local businesses, on iconic yellow paper.

> told him the ones I knew, and we consulted for a few minutes . . . Then he turns to me and he says, "The first thing I've got to do is to go down to Columbus Circle and get my Diner's Club in order." And I said, "What kind of a holy man is this? This is nothing like what I had expected!" He's been in this space for two hours and my whole mind is blown, my being was shattered, but it was the bridge of this love that made me go through all this and accept all this. And that was basically our first meeting . . .
>
> The next day . . . Murshid had a choice, he could have either gone to a meeting, like a lecture or *satsang* of Swami Muktananda, Satchitananda, Baba Ram Dass, Alan Ginsberg, Rudi, or go out to his cousin's in Queens, and he said that he thought he had to go out to his cousin in Queens. He said, "I know that they are going to feed me red meat, I know it, and I don't even want to eat it, but I'm going to eat it while I'm there."

Later at Shahabuddin's apartment, there was a fascinating and touching exchange when Murshid saw the picture of Shahabuddin's candidate for congress. Shahabuddin recounted:

> He looked at me, and he said, "How do I see her?" I said, "You see her in government." He said, "No." I don't remember exactly but it was something like, you see her in philosophy or helping the poor, or something, and he said, "No, no, no, no." . . . And he turned to Shabda and said, "How do I see her?" And Shabda said, "Dancing." Murshid said, "Right! That's how I see her; I see almost everybody dancing."

Shahabuddin described an encounter of one of his friends with Sam.

> [My friend] was supposed to meet me at my apartment at an appointed time, and nobody was at my apartment except Murshid, and he showed up early—he showed up like an hour early. I walked in and he had been alone with Murshid for an hour, and I thought, God knows what he thinks after spending an hour with Murshid. Now this man's hobby was cooking, really gourmet cooking. And finally we went out, the two of us together, and I said, "What did you talk about?" And he said, "It was the most amazing thing; that man knows more about gourmet cooking than anybody I know . . . We discussed it for a whole hour, and it was so interesting, and he asked me all the questions that nobody ever asked me and showed this interest."

Shahabuddin also spoke about a meeting between Murshid Sam and Pir Vilayat.

> Pir Vilayat had just flown in from Europe and was just spending the night there, and the previous three days, anytime anybody asked [Murshid] a question especially about the Sufi Order or anything like that, he would say, "We'll have to wait for the meeting with Pir Vilayat; that will clear all this up." And he was getting me so excited about this meeting with Pir Vilayat that I figured that this is going to be the big meeting—the essence of the essence! And whenever I asked him a question . . . about an experience I'd had when Murshid was leading a little meditation and he explained a little of it and then said, "You'll get the rest from Pir Vilayat." . . .
>
> And we get set to go to the meeting, and I think it was either Sitara, Shabda and I, or just Sitara and I—we were about to leave, and Murshid turns to me and says, "You can't go," and I said, "Alright." And I went down and I sat on the couch and he said, "It's not that I don't want you to go, but I don't think you should go." I said, "Alright," and inside, I was really starting to burn, you know. And I sat there on the couch and for the next ten minutes he didn't look at me, but he kept coming in and telling me, "It's just not quite right that you go," and on and on and on. And I kept feeling worse and worse and worse, and then he left and they went to the meeting. And I sat on the couch for the next two hours; I didn't move, and I got a deeper perspective into myself than I've ever had pretty much in my whole life! Of course he came back and he told me everything that happened there, at least from his eyes—which were pretty good eyes. And in a moment, any personal anger and anything that I had felt was gone. And somehow I knew that I had received a great blessing.

A similar situation arose on another occasion.

> We were going to see Clive Backster, who is the man who hooks up the plants to lie detectors, and the same thing, Murshid got me all psyched up for a few days and I was all set to go. And he said, "I don't think you can go; I don't know if you are scientific enough." And I said, "Alright," and went through the same thing again; he went, and he took Sitara [and Shabda], because I was thinking, "I'm more scientific than she is, you know." I went through the same thing, but this time the anger wasn't there. You know, I just didn't feel it; somehow it was just [all]

> right, even though I was feeling pretty sorry for myself. But he came back and reported everything that went on, and again I have the feeling that I really received something . . . I can't say that I consciously understood, yet I had received this—the minute I saw him it was like I had received all this love that somehow made it alright . . . I wouldn't be telling the truth if I said that I understood it . . . but I was much less angry in a deep place when it was all done. When these things happened, somehow, yes, I did understand—if not in my head, I understood it somewhere, someplace perhaps more important.

Shahabuddin was asked if Murshid Sam deliberately set up tests. This was his response:

> I can't answer that because I don't know. The best way I can answer that is by telling you another story. The day that Gamal Abdel Nasser died, I thought this was a pretty big event, and somehow I was up before Murshid got up—he was out late—and he came in I told him that Gamal Abdel Nasser had died, and he said, "I know." I don't know how he knew, but he knew! I said, "Murshid, what do you think about this?" He only ever raised his voice to me twice, but he turned around to me at this moment, and he started screaming, "I don't think, I don't think: I don't think!!!" And that is the answer to your question; I don't believe that Murshid consciously thought that this would be a good test, or that would be a good test. I don't think that God thinks, "I'll give this person syphilis; I'll give this person wealth." . . . It comes from a much greater consciousness. And I think that that is what happened. Murshid, just like us all, had the Guidance within him. The difference is that Murshid listened! . . . He wasn't afraid that this man who is my host is going to think ill of me if I don't let him come, or anything like that. I think he just acted from his heart, from his heart. Plus, the incredible aura of truth in everything that was done made it all acceptable, because that is true. I don't consider Murshid as a holy-man in a sense, because he was so regular, he was so normal.

Shahabuddin really felt that Murshid cared for him. He got a phone call from Murshid one day in the middle of the afternoon. Shahabuddin had been working for three days straight, 18 or 20 hours per day and had just kept going. Murshid called and told him the cats were fighting and he couldn't stand it. Shahabuddin relates,

> He said, "Come home right away!" And he hung up the phone. And I didn't think about can I or can't I? I just told them that I had to go home right away. It was about an hour from N.Y. City where I was working. I drove . . . to the house and it was just Murshid, and it was totally peaceful. There was no problem with the cats, and Murshid didn't say anything about the cats. Then I said, "Murshid, what about the cats?" and he said, "Right after I spoke to you, they all calmed down." And he said, "Here, sit down and have some lunch." And we sat down and had some lunch . . . I stayed at home for that afternoon and then the next day it was like a thought came into my head, "I think I'll take a day off." He said, "Good idea! Take a day off!"

Shahabuddin was the only one in his circle who felt their candidate was going to win. He asked Murshid Sam for help: "What shall I do?" Murshid replied, "It's very simple. You keep believing with all your heart that you are going to win; put all of your strength and all of your concentration into the fact that you are going to win. Then, if you lose, adjust!" And it was just a great lesson.

The Dances already had the beginnings of a presence on the East Coast. While Shabda was in New York caring for his father, before Murshid Sam arrived, Baba Ram Dass had a reunion weekend for all who had lived on or come through his father's property in Franklin, New Hampshire. The Dances of Universal Peace were shared there, captured by Amertat Cohn, who was filming the movie *Sunseed*.*

And there was a day when Shahabuddin was invited to go to Central Park, where Murshid and his new secretary Sitara, along with Shabda, would be presenting Dances. Murshid Sam often wore his dervish robe that had been given to him by Sufi Barkat Ali in Pakistan. Several decades later a woman who had become a follower of the Dances of Universal Peace described coming to Central Park and seeing this little old man wearing a burlap bag. She had met in Murshid Sam the life stream manifestation of the Dances she would later come to honor.

---

*Pir Shabda shared a letter he received from Murshid after sending him a picture of the gathering. Murshid's unfailing support and *kashf* were readily apparent. "Murshid has nothing but beautiful and fine feelings about you, and also about a lot of other young people here . . . Your pictures almost make me cry. Your reports are so wonderful that God himself told me they would be."

During his stay in the East Murshid was invited to the Rye, New York, estate of Charles Berner, a man who had been holding "Enlightenment Intensives." He had invited all of the gurus of the day who were in the West, hoping to promote a festival he had envisioned. Present were Yogi Bhajan, Swami Satchitananda, Rabbi Joseph Gelberman, Hilda Charlton, Amrit Desai, and of course Murshid Sam and Charles Berner. Each teacher had one or two attendants with them; Sitara and Shabda accompanied Murshid Sam.

Friday evening went smoothly enough with each teacher sharing a little about their life's path, their lineages and their work. The next morning Berner announced to the group, "I want to invite you all to join me in putting on a World Enlightenment Festival!"

Shabda writes,

> Traveling with Murshid always meant we were in for some surprises as his insight and reality were much deeper than ours. Indeed, Murshid nearly jumped out of his armchair, and in a loud voice exhorted, "World, world! We don't represent the world! Where are the Buddhists, the Muslims, the Christians?! Where are the Vietnamese, the Chinese, etc.?!" Then in a very pointed and penetrating voice he spoke directly to Charles Berner, "Is this Divine Guidance or is this your ego?[854]

The tone, temperature and overall atmosphere in the room dramatically changed and Berner was visibly shaken. First Yogi Bhajan spoke. His friendship with Murshid Sam had already been established early that summer in Golden Gate Park. He was many years Murshid Sam's junior, as were most of the others, and he said, "We should listen to Murshid. He is very deep, and he is our elder!"

Each leader chimed in with their response. Swami Satchitananda, 20 years Murshid's junior and much more of a romantic than Yogi Bhajan, offered his view. "This is such a beautiful idea. Let's develop it together."

After everyone spoke, they broke for lunch. Murshid Sam no longer felt his presence was welcomed or needed, so he, Shabda, and Sitara left the gathering. The festival never materialized.

Another meeting in New York was with Swami Muktananda at a luncheon set up for him. Sam arrived first and sat himself down in the seat intended for Muktananda. Although this caused some tension in the room, when Murshid and Muktananda were able to speak to one another, they had a joyful conversation about Mother Krishnabai. Both of them knew her personally and acknowledged her as a realized being who was easy to love and listen to.

Back in San Francisco

Murshid Sam returned to the Bay Area from his characteristically packed time on the East Coast in mid-November of 1970, resuming his many activities at home and never slowing down. He wrote to many friends of not having even an hour off per week and detailed some of his many activities: he now had over 100 disciples, which meant holding more interviews as well as more esoteric classes; he was holding several Dance classes per week, as well as general public meetings; universities were asking him to give talks; a long-awaited delegate with whom Murshid hoped to advance his Middle East peace plan arrived, requesting immediate and frequent meetings; Dances continued to appear, which then needed to be choreographed; and there was voluminous correspondence. Personal concerns figured in as well: social obligations to friends who visited from out of town, the properties needed maintenance, and friends in crisis turned to him.

Many acquaintances had told him or begged him to take it easy, but to no avail—his powerful motor would heat up and he would move forward instead. He was proud of what was coming to pass from his efforts. He was often known to say, "I planted seeds every year of my life, and nothing came up. Year after year, nothing came up—and now everything is coming up, and I can't keep up with the harvest. What am I to do? And God said to me, 'Harvest what you can and leave the rest to Me.'"[855] Sam was doing everything he could to reap the harvest.

Photo by Mansur Johnson

"I am not, Thou art"

He was spending most of his time at the Mentorgarten. In addition to everything else, he was finishing up significant esoteric writings. He had been energetically writing papers on *fana,* which included his *Sangatha* on *fana-fi-Sheikh,* and a *Sangatheka* on the same subject. After this came the *Sangitha* on *fana-fi-Rassoul,* to be followed by papers on *fana-fi-Muhammad.* The titles read "Teachings for the Murshid," "Instructions for the Pir," "On Being a Sheikh" (*Shuyukhuyat*—a paper that somehow showed up in the esoteric teachings in Germany), and finally, "*Malikiyyat:* The School of the Master. An Original *Sangatha.*" These papers along with many other writings and commentaries of Murshid Sam form an integral part of the Ruhaniat esoteric school.

When one deeply considers the processes taught in these papers one can get a very good view of Murshid Sam. From the standpoint of the Spiritual Hierarchy, including his own confirmation about the ultimate outcome as seen through his experiences in life, he was an *abdal,* one who has the spiritual gift of effacement in the essence of another being. If it was Prophet Muhammad, he was in oneness of attunement with this awakened being. If it was Hazrat Inayat Khan, he had already met him in eternity the day before he was initiated by him.

It was all embodied now in Sufi Ahmed Murad Chisti, who was attuned to the guidance of Inayat Khan for a large part of his life. To do this was to be in *fana-fi-Sheikh,* or in this case, *fana-fi-Pir.* He was one of the few disciples of Inayat who was able to follow the Pir-o-Murshid's request that his *mureeds* learn what he called *tasawwuri* Murshid (effacement in him).

In the greater community there was energy that year to have an event in December. The facility in Sausalito where weekly Sufi Dances were held was chosen as the venue for what was to be called the Whirling Dervish Bazaar. This took place the week of Christmas, 1970. It would embody many dimensions, including Dances and performances of the Sufi Choir.

It was here that Murshid, in addition to leading Dances, presented to Jiyu-Kennett Roshi one of the two green chairs in which Murshid and Phra Sumangalo had had their deep meetings together. These chairs were sacred to Sam. Jiyu-Kennett Roshi, English by birth, was the first woman in Japan to have received full acceptance of her role as a teacher in the lineage of Zen Buddhism. Years later Saul and other Dervish Healing Order companions were at her ashram near Shasta to pay their respects and to hold a retreat. Members of the Ashram returned the chair to Saul at that time to bring back to San Francisco.

There had been differences and conflicts within the circle of Hallelujah! The Three Rings. Murshid was trying to point the way. He had originally believed that their participation at the Bazaar was raising funds for Hallelujah! The Three Rings. That didn't turn out to be the case, so he took the funds and gave $100 to relief in East Pakistan. He was willing to take on the karma related to the money, thus protecting his *mureeds,* while supporting the work for peace in the Holy Land.

The Fateful Fall

Within a week of the conclusion of the Bazaar everything changed. Murshid Sam was not known for taking heed of his own physical health, although he was very vigorous. As Asha said when he was teaching at Lama, he would take them on a hike up the mountain and he always walked faster than all of them.

He was also quoted as saying that he had to check his body every two weeks since he no longer felt any pain, that God had removed his pain so that he could take on the pain of the world. I witnessed that he could indeed rise to a higher plane when exposed to pain. Once someone spilled boiling water on Murshid's hand. He stood upright, took several very deep breaths and transcended all pain. However, there were times he would lose touch with his everyday physical state. On a walk with me back from the Dented Can store (he liked to buy cheap) to the Mentorgarten, Murshid had a release of urine all over his pants and told me just to ignore it.

Murshid had a longstanding issue with itchy skin, especially on his arms, which constantly bothered him. Finally, following Saul's lead, he consulted a Chinese physician whose brother had been a doctor to Sam in previous years, so Sam was willing to accept this new physician. When he came back to the Mentorgarten from his appointment, Sam told me he had been informed that he had very high blood pressure. He was given medication for it, and the doctor said to leave the itching problem for some other time.

As it transpired, a number of Murshid's male disciples were staying at the house on Sunday night, December 27, 1970, for the men's Dance/Walk class that was to be held the next day. The visiting *mureeds*—including Shabda and Halim Frank Welsh, the treasurer—were spending the night in the front room. I was in my bedroom next door. In the very early morning Sam got up from sleep and visited the bathroom after having taken his blood pressure medication. In the bathroom, he filled the tub with hot water and took a bath. Murshid scrambled from the bathroom in his robe looking for the thermostat at the top of the stairs not far away.

I awoke to a thudding sound, and I knew something had gone wrong. Murshid had collapsed and fallen down the steep stairs. Frank was the first to reach him. Iqbal's car was near the house in Shabda's care, since Iqbal was on a 40-day retreat at the Dome of the Rock in Jerusalem. Shabda called Saul, head of the healing circle, who lived a block away, to come be of help. Saul walked down, not trusting himself to drive.

Shabda drove Murshid to the ER at San Francisco General Hospital along with Saul, Halim and me. He was put on a stretcher and was being restrained by Saul and Shabda as he became quite combative, or a "roaring borealis" as Shabda described him.* At one point one of Murshid's arms got free and he unintentionally hit Saul full in the face. Murshid

---

*Murshid had accepted that phrase earlier from me.

would alternate between chanting, "Allah, Allah Allah" or "*Allahu Akbar*" and "Let's get the hell out of here! What the hell are we doing here? Shut up!" This went on for some time until Murshid was taken for x-rays and found to have a broken arm.

During his hospital stay, Murshid continued alternating between reciting the prayers of Inayat Khan, or "All Powerful Creator, All Powerful Creator" and "Shut up! Let's get out of here." A round-the-clock vigil was set up for him with his disciples and friends taking turns staying with him. One disciple felt that with the gravity of Murshid's condition, people sobered up, came out of their fog and worked magnificently as a team, living the teachings he had given them. Many reported his coming back into lucidity, holding a normal conversation with them, then lapsing back into what was ultimately called a coma. Hospital staff who wanted him declared incompetent were held at bay with threats of a lawsuit made through legal friends. At one point, Murshid became totally lucid and called for dictation to be taken. He wrote his last letter to Sufi Barkat Ali:

Praise be to Allah!
This has been a glorious exit,
And one which will go down in history,
A sign of all the beauty, truth and goodness in the universe.
One has been truly saved from the jaws of death and adversity,
And may live on indefinitely as God wills.
It is the sign of all symbol and goodness,
And the establishment of God's message in the Western world forever,
Praise be to Allah!
For I am the first one born in the West to have received
the Divine Message, and believe to have representatives
in all the purity and goodness of which Allah is capable
and which will now be presumed done forever.[856]

During another lucid earth-plane moment, Murshid was told of all the people who had come to sit with him, keeping vigil. He cried when he heard of their gathering round, deeply touched that his friends thought that much of him. Murshid called his disciples "friends." Then he called me in and instructed me to pay the rent, refusing to listen to how all the funds were tied up in his name. "Now!" Heaven and Earth.

Murshid's *mureed* Mouni (Mary Sue) related that the feeling around Murshid's bed was full of light, that Murshid was surrounded by radiance, even when he was reaching through the rails of his bed, seemingly grabbing for something. After repeated questioning by Mouni if Murshid wanted something and being told very clearly "No!" repeatedly, finally Murshid answered, "Yes! You!" He pulled Mouni forward and gave her a kiss. They were both in a state of delight the rest of the afternoon. Mouni later described her understanding of the incident: "It's an example of how Murshid felt about us all. He really wanted us all, he just wanted us right in his heart. And that was how he taught us. That was really the center of his teaching more than anything else. He wanted everything for us. He wanted us to find Divine perfection. And he did everything he could for us to find that. But maybe more than wanting anything for us, he just reduced it to the simplest and most meaningful state of just wanting us."[857]

Murshid's light was seen by many. During our interview years later,[858] Murshida Vera shared this story:

> Wali Ali: "After Murshid fell down the stairs and was taken to the hospital, in the middle of the night a few days later I got a phone call from you, and I would like you to tell me—at the time I don't know if . . . someone else had told you about his accident?"
>
> Murshida Vera: "No, no, no. I knew nothing. I had no contact with anybody regarding what had happened to him. I called you at a horrible hour . . . 2:00 in the morning? . . . I woke up suddenly, and just sat up in bed and realized that Samuel was standing at the foot of my bed, and just as much in the flesh as he could ever be, in his robe, and looking right at me; and I addressed him; he called me; I heard his name; he called me three times. And I sat up and looked at the foot of the bed, and he was standing there. And I didn't realize it was the middle of the night, and I was just thrilled to death that he was there and began to talk to him, and then my conscious mind said, 'This is impossible!' I denied it, and immediately the manifestation in the physical body went into the spiritual body, into light; and I knew that he stood in the spirit body, talking to me. And that disappeared, and then just the feeling of ice [came] slowly down through each center of my body, and I thought, 'what has happened to Samuel? This is terrible.' I immediately got up . . . and called . . ."

> **Wali Ali**: "When I got to the telephone you said to me, 'Is Samuel all right?' . . . And I said, 'Well, he fell down the stairs.' I told you what had happened . . . This [appearance] is, of course, a very unusual experience—was this the first time that he had –"
> **Murshida Vera**: "It was not unusual in my life—unusual where Samuel was concerned, yes. But he always would come at the most amazing time. He just appeared in the flesh as if he was the answer to a call . . ."
> **Wali Ali**: "When you say, 'appeared in the flesh,' you mean actually physically—he would just come."
> **Murshida Vera** "He would appear at the house, yes. He would just come. He'd come to the door, or he'd come into the house and just be standing in the doorway. And it would be at a time when I was in trouble, when I needed him, for some reason, and he would be there . . . I'd been used to him coming in time of trouble, but I wasn't in trouble. There was no reason for him to come; the minute I began saying in my mind, 'This can't be. This is not possible,' then, of course, he went into the light. And I realized that he had come to inform me and to bid his farewells to me. And I felt very strongly his blessing."*

During his alert moments in the hospital, Murshid would demand to be moved to the Chinese hospital. Several of the *mureeds* as well as his niece Marilou, who was a nurse, also felt that his care was inadequate at SF General. No doctor wanted to take the responsibility for Murshid until finally one Chinese physician, called at random by Saul, was made to see the importance of this change for all concerned and agreed to take over, even though it meant risking his license. The transfer was ultimately made to a Chinese hospital, where his followers' vigil continued. Murshid Sufi Ahmed Murad Chisti, Samuel Leonard Lewis, left his body only a few days later on January 15th, 1971, at 1 a.m.

After Murshid Sam Leaves His Body: Early Days

In accordance with standard procedure, Murshid's body was moved to the morgue. There he continued to radiate blessings on his followers. Michael Gest reported that he and Banefsha spent a few hours with

---

* Murshida Vera was a lifelong friend and devotee. Her grave lies close to Murshid Sam's dargah, where their inner communication is said to continue.

Murshid in the morgue shortly after he was transferred from the Chinese hospital. "I really had this experience of him leaving his body, and infusing into the world and after that, that's when I understood Kabbalah, I finally understood these mysteries called *Merkaba**—and right after that I understood it not from a mental understanding and a kind of transcendental logic but direct understanding."[859] †

THREE-DAY VIGIL AFTER HIS DEATH
– Followers of Samuel Lewis considered him a saint
—Examiner photo by Paul Glines

Vigil Over Body

Samuel Lewis,
Sufi Saint Dies

By Dexter Waugh

Newspaper coverage from *San Francisco Examiner*

Surya, who had stayed outside the hospital and sung "Tis a Gift to Be Simple," found her grief upon learning of Murshid's death being transformed into laughter and then overwhelming joy. Likewise, Shahabuddin upon learning of Murshid Sam's passing reported that he was filled with tremendous joy that led him to dance in the streets of New York for four hours with a visiting friend who also knew Murshid.

Several followers who sat with Murshid Sam's body in the morgue—now surrounded by candles, flowers and incense—reported that his skin was translucent, radiant. They found the body before them different from the one they had experienced in life. Surya reported, "Murshid in life appeared much larger than he really was; he was shorter than I was, and I always thought he was taller . . . I just remember him as being huge."[860] She also found his features, which she had remembered as being rather large and coarse, to be quite the opposite: "While I sat by his body, there was this small, precise body with very delicate features, and a very beautiful aquiline nose. And the smoothest baby skin that I have ever seen. It really spoke of the spirituality of his being which had permeated even the flesh . . . There was nothing but joy there! . . . There

* In Kabbalah, *Merkaba* is the throne of God, or divine chariot; also associated practices.

† Murshid Sam had sponsored Michael and me to attend a class on Kabbalah at Berkeley. There we met the hero of Woodstock, Wavy Gravy, who was in attendance as an "expert" at the first class. He later became involved in leading a youth camp within the Mendocino camp sponsored by the Sufi Ruhaniat.

was just an incredible light about his body."[861] She too went dancing in the streets after leaving the morgue.

There was considerable disagreement as to the cause of Murshid Sam's death. Was it from a concussion sustained during the fall or was it from kidney damage related to long-undiagnosed high blood pressure, one sign of which is unrelenting itching? One family member (Marilou) felt that the purported uremia (buildup of toxins in the blood stream from kidney damage) was from dehydration related to poor care at San Francisco General Hospital.

Despite pleas not to perform an autopsy based on religious beliefs, an autopsy ultimately was conducted in conformance with State law due to the unexpected nature of the death. That autopsy reported the cause of death as a brain concussion. It was not a short journey from death to autopsy. The dispute ended up in Superior Court with the attorney employer of Vashist's wife Salima taking on the case *pro bono.* The headline in *The San Francisco Chronicle* referred to Murshid Sam as a Sufi saint who was being defended in court. Finally the body was released.

Asoka Edward Yerxa, a fairly new *mureed* who was also a carpenter, took it upon himself to build a coffin for Murshid Sam. Sam's body was wrapped in his dervish robe, placed in the coffin and flown to New Mexico accompanied by Mansur. They were picked up by Asha and then taken to Lama Foundation. Other disciples of Murshid Sam followed to help dig the grave in the frozen ground of Lama Mountain.

Asha shared her remembrance of what she witnessed when Sufi Ahmed Murad's body arrived at Lama.

> I walked into the huge Octagonal Dome. It was approaching dark. There was a palpable silence much like forest in late evening on a windless day. In the center of the room there was the coffin holding the body of Murshid Sam which had been brought from California by his disciples. The coffin did not reduce the spaciousness but expanded it. It seemed rather impolite to breathe, as though even breathing would crack the Holiness of the space.
>
> Piled up against all the eight walls were the boxes that held the texts, music and art of the book which would eventually become the iconic *Be*

Here Now composed by Ram Dass (Alpert) and members of the Lama Foundation. The four sides of the boxes alternated the words BE HERE NOW and BINDU TO OJAS. They were whispering through the room and it felt a bit as though Murshid was laughing from the diamond skylight above. I like to think Murshid's Baraka spread out with every copy of *Be Here Now.*

Several people were up the hill digging the grave early in the morning. A procession followed up the hill with his closer students as pall bearers. He was buried and dirt filled the grave. The dirt which his coffin replaced was piled above the ground and covered with large quartz rocks which are now still above that grave in the *dargah.** That evening there was a celebration of his life in the Dome, the *Be Here Now* boxes still in place. One of the remarkable shifts that was noticed was that his closest disciples seemed to have picked up or amplified certain qualities that Murshid had often displayed.[862]

Memorial service for Murshid Samuel Lewis at the Garden of Inayat

*Murshid Sam's tomb, also at Lama. Construction began in 2015, and the beautiful completed structure was dedicated in 2017.

Murshid had always said that he would be known for continuing to communicate with others after leaving the body. Many reported that Sam's voice in fact continued to be heard at the gravesite and in the retreat house where seekers would come to be near his grave at Lama. Over time, notebooks in the cabin were filled with people's experiences. To a large extent it is Murshid's voice found in those notebooks.

Surya, who was very much inwardly connected with Murshid Sam, shared a remembrance of two days before the memorial service.

> I was at that gathering at the Mentorgarten . . . It was the first gathering that we'd had after Murshid died. It just felt like after the disciples gathered after Christ died. It was just so very intensive, and we knew at that moment that Murshid was just so much more alive than ever. And it was such a triumphant gathering, although you could hear a few people here and there saying, "Oh, and well, he's passed, and we'll sort of pass too." And yet the people who were there who are really strong like Wali Ali and Moineddin (he had just come out of the hospital himself, and looked terrible). He was so strained and worn—but you felt the strength of these men, and of Murshid's being, that he had really and truly found [representatives on] earth.[863]

Surya went on to speak of the memorial service, which was held at the Garden of Inayat in Novato:

> I remember Joe Miller with that particular heart quality that just pierced right to the heart, to the core. What he said was so representative of Murshid's feelings, it was so very wonderful; and Pir had given so many teachings, and that great heart, which I felt, was part of his genius, and showed that side of his nature . . . [864]

Vocha Fiske

From *Sunseed*

Murshid's most respected lifelong friend, Vocha Fiske, eventually took the platform. Like her dear friend Sam, she was a doer. Here in this crowd of people she saw the opportunity to fully engage them and to arouse their energy and spiritual ideals. She stood before everyone and, extending her hands, said a phrase of Hazrat Inayat Khan, "May the message of God reach far and wide."

Mostly people just listened, but that wasn't what she wanted. Again this elderly lady stood up and said the words, but before expressing it through her arms, she spoke from the depth of her heart, "Do it! Do it! Do it!" In being so effaced in that, she inspired everyone.

I keenly remember a moment at the memorial service in a room full of people—Moineddin and I turned to look at each other and we said together, "He's still here."

He's still here. Murshid Sam's brilliant, magnetic voice can be heard through the lives of many to this day. This *Hadith* appears at his *dargah* at the Lama Foundation: "On that day the Sun will rise in the West, and all who see will believe." It clearly stands for the birth of the New Age in Murshid's realization.

The name Sufi Ahmed Murad signifies "one who is endeavoring to fulfill his life's purpose." After Sam's passing, Sufi Barkat Ali gave him a new name, Sufi Ba Murad, meaning "one who has accomplished his life's goals."

From *Sunseed*

Dargah of Murshid Samuel Lewis at Lama Foundation, New Mexico, completed 2017

Afterword

FOLLOWING THE MEMORIAL AND CARRIED BY THE FORCE of Murshid's presence that lived within them, Sam's disciples stepped forward to continue his legacy of promulgating universal truth. There was a group of young people waiting for the initiation Murshid had promised. Both Moineddin in Marin and I at the Mentorgarten conducted the initiations, calling forth not only God's name but that of great teachers and illuminated souls like Hazrat Inayat Khan and Sufi Ahmed Murad Chisti.

Murshid Sam's advanced Saturday night Dance class in the Mentorgarten meeting room continued under my leadership. In the past, no one but Murshid Sam had presented new Dances. Now it was viewed as appropriate to encourage the members of the class to come up with possible Dances. These would be danced and considered by the class, and often matured and became ready to offer publicly.

There were many skilled people in this class and much came out of their attempts to create beautiful Dances. In one class I mentioned something that Murshid Sam had said on several occasions years earlier: if you want to find a mantric way of presenting Christian Dances, you should learn the Lord's prayer in Aramaic, the actual language of Jesus. Saadi Neil Douglas-Klotz was one of the skilled dancers in the room and he immediately began to study Aramaic. Soon we had many Aramaic Dances, which eventually were led all over the world along with other Dances of Universal Peace.

It was well established and known that Moineddin would be Murshid's successor, as Sam had frequently made this announcement. Nevertheless, while Murshid Sam's legacy was being furthered by his disciples, there were rumblings behind the scenes. The unexpected nature of Sam's transition was taken advantage of by Neville Warwick, whom Murshid Sam had always defended. Warrick fabricated and spread the story around San Francisco to those who would listen that Samuel Lewis's disciples had pushed him down the stairs intending to kill him. Nothing could have been further from the truth, and Warrick was thus left, in a phrase Sam often used, to take on the karmic consequence that would come as a result of his lies.

There were several spiritual teachers who attempted in various ways to take over Murshid's following of engaged young people. Murshid Sam's close friend Joe Miller was a notable exception. He had been ordained as a Zen *roshi* by the same South Korean Master Seo as Sam and had his own following. Soon after Murshid's transition I invited Joe and his wife Guin to have dinner at the Mentorgarten. After the meal I asked Joe to be a helper. When Joe asked me how much I wanted him to take on, I replied, "All of it." But Joe and Guin had long made it clear that they fully supported the independence of Murshid's group of *mureeds*. Saul summarized Joe's approach fittingly:

> Joe Miller I remember most in particular. He came in and said, "I don't want anybody to take you guys over, Sam wouldn't want it that way, if he'd wanted it that way, he would have told you, so keep your own shot together; any help I can give you, ask, you don't want it, don't ask, I won't volunteer, I'm right here, all the time, constantly, I'm your friend, and your brother and don't worry about asking me, call me twenty-four hours a day, I'm always on call." I remember him coming to a couple of meetings (he really is a powerful man) and people would ask, "Wow, who are you, where do you teach?" And he would say, "It doesn't matter who I am, I don't teach, and you're here, and this is a good place to be. Stay with the Sufis. They got it." [865]

Joe and Guin Miller

When Pir Vilayat initiated Moineddin as a Murshid at a gathering at Hurkalya and somehow the word of what had happened got to Joe Miller, Joe did not wait for an invitation. He went immediately to

Hurkalya and made his way in to Pir Vilayat. He spoke to him in a Fudo-like manner saying that it was a mistake that Pir Vilayat had recognized Moineddin as a Murshid and had only initiated Sheikh Wali Ali to be a Khalif, and that it was a mistake because most everyone looked at the two of them as having the same realization. Pir Vilayat responded to Joe's advance and arranged for me, though I was content with things as they already stood, to come in to see him again. At that meeting the Pir gave me the equivalent degree as notated in Hazrat Inayat Khan's hierarchical writings, *Sheikh ul MaSheikh.*

Developments Inspired by Murshid Sam's Life

After Murshid Sam had said to me from his hospital bed, "What are you doing here? You should be at the house and paying the rent," I did what Murshid Sam had not done: I complained to the owner about the condition of the house. The owner responded that he had had enough of these hippies and that everyone there would be evicted, a pronouncement that shook up both Saul and me.

Fortunately, Saul knew an unusual man at a nearby office. Mr. Schwartz had a wooden leg and spoke very loudly. When Saul and I met up with him, he said something we liked: we should try to buy the place. Mr. Schwartz got on the telephone with the owner and in a wild manner started out by agreeing with the owner when he put down us young residents. He even cursed us. Then there would be a pause; he would cover the mouthpiece and curse the owner in a belligerent way. After another pause, he began to negotiate price. A give and take ensued, and eventually the owner accepted a price Schwartz offered on our behalf—about $35,000. When the owner responded positively to the bid, Schwartz shouted out, "Okay! It's a deal!"

As things progressed toward a mortgage agreement, we learned that the owner of the property was delinquent in taxes and was planning to pay them with the proceeds of the sale. As far as we were concerned, we were transparent with the lenders about our part in the exchange: none of us had full-time jobs. However, Allaudin Mathieu was an exception, and he and his wife Kathryn agreed to take on the loan. They only had to put up a dollar or two and never pay another cent on the loan. The young people involved were able to pay down the mortgage and thus retain the place that Murshid Sam had filled with his spiritual presence and tremendous atmosphere in general. It could not be given up.

A number of *mureeds* were interested in a *khankah.* They had filled a large apartment building and infused it with their practices. It became evident to them that, given the very low prices buildings were going for, they might be able to find a good place for a *khankah* for less than the rent they were paying at the apartments.

As time went on it became clear that more than one house would be needed for a real *khankah* in San Francisco. It seemed likely that suitable properties could be found near the Mentorgarten and that they might be secured at a good price. The search was broad and prices were indeed far lower than they would be in a few years. A favorable deal was made with the owner of two houses on Norwich Street, a five-minute walk from the Mentorgarten. The owner also owned a block of land connected to the property, but city restrictions prohibited him from selling it to someone else to build on. Instead, he sold it to the Sufis, who turned the area into a garden.

Khankah SAM, as it was called, went on to thrive and expand over the years. Sufis and those who knew about them came from all over the world as paying guests to the *Khankah* on their visits to San Francisco. Events such as the *Jamiat Khas,* led by Murshid Moineddin, Dance meetings, and other gatherings were held in the Mentorgarten meeting room. The *Khankah* continues to thrive after many years and still is very much blessed, reflecting Murshid Sam's ongoing presence in the neighborhood.

Wali Ali Meyer, Iqbal Lewis, Shahabuddin Less

There were many developments emanating from Murshid Sam's influence over the years. Hallelujah! The Three Rings expanded its activities, with its members holding different concentrations. Of its original five members, four of them soon traveled to the Middle East, beginning with Iqbal Jonathan Lewis, the group's president, in 1971. He focused on trade and proper business practices as universal and impersonal ways of creating peace: "Peace Through Business." He successfully developed and maintained trusting relationships for a decade with businessmen in Syria, Egypt, and Israel—Arabs and Jews alike—and had two flourishing businesses in the U.S. His first shop in San Francisco was initially funded in part by the Ruhaniat.

Two years later other members of the Three Rings also traveled to the Middle East and were introduced to the Palestinians Iqbal had met. With them was Khusro Howard Haas, who became a highlight of the group. His rise to prominence is worth sharing.

In 1970 at the California Mendocino Sufi camp, Pir Vilayat was putting together a pageant representing the Quest for the Holy Grail. When Pir Vilayat saw Howard, he immediately said, "That's Parsifal," and gave him that role in the pageant. A few months after the camp, an inspired Howard wrote the journey of *Parsifal the Clown* in one sitting on a park bench in San Francisco's Union Square. A Sufi-inspired journey of an old man, it began with the chant Om Mani Padme Hum. It was eventually performed in San Francisco's Dolores Park for hundreds of people.

I gave Howard the name Khusro, and he soon moved into the Hallelujah! The Three Rings house with Michael and Banefsha Gest, where gatherings of Christians, Muslims, and Jews had been hosted. Banefsha was already writing, directing and producing large pageants and she channeled what would happen in her presentations. When the Yom Kippur War broke out in 1973, Khusro had a vision of Parsifal leading a parade of Muslim, Christian, and Jewish children through the Old City of Jerusalem. He decided to travel to Israel during the war, but there was an immediate problem: at that point there were no direct passenger flights from the U.S. to Israel. Khusro made a fortunate connection with San Francisco's Senator Milton Marks, who set up passage for Khusro and Banefsha on a cargo flight. They settled in an Arab village on the Mount of Olives.

Thanks to Khusro's winning personality, deep sincerity, and ability to relate well to new people, he was able to arrange for Michael Gest to set up an area on a university campus there to develop seeds that would be ideal for planting in a dry environment. Unfortunately for Michael's plans, the seeds did not sprout.

After Khusro arrived in Jerusalem, the Parsifal show was phonetically translated into Hebrew and received broad appreciation by all denominations. Following up on his vision of working with young people in the Holy Land, he soon put together a group of 11 youths (most in their early twenties) who were a mixture of Muslims, Christians, and Jews. They took on the name "The Gypsies" and danced, sang, and held workshops throughout Israel, performing in Hebrew and Arabic. It was perhaps the first time these Muslim and Jewish young people had a positive interaction with each other. One time the group bussed Arab children into the "New City" to join Jewish children for a performance. The show was called *Kippot and Kafiya,* after the traditional head coverings of the two peoples. Once again, the various religions embraced a common experience.

Israel's President Ephraim Katzir and Jerusalem Mayor Teddy Kollek were notable supporters of The Gypsies. In 1974, The Gypsies won the prestigious Israeli Interfaith Award, an honor that did not go unnoticed stateside. Upon his return to America, Khusro was called in by Secretary of State Henry Kissinger's office for an interview with a staff member. The office was eager to learn how The Gypsies had made their work so successful.

While in Jerusalem, Khusro forged a strong relationship with Rabbi Shlomo Carlebach and Sufi Sheikh Hassan Moumani. Banefsha had originally met Sheikh Hassan on a bus in the mid-1970s and brought him back to America, where he met Iqbal. On one of Iqbal's subsequent business trips, he met Sheikh Hassan again and brought him back to the U.S., although his return visit was not universally supported. He lived with Iqbal and Sitara in Marin County, forming a deep impression on his hosts, and ultimately initiated Iqbal and Shabda as sheikhs in the Rifa'i Order. The *hadrat* zikrs learned from Sheikh Hassan are still being led by Iqbal today. Sheikh Hassan ultimately married a young woman from Berkeley. After their child was born they moved to the Middle East into one of the camps set aside for Palestinians. Sheikh Hassan spent much time with The Gypsies in the home of Khusro and his wife Shareen.

Khusro spent three years in Jerusalem entertaining, educating, and bringing people young and old together. When he returned to the United States, he dedicated his time to education in both public and private institutions. As head of a Jewish school in Kansas, his school was in partnership with a Christian school and a Muslim school.

Another initiative started later in the Middle East was called the Abrahamic Reunion. Shahabuddin Less created a website* that describes the activities of this group. Here is a description from the site:

> The Abrahamic Reunion is a team of religious & spiritual leaders—men, women, Jewish, Muslim, Christian, & Druze—dedicated to uplifting human consciousness and building peace in the Holy Land by opening hearts to the love and wisdom of all spiritual traditions . . .
>
> Founded in 2004, The Abrahamic Reunion has been to two Parliaments of The Worlds' Religions as featured presenters, and has convened inter-religious peacemaking dinners every year since 2004. During the 50-Day Gaza War of 2014, AR leaders decided to begin organizing one event every month to bring more people together to fuel the causes of tolerance, amity, understanding, and harmonious coexistence† . . .
>
> The Abrahamic Reunion seeks to be a living example of our values and beliefs; to find and support other spiritual peace makers and organizations; to provide training for those interested in spiritual peacemaking; and to create and implement interfaith programs, celebrations, youth activities and other educational initiatives. [866]

Other disciples of Murshid Sam carried the soul awakening he had imparted in other directions. His followers continued to lead Walks and Dances at various locations in the U.S. as well as abroad. A project of *Khankah* SAM in San Francisco centered around providing an on-site, live-in training program for those who wanted to study the Dances and Walks intensively in month-long modules. It was called the Center for the Study of Spiritual Dance and Walk and ultimately morphed into the

---

* Abrahamicreunion.org.

† Murshid Sam set the example here in launching a practice of eating, dancing, and praying together, exchanging feelings across any restrictive guidelines. Even before 2004, when the Abrahamic Reunion was formally launched, there were representatives of multiple religions who began to hold events there for harmony, inspired by the example of Samuel Lewis.

Dances of Universal Peace, which was founded on a global level by Dance leaders Saadi Neil Douglas-Klotz and Tasnim Hermila Fernandez.* The organization saw many permutations over the years. Now known as Dances of Universal Peace International,† it is approaching 1200 certified Dance leaders in 50 countries. The website of the Dances of Universal Peace operates in up to seven languages (English, French, German, Dutch, Spanish, Portuguese, and Russian), and its staff manages to correspond in many others. A process is beginning to translate key documents such as the Leader Guidelines into Farsi and other languages relevant to the expanding Dance family.

A few early noteworthy journeys abroad included pilgrims who traveled to share the Dances of Universal Peace in Russia in 1989 (led by Khalif Saadi) and the Middle East in 1993 (also led by Saadi, who had been made a Murshid in 1990). The pilgrims would begin dancing in public and invite onlookers to join them with invitations printed and handed out in the languages of the respective countries. The scope of the Dances was broad. In the Middle East, Dances in Aramaic (Jesus's native language) often opened the program; because Aramaic has similarities to both Hebrew and Arabic, those who heard the circle chanting registered no immediate objection and were more likely to join in.

In the new millennium the work expanded considerably when leaders in Latin America began working with the Global Ecovillage Network as well as with Sun (men) and Moon (women) dancers in the Lakota tradition. This brought into the Dance circles and Leaders Guild a huge influx of young people with a concentration on sustainability and indigenous roots. In turn, some of these people began taking the Dances and Walks into new and more remote regions: the Middle East, Africa and Asia-Pacific, areas where peace seems particularly needed and where the local residents might not otherwise have the opportunity to experience the Dances. The younger generation mentors who hold this focus today are naturally attracting youth of similar age. We now have Dance leaders, the future of our family, who are seven generations from

---

* See dancesofuniversalpeace.org/duphistory.shtm for a full account.

† Dancesofuniversalpeace.org.

Murshid Sam in lineage descent. Through mentoring, *inshallah* the essence of the Dances as spiritual practice will continue to be transmitted.

The Dances and Walks are overseen by the Guidance Council of the Ruhaniat. It holds in trust the transmission of the Dances of Universal Peace and Walking Meditations in the lineage of Murshid Samuel L. Lewis. The Pir of the Sufi Ruhaniat International is the Spiritual Director of the Dances worldwide. Four to six Senior Mentors, appointed by the Pir on a rotating basis, have the responsibility of guiding leaders and mentors by encouraging their spiritual expansion and personal development, supporting educational opportunities, setting guidelines for certification and for mentor acknowledgements, recognizing mentors, and upholding standards of conduct and human relationship that are in keeping with the transmission of the Dances of Universal Peace.

The Sufi Ruhaniat International became an organization independent from the Sufi Order in 1977 while under Pir Moineddin's guidance (1971–2001) and has continued to grow under the guidance of Moineddin's successor, Pir Shabda Kahn. The Ruhaniat holds several spiritual concentrations that mirror the diversity of Murshid Sam's life and that continue to develop through the inspired leadership of many devotees: Esoteric School, Dances of Universal Peace and Walking Concentrations, Dervish Healing Order, Service of Universal Peace, Spiritual Psychology and SoulWork, Wisdom of the Feminine, *Ziraat* (Spiritual Ecology), and *Khilvat* (Spiritual Retreat). Further detail on these concentrations can be found at the Ruhaniat.org website.

At the time of this writing, the Sufi Ruhaniat International has approximately 3,000 members and is guided by a Murshids' Circle with equal representation of women and men. Of the total Ruhaniat membership, nearly 350 have been given initiations that allow them to teach and carry forth the message of Love, Harmony, and Beauty brought to the West in 1910 by Hazrat Inayat Khan and lovingly, masterfully transmitted by Sufi Ahmed Murad Chisti.

Murshid Sam's universal approach opened the doors for many deep Ruhaniat affiliations to flourish. Suleyman Dede was the Sheikh of Konya and the caretaker of the Mevlana (Jelaluddin Rumi) Museum in

Turkey. During one of his many visits to the U.S. in the 1970s he performed the Whirling Dervish Sheikh's turn at Hurkalya, deeply moving all present. A few years later, in 1978, Sheikh Dede sent his son Jelaluddin Loras to continue the Mevlevi tradition in the West. Attuning the tradition to the Western heart and at his father's recommendation, Jelaluddin opened up the turning practice equally to women (which at that time was forbidden in Turkey). He then advanced one giant step further toward mutual acceptance with the Ruhaniat by inviting all Ruhaniat teachers to stand with him during the Sema program.

Many Ruhaniat initiates joined The Mevlevi Order of America, which remains quite active. Ruhaniat Sheikha Khadija Radin is one of these and appears on the cover of the book *Women Called to the Path of Rumi.*[*] She has traveled to Israel and Palestine numerous times over the decades, teaching turning and leading retreats. She is warmly accepted by both cultures as she focuses on Mevlana and love. Where certain Arabic phrases are traditional to recite, she substitutes the words of Rumi: "Only Love. Only Love."[†]

Despite differences that initially caused friction between the various Inayati orders (those which trace their lineage back to Hazrat Inayat Khan), bridges were built that ultimately led to the formation of the Federation of the Sufi Message. This rapprochement was furthered by Inayat's younger son Hidayat Khan, who became Pir of the Sufi Movement, and who asked for assistance from the Ruhaniat while at a Ruhaniat camp at the Lama Foundation. One of the Ruhaniat teachers, Khalif Saadi, agreed to serve as the Sufi Movement's *peshkar*.[‡]

After long discussions, the Federation formed in the year 2000. Its current members are the International Sufi Movement, the Inayatiyya (formerly the Sufi Order), the Sufi Ruhaniat International, Sufi Contact, the Fraternity of Light, the Sufi Way and the Inayati-Maimuni Order.

---

*Shakina Reinhertz, *Women Called to the Path of Rumi: The Way of the Whirling Dervish* (Prescott, AZ: Hohm Press, 2001).

†For more information about Sheikha Khadija's work, see whirling-dervish.org.

‡In this role, Saadi functioned as the head of the Brotherhood/Sisterhood work in the Sufi Movement. This work ended up being key in forming a bridge between the Sufi Movement and the Ruhaniat, and helped open the way for the formation of the Federation.

Hazrat Inayat Khan's message of Love, Harmony, and Beauty continues to spread far and wide, uniquely yet universally expressed through his lineage.

Murshid Sam's manifestation of inclusive universal spirituality was and is a beacon that continues to light the way for old and young, seekers from any religious background or none—followers all of the path of truth and love.

for Khankah files - esp. Hasan to read

Saturday, February 14, 1969. San Francisco (unedited) by Melvin F. Meyer

This is the first entry in this diary. I have read recently five or six volumes in the "diary of a devotee" which describes the daily life of Anandashram, focusing particularly on Swami Ram Das and Mataji Krishnabai. It made a deep impression on me as I was able to make contact with these self-realized souls as they actually lived. Also the writer was very careful to give a total picture, to present their 'weaknesses' and not mould them to fit some saintly stereotype. This too was very helpful to me.

Our Murshid, Samuel Lewis (Sufi Ahmed Murad Chisti) often speaks of living in the world of reality and not 'realism'. Most of his life he has been rejected because he did not fit somebody's idea of what a mystic should be like though he has had the real experiences. I have the good fortune to be living in the house with Murshid and now I shall use this opportunity to give the same kind of objective report on him as was given by the devotee at Anandashram. Inshallah, it will help those who read it to partake of some of the reality of the man and those close to him. If it helps unveil some of the delusions and preconceptions we have about enlightened men I will be satisfied.

Murshid was up before anyone else. Went to the bakery and bought some apple strudel and banana cream pie (especially for Mansur who has been spending the night here on Fridays and staying over for the dance class.).

He answered some correspondence. Wrote one of his frequent letters to Art Hoppe, describing briefly the wonderful reception he got on Haight Street Friday afternoon and taking a few jabs at "General" S.I. Hayakawa.

We drove to U.C. extension center where we are taking a course on The Influence of Traditional Religions on Politics of Contemporary Asia. The professor Mrs. Nottingham has been cordial--accepting Murshid's reports on the people he knows and the experiences he has had! Murshid spoke up strongly several times in class--particularly on one of his favorites subjects, how we don't listen to Asians (they are thought forms not realities.). Somebody volunteered, Americans don't know how to listen period. Someone asked about information on area Buddhist organizations and Sam popped up with some places to go and get it. Some people were taken aback by his vociferousness. Later he said, "These people just want to ask questions, they don't want the answers."

Back to the house for lunch. Dancing class to start at 2. Murshid brought school catalog with numerous courses he may sponsor people to take.

About 20 disciples here for closed dancing class. His most advanced disciples. Stiff training. Today we walked up the hill here, doing the fire breath and down with gentle inhalation, heavy exhalation. He introduced today the women's Zikar dance which men may join in too. We say the Kalama: LA EL LA HA EL IL ALLAH HU, then EL ALLAH HU, ALLAH HU, and HU. Then IL ALLAH HA EL IL ALLAH HU, etc. Then HU ALLAH HA...etc. The mantra which we sung has a very powerful effect tho Fatima for one was not satisfied with the dance movements which Murshid introduced. They were a bit awkward but today was the first time--we will have to see.

David took a call from Michael saying Banefsha needed Murshid's help, an emergency. She is pregnant. Murshid waited until after the class to call and then told her to contact his god-daughter Nancy who just recently had a child. Murshid did not interrupt the class to return the call. "My work is not primarily that of a healer," he said. Later he also said, "They call me when they are in these high emotional states and not when I can really help them."

First page of Wali Ali's Diary

APPENDIX

Wali Ali's Diary of Life with Murshid Sam

Editors' Note: In late 2022, Hassan Herz brought to the editorial team an item he had found among papers originating with Wali Ali. This prized discovery is a diary that Wali Ali maintained during February and March of 1969, when he had begun to function as one of Murshid Sam's esoteric secretaries. It gives a unique close-up of the texture of Murshid Sam's life during that period. Original typography has been preserved as much as possible; the text has been lightly edited for clarity.

Saturday, February 14, 1969. San Francisco by Melvin F. Meyer

This is the first entry in this diary. I have read recently five or six volumes in the "diary of a devotee" which describes the daily life of Anandashram, focusing particularly on Swami Ram Das and Mataji Krishnabai. It made a deep impression on me as I was able to make contact with these self-realized souls as they actually lived. Also the writer was very careful to give a total picture, to present their 'weaknesses' and not mould them to fit some saintly stereotype. This too was very helpful to me.

Our Murshid, Samuel Lewis (Sufi Ahmed Murad Chisti) often speaks of living in the world of reality and not 'realism'. Most of his life he has been rejected because he did not fit somebody's idea of what a mystic should be like though he has had the real experiences. I have the good fortune to be living in the house with Murshid and now I shall use this opportunity to give the same kind of objective report on him as was given by the devotee at Anandashram. Inshallah, it will help those who read it to partake of some of the reality of the man and those close to him. If it helps unveil some of the delusions and preconceptions we have about enlightened men I will be satisfied.

Murshid was up before anyone else. Went to the bakery and bought some apple strudel and banana cream pie (especially for Mansur who has been spending the night here on Fridays and staying over for the dance class.).

He answered some correspondence. Wrote one of his frequent letters to Art Hoppe, describing briefly the wonderful reception he got on Haight Street Friday afternoon and taking a few jabs at "General" S.I. Hayakawa.

We drove to U.C. extension center where we are taking a course on The Influence of Traditional Religions on Politics of Contemporary Asia. The professor Mrs. Nottingham has been cordial—accepting Murshid's reports on the people he knows and the experiences he has had! Murshid spoke up strongly several times in class—particularly on one of his favorite subjects, how we don't listen to Asians (they are thought forms not realities.). Somebody volunteered, Americans don't know how to listen period. Someone asked about information on area Buddhist organizations and Sam popped up with some places to go and get it. Some people were taken aback by his vociferousness. Later he said, "These people just want to ask questions, they don't want the answers."

Back to the house for lunch. Dancing class to start at 2. Murshid brought school catalog with numerous courses he may sponsor people to take.

About 20 disciples here for closed dancing class. His most advanced disciples. Stiff training. Today we walked up the hill here, doing the fire breath and down with gentle inhalation, heavy exhalation. He introduced today the women's Zikar dance which men may join in too. We say the Kalama: LA EL LA HA EL IL ALLAH HU, then EL ALLAH HU, ALLAH HU, and HU. Then IL ALLAH HA EL IL ALLAH HU, etc. Then HU ALLAH HA...etc. The mantra which we sung has a very powerful effect tho Fatima for one was not satisfied with the dance movements which Murshid introduced. They were a bit awkward but today was the first time—we will have to see.

David took a call from Michael saying Banefsha needed Murshid's help, an emergency. She is pregnant. Murshid waited until after the class to call and then told her to contact his god-daughter Nancy who just recently had a child. Murshid did not interrupt the class to return the call. "My work is not primarily that of a healer," he said. Later he also said, "They call me when they are in these high emotional states and not when I can really help them."

After class he watched Perry Mason as usual, to come down, cracking nuts all the while.

Frank has called to say he is coming over tonite. He has told me that he is going to tell Murshid he can no longer be his disciple. Many past incidents which I won't go into here. Murshid is very strict with him trying to help him make his own decisions and not be wishy-washy. Frank keeps bringing his discriminating intellect into play. Murshid has lost his temper with him several times for interrupting his work in various ways. Recently Frank gave him $200 to put in a savings account, then he decides he wants the money back now. Murshid has classes 7 days a week: "He's got to learn I'm not his errand boy."

After the dance class a Vietnamese Buddhist from Monterey who Murshid had mentioned in class today—An The (who gave him his copy of "Lotus in a Sea of Fire") called. He wants Sam to come to Monterey and speak on Zen. Sam was receptive.

I can't say how thorough this diary will be, but Allah willing it will continue and I intend to keep 'balanced' what I do present.

10p.m. Frank came and went. Long discussion between he and Murshid. Later Murshid said "I told him if he could stick to something for 6 months, anything, then that would be progress.... I asked him not to run around and see a lot of spiritual teachers. That will only get him more confused. I must be firm with him. That is compassion. Someone else and I might have acted completely differently." Murshid says one cannot be ruled by principles, one should rule them. "I give him practices which will solve his problems, but he doesn't do them. Well let him run away; he will come back and apologize some day and I will accept him."

He wrote another letter, then to bed.

———*———

Sunday.

This morning our household, David, Gwen, Murshid and myself joined Rev. Eugene Wagner in Golden Gate Park to pay our respects to the Buddha in the Japanese Tea Garden. A beautiful day especially after a particularly long rainy season. Trees just beginning to blossom.

We all chanted the Tri-Ratna. NAMO TASO BHAGAVATO ARAHATO SAMMA SAMBUDDHASA. BUDDHAM SARANAM GACCHAMI, DHARMAM SARANAM GACCHAMI, SANGAM SARANAM GACCHAMI. DUTIAMPI...TATIAMPI, etc. Murshid read a short prayer, it being the 5 things which a follower of the dharma avoids. That was all. Short and very sweet. Murshid told Rev. Wagner he wanted to do this at least once each year and he intends to leave it in his will to that effect. They talked of other news—the article in Playboy on Murshid—"It's not that it's personally derogatory at all but they have no idea what Sufism is, they lump it in with the cults of California." He said he was feeling mentally very fit and working like crazy. "You can ask him" he said, pointing to me. "I don't need to ask; I can look at you and tell," Wagner said.

Back here for a gourmet lunch—Murshid cooking much of it. Inexpensive food as always but elegantly prepared.

Nancy called. She and a visiting friend are coming to the meeting tonite.

10:30pm. 20 people at meeting. Totally on Lord Buddha, being our celebration of pari-nirvana day. Murshid wore his Buddhist robe which I have never seen him do before. In the basement we did two new walks. Bodhisattva walks—Avalokita and Kwon Yin. And then feeling oneself becoming the embodiment of those qualities—the Maitreya walk. He read some Zen stories one about a master who whacked his disciple quite a bit and gave him one last whack for good measure before he left on a pilgrimage because he said he wouldn't get another chance.

Also story of master who taught swordsmanship by sneaking up behind disciple and whacking him. Then Murshid say "Does anybody want me to do that to him?" I quickly raised my hand. "This is no joke" he said. I looked happily in his eyes. "He's going to flunk his first test;" he repeated this several times. Then he took someone in the next room to tell them what that test was going to be. "See, she knows he's going to flunk his first test.... You better look out." Joking air but a steely expression in his eyes during all this. After meeting over he took down his Zen stick and came threateningly up to me as if to hit me hard on the head. I sat waiting smiling up at him. Instead he tapped me gently on the left shoulder. "That cherubic smile isn't going to help you a bit," he said. Earlier in the evening he had spoken about masters who whack students have to pay the karmic price if the students don't attain enlightenment.

Nancy and party didn't show up. David and Gwen had automobile accident earlier in evening. Someone ran them off the road. Car rolled over. Neither was hurt. At the time they were chanting EL ALLAH HU.

———*———

MONDAY

Murshid <u>as usual</u> writing reams of correspondence. Hitting hard on the rejection by S.I. Hayakawa of his work in G.S. (General Semantics). He had presented papers to him in the past of the nature of an excerpt from "The Awakening of Faith" describing the word <u>tathata</u> (suchness), which puts an end to words, pointing to that reality beyond verbalization—both sūnya and a-sūnya. He is having this xeroxed by Rev. Wagner and sent out. "I never have gotten anywhere when I followed the advice of the 'good' people and acted Gandhi-like. Every time I've fought I've succeeded.... Hayakawa turns this down in favor of Alan Watts on Zen.... These people reject me anyway, so what have I got to lose." He was also thinking of the <u>Playboy</u> article; most people are recommending that he not sue.

Murshid took Nancy, Ralph and friend to lunch at a Japanese restaurant. "When we got there the girls told me they were both dieting."

______*______

Tuesday.

Gwen: (seeing something about Lent) When is Lent?

Sam: Starts Wednesday, tomorrow. Now you're going to have to give up bananas on your apple fritters and apples on your banana fritters. Have to have a spirit of sacrifice.

Working like crazy all morning. Numerous letters. Sam wrote Playboy thanking them for recognizing that Sufis exist and mentioning a couple of inaccuracies in the article. A light letter. He said he would do as Rev. Warwick suggested and this was his suggestion. Nevertheless Sam is using this Playboy thing as a lever for getting attention, e.g., Philip Burton, State Dept.

Late in the morning we climbed up the hill and picked some wild turnip greens. I washed and chopped them. Sam mixed them with yogurt, milk, soy flour, and fryed them. Delicious.

After lunch Ed came over to see Murshid. He has been a ballet dancer and is now living and studying with Gavin Arthur the astrologer. Murshid told him the purpose of dance as we know it is to produce an aesthetic effect in the audience and the performer. This has nothing to do with awakening the inner life. He was showing him movements and concentrations in the front room. Then he gave Ed something from Inayat Khan to read and came into the office. He told me, "This does not necessarily make me feel good. I can see now so much work to be done; sometimes it makes me dizzy. Even for a man in his 20s but to undertake all this in your 70s..." He wrote a letter then went back in the front room to work some more with Ed.

Our cars being out of commission he got Ed to take him to his afternoon lecture on Christian Mysticism at the Church of the Children. He was to stop off first at UC Extension and pay $75 to register Jemila in a course on Raku Pottery. I stayed home to cover the house and prepare supper.

______*______

Wed. Murshid taking "day off." He called off his meeting in Corte Madera in order to go to show at Academy of Sciences about a pilgrimage to Iran. He typed some letters and did some commentary work this morning. Then went downtown to do some errands.

In the afternoon Murshid did more errands. Coming back took short siesta. Up—"Allah told me not to work at the typewriter." (His enforced not working over New Years had been something of an ordeal as I can testify. But this turned out different.) He decided to go into the kitchen and work on supper. He had been there only a short time when Ruthie called from Corte Madera, "Carol Ann (a disciple) is stranded at the Greyhound Station with lots of bags and no money." We got her pay phone number and Murshid said to tell her to get a taxi over here. Which she did. Shirin was with her. They both coming from 5 days at Mount Shasta.

There followed an incredible supper preparation scene. When Murshid gets going in the kitchen there is so much activity so fast everybody around either grooves with it and gets high or gets the hell out of there. 6 people in the kitchen so you can imagine.

"You're so lucky to be coming on a night when we're having guests for dinner." "Oh, who are the guests?" "YOU."

Wonderful meal, everyone got stuffed. They were so happy to step into so much JOY after the downer at the bus station and no money for a while.

Carol Ann's boyfriend coming to pick them up from Corte Madera. Murshid said he and David would wait and ride to the lecture with him. He was expected at 7. I said he wouldn't be here til 20 to 8 which proved correct to the minute. Gypsy (Carol Ann) got impatient. Murshid told her someone in her condition should learn patience which is exactly what Mother Mary told her at Shasta.

Then for non-dualistic teaching he said "I want to get you into the heart-body—Have you read "The Rejected Avatar"? the last part?"—He then gave her a Krishna Darshan which made a visible change in her. "I don't like to do this very often." ... "Even when I play games I'm not playing games." Next Wednesday at Corte Madera Murshid said he was giving Darshan.

James arrived at 20 to 8 amidst much laughter.

*

Thurs.

Murshid usually is in Novato on Thurs where he has a closed class. This week, however, he's here. (It should be noted that most of the quotes and conversations are not exact, it being some time before I write them down. However unless I'm sure I've got the sense of it I don't try to paraphrase.)

Walking to the Big Bonus this morning, the subject of Gurdjieff-ites came up. Murshid deprecatingly mentioned their thing "of looking for the real self." I said, "As soon as I see one follower of Gurdjieff who's attained some kind of peace I'll show it some respect." Murshid: "They love complexities.... That's why Paul Reps never loses a debate. Everything, the other fellow says—'concept', 'abstraction.' And they give in. But if they'd demonstrate it wasn't an abstraction he'd accept it. He would too."

Later in the morning Akbar came over for some private instruction. Murshid showed him some walks we've had at meetings during the week. Akbar reads 2nd year gathas and Murshid asked him to arrange for more meetings. "I'm going to give bayat again soon." He also asked me to give Akbar a copy of the commentary on "The Inner Life" when I finish typing it. Murshid is almost thru with this work now. After meeting privately with Akbar Murshid came in kitchen and said "He's making excellent progress."

In the afternoon Murshid worked on the commentary. Later Nancy sent over a couple to see Sam. She was scared, shy, intelligent, under observation psychiatric hospital. Sam said her mind and breathing weren't coordinated. He told her to watch her children breathe and learn from them. Come to meeting Sunday night and get more breathing practices.

At supper David suggested she might be Gemini with her breath and mind uncoordinated. Sam said she might be. Agreed Geminis often like that. We discussed some Geminis we knew. Gwen was asking about her rising sign Libra (sun in Scorpio). Sam said, "I don't know what you get your plumpness from." I said, "From your cooking; there are some truths beyond astrology." (She's gained 30 pounds since she moved in here.)

*

Friday.

Murshid up very early writing letters and working on commentary on "Inner Life" which is very near completion. Later in the day he got the statement from his estate of his yearly earnings. Glancing at it it appeared to him that he would have to take out a loan to pay his income tax. A bit upset over finances—David has just started back to work and hasn't gotten a check yet so behind on paying Sam for rent, etc.

Mansur, Murshid's chief esoteric secretary, came in today. He drove Sam over to his talk at the Brother Juniper Cafe on Haight St. in the afternoon. I stayed home to catch up typing "The Inner Life."

Daniel, who doubles as an esoteric secretary and financial secretary, unexpectedly came in during the interval. He calculated the income tax—standard deduction coming to $72, good chance of getting it much lower using long form. (Murshid being 72, he gets extra deductions.)

The meeting was very fiery. Murshid said there was a person who said he was half Negro and half Jew who kept breaking up the meeting and attacking him—saying he was preaching hate (!). "He had a regular Hitler mind," Murshid said. "I was firm with him—none of this namby-pamby 'love'....they (the audience) can respect that. Some said I wasn't rough enough....One is of two minds, to deal with the troublemaker or to ignore and build up good will with those who are willing to listen."

They brought a girl home with them from the meeting who had supper with us. Murshid to her at supper: "I give people a choice, they can get hot under the collar or warm in the heart. Take your pick." "You mean you can choose." "Oh yes there's free choice." "I'll take warm in the heart." (Laughter) (pause) "Sure you don't want to change your mind?" At the end of the meal he held her hand and spoke to her for a while.

She, Mansur, Gwen and Murshid went over to Gavin Arthur's tonite to attend his weekly lecture on astrology. Gavin is in a running debate that the Aquarian Age has not yet come and is indeed a good ways off. Murshid recently wrote him that this new spiritual generation may—a la Edward Carpenter—be astrologically explained by an influx of many Uranians and Neptunians occurring since the discovery of those planets. On this basis one could look for Plutonians in 200 years. Gavin called today saying he like the explanation.

———*———

Saturday. At the dance class in the first half we did the Avalokita and Kwon Yin walks. Also the dhiranis with the wasifas and attributes of God. And the aklak allah walk where one feels perfectly free having his being totally in God. Murshid spent much time 'jawing' as he calls it and I for one was rather restless and know that others often feel that way. Then, bang, after our recess—back into the basement and Murshid instituted—saw on the spot—a new dervish dance. Basically the circle moves saying ALLAH-ALLAH-ALLAH.....then stops... YA HAYY, YAHAAK, salaaming 4 times around and around. In the center two people whirling—ALLAH—then facing each other YA HAYY YA HAKK. Everyone became so joyful and the magnetic energy level went way way up and quickly. Murshid says the difference between his dances and those of many others is that while one may develop magnetism during the dance of these others when it's over one loses it and gets tired; his dances leave one fresher more magnetic than before and this magnetism (baraka) endures.

———*———

Sunday. Walking and OM SRI RAM JAI RAM JAI JAI RAM dances at meeting.

Banefsha—a beautiful newly pregnant Jewish disciple got very upset. Some one came into the meeting who she disliked intensely because of past injustice done to her. After the meeting she exploded at Sam about how she "has to tell the truth, tell it like it is man, bluntly. You say no body listens to you but you won't listen to anybody. You talk about hypocrites but you're the worst hypocrite there is...sometimes." And so on for a while in this vein.

They talked for a long time and as it turned out Sam said he was reminded of the Zen story where the guy walks into the meeting and assails the teacher—who says 'Won't you step over here..., no, no over here might be better, ...no I guess over here.... There you're listening to me already and I think at heart you're a very gentle fellow.' That's the way it turned out. Sam said he would be her 'grandfather' (she's never had anyone to lean on) and this made her very very happy. She and her boy friend stayed over quite late talking—till well past midnight. Sam went to bed shortly before midnight.

At the end of the meeting, to jump back, we had a very fine kirtan.—something that hasn't happened in some time. Daniel playing his guitar beautifully as usual. Many people caught up in the ecstasy. (Krishna Das and Suzanne dancing—they went over to the Fillmore afterwards to perform.) Particularly wonderful was the long HARI KRISHNA...singing.

______*______

<u>Monday.</u>

As far as is possible a "normal" day in this house. Murshid did some commentary work, wrote some letters. Picked greens on the hill, played canasta with me. Read from Inayat Khan at meeting, told stories, then in 2nd half we did Dervish Dancing.

Mansur came up and took Murshid to Novato after the meeting.

______*______

<u>Wed.</u>

Gwen and I hitchhiked to the meeting in Corte Madera—I wanted to go in particular because Murshid was giving Darshan. We had an exciting time hitchhiking having little hope in one sense that we could make it in time and in another sense great confidence. Someone we were hitching with gave us pot to smoke which we did. Due to combinations of fortuitous circumstances—the last being Daniel's car from Lagunitas was late and came in time to give us a ride up the <u>long</u> hill to Amin's house. Enormous crowd—60 people easy. All 'young' (between 20 and 30) except for a few babies and Krishna Das—our hatha yoga teacher whose body easily falls in that range. We came in just as they were finishing one series of dances. Murshid told some stories—one could look in his eyes and see how drunk with ecstasy he was. Mansur brought his tape recorder.

Then Murshid selected 5 girls and 1 volunteer to do the Krishna dance. Gypsy, Fatima, Ruth (Parisa), Jayonara, and Jemila (who plays Radha) and Claire (Salima) volunteered. Murshid assumed the role of Krishna and I mean just that. There was Krishna dancing with the Gopis—all one needed was faith to see, especially if one accepts Ram Das' "Guru is God." Krishna dances with each of the Gopis in turn transfixing them with his loving attention and Darshan. All the while the Gopis and many in the audience were rhythmically chanting "Krishna, Krishna, Krishna..." to the music. Then when Krishna comes to Radha—he falls in love and begins chanting her name. Then each of the remaining Gopis select their own 'Krishna' from the audience and Krishna and Radha dance in the middle of the circle while each of the other partners follow their steps.

After this dance Murshid gave Darshan to all those present—passing around the room blessing each person, holding his hands to their foreheads; some he kissed men or women.

After recess came a lesson from Inayat Khan and more dancing. We did the Allah-Allah-Allah- Ya Hayy Ya Hakk dance Murshid had seen at the dancing class last week. The house was electric and alive and joyful. We did the dance by signs of the Zodiac—Earth signs together, air, water, and fire. The water signs were most numerous and the fire signs very small. To get the fire sign circle to workable size Murshid asked those who had Sagitarrius, Aries or Leo rising to join in.

______*______

Friday, Feb. 28.

Murshid came in with Mansur and Moin-ed-din for lunch. Later this afternoon to the Brother Juniper Cafe on Haight St. for a talk.

About Wed. night meeting he said: "I'm glad you came; I had a hunch you were coming." Mel: "We're glad we came too, it was wonderful...I mean it was really wonderful." Murshid: "I got so high I don't even know... That Krishna dance was the best I've ever done. Jemila was in both those dances and she was really in fine form; it's truly wonderful for me spiritually. Did you see the new Ram dance I put on first?" Mel: "No, we came in just as it was ending." Murshid: "Well it's new. At the end each person grabs a partner and it ends up the men saying Sita and the women Rama."

"I went around kissing all the girls. I haven't done that since the New Year's Eve Party, but that was a party. People may think I'm being amorous but it's really the most serious thing I do. To wake up people's hearts it's not necessary to put out a lot of prohibitions and inhibitions—one works with what's there."

Later in the afternoon—Frank came over again to get some money back that he had given Murshid. Murshid didn't want to take it ($200) but Frank insisted. He had put it in a special savings acct in Fairfax. Now Frank has spent all the rest of the $1000 school loan (he dropped out of school) and has been pestering Murshid for this money. Murshid has said several times in the past "I'm not his errand boy." Today he gave him a check for $50 on his own account—he hadn't gotten to Fairfax. Frank was worrying about when he'd get the rest of it. "Next week I hope—now get out of my house." A scene ensued. Murshid repeated the above—"get out." Later he told me: "There's a man who's going to have to learn the hard way. He's never taken my advice. He just takes up my time. Five separate occasions on courses of study and Harvard and then never followed thru. About girls, then never followed thru. And now this—He told me to keep it so he wouldn't splurge it away."

(Speaking with Moineddin—he told me that those at the Khankah could feel the atmosphere building for the Wednesday meeting long beforehand and that riding to the meeting in the car there was perfect quiet and unity and love. He said one of the few things he remembered thinking was "I sure hope we don't end up talking about this." We both laughed.)

Later Friday to Haight St. where Murshid addressed a fairly small—compared to previous meetings—crowd—at the cafe. (They had forgotten to put out the sign announcing his talk.) Very peaceful. We did "Buddha's Yoga" that he gives. When the weather clears to Golden Gate Park for free Dervish Dancing.

Stopped by Sunset Health Foods (run by spiritual brothers.) Now called New Age Natural Foods. Murshid bought the last of their pecans for Fatima. Also he brought back catered Chinese dinners for supper at the Khankah.

In the evening to U. of Marin for lecture by Sen. Church on U.S. foreign policy, which when we arrived and paid our money and sat down the m.c. announces "and now our speaker for the evening Mr. Ansel Adams." The other lecture had been the previous week. We enjoyed it however—on photography.

Left halfway thru to go to Geo. Matthews house for his birthday party. Everyone including Murshid enjoyed themselves in very human ways.

_____*_____

Saturday. We came back in time for our morning class. Lecture on Confucianism by bright young man. Murshid made point that Confucianism can hardly be separated from China-ism which prof. accepted. Also Murshid said he had been in San Yat Sen's movement.

Back here for dancing class which was excellent as usual. Preparations being made for Spring celebration at Khankah. Many disciples have birthdays around that time. David H. and Suzanne M. will be the pivots in the birthday dance which we did today.

There are 10 pairs of men and women and two men musicians in this class and everybody loves each other. Not only the teacher but each other as well. What is a new age anyway?

_____*_____

Sunday.

One must admit to being lax in making diary entries. It is now Tuesday. Also details of daily life are being left out. After catching up I hope to remedy this.

At the meeting Sun. nite Gavin Arthur and friends showed up and much later Schattsie Wallace who had been at the Temple of Understanding Summit Conference in Darjeeling. Murshid stalled waiting for Schattsie to show up—jawing—as he puts it—for close to an hour. Some people—myself included—get restless at such times anxious to be dancing or doing breathing practices. When Schattsie arrived she spoke quite glowingly of Julie Medlock at Auroville. She indicated however that she was not spiritually prepared for India and did not necessarily relate favorably to much of this aspect.

After this we went downstairs and did an OM SRI RAM JAI RAM JAI JAI RAM dance which impressed Gavin quite favorably. (He should see the dancing class.) Even when the group is largely strangers always the dances increase the level of joy and draw the people somewhat together. Murshid calls them communal dances.

Monday.

The meeting tonite was mostly an initiation—Gwen, Greg H., and Keith. We had ice cream afterwards. No dancing. Very relaxed atmosphere. 3 Scorpios!

The day itself was extraordinarily busy from an office work standpoint. Murshid and I were both going full speed all day. He dictated numerous letters, wrote others, did commentary work. Saw briefly a disciple—Richard Gorin—and made suggestions to him and analysis from his astrological chart. The amount of work that gets turned out on days like this is simply inconceivable to those who haven't seen it. I can't stress this enough.

*

Friday.

Murshid back in the afternoon. Report on lecture at Sonoma State--very successful. 100-150 people. Mansur taped it.

This afternoon to Bro. Junipers on Haight St. Several 'live' people in the audience which always perks Murshid up. One drunk Negro man came in late in the program started to interrupt—not hostile but raucous. Murshid cut him off instantly—"Be quiet, I'm speaking to someone else." Again he interrupted and again the same response. Then the 3rd time Murshid said, "I stop speaking until he's taken out." Which happened. He was never allowed to destroy the meeting. Murshid is very firm in not making the same mistake twice.

Murshid said already in the day he'd had 7 interviews. Tom Sager came to supper from the meeting. He's a peaceful revolutionary completely at odds with both sides at S.F. State where he's been a student and frustrated that he's incapable of helping the situation. He's withdrawn and is going to San Bernadino to school. After supper Murshid spent some time alone with him. Came back in "tired." By-passing Gavin's. Got some ice cream at Baskin-Robbins—someone in the dancing class, Ruthie (now Parisa) has birthday tomorrow.

Frank called late in the evening. Wants his money. Murshid is making him sweat. "Not until I get a written apology," I conveyed to him from Murshid. Frank feels the money should be separated from the Guru-disciple relationship problem. Murshid is determined to teach him a lesson one way or another.

(Report on the meeting in Corte Madera this Wednesday—many more people than even last week. Celebrated Amin's birthday with ice cream. Murshid being partially tired from Sonoma State had Moin-ed-din lead many of the dances which "He did perfectly.")

Saturday.

To our class at the University. Riding over Murshid said (about Frank in particular who had called in the morning) "I'm definitely not mad at him.... Being negative isn't showing love.... If I make mistakes I'm not going to make the same ones Inayat Khan made— I'm going to make my own—he came to the West and was incapable of dealing with organizations."

Murshid wore his Dervish Robe and Bernousse to class where a prof. was lecturing on Islam. Anything could have happened—but actually they made friends, the professor accepting every remark and suggestion Murshid made.

At the dancing class we did first of all the Moses walk—breath full in the upper chest, invocation: Toward the one, the perfection of love, harmony, and beauty. (period). Right hand index finger up, left hand palm receptive; an example to the world. Then we walked up the hill in this breath (no hand motions.)

A photographer from The Oracle came to take pictures of the dancing.

We then had ice cream—Ruthie's birthday, but she stayed home to look over a new sitar she might be getting—we had the ice cream anyway. More Dervish Dancing afterwards. The Dance of Love and Brotherhood. Ram-Nam Dance. As usual the dances quite effective.

Then Murshid had some interviews. Fatima had been lying on my bed—slightly sick (she's pregnant) and he saw her before they returned to Novato. Then watched Perry Mason. Wrote several letters before supper—one to Reps.

_____*_____

Sunday.

Woken up at 6:15 this morning by Eric from Father Blighton's place. He'd asked to see Sam. Surprise—Sam was asleep. Spent an hour or so here. Sam spoke about breathing and many other things. I gave him some Candidates Gathekas. Murshid told him his examination would be to ask three questions on the basis of the material. He gave him a breathing practice which he asked for.

At the meeting in the evening George Hoyt—magazine publisher friend of Reps showed up. Sam told him that Reps wrote some excellent things 20-30 years before on achieving heart-awakening etc., but now he won't stick by them or make them available. "I stand by materials I wrote 20 or 30 years ago. I respect the state of consciousness I was in when I wrote them. It's too bad Reps won't stand by his old stuff." Hoyt: "Perhaps he's growing simpler." Sam: "I'm not saying anything about that, only that he should stand by his earlier work."

Hoyt wants Sam to give him stories of living Sufis which Sam is in the process of doing. Nothing was done about this tonight as Hoyt had to leave before the meeting was over.

Some people from the Living Theatre (from Kansas) came in during the dancing. Nobody knows how they got wind of the place. Sam: "The only thing I know about Kansas is it has a wonderful Oriental art museum." One of the boys agreed. "I knew Prendergast too."

_____*_____

Monday.

Murshid went with Daniel to Berkeley in the morning to talk to people in the Oriental Studies Department about the possibility of Korean Grand Master Seo coming here to teach. Master Seo had asked Sam to perform this errand for him. He is Sam's Roshi in a sense; he granted Sam the Zen stick and authority. He is now at Temple U. Murshid said later in the day that he would probably be here for the

Wesac- May day celebration. The professor Sam wanted to see was unavailable but Sam talked to other people and students and came back satisfied with the venture. At the meeting in the evening he said "We met some 3rd world students. Leaving out whether they're right or wrong which I don't know anything about, they're serious, while the newspaper reporters are superficial." He was relating it to the distinction between Saturn as deep minded (not malefic) and Mercury as skimming the surface.

______*______

Tues. I don't remember much what happened Tuesday but to fill in I'll mention a couple of incidents I do remember from the last few days.

At supper one night (Mansur was here) Murshid said he had gotten two dates for his passing both of which are at least 20 years away--barring an accident, he said.

As usual he went to Father Blighton's for his lecture on Christian mysticism today—then to Novato. After this week these meetings will be on Mondays, giving Murshid at least one theoretical day-off.

______*______

Friday

Murshid came back from Novato with a bad flu-type cold.

Told story of Fatima and the ice cream. He had bought 2 kinds of ice—strawberry and mandarin chocolate (which he had been touting). He said he got it for Amin. Fatima says—"You get this ice cream nobody wants...See you don't even eat it yourself. Nobody likes it." "Amin likes it." "Let Amin speak for himself. Do you like it?" "Yes." "You do. Better than the other kind?" "Yes." "You get all that ice cream just for one person, nobody else likes it...etc." I said "You and Fatima agree on all the little things like religion and spirituality but on the big things like ice cream..." There has been a long feud between the two of them over ice cream.

Murshid wrote a very firm letter to Prof. Archie Baum who had sent him his latest book. The latter was in praise of those who have had awakening experiences and against self-styled professor type 'experts'.

To Brother Juniper Cafe where Murshid 'croaked' his lecture. We did breathing practices. Postponed doing dancing until next week. They are doing a lively business there.

Stopped off afterwards at New Age Natural Food where we got brown rice and a bottle of vitamin C (rose hips condensed) for Murshid.

______*______

diary breaks off at this point

Glossary

Language abbreviations:

Ar. Arabic
Gr. Greek
Heb. Hebrew
Hin. Hindi
Jap. Japanese
Lat. Latin
OA Old Avesta
Pal. Pali
Per. Persian
Skt. Sanskrit
Tib. Tibetan
Ur. Urdu

abdal (Ar.) Literally "substitutes." In Sufi tradition, a group of saints known only to and appointed by Allah, keepers of equilibrium in the world. They are said to be God's merciful subjects, with the mission of giving aid and blessing to all of God's creatures. The *abdal* are considered in classical Sufi writings to be among the Spiritual Hierarchy, which is characterized by increasing degrees of responsiveness or effacement in the One.

abdallah (Ar.) One whose life path is to efface all ego claims and work tirelessly as a satisfied servant of God. (Also *abdullah.*)

akasha (Skt.) The primordial element of ether; also sky, space. As used in Theosophy, this term refers to a universal etheric field storing a record of all events, thoughts, and emotions.

akhlak Allah (Ar.) Freely moving in the manner or presence of God; feeling the presence of the God reality.

alaya vijnana (Skt.) Buddhist term translated as "fundamental storehouse consciousness."

alhamdulillah (Ar.) Traditionally translated "All praise to God." Scholarship suggests it may also be understood as "All gratitude belongs to God."

Allahu Akbar (Ar.) God is the most great; often rendered in Murshid Sam's attunement as "Peace is power." (Also *Allaho Akbar.*)

amal (Ar.) Absorption of self in the Absolute. (Also see *samadhi.*)

amr (Ar.) Divine command.

amrita (Skt.) Literally "immortality;" also referred to as a nectar.

ananda (Skt.) Pure bliss; infinite love, infinite bliss; joy.

anatta (Pal.) Buddhist doctrine that there is no "self" in the sense of a permanent, integral, autonomous being within an individual existence. (Also *an-atta.*)

anjuman (Per.) Gathering or gathering place, often educational.

arhat (Skt.) One who has attained release from the cycle of death and rebirth, the highest state in early Buddhism.

asana (Skt.) Yogic posture.

auliya (Ar.) Protectors, helpers, or friends (more specifically, friends of God); commonly used by Muslims to refer to an Islamic saint or saints. (Also *aulia, awliya*; sing. *wali.*)

bakshish (Per.) Bribe, tip, or alms.

baqa (Ar.) After emptying/annihilation of the self (*fana*), the state of living as a purer, truer manifestation of God: with, through, in, and for God.

baraka (Ar.) Blessing.

bayat (Ar.) Sufi ritual of initiation.

bhakti (Skt.) Yoga of devotion.

bhikku (Pal.) Buddhist Monk.

bodhisattva (Skt.) Enlightened being who is able to reach nirvana but, out of compassion, remains on the wheel of incarnation to save all beings.

cherag (Per.) Literally, "lamp." The word is used in the Inayati schools to indicate a leader of the Service of Universal Peace.

dajjal (Ar.) One whose ego proclaims itself as a savior.

dargah (Ar.) Saint's tomb.

darood (Ar.) A Sufi practice of concentration in which a sacred phrase is repeated in the mind; the breath becomes rhythmic and attunement is deepened.

darshan (Hin.) Soul-to-soul transmission via the glance from one person (typically a teacher) to another.

dharma (Skt.) Nature of reality regarded as a universal truth, as taught by the Buddha; the teaching of Buddhism.

dharmakaya (Skt.) Body of Dharma, body of law; the essential mind of Buddha. One of the three bodies (*trikaya*) of Buddha: the ideal body or the essence of the Absolute. Also characterized as "Limitless Freedom."

dhikr (Ar.) See *zikr*.

dhyana (Skt.) Meditation.

fana (Ar.) Sufi practice of effacement (emptying or annihilation of oneself) in a higher spiritual figure or the Absolute. The classical stages are *fana-fi-Sheikh, fana-fi-Rassoul, fana-fi-Lillah,* and *fana-i-baqa,* with a possibility of *fana-fi-Pir* between the first and second.

faqr (Ar.) A path of "poverty" chosen to attain mystical knowledge and intimacy with Allah. One who chooses such a path is referred to as a *faqir*.

fikr (Ar.) The practice of silently following a sacred phrase in thought on the breath.

Fudo Bosatsu (Jap.) Masculine *bodhisattva* of compassion. An emanation of Buddha that burns through all ignorance for the sake of the Dharma, appearing in the hell realms to bring light, hope, and guidance to those who have become stuck there in confusion and pain. Protector of the Dharma.

garuda (Skt.) In Hindu mythology, a sacred bird ridden by Vishnu.

Gathas (OA) A collection of beginning teachings of Hazrat Inayat Khan for *mureeds;* classically a short verse form.

Gayan (Hin.) Literally "song," the *Gayan* is a collection of short lyrical sayings of Hazrat Inayat Khan.

Githas (OA) A collection of intermediate teachings of Hazrat Inayat Khan for *mureeds*.

Ghaus (Ar.) In Sufi tradition, an advanced grade within the Spiritual Hierarchy.

gopis (Skt.) Milkmaids of Krishna's acquaintance. Primary among these is Radha, Krishna's consort.

Hadith (Ar.) Remembrances of the life and sayings of Prophet Muhammad.

Hakeekat (Ar.) The third stage of the Sufi path as explained by Hazrat Inayat Khan. *Hakeekat* is the mystery of God's own self-knowing without any intermediary to reflect upon. (Also *haqiqat.*)

Hakim (Ar.) Wise leader.

hal (Ar.) Transient mystical state. (Also see *makam.*)

hamsa (Skt.) White Swan. A bird of Hindu mythology. In yoga it represents the breath.

Hazrat (Ar.) An honorific title for a deeply respected and beloved Sufi teacher whose spiritual presence is always available to *mureeds*, whether at a distance or no longer in the body.

hikmat (Ar.) Truth.

Hurkalya (Ar.) The archetypal realm underlying all forms observed on earth; it carries the connotation that what we witness is to remind us of the Source of all, taking us back to the form's purest manifestation. Name given to Pir Vilayat and Taj Inayat's gathering house in San Anselmo, CA.

ijazat (Ur.) Formal recognition giving permission to teach.

insaan-i-kamil (Ar.) The complete/perfected human being.

inshallah (Ar.) If it be the will of Allah.

irfan (Ar.) Literally "knowledge," especially Gnosis. An applied spiritual science through which breath and the name Allah are used to direct the life force anywhere needed.

ishk (Ar.) The non-rational, all-inclusive, overwhelming divine love that binds the atoms of the universe together. Murshid Sam said, "*Ishk* is the essence of our existence." (Also *ishq.*)

Jalali (Ar.) One who has mastered power/strength for the benefit of all.

jamia (Ar.) Gathering or gathering place, often educational.

Jamiat Aam (Ar.) A gathering for all members of a Sufi lineage.

Jamiat Khas (Ar.) A gathering for the designated spiritual and organizational leaders of a Sufi lineage.

jelal (Ar.) Strength or power like the Sun. (Also *jalal.*)

jemal (Ar.) Empathy or beauty like the moon. (Also *jamal.*)

jhana (Pal.) See *dhyana.*

ji ji mu ge (Jap.) Zen teaching that there is no disconnection between events; "every thing is everything."

Kabbalah (Heb.) Foundational text of Jewish mysticism.

kalama (Ar.) Islamic declaration of faith, which is variously transliterated, for example, as "La ilaha illa'llah, Muhammad ar-Rassoul Lillah" or "La ilaha el Allahu, Muhammad ar-Rassoul Lillah."

karuna (Skt.) Compassion.

kasab (Ar.) A Sufi breath practice.

kashf (Ar.) Faculty of insight.

kemal (Ar.) Literally "perfection," "completeness." Pure potentiality which contains the perfection, the completion of both the creative force and the destructive force.

Khalandar (Ar.) A person with the gift of insight who has achieved Oneness with all that is; saint.

Khalif (Ar.) In Sufi usage, *Khalif* is a teaching rank; the feminine form is *Khalifa.* The specific obligations and authority of this rank vary among Sufi lineages and over time. In common Arabic the term refers to the civil and spiritual leader of an Islamic state or region.

khankah (Ar.) Gathering place or residence of Sufi students.

khawwali (Ar.) (See *qawwali.*)

khilafat (Ar.) Leadership succession in an Islamic or Sufi community/lineage.

khilvat (Ar.) Spiritual retreat.

khirkah (Ar.) Robe.

Khwaja (Per.) An honorific title particularly used for Sufi teachers; literally "lord" or "master."

koan (Jap.) Paradoxical anecdote or riddle, used in Zen Buddhism to demonstrate the inadequacy of logical reasoning and to provoke enlightenment.

Kwannon (Jap.) Feminine *bodhisattva* of compassion. (Known as Quan Yin in China and Kwan Zeon in Korea.)

Kutb, Kutub (Ar.) See *Qutub.*

kwancho (Jap.) Buddhist priest.

lila (Skt.) Divine play of creation.

madzub (Ar.) A God-intoxicated being, whose behavior may appear strange or incoherent.

mahamudra (Skt.) Literally "great seal." Meditation practice of mystical union originating in Tibetan (Vajrayana or Tantric) Buddhism.

makam (Ar.) Mystical station; a stable state of spiritual attainment, not transient (Also see *hal*).

Malamatiyya (Ar.) Iranian Sufi sect of the 8th–9th centuries that engaged in self-blame to detach from worldly things.

manas (Skt.) Mind-stuff. The perceiving mind.

mantra, mantram (Skt.) A word, phrase, or sound repeated to aid concentration or alter consciousness in meditation. The two words are sometimes used with this distinction: a *mantram* is vocalized, a *mantra* is silent.

marefat (Ar.) Direct knowledge of spiritual truth. (Also *marifat.*)

Masheikh (Ar.) Equivalent of *murshid.*

mast (Ar.) See *madzub.*

maya (Skt.) Illusion.

Merkaba (Heb.) In Jewish mysticism, the essential inner wisdom vehicle (classically envisioned as a chariot) that transports one's consciousness to higher dimensions.

mujahida (Ar.) A Sufi practice used to clear false impressions from the heart to allow the light of the soul to shine through.

Munshi (Ar.) Honorific indicating respect for an educated person such as a secretary, teacher, or writer.

murakkabah (Ar.) Sufi science of concentration.

mureed (Ar.) A disciple on the Sufi path.

Murshid (Ar.) Sufi guide or teacher. (Feminine *Murshida.*)

mushahida (Ar.) A practice of contemplation in which a devotee who has cleared away all impressions is able to be God's representative in humanity in an area close to one's heart. Also understood as attainment in *shahud.*

nachash (Heb.) An encoiling around one's constructed idea of self, a force of taking, not giving. Rendered in English translations of the Bible as "serpent."

nasoul (Ar.) In Sufi breath practice, the offering of the exhalation.

nirmanakaya (Skt.) One of the three bodies (*trikaya*) of Buddha: the body of transformation.

nirvana (Skt.) Release into unity.

nufs (Ar.) Islamic term for the incarnated and developing soul, often rendered as "ego." (Also *nafs.*)

parinirvana (Skt.) Nirvana after death.

Pir (Ar.) Lineage holder and head of a Sufi order.

Pir-o-Murshid (Ar.) Literally "*Pir* and *Murshid.*" One who is head of a Sufi order and its lead teacher or Sufi guide; a term of deep respect.

prajna (Skt.) Spiritual insight, perfect wisdom; intuiting beyond form, thought, impression and mind stuff, and awakening in the heart of perfect wisdom.

prasad (Skt.) Sacred offering of food.

qawwali (Ar.) Sufi spiritual singer. (Also *kawwali, khawwali.*)

Qutub (Ar.) Living head of the Spiritual Hierarchy for a country or nation. (Also *Qutb.*)

rakat (Ar.) A single iteration of prescribed movements and supplications performed by Muslims as part of the prescribed obligatory prayer known as *salat.*

ras lila (Hin.) Dance of divine love.

Rassoul (Ar.) Prophet; world-messenger. In the Meher Baba tradition, *Rasul* refers to Baba as the Avatar.

ryazat (Ur.) Spiritual practice.

Roshi (Jap.) Zen master; used as an honorific or title.

sama drishti (Skt.) Supreme, universal, or cosmic outlook.

samadhi (Skt.) State in which the individual and universal consciousness unite.

sambhogakaya (Skt.) The body of bliss. One of the three bodies (*trikaya*) of Buddha.

samsara (Skt.) Eternal round of birth and death.

samskara (Skt.) Karmically inherited obstructive mental and emotional pattern.

sanatana dharma (Skt.) The eternal teachings or perennial philosophy. (Also *dhamma.*)

Sangha (Skt.) Brotherhood; more generally, a spiritual community. One of the Three Jewels of Buddhism, along with Buddha and Dharma.

Sarkar (Ar.) Honorific indicating respect for a person in authority. (Also *Sirkar.*)

satori (Jap.) Sudden Enlightenment, a moment of total Presence.

shaghal (Per.) Sufi/yogic practice in which any or all of the 7 openings of the head are covered, to draw the attention from the outer 5 senses to the experience of inner realms. In Yoga this practice is called *shanmukhi mudra.*

shahud (Ar.) Direct or deep sight. (Also *shahid.*)

Shari'at (Ar.) The first stage of the Sufi path, living appropriately, as explained by Hazrat Inayat Khan. *Shari'at* expresses laws drawn from the Qur'an.

Sheikh (Ar.) Muslim or Sufi religious leader, initiator, teacher, or guide; may be a formal title or an honorific. (Feminine *Sheikha.*)

Sidi (Ar.) Title of respect often used to mean "saint."

silsila (Ar.) Historical chain of leaders in a spiritual lineage; "spiritual genealogy."

simurgh (Per.) Wise and benevolent bird in Persian mythology and literature.

sifat (Ar.) Divine attribute.

Sirkar (Ar.) (See *Sarkar.*)

sirr (Ar.) Literally "secret," the intimate and ineffable "point of contact" between the individual and the Divine, often referred to as the heart of hearts.

soma (Skt.) Sacred intoxicating drink used in Vedic ritual.

sojo (Jap.) Approximate equivalent of Bishop in Zen hierarchy.

Subhanallah (Ar.) Sufi expression of praise and surrender, literally "Glory be to God."

talib (Ar.) Seeker of knowledge, student.

tarik (Ar.) Esoteric path; inner school. (Also *tarika.*)

Tarikat (Ar.) The second stage of the Sufi path as explained by Hazrat Inayat Khan. *Tarikat* refers to the path or steps in the spiritual journey leading toward unity, and often is synonymous with Sufism. (Also *tareekat.*)

tasawwuf (Ar.) Sufism and its teachings.

tasawwuri (Ar.) Oneness in feeling, attunement, with the teacher.

taubah (Ar.) Turning, especially toward loving forgiveness.

tawwajeh (Ar.) Spiritual merging of soul to soul and heart to heart through the glance; for example, the *mureed*'s experience of merging with their Murshid's vibration.

tulku (Tib.) Reincarnate custodian of a specific lineage of teachings in Tibetan Buddhism; reborn Tibetan Buddhist master.

urs (Ar.) Anniversary of the death of a Sufi saint; literally "wedding."

urouj (Ar.) Rising energy of the inhalation.

vijnana (Skt.) Cosmic awareness; life force, discernment, powers of mind.

walayat (Ar.) Absorption of self in the absolute.

waliyat (Ar.) Sainthood.

wazifah (Ar.) Divine Name or attribute of Allah. The practice is to invoke a Name as a prayer. (Pl. *wazaif.*)

zaval (Ar.) The ceasing of activity, as at the end of exhalation.

zikr (Ar.) Form of devotion, chiefly associated with Sufism, in which the worshiper is absorbed in the rhythmic repetition of a sacred phrase or name or attribute of Allah. (Also *dhikr.*)

Ziraat (Ar.) Sufi meditational practice focusing on nature and the five elements.

Endnotes

The Murshid Samuel Lewis Archives, murshidsam.org, are here referred to simply as Archives.

1. New Age Productions, *Sunseed,* 1973.
2. W.S. Gilbert and Arthur Sullivan, "The Law Is the True Embodiment," in *Iolanthe* (D'Oyly Carte Opera Company, premiered New York, London, 1882).
3. Gustav Luders and Frank Pixley, *King Dodo* (New York: M. Witmark & Sons, 1901).
4. Psalm 118:21–23, *New American Standard Bible.*
5. Samuel Lewis to Florie (Leonard), January 9, 1961.
6. Mildred White, "Remembrance," 1977, Archives.
7. Vera Van Voris, "Remembrance," 1972, Archives.
8. Samuel Lewis, "My Lesson in Spiritual Cosmogony and Astronomy," undated, Archives.
9. Samuel Lewis, "Intimations of Immortality from Juvenile Reminiscences," undated, Archives.
10. Inayat Khan, "The Phenomenon of the Soul," in *The Sufi Message of Hazrat Inayat Khan* (Delhi: Motilal Banarsidass, 2011), vol. V, part III. Available at Wahiduddin's Web, wahiduddin.net/mv2/V/V_10.htm.
11. Inayat Khan, "The Soul, Whence and Whither," in *The Sufi Message of Hazrat Inayat Khan* (Delhi: Motilal Banarsidass, 2011),vol. I, part III. Available at Wahiduddin's Web, wahiduddin.net/mv2/I/I_III_0.htm.
12. Mary Lou ([*sic*]; correctly Marilou) Foster, "Remembrance," March 22, 1976, Archives.
13. Samuel Lewis, "God, My Mother," in "The Diwan of Samuel Leonard Lewis," March 17, 1925, Archives.
14. Samuel Lewis, "The Degeneration Gap," letter to Art (Hoppe), May 6, 1969, Archives.
15. Samuel Lewis, "The Day of the Lord Cometh," in *Jerusalem Trilogy,* 38 (see n. 249).
16. Samuel Lewis, "Dharma Transmission," undated, Archives. Authorship is also given in Samuel Lewis's Zen name, He Kwang.
17. Whiteman and Lewis, *Glory Roads,* 247 (see n. 175).
18. Jackson Stitt Wilson, "Moses: The Greatest of Labour Leaders," in *How I Became a Socialist and Other Papers* (Berkeley, CA: published by the author, 1912). Available in facsimile through Google Books, play.google.com/books/reader?id=FNBIAAAAIAAJ&pg=GBS.PP9, 91–92.
19. Lewis, *Jerusalem Trilogy,* 44–45 (see n. 249).
20. Ibid., 97–98 (see n. 249).
21. Samuel Lewis, "In Quest of the Super Miraculous," Archives.
22. Samuel Lewis to Chitrabhanu (H. H. Muni Shri Chandraprabh Sagar), undated, Archives.
23. Frank Morton Todd, *The Story of the Exposition* (New York: G. P. Putnam's Sons, 1921) vol. 5, chap. 1.

24. Samuel Lewis to Norman (McGhee), May 2, 1963, Archives.
25. Lewis, "Dharma Transmission" (see n. 16).
26. Cassius J. Keyser, *Science and Religion: The Rational and the Super-Rational* (New Haven: Yale University Press, 1914), 34.
27. Cassius J. Keyser, *The New Infinite and the Old Theology* (New Haven: Yale University Press, 1915), Preface.
28. Lewis, "Degeneration Gap" (see n. 14).
29. Samuel Lewis, "The Lotus and the Universe," undated, Archives.
30. Lewis, "Quest" (see n. 21).
31. Samuel Lewis to Mr. (A.L.) Rogers, January 23, 1965, Archives.
32. Soyen Shaku, *Sermons of a Buddhist Abbot: Addresses on Religious Subjects,* trans. Daisetz Teitaro Suzuki (Chicago: Open Court, 1906). Available in facsimile through Google Books, books.google.com/books/about/Sermons_of_a_Buddhist_Abbot.html?id=emVRAAAAYAAJ, 25–26.
33. Ibid., 169.
34. Samuel Lewis, "Incense from Roshis," undated, Archives.
35. Ibid.
36. Ibid.
37. Lewis, "Lotus" (see n. 29).
38. Lewis, "Incense" (see n. 34).
39. Nyogen Senzaki, ed. and trans., *The Iron Flute: 100 Zen Koans* (Boston: Tuttle Publishing, 2000), 135.
40. Kazuaki Tanahashi and Roko Sherry Chayat, *Endless Vow: The Zen Path of Soen Nakagawa* (Boulder, CO: Shambhala, 1996), 145, quoted in Wikipedia, "Nyogen Senzaki," last modified January 9, 2019, en.wikipedia.org/wiki/Nyogen_Senzaki.
41. Lewis, "Incense" (see n. 34).
42. Lewis, "Lotus" (see n. 29).
43. Ibid.
44. Lewis, "Dharma Transmission" (see n. 16).
45. Lewis, "Incense" (see n. 34).
46. *The Sufi Call* (London: The Sufi Publishing Society, 1916), 5–6.
47. Inayat Khan, "Autobiographical notes for America, 1910–1912," in Edward E. Curtis, *The Columbia Sourcebook of Muslims in the United States* (New York: Columbia University Press, 2009), 50–51.
48. Rabia Martin, autobiographical sketch, in Nekbakht Foundation, *Biography of Pir-O-Murshid Inayat Khan* (Suresnes, France: Nekbakht, 1979), 520–521.
49. Samuel Lewis, Diary, March 26, 1967, Archives.
50. Samuel Lewis, "Communications with Inayat Khan," January 31, 1930, Archives.
51. Samuel Lewis, "Genuine Mystical Experience versus Pseudo-Mystical Experience," November 18, 1966, Archives.
52. Ibid.
53. Samuel Lewis, "Six Interviews with Hazrat Inayat Khan," 1970, Archives.
54. White, "Remembrance" (see n. 6).
55. Ibid.
56. Foster, "Remembrance" (see n. 12).
57. Hafiz, *Ghazels from the Divan of Hafiz,* trans. Justin Huntly McCarthy (London: David Nutt, 1893), 17.
58. Samuel Lewis, "Hafiz," March, 1925, Archives.
59. Ibid.
60. Lewis, "Six Interviews" (see n. 53).
61. Samuel Lewis to Beloved One of Allah (Shams-ed-din), March 6, 1966, Archives.
62. Samuel Lewis, "Initiation," March, 1925, Archives.
63. Samuel Lewis, "The Art of Creation," March, 1925, Archives.
64. Lewis, "Initiation" (see n. 62).
65. Lewis, "Mystical Experience" (see n. 51).
66. Lewis, "Initiation" (see n. 62).
67. Samuel Lewis, "The Diwan of Samuel Leonard Lewis," Archives.
68. Lewis, "Initiation" (see n. 62).
69. Ibid.
70. Samuel Lewis, "Paper IV: Pesach Passover," Archives.
71. Samuel Lewis to Pir-o-Murshid Sufi Sahib (Barkat Ali), July 13, 1966, Archives.

72. Lewis, "Initiation" (see n. 62).
73. Lewis, "Six Interviews" (see n. 53).
74. Hugh Talat Halman, *Where the Two Seas Meet* (Louisville, KY: Fons Vitae, 2013), 222–223.
75. The Qur'an 18:65.
76. Halman, *Two Seas,* 241 (see n. 74).
77. Documents #55 and #95, Sufi Ruhaniat International unpublished collection.
78. Samuel Lewis to My Aunt (Hatty Davis), March 31, 1925, Archives.
79. Paul Reps, "Remembrance," undated, Archives.
80. Ibid.
81. Rabia Martin, "Mrs. A. Martin (Murshida Rabia)," in "Biographical Sketches," Wahiduddin's Web, accessed July 14, 2016, wahiduddin.net/mv2/bio/Sketches.htm.
82. Lewis, "Six Interviews" (see n. 53).
83. Samuel Lewis to Beloved Ones (likely Saadia Khawar Khan and Bibijan), March 26, 1967, Archives.
84. Ibid.
85. Ibid.
86. Theodoor van Hoorn, *Recollections of Inayat Khan and Western Sufism,* trans. and ann. Hendrik J. Horn (Leiden, Netherlands: Foleor Publishers, 2010).
87. Mysore *Herald,* November 28, 1907, 70, cited in Khan, "A Hybrid Sufi Order," 301 (see n. 89).
88. Raden Mas Jodjana, *A Book of Self Re-Education* (Essex: L.N. Fowler and Co., 1981), 172.
89. Zia Inayat Khan, "A Hybrid Sufi Order at the Crossroads of Modernity: The Sufi Order and Sufi Movement of Pir-O-Murshid Inayat Khan" (Ph.D. diss., Duke, 2006), 84.
90. Ibid., 85.
91. van Hoorn, *Recollections,* 83 (see n. 86).
92. Khan, "A Hybrid Sufi Order," 109 (see n. 89).
93. Inayat Khan, "The Masters," in *The Sufi Message of Hazrat Inayat Khan* (Delhi: Motilal Banarsidass, 2011),vol. I, sec. I, part II. Available at Wahiduddin's Web, wahiduddin.net/mv2/I/I_I_2.htm.
94. Inayat Khan, "The Mystical Life of the Prophet Muhammad,"1919, Sufi Ruhaniat International unpublished collection, 36.
95. Khan, "A Hybrid Sufi Order," 103 (see n. 89).
96. Ibid., 106–7.
97. *The Sufi,* January 1919, cited in Khan, "A Hybrid Sufi Order," 109 (see n. 89).
98. van Hoorn, *Recollections,* 166–167 (see n. 86).
99. Ibid., 135–136.
100. Ibid., 59.
101. Khan, "A Hybrid Sufi Order," 178–181 (see n. 89).
102. Ibid., 190.
103. Reps, "Remembrance," Archives (see n. 79).
104. Ibid.
105. Ada Martin to Inayat Khan, April 17, 1911 (Sufism Reoriented unpublished archives).
106. Inayat Khan to Ada Martin (Sufism Reoriented unpublished archives).
107. Samuel Lewis, "Commentary on *The Bowl of Saki* of Hazrat Inayat Khan," January 22 entry, Archives. The title of the present section is Inayat Khan's text given for that date, and the subject of this commentary (see also n. 424).
108. Lewis to Beloved Ones (see n. 83).
109. Reps, "Remembrance" (see n. 79).
110. van Hoorn, *Recollections,* 132 (see n. 86).
111. Inayat Khan to Rabia Martin, November 6, 1924 (Sufism Reoriented unpublished archives).
112. Khan, "A Hybrid Sufi Order," 195 (see n. 89).
113. Ibid., 195–196.
114. Ibid., 196.
115. Lewis to Beloved Ones (see n. 83).
116. Ibid.
117. Lewis, "Six Interviews" (see n. 53).
118. Lewis to Beloved Ones (see n. 83).
119. Samuel Lewis to Beloved One of Allah (Saadia Khawar Khan), undated (likely 1967), Archives.
120. Inayat Khan, *Bowl of Saki,* February 27 entry, Archives (see also n. 424).
121. Lewis, "Commentary on *Bowl of Saki,*" February 27 entry, Archives (see also n. 424).
122. Khan, "A Hybrid Sufi Order," 196 (see n. 89).

123. Ibid., 204.
124. Ibid., 208.
125. Inayat Khan to Rabia Martin, February 8, 1915 (Sufism Reoriented unpublished archives).
126. Khan, "A Hybrid Sufi Order," 206 (see n. 89).
127. Ibid., 206–207.
128. Ibid., 210.
129. Ibid., 217.
130. Ibid., 216.
131. Samuel Lewis to John (surname unknown), November 6, 1961, Archives.
132. Samuel Lewis to World Congress of Faiths, December 15, 1970, Archives.
133. Carnegie Council for Ethics in International Affairs, "Henry A. Atkinson," retrieved October 19, 2019, www.carnegiecouncil.org/about/history/timeline/1918.
134. Samuel Lewis to Rev. Joseph Masson, May 24, 1970, Archives.
135. Samuel Lewis to A. B. Patel, December 24, 1969, Archives.
136. Samuel Lewis to Rt. Rev. James A. Pike, October 29, 1967, Archives.
137. Samuel Lewis to Gerald Yoachum, September 6, 1970, Archives.
138. Samuel Lewis to Charles Y. Glock, March 12, 1967, Archives.
139. Lewis, "Dharma Transmission" (see n. 16).
140. Samuel Lewis to Bill (Hathaway?), April 22, 1961, Archives.
141. Samuel Lewis, "Learning Zen from Zen Teachers," in "The Lotus and the Universe," undated, Archives.
142. Samuel Lewis to Bodhisattva, October 7, 1965, in "Buddhists Correspondence," Archives.
143. Samuel Lewis, commentary on "Number 1: Attitude" in *Gatha with Commentary: Tasawwuf: Metaphysics Series III of Pir-o-Murshid Hazrat Inayat Khan,* undated, Archives.
144. Samuel Lewis, "Social *Githekas,*" Series XXXII: Number 9, undated, Archives.
145. Samuel Lewis, "Rhapsodiae Coronae Mundi," Archives.
146. Ibid.
147. Lewis, "Learning Zen" (see n. 141).
148. Lewis, "Dharma Transmission" (see n. 16).
149. Lewis, "Learning Zen" (see n. 141).
150. Lewis, "Dharma Transmission" (see n. 16).
151. Ibid.
152. Lewis, "Incense" (see n. 34).
153. Lewis, "Dharma Transmission" (see n. 16).
154. Lewis, "Lotus" (see n. 29).
155. Buddhist Society of America, *Cat's Yawn: The Thirteen Numbers Published From 1940 To 1941* (Whitefish, MT: Literary Licensing, 2011).
156. Sokei-an Sasaki, *Holding the Lotus to the Rock: The Autobiography of Sokei-an, America's First Zen Master,* ed. Michael Hotz (New York: Four Walls Eight Windows, 2003).
157. Lewis, "Dharma Transmission" (see n. 16).
158. Sokei-An Sasaki, *The Zen Eye: A Collection of Zen Talks,* ed. Mary Farkas (Tokyo: Weatherhill, 1993), 147.
159. Ibid., 149.
160. Samuel Lewis, Commentary on Inayat Khan, "Mental Purification," Archives.
161. Peter Harvey, *An Introduction to Buddhism: Teachings, History and Practices* (Cambridge, UK: Cambridge University Press, 1995), 126–128.
162. Sasaki, *Lotus,* 117–118 (see n. 156).
163. Buddhist Society of America, "Eno," in *Cat's Yawn,* April, 1941 (see also n. 155).
164. Sasaki, "This Life is Life after Death," in *Lotus,* 117 (see n. 156).
165. Lewis, "Dharma Transmission" (see n. 16).
166. Samuel Lewis, "What did Sokei-an Teach You," in "Incense from Roshis," undated, Archives.
167. Lewis, "Dharma Transmission" (see n. 16).
168. Sasaki, *Lotus,* 124–125 (see n. 156).
169. Lewis, "Dharma Transmission" (see n. 16).
170. Samuel Lewis, "Sokei-an" (see n. 166).
171. Lewis, "Incense" (see n. 34).
172. Ibid.
173. Samuel Lewis, "The Book of Cosmic Prophecy," Archives.
174. Lewis, "Mystical Experience" (see n. 51).

175. Luther Whiteman and Samuel L. Lewis, *Glory Roads: The Psychological State of California* (New York: Thomas Y. Crowell, 1936).
176. Samuel Lewis to Gorham Munson, November 8, 1938 (Wesleyan University, Munson Collection).
177. Whiteman and Lewis, *Glory Roads,* v–vi (see n. 175).
178. Ibid., 1–5.
179. Ibid., 62–145.
180. Ibid., v–vi.
181. Ibid., 127.
182. Alexander Meiklejohn, "Adult Education: A Fresh Start," in *The New Republic,* August 15, 1934, 15–17.
183. Document #105, June 2, 1942, Sufi Ruhaniat International unpublished collection.
184. Meiklejohn, "Adult Education," 15–17.
185. StateUniversity.com, "Alexander Meiklejohn (1872–1964)," accessed October 07, 2016, education.stateuniversity.com/pages/2215/Meiklejohn-Alexander-1872–1964.html.
186. Document #95, October 17, 1942, Sufi Ruhaniat International unpublished collection.
187. Vocha Fiske, "Remembrance," 2016, Archives.
188. Samuel Lewis, "Aid and Comfort to the Elderly," in *Controversy,* 2.3, February 1, 1935, 5.
189. Wikipedia, "Social credit," as modified November 18, 2019, 20:00, en.wikipedia.org/wiki/Social_credit.
190. Lewis, "Aid and Comfort" (see n. 188).
191. Ibid.
192. Samuel Lewis to Gorham Munson, December 30, 1935 (Wesleyan University, Munson Collection).
193. Gorham Munson to Samuel Lewis, January 13, 1936 (Wesleyan University, Munson Collection).
194. Samuel Lewis, "Mint's Meat," in *Controversy,* VI.1, March, 1936, 8–9.
195. Gorham Munson to Samuel Lewis, February 3, 1936 (Wesleyan University, Munson Collection).
196. Andrew Salinas, "Munson, Gorham Bert," retrieved 6/7/20 from Amistad Research Center, amistadresearchcenter.tulane.edu/archon/index.php?p=creators/creator&id=749.
197. Samuel Lewis to Gorham Munson, January 30, 1936 (Wesleyan University, Munson Collection).
198. Gorham Munson to Samuel Lewis, March 30, 1936 (Wesleyan University, Munson Collection).
199. Gorham Munson to Samuel Lewis, June 22, 1936 (Wesleyan University, Munson Collection).
200. Samuel Lewis to Gorham Munson, June 17, 1936 (Wesleyan University, Munson Collection).
201. Samuel Lewis to Gorham Munson, July 18, 1936 (Wesleyan University, Munson Collection).
202. Samuel Lewis to Gorham Munson, September 4, 1936 (Wesleyan University, Munson Collection).
203. Samuel Lewis to the Editor, London *New English Weekly,* June 8, 1936 (Munson Collection).
204. Samuel Lewis to Gorham Munson, September 28, 1938 (Wesleyan University, Munson Collection).
205. Samuel Lewis, postcard to Gorham Munson, October 16, 1938 (Wesleyan University, Munson Collection).
206. Gorham Munson to Samuel Lewis, 26 October 1938 (Wesleyan University, Munson Collection).
207. Lewis to Munson (see n. 176).
208. Ibid.
209. Samuel Lewis to Gorham Munson, June 15, 1939 (Wesleyan University, Munson Collection).
210. Gorham Munson to Samuel Lewis, June 23, 1939 (Wesleyan University, Munson Collection).
211. Gavin Arthur, "Remembrance," Archives.
212. Lewis to Munson (see n. 209).
213. Ibid.

214. White, "Remembrance" (see n. 6).
215. Samuel Lewis to Gorham Munson, June 27, 1939 (Wesleyan University, Munson Collection).
216. Gorham Munson to Samuel Lewis, July 8, 1939 (Wesleyan University, Munson Collection).
217. Inayat Khan, *Bowl of Saki,* May 10 entry, Archives (see also n. 424).
218. Lewis, "Commentary on *Bowl of Saki,*" May 10 entry, Archives (see also n. 424).
219. Samuel Lewis, "*Githekas* on: Self Protection: Series 1," undated, Archives.
220. Samuel Lewis, *This is the New Age, In Person* (Tucson, AZ: Omen Press, 1972). A version is also available in Archives.
221. Samuel Lewis, "*Sangatheka* Number 8" in "Addresses to Khalifs and Sheikhs," undated, Archives.
222. "Lewis to Lecture," *Oakland Tribune,* October 15, 1932, 4.
223. *Oakland Tribune,* September 3, 1932, 9.
224. *Oakland Tribune,* July 9, 1932, 4.
225. *Oakland Tribune,* March 4, 1933, 9.
226. Samuel Lewis, *Spiritual Dancing,* Archives.
227. Samuel Lewis, "On the Control and Sublimation of Vital Force," Archives.
228. Inayat Khan, *Bowl of Saki,* May 20 entry, Archives (see also n. 424).
229. Lewis, "Commentary on *Bowl of Saki,*" May 20 entry, Archives (see also n. 424).
230. Samuel Lewis to Gorham Munson, March 12, 1937 (Wesleyan University, Munson Collection).
231. Vera Corda, "Biography," veracorda.com/biography.php, retrieved 4/13/21.
232. Van Voris, "Remembrance" (see n. 7).
233. Ivy Duce, "Remembrance," Archives.
234. Wali Ali Meyer, "A Sunrise in the West: Hazrat Inayat Khan's Legacy in California," in *A Pearl in Wine: Essays on the Life, Music, and Sufism of Hazrat Inayat Khan,* ed. Zia Inayat Khan (New Lebanon, NY: Omega Publications, 2001), 411–412.
235. UrduPoint, urdupoint.com/dictionary/roman-urdu-to-english/ijazat-roman-urdu-meaning-in-english/69139.html, retrieved 10/23/2020.
236. Meyer, "Hazrat Inayat Khan's Legacy" (see n. 234).
237. Celia Genn, "Exploration and Analysis of the Origins, Nature and Development of the Sufi Movement in Australia" (Ph.D. thesis, University of Queensland, 2004), 134–139, 143–144.
238. Ibid.
239. Ibid.
240. Inayat Khan, *Bowl of Saki,* October 13 entry, Archives (see also n. 424).
241. Lewis, "Commentary on *Bowl of Saki,*" October 13 entry, Archives (see also n. 424).
242. Reps, "Remembrance" (see n. 79).
243. Van Voris, "Remembrance" (see n. 7).
244. Inayat Khan, "Number 6: Be Conscious of Every Breath" in *Gatha with Commentary: Pasi Anfas: Breath, Series II of Pir-o-Murshid Hazrat Inayat Khan,* undated, Archives.
245. Samuel Lewis, commentary on "Be Conscious of Every Breath" (see n. 244).
246. Samuel Lewis, "Purification of the Body, Part 2," in "Sixty Four Recorded Talks," (audio, timestamp 15:00), Archives.
247. Samuel Lewis to Shamcher (Bryn Beorse), undated (likely 1969), Archives.
248. Samuel Lewis, "Purification" (see n. 246).
249. Samuel Lewis, *The Jerusalem Trilogy: Song of the Prophets* (Novato, CA: Prophecy Pressworks, 1975). Also in Archives.
250. Samuel Lewis, Diary, March 31, 1965.
251. Lewis, *Jerusalem Trilogy* (see n. 249).
252. Samuel Lewis to Shamcher (Bryn Beorse), November 19, 1969, Archives.
253. Samuel Lewis to Senator Thomas Kuchel, September 23, 1966, Archives.
254. Samuel Lewis to Stewart Alsop, March 25, 1967, Archives.
255. *Publishers Weekly,* "Landsdale Unquiet American," retrieved December 22, 2019, www.publishersweekly.com/9780395385104.
256. Edward Lansdale to Samuel Lewis, May 4, 1969, Sufi Ruhaniat International unpublished collection.

257. Lydia M. Fish, "General Edward G. Lansdale and the Folksongs of Americans in the Vietnam War," *The Journal of American Folklore*, 102.406, Vietnam (Oct.–Dec., 1989), 390–411.
258. Samuel Lewis to Rosemary Benton, August 29, 1961, Archives.
259. Inayat Khan, *Bowl of Saki*, December 22 entry, Archives (see also n. 424).
260. Lewis, "Commentary on *Bowl of Saki*," December 22 entry, Archives (see also n. 424).
261. Samuel Lewis to Murshida (Ivy Duce), February 3, 1948, Archives.
262. Bhau Kalchuri, *Lord Meher*, lordmeher.org/rev/index.jsp, 2470.
263. Ibid.
264. Lewis to Sufi Sahib (see n. 71).
265. Foster, "Remembrance" (see n. 12).
266. Lewis, "Lotus" (see n. 29).
267. Lewis, "Cosmic Prophecy" (see n. 173).
268. Samuel Lewis to Laura DeLavigne, February 13, 1942 (Meher Spiritual Center at Myrtle Beach, SC, unpublished collection).
269. Ibid.
270. Samuel Lewis to American Friends of the Middle East, October 21, 1963, Archives.
271. Samuel Lewis to Rev. Lowell R. Ditzen, May 17, 1970, Archives.
272. Samuel Lewis to Aramdarya (Luise Berrenberg), May 21, 1964, Archives.
273. Samuel Lewis to Elizabeth Patterson, August 25, 1969, Archives.
274. Samuel Lewis to Laura DeLavigne, May, 1946 (Meher Center collection).
275. Ibid.
276. Samuel Lewis to Laura DeLavigne, August 5, 1946 (Meher Center collection).
277. Ibid.
278. Samuel Lewis to Laura DeLavigne, September 9, 1946 (Meher Center collection).
279. Ibid.
280. Samuel Lewis to Laura DeLavigne, October 1, 1946 (Meher Center collection).
281. Ibid.
282. Rudyard Kipling, "Recessional," in *A Choice of Kipling's Verse*, T. S. Eliot, ed. (New York: Scribners, 1943).
283. Samuel Lewis to Laura DeLavigne, February 26, 1947 (Meher Center collection).
284. Meher Baba, postcard to Samuel Lewis, March, 1947 (Meher Center collection).
285. Meher Baba, quoted in "Blue Bus Tours," retrieved June 28, 2020, lordmeher.org/rev/index.jsp, 2021.
286. Gina Cerminara, "Remembrance," October 10, 1975, Archives.
287. Filis Fredericks, article in *Awakener*, 20.2, 1983, 35.
288. Paula Saffire, personal conversation with Wali Ali Meyer.
289. Ross Keating, *Francis Brabazon: Poet of the Silent Word—A Modern Hafiz* (Beacon Hill, Australia: World Axis Press, 2002), 63–68.
290. Saffire, conversation with Meyer.
291. Ibid.
292. Ibid.
293. Ibid.
294. Keating, *Brabazon*, 68 (see n. 289).
295. Ibid.
296. Margaret Albanese, "Remembrance," February 5, 1976, Archives.
297. Francis Brabazon, in *7 Stars to Morning* (Sydney: Morgan's Bookshop, 1956), 59.
298. Don Stevens, *Some Results* (Companion Enterprises, 1995), 4.
299. Ibid.
300. Ibid., 6.
301. Samuel Lewis, Diary, July 26, 1963, Archives.
302. Samuel Lewis to Shams-ed-din Ahmed, May 14, 1967, Archives.
303. Stevens, *Results* (see n. 298).
304. Ibid.
305. Samuel Lewis, Diary, April 4, 1963, Archives.
306. Samuel Lewis, Diary, August 16, 1963, Archives.
307. Lewis to Murshida (see n. 261).
308. Ibid.
309. Ibid.
310. Samuel Lewis to S.A. Ataullah Shuttari, November 7, 1963, Archives.

311. Ivy Duce, "Remembrance," Archives.
312. Samuel Lewis to Meher Baba, May 12, 1948, Archives.
313. Samuel Lewis to John (surname unknown), November 11, 1963, Archives.
314. *Daily Independent Journal,* San Rafael, California, January 3, 1950, 1.
315. Murshida (Ivy Duce) to Samuel Lewis, January 9, 1950, Archives.
316. Ibid.
317. Lewis to Beloved Ones (see n. 83).
318. Lewis to Beloved One (see n. 119).
319. Lewis, "Commentary on *Bowl of Saki,*" October 13 entry, Archives (see also n. 424).
320. Reps, "Remembrance" (see n. 79).
321. Elliott Lewis to Samuel Lewis, October, [1948], Archives.
322. Samuel Lewis to Marion (Mann), December 27, 1962, Archives.
323. Samuel Lewis to C. R. Cutright, May 14, 1961, Archives.
324. Samuel Lewis to Harry (Nelson), March 1, 1962, Archives.
325. Harry Nelson, "Remembrance," August 12, 1976, Archives.
326. Ibid.
327. Ibid.
328. Hilda Galbraith, "Remembrance," April 21, 1976, Archives.
329. Constance Luick, "Remembrance," September, 1975, Archives.
330. Ibid.
331. Ibid.
332. Van Voris, "Remembrance" (see n. 7).
333. Arthur, "Remembrance" (see n. 211).
334. Ibid.
335. Ibid.
336. Samuel Lewis to Shamcher (Bryn Beorse), September 26, 1970, Archives.
337. Samuel Lewis to Gavin (Arthur), October 20, 1960, Archives.
338. Florence Leonard, "Remembrance," November 18, 1976, Archives.
339. Albanese, "Remembrance" (see n. 296).
340. Arthur, "Remembrance" (see n. 211).
341. Ibid.
342. Will Fellows, *Gay Bar: The Fabulous, True Story of a Daring Woman and Her Boys in the 1950s* (Madison, WI: University of Wisconsin Press, 2010), 14.
343. Samuel Lewis to Gavin (Arthur), December 31, 1960, Archives.
344. Samuel Lewis to Walt and Magana (Baptiste), January 16, 1961, Archives.
345. *ONE Institute Quarterly: Homophile Studies,* VII.3–4, 1967.
346. Arthur, "Remembrance" (see n. 211).
347. Samuel Lewis, Diary, April 3, 1963, Archives.
348. Ibid.
349. Leonard, "Remembrance" (see n. 338).
350. Ibid.
351. Ibid.
352. Ibid.
353. Crist Lovdjieff and Yvonne Childs, "Remembrance," November 21, 1976, Archives.
354. Ibid.
355. Swami Ramdas, *World Is God* (Bombay: Bhavan Book University, 1967), 116–128.
356. Lovdjieff and Childs, "Remembrance" (see n. 353).
357. Ibid.
358. Samuel Lewis to Margaret (Albanese), January 29, 1955, Archives.
359. Saladin (Paul Reps) to Samuel Lewis, December 3, 1955, Archives.
360. Saladin (Paul Reps) to Samuel Lewis, December 19, 1955, Archives.
361. Samuel Lewis to Margaret (Albanese), January 24, 1955, Archives.
362. Lewis to Margaret (see n. 358).
363. Ibid.
364. Robert Stuart Clifton to Samuel Lewis, November 16, 1953, Archives.
365. Robert Stuart Clifton to Samuel Lewis, June 26, 1954, Archives.
366. Robert Stuart Clifton to Samuel Lewis, January 18, 1955, Archives.
367. Samuel Lewis to Sumangalo (Robert Clifton), August 7, 1955, Archives.
368. Foster, "Remembrance" (see n. 12).
369. John Rockwell to Samuel Lewis, June 24, 1965

370. (Papa) Ramdas to Samuel Lewis, July 15, 1955, Archives.
371. (Papa) Ramdas to Samuel Lewis, September 1, 1955, Archives.
372. RSC (Robert Clifton) to Samuel Lewis, August 29, 1955, Archives.
373. Lewis to Sumangalo (see n. 367).
374. Samuel Lewis to Sumangalo (Robert Clifton), May 24, 1956, Archives.
375. K.R. Patel to Samuel Lewis, August 10, 1955, Archives.
376. Ibid.
377. Viola Harris to Samuel Lewis, November 7, 1953, Archives.
378. Samuel Lewis to Mr. (William?) Winter, June 17, 1956, Archives.
379. Samuel Lewis to Tony (Leonard Austin), May 28, 1956, Archives.
380. Samuel Lewis, Diary, May 29, 1956, Archives.
381. Samuel Lewis to David W. Brokensha, January 14, 1965, Archives.
382. Samuel Lewis to James A. Michener, June 15, 1956, Archives.
383. Samuel Lewis to E.W. Strong (Chancellor, UC Berkeley), November 10, 1964, Archives.
384. Samuel Lewis, Diary, May 31, 1956, Archives.
385. Samuel Lewis to Harry (Nelson), June 9, 1956, Archives.
386. Samuel Lewis to S.D. (Stanton Delaplane), June 7, 1956, Archives.
387. Samuel Lewis to Evelyn, Grace, and Jim (surnames unknown), June 7, 1956, Archives.
388. Samuel Lewis, Diary, May 30, 1956, Archives.
389. Samuel Lewis to Lois (surname unknown) et al., May 21, 1956, Archives.
390. Samuel Lewis to Carroll Parrish, December 10, 1964, Archives.
391. Lewis, "Incense" (see n. 34).
392. Ibid.
393. Samuel Lewis, Diary, June 14, 1956, Archives.
394. Lewis, "Incense" (see n. 34).
395. Ibid.
396. Ibid.
397. Samuel Lewis, Diary, May 24, 1956, Archives.
398. Lewis, "Lotus" (see n. 29).
399. Lewis to Michener (see n. 382).
400. Samuel Lewis to Harry (Nelson), June 10, 1956, Archives.
401. Samuel Lewis to James O. Kinoshita, June 16, 1956, Archives.
402. Ibid.
403. Ibid.
404. Lewis to Winter (see n. 378).
405. Samuel Lewis to Rudolph (Olsen), July 11, 1956, Archives.
406. Samuel Lewis to Bryn Beorse, July 6, 1956, Archives.
407. Samuel Lewis, Diary, June 28–July 1, 1956, Archives.
408. Samuel Lewis to Mr. (William?) Winter, July 1, 1956, Archives.
409. Samuel Lewis, Diary, June 27, 1956, Archives.
410. Samuel Lewis to Jack (Betts?), July 2, 1956, Archives.
411. Samuel Lewis, Diary, July 3, 1956, Archives.
412. Samuel Lewis to S.D. (Stanton Delaplane), July 2, 1956, Archives.
413. Lewis to Beorse (see n. 406).
414. Samuel Lewis to Bryn (Beorse), July 20, 1956, Archives.
415. Lewis to Rudolph (see n. 405).
416. Ibid.
417. Samuel Lewis to George & Paul (surnames unknown), July 13, 1956, Archives.
418. Samuel Lewis to Paul & George (surnames unknown), July 14, 1956, Archives.
419. Samuel Lewis to Winter (see n. 408).
420. Ibid.
421. Samuel Lewis to S.D. (Stanton Delaplane), July 10, 1956, Archives.
422. Lewis to Paul & George (see n. 418).
423. Samuel Lewis to John (surname unknown), July 20, 1956, Archives.
424. Inayat Khan, *The Bowl of Saki* (Delhi: Motilal Banarsidass, 1996), July 18 entry. All entries available with commentary by Samuel Lewis in Archives.
425. Lewis to John (see n. 423).
426. Ibid.

427. Samuel Lewis to Bashir Ahmed Minto, July 24, 1956, Archives.
428. Ibid.
429. Ibid.
430. Samuel Lewis, Diary, July 27, 1956, Archives.
431. Samuel Lewis, Diary, July 29, 1956, Archives.
432. Ibid.
433. Ibid.
434. Samuel Lewis, "Purna Vedanta Yoga Gita," August 9, 1956, Archives.
435. Samuel Lewis to Rudolph (Schaeffer), July 29, 1956, Archives.
436. Ibid.
437. Samuel Lewis, Diary, undated (likely late July, 1956), Archives.
438. Samuel Lewis to Quantz (Crawford), October 6, 1956, Archives.
439. Samuel Lewis to Professor (Pitrim) Sorokin, August 27, [1956,] Archives.
440. Samuel Lewis to Vilayat (Khan), August 5, 1956, Archives.
441. Samuel Lewis to Quantz (Crawford), August 3, 1956, Archives.
442. Samuel Lewis to World Affairs Council, August 28, 1956, Archives.
443. Ibid.
444. Hasan Sani Nizami and Shabda Kahn, 2007, interview transcripts in Sufi Ruhaniat International unpublished collection.
445. Lewis to World Affairs Council (see n. 442).
446. Samuel Lewis, Diary, August 29, 1956, Archives.
447. Ibid.
448. Samuel Lewis to Mac (surname unknown), September 3, 1956, Archives.
449. Samuel Lewis to Chris (surname unknown), September 13, 1956, Archives.
450. Lewis to Mac (see n. 448).
451. Samuel Lewis to Fred (surname unknown), September 5, 1956, Archives.
452. Ibid.
453. Ibid.
454. Samuel Lewis to Quantz (Crawford), September 5, 1956, Archives.
455. Samuel Lewis to Rudolph (Schaeffer), undated (likely 1956), Archives.
456. Lewis to Chris (see n. 449).
457. Samuel Lewis to Gavin (Arthur), undated (likely 1956), Archives.
458. Samuel Lewis to Mr. (William?) Winter, September 17, 1956, Archives.
459. Ibid.
460. Samuel Lewis to Harry (Nelson), September 19, 1956, Archives.
461. Lewis to Gavin (see n. 457).
462. Samuel Lewis to Rudolph (Schaeffer), September 22, 1956, Archives.
463. Lewis to Vilayat (see n. 440).
464. Ibid.
465. Vilayat Khan to *Mureeds,* August 11, 1956, Archives.
466. Samuel Lewis to Pir Zade Vilayat Inayat Khan, September 17, 1956, Archives.
467. Samuel Lewis, from "Sand and Glass," Archives.
468. Inayat Khan, *Bowl of Saki,* July 17 entry, Archives (see also n. 424).
469. Lewis, "Commentary on *Bowl of Saki,*" July 17 entry, Archives (see also n. 424).
470. Samuel Lewis to Professor Seroking (Sorokin?) of Harvard, October 1, 1956, Archives.
471. Samuel Lewis to Fred (surname unknown), October 3, 1956, Archives.
472. Samuel Lewis to Mac (surname unknown), September 3, 1956, Archives.
473. Lewis, "Lotus" (see n. 29).
474. Ibid.
475. Ibid.
476. Ibid.
477. Samuel Lewis, "Vision and Ritual in Sufism," undated, Archives.
478. Ibid.
479. Ibid.
480. Samuel Lewis to Nuria (surname unknown), October 25, 1956, Archives.
481. Samuel Lewis to Beloved One of Allah (Saadia Khawar Khan), July 25, 1966, Archives.
482. Samuel Lewis, Diary, October 22, 1956, Archives.
483. Lewis to Nuria (see n. 480).
484. Ibid.

485. Samuel Lewis to Jim (surname unknown), October 25, 1956, Archives.
486. Ibid.
487. Samuel Lewis to E. T. Bell, October 25, 1956, Archives.
488. Lewis to Nuria (see n. 480).
489. Samuel Lewis to James and Ruth (surnames unknown), December 3, 1956, Archives.
490. Lewis to Nuria (see n. 480).
491. Ibid.
492. Ibid.
493. Samuel Lewis, Diary, November 4, 1956, Archives.
494. Samuel Lewis to Harry (Nelson), November 6, 1956, Archives.
495. Ibid.
496. Samuel Lewis, Diary, November 12, 1956, Archives.
497. Ibid.
498. Samuel Lewis to Pres (surname unknown), November 14, 1956, Archives.
499. Samuel Lewis, Diary, November 18, 1956, Archives.
500. Samuel Lewis to Gavin (Arthur) and Myra (Kingsley), November 20, 1956, Archives.
501. Samuel Lewis to Quantz (Crawford), November 27, 1956, Archives.
502. Lewis to James and Ruth (see n. 489).
503. Samuel Lewis to Joe and Margaret (surnames unknown), December 3, 1956, Archives.
504. Samuel Lewis to Gavin (Arthur), December 13, 1956, Archives.
505. Ibid.
506. Samuel Lewis to Harry (Nelson), December 14, 1956, Archives.
507. Samuel Lewis to Robert (Clifton), December 17, 1956, Archives.
508. Ibid.
509. Lewis to Joe and Margaret (see n. 503).
510. Samuel Lewis to Edna (Bellefontaine), November 14, 1957, Archives.
511. Samuel Lewis to Sumangalo (Robert Clifton), September 13, 1956, Archives.
512. Samuel Lewis to Leonora (Ponti), April 5, 1958, Archives.
513. Arthur, "Remembrance" (see n. 211).
514. *North Tonawanda NY Evening News,* February 26, 1970.
515. Samuel Lewis, "Siva! Siva!," undated, Archives.
516. Ibid.
517. Samuel Lewis, "Crescent and Heart," XI, undated, Archives.
518. Lewis, "Saladin," in *Jerusalem Trilogy,* 196–217 (see n. 249).
519. Samuel Lewis to A. A. Siddiqui, April 18, 1959, Archives.
520. Ibid.
521. Samuel Lewis to Norman (McGhee), December 16, 1959, Archives.
522. Samuel Lewis to Willie (Wise), January 29, 1961, Archives.
523. Samuel Lewis to Morris W. Hirsch, May 2, 1965, Archives.
524. Samuel Lewis to Gavin (Arthur), March 27, 1966, Archives.
525. Samuel Lewis to Gavin (Arthur), June 6, 1966, Archives.
526. Viola Harris to Samuel Lewis, May 3, 1958, Archives.
527. Samuel Lewis, Diary, March 22, 1960, Archives.
528. Ibid.
529. Samuel Lewis to Blanche (Baker), March 26, 1960, Archives.
530. Ibid.
531. Samuel Lewis, "How to be a Buddhist? How to be a Buddha?," 1959, Archives.
532. Samuel Lewis to Charles Siegferth, April 2, 1960, Archives.
533. Samuel Lewis to Walter J. Fischel, April 3, 1960, Archives.
534. Samuel Lewis to Franz Rosenthal, undated, Archives.
535. Samuel Lewis to Charles Morris, September 12, 1954, Archives.
536. Samuel Lewis, Diary, April 26, 1960, Archives.
537. Samuel Lewis to Hugo (Selig), January 15, 1960, Archives.
538. Oliver Reiser to Samuel Lewis, December 24, 1958, Archives.

539. Mary Farkas to Samuel Lewis, June 2,1958, Archives.
540. Mary Farkas to Samuel Lewis, October 30, 1958, Archives.
541. Mary Farkas to Samuel Lewis, November 11, 1959, Archives.
542. Gwyn (surname unknown) to Samuel Lewis, July 28, 1959, Archives.
543. Samuel Lewis, Diary, April 26, 1960, Archives.
544. Samuel Lewis to Murshida (Ivy Duce), April 27, 1960, Archives.
545. Samuel Lewis to Dorothy (Schueler?), May 31, 1960, Archives.
546. Samuel Lewis to Ruth (surname unknown), June 5, 1960, Archives.
547. Samuel Lewis to Charlie (Siegferth), June 8, 1960, Archives.
548. Samuel Lewis to Rudolph (Schaeffer), July 4, 1960, Archives.
549. Samuel Lewis to Mr. and Mrs. (Russell) Smith, August 7, 1960, Archives.
550. Ibid.
551. Samuel Lewis to Fred and Corinne (Reinhold), August 9, 1960, Archives.
552. Lewis to Ruth (see n. 546).
553. Samuel Lewis to Bill (Hathaway?), August 18, 1960, Archives.
554. Samuel Lewis to Leonora (Ponti), August 27, 1960, Archives.
555. Samuel Lewis to Gavin (Arthur), August 28, 1960, Archives.
556. Ibid.
557. Samuel Lewis, Diary, September 2, 1960, Archives.
558. Samuel Lewis to Rudy (Olsen), September 3, 1960, Archives.
559. Samuel Lewis, "The Pukhtunistan Special," Diary, ca. September 2, 1960, Archives.
560. Samuel Lewis to Harry (Nelson), September 7, 1960, Archives.
561. Samuel Lewis to Harry (Nelson), September 9, 1960, Archives.
562. Samuel Lewis to Jack (Betts?), September 8, 1960, Archives.
563. Samuel Lewis to Jane and Vince (surnames unknown), September 10, 1960, Archives.
564. Samuel Lewis to Mac (surname unknown), September 14, 1960, Archives.
565. Ibid.
566. Samuel Lewis to Florie (Leonard), September 18, 1960, Archives.
567. Samuel Lewis to Harry (Nelson), September 20, 1960, Archives.
568. Ibid.
569. Samuel Lewis to Professor Cutright, September 21, 1960, Archives.
570. Samuel Lewis to Rudy (Schaeffer), September 21, 1960, Archives.
571. Ibid.
572. Samuel Lewis to Florie (Leonard), September 25, 1960, Archives.
573. Samuel Lewis to Florie (Leonard), September 26, 1960, Archives.
574. Samuel Lewis to Jack (Betts?), September 27, 1960, Archives.
575. Samuel Lewis to Willie Wise and William Gaskin, September 28, 1960, Archives.
576. Samuel Lewis to Abdul Sattar, October 2, 1960, Archives.
577. Samuel Lewis to Florie (Leonard), October 4, 1960, Archives.
578. Lewis, "Incense" (see n. 34).
579. Samuel Lewis to Quazi Mehay Allum, October 10, 1960, Archives.
580. Samuel Lewis to Rudolph Schaeffer, October 14, 1960, Archives.
581. Samuel Lewis to Florie (Leonard), October 12, 1960, Archives.
582. Ibid.
583. Samuel Lewis to Harry (Nelson), October 16, 1960, Archives.
584. Samuel Lewis to Clifford Cutright, October 18, 1960, Archives.
585. Samuel Lewis to Florie (Leonard), October 19, 1960, Archives.
586. Samuel Lewis to Max and Winnie (surnames unknown), October 19, 1960, Archives.
587. Samuel Lewis to Peg (Allmond), December 12, 1960, Archives.
588. Ibid.

589. Samuel Lewis to Peggy (Allmond), January 17, 1961, Archives.
590. Ibid.
591. Samuel Lewis to Florie (Leonard), January 8, 1961, Archives.
592. Samuel Lewis to Florie (Leonard), December 31, 1960, Archives.
593. Ibid.
594. Ibid.
595. Samuel Lewis to Ruth (surname unknown), January 4, 1961, Archives.
596. Ibid.
597. Samuel Lewis to Florie (Leonard), January 5, 1961, Archives.
598. Ibid.
599. Ibid.
600. Lewis to Walt and Magana (see n. 344).
601. Inayat Khan, *Bowl of Saki,* July 16 entry, Archives (see also n. 424).
602. Lewis, "Commentary on *Bowl of Saki,*" July 16 entry, Archives (see also n. 424).
603. Samuel Lewis to Ruth (surname unknown) et al., January 18, 1961, Archives.
604. Ibid.
605. Ibid.
606. Samuel Lewis to Rudolph Schaeffer School of Design, January 19, 1961, Archives.
607. Samuel Lewis to Tony (Leonard Austin), January 24, 1961, Archives.
608. Samuel Lewis to Jim (surname unknown), January 29, 1961, Archives.
609. Ibid.
610. Ibid.
611. Samuel Lewis to Beloved Ones of God, January 30, 1961, Archives.
612. Ibid.
613. Ibid.
614. Ibid.
615. Samuel Lewis to Pir-o-Murshid Maulana Abdul Ghafoor, January 24, 1961, Archives.
616. Samuel Lewis to Rudolph (Schaeffer), February 2, 1961, Archives.
617. Ibid.
618. Samuel Lewis to Rudy (Schaeffer), February 6, 1961, Archives.
619. Lewis to Rudolph (see n. 616).
620. Lewis to Rudy (see n. 618).
621. Ibid.
622. Ibid.
623. Ibid.
624. Ibid.
625. Samuel Lewis to Abdul Rachman, February 7, 1961, Archives.
626. Ibid.
627. Ibid.
628. Ibid.
629. Ibid.
630. Samuel Lewis, Diary, February 9, 1961, Archives.
631. Samuel Lewis to Harry (Nelson), February 13, 1961, Archives.
632. Samuel Lewis to Jack (Betts?), February 17, 1961, Archives.
633. Samuel Lewis to Rudy (Schaeffer), February 20, 1961, Archives.
634. Samuel Lewis, Diary, February 25, 1961, Archives.
635. Samuel Lewis to Gavin (Arthur), February 22, 1961, Archives.
636. Ibid.
637. Ibid.
638. Ibid.
639. Samuel Lewis to John (surname unknown), February 28, 1961, Archives.
640. Lewis to Rudy (see n. 633).
641. Samuel Lewis to World Affairs Council of Northern California, March 4, 1961, Archives.
642. Ibid.
643. Samuel Lewis to Rudy (Schaeffer), March 7, 1961, Archives.
644. Samuel Lewis to American Friends of the Middle East, March 8, 1961, Archives.
645. Ibid.
646. Ibid.
647. Samuel Lewis to Magana (Baptiste), March 12, 1961, Archives.
648. Samuel Lewis to Professor Cutright, March 12, 1961, Archives.
649. Lewis to Magana (see n. 647).
650. Ibid.
651. Ibid.

652. Samuel Lewis to Florie (Leonard), March 18, 1961, Archives.
653. Samuel Lewis to Florie (Leonard), "March, 28"[*sic*], 1961, Archives.
654. Samuel Lewis to Pakistan House, March 16, 1961, Archives.
655. Lewis to Florie (see n. 652).
656. Ibid.
657. Lewis to Pakistan House (see n. 654).
658. Samuel Lewis to Harry (Nelson), March 16, 1961, Archives.
659. Lewis to Pakistan House (see n. 654).
660. Samuel Lewis to American Friends of the Middle East, March 23, 1961, Archives.
661. Samuel Lewis, Diary, March 27, 1961, Archives.
662. Samuel Lewis to Jack (Betts?), March 29, 1961, Archives.
663. Samuel Lewis to Barry (surname unknown), April 25, 1961, Archives.
664. Samuel Lewis, Diary, "March, 28" [*sic*], 1961, Archives.
665. Samuel Lewis, Diary, March 27, 1961, Archives.
666. Ibid.
667. Ibid.
668. Samuel Lewis to Dan (surname unknown), April 5, 1961, Archives.
669. Samuel Lewis to Horace (Hair), April 1, 1961, Archives.
670. Samuel Lewis to Horace (Hair), April 6, 1961, Archives.
671. Samuel Lewis to Joan and Harold (surnames unknown), March 30, 1961, Archives.
672. Ibid.
673. Lewis to Jack (see n. 662).
674. Lewis to Joan and Harold (see n. 671).
675. Samuel Lewis to Bill (Hathaway?), April 4, 1961, Archives.
676. Samuel Lewis to Fred and Corinne (Reinhold), May 7, 1961, Archives.
677. Samuel Lewis to Jack (Betts?), April 20, 1961, Archives.
678. Lewis to Bill (see n. 140).
679. Samuel Lewis to Jack (Betts?), April 26, 1961, Archives.
680. Samuel Lewis to Madelynne (Greens), May 1, 1961, Archives.
681. Lewis to Barry (see n. 663).
682. Ibid.
683. Samuel Lewis to Wesley (Miller), May 9, 1961, Archives.
684. Ibid.
685. Samuel Lewis to Lemanda (surname unknown), May 18, 1961, Archives.
686. Lewis to Fred and Corinne (see n. 676).
687. Lewis to Wesley (see n. 683).
688. Ibid.
689. Samuel Lewis to Lemanda (see n. 685).
690. Lewis to Wesley (see n. 683).
691. Lewis to Fred and Corinne (see n. 676).
692. Samuel Lewis to Lemanda (see n. 685).
693. Samuel Lewis to UC Department of South Asian Studies, May 8, 1961, Archives.
694. Lewis to Wesley (see n. 683).
695. Samuel Lewis to Pir-O-Murshid (Barkat Ali), June 14, 1961, Archives.
696. Saadia Khawar Khan Chishti, *Voice of the Heart: A Gathering in Remembrance of the Life and Spiritual Practices of Sufi Ahmed Murad Chishti, Murshid Samuel Lewis,* (2000, video in Sufi Ruhaniat International unpublished collection).
697. Seyyed Hossein Nasr to Samuel Lewis, August 25, 1963, Archives.
698. Samuel Lewis, "Vision and Ritual" (see n. 477).
699. Ibid.
700. Samuel Lewis to Saadia Khawar Khan, August 21, 1970, Archives.
701. Samuel Lewis to Q. U. Shahab, September 9, 1961, Archives.
702. Lewis to Pir-O-Murshid (see n. 695).
703. Asim Chisti, interview with Wali Ali Meyer, 2014, Sufi Ruhaniat International unpublished collection.
704. Lewis, "Lotus" (see n. 29).
705. Ibid.
706. Samuel Lewis, "Path of Initiation and Discipleship, Part 2," in "64 Talks," Archives, 4:34 ff.

707. Samuel Lewis to Norman (McGhee), May 14, 1961, Archives.
708. Samuel Lewis to Norman (McGhee), June 28, 1961, Archives.
709. Samuel Lewis to Ian Stevenson, undated (likely 1967), Archives.
710. Lewis, "Lotus" (see n. 29).
711. Ibid.
712. Ibid.
713. Ibid.
714. Ibid.
715. Lewis to Norman (see n. 708).
716. Ibid.
717. Satchidananda to Samuel Lewis, January 18, 1962, Archives.
718. Samuel Lewis to Swami Akhilananda, January 29, 1962, Archives.
719. Samuel Lewis to LeonaraH ([*sic*]; Leonora Ponti), January 23, 1962, Archives.
720. Lewis to Akhilananda (see n. 718).
721. Samuel Lewis to Willie (Wise), January 26, 1962, Archives.
722. Lewis to Akhilananda (see n. 718).
723. Samuel Lewis to Grace and Nick (surnames unknown), February 20, 1962, Archives.
724. Lewis to Harry (see n. 324).
725. Samuel Lewis to Willie (Wise), March 27, 1962, Archives.
726. Samuel Lewis to Friends (Norman McGhee), April 8, 1962, Archives.
727. Ibid.
728. Samuel Lewis to Willie (Wise), April 14, 1962, Archives.
729. Samuel Lewis to Leonora (Ponti), April 11, 1962, Archives.
730. Samuel Lewis to Willie (Wise), April 13, 1962, Archives.
731. Samuel Lewis to Gordon (Onslow-Ford), October 10, 1962, Archives.
732. Saadia Khawar Khan, *Voice of the Heart* (see n. 696).
733. Samuel Lewis to Saadia (Khawar Khan), September 27, 1962, Archives.
734. Ibid.
735. Samuel Lewis to Khawar Saadia (Khan), September, 1962, Archives.
736. Ted Reich, "Remembrance," April 30, 1971, Archives.
737. Samuel Lewis, Diary, January 9, 1963, Archives.
738. Ibid.
739. Ibid.
740. Samuel Lewis, Diary, January 11, 1963, Archives.
741. Samuel Lewis, Diary, January 15, 1963, Archives.
742. Samuel Lewis to Fred (surname unknown), January 20, 1963, Archives.
743. Gene Wagner to Samuel Lewis, February 3, 1964, Archives.
744. Gene Wagner to Samuel Lewis, October 8, 1964, Archives.
745. Samuel Lewis to Edward & Angela (surnames unknown), January 28, 1965, Archives.
746. Eugene (Wagner) to Samuel Lewis, September 30, 1965, Archives.
747. Mansur Johnson, *Murshid: A Personal Memoir of Life with American Sufi Samuel L. Lewis* (Seattle: PeaceWorks Publications, 2006), 125–126.
748. Samuel Lewis to Neville Warwick, September 7, 1968, Archives.
749. Ibid.
750. Ibid.
751. Samuel Lewis to Pir-O-Murshid (Barkat Ali), November 17, 1963, Archives.
752. Samuel Lewis to Beloved One of God, May 23, 1963, Archives.
753. Samuel Lewis to Ruth (surname unknown), August 23, 1961, Archives.
754. Barkat Ali to Samuel Lewis, undated, Archives.
755. Samuel Lewis to Pir-O-Murshid (Barkat Ali), March 1, 1965, Archives.
756. Samuel Lewis to Gavin (Arthur), June 23, 1966, Archives.
757. Ralph and Nancy Silver, "Remembrance," January 28, 1976, Archives.
758. Samuel Lewis to Sharab (Harris), September 1, 1964, Archives.
759. Reich, "Remembrance" (see n. 736).

760. Samuel Lewis to Aramdarya (Luise Berrenberg), November 13, 1966, Archives.
761. Samuel Lewis to Vocha (Fiske), November 21, 1966, Archives.
762. Lewis to Aramdarya (see n. 760).
763. Samuel Lewis to Beloved one of God (Cecil Gibbings), November 19, 1966, Archives.
764. Samuel Lewis to Saadia Khawar Khan, January 13, 1967, Archives.
765. Samuel Lewis to Beloved One of Allah (Saadia Khawar Khan), April 4, 1967, Archives.
766. Silver and Silver, "Remembrance" (see n. 757).
767. Samuel Lewis, "The Relevance of Eastern Religions to Western Youth," Feb. 26, 1968, Archives.
768. Moineddin and Fatima Jablonski, "Remembrance," undated, Archives.
769. Reich, "Remembrance" (see n. 736).
770. Devi Rudman (Deborah Churney Lewis), "Remembrance," December 23, 1976, Archives.
771. Inayat Khan, *Bowl of Saki,* May 13 entry, Archives (see also n. 424).
772. Lewis, "Commentary on *Bowl of Saki,*" May 13 entry, Archives (see also n. 424).
773. Samuel Lewis to Saadia (Khawar Khan), October 18, 1962, Archives.
774. Samuel Lewis to Norman (McGhee), December 6, 1963, Archives.
775. Samuel Lewis to Beloved One of God (Saadia Khawar Khan), April 4, 1967, Archives.
776. Samuel Lewis to Ruth (surname unknown), May 28, 1963, Archives.
777. Samuel Lewis, Diary, July 27, 1963, Archives.
778. Lewis to Ruth (see n. 776).
779. Samuel Lewis, Diary, July 27, 1963, Archives.
780. Samuel Lewis to LeonaraH (see n. 719).
781. Mariam Baker, *Sacred Voices: Stories from the Caravan of Women* (Indianapolis: Dog Ear Publishing, 2018).
782. Samuel Lewis, Diary, May 15, 1963, Archives.
783. Samuel Lewis, Diary, April 18, 1963, Archives.
784. Lewis, Diary (see n. 782).
785. Samuel Lewis to Shamcher (Bryn Beorse), June 25, 1968, Archives.
786. Zeinob Burnham, "Remembrance," September 2, 1976, Archives
787. Samuel Lewis to Beloved One of God (Saadia Khawar Khan), June 17, 1969, Archives.
788. Ruth St. Denis, *Wisdom Comes Dancing: Selected Writings of Ruth St. Denis on Dance, Spirituality, and the Body,* ed. Kamae A. Miller (Seattle: PeaceWorks Publications, 2006), 30.
789. Ibid., 55.
790. Samuel Lewis to Julie Medlock, May 8, 1968, Archives.
791. Lewis, *Spiritual Dancing,* ch. 13 (see n. 226).
792. Samuel Lewis to Beloved Ones of Allah, September 6, 1963, Archives.
793. Samuel Lewis to My Dear Brother, November 3, 1963, Archives.
794. Samuel Lewis to Dear Heart, January 14, 1964, Archives.
795. Samuel Lewis to Beloved One of Allah (Saadia Khawar Khan), June 24, 1966, Archives.
796. Samuel Lewis to Norman (McGhee), May 26, 1968, Archives.
797. Samuel Lewis to Shamcher (Bryn Beorse), September 1, 1967, Archives.
798. Lewis to Shamcher (see n. 785).
799. Samuel Lewis to Rudy (Olsen), September 28, 1968, Archives.
800. Samuel Lewis to Suzanne D'Mitrieff, October 29, 1968, Archives.
801. Samuel Lewis to Paul Reps, January 27, 1969, Archives.
802. Samuel Lewis to Shamcher (Bryn Beorse), May 8, 1969, Archives.
803. Lewis to Reps (see n. 801).
804. Samuel Lewis to Pir Vilayat (Khan), February 26, 1969, Archives.
805. Ibid.
806. Vilayat Inayat Khan to Samuel Lewis, May 16, 1969, Archives.
807. Samuel Lewis to Pir Vilayat (Khan), May 19, 1969, Archives.
808. Samuel Lewis, Diary, June 17, 1969, Archives.

809. Samuel Lewis to Pir Vilayat I. Khan, July 19, 1969, Archives.
810. Samuel Lewis to Atiya (Brautlacht), November 8, 1969, Archives.
811. Hassan Herz, "Remembrance," August 31, 2021, Sufi Ruhaniat International unpublished collection.
812. Ibid.
813. Samuel Lewis, Diary, January 17, 1968, Archives.
814. Samuel Lewis to Shamcher (Bryn Beorse), February 12, 1968, Archives.
815. Jacob Needleman, jacket blurb for Mansur Johnson, *Murshid* (Seattle: Peaceworks Publications, 2006), back cover.
816. Samuel Lewis to Paul Reps, July 15, 1968, Archives.
817. William Brinner, "Remembrance," December 6, 1976, Archives.
818. Samuel Lewis to Reps San (Paul Reps), April 20, 1969, Archives.
819. Samuel Lewis to Shamcher (Bryn Beorse), November 23, 1969, Archives.
820. Andreina Leanza Becker-Colonna to Sabira Scott, May 31, 1976, Archives.
821. Kyung-Bo Seo, "Remembrance," April 25, 1976, Archives.
822. Lewis to Pir Vilayat (see n. 804).
823. Lewis, *Spiritual Dancing* (see n. 226).
824. Johnson, *Murshid,* 337–338 (see n. 747).
825. Ibid., 404.
826. Saadia Khawar Khan, *Voice of the Heart* (see n. 696).
827. Asha Greer, personal communication to Barakat Bryan, March, 2020, Sufi Ruhaniat International unpublished collection.
828. Samuel Lewis to Frances (van Briesen), December 14, 1970, Archives.
829. Samuel Lewis, "Draft: Integrative Program for Peace in the Near East," undated, Archives.
830. Inayat Khan, *Bowl of Saki,* March 20 entry, Archives (see also n. 424).
831. Lewis, "Commentary on *Bowl of Saki,*" March 20 entry, Archives (see also n. 424).
832. Samuel Lewis to U. Darrani, June 22, 1970, Archives.
833. Samuel Lewis to Khankah, June 3, 1970, Archives.
834. Samuel Lewis to Anandashram, June 3, 1970, Archives.
835. Samuel Lewis to Finley Dunne, June 3, 1970, Archives.
836. Silver and Silver, "Remembrance" (see n. 757).
837. Ibid.
838. Ibid.
839. Ibid.
840. Lewis to Darrani (see n. 832).
841. Greer to Bryan (see n. 825).
842. Samuel Lewis to Uncle (Harry Rosenthal), June 27, 1970, Archives.
843. Shahabuddin and Surya Less, "Remembrance," April 15, 1976, Archives.
844. Samuel Lewis to Ram, September 24, 1970, Archives.
845. Samuel Lewis to Saadia Khawar Khan and Bibijan, September 6, 1970, Archives.
846. Bibijan to Pir-O-Murshid (Samuel Lewis), April 26, 1970, Archives.
847. Samuel Lewis to Bibijan, April 29, 1970, Archives.
848. Samuel Lewis to Shamcher Bryn Beorse, September 26, 1970, Archives.
849. Samuel Lewis to Gavin (Arthur), September 27, 1970, Archives.
850. Samuel Lewis to W. D. Begg, October, 1970, Archives.
851. Samuel Lewis to Shamcher Bryn Beorse, October 2, 1970, Archives.
852. Samuel Lewis, Selections From "The Black Christ," undated, Archives.
853. Less, "Remembrance" (see n. 841).
854. Shabda Kahn, personal communication to Barakat Bryan, Sufi Ruhaniat International unpublished collection.
855. Lewis, *New Age* (see n. 220).
856. Samuel Lewis to Barkat Ali, January 2, 1971, Archives.
857. Iqbal Lewis and Mouni Akbar Saul, "Remembrance," undated, Archives.

858. Van Voris, "Remembrance" (see n. 7).
859. Michael Suleiman, "Remembrance," October 28, 1976, Archives.
860. Less, "Remembrance" (see n. 843).
861. Ibid.
862. Greer to Bryan (see n. 827).
863. Less, "Remembrance" (see n. 843).
864. Ibid.
865. Saul Barodofsky, "Remembrance," undated, Archives.
866. Abrahamic Reunion, retrieved August 3, 2020, Abrahamicreunion.org.

Image Credits

Credits for the images used in this book are listed below by page number. Images not listed are either in the public domain or by unknown photographers. We apologize for any oversights.

Facing page 1: by permission of Baraka Carol Russell. **3**: courtesy of Mrs. Theresa Henderson and Samuel Lewis's family. **32, 35**: by permission of the Zen Studies Society. **38**: courtesy of the Nekbakht Foundation. **42**: courtesy of the Nekbakht Foundation and Sufism Reoriented. **61, 62, 66, 87**: courtesy of the Nekbakht Foundation. **77**: courtesy of Shahnoor Habib Munmun (CC BY 3.0). **94**: courtesy of the Roerich Museum, New York. **99, 101**: by permission of the First Zen Institute of America. **107, 114**: by permission of Alamy.com. **138**: by permission of the Paul Brunton Philosophic Foundation. **140**: courtesy of Muhaima Janet Startt. **152, 159**: by permission of Holistic Human Development, Inc. **174, 188, 191, 224**: by permission of Sufism Reoriented. **203**: courtesy of Vysotsky (CC BY-SA 3.0). **209, 234**: by permission of Meher Nazar Publications. **247**: by permission of Mansur Johnson. **248**: courtesy of ONE Archive, University of Southern California Library. **270**: by permission of Anandashram. **272**: by permission of Baraka Carol Russell. **276**: courtesy of Irina Gelbukh (CC BY-SA 3.0). **280**: by permission of University of Washington Libraries, Special Collections, INC0112. **284**: by permission of Philip Pascuzzo. **295**: courtesy of tawatchai07 (Freepik.com). **298, 309, 318**: courtesy of Khwaja Hasan Sani Nizami. **311**: courtesy of Aiwok (CC BY-SA 3.0). **313**: by permission of Shabda Kahn. **317**: courtesy of Suprateek Choudhury (CC BY-SA 3.0). **336, 350, 353**: by permission of Anandashram. **338**: courtesy of Varun Shiv Kapur (CC BY 2.0). **341**: by permission of David Harper. **356**: by permission of Jelaluddin Hauke Sturm. **368**: courtesy of David Iliff (CC BY-SA 3.0). **378**: courtesy of Edna Bellefontaine (CC0 1.0). **390**: courtesy of justsitting (CC BY-SA 4.0). **395**: courtesy of Imam Khairul Annas (CC BY-SA 3.0). **399**: by permission of Cynthia MacAdams. **412**: by permission of Baraka Carol Russell. **417**: courtesy of A. K. Khalifeh (CC BY-SA 3.0). **421**: courtesy of Samir I. Sharbaty (CC BY-SA 3.0). **426**: courtesy of Daniel Mayer (CC BY-SA 4.0). **427**: courtesy of Shamcher Archives (CC BY-SA 3.0). **445**: courtesy of Joelsuganth (CC BY-SA 3.0). **464**: courtesy of Gérard Ducher (CC BY-SA 2.5). **465**: courtesy of Clemens Schmillen (CC BY-SA 4.0). **491**: courtesy of Pale Blue Dot (CC BY-SA 3.0). **502**: courtesy of Osama Shukir Muhammed Amin FRCP(Glasg) (CC BY-SA 4.0). **513**: by permission of Fatima Lassar. **547** by permission of Mansur Johnson. **554**: by permission of Amertat Cohn: from the movie *Sunseed*. **573**: by permission of Mansur Johnson. **574**: by permission of Amertat Cohn: from the movie *Sunseed*. **584**: attributed to Jelaluddin Cave, by permission of Joe and Sitara Cave. **586**: by permission of Amertat Cohn: from the movie *Sunseed*. **587**: by permission of Mansur Johnson. **590**: courtesy of Mansur Johnson. **596**: courtesy of Mansur Johnson. **604**: by permission of Shabda Kahn. **606**: by permission of Amertat Cohn: from the movie *Sunseed*. **608**: by permission of Mansur Johnson. **609**: courtesy of Mansur

Johnson. **612, 613**: attributed to Jelaluddin Cave, by permission of Joe and Sitara Cave. **618**: by permission of Mansur Johnson. **619**: by permission of the United Nations Archives at Geneva. **620**: by permission of Lama Foundation. **621**: courtesy of Mansur Johnson. **623**: by permission of Allaudin Mathieu. **626**: by permission of Hakim Saul-uddin Barodofsky. **628, 646**: attributed to Jelaluddin Cave, by permission of Joe and Sitara Cave. **647**: by permission of Mansur Johnson. **653**: by permission of *The San Francisco Examiner.* **655**: attributed to Jelaluddin Cave, by permission of Joe and Sitara Cave. **656, 657**: by permission of Amertat Cohn: from the movie *Sunseed.* **658**: by permission of Shabda Kahn. **667**: by permission of Fatima Lassar.

Index